Linux® All-in-One Desk Reference For Dummies®

Cheat Sheet

Bash Shell

- Pipe:
  - *command1 | command2*
- Redirections:
  - *command > file* (output goes to file)
  - *command < file* (input from file)
  - *command > file* (append to file)
  - *command 2> file* (errors go to file)
- Commands:
  - *alias* (Defines shortcut for a long command)
  - *apropos* (Searches the manpages for keywords)
  - *history* (Displays most recent commands)
  - *locate* (Finds files)
  - *whereis* (Finds ... les for a com...
  - ... r a command)
  - ... ment
  - ... user's home directory)
  - *PATH* (Directories to search for commands)
  - *TERM* (Name of terminal type)

D0870986
WITHDRAWN

File System

- Key directories in the file system:
  - */* Root directory (base of file system)
  - */bin* (Executable programs)
  - */boot* (Linux kernel and boot loader)
  - */dev* (Special device files)
  - */etc* (System configuration files)
  - */home* (Home directories of all users)
  - */lib* (Library files for programs)
  - */media* (Mount points for CD-ROM, floppy)
  - */root* (Home directory of the *root* user)
  - */sbin* (System administration commands)
  - */srv* (Data for services such as Web and FTP)
  - */tmp* (Temporary directory)
  - */usr* (Many important programs)
  - */var* (Various system files, such as logs)
- Commands:
  - *cat* Copies a file to the standard output
  - *cd* Changes current directory
  - *chmod* Changes file permissions
  - *chown* Changes file ownerships
  - *cp* Copies files
  - *dd* Copies blocks of data
  - *df* Reports disk space usage by device
  - *diff* Compares two text files
  - *du* Reports disk space usage by directory
  - *file* Displays the type of data in a file
  - *find* Finds files based on specified criteria
  - *grep* Searches for text in a file
  - *ln* Links a filename to a link name
  - *ls* Displays the contents of a directory
  - *mkdir* Creates a directory
  - *more* Displays a text file, one page at a time
  - *mount* Mounts a file system
  - *mv* Renames or moves file
  - *pwd* Displays the current directory
  - *rm* Deletes files
  - *rmdir* Deletes directories
  - *sort* Sorts lines in a text file
  - *split* Splits a file into smaller parts
  - *umount* Unmount a file system
  - *wc* Counts words and lines in a file
- File permissions:
  - *rwxrwxrwx* 3 groups of *rwx*, leftmost is for owner, middle for group, rightmost for others; *rwx* stands for read (*r*), write (*w*), execute (*x*); dash (-) means no permission
  - *rwx------* Only owner can read, write, execute
  - *rw-r--r--* Everyone can read, owner can write
  - *rw-------* Only owner can read and write
  - *r--r--r--* Read-only file (everyone can read)

For Dummies: Bestselling Book Series for Beginners

Linux® All-in-One Desk Reference For Dummies®

Cheat Sheet

GNOME and KDE Desktops

- Click the Main Menu button in GNOME or KDE and then select applications to run.
- Always right-click for a context menu of options.
- Right-click on the GNOME panel to add applets to the panel.
- To run OpenOffice.org applications, choose Main Menu⇨Office.

Linux Installation

1. Resize disk partition using partitioning tool such as PartitionMagic or get a second hard drive.
2. Burn CDs for your distribution and boot PC from CD.
3. Go through graphical installation steps.
4. Configure other hardware when system first boots up.

System Administration

Debian: *dpkg -l keyword* (check package status), *apt-cache search package* (search for package), *apt-get install package* (install package), *apt-get update* (update package list), *apt-get upgrade* (upgrade the packages)

Fedora Core: Look for options in Main Menu⇨System Settings and Main Menu⇨System Tools, *rpm -q rpmname* (check package), *rpm -ivh package file* (install package)

SUSE: Main Menu⇨System⇨YaST

Xandros: Main Menu⇨Control Center, Main Menu⇨Xandros File Manager, Main Menu⇨Xandros Networks (for software updates)

Unpack compressed tar files: *tar zxvf file name.tgz*

Unpack bz2 compressed files: *bzip2 -d file name.bz2*

GUI Configuration Tools

- **Fedora Core:** Main Menu⇨System Settings
- **SUSE:** Main Menu⇨System⇨YaST
- **Xandros:** Main Menu⇨Control Center

Commands to check network:

- *ping* — Checks network connectivity
- *ifconfig* — Configures network interface
- *iwconfig* — Configures wireless network interface
- *netstat* — Displays network status

Wiley, the Wiley Publishing logo, For Dummies, the Dummies Man logo, the For Dummies Bestselling Book Series logo and all related trade dress are trademarks or registered trademarks of John Wiley & Sons, Inc. and/or its affiliates. All other trademarks are property of their respective owners.

Copyright © 2005 Wiley Publishing, Inc.
All rights reserved.

Item 7936-3.

For more information about Wiley Publishing, call 1-800-762-2974.

SCC
39.99

Linux®
All-in-One DESK REFERENCE
FOR DUMMIES®

Learning Resources Center
Collin County Community College District
Spring Creek Campus
Plano, Texas 75074

WITHDRAWN

Linux® All-in-One DESK REFERENCE FOR DUMMIES®

by Naba Barkakati

WILEY

Wiley Publishing, Inc.

Linux® All-in-One Desk Reference For Dummies®

Published by
Wiley Publishing, Inc.
111 River Street
Hoboken, NJ 07030-5774

Copyright © 2005 by Wiley Publishing, Inc., Indianapolis, Indiana

Published by Wiley Publishing, Inc., Indianapolis, Indiana

Published simultaneously in Canada

No part of this publication may be reproduced, stored in a retrieval system or transmitted in any form or by any means, electronic, mechanical, photocopying, recording, scanning or otherwise, except as permitted under Sections 107 or 108 of the 1976 United States Copyright Act, without either the prior written permission of the Publisher, or authorization through payment of the appropriate per-copy fee to the Copyright Clearance Center, 222 Rosewood Drive, Danvers, MA 01923, (978) 750-8400, fax (978) 646-8600. Requests to the Publisher for permission should be addressed to the Legal Department, Wiley Publishing, Inc., 10475 Crosspoint Blvd., Indianapolis, IN 46256, (317) 572-3447, fax (317) 572-4355, e-mail: `brandreview@wiley.com`.

Trademarks: Wiley, the Wiley Publishing logo, For Dummies, the Dummies Man logo, A Reference for the Rest of Us!, The Dummies Way, Dummies Daily, The Fun and Easy Way, Dummies.com, and related trade dress are trademarks or registered trademarks of John Wiley & Sons, Inc. and/or its affiliates in the United States and other countries, and may not be used without written permission. Linux is a registered trademark of Linus Torvalds. All other trademarks are the property of their respective owners. Wiley Publishing, Inc., is not associated with any product or vendor mentioned in this book.

LIMIT OF LIABILITY/DISCLAIMER OF WARRANTY: THE PUBLISHER AND THE AUTHOR MAKE NO REPRESENTATIONS OR WARRANTIES WITH RESPECT TO THE ACCURACY OR COMPLETENESS OF THE CONTENTS OF THIS WORK AND SPECIFICALLY DISCLAIM ALL WARRANTIES, INCLUDING WITHOUT LIMITATION WARRANTIES OF FITNESS FOR A PARTICULAR PURPOSE. NO WARRANTY MAY BE CREATED OR EXTENDED BY SALES OR PROMOTIONAL MATERIALS. THE ADVICE AND STRATEGIES CONTAINED HEREIN MAY NOT BE SUITABLE FOR EVERY SITUATION. THIS WORK IS SOLD WITH THE UNDERSTANDING THAT THE PUBLISHER IS NOT ENGAGED IN RENDERING LEGAL, ACCOUNTING, OR OTHER PROFESSIONAL SERVICES. IF PROFESSIONAL ASSISTANCE IS REQUIRED, THE SERVICES OF A COMPETENT PROFESSIONAL PERSON SHOULD BE SOUGHT. NEITHER THE PUBLISHER NOR THE AUTHOR SHALL BE LIABLE FOR DAMAGES ARISING HEREFROM. THE FACT THAT AN ORGANIZATION OR WEBSITE IS REFERRED TO IN THIS WORK AS A CITATION AND/OR A POTENTIAL SOURCE OF FURTHER INFORMATION DOES NOT MEAN THAT THE AUTHOR OR THE PUBLISHER ENDORSES THE INFORMATION THE ORGANIZATION OR WEBSITE MAY PROVIDE OR RECOMMENDATIONS IT MAY MAKE. FURTHER, READERS SHOULD BE AWARE THAT INTERNET WEBSITES LISTED IN THIS WORK MAY HAVE CHANGED OR DISAPPEARED BETWEEN WHEN THIS WORK WAS WRITTEN AND WHEN IT IS READ. FULFILLMENT OF EACH COUPON OFFER IS THE SOLE RESPONSIBILITY OF THE OFFEROR.

For general information on our other products and services, please contact our Customer Care Department within the U.S. at 800-762-2974, outside the U.S. at 317-572-3993, or fax 317-572-4002.

For technical support, please visit `www.wiley.com/techsupport`.

Wiley also publishes its books in a variety of electronic formats. Some content that appears in print may not be available in electronic books.

Library of Congress Control Number: 2004116155

ISBN: 0-7645-7936-3

Manufactured in the United States of America

10 9 8 7 6 5 4 3 2

1O/QU/QR/QV/IN

WILEY

About the Author

Naba Barkakati is an electrical engineer and a successful computer-book author who has experience in a wide variety of systems, ranging from MS-DOS and Windows to UNIX and Linux. He bought his first personal computer — an IBM PC-AT — in 1984 after graduating with a PhD in electrical engineering from the University of Maryland at College Park. While pursuing a full-time career in engineering, Naba dreamed of writing software for the emerging PC software market. As luck would have it, instead of building a software empire like Microsoft, he ended up writing successful computer books. Currently, Naba is a Senior Level Technologist at the Center for Technology and Engineering in the U.S. Government Accountability Office (GAO).

Over the past 15 years, Naba has written over 25 computer books on a number of topics, ranging from Windows programming with C++ to Linux. He has authored several best-selling titles, such as *The Waite Group's Turbo C++ Bible, Object-Oriented Programming in C++, X Window System Programming, Visual C++ Developer's Guide, Borland C++ 4 Developer's Guide,* and *Linux Secrets.* His books have been translated into many languages, including Spanish, French, Polish, Greek, Italian, Chinese, Japanese, and Korean. Naba's most recent book is *Red Hat Fedora Linux 2 All-in-One Desk Reference For Dummies*, also published by Wiley Publishing, Inc.

Naba lives in North Potomac, Maryland, with his wife Leha, and their children, Ivy, Emily, and Ashley.

Dedication

I would like to dedicate this book to my wife Leha, and daughters Ivy, Emily, and Ashley.

Author's Acknowledgments

I am grateful to Terri Varveris for getting me started on this book — a set of eight quick reference guides about Linux that focuses on several major Linux distributions. As the project editor, Paul Levesque guided me through the manuscript-submission process and kept everything moving. I appreciate the guidance and support that Terri and Paul gave me during this project.

I would like to thank Jason Luster for reviewing the manuscript for technical accuracy and providing many useful suggestions for improving the book's content.

Thanks to everyone at Wiley Publishing for transforming my raw manuscript into this well—edited and beautifully packaged book.

Of course, there would be no reason for this book if it were not for Linux. For this, we have Linus Torvalds and the legions of Linux developers around the world to thank. Finally, and as always, my greatest thanks go to my wife, Leha, and our daughters, Ivy, Emily, and Ashley — it is their love and support that keeps me going. Thanks for being there!

Publisher's Acknowledgments

We're proud of this book; please send us your comments through our online registration form located at www.dummies.com/register/.

Some of the people who helped bring this book to market include the following:

Acquisitions, Editorial, and Media Development

Project Editor: Paul Levesque

Acquisitions Editor: Terri Varveris

Copy Editor: Jean Rogers

Technical Editor: Jason Luster

Editorial Manager: Kevin Kirschner

Permissions Editor: Laura Moss

Media Development Specialist: Travis Silvers

Media Development Manager: Laura VanWinkle

Media Development Supervisor: Richard Graves

Editorial Assistant: Amanda Foxworth

Cartoons: Rich Tennant (www.the5thwave.com)

Production

Project Coordinator: Nancee Reeves

Layout and Graphics: Andrea Dahl, Denny Hager, Joyce Haughey, Stephanie D. Jumper, Heather Ryan, Jacque Roth

Proofreaders: Laura Albert, John Greenough, Jessica Kramer, Arielle Mennelle, Carl Pierce, Dwight Ramsey

Indexer: Sherry Massey

Special Help: Teresa Artman, Virginia Sanders

Publishing and Editorial for Technology Dummies

Richard Swadley, Vice President and Executive Group Publisher

Andy Cummings, Vice President and Publisher

Mary Bednarek, Executive Acquisitions Director

Mary C. Corder, Editorial Director

Publishing for Consumer Dummies

Diane Graves Steele, Vice President and Publisher

Joyce Pepple, Acquisitions Director

Composition Services

Gerry Fahey, Vice President of Production Services

Debbie Stailey, Director of Composition Services

Contents at a Glance

Table of Contents

Introduction

Linux is truly amazing when you consider how it originated and how it continues to evolve. From its modest beginning as the hobby of one person — Linus Torvalds of Finland — Linux has grown into a full-fledged operating system with features that rival those of any commercial UNIX operating system. To top it off, Linux — with all of its source code — is available free of cost to anyone. All one has to do is download it from an Internet site or get it on CDs or a DVD for a nominal fee from one of many Linux CD vendors.

Linux certainly is an exception to the rule that "you get what you pay for." Even though Linux is free, it is no slouch when it comes to performance, features, and reliability. The robustness of Linux has to do with the way it is developed and kept updated. Many developers around the world collaborate to add features. Incremental versions are continually being downloaded by users and tested in a variety of system configurations. Linux revisions go through much more rigorous beta testing than any commercial software does.

Since the release of Linux kernel 1.0 on March 14, 1994, the number of Linux users around the world has grown exponentially. Many Linux distributions — combinations of the operating system with applications and installation tools — have been developed to simplify the installation and use. Some Linux distributions are commercially sold and supported, while many continue to be freely available.

Unlike many freely available software programs, Linux comes with extensive online information on topics such as installing and configuring the operating system for a wide variety of PCs and peripherals. A small group of hard-core Linux users are expert enough to productively use Linux with the online documentation alone. A much larger number of users, however, move to Linux with some specific purpose in mind (such as setting up a World Wide Web server or learning Linux). Also, a large number of Linux users use their systems at home. For these new users, the online documentation is not easy to use, and the documentation typically does not cover the specific uses of Linux that the user may have in mind.

If you are beginning to use Linux, what you need is a practical guide that not only gets you going with the installation and setup of Linux, but also shows you how to use Linux for a specific task, such as a Web server or to develop software. You may also want to try out different Linux distributions before settling on one that you like.

Accordingly, *Linux All-in-One Desktop Reference For Dummies* comes with a DVD that includes five different Linux distributions — Debian GNU/Linux (Sarge), Fedora Core 3, Knoppix 3.6, SUSE Linux 9.1, and Xandros Open Circulation Edition — and the instructions to install and use any of these distributions. (*Hint*: Use Knoppix Live CD for a quick, no-risk Linux experience.)

About This Book

Linux All-in-One Desk Reference For Dummies gives you eight different quick-reference guides in a single book. Taken together, these eight minibooks provide detailed information on installing, configuring, and using Linux.

What you'll like most about this book is that you don't have to read it sequentially chapter by chapter, or, for that matter, even the sections in a chapter. You can pretty much turn to the topic you want and quickly get the answer to your pressing questions about Linux, be it about using the OpenOffice.org word processor or setting up the Apache Web server.

Here are some of the things you can do with this book:

- Install and configure Linux — Debian, Fedora Core, Knoppix, SUSE, or Xandros — from the DVD-ROM included with the book.
- Connect the Linux PC to the Internet through a DSL or cable modem.
- Set up dialup networking with PPP.
- Add a wireless Ethernet to your existing network.
- Get tips, techniques, and shortcuts for specific uses of Linux, such as
  - Setting up and using Internet services such as Web, Mail, News, FTP, NFS, and DNS.
  - Setting up a Windows server using Samba.
  - Using Linux commands.
  - Using Perl, shell, and C programming on Linux.
  - Using the OpenOffice.org office suite and other applications that come with Linux.
- Understand the basics of system and network security.
- Perform system administration tasks.

Conventions Used in This Book

I use a simple notational style in this book. All listings, filenames, function names, variable names, and keywords are typeset in a `monospace` font for ease of reading. I *italicize* the first occurrences of new terms and concepts, and then provide a definition right there. I show typed commands in **boldface**. The output of commands and any listing of files is shown in a `monospace` font.

What You Don't Have to Read

Each mini reference book zeros in on a specific task area — such as using the Internet or running Internet servers — and then provides hands-on instructions on how to perform a series of related tasks. You can jump right to a section and read about a specific task. You don't have to read anything but the few paragraphs or the list of steps that relate to your question. Use the Table of Contents or the Index to locate the pages relevant to your question.

You can safely ignore text next to the Technical Stuff icons as well as the sidebars. However, if you are the kind of person who likes to know some of the hidden details of how Linux works, by all means, dig into the Technical Stuff icons and the sidebars.

Who Are You?

I assume that you are somewhat familiar with a PC — you know how to turn it on and off and you have dabbled a bit with Windows. Considering that most new PCs come preloaded with Windows, this assumption is safe, right? And you know how to use some of the Windows applications such as Microsoft Office.

When installing Linux on your PC, you may want to retain your Windows 2000 or Windows XP installations intact. I assume you don't mind investing in a good disk-partitioning tool such as PowerQuest's PartitionMagic, available at `www.powerquest.com/partitionmagic`. (No, I don't have any connections with PowerQuest.)

I also assume that you are willing to accept the risk that when you try to install Linux, some things may not quite work. Problems can happen if you have some uncommon types of hardware. If you are afraid of ruining your system, try finding a slightly older spare Pentium PC that you can sacrifice and then install Linux on that PC. Or simply boot your PC with the Knoppix Live CD in the CD-ROM drive.

How This Book Is Organized

Linux All-in-One Desk Reference For Dummies has eight minibooks, each of which focuses on a small set of related topics. If you are looking for information on a specific topic, check the minibook names on the spine or consult the Table of Contents.

This desk reference starts with a minibook that explains the basics of Linux and guides you through the installation process (a very useful aspect of this book because you typically do not purchase a PC with Linux preinstalled). The second minibook serves as a user's guide to Linux — it focuses on exploring various aspects of a Linux workstation, including the GNOME and KDE GUIs and many of the applications that come bundled with Linux. The third minibook covers networking and the fourth minibook goes into using the Internet. The fifth minibook introduces system administration. The sixth minibook turns to the important subject of securing a Linux system and its associated network. The seventh minibook shows you how to run a variety of Internet servers from mail to a Web server. The eighth and final minibook introduces you to programming.

Here's a quick overview of the eight books and what they contain:

Book I: Linux Basics: What is Linux? Understanding what's new in the Linux 2.6 kernel. Installing, configuring, and troubleshooting different Linux distributions (Debian, Fedora Core, Knoppix, SUSE, and Xandros). Taking Linux for a test drive.

Book II: Linux Desktops: Exploring GNOME and KDE. Using the shell (what's a shell anyway?). Navigating the Linux file system. Exploring the applications such as multimedia software as well as the text editors (`vi` and `emacs`).

Book III: Networking: Connecting the Linux PC to the Internet through a dialup connection or a high-speed always-on connection such as DSL or cable modem. Configuring and managing TCP/IP networks, including wireless networks.

Book IV: Internet: Using various Internet services such as e-mail, Web surfing, and reading newsgroups. Transferring files with FTP.

Book V: Administration: Performing basic system administration. Managing user accounts and the file system. Installing applications. Working with devices and printers. Using USB devices. Upgrading and customizing the Linux kernel.

Book VI: Security: Understanding network and host security. Securing the host and the network. Performing security audits.

Sidebars

Sometimes, I use sidebars to highlight interesting, but not critical, information. Sidebars explain concepts you may not have encountered before or give a little insight into a related topic. If you're in a hurry, you can safely skip the sidebars.

Book VII: Internet Servers: Managing the Internet services. Configuring the Apache Web server. Setting up the FTP server. Configuring the mail and news servers. Providing DNS. File sharing with NFS. Using Samba to set up a Windows server.

Book VIII: Programming: Finding out the basics of programming. Exploring the software development tools in Linux. Writing shell scripts. Learning C and Perl programming.

Appendix: About the DVD: Summarizes the contents of the book's companion DVD-ROM.

What's on the DVD?

The DVD contains five Linux distributions — it's a Fedora Core 3 DVD that contains four folders, one for each of Debian, Knoppix, SUSE, and Xandros. Knoppix is a Live CD distribution and Xandros is in the form of the Open Circulation Edition CD. You may use the DVD in accordance with the license agreements accompanying the software. To find out more about the contents of the DVD, please consult the appendix.

Icons Used in This Book

Following the time-honored tradition of the *All-in-One Desk Reference For Dummies* series, I use icons to help you quickly pinpoint useful information. The icons include the following:

The Distribution Specific icon points out information that applies to specific distributions — Debian, Fedora Core, Knoppix, SUSE, and Xandros — that this book covers.

The Remember icon marks a general interesting fact — something that you want to know and remember.

The Tip icon marks things that you can do to make your job easier.

The Warning icon highlights potential pitfalls. With this icon, I'm telling you: "Watch out! This could hurt your system!"

The Technical Stuff icon marks technical information that could be of interest to an advanced user (or those of us aspiring to be advanced users).

Where to Go from Here

It's time to get started on your Linux adventure. Take out the DVD and install Linux — pick a distribution, any distribution (as long as it's Debian, Fedora Core, Knoppix, SUSE, or Xandros). Then, turn to a relevant chapter and let the fun begin. Use the Table of Contents and the Index to figure out where you want to go. Before you know it, you'll become an expert at Linux!

I hope you enjoy consulting this book as much as I enjoyed writing it!

Book I

Linux Basics

The 5th Wave   By Rich Tennant

WANDA HAD THE DISTINCT FEELING HER HUSBAND'S NEW SOFTWARE PROGRAM WAS ABOUT TO BECOME INTERACTIVE.
MANUAL

Contents at a Glance

Chapter 1: Introducing Linux

In This Chapter

- **Explaining what Linux is**
- **Going over what Linux distributions typically include**
- **Discovering what Linux helps you manage**
- **Getting started**

I bet you've heard about Linux. If you're wondering what exactly Linux is and what it can help you do, this chapter is all about answering those questions. Here I provide a broad-brushstroke picture of Linux and tell you how you can start using it right away.

By the way, this book covers Linux for Intel 80x86 and Pentium processors (basically any PC that can run any flavor of Windows).

What Is Linux?

You know that your PC is a bunch of *hardware* — things you can touch, like the system box, monitor, keyboard, and mouse. The system box contains the most important hardware of all — the *central processing unit* (CPU), the microchip that runs the *software* (any program that tells the computer how to do your bidding), which you actually *can't* touch. In a typical Pentium 4 PC, the Pentium 4 microprocessor is the CPU. Other important hardware in the system box includes the memory (RAM chips) and the hard drive — and one program has to run all this stuff and get it to play nice: the operating system.

The *operating system* is software that manages all the hardware and runs other software at your command. You, the user, provide those commands by clicking menus and icons or by typing some cryptic text. Linux is an operating system — as are UNIX, Windows 98, Windows 2000, and Windows XP. The Linux operating system is modeled after UNIX; in its most basic, no-frills form, the Linux operating system also goes by the name *Linux kernel*.

The operating system is what gives a computer — any computer — its personality. For example, you can run Windows 98 or Windows XP on a PC — and on that same PC, you can *also* install and run Linux. That means, depending on which operating system is installed and running at any particular time, *the same PC* can be a Windows 98, Windows XP, or Linux system.

Does Linux really run on any computer?

Linux runs on many different types of computer systems — and it does seem able to run on nearly any type of computer. Linus Torvalds and other programmers originally developed Linux for the Intel 80x86 (and compatible) line of processors. Nowadays, Linux is also available for systems based on other processors — such as those with AMD's 64-bit AMD64 processors, the Motorola 68000 family; Alpha AXPs; Sun SPARCs and UltraSPARCs; Hewlett-Packard's HP PA-RISC; the PowerPC and PowerPC64 processors; and the MIPS R4x00 and R5x00. More recently, IBM has released its own version of Linux for its S/390 mainframe. This book covers Linux for Intel 80x86 and Pentium processors (these have in common a basic physical structure known as *IA-32 architecture*).

The primary job of an operating system is to load software (computer programs) from the hard drive (or other permanent storage) into the memory and get the CPU to run those programs. Everything you do with your computer is possible because of the operating system — so if the operating system somehow messes up, the whole system freezes up. You know how infuriating it is when your favorite operating system — maybe even the one that came with your PC — suddenly calls it quits just as you were about to click the Send button after composing that long e-mail to your friend. You try the three-finger salute (pressing Ctrl+Alt+Del), but nothing happens. Then it's time for the Reset button (provided your computer's builders were wise enough to include one). Luckily, that sort of thing almost never happens with Linux — it has a reputation for being a very reliable operating system.

TECHNICAL STUFF

In technical mumbo jumbo, Linux is a *multiuser, multitasking operating system*. All this means is that Linux enables multiple users to log in, and Linux can run more than one program at the same time. Nearly all operating systems are multiuser and multitasking these days, but when Linux first started in 1994, *multiuser* and *multitasking* were big selling points.

Linux distributions

A *Linux distribution* consists of the Linux *kernel* (the operating system) and a collection of applications, together with an easy-to-use installation program. By the way, most people just say *Linux* to refer to a specific Linux distribution.

You find many Linux distributions, and each includes the standard Linux operating system and the following major packages:

- **The X Window System:** The graphical user interface.
- **One or more graphical desktops:** Among the most popular are GNOME and KDE.

✦ **A selection of applications:** Linux programs come in the form of ready-to-run software, but the *source code* (the commands we humans use to tell the computer what to do) is included (or easily available), as is its documentation.

Current Linux distributions include a huge selection of software — so much that it usually requires multiple CD-ROMs or a single DVD-ROM (which this book includes).

The development and maintenance of the Linux kernel, software packages in a Linux distribution, and the Linux distributions themselves are organized as open source projects. In a nutshell, *open source* means access to the source code and the right to freely redistribute the software without any restrictions. There's a lot more to the definition than my succinct note. To find out more about the details of what open source means and the acceptable open source licenses, you can visit the Open Source Initiative Web site at `www.opensource.org`.

Table 1-1 lists a few major Linux distributions along with a brief description for each. There are many more Linux distributions besides the ones I show in Table 1-1.

To find out more about Linux distributions, visit DistroWatch.com at `www.distrowatch.com`. At that Web site, you can read up on specific distributions as well as find links for ordering CDs for specific distributions.

Table 1-1 Major Linux Distributions

Distribution	*Description*
Debian GNU/Linux	This non-commercial distribution started in 1993 and continues to be a popular distribution with many volunteer developers around the world contributing to the project. The installation is harder because in addition to the basic steps you'd expect, you also need to provide information about your PC's hardware. However, after you have installed the basic Debian system, you can install and upgrade Debian packages easily with a package installer called `apt-get` where `apt` stands for the Advanced Package Tool. Debian is available free of charge from `www.debian.org`.
Fedora Core	This distribution is the successor to Red Hat Linux — the Linux distribution from Red Hat. Fedora Core 1, released in November 2003, was the successor to the Red Hat Linux 9. Fedora Core is freely available. Fedora Core uses the Red Hat Package Manager (RPM) format for its software packages. You can download Fedora Core from `fedora.redhat.com`.

(continued)

Table 1-1 *(continued)*

Distribution	*Description*
Gentoo Linux	This is a non-commercial, source-based (meaning that all software is provided in source code form) distribution that first appeared in 2002. The installer provides some binary packages to get the Linux going, but the idea is to compile all source packages on the user's computer. This makes it time-consuming to build a full-fledged Gentoo system with the latest graphical desktops, multimedia, and development tools because all the packages have to be downloaded and compiled. Gentoo Linux is freely available from `www.gentoo.org`.
Knoppix	This Live CD distribution is based on Debian and named after its developer Klaus Knopper of Germany. Knoppix can be used as a recovery tool (to fix problems with an already-installed Linux system) because you can run Knoppix directly from the CD without having to first install it on the hard drive. The Knoppix CD stores software in compressed format and Knoppix decompresses the programs on the fly. Using this approach, Knoppix can pack up to 2GB of software on a CD. Knoppix uses the Debian package management. For information on downloading Knoppix free of charge, visit the Knoppix Web site at `www.knopper.net/knoppix/index-en.html`.
Linspire	This commercial distribution was first released in 2002 under the name LindowsOS. Linspire uses the Debian package format and offers software download, for a fee, through what it calls the Click-N-Run Web-based interface. You can download a Live CD version called LindowsLive! via BitTorrent, a peer-to-peer file sharing system. For more information about Linspire, visit `www.linspire.com`.
Mandrakelinux	This popular distribution began life as a 1998 release of Red Hat Linux with an easy-to-use installer and with KDE as the default desktop. Mandrake Linux is freely available. Mandrake software packages use the Red Hat Package Manager (RPM) format. You can download Mandrake Linux from `www.mandrakelinux.com`.
MEPIS Linux	This Debian-based Live CD distribution was first released in July 2003. It also includes a graphical installer that can be launched from the CD to install MEPIS on the hard drive. MEPIS has good hardware detection and it comes with Java and multimedia software, which makes it popular. MEPIS uses the Debian package format. You can download slightly older versions of MEPIS free of charge from `www.mepis.org`.
Slackware Linux	This is one of the oldest distributions, having been first released in 1992. Slackware uses compressed tar files for its packages and provides a text-based installer with limited automatic detection of hardware. All software configurations are done by editing text files. Slackware is freely available from `www.slackware.com`.

Distribution	Description
SUSE Linux	This commercial distribution focuses on the desktop and includes some proprietary components that prevent its redistribution. SUSE comes with the YaST installation and configuration tool. SUSE Linux uses Red Hat Package Manager (RPM) packages. Although SUSE does not provide ISO image files for SUSE Linux, you can install it via FTP over the Internet. Also, a Live CD version of SUSE called SUSE Live Eval is available free of charge from the SUSE Web site. Visit `www.suse.com` for more information about SUSE Linux.
Xandros Desktop	This distribution is the successor to Corel Linux and is based on Debian. Xandros is aimed at first-time Linux users with an installer that can repartition the hard drive. The versatile Xandros File Manager is a key selling point of Xandros. However, Xandros includes some proprietary components that prevent redistribution. A limited version of Xandros Desktop called the Open Circulation Edition is available for free through BitTorrent. Visit `www.xandros.com` for more information about Xandros.

As you can see from the brief descriptions in Table 1-1, some of the Linux distributions such as Knoppix and MEPIS are in the form of Live CDs. A *Live CD* includes a Linux kernel that you can boot and run directly from the CD, without having to first install it on your hard drive. Such Live CD distributions can be handy if you want to try out a distribution before you decide whether to install it or not.

Many Linux distributions, such as SUSE Linux and Xandros Desktop, are commercial products that you can buy online or in computer stores and bookstores. If you have heard about *open source* and the *GNU (GNU's Not UNIX)* license, you may think that no one can sell Linux for profit. Luckily for companies that sell Linux distributions, the GNU license — also called the GNU General Public License (GPL) — does allow commercial, for-profit distribution, but requires that the software be distributed in source-code form, and stipulates that anyone may copy and distribute the software in source-code form to anyone else. Several Linux distributions are available free of charge under the GPL, which means that the publisher may include these distributions on a DVD-ROM with this book and that you may make as many copies of the DVD as you like.

Making sense of version numbers

Both the Linux kernel and a Linux distribution have their own version numbers, not to mention the many other software programs (such as GNOME and KDE) that come with the Linux distribution. The version numbers for the Linux kernel and the Linux distribution are unrelated, but each has particular significance.

Linux-kernel version numbers

After Linux kernel version 1.0 was released on March 14, 1994, the loosely knit Linux development community adopted a version-numbering scheme. Version numbers such as 1.*X*.*Y* and 2.*X*.*Y*, where *X* is an even number, are considered the stable versions. The last number, *Y*, is the patch level, which is incremented as problems are fixed. For example, 2.6.7 is a typical, stable version of the Linux kernel. Notice that these version numbers are in the form of three integers separated by periods — *Major.Minor.Patch* — where *Major* and *Minor* are numbers denoting the major and minor version numbers, and *Patch* is another number representing the patch level.

Version numbers of the form 2.*X*.*Y* with an odd *X* number are beta releases for developers only; they may be unstable, so you should not adopt such versions for day-to-day use. For example, when you look at version 2.5.75 of the Linux kernel, notice the *5* — that tells you it's a beta release. Developers add new features to these odd-numbered versions of Linux.

You can find out about the latest version of the Linux kernel online at `www.kernel.org`.

Distribution-specific version numbers

Each Linux distribution has a version number as well. These version numbers are usually of the form *X*.*Y*, where *X* is the major version and *Y* the minor version. Nowadays, if the minor version number is zero, it's simply dropped — as in Fedora Core 1 and Fedora Core 2. Unlike with the Linux-kernel version numbers, no special meaning is associated with odd and even minor versions. Each version of a Linux distribution includes specific versions of the Linux kernel and other major components, such as GNOME, KDE, and various applications.

The developers of active Linux distributions usually release new versions of their distribution on a regular basis — every six months or so. For example, SUSE Linux 9.0 was released in October 2003 and 9.1 was released in April 2004. Typically, each new major version of a Linux distribution provides significant new features.

Debian always has at least three releases at any time — *unstable, testing,* and *stable.* The *stable* release is the latest officially released distribution that most users would use. The *unstable* version is the distribution being worked on by developers. The *testing* distribution contains packages that have gone through some testing, but are not ready for inclusion in the stable release yet.

Linux Standard Base (LSB)

Linux has become important enough that there is a standard for Linux called the Linux Standard Base (or LSB, for short). LSB is a set of binary standards that should help reduce variations among the Linux distributions and promote portability of applications. The idea behind LSB is to provide application binary interface (ABI) so that software applications can run on any Linux (or other UNIX) systems that conform to the LSB standard. The LSB specification references the POSIX standards as well as many other standards such as the C and C++ programming language standards, the X Window System version 11 release 6 (X11R6), and the Filesystem Hierarchy Standard (FHS). LSB version 1.2 (commonly referred to as LSB 1.2) was released on June 28, 2002. LSB 1.3 came out in January 2003, and LSB 2.0 was released on August 30, 2004.

The LSB specification is organized into two parts — a common specification that remains the same across all types of processors and a set of hardware-specific specifications, one for each type of processor architecture. For example, LSB 1.2 has architecture-specific specifications for Intel 32-bit (IA32) and Power PC 32-bit (PPC32) processors. LSB 1.3 adds a specification for the Intel 64-bit (IA64) architecture and IBM S390 processors, in addition to the ones for IA32 and PPC32. LSB 2.0 includes specification for the AMD 64-bit (AMD64) processors.

An LSB certification program exists, and by now, several Linux distributions (such as Red Hat Linux 9, Red Hat Enterprise Linux 3 for x86, SUSE Linux 9.1, and Sun Wah Linux Desktop 3.0) are certified to be LSB 1.3 compliant IA32 runtime environments. You can expect more distributions to be LSB 2.0 certified in the near future.

To discover more about LSB, visit `www.linuxbase.org`. The latest list of LSB-certified systems is available at `www.opengroup.org/lsb/cert/cert_prodlist.tpl`.

What a Linux Distribution Includes

A Linux distribution comes with the Linux kernel and a whole lot more software. These software packages include everything from the graphical desktops to Internet servers to programming tools to create new software. In this section, I briefly describe some major software packages that come bundled with typical Linux distributions. Without this bundled software, Linux wouldn't be as popular as it is today.

GNU software

At the heart of a Linux distribution is a collection of software that came from the GNU Project. You get to know these GNU utilities only if you use your Linux system through a text terminal (or a graphical window that mimics one) — a basic *command-line interface* that puts nothing much on-screen but a prompt at which you type in your commands. The GNU software is one of the basic parts of any Linux distribution.

What is the GNU Project?

GNU is a recursive acronym that stands for *GNU's Not UNIX*. The GNU Project was launched in 1984 by Richard Stallman to develop a complete UNIX-like operating system. The GNU Project developed nearly everything needed for a complete operating system except for the operating system kernel. All GNU software was distributed under the GNU General Public License (GPL). GPL essentially requires that the software is distributed in source-code form and stipulates that any user may copy, modify, and distribute the software to anyone else in source-code form. Users may, however, have to pay for their individual copies of GNU software.

The Free Software Foundation (FSF) is a tax-exempt charity that raises funds for work on the GNU Project. To find out more about the GNU Project, visit its home page at `www.gnu.org`. You can find information about how to contact the Free Software Foundation and how to help the GNU Project.

As a Linux user, you may not realize the extent to which all Linux distributions rely on GNU software. Nearly all the tasks you perform in a Linux system involve one or more GNU software packages. For example, the GNOME graphical user interface (GUI) and the command interpreter (that is, the Bash shell) are both GNU software programs. By the way, the *shell* is the command-interpreter application that accepts the commands you type and then runs programs in response to those commands. If you rebuild the kernel or develop software, you do so with the GNU C and C++ compiler (which is part of the GNU software that accompanies Linux). If you edit text files with the `ed` or `emacs` editor, you're again using a GNU software package. The list goes on and on.

TECHNICAL STUFF

Table 1-2 lists some of the well-known GNU software packages that come with most Linux distributions. I show this table only to give you a feel for all the different kinds of things you can do with GNU software. Depending on your interests, you may never need to use many of these packages, but knowing they are there in case you ever need them is good.

Table 1-2 Well-Known GNU Software Packages

Software Package	*Description*
Autoconf	Generates shell scripts that automatically configure source-code packages
Automake	Generates `Makefile.in` files for use with Autoconf
Bash	The default shell — command interpreter — in Linux
Bc	An interactive calculator with arbitrary precision numbers

Software Package	*Description*
Binutils	A package that includes several utilities for working with binary files: `ar`, `as`, `gasp`, `gprof`, `ld`, `nm`, `objcopy`, `objdump`, `ranlib`, `readelf`, `size`, `strings`, and `strip`
Coreutils	A package that combines three individual packages called Fileutils, Shellutils, and Textutils and implements utilities such as `chgrp`, `chmod`, `chown`, `cp`, `dd`, `df`, `dir`, `dircolors`, `du`, `install`, `ln`, `ls`, `mkdir`, `mkfifo`, `mknod`, `mv`, `rm`, `rmdir`, `sync`, `touch`, `vdir`, `basename`, `chroot`, `date`, `dirname`, `echo`, `env`, `expr`, `factor`, `false`, `groups`, `hostname`, `id`, `logname`, `nice`, `nohup`, `pathchk`, `printenv`, `printf`, `pwd`, `seq`, `sleep`, `stty`, `su`, `tee`, `test`, `true`, `tty`, `uname`, `uptime`, `users`, `who`, `whoami`, `yes`, `cut`, `join`, `nl`, `split`, `tail`, `wc`, and so on
Gnuchess	A chess game
GNU C Library	For use with all Linux programs
Cpio	Copies file archives to and from disk or to another part of the file system
Diff	Compares files, showing line-by-line changes in several different formats
Ed	A line-oriented text editor
emacs	An extensible, customizable full-screen text editor and computing environment
Findutils	A package that includes the `find`, `locate`, and `xargs` utilities
Finger	A utility program designed to enable users on the Internet to get information about one another
Gawk	The GNU Project's implementation of the AWK programming language
GCC	Compilers for C, C++, Objective C, and other languages
Gdb	Source-level debugger for C, C++, and Fortran
Gdbm	A replacement for the traditional `dbm` and `ndbm` database libraries
Gettext	A set of utilities that enables software maintainers to internationalize (that means make the software work with different languages such as English, French, Spanish, and so on) a software package's user messages
Ghostscript	An interpreter for the Postscript and Portable Document Format (PDF) languages
Ghostview	An X Window System application that makes Ghostscript accessible from the GUI, enabling users to view Postscript or PDF files in a window
The GIMP	The GNU Image Manipulation Program is an Adobe Photoshop-like image-processing program

(continued)

WITHDRAWN

SPRING CREEK CAMPUS

Table 1-2 (continued)

Software Package	***Description***
GNOME	Provides a graphical user interface (GUI) for a wide variety of tasks that a Linux user may perform
Gnumeric	A graphical spreadsheet (similar to Microsoft Excel) that works in GNOME
`grep` package	Includes the `grep`, `egrep`, and `fgrep` commands that are used to find lines that match a specified text pattern
Groff	A document-formatting system similar to `troff`
GTK+	A GUI toolkit for the X Window System (used to develop GNOME applications)
Gzip	A GNU utility for compressing and decompressing files
Indent	Formats C source code by indenting it in one of several different styles
Less	A page-by-page display program similar to `more`, but with additional capabilities
Libpng	A library for image files in the Portable Network Graphics (PNG) format
m4	An implementation of the traditional UNIX macro processor
Make	A utility that determines which files of a large software package need to be recompiled, and issues the commands to recompile them
Mtools	A set of programs that enables users to read, write, and manipulate files on a DOS file system (typically a floppy disk)
Ncurses	A package for displaying and updating text on text-only terminals
Patch	A GNU version of Larry Wall's program to take the output of diff and apply those differences to an original file to generate the modified version
RCS	The Revision Control System is used for version control and management of source files in software projects
Sed	A stream-oriented version of the `ed` text editor
Sharutils	A package that includes `shar` (used to make shell archives out of many files) and `unshar` (to unpack these shell archives)
Tar	A tape archiving program that includes multivolume support; the capability to archive sparse files (files with big chunks of data that are all zeros), handle compression and decompression, and create remote archives; and other special features for incremental and full backups
Texinfo	A set of utilities that generates printed manuals, plain ASCII text, and online hypertext documentation (called Info), and enables users to view and read online Info documents
Time	A utility that reports the user, system, and actual time that a process uses

GUIs and applications

Face it — typing cryptic Linux commands on a terminal is boring. For average users, using the system through a *graphical user interface* (*GUI*, pronounced "gooey") — one that gives you pictures to click and windows (small *w*) to open — is much easier. This is where the X Window System, or X, comes to the rescue.

X is kind of like Microsoft Windows, but the underlying details of how X works is completely different from Windows. Unlike Windows, X provides the basic features of displaying windows on-screen, but it does not come with any specific look or feel for graphical applications. That look and feel comes from GUIs, such as GNOME and KDE, which make use of the X Window System.

Most Linux distributions come with the X Window System in the form of XFree86 or X.Org X11 — implementations of the X Window System for 80x86 systems. XFree86 and X.Org X11 work with a wide variety of video cards available for today's PCs.

REMEMBER

Until recently, XFree86 from the XFree86 Project (`www.xfree86.org`) was the most commonly used X Window System implementation for x86 systems. However, around version 4.4, some changes to the XFree86 licensing terms caused concerns to many Linux and UNIX vendors — they felt that the licensing terms were no longer compatible with the GNU General Public License (GPL). In January 2004, several vendors formed the X.Org Foundation (`www.x.org`) to promote continued development of an open source X Window System and graphical desktop. The first release of X.Org X11 uses the same code that was used by XFree86 4.4, up until the time when the XFree86 license changes precipitated the creation of X.Org Foundation.

As for the GUI, Linux distributions include one or both of two powerful GUI desktops: KDE (K Desktop Environment) and GNOME (GNU Object Model Environment). If both GNOME and KDE are installed on a PC, you can choose which desktop you want as the default — or switch between the two. KDE and GNOME provide desktops similar to those of Microsoft Windows and the Mac OS. GNOME also comes with the Nautilus graphical shell that makes finding files, running applications, and configuring your Linux system easy. With GNOME or KDE, you can begin using your Linux workstation without having to know cryptic Linux commands. However, if you ever need to use those commands directly, all you have to do is open a terminal window and type them at the prompt.

Linux also comes with many graphical applications. The most noteworthy program is the GIMP (GNU Image Manipulation Program), a program for working with photos and other images. The GIMP's capabilities are on a par with Adobe Photoshop.

Providing common productivity software — such as word-processing, spreadsheet, and database applications — is an area in which Linux used to be lacking. This situation has changed, though. Linux comes with the OpenOffice.org office productivity applications. In addition, you may want to check out these prominent, commercially available office productivity applications for Linux that are not included on this book's companion DVD-ROM:

- **Applixware Office:** Now called Anyware Desktop for Linux, this office package is a good example of productivity software for Linux. You can find it at `www.vistasource.com`.
- **StarOffice:** From Sun Microsystems (`www.sun.com/staroffice`), StarOffice is another well-known productivity software package.
- **CrossOver Office:** From CodeWeavers (`www.codeweavers.com/site/products`), you can use CrossOver Office to install your Microsoft Office applications (Office 97, Office 2000, and Office XP) in Linux.

As you can see, there's no shortage of Linux office applications that are compatible with Microsoft Office.

Networks

Linux comes with everything needed to use the system in networks so that the system can exchange data with other systems. On networks, computers that exchange data have to follow well-defined rules or protocols. A *network protocol* is a method that the sender and receiver agree upon for exchanging data across a network. Such a protocol is similar to the rules you might follow when you're having a polite conversation with someone at a party. You typically start by saying hello, exchanging names, and then taking turns talking. That's about the same way network protocols work. The two computers use the protocol to send bits and bytes back and forth across the network.

One of the most well known and popular network protocols is Transmission Control Protocol/Internet Protocol (TCP/IP). TCP/IP is the protocol of choice on the Internet — the "network of networks" that now spans the globe. Linux supports the TCP/IP protocol and any network applications that make use of TCP/IP.

Internet servers

Some popular network applications are specifically designed to deliver information from one system to another. When you send electronic mail (e-mail) or visit Web sites using a Web browser, you use these network applications (also called Internet services). Here are some common Internet services:

- Electronic mail (e-mail) that you use to send messages to any other person on the Internet using addresses like `joe@someplace.com`.
- World Wide Web (or simply, Web) that you browse using a Web browser.

- News services, where you can read newsgroups and post news items to newsgroups with names such as `comp.os.linux.networking` or `comp.os.linux.setup`.
- File-transfer utilities that you can use to upload and download files.
- Remote login that you can use to connect to and work with another computer (the remote computer) on the Internet — assuming you have the required username and password to access that remote computer.

Any Linux PC can offer these Internet services. To do so, the PC must be connected to the Internet and it must run special server software called *Internet servers*. Each of the servers uses a specific protocol for transferring information. For example, here are some common Internet servers that you find in Linux:

- `sendmail` is the mail server for exchanging e-mail messages between systems using SMTP (Simple Mail Transfer Protocol).
- Apache `httpd` is the Web server for sending documents from one system to another using HTTP (Hypertext Transfer Protocol).
- `vsftpd` is the server for transferring files between computers on the Internet using FTP (File Transfer Protocol).
- `innd` is the news server for distribution of news articles in a store and forward fashion across the Internet using NNTP (Network News Transfer Protocol).
- `in.telnetd` allows a user on one system to log in to another system on the Internet using the TELNET protocol.
- `sshd` allows a user on one system to securely log in to another system on the Internet using the SSH (Secure Shell) protocol.

Software development

Linux is particularly well suited to software development. Straight out of the box, it's chock-full of software-development tools such as the compiler and libraries of code needed to build programs. If you happen to know UNIX and the C programming language, you will feel right at home programming in Linux.

As far as the development environment goes, Linux has the same basic tools (such as an editor, a compiler, and a debugger) that you might use on other UNIX workstations, such as those from IBM, Sun Microsystems, and Hewlett-Packard (HP). What this means is that if you work by day on one of these UNIX workstations, you can use a Linux PC in the evening at home to duplicate that development environment at a fraction of the cost. Then you can either complete work projects at home or devote your time to software you write for fun and to share on the Internet.

Just to give you a sense of Linux's software-development support, here's a list of various features that make Linux a productive software-development environment:

- ✦ GNU C compiler, `gcc`, can compile ANSI-standard C programs.
- ✦ GNU C++ compiler (`g++`) supports ANSI-standard C++ features.
- ✦ The GNU compiler for Java (`gcj`) can compile programs written in the Java programming language.
- ✦ The GNU `make` utility enables you to compile and link large programs.
- ✦ The GNU debugger, `gdb`, enables you to step through your program to find problems and to determine where and how a program failed. (The failed program's memory image is saved in a file named `core`; `gdb` can examine this file.)
- ✦ The GNU profiling utility, `gprof`, enables you to determine the degree to which a piece of software uses your computer's processor time.
- ✦ Subversion, Concurrent Versions System (CVS), and Revision Control System (RCS) maintain version information and control access to the source files so that two programmers don't inadvertently modify the same source file at the same time.
- ✦ The GNU `emacs` editor prepares source files and even launches a compile-link process to build the program.
- ✦ Perl is a scripting language that you can use to write scripts to accomplish a specific task, tying together many smaller programs with Linux commands.
- ✦ The Tool Command Language and its graphical toolkit (`Tcl/Tk`) enable you to build graphical applications rapidly.
- ✦ Python is an interpreted programming language comparable to Perl and Tcl (for example, the Fedora Core installation program, called `anaconda`, is written in Python).
- ✦ Dynamically linked shared libraries allow your actual program files to be much smaller because all the library code that several programs may need is shared — with only one copy loaded in the system's memory.

Online documentation

As you become more adept at using Linux, you may want to look up information quickly — without having to turn the pages of (ahem) this great book, for example. Luckily, Linux comes with enough online information to jog your memory in those situations when you vaguely recall a command's name, but can't remember the exact syntax of what you're supposed to type.

If you use Linux commands, you can view the manual page — commonly referred to as the *man page* — for a command by using the `man` command. (You do have to remember that command in order to access online help.)

You can also get help from the GUI desktops. Both GNOME and KDE desktops come with help viewers to view online help information. In both GNOME and KDE, select Main Menu⇨Help. You can then browse the help information by clicking the links on the initial help window. Figure 1-1 shows a typical help window — this one from a KDE desktop.

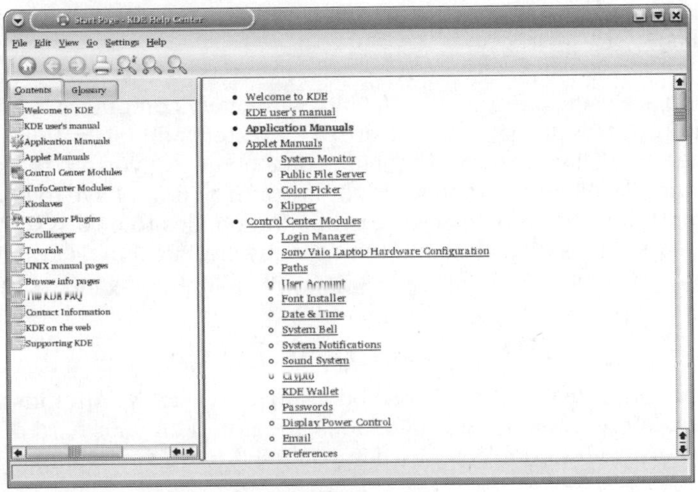

Figure 1-1: Online help is available from the GUI desktops.

What Linux Helps You Manage

As an operating system, Linux acts as the intermediary through which you, as the "lord of the system," manage all the hardware. The hardware includes the system box, the monitor, the keyboard, the mouse, and anything else connected to the system box. The catchall term *peripheral* refers to any equipment attached to the system. If you use a laptop computer, all your hardware is packaged into the laptop.

Inside that system box is the system's brain — the microprocessor (Intel Pentium 4, for example) or the central processing unit (CPU) — that performs the instructions contained in a computer program. When the microprocessor is running a computer program, that program's instructions are stored in the memory or RAM. RAM stands for *Random Access Memory* (that means any part of the memory can be accessed randomly — in arbitrary order).

The system box has another crucial component — the hard drive (or hard disk, as it is sometimes called). The hard drive is the permanent storage space for computer programs and data. It's permanent in the sense that the contents don't disappear when you power off the PC. The hard drive is organized into files, which are in turn organized in a hierarchical fashion into directories and subdirectories (somewhat like organizing papers in folders inside the drawers of a file cabinet).

To keep a Linux system running properly, you or someone else has to make sure that the hardware is working properly and that the files are backed up regularly. There is also the matter of security — making sure that only legitimate people can access and use the system. These tasks are called *system administration*.

If you are using Linux at a big facility with many computers, a full-time system administrator probably takes care of all system administration tasks. On the other hand, if you are running Linux on a home PC, you are the system administrator. Don't let the thought frighten you. You don't have to know any magic incantations or prepare cryptic configuration files to be a system administrator. Most Linux distributions include many graphical tools that makes system administration a "point-and-click" job, just like running any other application.

Disks, CD-ROMs, and DVD-ROMs

Some Linux distributions come on a single DVD-ROM. After installation, the Linux kernel and all the applications are stored on your hard drive — which is where your PC looks first when you tell it to do something.

Typically, the hard drive is prepared to use Linux during the installation process. After that, you usually leave the hard drive alone except to back up the data stored there or (occasionally) to install new applications.

Using CD-ROMs or DVD-ROMs in Linux is easy. While you are logged in at the GNOME or KDE desktop, just pop in a CD or DVD in the drive, and the system should automatically detect the DVD/CD-ROM. Depending on the Linux distribution, either a DVD/CD-ROM icon appears on the desktop or a file manager automatically opens and displays the contents of the DVD/CD-ROM. If all else fails, you can type a simple `mount` command to associate the DVD/CD-ROM with a directory on your system. This whole process of accessing the files on a CD or a DVD from Linux is called *mounting the CD or the DVD*.

Besides the hard drive and DVD/CD-ROM drive, of course, your PC may have other drives, such as a floppy disk or Zip drive, and using those disks in Linux is also simple: You insert a disk and double-click the icon that represents the disk drive on the GUI desktop. Doing so mounts the disk so that you can begin using it.

Peripheral devices

Anything connected to your PC is a peripheral device, and so are some components like sound cards that are installed inside the system box. You can configure and manage these peripheral devices in Linux.

One of the common peripherals is a printer, typically hooked up to the parallel port of your PC. (Many distributions come with a graphical Printer Configuration tool that you can use to configure the printer.)

Another peripheral device that needs configuration is the sound card. Most Linux distributions detect and configure sound cards, just as Windows does. However, if Linux cannot detect the sound card correctly, you may have to run a text-mode or graphical tool to configure the sound card.

Linux configures other peripheral devices such as the mouse and keyboard at the time of installation. You can pretty much leave them alone after installation.

Nowadays, PCs come with the USB (Universal Serial Bus) interface; many devices, including printers and scanners, plug into a PC's USB port. One nice feature of USB devices is that you can plug them into the USB port and unplug them at any time — the device does not have to be connected when you power up the system. These devices are called *hot plug* because you can plug in a device when the system is hot, meaning while it's running. Linux supports many hot plug USB devices. When you plug in a device into the USB port, Linux loads the correct driver and makes the device available to applications.

File systems and sharing

The whole organization of directories and files is called the *file system*. You can, of course, manage the file system using Linux. When you browse the files from the GNOME or KDE graphical desktop, you work with the familiar folder icons.

REMEMBER

A key task in caring for a file system is to back up important files. In Linux, you can use the `tar` program to archive one or more directories on a floppy or a Zip drive. You can even back up files on a tape (if you have a tape drive). If you have a CD burner, you can also burn a CD with the files you want to back up or save for posterity.

Linux can also share parts of the file system with other systems on a network. For example, you can use the Network File System (NFS) to share files with other systems on the network. To a user on the system, the remote system's files appear to be in a directory on the local system.

Linux also comes with the Samba package, which supports file sharing with Microsoft Windows systems. Samba makes a Linux system work just like a Windows file or print server. You can also access shared folders on other Windows systems on your network.

Network

Now that most PCs are either in a local area network or connected to the Internet, you need to manage the network as well. Linux comes with a Network Configuration tool to set up the local area network. For connecting to the Internet using a modem, there is usually a GUI Internet Dialup Tool.

If you connect to the Internet using DSL (that's the fast Internet connection from the phone company) or cable modem, you need a PC with an Ethernet card that connects to the cable or DSL modem. It also means that you have to set up a local area network and configure the Ethernet card. But fortunately, these steps are typically a part of Linux installation. If you want to do the configurations later, you can by using a GUI network configuration tool.

Linux also includes tools for configuring a *firewall,* a protective buffer that helps keep your system relatively secure from anyone trying to snoop over your Internet connection. You can configure the firewall by using `iptables` commands or by running a GUI firewall configuration tool.

Getting Started

Based on my personal experience in learning new subjects, I prescribe a four-step process to get started with Linux:

1. **Install** Linux on your PC.
2. **Configure** Linux so that everything works to your liking.
3. **Explore** the GUI desktops and the applications.
4. **Learn** the details of specific subjects such as Internet servers.

In the following sections, I explain this prescription a bit more.

Install

Microsoft Windows comes installed on your new PC, but Linux usually doesn't. So your first hurdle is to get Linux onto your PC.

After you overcome that initial human fear of the unknown, I'll bet you find Linux fairly easy to install — but where do you *get* it in the first place? Well, the good news is that it's free — available just for the downloading. For example, you can visit the Linux Online Web site at `www.linux.org` and click the Download button.

TIP

Because the complete distribution is *huge* — it takes up several CDs or a single DVD — your best bet is to buy a book (such as this one) that comes with Linux on a DVD-ROM. You can then do the installation by following the instructions in the book.

Just to pique your curiosity, installation involves creating space on the hard drive for both Windows and Linux. Then a step creates the Linux partitions and installs Linux from the DVD. Along the way, you configure many items — from the Ethernet card (if any) to the X Window System.

Configure

When you finish installing Linux, the next step is to configure individual system components (for example, the sound card and the printer) and tweak any needed settings that aren't configured during installation.

If you aren't getting a graphical login screen, for example, Linux comes with tools that help you troubleshoot that problem (typically by configuring the X Window System).

You also want to configure your GUI desktop of choice — GNOME or KDE. Each has configuration tools. You can use these tools to adjust the look and feel of the desktop (background, title fonts, even the entire color scheme).

After you're through with the configuration step, all the hardware on your system and the applications run to your liking.

Explore

With a properly configured Linux PC at your disposal, you are ready to explore Linux itself. You can begin the exploration from the GUI desktop that you get after logging in.

Explore the GUI desktops — GNOME and KDE — and the folders and files that make up the Linux file system. You can also try out the applications from the desktop. You find office and multimedia applications and databases to explore.

Also try out the *shell* — open up a terminal window and type some Linux commands in that window. You can also explore the text editors that work in text mode. Knowing how to edit text files without the GUI just in case the GUI is not available is a good idea. At least you won't be helpless.

Learn

After you explore the Linux landscape and know what is what, you can then dig in deeper and find out more about specific subject areas. For example, you may be interested in setting up Internet servers. You can then learn the details of setting up individual servers such as `sendmail` for e-mail, Apache for a Web server, and the INN server for news.

You can choose to find out about many more areas, such as security, programming, and system administration.

Of course, you can expect this step to go on and on, even after you have your system running the way you want it — for now. After all, learning is a lifelong journey.

Bon voyage!

Chapter 2: Installing Linux

In This Chapter

- **Understanding the installation steps**
- **Burning CDs for your distribution**
- **Trying out the Knoppix Live CD**
- **Making a list of your PC's hardware**
- **Setting aside hard drive space for Linux**
- **Installing Debian**
- **Installing Fedora Core**
- **Installing SUSE Linux**
- **Installing Xandros Desktop**

PCs come with Microsoft Windows preinstalled. If you want to use Linux, you first have to install it. This book comes with a DVD-ROM that contains several Linux distributions — Debian, Fedora, Knoppix, SUSE, and Xandros. Some are full distributions and a few are Live CDs that you can try without installing on the hard drive. (*Full distributions* mean everything you expect to get in those distributions, whereas *Live CDs* mean CDs from which you can directly boot Linux.) The version of Xandros on the DVD is a limited version of Xandros Desktop called the Open Circulation Edition. All you have to do to install or try any of these distributions is follow the steps in this chapter.

You may feel a tad worried about installing a new operating system on your PC because it's a bit like brain surgery — or, rather, more like grafting on a new brain because you can install Linux in addition to Microsoft Windows. When you install two operating systems like that, you can choose to start one or the other as you power up the PC. The biggest headache in adding Linux to a PC with Windows is creating a new *disk partition* — basically setting aside a part of the hard drive for Linux. The rest of the installation is fairly routine — just a matter of following the instructions. If you want to try any of the Live CDs, you don't have to do any disk partitioning — just boot your PC from the Live CD. But most of all, just take a deep breath and exhale slooowwwly. You have nothing to worry about because I explain everything in this chapter.

Following the Installation Steps

Installing any Linux distribution involves a number of steps — and I want to walk you through them briefly, without the details. Then you can follow the detailed steps for the specific distributions and install what you want from this book's companion DVD-ROM.

Before I explain the details of installing Linux, I want to explain how we have packed several Linux distributions on the DVD. Here's the scoop on the companion DVD:

- It's a Fedora Core DVD together with Knoppix, which means you can boot your PC from the DVD and either run Knoppix Live CD or install Fedora Core directly from the DVD.
- In addition to the Fedora Core files, the DVD contains a folder within which there are several folders, one for each of the distributions — Debian, Knoppix, SUSE, and Xandros. In each folder, you find that distribution's ISO image files. You have to burn these ISO images onto CDs before using them to install that distribution.
- SUSE is also in the form of a Live CD that you can use to boot your PC and run directly from the CD (that is, the CD you burned with the SUSE ISO image).

Some Linux distributions require that you have quite a bit of information about your PC's hardware on-hand before installation. If you are planning to install Debian, you should go ahead and gather information about your PC and its peripheral components prior to starting the installation. Luckily, most other Linux installation programs can detect and work with most PC peripherals. Nevertheless, it's a good idea to figure out your PC's hardware so that you can troubleshoot in case something goes wrong with the installation.

The very first step is to burn the CDs for your distribution, unless you are planning to install Fedora Core. You can burn the CDs on any system that has a CD burner. Typically, if you already have a Windows PC with a CD burner, you can simply use that system to burn the CDs. Remember that you must have a DVD drive as well because you have to burn the CDs from this book's companion DVD-ROM. A PC with a combination DVD-ROM and CD burner would be adequate for this task.

The second step is to make sure that your PC can boot from the DVD/CD-ROM drive. Most new PCs can boot directly from the DVD/CD-ROM drive, but some PCs may require intervention from you. Typically, the PC may be set to boot from the hard drive before the DVD/CD drive, and you have to get into SETUP to change the order of boot devices. To set up a PC to boot from the DVD drive, you have to go into SETUP as the PC powers up. The exact steps for entering SETUP and setting the boot device vary from one PC to the next, but typically they involve pressing a key such as F2. As the PC powers up, a brief message tells you what key to press to enter SETUP. When you're in SETUP, you can designate the DVD/CD drive as the boot device. After your PC is set up to boot from the DVD/CD drive, simply put the DVD or CD in the DVD/CD drive and restart your PC.

If you are planning to try the Live CD distributions such as Knoppix or SUSE Live Eval, then the third step is to boot your PC from the Live CD. Otherwise, the third step is to make room for Linux on your PC's hard drive. If you're running Microsoft Windows, this step can be easy or hard, depending on whether you want to *replace* Windows with Linux or keep *both* Windows and Fedora Core.

If you want to install Linux without removing (or disturbing) Windows, remember that your existing operating system — which is, I assume, Windows 95, 98, Me, NT, 2000, or XP — is currently using the entire hard drive. That means you have to *partition* (divide) the hard drive so that Windows can live on one part of it and Linux can live on the other. Doing so can be a scary step because you run the risk of ruining the hard drive and wiping out whatever is on the drive.

To set aside space on your hard drive that the Linux installation program can use, you should use a partitioning program to help you create the partition. If your PC runs Windows NT, 2000, or XP, consider investing in a commercial hard drive partitioning product such as Symantec's Norton PartitionMagic (`www.powerquest.com/partitionmagic`), which works for Windows 95/98/Me systems as well.

Note that the installers for some Linux distributions such as Xandros Desktop can automatically create partitions for Linux by reducing the size of a Windows partition. In that case, you do not need to use a tool such as PartitionMagic to shrink the size of the existing Windows partition on your hard drive.

After you set aside a hard drive partition for Linux, you can boot the PC from the selected distribution's CD and start the Linux installation. Quite a few steps occur during installation and they vary from one distribution to another, but, when you've come this far, it should be smooth sailing. Just go through the installation screens and you are done in an hour or two. Most installers bring up a graphical user interface (GUI) and guide you through all the steps. One key step during installation involves partitioning the hard drive again, but this time you simply split the extra partition you created earlier. After a few configuration steps, such as setting up the network and the time zone, you select the software packages to install and then let the installer complete the remaining installation chores.

At the end of the installation, you reboot the PC and when Linux runs for the first time, you get a chance to perform some more configuration steps and install additional software packages.

Burning CDs from ISO Images

This book's companion DVD includes Debian, Knoppix, SUSE, and Xandros distributions in the form of ISO images, organized into separate folders. To install any of these distributions, you must first burn the selected distribution's ISO images onto CDs. You can typically perform this step on a PC with a CD burner, most likely under Microsoft Windows because most new PCs come with Windows preinstalled.

The exact steps for burning a CD from an ISO image depends on the CD burning application that you use. The general steps are as follows:

1. **Place the companion DVD-ROM into the PC's DVD drive.**

   If your DVD drive is a combination DVD/CD burner, you have to first copy the ISO image files of the Linux distribution from the DVD to the PC's hard drive so that you can use the same drive to burn the CDs.

2. **Start the CD burner application.**
3. **From the CD burner application, open the image file.**

   The exact steps depend on the CD burner application. Typically, you do this by selecting File⇨Open. From the Open dialog box, select the ISO image file for the distribution. If you are unsure, search the application's online help for information on burning a CD from an ISO image.

4. **Place a blank recordable CD in the CD burner.**
5. **Burn the ISO image onto the recordable CD.**

   Typically, the CD burner application has a toolbar button that you can click to start burning the ISO image onto the blank CD.

6. **If the distribution has more ISO images, repeat Steps 2 through 4 for the remaining ISO images.**

   Live CD distributions such as SUSE Live Eval come in a single ISO image that you can burn on a single CD. Other distributions typically come in multiple ISO images and you have to burn each image file onto a separate CD.

Checking Your PC's Hardware

If you're concerned that your PC may not be able to run Linux, here are some of the key components in your PC that you need to consider before you start the Linux installation:

✦ **DVD/CD-ROM:** You must have a DVD/CD-ROM drive and the PC must be able to boot from that drive. The exact model doesn't matter. What matters is how the DVD/CD-ROM drive connects to the PC. Most new PCs have DVD/CD-ROM drives that connect to the hard drive controller (called IDE for Integrated Drive Electronics or ATA for AT Attachment). If you add an external DVD/CD drive, it most likely connects to the USB port. Any IDE/ATA or USB DVD/CD-ROM works in Linux.

- **Hard drives:** Any IDE disk drive works in Linux. Another type of hard drive controller is SCSI (Small Computer System Interface), which Linux also supports. To comfortably install and play with Linux, you need about 5GB of hard drive space. On the other hand, to try the Live CD versions of Linux such as Knoppix, you don't need any space on the hard drive.
- **Keyboard:** All keyboards work with Linux and the X Window System.
- **Modem:** If you plan to dial out to the Internet, you need a modem that Linux supports. For software-based modems, called *soft modems* or *win-modems,* you may have to download a driver from the manufacturer (it may or may not be freely available).
- **Monitor:** The kind of monitor is not particularly critical except that it must be capable of displaying the screen resolutions that the video card uses. The screen resolution is expressed in terms of the number of picture elements (pixels), horizontally and vertically (for example, 1024 x 768). The installer can detect most modern monitors. If it does not detect your monitor, you can select a generic monitor type with a specific resolution such as 1024 x 768. You can also specify the monitor by its make and model (which you can find on the back of the monitor).
- **Mouse:** The installation program can detect the mouse. All types of mouse (such as PS/2 or USB) work with Linux and the X Window System.
- **Network card:** Not all PCs have network cards, but if yours does, the installer can probably detect and use it. If you have problems, try to find the make and model (such as *Linksys LNE100TX Fast Ethernet Adapter*) so that you can search for information on whether Linux supports that card or not.
- **Processor:** A 400 MHz Pentium II or better is best. The processor speed, expressed in MHz (megahertz) or GHz (gigahertz), is not that important as long as it's over 400 MHz, but the faster the better. Linux can run on other Intel-compatible processors such as AMD, Cyrix, and VIA processors.
- **RAM:** RAM is the amount of memory your system has. As with processing speed, the more RAM, the better. You need 256MB to install both Linux and the X Window System and to comfortably run a GUI desktop.
- **SCSI controller:** Some high-performance PCs have SCSI controllers that connect disk drives and other peripherals to a PC. If your PC happens to have a SCSI controller, you might want to find out the make and model of the controller.

- **Sound card:** If your PC has a sound card and you want to have sound in Linux, you have to make sure it's compatible. You can configure the sound card after successfully installing Linux.
- **Video card:** Linux works fine with all video cards (also known as *display adapters*) in text mode, but if you want the GUI, you need a video card that works with the X Window System. The installer can detect a supported video card and configure the X Window System correctly. However, if the installer cannot detect the video card, it helps if you know the make and model of your video card.

In addition to this hardware, you also need to find out the make and model of any printer you plan to use in Linux.

TIP

Many distributions, such as Debian GNU/Linux, will work on any hardware that's compatible with the Linux kernel. For information on Linux-compatible hardware, see `www.tldp.org/HOWTO/Hardware-HOWTO`.

DISTRIBUTION SPECIFIC

To check if your PC's hardware is compatible with SUSE Linux, visit the SUSE Linux Hardware Database at `hardwaredb.suse.de`. For Xandros Desktop, you can find the hardware compatibility list at `www.xandros.com/support/hcl.html`.

Setting Aside Space for Linux

In a typical Windows PC, Windows is sitting on one big partition, taking over the whole hard drive. You want to shrink that partition and create room for Linux. During Linux installation, the installation program uses the free space for the Linux partitions.

DISTRIBUTION SPECIFIC

To try out any of the Live CD distributions — Knoppix or SUSE Live Eval — you don't have to repartition your hard drive. Just boot your PC from the Live CD and you can start using these distributions. The Xandros installer can repartition a Windows partition (performing the same task as a tool such as PartitionMagic), so you do not need to perform the repartitioning step beforehand. If you are planning to install Fedora Core, Debian, or any other Linux distribution on the hard drive, then you have to repartition your hard drive.

Norton PartitionMagic, from Symantec, can resize and split disk partitions in all Microsoft operating systems from Windows 95/98/Me to Windows NT/2000/XP. It's a commercial product, so you have to buy it to use it. At the time I'm writing this, the list price of Norton PartitionMagic 8.0 is $69.95. You can read about it and buy it at `www.powerquest.com/partitionmagic`.

Resizing the disk partition always involves the risk of losing all data on the hard drive. Therefore, before you resize hard drive partitions using a disk-partitioning tool such as PartitionMagic, *back up your hard drive*. After making your backup — and before you do *anything* to the partitions — please make sure that you can restore your files from the backup.

When you run PartitionMagic, it shows the current partitions in a window. If you're running Windows XP, your hard drive typically has two partitions: one small, hidden partition that contains Windows XP installation files, and a huge second NTFS partition that serves as the C: drive. You have to reduce the size of the existing C: drive. Doing so creates unused space following that partition. Then, during Fedora Core installation, the installation program can create new Linux partitions in the unused space.

To reduce the size of the Windows partition using PartitionMagic, follow these steps:

1. **In the partition map in PartitionMagic's main window, right-click the partition and select Resize/Move from the context menu.**

   The Resize Partition dialog box appears.

2. **In the Resize Partition dialog box, click and drag the right edge of the partition to a smaller size.**

   For a large hard drive (anything over 10GB), reduce the Windows partition to 5GB and leave the rest for Fedora Core. If you have to live with a smaller drive, try to create at least 4GB of space for Linux.

3. **Click OK and then Apply to apply the changes. After PartitionMagic has made the changes, click OK.**

4. **Reboot the PC.**

You don't have to do anything with the hard drive space left over after shrinking the partition that used to be the C: drive. During installation, the Linux installer uses that free space to install Linux.

If you don't want to buy PartitionMagic, you could install a Linux distribution such as Xandros that comes with an installer that can perform this step. If you don't feel comfortable mucking around with the hard drive partitions, you can always try Linux with the Knoppix Live CD.

Trying Out Knoppix Live CD

To try out Knoppix, follow these steps:

1. **Boot your PC from this book's companion DVD.**

A `boot:` prompt appears. At this prompt, you can enter various commands to control the boot process. In particular, you can type commands to disable some types of hardware detection that may be causing the installation to fail.

2. **A few minutes later, you should see the KDE GUI desktop that Knoppix uses.**

   You can now start using Knoppix.

TIP

If you are trying Knoppix on a laptop and it hangs after displaying a message about probing SCSI (that's the name of a type of interface), then reboot and when the boot prompt appears, type **knoppix noscsi**. That should get you through the problem.

After you get the Knoppix desktop, you can begin exploring Knoppix. Consult Chapter 4 of this minibook for more information on trying out Linux.

Installing Debian GNU/Linux

To install Debian GNU/Linux, you first have to burn the CDs from the ISO images in the Debian folder of the companion DVD (see the "Burning CDs from ISO Images" section, earlier in this chapter).

REMEMBER

Note that the Debian installer does not install the X Window System. You have to install X as a separate package after you finish installing the base operating system.

Getting an overview of the installation

When you have the Debian CDs in hand, you are ready to install Debian GNU/Linux. Before you dive into the installation, here is an overview of the major steps in installing Debian:

1. Before you begin the installation, remember to gather information about your computer's hardware because you may need to provide some details if the Debian installer cannot detect some peripheral on your PC.
2. Boot the PC from the first Debian CD. You can also boot from an installer boot CD that's available in ISO image form at `www.debian.org/devel/debian-installer`. After the PC boots, you see a boot screen with a `boot:` prompt. You can press Enter to proceed, but if the system hangs, you may need to reboot again and enter some boot options such as `linux acpi=off` at the boot prompt. The Linux kernel then boots and starts the Debian installer.
3. Select the installation language.

4. Configure the network interface.
5. Create the hard drive partitions that will be used by Debian. At a minimum, you have to create a swap partition and a partition for the root file system.
6. Install and set up the base system that includes the Linux kernel and GNU utilities.
7. Configure and install the GRUB boot loader so that it can start up Debian as well as other operating systems installed on your hard drive.
8. Reboot the PC to start the base Debian system and finish the configuration steps — setting the time zone, setting the `root` password, and creating a normal user account, for example.
9. Configure the Advanced Package Tool (APT) for further package installations. You have to identify sources such as the CDs (if you have them) and Internet sites where Debian packages can be found. The installer provides suggestions; all you have to do is select the sources.
10. Select software packages to install, including the desktop and various servers.
11. The installer either downloads the files from the Internet or gets what it needs from the CD, installs all selected software, and then configures all packages, including the X Window System. After completing the configurations, the installer starts X and displays a graphical login screen.

After you install Debian GNU/Linux, you can use the `apt-get` command-line tool to install other packages and even upgrade the entire distribution.

Completing the Debian installation

Start by inserting the first CD into your PC's DVD/CD drive and then reboot the PC. The PC boots from the CD and displays a screen that says `Press F1 for help`. It's a good idea to press F1 and see the Help index, which tells you what information you can get by pressing various function keys from F1 through F10. Table 2-1 summarizes the help information that the function keys provide.

Table 2-1 Function Keys at Debian Installer Boot Screen

Function Key	*What It Displays*
F1	Help index
F2	What your PC must have in terms of memory and hard drive space for installing Debian (at least 32MB of memory and 256MB hard drive space for a minimal installation, but this could change in the future)

(continued)

Table 2-1 *(continued)*

Function Key	*What It Displays*
F3	The ways you can boot Linux from the CD (for example, by typing **linux** or **expert** or **linux26** or **expert26**, with each loading a different kernel)
F4	An overview of the boot parameters you can enter and the details you can get by pressing the function keys F5, F6, and F7
F5	Boot parameters for special machines, such as some IBM Thinkpads and laptops with display problems
F6	Boot parameters for special disk controllers, such as Adaptec 151x, 152x, 1542, 274x, and 284x
F7	Boot parameters for use by the installer (for example, if you don't want the installer to probe for USB, add the parameter `debian-installer/probe/usb=false`)
F8	Points you to `www.debian.org` and tells you how to get help
F9	Brief mention of the Debian project
F10	Information about copyrights and warranties that apply to Debian GNU/Linux

After reading the help information, you can either press Enter to start or enter any boot parameters that you need for your PC. After the Linux kernel loads, follow these steps to complete the Debian GNU/Linux installation (make sure your PC has a broadband Internet connection such as DSL or cable modem):

1. **Select the language, the country or region, and the keyboard layout from the initial text-mode screens.**

   Use the arrow keys to make your selection and press Enter after each selection. The installer then detects the hardware and loads components of the Debian installer from the CD-ROM. Then the installer prompts for parameters to configure the network.

2. **Enter the host name for your computer and select whether you want to automatically configure the network with Dynamic Host Configuration Protocol (DHCP).**

   If your network does not have a DHCP server, you have to specify the IP addresses of the network interface and the name server. With DHCP, the installer gets the required network parameters from a local DHCP server. Then the Debian installer starts the disk partitioning tool that displays several options, as shown in Figure 2-1.

3. **If you have created free space for Debian, select the default choice of Use the Largest Continuous Free Space and press Enter.**

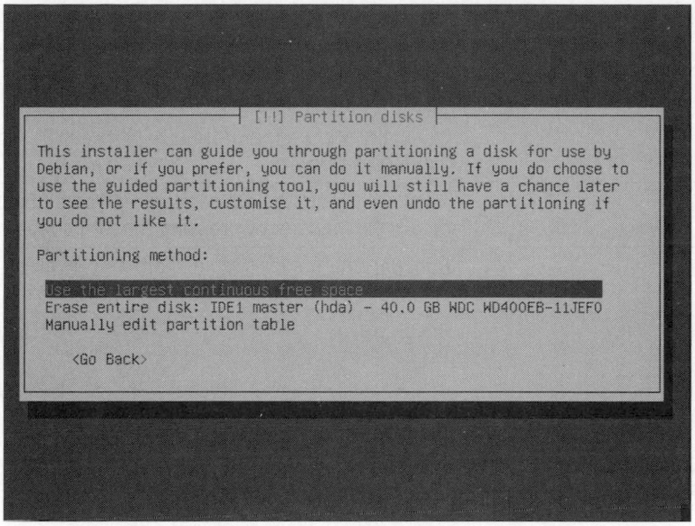

Figure 2-1: Debian installer displays these initial disk partitioning options.

If your hard drive already has partitions that you want to use for Debian, select the Manually Edit Partition Table option and press Enter. The installer displays further options together with the list of existing partitions, as shown in Figure 2-2.

You can click on one of the partitions and then edit its characteristics — what file system to use, for example — and select a mount point for the partition. When you're done, you can finish partitioning and write the partition table to the hard drive. (See Figure 2-3.)

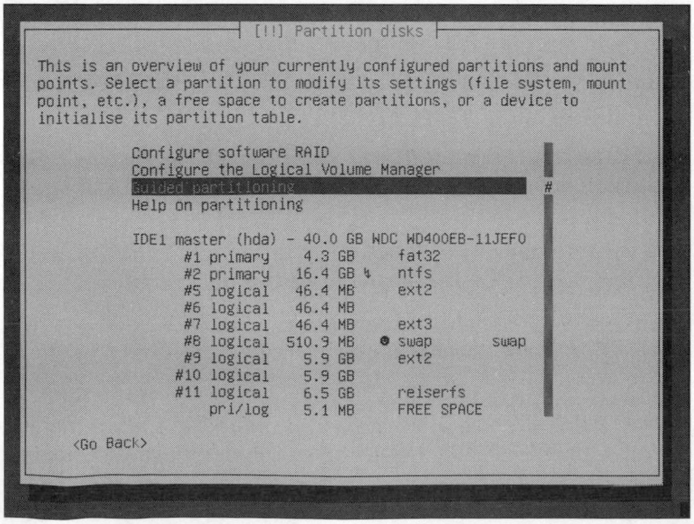

Figure 2-2: You can manually edit disk partitions from this screen.

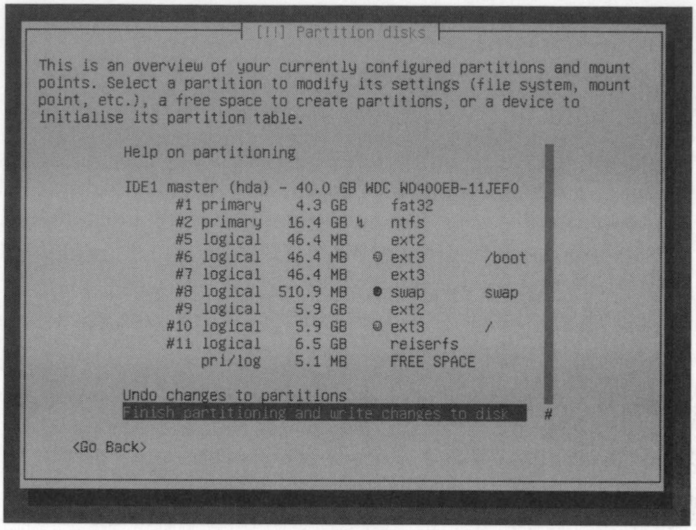

Figure 2-3: When you're done, write the partition table to the hard drive.

The installer warns you that data on the selected partitions will be destroyed, and after you select Yes, it completes the partitioning and begins installing the base system.

After installing the base operating system, the installer detects other operating systems on any of the disk partitions and recommends installing the GRUB boot loader on the hard drive's first sector, called the *Master Boot Record (MBR)*.

4. **Install the GRUB boot loader and reboot the PC.**

   The installer finishes installing the boot loader. Then it ejects the CD and reboots the PC. When the PC reboots, Debian starts and guides you through a number of configuration steps.

5. **Select the time zone and indicate if the PC's hardware clock is set to Greenwich Mean Time (GMT).**

   The answer is usually no.

6. **Enter the `root` (the super user) password.**

7. **Set up a normal user account by entering the requested information: the username, the full name, and the password.**

8. **Configure APT by indicating sources from where you want Debian to download software packages.**

   You have to pick a country — and a server in that country — identifying the FTP and Web repositories containing the Debian packages. If your PC is behind a HTTP proxy, you can specify the proxy as well (if not, just ignore this part). Later on, you can use the `apt-get` command to install or update various software packages that are available in the Debian format. You can also identify a CD as a source of Debian packages, but you can always get the latest software if you identify a server as the source.

9. **Select the software packages to install.**

   You can pick from preconfigured packages that include: Desktop environment, Web server, Print server, DNS server, File Server, Mail server, and SQL database. You can also manually select packages. If you select the Desktop environment package, you'll get the X Window System and the KDE desktop.

   The installer then begins to download and install the selected packages.

10. **Answer configuration questions as the installer prompts for information to configure the software packages it has downloaded and installed.**

    The XFree86 package (the X Window System) is one of the packages the installer configures. After finishing all the configurations, the installer starts X and you get a graphical login prompt.

11. **Log in at the graphical login screen.**

    By default, the Debian installer installs the GNOME Desktop Manager (gdm), which starts the KDE desktop. That's why the login screen says GNOME Desktop Manager, but after you log in, you get the KDE desktop.

That's it! You have Debian up and running now. You can explore it at your leisure and install more software packages as you need them and as you become more knowledgeable about Debian.

Installing Fedora Core

To install Fedora Core, insert this book's companion DVD in the DVD drive and restart your PC. (In Windows, choose Start➪Shutdown and then select Restart from the dialog box.) If you are using CDs, the installation steps are the same as that for the DVD except that you have to swap CDs when prompted by the installation program.

If your PC isn't already set to boot from DVD drive, you have to get into SETUP to change the order of boot devices.

After your PC powers up, it loads the Linux kernel from the DVD and the Linux kernel starts running the Fedora Core installation program. For the rest of the installation, you work with the installation program's GUI screens.

After a few moments, the text screen displays a Welcome message and a `boot:` prompt. The Welcome message tells you that help is available by pressing one of the function keys F1 through F5. To start installing Fedora Core immediately, press Enter. You can also enter other options at the `boot:` prompt. For example, if you think the DVD might be corrupted, type **linux mediacheck** to test the DVD media for any problems. Press Enter to perform the media check. After the media check, you can continue with the installation.

Installing Fedora Core from the companion DVD-ROM on a fast (400MHz or better) Pentium PC takes about an hour or so, if you install nearly all packages.

The Fedora Core installation program *probes* — attempts to determine the presence of — specific hardware and tailors the installation steps accordingly. For example, if the installation program detects a network card, the program automatically displays the screens needed to configure your PC to work with the network in Linux. You may see a different sequence of screens from what I show in the following sections; the exact sequence depends on your PC's specific hardware configuration.

If you run into any problems during the installation, turn to Chapter 3 of this minibook. That chapter shows you how to troubleshoot common installation problems.

Selecting keyboard and installation type

This first phase of the installation is where you go through a number of steps before moving on to create the disk partitions for Fedora Core. Here are the steps in the first phase:

1. **Select the language you want from the list of languages on-screen, and then click Next to proceed to the next step.**

   Each screen has online help available on the left side of the screen. You can read the Help message to find out more about what you're supposed to do in a specific screen. After you select the language, the installer displays a list of keyboard layouts.

2. **Select a keyboard layout suitable for your language's character set (for example, U.S. English in the United States), and then click Next.**

   The installation program next displays a screen asking whether you want to install a new system or upgrade an older Fedora Core installation.

3. **For a new Fedora Core installation, click Install and then select the installation type.**

   For a new installation, you have to select one of the following installation types — Personal Desktop, Workstation, Server, or Custom. The Personal Desktop, Workstation, and Server installations simplify the installation process by partitioning the hard drive in a predefined manner. The Personal Desktop installation creates a Fedora Core system with a graphical environment along with productivity applications.

A Workstation-class installation installs a graphical environment as well as software development tools. This type of installation also deletes all currently existing Linux-related partitions, creating a set of new partitions for Linux.

WARNING!

A Server-class installation deletes *all* existing disk partitions, including any existing Windows partitions, and creates a whole slew of Linux partitions. Server-class installation does not install the graphical environment.

TIP

For maximum flexibility, select the Custom installation. That way you can select only the packages you want to try out.

The next major phase of installation involves partitioning the hard drive for use in Fedora Core.

Partitioning the hard drive for Fedora Core

The Fedora Core installer displays a screen that gives you the following options for partitioning and using the hard drive:

- **Automatically Partition:** This option (the one most users choose) causes the Fedora Core installation program to create new partitions for installing Linux according to your chosen installation type, such as workstation or server. After the automatic partitioning, you get a chance to customize the partitions.
- **Manually Partition with Disk Druid:** With this option, you can use the Disk Druid program that lets you partition the hard drive and, at the same time, specify which parts of the Linux file system to load, and on which partition(s).

TIP

From the disk-partitioning strategy screen, select the first option to have the installer automatically partition the hard drive for you. The Fedora Core installer then displays another screen (see Figure 2-4) that asks you how you want the automatic partitioning to be done.

You can select from three options:

- **Remove All Linux Partitions on This System:** This option causes the Fedora Core installer to remove all existing Linux partitions and to create new partitions for installing Fedora Core. You can use this option if you already have any version of Linux installed on your PC and want to wipe it out and install the latest version of Fedora Core.
- **Remove All Partitions on This System:** This option is similar to the first option, except that the installation program removes all partitions, including those used by other operating systems such as Microsoft Windows. *Use this only if you want Fedora Core as the only operating system for your PC.*

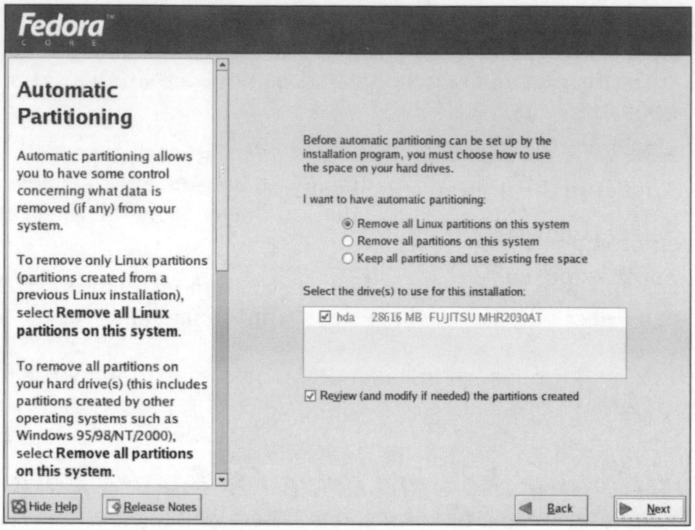

Figure 2-4: Select an automatic partitioning option from this screen.

✦ **Keep All Partitions and Use Existing Free Space:** If you created space for Linux by using PartitionMagic or the FIPS utility, select this option to create the Linux partitions using the free space on the hard drive. If you are installing Fedora Core on a new PC after resizing the partition, this option is the right one to choose.

Select the appropriate option and click Next. For example, if you select the first option, the Fedora Core installation program displays a dialog box to confirm your choice and to point out that all data in the existing Linux partitions will be lost. Click Yes to continue. The installation program shows the partitions it has prepared, as shown in Figure 2-5. The exact appearance of this screen depends on your hard drive's current partitions.

This Disk Setup screen displays a list of disk drives and the current partition information for one of the drives. If you want to accept these partitions as is, click Next to proceed.

WARNING! If your PC doesn't have enough memory (typically less than 128MB), the installer asks if it can write the partition table and activate the swap partition. After you do this, your hard drive partitions are changed. Click Yes *only* if you are committed to the new partitions and definitely want to install Fedora Core.

Setting up key system parameters

With the disk partitioning out of the way, you're almost ready to begin installing the software packages. First, the Fedora Core installer prompts you to set up some key system parameters. Specifically, you have to do the following:

- ✦ Install the boot loader
- ✦ Configure the network
- ✦ Configure the firewall and SELinux
- ✦ Select languages to support
- ✦ Set the time zone
- ✦ Set the `root` password

You can go through these steps fairly quickly.

Installing the boot loader

The installer displays a screen from where you can install the GRUB boot loader. (GRUB stands for *GRand Unified Bootloader.* There is another boot loader named LILO — *Linux Loader,* but Fedora Core uses GRUB by default.) The *boot loader* is a tiny program that resides on the hard drive and starts an operating system when you power up your PC. If you have Windows on your hard drive, you can configure the boot loader to load Windows or any other installed operating systems as well.

You can skip the boot loader installation entirely. However, if you choose not to install any boot loader, definitely create a boot disk later on. Otherwise, you cannot start Fedora Core when you reboot the PC even though Fedora Core would be installed on the hard drive. You get a chance to create the boot disk at the very end of the installation.

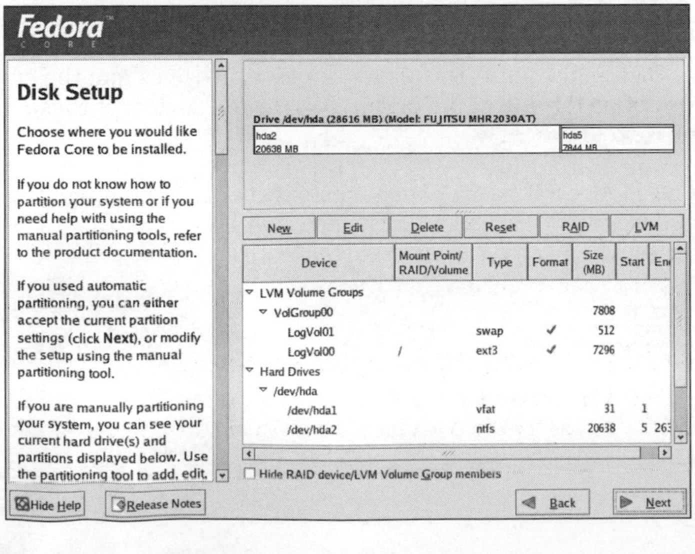

Figure 2-5: Disk partitions created by the Fedora Core installer.

For greater security (so no one can boot your system without a password), select the Use a Boot Loader Password check box. The installer displays a dialog box in which you can specify a password for GRUB.

After making your selections, click Next to continue.

Configuring the network

Assuming that your PC has a network card and the Linux kernel detects that card, the Fedora Core installer displays the network configuration screen (as shown in Figure 2-6).

From this screen, you can set up your network card's IP address (so other PCs in the network can talk to your PC). This screen displays a list of the network devices (for example, Ethernet cards) installed in your PC. For each network device, you can indicate how the IP address is set. Click the Edit button next to the list and a dialog box appears; there you can specify the options.

You can specify the IP (Internet Protocol) address for the network card automatically using DHCP, where your PC gets its IP address and other network information from a DHCP server. This is often the case if your PC is connected to a DSL or cable modem router.

Select DHCP only if a DHCP server is running on your local area network. If you choose DHCP, your network configuration is set automatically and you can skip the rest of this section.

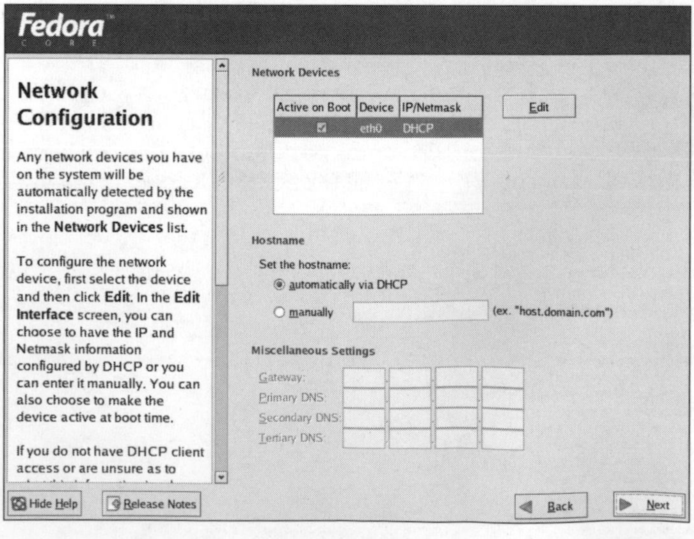

Figure 2-6: Configure the network options from this screen.

If you do not configure the network using DHCP, you have to provide an IP address and other network information such as the IP addresses of the primary DNS and the secondary DNS (the name servers that translate machine names such as `www.amazon.com` into IP addresses). Enter any needed parameters and click Next to continue.

Configuring the firewall and SELinux

In this step, select a predefined level of security and the level of Security Enhanced Linux (SELinux) access control and customize these security levels to suit your needs. Note that SELinux is a mandatory access control framework developed by the National Security Agency (NSA), a U.S. government agency, and is included in Linux kernel 2.6. You can find more about SELinux at the NSA's Web site, `www.nsa.gov/selinux`. To explain briefly, SELinux access control goes beyond the traditional access control in Linux, which is based on the user and group ID that owns a process or a file. SELinux views the system in terms of *subjects* (users or processes) and *objects* (files, devices, any system resources). Subjects can take on different *roles,* such as normal user or system administrator. Each subject also has a *domain* and each object has a *type*. SELinux provides fine-grained control over who can access what in a Linux system by defining what domains can access what types and how one domain can transition into another when programs execute. It sounds confusing, but you don't need to understand everything to enjoy the increased security provided by SELinux.

For the firewall, you have to select one of the following options:

- **No firewall** means that your system accepts all types of connections and does not perform any security checking. Use this option only if your system runs in a trusted network or if you plan to set up a firewall configuration later on (the sooner the better).
- **Enable firewall** means that you want to set up a firewall. You can then select the services such as Mail and FTP that are allowed to pass through the firewall. You can also enter port numbers that are allowed through the firewall. You can also allow all traffic from a specific network interface card.

Additionally, you can also enable selected services to pass through the firewall.

For the SELinux access control configuration, leave the SELinux access control set at its default setting.

When you're done configuring the firewall and setting SELinux, click Next to continue.

Selecting languages to support

In this step, you select one or more languages that your Fedora Core system must support when the installation is complete. These are the languages that the system supports when you reboot the PC after completing your Fedora Core installation. From the Language Support Selection screen, select one or more languages to support. You must also select a default language. Then click Next to continue.

Setting the time zone

After completing the network configuration, select the time zone — the difference between the local time and the current time in Greenwich, England, which is the standard reference time (also known as *Greenwich Mean Time* or GMT as well as UCT or *Universal Coordinate Time*). The installer shows you a GUI from which you can select the time zone in terms of a geographic location. After you select your time zone, click Next to continue.

Setting the root password

The installer displays the Set Root Password screen from which you can set the `root` password. Earlier versions of the Fedora Core installer enabled you to add one or more user accounts at this step, but now you get a chance to add user accounts when you run Fedora Core for the first time. (See Chapter 4 of this minibook.)

The *`root` user* is the *superuser* in Linux — the one who can do anything in the system. You're better off reserving that account for your own exclusive use. You need to assign a password that you can remember but that others cannot guess easily. Make the password at least eight characters long, include a mix of letters and numbers, and (for good measure) throw in some special characters, such as + or *.

Type the password on the first line and re-enter the password on the next line. Each character in the password appears as an asterisk (*) on-screen. You have to type the password twice, and both entries must match before the installation program accepts it. This feature ensures that a mistyped (or guessed) password doesn't work.

You must enter the `root` password before you can proceed with the rest of the installation. After you have done so, click the Next button to continue with the installation.

Selecting and installing the package groups

After you set up the key system parameters, the installer displays a screen from which you can select Fedora Core package groups to install. After you select the package groups, you can take a coffee break and let the Fedora

Core installation program get busy formatting the disk partitions and copying all your selected files to those partitions.

A *package group* is made up of several Fedora Core packages. Each Fedora Core package, in turn, includes many files that make up specific software.

Figure 2-7 shows the screen with the list of package groups (in effect, the software components) that you can choose to install. An icon, a descriptive label, and a check box identify each package group.

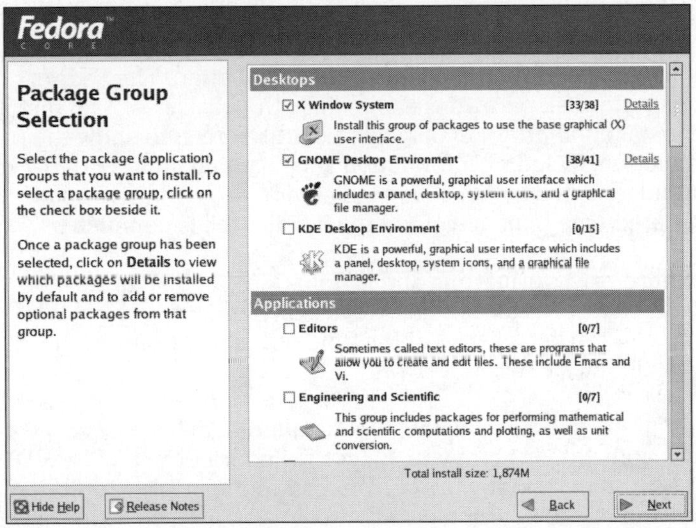

Figure 2-7: Select the package groups to install from this screen.

Some package groups are already selected, as indicated by the check marks in the check boxes. Think of the selected package groups as the minimal set of packages for the class of installation (workstation, server, or custom) that you've chosen. You can, however, choose to install any or all components. Use the mouse to move up and down in the scrolling list, clicking a check box to select or deselect each package group as appropriate.

In an actual production installation of Fedora Core, you install exactly the package groups you need. However, when you're trying to learn everything about Fedora Core, you need many different packages. If you have enough hard drive space (at least 6GB) for the Linux partition, select the Everything package group — all the package groups install so that you can try out the whole nine yards.

In addition to the package groups that you select from the screen shown in Figure 2-7, the Fedora Core installer automatically installs a large number of packages needed to run the Linux kernel and the applications you select.

Even if you don't select a single package group from this screen, the installation program installs a plethora of packages — and they're all needed simply to run the core Linux operating system and a minimal set of utilities.

TIP

Each package group requires specific packages to run. The Fedora Core installation program automatically checks for any package dependencies and shows you a list of any required packages you haven't selected. In this case, install the required packages.

After you select the package groups you want to install, click Next to continue.

The installer then displays a screen informing you that installation is about to begin. Click Next to proceed with the installation. The Fedora Core installer formats the disk partitions and installs the packages. As it installs packages, the installation program displays a status screen to show the progress of the installation, including information such as total number of packages to install, number installed so far, estimated amount of hard drive space needed, and estimated time remaining until the installation is complete.

TIP

The hard drive formatting and installation can take quite a bit of time — so you can take a break and check back in 15 minutes or so. When you come back, you can get a sense of the time remaining from the status screen, which updates continuously.

After all the packages install, the installer displays a message informing you that installation is complete. Eject the Fedora Core DVD or CD and click the Exit button to reboot your PC. You can then perform additional configurations and install additional software.

Installing SUSE Linux

The companion DVD does not include the full SUSE Linux distribution because it's a commercial product. Instead, the DVD includes the ISO image for a SUSE Live CD that enables you to try out the SUSE desktop before you decide whether to buy the full distribution. In this section, I describe the installation process for the full distribution.

TIP

To try the SUSE Linux Live CD version, simply burn a CD from the SUSE Live Eval ISO image on this book's companion DVD and then boot your PC from that CD.

To install the full SUSE distribution, you have two options:

- Install the full distribution free of charge directly over a high-speed Internet connection from one of the FTP servers that mirror the SUSE Linux distribution.

✦ Order the latest release of the full distribution from SUSE (`www.suse.com`) or buy it at a retail computer store. The personal edition of SUSE Linux 9.1 costs approximately $30 U.S.

In the following sections, first I go over the steps for performing an FTP install, and then I describe the full SUSE install from CDs or a DVD.

Performing an FTP install

To install SUSE Linux from one of many FTP servers that mirror the SUSE distribution, you have to perform the following major steps:

1. Download the SUSE boot image from the FTP server and burn a CD with that image.
2. Make a note of the FTP server's IP address and the directory where the SUSE distribution's files are located.
3. Boot the PC with the boot CD and then type a command at the boot prompt to begin an FTP install from the FTP server that you identify by its IP address.

If you have a PC that runs Windows and has a high-speed Internet connection, you can use that PC to download the boot image and burn the boot CD. You can also use the PC to look up the IP address of the FTP server.

REMEMBER

You also need to know the name of the network card installed in your PC because you have to manually load the driver before you can start the SUSE FTP install. You can find the FTP server's IP address at the same time when you download the SUSE installer's boot image. I explain the steps in this section.

Installing SUSE from an FTP server can take two hours or more over a typical broadband DSL or cable modem connection to the Internet. Follow these steps to do an FTP install from an FTP server over the network:

1. **Use a Web browser to open the list of FTP servers at** `www.suse.com/us/private/download/ftp/int_mirrors.html` **and find a FTP server near you that's marked** `complete` **(that means the server has the complete SUSE distribution and all updates).**

   The list of servers is organized by country and it includes both FTP and HTTP (Web) servers. Go to your nearest country and then pick the nearest server that's marked `complete`.

   TIP

   If you are performing this step in Microsoft Windows, open a Command Prompt window (choose Start⇨Run and type **cmd** and press Enter) and type **ping** followed by the name of the FTP server (for example, **mirror.mcs.anl.gov**). You'll then see the IP address of the FTP server on the next line (for example, 140.221.9.138). Write down that IP address for use later on.

2. **Click your FTP server link and find the directory that contains the `boot.iso` file — that's the SUSE installer's boot image.**

   The directory depends on the version of SUSE. For example, for version 9.1, the `boot.iso` file is in the FTP server's `pub/suse/i386/9.1/boot/` directory. The file is about 23MB in size.

3. **Download the `boot.iso` file and save it.**

4. **Burn the `boot.iso` image onto a CD.**

   Use your PC's CD burner application to burn the ISO image named `boot.iso`.

5. **Go to the PC on which you want to do the SUSE FTP install, insert the boot CD, and restart the PC.**

   If your PC isn't set up to boot from the CD drive, you have to enter SETUP (by pressing a key such as F2 as the PC powers up) and change the order of the boot devices.

   The PC reboots and after a few moments, a text screen displays a screen with a number of options. Use the arrow keys to move between list items and the buttons on the screen.

6. **Use the arrow keys to select the Manual Installation option and press Enter.**

   The installer shows a list of languages.

7. **Select the language and press Enter.**

   The installer displays a list of keyboard maps — the language-dependent layouts for the keyboard.

8. **Select the keyboard language and press Enter.**

   The installer displays the Main menu.

9. **Use the arrow keys to select Kernel Modules (Hardware Drivers) and press Enter.**

   The installer displays a list of choices that includes options to load driver modules as well as view names of loaded modules.

10. **Use the arrow keys to select Load Network Card Modules and press Enter.**

    The installer displays a list of network driver modules, organized by the name of the network card.

11. **Use the arrow keys to select your network card and press Enter.**

    The installer prompts for any parameters for the driver. Press Enter if there are no parameters. If all goes well, the installer successfully loads the network driver module and displays a message. Press Enter to continue.

12. **Press the right-arrow key to select Back and press Enter.**

    You will be back at the Main menu.

13. **Use arrow keys to select Start Installation/System and press Enter. On the next screen, select Start Installation/Update and press Enter.**

    The installer displays a list of source mediums — this is where you indicate where the installer can find the files it needs to perform the installation.

14. **Select Network as the source medium and press Enter.**

    The installer prompts you for the network protocol.

15. **Select FTP as the network protocol and press Enter.**

    A dialog box prompts you to determine whether to configure the network automatically by using the Dynamic Host Configuration Protocol (DHCP). If your network uses DHCP as most do, select Yes and press Enter. Otherwise, you have to enter the IP address and the name server's IP address at this step. The installer then prompts for the IP address of the FTP server.

16. **Enter the IP address of the FTP server that you found in Step 1 (for example, enter** 140.221.9.138 **for the FTP server** `mirror.mcs.anl.gov`**).**

    The installer prompts you if you want to use a username and password to connect to the FTP server. Because the FTP servers support anonymous FTP — which means anyone can log in with the username `anonymous` — select No and press Enter. The installer also prompts if you want to use a HTTP proxy. Unless your PC is behind a proxy (which may be the case at some organizations), select No and press Enter. The installer then prompts for the name of the directory where the SUSE files are located.

17. **Enter the name of the directory on the FTP server where the SUSE Linux files are located and press Enter.**

    The directory name would be the parent directory of the location where you found the `boot.iso` file in Step 1. For example, if the `boot.iso` file is in `pub/suse/i386/9.1/boot/`, then you should type **pub/suse/i386/9.1/** and press Enter.

    The installer displays a message informing you that it is loading data into ramdisk (which refers to an area of memory that acts as a hard drive). When the installer finishes downloading data, the YaST (that's what the SUSE installer is called) installer starts and displays its initial GUI screen.

From this point on, the installation steps are the same as the ones for CD/DVD install, which I explain in the next section. You should jump to the point where the YaST installer displays its initial GUI screen.

Installing SUSE Linux from CDs or DVD

To install SUSE Linux from CDs or DVD that you have ordered from SUSE, simply insert the first CD or the DVD into your PC's CD/DVD drive and restart your PC (in Windows, choose Start⇨Shutdown and then select Restart from the dialog box). Note that you may have to enter SETUP and make sure that your PC is set to boot from the CD/DVD drive. If you are using CDs, the installation steps are the same as that for the DVD except that you have to swap CDs when prompted by the installation program.

After your PC powers up, a boot loader starts and displays an initial boot screen with a menu of items. Table 2-2 lists these boot menu items and their meaning. As you can see, you can perform a number of tasks from the boot screen, including booting an existing installation from the hard drive and starting a rescue system.

Table 2-2 SUSE Installer Boot Menu Items

Select This Item	*To Do This*
Boot from Hard Disk	Boot the PC from a previously installed operating system from the hard drive.
Installation	Automatically detect hardware and then begin installing SUSE Linux.
Installation — ACPI Disabled	Disable support for ACPI (Advanced Configuration and Power Interface), but otherwise detect hardware and start SUSE installation.
Installation — Safe Settings	Disable potentially troublesome features such as ACPI, APM (Advanced Power Management), and DMA (direct memory access) for IDE interface and start installing SUSE. Select this option if the installation hangs with any of the other options.
Manual Installation	Control all aspects of installation, including loading device driver modules for your PC's hardware.
Rescue System	Start a small Linux system in memory so that you can troubleshoot by logging in as `root`.
Memory Test	Check to see if there is any problem with the PC's memory.

Along the bottom of the SUSE installer boot screen, you see some information about using the function keys F1 through F6. Table 2-3 explains what each of these functions does.

You can also provide other installer options — as well as Linux kernel options — at the Boot Options text box below the boot menu. The installer options control some aspects of the installer's behavior, whereas the kernel options are passed to the Linux kernel that starts when you start the installation. I explain many of these boot options in Chapter 3 of this minibook.

Table 2-3 Using Function Keys at the SUSE Installer Boot Screen

Press This Function Key	*To Do This*
F1	Get *context-sensitive* help — help information that depends on the currently selected item. Use the up- and down-arrow keys to read the Help screen and the left- and right-arrow keys to jump between topics. You can dismiss the Help screen by pressing Escape.
F2	Select a screen resolution that you want the YaST installer to use for its GUI. If the GUI screen fails to appear, you can select Text Mode for a text mode interface.
F3	Select the source from where you want to install. The choices are: CD or DVD, network sources with different protocols such as FTP, HTTP, NFS, and SLP (Service Location Protocol).
F4	Select the language and keyboard mapping to be used by the boot loader.
F5	View kernel messages as the Linux kernel loads. This could help you identify problems if the installation hangs.
F6	Update a driver module for new hardware for which drivers may not be on the CD or DVD. You will be prompted to insert the updated driver module on a floppy or CD-ROM after you start the installation.

TIP

The installer initially picks a rather high screen resolution for the GUI screen (typically, 1280 x 1024 pixels). You should press F2, which brings up a menu from which you can select a more reasonable screen resolution, such as 1024 x 768 pixels.

After setting the screen resolution by pressing F2, select Installation from the boot menu and press Enter. This loads the Linux kernel from the DVD and the Linux kernel starts running the YaST installation program. For the rest of the installation, you work with YaST's GUI screens.

TIP

If you run into any problems during the installation, turn to Chapter 3 of this minibook. That chapter shows how to troubleshoot common installation problems.

Starting the SUSE install in YaST

YaST — the SUSE installer — displays a GUI screen (see Figure 2-8) from which you install SUSE Linux on your PC's hard drive and configure it.

The left-hand side of the YaST screen shows the list of installation steps, organized into two broad categories of tasks — Base Installation and Configuration. An arrow marks the current step. For example, in Figure 2-8, the arrow marks the language selection step. After the step is complete, YaST displays a check mark next to the step.

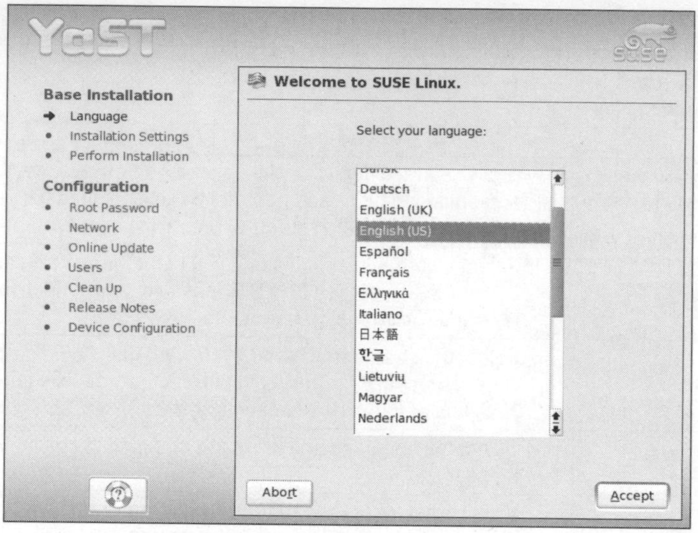

Figure 2-8: The YaST installer's main GUI screen.

On the right-hand side of the YaST screen (see Figure 2-8), you see the options for the current step. You have to select options and then click Accept to proceed to the next installation step. You can abort the installation at any time by clicking the Abort key up until you confirm that you want to really proceed with the installation.

TIP: At any installation step, click the lifebuoy button at the lower-left corner of the YaST screen (refer to Figure 2-8) to view context-sensitive help information for the current step. The help appears in the left-hand side of the YaST screen. Press the button again to return to view the list of installation steps.

Follow these steps to complete the base installation tasks in the YaST installer:

1. **Select the language to be used during installation and for use in the installed SUSE Linux system. Then click Accept.**

   YaST probes the hardware and loads driver modules. YaST may prompt you to confirm that it should load some driver modules. Then YaST displays a dialog box (shown in Figure 2-9) that prompts you for the next step.

2. **Assuming that you are installing SUSE for the first time, select New Installation and click OK.**

   YaST gathers information about the system and prepares a list of all the installation settings, organized by category, as shown in Figure 2-10.

Table 2-4 summarizes the installation settings categories. Note that you have to scroll down to see all the installation settings in the screen shown in Figure 2-10.

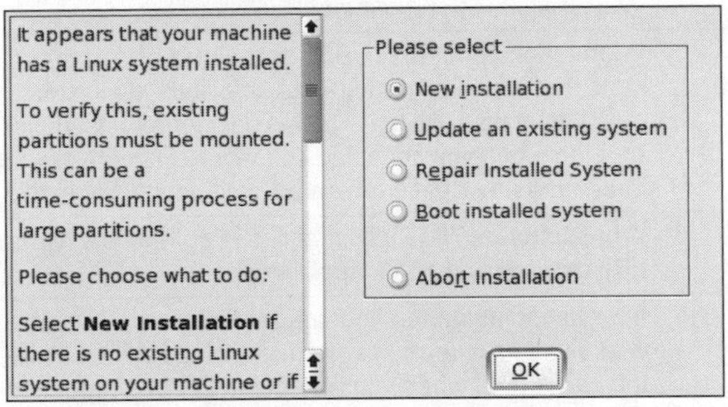

Figure 2-9: Select whether you want a new installation or not.

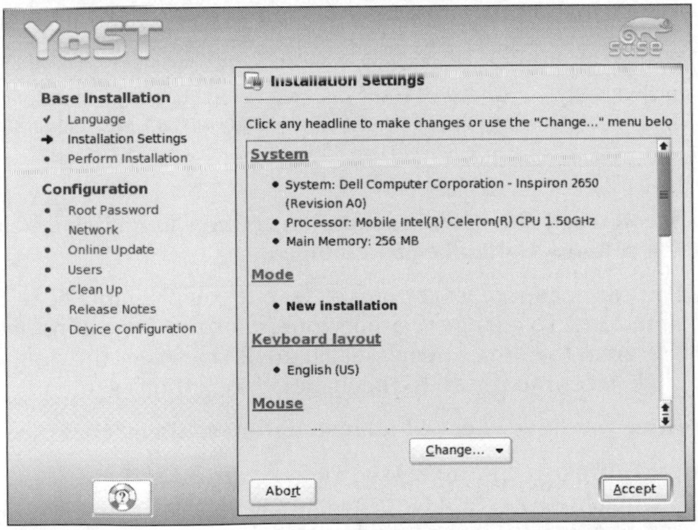

Figure 2-10: Click a heading to make changes to that category of settings.

Table 2-4 Installation Settings Categories

Category	*What These Settings Specify*
System	Information about the PC's hardware, including the processor type, amount of memory, hard drive, keyboard, mouse, graphics card, sound, and Ethernet card.
Mode	Whether this is a new installation or an update.

(continued)

Table 2-4 (continued)

Category	*What These Settings Specify*
Keyboard Layout	Language and layout of the keyboard.
Mouse	Type of mouse (for example, PS/2 mouse).
Partitioning	Information about the partitions that will be formatted and any partitions that would be mounted on the Linux file system. You should check to make sure that YaST is using the unused disk partitions you created when you set aside space for Linux (as explained in the "Setting Aside Space for Linux" section, earlier in this chapter).
Software	What software YaST will install. The default is a typical system with KDE desktop and office applications.
Booting	Information about the boot loader that takes care of starting Linux (as well as other operating systems, such as Windows XP, that may be on the hard drive) when you reboot the PC. The default is the GRUB boot loader, installed on the hard drive's master boot record (MBR).
Time Zone	Current time zone and how the hardware clock stores time. The default is the USA/Pacific time zone, which you may need to change.
Language	The language to be used by the installed SUSE Linux system.
Default Runlevel	What processes Linux starts after booting. The default runlevel is 5, which gives you a full multiuser system with networks enabled and a graphical login screen.

3. **Scroll down the list of installation settings and click a heading to view the settings and make any changes.**

   You can accept most settings as is, but you probably need to change the time zone. To change the time zone, click the Time Zone section heading. From the next screen (see Figure 2-11), select the time zone and click Accept to return to the Installation Settings screen.

4. **After you have checked all installation settings, click Accept.**

   YaST displays a warning (shown in Figure 2-12) that tells you that this is the point of no return and you can commit to the installation by clicking Yes or return to the installation settings by clicking No.

5. **If you are certain that you want to continue with the installation, click the Yes, Install button.**

   YaST then begins the installation, which includes formatting and preparing the hard drive partitions and copying SUSE Linux files to the hard drive.

As YaST installs the software packages, it displays a slide show that introduces various features of SUSE Linux. After the base installation is complete,

YaST installs the boot loader and reboots the system. At the boot screen, you should select to boot Linux so that you can complete the remaining SUSE installation steps.

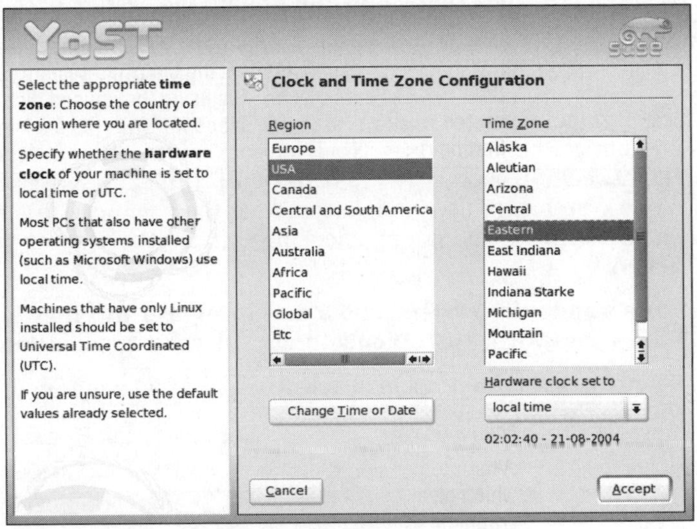

Figure 2-11: Select the time zone and click Accept.

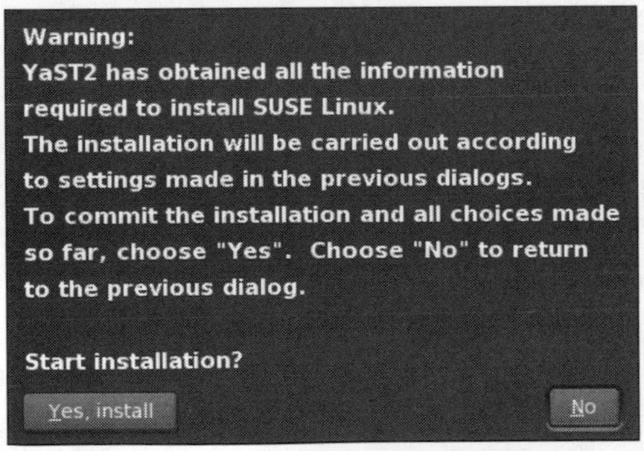

Figure 2-12: Click the Yes, Install button only if you are sure.

Completing the SUSE Linux configuration

After you reboot the base SUSE system, YaST guides you through some configuration steps, as follows:

1. **Enter the password for the `root` user.**

   The `root` user is the administrator account that you can use to do anything on the system — from installing software to adding new user accounts.

2. **Accept or change the network configuration.**

   YaST displays the current settings (see the example in Figure 2-13). If the settings are correct, you can simply click Next to continue.

3. **Test the Internet connection and update the system with the YaST online update service.**

4. **Select whether your PC is a standalone machine or a network client.**

   If you select network client, you have to select one of two network authentication methods — NIS (Network Information System) or LDAP (Lightweight Directory Access Protocol). Typically, most PCs are standalone systems. (This simply means that the user accounts are authenticated on the PC and not by checking with another server on the network.)

5. **For a standalone system, add a new local user by entering the username, password, and other settings. Click Next to continue.**

   If you mark the Auto Login check box, SUSE Linux automatically logs in this user when it starts.

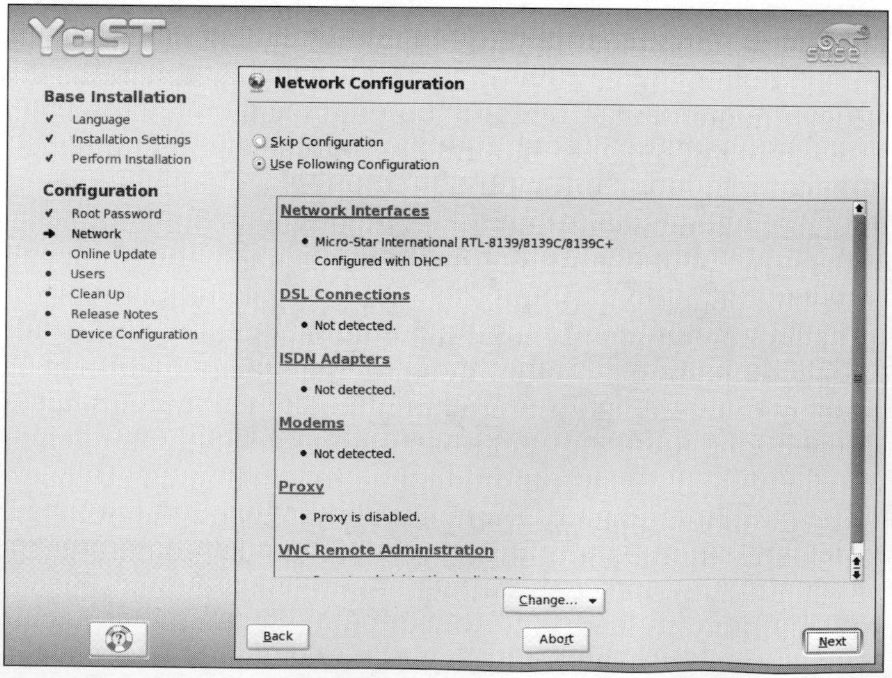

Figure 2-13: Accept or change the network configuration from this screen.

6. **Read the release notes and click Next.**

   The release notes contain last-minute information about the SUSE Linux distribution, including any known problems and workarounds. It's worth glancing through so that you know about anything that might apply to your PC's hardware configuration.

7. **Accept or change the displayed hardware configuration for your PC.**

   The configuration includes information about specific hardware such as your graphics card, monitor, sound card, printing system, and so on. Typically, the displayed configuration should be acceptable. If not, you can make changes by clicking the name of the device. After the configuration steps are complete, YaST informs you that the installation is complete, as shown in Figure 2-14.

8. **Click Finish to complete the installation.**

   The installer then reboots the system. When you see the graphical login screen, you can log into the system and start using it.

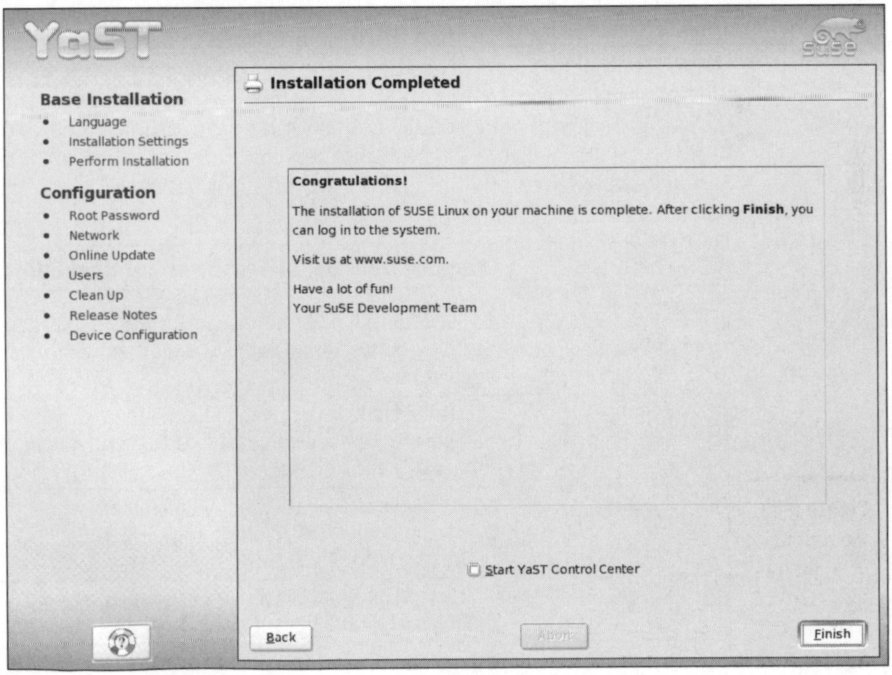

Figure 2-14: Click Finish to reboot and begin using your SUSE system.

Installing Xandros Desktop

The companion DVD does not include the full Xandros Desktop distribution because it's a commercial product. Instead, the DVD includes the ISO image for a limited version called Xandros Open Circulation Edition (OCE). You can install the Xandros OCE to try out the Xandros Desktop before you decide whether to buy the full distribution. In this section, I describe the installation process for Xandros OCE, which is similar to that for the full distribution except that the full distribution includes lots more software packages.

To install the Xandros OCE, burn a CD from the Xandros OCE ISO image on this book's companion DVD and then boot your PC from that CD. See the section, "Burning CDs from ISO Images," earlier in this chapter, for instructions.

The initial Xandros boot screen displays a logo and a message that says `Press Shift for troubleshooting options`. If you do nothing, the Linux kernel loads and starts a GUI installer. However, if the installation seems to hang, reboot the PC and this time press Shift at the boot screen. You then see a number of options for starting the Linux kernel. The default is marked the Default Setup, but you have options to try various levels of APM and ACPI support. Use the up- and down-arrow keys to select one of these alternatives and press Enter to get around problems with the installation process. Also, if you can't seem to get the GUI screen, try selecting the VESA Mode Setup. That could get around any problems in starting the X Window System. Table 2-5 summarizes the Xandros boot options that you can access by pressing Shift at the initial boot screen.

Table 2-5 Xandros Boot Options at the Initial Boot Screen

This Option	*Does the Following*
Default Setup	Starts the Linux kernel with the option `acpi=on`, which enables support for ACPI.
ACPI 2 Setup	Starts the Linux kernel with the options `acpi=on noapic` (enables ACPI, but disables the APIC — Advanced Programmable Interrupt Controller).
ACPI 3 Setup	Starts the Linux kernel with the options `acpi=on pci=biosirq` (enables ACPI, but uses BIOS settings to route interrupt requests or IRQs).
ACPI 4 Setup	Starts the Linux kernel with the options `acpi=on pci=noacpi` (enables ACPI and does not use ACPI to route interrupt requests).
APM Setup	Starts the Linux kernel with the option `acpi=off` (disables ACPI).
APM 2 Setup	Starts the Linux kernel with the options `acpi=off noapic` (disables both ACPI and APIC).
APM 3 Setup	Starts the Linux kernel with the options `acpi=off pci=biosirq` (disables ACPI and uses BIOS settings to route interrupt requests).

This Option	*Does the Following*
256-Color Setup	Starts X Window System with the video card in a 256-color mode, which should work on nearly all video cards.
VESA Mode Setup	Starts the X Window System with the VESA (Video Electronics Standards Association) driver.
Custom Setup	Starts the Linux kernel with the option `vga=normal` (the screen appears in 80x25 text mode).
Restore Xandros	Enables you to restore Xandros and fix problems.
Rescue Console	Starts the Linux kernel in single user mode in a 80x25 text screen where you can log in as `root` and fix problems.
International	Enables you to pick non-U.S. keyboard and language.

Usually, you don't have to do anything because the boot loader automatically loads the Linux kernel and the driver modules. Then it reads the CD, detects and configures hardware, and starts the X Window System and the GUI installer. If all goes well, you should see the initial GUI screen, as shown in Figure 2-15, where you should click Next to continue with the installation.

The next screen displays the infamous EULA — End User License Agreement — of the commercial software world. If you decide to continue, read the EULA, click I Accept the Agreement to accept the agreement, and then click Next.

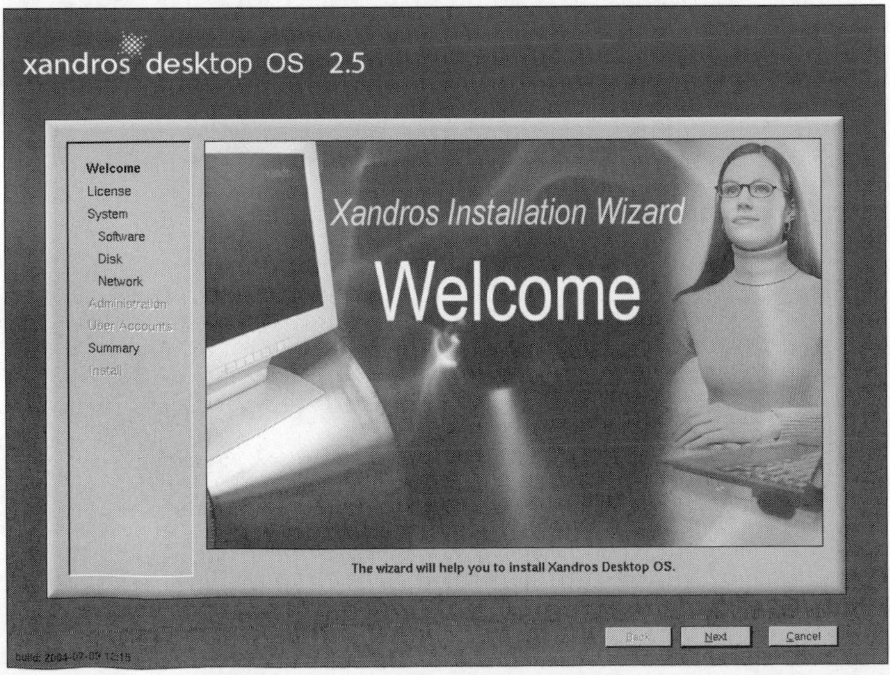

Figure 2-15: Start the Xandros installation at this GUI screen.

The Xandros installer then displays two choices for installation:

- ✦ **Express Install:** Installs Xandros on your PC with default settings and a selection of commonly used software.
- ✦ **Custom Install:** Enables you to control some of the steps in installing Xandros, including the selection of software, the disk partitions used by Xandros, and the network configuration.

I describe both install methods in the following sections.

Using Xandros Express Install

Xandros Express Install is very simple — provided you want Xandros to use the entire hard drive or take over an unused partition. In a nutshell, you enter the `root` password and create a normal user account. Then review the installation summary, click Finish, and the installer does the rest.

If you have Windows installed on your PC, the Xandros installer displays a screen (see Figure 2-16) that prompts you whether you want to keep Windows or overwrite it. The default is to keep Windows. You can indicate your choice and click Next to continue.

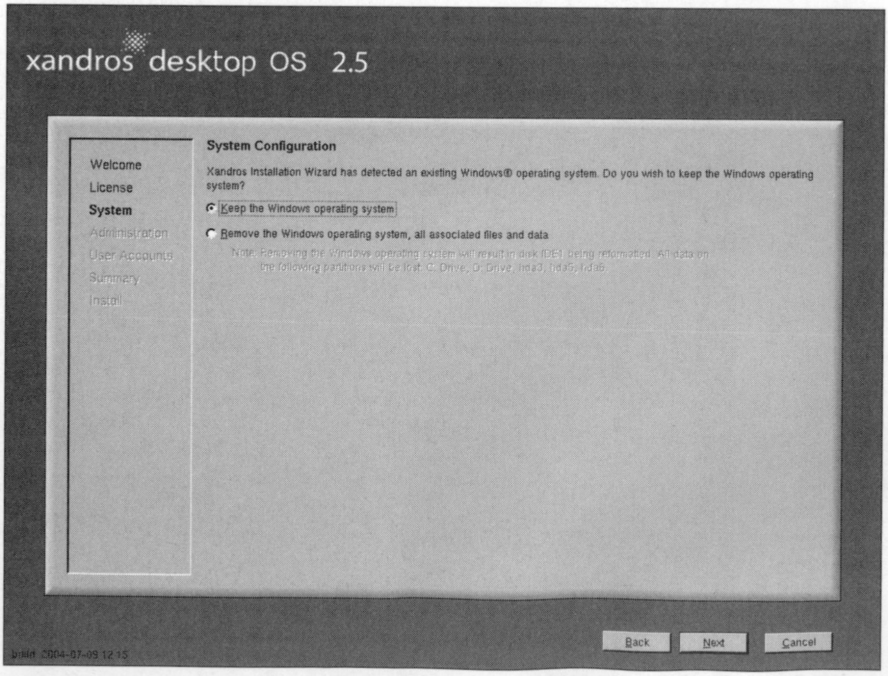

Figure 2-16: The Xandros installer prompts whether you want to keep or overwrite Windows.

The next screen asks for the `root` (administrator) password and the name of the computer. Enter the `root` password and confirm it by typing it again. For the computer name, you can accept the name concocted by the Xandros installer or type in something more meaningful to you. Then click Next.

Next, you get the chance to create a normal user account. Type in the requested information, which includes the username and password, and then click Next. This username is used to log into Xandros.

The installer displays an installation summary screen (shown in Figure 2-17) for your review. Carefully check the information, in particular whether the installation is going to take over a partition or the whole hard drive. If you need to make changes, click Back. Otherwise, click Finish to start the installation.

After the installer finishes installing Xandros, it prompts you to create a rescue disk — a disk that enables you to start Xandros in case you have problems with booting Xandros directly from the hard drive. Insert a floppy disk and follow the instructions to complete this step.

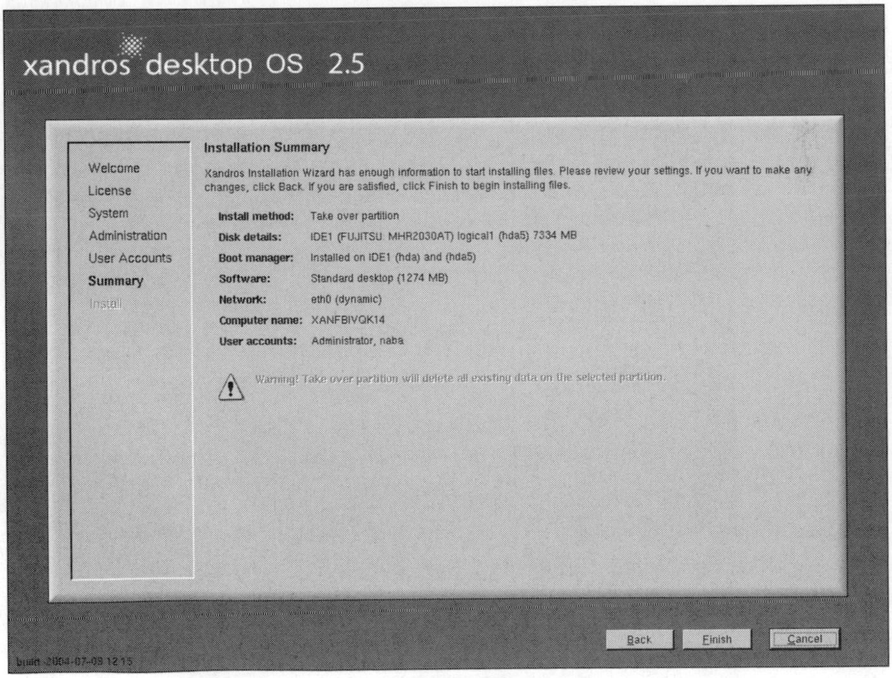

Figure 2-17: Review the installation summary and click Finish to install Xandros.

Using Xandros Custom Install

The Custom Install method gives you some control over what software gets installed. It also lets you identify specific disk partitions for the installation, configure the network, and add multiple user accounts. To use Custom Install, select the option from the Installation Selection screen — the screen that appears right after you accept the EULA agreement — and then click Next, as shown in Figure 2-18.

The installer displays the Software Selection screen (see Figure 2-19), where you can select the applications that you want to install.

You can pick from four predefined sets of applications:

- **Minimal desktop:** Installs a basic set of applications.
- **Standard desktop:** Installs a recommended set of commonly used applications.
- **Complete desktop:** Installs all standard applications plus some more applications such as some server software.
- **Custom desktop:** Installs a base set of software, and you can then select applications a la carte from the list that appears below these choices.

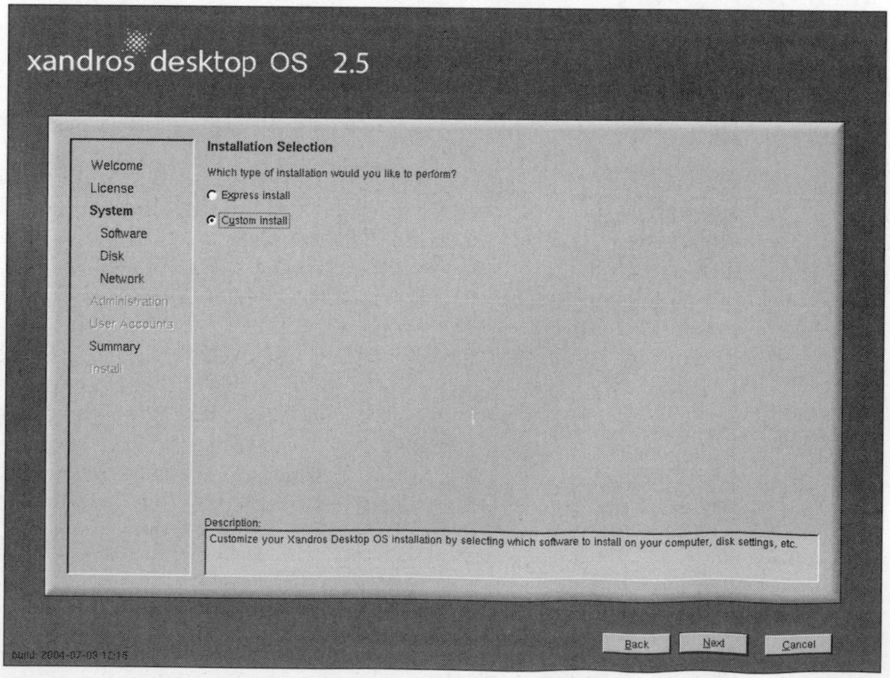

Figure 2-18: Select Custom Install from this screen.

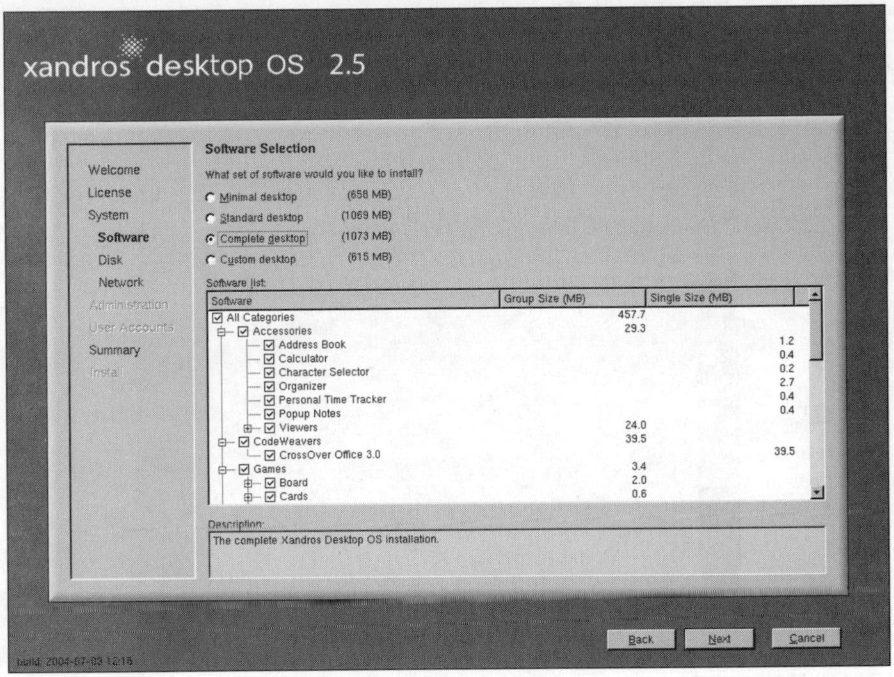

Figure 2-19: From this screen, you can select the applications to install.

As you click to select any of these sets, you can see the detailed selections in the list that appears below these choices. You can also add or delete anything you want from the list, so the predefined sets should not constrain your choices. Click Next after selecting the software that you want to install.

The installer then guides you through the disk configuration steps. The next screen, shown in Figure 2-20, shows what the installer suggests. If you have an available disk partition, the installer suggests taking over the hard drive or a partition. (Don't worry, you get to see exactly how the installer wants to use the disk partitions and you can intervene, if necessary.)

If you want to manage the disk partitions, click the Manage Disks and Partitions item and then click Next. The installer displays an editor where you can delete and add partitions and assign mount points for partitions. For example, you could assign a small 50MB partition to the `/boot` mount point and assign a multi-gigabyte partition to the root file system (/). You can also identify a swap partition approximately twice the size of available memory. Linux uses the swap partition as virtual memory — a hard drive-based extension of the PC's memory.

Table 2-6 summarizes the possible options available in the Disk Configuration screen. (Refer to Figure 2-20.) Note that only the options applicable to your PC are available for selection. The others are grayed out.

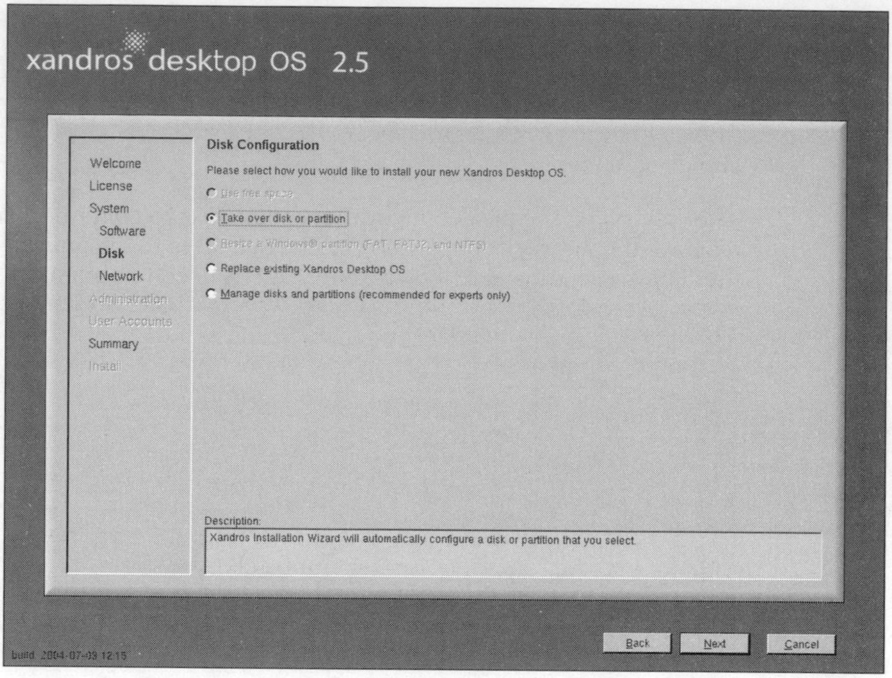

Figure 2-20: Xandros installer suggests how it plans to use the hard drive.

Table 2-6 Options for Disk Configuration

This Option	*Does the Following*
Use Free Space	Uses the largest unallocated block of space on the hard drive
Take Over Disk or Partition	Takes over an entire hard drive, a specific partition, or a previous version of Xandros and erases all data
Resize a Windows Partition	Reduces the size of a Windows partition and installs Xandros in the space that's freed up
Replace Existing Xandros Desktop OS	Upgrades a previous version of Xandros (keeps user accounts, renames directories with an `_old` suffix, and retains some default settings)
Manage Disks and Partitions	Enables you to create one or more disk partitions and specify the mount points for the partitions

If you decide to go with the default Take Over Disk or Partition selection and click Next, the Xandros installer shows you the partition it plans to take over. If you agree, click Next. The installer then displays the disk configuration in the form of the location of the swap partition and the root file system, as shown in Figure 2-21. A check box shows that the installer will load the boot manager on the master boot record of the first IDE hard drive.

Note that the Xandros installer uses the ReiserFS file system for the disk partition. Other file system choices are Ext2 or Ext3. You can go with the default choice of ReiserFS.

After reviewing the disk configuration, click Next to continue. The installer displays the network configuration. The default is to dynamically configure the Ethernet card, which means that DHCP is used to obtain the IP addresses of the network interface and the name servers. If this works for your network, click Next. Otherwise, you have to click Edit and enter a static IP address for the network. You can also choose not to configure the network. Click Next after completing the network configuration step.

The installer prompts for the `root` user password. You can also enter a computer name. After you click Next to continue, the installer displays the User Account Configuration screen, where you can define multiple user accounts. For each user account, click Add and then enter the required information. After you are done adding user accounts, click Next.

The installer displays the installation summary screen (see Figure 2-22).

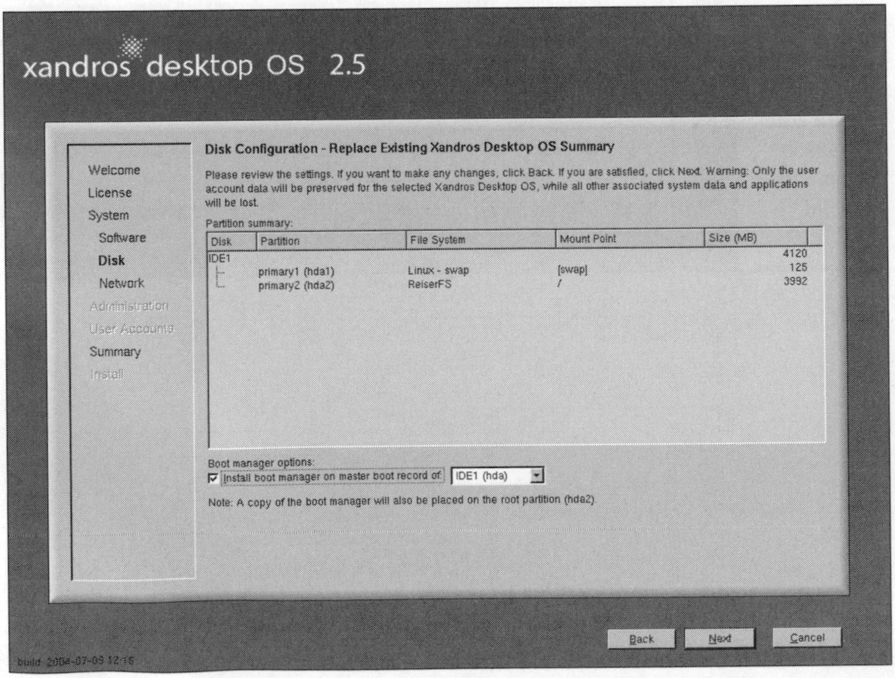

Figure 2-21: Xandros installer displays the disk configuration.

Review the information carefully and click Back to correct any errors. When you are sure that the selections are acceptable, click Finish. The installer finishes installing Xandros and prompts you to create rescue disk. Insert a blank formatted floppy and follow the instructions to complete this final step. You need the rescue disk to start Xandros in case you have any problem booting Xandros from the hard drive.

Congratulations! You can now reboot your PC and start using Xandros Desktop.

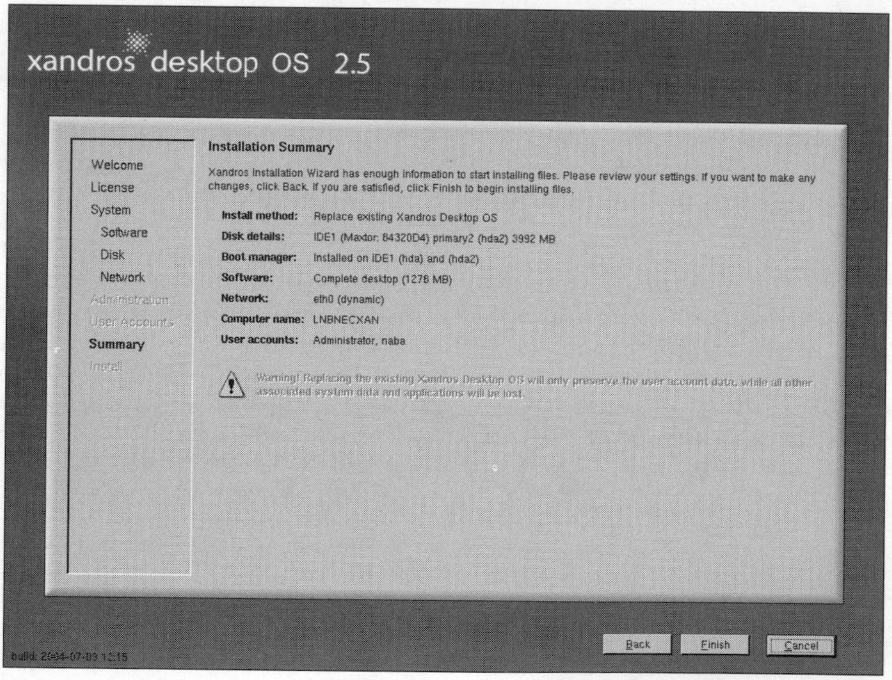

Figure 2-22: Installation summary for custom install.

Chapter 3: Troubleshooting and Configuring Linux

In This Chapter

- Troubleshooting the installation
- Configuring the X Window System
- Setting up printers
- Managing DVDs and CD-ROMs
- Installing additional software packages

During the installation of Linux, the installer attempts to detect key hardware components, such as the SCSI controller and network card. According to what it detects, the installer takes you through a sequence of installation steps. For example, if the installer cannot detect the network card, it skips the network configuration step. This is perfectly okay if you don't in fact have a network card, but if you do have one and the installer mistakenly insists that you don't, you have an installation problem on your hands.

Another installation problem that might crop up occurs when you restart the PC and, instead of a graphical login screen, you get a text terminal — which means something is wrong with the X Window System (or X) configuration.

Also, typically the Linux installation doesn't include configuration procedures for every piece of hardware in your PC system. For example, most installations do not set up printers during installation.

In this chapter, I show you some ways to troubleshoot installation problems. I show you how to configure X to get started with a GUI screen and how to configure a printer.

You may also have to install additional software packages from the companion DVD-ROM. I show you how to install packages in different formats such as the Red Hat Package Manager (RPM) and Debian package — the two formats in which most Linux software is distributed.

Using Text Mode Installation

Most Linux installers attempt to use the X Window System (X) to display the graphical installation screens. If the installer fails to detect a video card, X does not start. If — for this reason or any other reason — the installer fails to start X, you can always fall back on a text mode installation. Then you can specify the video card manually or configure X later on by using a separate configuration program. You can also configure X by editing its text configuration file.

Table 3-1 lists how you can get to the text mode installation from the initial installer screen for the Linux distributions included in this book's DVD. Typically, the text mode installation sequence is similar to that of the graphical installation that I outline in Chapter 2 of this minibook. You respond to the prompts and perform the installation.

Table 3-1 Text Mode Installation in Some Linux Distributions

Distribution	*How to Get to Text Mode Installer*
Debian	The Debian installer works in text mode.
Fedora Core	Type **text** at the `boot:` prompt after you start the PC from the Fedora Core CD or DVD.
Knoppix	Start Knoppix in text mode by typing **knoppix 2** at the `boot:` prompt (because Knoppix is a Live CD distribution, you do not have to install it).
SUSE	In the first installation screen, press F2, and then use the arrow keys to select the text mode option and press Enter.
Xandros	Hold down the Shift key while booting the CD and select Rescue Console. When the `bash-2.05a#` prompt appears, type **quick_install** and follow the instructions.

Disabling Hardware Probing in Fedora

Linux installers try to detect hardware in your PC by a method known as *hardware probing,* which involves accessing the hardware. Sometimes the probing causes the installation to hang or the probing fails to detect the hardware. If problems occur with hardware probing, you can disable probing.

If the Fedora Core installer does not detect the SCSI controller or network card, you can specify these devices manually by typing **linux noprobe** at the `boot:` prompt.

To see whether the installer detected the hardware, look for any indication of SCSI or network devices in the messages the Linux kernel displays as it boots. To view these messages during installation, press Ctrl+Alt+F4. The display switches to a virtual console in text mode on which the messages appear. (A *virtual console* is a screen of text or graphical information stored in memory that you can view on the physical screen by pressing a specific key sequence.)

Another sign of undetected hardware is when the installation program skips a step. For example, if the Linux kernel does not detect the network card, the installation program skips the network configuration step.

To manually install devices, follow these steps:

1. **Type** linux noprobe **at the** `boot:` **prompt in the initial text screen.**

   The installer then displays a dialog box that shows you the devices that are detected and gives you the opportunity to add other devices.

2. **Press Tab to highlight the Add Device button, and then press Enter.**

   The installer displays a dialog box that prompts you for the type of device — SCSI or Network.

3. **If you have any SCSI device, such as a SCSI hard drive, select SCSI and press Enter.**

   The installer displays a list of SCSI controllers. When you select the one on your system and press Enter, the installer then loads the appropriate driver module. The SCSI driver automatically probes and determines the SCSI controller's settings.

   After you add any SCSI controllers, you're back at the initial dialog box — and from there you can add network cards.

4. **If you select Network from the list and press Enter, the installation program displays a list of network cards from which you can select your network card.**

   When you press Enter, the installation program loads the driver module for the selected network card. That driver then probes and determines the network card settings.

5. **[Optional] If you need a Linux device driver that does not come with Fedora Core, try checking the vendor's Web site or using a search engine (such as Google —** `www.google.com`**) to find a Linux driver.**

   TIP

   Many hardware vendors provide Linux device drivers for download, just as they do Windows drivers.

   After you finish adding the SCSI controllers and network cards, the installer switches to graphics mode and guides you through the rest of the installation.

Troubleshooting X

I had this problem on an older PC every time I installed Linux: During installation, the GUI installation worked fine — but when I rebooted the PC for the first time after installation, the graphical login screen would not appear. Instead, I would end up with a text login screen or the boot process might seem to hang with a gray screen. If this problem happens to you, here's how you can troubleshoot the problem:

1. **Press Ctrl+Alt+Del to reboot the PC.**

   The PC starts to boot and you get to a screen where the GRUB boot loader prompts you for the operating system to boot. (If you are using LILO, you get a text prompt.)

2. **For GRUB, press the A key to add an option for use by the Linux kernel. For LILO, skip this step.**

   The GRUB boot loader then displays a command line for the Linux kernel and prompts you to add what you want.

3. **For GRUB, type a space followed by the word** single **and then press Enter. For LILO, type** linux single **and press Enter.**

   The Linux kernel boots in a single-user mode and displays a prompt that looks like the following:

   ```
   sh-2.05b#
   ```

   Now you're ready to configure X.

X uses a configuration file — depending on your distribution the file is called `XF86Config`, `XF86Config-4`, or `xorg.conf` — to figure out the type of display card, monitor, and the kind of screen resolution you want. The Linux installer prepares the configuration file, but sometimes the configuration isn't correct.

To quickly create a working configuration file, follow these steps:

1. **Type the following command:**

   ```
   X -configure
   ```

   This causes the X server to run and create a configuration file. The screen goes blank and then the X server exits after displaying some messages. The last line of the message says the following in Fedora Core:

   ```
   To test the server, run 'X -xf86config //xorg.conf.new'
   ```

2. **On Fedora Core, use a text editor such as `vi` to edit the `//xorg.conf.new` file and change `/dev/mouse` to `/dev/input/mice`.**

3. **On Debian, SUSE, and Xandros, try the new configuration file by typing** X -xf86config //XF86Config.new. **On Fedora Core, try the new configuration file by typing** X -xf86config //xorg.conf.new.

   If you see a blank screen with an X-shaped cursor, the configuration file is working fine.

4. **Press Ctrl+Alt+Backspace to kill the X server.**
5. **Copy the new configuration file to the** `/etc/X11` **directory with the following command (on Fedora Core systems, change the filename to** xorg.conf.new**):**

   ```
   cp //XF86Config.new /etc/X11/XF86Config
   ```

   You now have a working X configuration file.
6. **Reboot the PC by pressing Ctrl+Alt+Del or typing** reboot.

   If all goes well, you go through the normal Fedora Core initial setup screens and (finally) get the graphical login screen.

TIP: The X configuration file created by using the `-configure` option of the X server does not display at the best resolution possible. To fine-tune the configuration file, you have to run a utility to adjust the display settings after you reboot the system. The exact utility depends on your Linux distribution, but most distributions include a utility that enables you to configure the video card, monitor, and display settings through a graphical user interface.

Resolving Other Installation Problems

I'm sure I haven't exhausted all the installation problems that are lurking out there. Nobody can. There are so many different combinations of components in Intel x86 PCs that Murphy's Law practically requires some combination of hardware to exist that the installation program can't handle. This section lists a few known problems. For others, I advise you to go to Google Groups (`groups.google.com`) and type in some of the symptoms of the trouble. Assuming that others are running into similar problems, you can get some indication of how to troubleshoot your way out of your particular predicament.

Using Knoppix boot commands

The Knoppix Live CD can be a great troubleshooting tool because Knoppix is good at detecting hardware and you can run it directly from the CD. Of course, sometimes you may have trouble getting Knoppix itself started. If that happens, you can try entering Knoppix boot commands at the `boot:` prompt that appears after you boot your PC from the Knoppix Live CD. For example, if Knoppix seems to hang when trying to detect a SCSI card, you can disable SCSI probing by typing **knoppix noscsi** at the `boot:` prompt. Or, if you want the X server to load the `nv` module (for graphics cards based on the NVIDIA chipset), you can type **knoppix xmodule=nv** at the `boot:` prompt. Table 3-2 lists some common Knoppix boot commands.

Table 3-2 Some Common Knoppix Boot Commands

Boot Command	*What It Does*
`expert`	Starts in expert mode, which enables the user to interactively set up and configure Knoppix.
`failsafe`	Boots without attempting to detect hardware (except for the bare minimum needed to start Linux).
`fb1280x1024`	Uses fixed framebuffer graphics at the specified resolution (specify the resolution you want such as 1024x768, 800x600, and so on).
`knoppix 1`	Starts Knoppix in run level 1 (single-user mode), which can be used to perform rescue operations.
`knoppix 2`	Starts at run level 2, which provides a text mode shell prompt only.
`knoppix acpi=off`	Disables ACPI (Advanced Configuration and Power Interface) completely.
`knoppix atapicd`	Uses the ATAPI CD-ROM interface instead of emulating a SCSI interface for IDE CD-ROM drives.
`knoppix desktop=`*`wmname`*	Uses the specified Window Manager instead of the default KDE (*`wmname`* can be one of: `fluxbox`, `icewm`, `kde`, `larswm`, `twm`, `wmaker`, or `xfce`).
`knoppix dma`	Enables direct memory access (DMA) for all IDE drives.
`knoppix floppy config`	Runs the shell script named `knoppix.sh` from a floppy (the shell script contains Linux commands that you want to run).
`knoppix fromhd=/dev/hda1`	Boots from a previously copied image of Live CD that's in the specified hard drive partition.
`knoppix hsync=80`	Uses a 80 kHz horizontal refresh rate for X (enter the horizontal refresh rate you want X to use).
`knoppix lang=`*`XX`*	Sets the keyboard language as specified by the two-letter code *`XX`* (use one of the following for *`XX`*: `cn` = Simplified Chinese, `de` = German, `da` = Danish, `es` = Spanish, `fr` = French, `it` = Italian, `nl` = Dutch, `pl` = Polish, `ru` = Russian, `sk` = Slovak, `tr` = Turkish, `tw` = Traditional Chinese, or `us` = U.S. English).
`knoppix mem=256M`	Specifies that the PC has the stated amount of memory (in megabytes).
`knoppix myconf=/dev/hda1`	Runs shell script `knoppix.sh` from the `/dev/hda1` partition (enter the partition name where you have the `knoppix.sh` file).
`knoppix myconf=scan`	Causes Knoppix to search for the file named `knoppix.sh` and execute the commands in that file, if any.
`knoppix noeject`	Does not eject the Live CD after you halt Knoppix.
`knoppix noprompt`	Does not prompt to remove the Live CD after you halt Knoppix.

Boot Command	*What It Does*
`knoppix nowheel mouse`	Forces PS/2 protocol for a PS/2 mouse or touchpad (as opposed to being detected automatically).
`knoppix no`*`XXX`*	Causes Knoppix to skip specific parts of the hardware detection (where *`XXX`* identifies the hardware or server that should not be probed: `apic` = Advanced Programmable Interrupt Controller, `agp` = Accelerated Graphics Port, `apm` = Advanced Power Management, `audio` = sound card, `ddc` = Display Data Channel, `dhcp` = Dynamic Host Configuration Protocol, `fstab` = file system table, `firewire` = IEEE 1394 high-speed serial bus, `pcmcia` = PC Card, `scsi` = Small Computer System Interface, `swap` = hard drive space used for virtual memory, `usb` = Universal Serial Bus).
`knoppix pci=bios`	Uses BIOS directly for bad PCI controllers.
`knoppix pnpbios=off`	Skips the plug-and-play (PnP) BIOS initialization.
`knoppix screen=1280x1024`	Sets screen resolution to 1280 x 1024 pixels (enter whatever resolution you want, such as `1024x768`, `800x600`, `640x480`, and so on).
`knoppix testcd`	Checks the data integrity of the Live CD by using the MD5 sum.
`knoppix tohd=/dev/hda1`	Copies the Live CD to the specified hard drive partition and runs from there.
`knoppix toram`	Copies the Live CD to RAM (memory) and runs from there.
`knoppix vga=ext`	Uses 50-line text mode display.
`knoppix vsync=60`	Uses a vertical refresh rate of 60 Hz for X (enter the vertical refresh rate you want X to use).
`knoppix wheelmouse`	Enables the IMPS/2 protocol for wheel mice.
`knoppix xmodule=`*`modname`*	Causes the X server to load the module specified by *`modname`* so that X works on your video card (*`modname`* can be one of `ati`, `fbdev`, `810`, `mga`, `nv`, `radeon`, `savage`, or `s3`).
`knoppix xserver=`*`progname`*	Starts the X server specified by *`progname`* (can be one of `XFree86` or `XF86_SVGA`).

TIP

When you have multiple Knoppix boot commands, simply combine them into a single line. For example, to specify that you want to skip the SCSI auto detection, use the U.S. keyboard, a wheelmouse, and require the X server to load the `nv` module, you would enter the following at the `boot:` prompt:

```
knoppix noscsi lang=us wheelmouse xmodule=nv
```

The fatal signal 11 error

Some people get a fatal `signal 11 error` message during installation — and it stops the process cold. This error usually happens past the initial boot screen as the `anaconda` installer is starting its GUI or text interface.

The most likely cause of a `signal 11 error` during installation is a hardware error related to memory or the cache associated with the CPU (microprocessor).

Signal 11, also known as SIGSEGV (short for Segment Violation Signal), can occur in other Linux applications. A *segment violation* occurs when a process tries to access a memory location that it's not supposed to access. The operating system catches the problem before it happens and stops the offending process by sending it a signal 11. When that happens during installation, it means the installer made an error while accessing memory, and the most likely reason is some hardware problem. A commonly suggested cure for the signal 11 problem is to turn off the CPU cache in the BIOS. To do so, you have to enter SETUP while the PC boots (by pressing a function key such as F2) and then turn off the CPU cache from the BIOS setup menu.

If the problem is due to a hardware error in memory (in other words, the result of bad memory chips), you could try swapping the memory modules around in their slots. You may also consider replacing an existing memory module with another memory module, if you have one handy.

You can read more about the signal 11 problem at `www.bitwizard.nl/sig11`.

Using Linux kernel boot options

When you boot the PC for Linux installation, either from the DVD or the first CD-ROM, you get a text screen with the `boot:` prompt. Typically, you press Enter at that prompt or do nothing and the installation begins shortly. You can, however, specify quite a variety of options at the `boot:` prompt. The options control various aspects of the Linux kernel startup, such as disabling support for troublesome hardware or starting the X server using a specific X driver module. Some of these boot options can be helpful in bypassing problems that you may encounter during installation.

To use these boot options, typically you type **linux** followed by the boot options. For example, to perform text mode installation and tell the kernel that your PC has 256MB of memory, you type the following at the `boot:` prompt:

```
linux text mem=256M
```

Consult Table 3-3 for a brief summary of some of the Linux boot options. You can use these commands to turn certain features on or off.

Although I mention these Linux kernel boot commands in the context of troubleshooting installation problems, you can use many of these commands anytime you boot a PC with any Linux distribution and you want to turn specific features on or off.

Table 3-3 Some Linux Boot Options

Use This Boot Option	*To Do This*
`askmethod`	Prompts you for other installation methods, such as installing over the network using NFS, FTP, or HTTP.
`apic`	Works around a bug commonly encountered in the Intel 440GX chipset BIOS and only executes with the installation program kernel.
`acpi=off`	Disables ACPI in case there are problems with ACPI.
`dd`	Prompts for a driver disk during the installation of Red Hat Linux.
`display=IP_address:0`	Causes the installer GUI to appear on the remote system identified by the IP address. (Make sure that you run the command `xhost +`*`hostname`* on the remote system where *`hostname`* is the host where you are running the installer.)
`driverdisk`	Performs the same function as the `dd` command.
`enforcing=0`	Turns off Security Enhanced Linux (SELinux) mandatory access control.
`expert`	Enables you to partition removable media and prompts for a driver disk.
`ide=nodma`	Disables DMA (direct memory access) on all IDE devices and can be useful when you are having IDE-related problems.
`ks`	Configures the Ethernet card using DHCP and then runs a kickstart installation by using a *kickstart* file from an NFS server identified by the `bootServer` parameters provided by the DHCP server.
`ks=`*`kickstartfile`*	Runs a kickstart installation by using the kickstart file specified by *`kickstartfile`*. (The idea behind kickstart is to create a text file with all the installation options and then "kick start" the installation by booting and then providing the kickstart file as input.)
`lowres`	Forces the installer GUI to run at a lower resolution (640 x 480).
`mediacheck`	Prompts you if you want to check the integrity of the CD image (also called the ISO image). Checking the image is done by computing the MD5 `checksum` and comparing that with the official Fedora Core value. It can take a few minutes to check a CD-ROM.
`mem=`*`xxx`*`M`	Overrides the amount of memory the kernel detects in the PC (some older machines could detect only 16MB of memory, and on some new machines, the video card may use a portion of the main memory). Replace *`xxx`* with the number representing the megabytes of memory in your PC.
`nmi_watchdog=1`	Enables the built-in kernel deadlock detector that makes use of Non Maskable Interrupt (NMI).
`noapic`	Prevents the kernel from using the Advanced Programmable Interrupt Controller (APIC) chip. (Use this command on motherboards known to have a bad APIC.)

(continued)

Table 3-3 *(continued)*

Use This Boot Option	*To Do This*
`nofirewire`	Does not load support for FireWire.
`noht`	Disables *hyperthreading* (a feature that enables a single processor to act as multiple virtual processors at the hardware level).
`nomce`	Disables self-diagnosis checks performed on the CPU by using Machine Check Exception (MCE). On some machines, these checks are performed too often and need to be disabled.
`nomount`	Does not automatically mount any installed Linux partitions in rescue mode.
`nopass`	Does not pass the keyboard and mouse information to stage 2 of the installation program.
`nopcmcia`	Ignores any PCMCIA controllers in system.
`noprobe`	Disables automatic hardware detection and instead prompts the user for information about SCSI and network hardware installed on the PC. You can pass parameters to modules by using this approach.
`noshell`	Disables shell access on virtual console 2 (the one you get by pressing Ctrl+Alt+F2) during installation.
`nousb`	Disables the loading of USB support during the installation (may be useful if the installation program hangs early in the process).
`nousbstorage`	Disables the loading of the `usbstorage` module in the installation program's loader. It may help with device ordering on SCSI systems.
`reboot=b`	Changes the way the kernel tries to reboot the PC so that it can reboot even if the kernel hangs during system shutdown.
`pci=noacpi`	Causes the kernel to not use ACPI to route interrupt requests.
`pci=biosirq`	Causes the kernel to use BIOS settings to route interrupt requests (IRQs).
`rescue`	Starts the kernel in rescue mode where you get a shell prompt and can try to fix problems.
`resolution=`*`HHH`*`x`*`VVV`*	Causes the installer GUI to run in the specified video mode (replace *`HHH`* and *`VVV`* with standard resolution numbers, such as `640x480`, `800x600`, `1024x768`, and so on).
`selinux=0`	Disables the SELinux kernel extensions.
`serial`	Turns on serial console support during installation.
`skipddc`	Skips the Display Data Channel (DDC) probe of monitors (useful if the probing causes problems).
`vnc`	Starts a VNC (Virtual Network Computing) server so that you can control the GUI installer from another networked system that runs a VNC client.
`text`	Runs the installation program in text mode.

Setting Up Printers

In most Linux distributions, you have to set up any printers after you install the distribution. The following sections outline the printer configuration steps for each of the distributions on this book's DVD — Debian, Fedora Core, SUSE, Knoppix, and Xandros.

Configuring printers in Debian

Debian comes with the foomatic-gui utility that enables you to configure a printer through a graphical interface, as shown in Figure 3-1. To configure a printer, connect the printer to the appropriate port — parallel or USB — and turn it on. Then follow these steps:

1. **Select Main Menu⇨System⇨Printers from the GUI desktop to start the foomatic-gui.**

   If you are not logged in as `root`, a dialog box prompts you for the `root` password. If you cannot find the menu item, open a terminal window, type **su -** to become `root`, and then type **export DISPLAY=:0.0; foomatic gui**. The foomatic-gui utility displays its main window, as shown in Figure 3-1.

2. **Click Add on the toolbar. (Refer to Figure 3-1.)**

   The foomatic-gui tool starts the Add Printer wizard (see Figure 3-2) that guides you through the process of adding a new printer to your system.

3. **Click Forward.**

   The Add Printer wizard displays a number of different connection types for the printer. Select your printer connection from the list.

   To add a network-connected printer, click Detect Network Printers, and you should see a list of printers, including Windows printers, available on your network. After you select the printer connection, foomatic-gui requests a name for the queue used to hold print jobs for that printer.

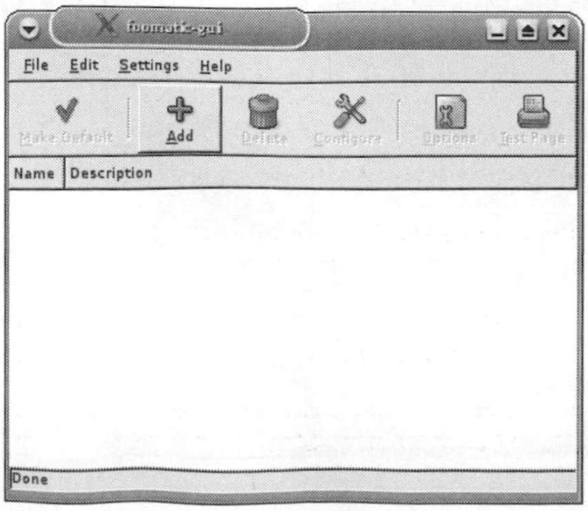

Figure 3-1: Use the foomatic-gui to configure and manage printers in Debian.

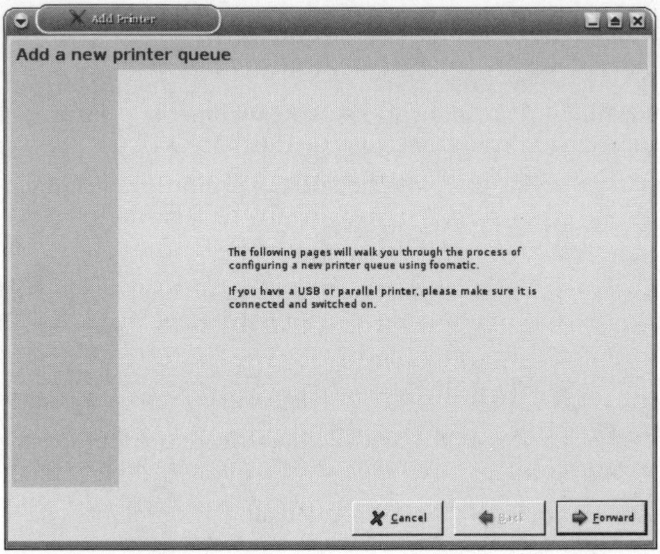

Figure 3-2: The Add Printer wizard guides you through the steps.

4. **Enter a name for the printer queue as well as identifying information about the printer (the location and a brief description) and click Forward.**

   The foomatic-gui tool displays a list of printer make and models, as shown in Figure 3-3.

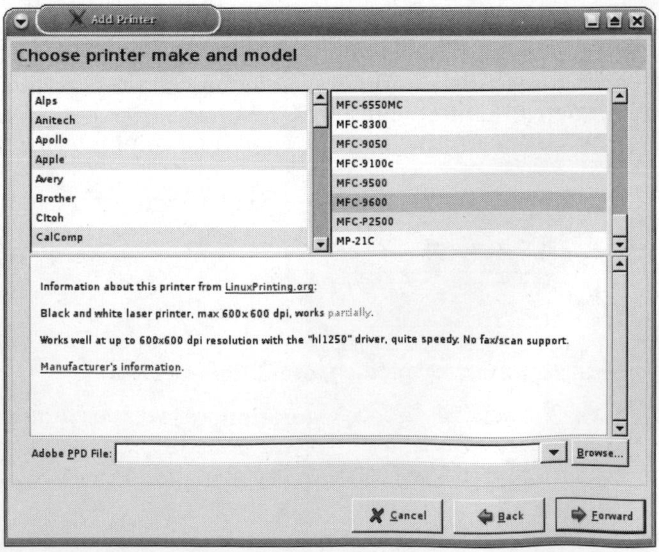

Figure 3-3: Select your printer make and model from this foomatic-gui screen.

5. **Select the printer's make and model and click Forward.**

   The foomatic-gui tool displays the drivers that apply to this printer.

6. **Select the driver you want to use and click Forward.**

   Pick the driver marked `recommended`. The foomatic-gui tool displays a message saying that you can add the printer by clicking Apply.

7. **Click Apply to add the printer.**

From the foomatic-gui window (refer to Figure 3-1) you can select a printer and click the Test Page button to print a test page.

Configuring printers in Fedora Core

The Fedora Core installer does not include a printer configuration step, but you can easily configure a printer from a graphical utility program. To set up printers, follow these steps:

1. **From the graphical login screen, log in as `root`.**

   If you're not logged in as `root`, proceed to the next step and the printer configuration tool prompts you for the `root` password.

2. **From the GNOME or KDE desktop, choose Main Menu➪System Settings➪Printing.**

   The printer configuration tool is called `system-config-printer`. Figure 3-4 shows its main window.

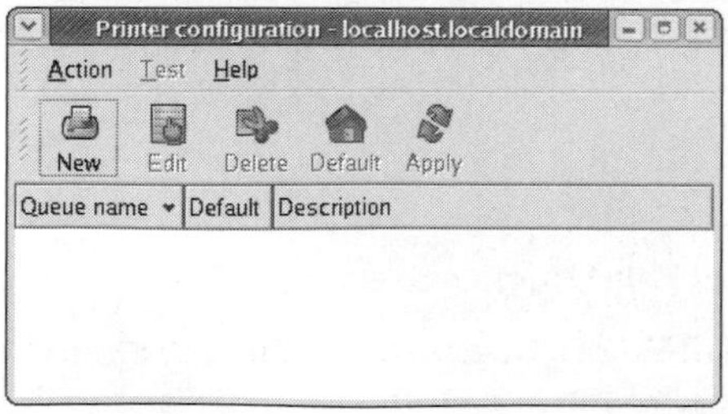

Figure 3-4: Configure and manage printers from the Printer Configuration tool.

3. **Click the New button to configure a new printer.**

   The Fedora Core's Printer Configuration wizard starts. The initial window displays a message that assures you that nothing changes until you click the Apply button at the end of all the steps. Click Forward to continue.

4. **Enter the name for the print queue and a short description of the print queue; then click Forward.**

   Use some systematic approach when naming the print queue. For example, if I have a HP Laserjet 5000 printer on the second floor in Room 210, I might name the queue `Room210HPLJ5000` because this name makes finding the printer easier. Sometimes systems administrators choose cute names such as `kermit`, `piggy`, `elmo`, `cookiemonster`, and so on, but after you have too many printers, such cute schemes don't work well. Providing a clue about the printer's location as well as the make and model in the print queue's name is best.

5. **In the next screen (see Figure 3-5), select a queue type from the drop-down list; then click Forward.**

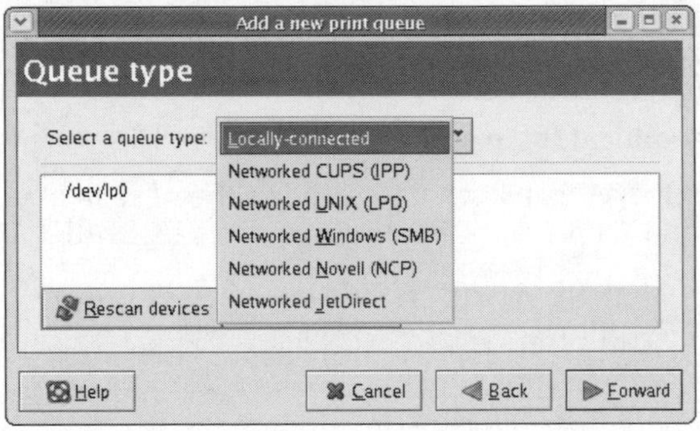

Figure 3-5: Select the print queue type from this window.

TIP

Select the print queue type that applies to your situation. For example, if you want to print on a shared Windows printer, select Networked Windows (SMB).

To set up a printer connected to your PC's parallel port, select Locally-connected.

The following types of print queues are available:

- **Locally-connected:** Refers to a printer connected directly to the serial, parallel, or USB port of your PC.
- **Networked CUPS (IPP):** Refers to a Common UNIX Printing System (CUPS) print queue at another server on the network (IPP refers to the Internet Printing Protocol used to communicate with the remote CUPS server).
- **Networked UNIX (LPD):** Refers to a print queue managed by the LPD server on another UNIX system on the local network (LPD refers to Line Printer Daemon — another print spooler for UNIX systems).

- **Networked Windows (SMB):** Refers to a printer connected to another PC on the local network that uses the Server Message Block (SMB) protocol, the underlying protocol in Windows file and print sharing.
- **Networked Novell (NCP):** Refers to a printer connected to a Novell Netware server on the local network.
- **Networked JetDirect:** Refers to a HP JetDirect printer connected directly to the local network.

6. **If you select Locally-connected, the next screen displays information about the detected parallel port; click Forward to continue.**

   For other options, you get a screen that prompts you to identify the network printer. The way you specify a network printer depends on the network type. For example, to use a networked CUPS printer on a host with the IP address 192.168.0.8 on your local area network, you have to type a name such as **http://192.168.0.8:631/printers/HPLaserjetRoom210** where *HPLaserjetRoom210* is the name of the networked printer.

7. **Select the make and model of your printer, and then click Forward.**

   Click the drop-down list (above the scrolling list) to display a list of printer manufacturers. When you choose a printer manufacturer from this list, the scrolling list displays the names of different printer models from that manufacturer. If you have a PostScript printer, you can simply go to the Generic list (Generic is one of the choices in the manufacturer list) and select PostScript printer.

   The last screen shows information about the new print queue.

8. **Review all information to make sure it's correct, and then click Finish to create the print queue.**

9. **When a dialog box appears, asking whether you want to print a test page, click Yes.**

   Doing so applies all changes and restarts the print-scheduler program that takes care of printing. The printer now prints a test page, after which a message box appears and asks you to check the test page.

10. **Click OK to dismiss the message box.**

    The new print queue appears in the printer configuration window, and you can submit print jobs to this queue.

11. **Quit the printer configuration tool.**

    You can do so by choosing Action➪Quit, or by closing the printer configuration window (click the X button in the upper-right corner of the window's frame). You are prompted to save the printer information.

Configuring printers in Knoppix

To add a printer in Knoppix, follow these steps:

1. **From the Knoppix desktop, choose Main Menu⇨KNOPPIX⇨Configure⇨Configure printer(s).**

   The Configure Printers wizard appears. Figure 3-6 shows its main window.

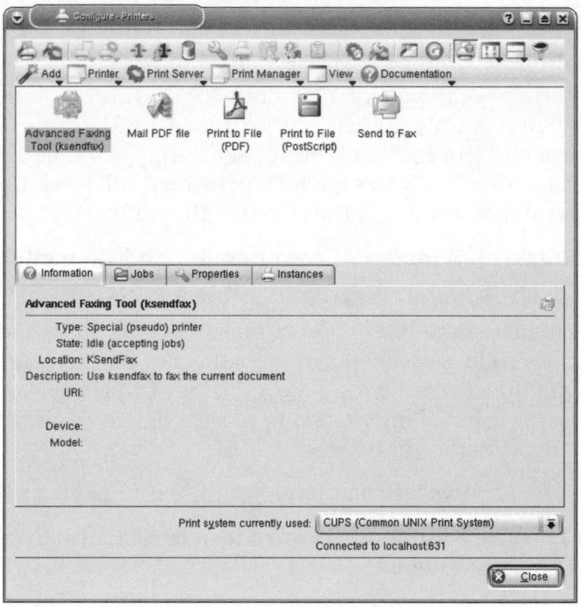

Figure 3-6: In Knoppix, configure and manage printers from this GUI tool.

2. **Click Add on toolbar and select Add Printer/Class from the drop-down menu.**

   The Printer Configuration wizard starts the Add Printer Wizard (see Figure 3-7) that guides you through the steps.

3. **Click Next and from the next screen select the type of printer connection.**

   This can be a local parallel, serial, or USB port, as well as a network printer supporting different protocols such as TCP or IPP. Select your printer type and click Next. Depending on your printer's connection type, the wizard prompts for more information. For example, for a local printer, you have to select the parallel, serial, or USB port from a list.

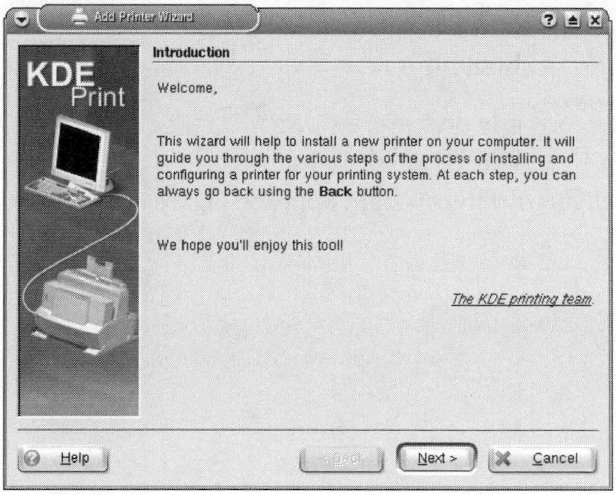

Figure 3-7: Add a new printer through the Add Printer Wizard.

4. **Provide information about the printer connection — the local port or the URL identifying the network printer. Then click Next.**

   The wizard displays a list of printer makes and models, as shown in Figure 3-8.

5. **Select your printer's make and model and click Next.**

   The wizard displays a list of drivers along with its recommendation.

6. **Select the printer driver and click Next.**

   The wizard displays a screen (see Figure 3-9) from which you can test the printer settings.

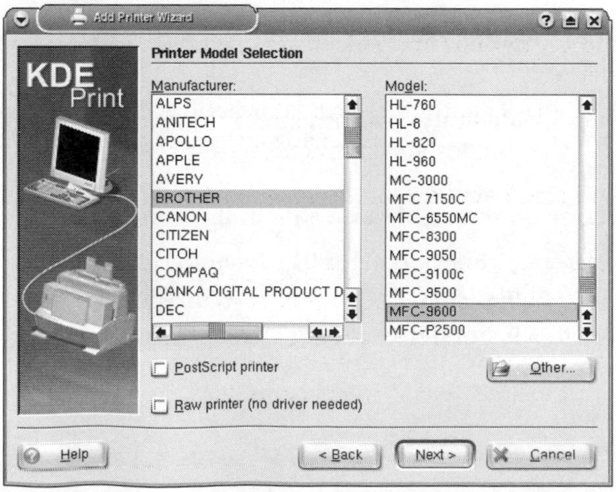

Figure 3-8: Select the printer's make and model.

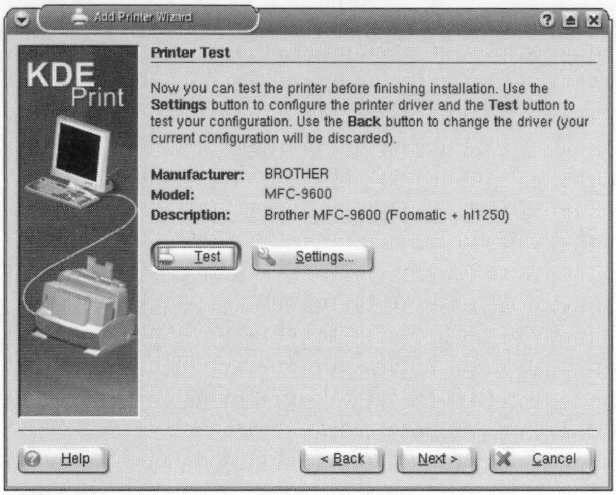

Figure 3-9: Test the printer settings before installing a printer.

7. **Select whether you want banners after each print job and click Next.**
8. **Set any quotas such as page limit or limit on the size of files sent to the printer and click Next.**
9. **Specify user access settings such as users who can access the print queue and click Next.**
10. **Name the print queue and add printer description. Click Next.**
11. **Review printer settings and click Finish to add the printer.**

Configuring printers in SUSE

To add a printer in SUSE, follow these steps:

1. **Select Main Menu⇨System⇨YaST and click Hardware on the left-hand side of the window.**

   The YaST control center displays information about various hardware, as shown in Figure 3-10. As you can see, you can configure various hardware from YaST.

2. **Click Printer on the right-hand side of the window.**

   YaST opens the Printer Configuration window and displays information about any printers that it detects, as shown in Figure 3-11.

3. **If your printer is not detected, click Other and then click Configure.**

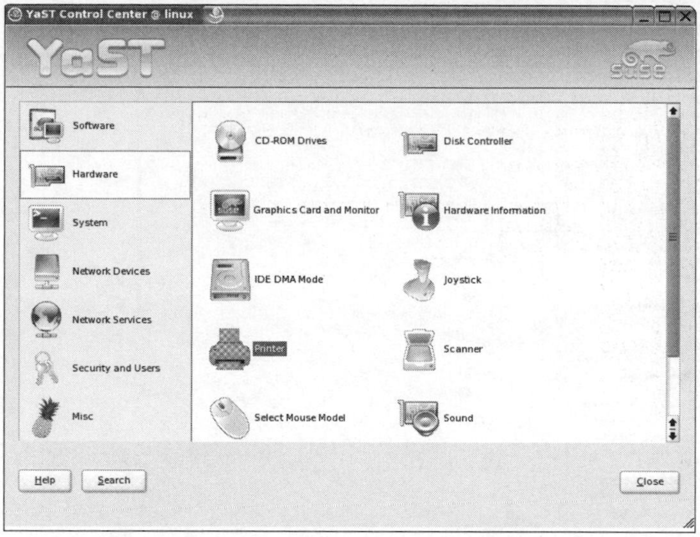

Figure 3-10: To configure anything, start with the YaST Control Center.

YaST displays a list of printer types (see Figure 3-12) from which you can select your printer. The type depends on how your printer is connected to your PC (through parallel, serial, USB, or network).

4. **Select your printer type and click Next.**

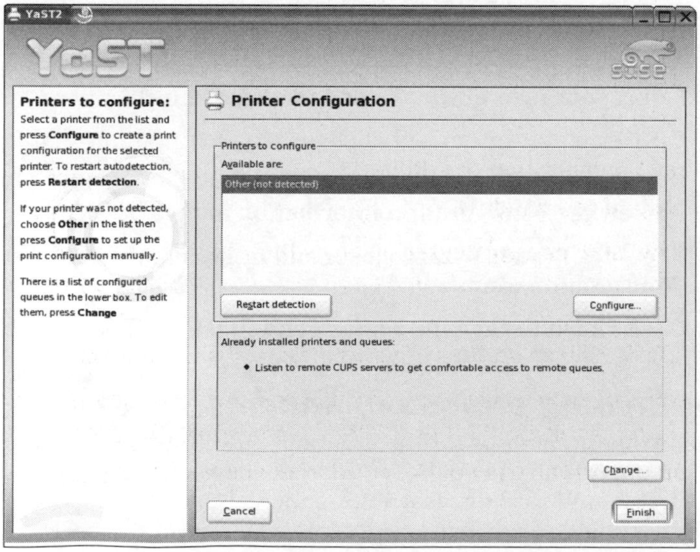

Figure 3-11: YaST displays this Printer Configuration window.

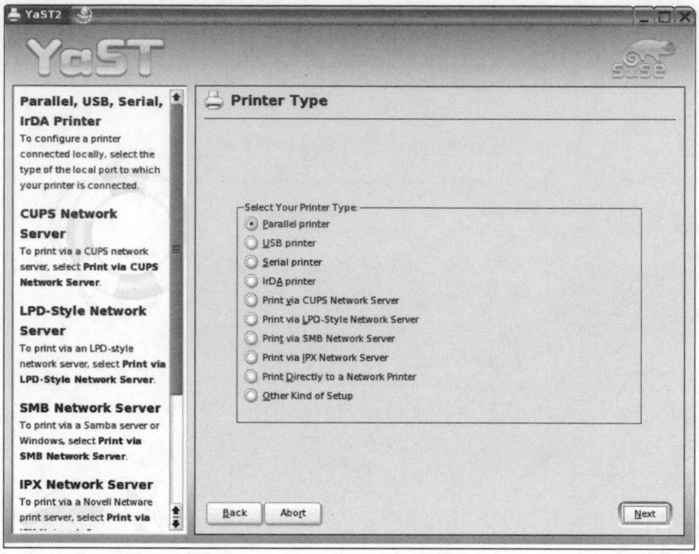

Figure 3-12: Select your printer type from this window.

YaST prompts for more information, depending on the printer type you selected. For example, for a parallel printer, you have to identify the parallel port to which the printer is attached.

5. **Provide information about the printer connection and click Next.**
6. **Enter the name of the print queue as well as some descriptive information about the printer and click Next.**

   YaST displays a list of printer makes and models.
7. **Select your printer's make and model. Then click Next.**

   YaST displays the current configuration information so that you can test the configuration or edit it.
8. **Review the configuration information and click OK.**

   The Adds Printer Wizard closes and returns to the YaST Printer Configuration window.
9. **Click Finish to save the settings and finish adding the printer.**

Configuring printers in Xandros

When you run Xandros for the first time, the First Run Wizard runs and gives you an opportunity to configure printers. Figure 3-13 shows the screen where the First Run Wizard displays information about printers and also gives you an opportunity to add a new printer.

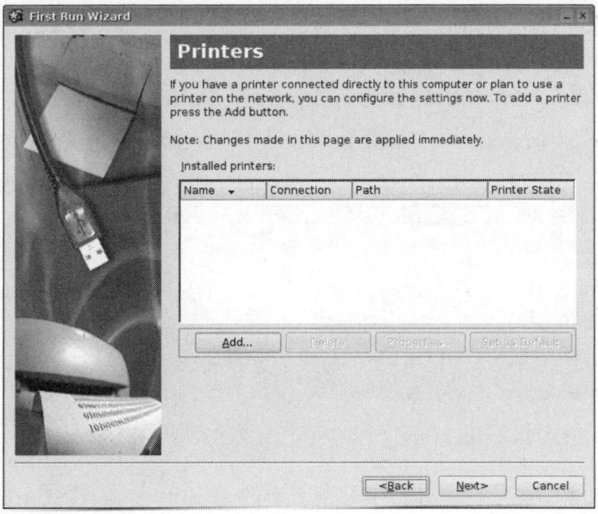

Figure 3-13: The printer configuration step in Xandros.

If you skipped it during the first reboot, you can always start the First Run Wizard by selecting Main Menu➪Applications➪System➪First Run Wizard.

From the First Run Wizard's Printer screen, follow these steps to configure a printer:

1. **Click Add in First Run Wizard's Printer screen (refer to Figure 3-13).**

   The Add Printer Wizard starts, as shown in Figure 3-14.

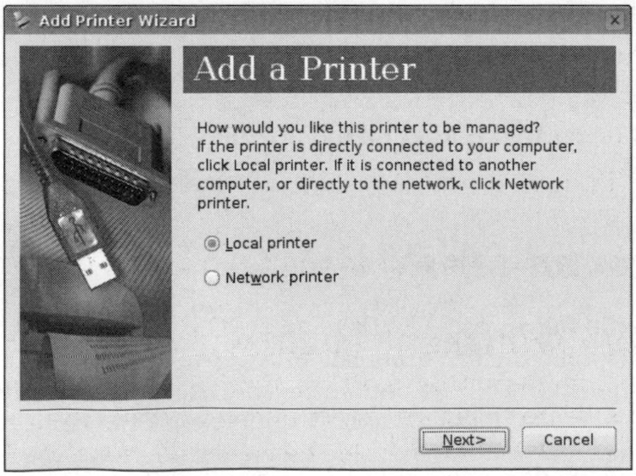

Figure 3-14: The Add Printer Wizard in Xandros prompts you for printer details.

2. **Select the type of printer — Local Printer or Network Printer — and then click Next.**

   The wizard prompts for more information about the printer's connection.

3. **Provide information about the printer's connection and click Next.**

   For example, for a local printer, specify whether it's a parallel or USB printer. The wizard displays a screen from where you can select the printer's make, model, and a driver.

4. **Select your printer's make, model, and driver, as shown in Figure 3-15. Click Next.**

   The wizard gives you the option of printing a test page and completing the printer configuration.

5. **Click Finish to complete printer configuration.**

After finishing printer configuration, the First Run Wizard continues with other configuration tasks.

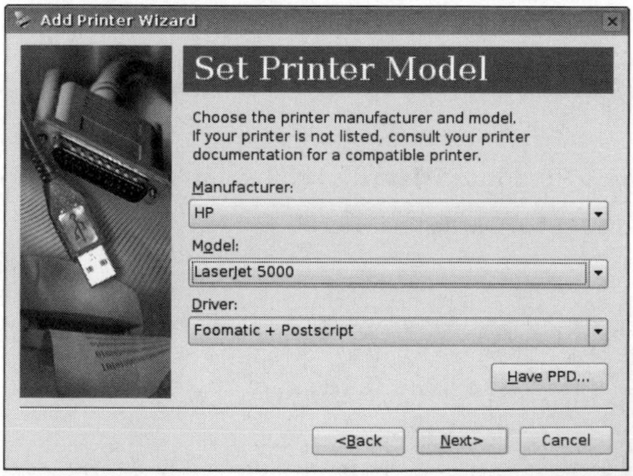

Figure 3-15: Select the printer's make, model, and a driver.

Managing DVDs and CD-ROMs

The GUI desktop makes using DVDs and CD-ROMs in Linux easy. Just place a DVD or a CD-ROM in the drive, and an icon appears on the desktop. You can then access the CD or DVD by double-clicking the icon on the desktop. To access the files and folders, you simply double-click the icons that appear in a GUI file manager window. In some Linux distributions, the GUI even automatically opens the contents of a CD or DVD in a file manager window soon after you insert the CD or DVD in the drive.

If you see a DVD/CD-ROM icon, right-click that icon for a context menu. From that menu, you can eject the CD or DVD when you are done.

The Knoppix desktop has icons for each detected drive. To open a CD or DVD, simply click the icon for that drive. In SUSE, click the My Computer icon, and then click the icon for the DVD/CD drive. Xandros Desktop opens the CD/DVD in a Xandros File Manager window.

Installing Other Software

The exact steps for installing software depends on the type of package in which the software is distributed. Most Linux software comes in either a Red Hat Package Manager (RPM) file or a Debian package file. The RPM files have a `.rpm` extension, and the Debian packages have `.deb` extension.

Most distributions provide GUI installers to ease the process of installing new software packages. In this section, I provide a quick overview of adding software in Debian, Fedora Core, SUSE, and Xandros. You typically do not add software to Knoppix because Knoppix is a Live CD distribution that runs from the CD-ROM.

Fedora Core and SUSE uses RPM packages. Debian and Xandros are all Debian-based distributions and, as expected, they typically use Debian packages (also called DEB). However, both RPM and DEB packages can be installed in any Linux distribution. SUSE is Debian-based, but it uses RPM packages.

Installing software in Debian

The best way to manage software packages in Debian is to use APT — the Advanced Packaging Tool — that you usually control through the `apt-get` command.

When you install Debian, one of the last steps is to configure the sources for APT. The APT sources are the Internet servers (both FTP and Web) where APT looks for software packages to download and install on your system. Assuming that APT is properly configured and that your system has a high-speed Internet connection, you can install any package by typing the following command in a terminal window:

```
apt-get install pkgname
```

where *pkgname* is the name of the package that you want to install. If you do not know the package name, start by typing the following command in the terminal window:

```
apt-cache search keyword
```

where *keyword* is related to the package you want to install. For example, to search for a package that has the word "screenshot" in its description and also contains the word "KDE," I would type the following (I use `grep` to search the output for occurrences of the text KDE):

```
apt-cache search screenshot | grep KDE
```

This command then prints the following line as the result:

```
ksnapshot - Screenshot application for KDE
```

This shows that the `ksnapshot` package is what I need. If this package was not yet installed, I could then install it by typing the following command:

```
apt-get install ksnapshot
```

That, in a nutshell, is how you can use the command-line tools to look for and install packages in Debian.

Debian also includes a GUI package installer for KDE called KPackage. KPackage is quite intuitive to use. To try it, select Main Menu⇨System⇨Package Manager from the KDE desktop in Debian. KPackage displays its main window, shown in Figure 3-16, with information about packages.

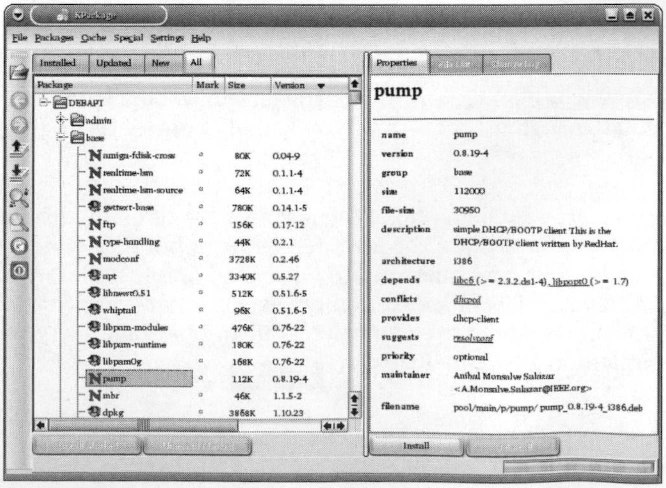

Figure 3-16: You can install and remove packages by using KPackage.

By clicking the tabs — Installed, Updated, New, All — you can view lists of various types of packages, ranging from ones already installed on your system to new ones. Each package list is organized into groups. You can open and close the groups to see individual package names.

When you click on a package, KPackage displays information about the selected package in the right-hand side of the window. You can install any uninstalled package by clicking the Install button in the lower-right corner of the window.

Installing software in Fedora Core

Most Fedora Core software comes in the form of Red Hat Package Manager (RPM) files. An RPM file is basically a single package that contains everything — all the files and configuration information — needed to install a software product.

From the GNOME desktop, use the Add and Remove Packages utility — a graphical utility for installing and uninstalling RPMs. Follow these steps:

1. **Choose Main Menu⇨System Settings⇨Add/Remove Applications.**

   If you're not logged in as `root`, a dialog box prompts you for the `root` password. The Add and Remove Packages utility starts and gathers information about the status of packages installed on your system. After it sorts through the information about all the installed packages, the utility displays the Package Management dialog box, which contains a list of all the packages. (See Figure 3-17.)

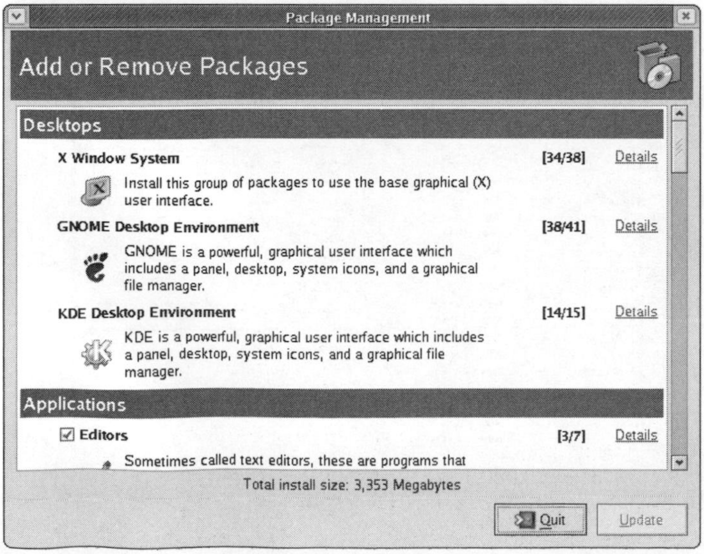

Figure 3-17: Use the Add and Remove Packages to manage software in Fedora Core.

2. **To install an uninstalled package group, select the check box to the left of that package group's name. For partially uninstalled package groups, click the Details hyperlink next to that package.**

   A dialog box appears with details of the packages in the package group.

3. **In the dialog box, select the packages that you want to install or remove by clicking the names, and then click Close to exit the dialog box.**

   You return to the Package Management dialog box and, if you added or removed any package, the Update button becomes active.

4. **Click the Update button to update the packages based on any additions or removals you made in the lists of packages.**

Installing software in SUSE

In SUSE, follow these steps to install or remove software:

1. **Select Main Menu⇨YaST to start the YaST Control Center, as shown in Figure 3-18.**

   The YaST Control Center displays categories of tasks on the left-hand side and specific tasks for that category on the right-hand side. Make sure that you click the Software category on the left-hand side so that the right-hand side shows the options for software.

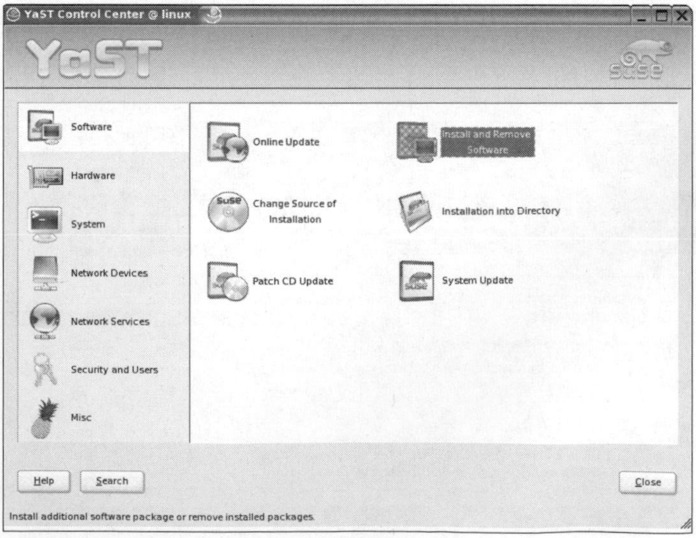

Figure 3-18: Start software installation or removal from the YaST Control Center.

2. **Click the Install and Remove Software icon on the right-hand side (refer to Figure 3-18).**

   YaST displays information about available software packages in a new window, as shown in Figure 3-19.

3. **Select packages to install or search for a package by name.**

   To search for a package by name, click Filter in the upper-left corner, select Search from the drop-down list, and enter a keyword to look for matching package names.

4. **Click the Accept button in the bottom-right corner to begin installing selected packages.**

   YaST checks for *dependencies* — whether a package requires other packages to install correctly — before installing packages. If you want to view what changes would occur when you click Accept, click Filter and select Installation Summary.

Installing software in Xandros

Xandros Desktop OS comes with Xandros Networks, which enables you to buy software online as well as install software from a CD or DVD. To start Xandros Networks, double-click the Xandros Networks icon on the Xandros desktop. Xandros Networks starts, connects to a Xandros server, and displays information about installed, updated, and new applications, as shown in Figure 3-20.

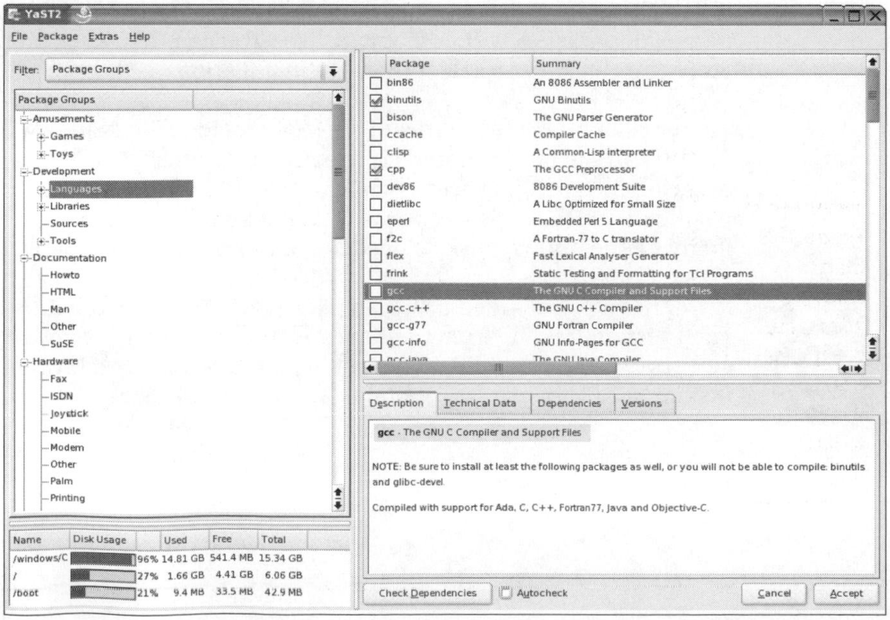

Figure 3-19: Install or remove software from this YaST window.

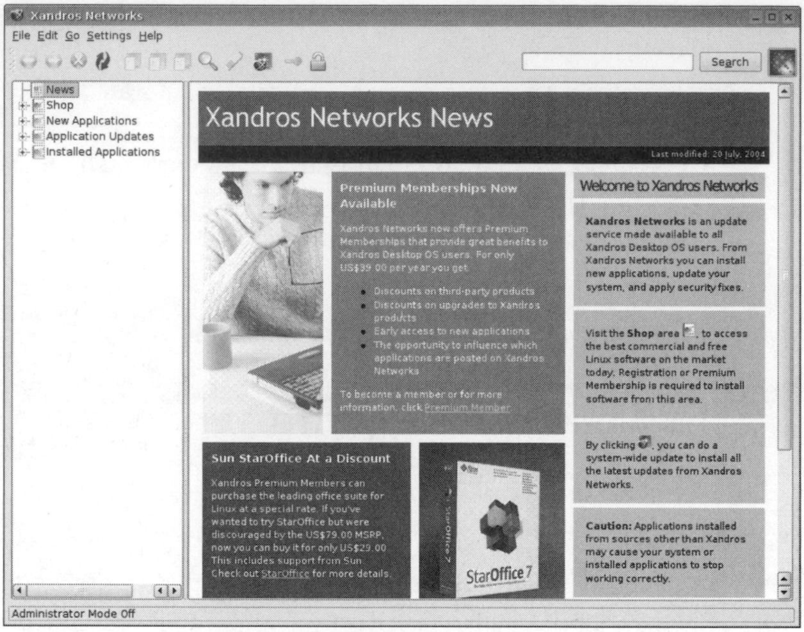

Figure 3-20: Use Xandros Networks to install or upgrade software.

To look at the list of new applications, click the plus sign to the left of the New Applications label on the left-hand side of the Xandros Networks window (see Figure 3-21). You get a further list of application categories. If you click on a category, the right-hand side of the window shows the names of packages within that category. You can then click on packages or an entire category to select them for installation.

To install any selected software packages, select File⇨Enter Administrator Mode. You will be prompted for the Administrator (`root`) password. After entering the `root` password, you can select File⇨Install All Selected New Applications. Xandros Networks will check for dependencies, prompt you if any further information is needed, and install the new software.

TIP

If you have downloaded a Debian package, you can install it by selecting File⇨Install DEB File from the Xandros Networks menu. Similarly, the menu selection File⇨Install RPM File installs an RPM package. (For more about installing RPM packages, see Book V, Chapter 4.)

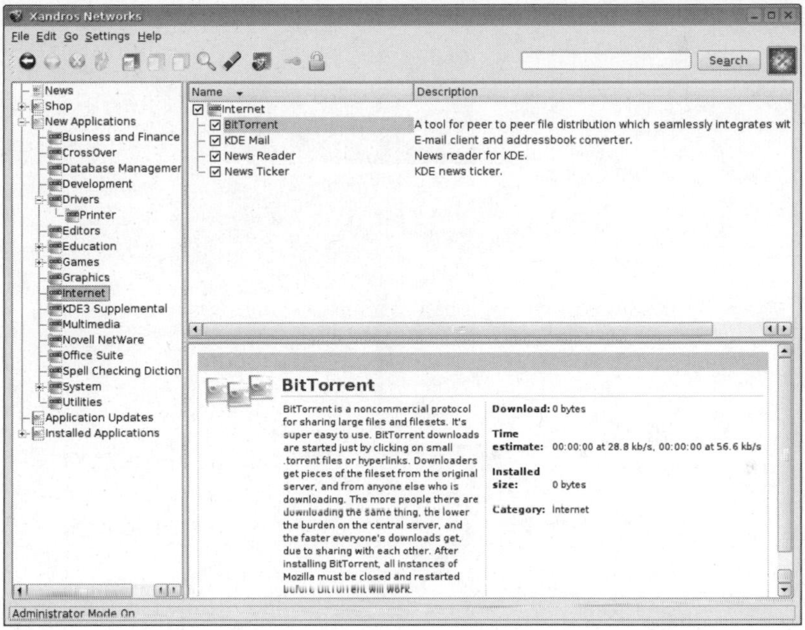

Figure 3-21: Select the packages to install.

Chapter 4: Trying Out Linux

In This Chapter

- **Starting Linux**
- **Logging in**
- **Checking out the GUI desktops**
- **Playing with the shell**
- **Shutting down**

You're sitting in front of your PC about to turn it on. You know that the PC has Linux installed (maybe you did the installing yourself, but who's keeping track?). You're wondering what to expect when you turn it on and what you do afterward. Not to worry. If you're using Linux for the first time, this chapter shows you how to log in, check out the graphical desktops, try out some cryptic Linux commands, and finally, shut down the PC.

If you are trying out the Knoppix Live CD, all you have to do is boot from the Knoppix Live CD — as explained in Book I, Chapter 2 — and then you can try it just like any other Linux distribution.

For those of you who already know something about Linux, flip through this chapter to see if anything looks new. You never know what you may not know!

Starting Linux

When you power up the PC, it goes through the normal power-up sequence and loads the boot loader — GRUB or LILO, depending on your Linux distribution and what you selected during installation. The *boot loader* (once known as the bootstrap loader) is a tiny computer program that loads the rest of the operating system from the hard drive into the computer's memory. The whole process of starting up a computer is called *booting*.

For Live CDs such as Knoppix that boot from a CD, the boot loader is typically ISOLINUX, a boot loader designed to work from an ISO 9660 CD-ROM.

The LILO and GRUB boot loaders display a graphical screen with the names of the operating systems that the boot loader can load. For example, if your PC has Windows and Linux, you see both names listed. You can then use the up- and down-arrow keys to select the operating system you want to use. If the PC is set up to load Linux by default, wait a few seconds, and then the boot loader starts Linux. To be more precise, the boot loader loads the *Linux kernel* — the core of the Linux operating system — into the PC's memory.

Other boot loaders such as ISOLINUX may display a text `boot:` prompt at which you can type boot commands to load specific operating systems and pass options to that operating system.

As the Linux kernel starts, you see a long list of opening messages, often referred to as the *boot messages.* (You can see these messages at any time by typing the command **dmesg** in a terminal window.) These messages include the names of the devices that Linux detects. One of the first lines in the boot messages reads

```
Calibrating delay loop... 2981.88 BogoMIPS
```

BogoMIPS is Linux jargon (explained in this chapter in a handy sidebar) for a measure of time. The number that precedes BogoMIPS depends on your PC's processor speed, whether it's an old 200 MHz Pentium or a new 4 GHz Pentium 4. The kernel uses the BogoMIPS measurement when it has to wait a small amount of time for some event to occur (like getting a response back from a disk controller when it's ready).

What is BogoMIPS?

As Linux boots, you get a message that says `Calibrating delay loop... 421. 23 BogoMIPS`, with some number before the word *BogoMIPS.* BogoMIPS is one of those words that confounds new Linux users, but it's just jargon with a simple meaning.

BogoMIPS is Linus's invention (yes, the same Linus Torvalds who started Linux), and it means *bogus MIPS.* As you may know, MIPS is an acronym for *millions of instructions per second* — a measure of how fast your computer runs programs. Unfortunately, MIPS isn't a very good measure of performance; the MIPS measurements of different types of computers are difficult to compare accurately. BogoMIPS is basically a way to measure the computer's speed that's independent of the exact processor type. Linux uses the BogoMIPS number to calibrate a *delay loop,* in which the computer keeps running some useless instructions until a specified amount of time passes. Of course, the reason for killing valuable processor time like this is to wait for some slowpoke device to get ready for work.

After the boot messages, some Linux distributions such as Fedora Core switch to a graphical boot screen that shows information about the progress of system startup. When you boot some Linux distributions such as Fedora Core and Xandros Desktop OS for the first time after installation, you get an initial configuration program that guides you through some configuration steps such as setting the date and time and adding user accounts. To complete such first-time configuration steps, all you have to do is enter the requested information.

After Linux boots, you typically get a graphical login screen. For a Live CD distribution such as Knoppix, you get the desktop without having to log in as a user. Figure 4-1 shows the Knoppix desktop after you boot your PC from the Knoppix Live CD.

For other distributions such as SUSE, a typical graphical login screen looks similar to the one shown in Figure 4-2.

The login window in the middle of the screen displays a Welcome message and has a text input field where you can type your username and password.

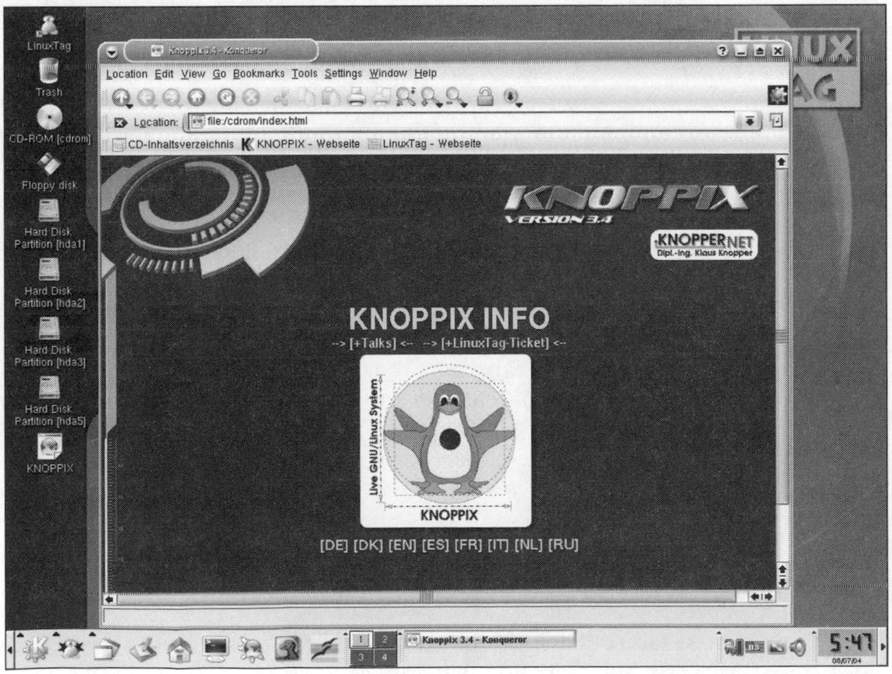

Figure 4-1: After booting from Knoppix Live CD, you get the Knoppix desktop.

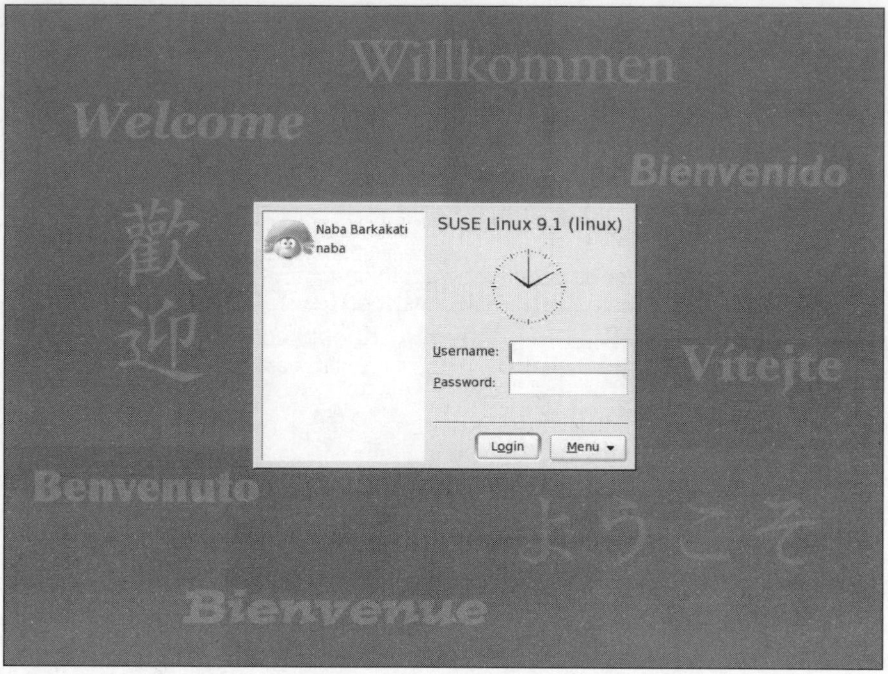

Figure 4-2: The graphical login screen is where you log in as a user.

You can log in using any of the accounts you define during or after the installation. There is always the `root` username, which happens to be the superuser or the administrator account. Whether you install Linux yourself or someone installs it for you, you need to know the `root` password. Without that, you cannot do many of the tasks necessary to find out how Linux works.

For example, to log in as user `spiderman`, type **spiderman** in the first text field and press Enter. (Move the mouse over the login dialog box before you begin typing.) Then type `spiderman`'s password and press Enter. You then see the initial graphical user interface (GUI — pronounced *gooey* for short) appear. What you get depends on your choice of GUI — GNOME or KDE. If someone made the choice for you, don't worry — GNOME and KDE are both quite good and versatile.

Exploring GUI Desktops

Most Linux distributions come with one or both of two GUI desktops — GNOME and KDE. If you install both, you can try them out one by one. Each distribution has its default GUI. Table 4-1 lists the default GUI desktops of some Linux distributions. I provide an overview of the two major GUI desktops — GNOME and KDE — in the following sections.

Table 4-1 Default GUI Desktops for Some Linux Distributions

Distribution	*Default GUI Desktop*
Debian	User can install any GUI desktop: GNOME, KDE, or XFCE. (XFCE is another GUI desktop for UNIX systems. You can find more information about XFCE at `www.xfce.org`.) Typically, Debian installs KDE by default.
Fedora Core	GNOME, but a user can install KDE as well and easily switch between the two.
Knoppix	KDE.
SUSE	KDE.
Xandros	KDE with enhancements (it's called Xandros Desktop).

GNOME

GNOME stands for *GNU Network Object Model Environment* (and GNU, as you probably know, stands for *GNU's Not UNIX*). GNOME is a graphical user interface (GUI) and a programming environment. From the user's perspective, GNOME is like Microsoft Windows. Behind the scenes, GNOME has many features that allow programmers to write graphical applications that can work together well. In this chapter, I point out only some key features of the GNOME GUI, leaving the details for you to explore on your own at your leisure.

If you're curious, you can always find out the latest information about GNOME by visiting the GNOME home page at `www.gnome.org`.

If GNOME is the default desktop, after you log in, you see the GNOME GUI desktop. Figure 4-3 shows the GNOME desktop for a typical user.

WARNING!

You should not normally log in as `root`. When you log in as `root`, you could accidentally damage your system because you can do anything when you're `root`. Always log in as a normal user. When you need to perform any task as `root`, type **su -** in a terminal window and enter the `root` password.

The exact appearance of the GNOME desktop depends on the current *session* — the set of applications running at that time — and your Linux distribution. As you can see, the initial GNOME desktop, shown in Figure 4-3, is very similar to the Windows desktop. It has the GNOME panel, or simply the panel (similar to the Windows taskbar) along the bottom and icons for folders and applications appear directly on the desktop. You can place icons directly on the Windows desktop in a similar way.

You can move and resize the windows just as you do in Microsoft Windows. Also, as in the window frames in Microsoft Windows, the right-hand corner of the window's title bar includes three buttons. The leftmost button reduces the window to an icon, the middle button maximizes the window to fill up the entire screen, and the rightmost button closes the window.

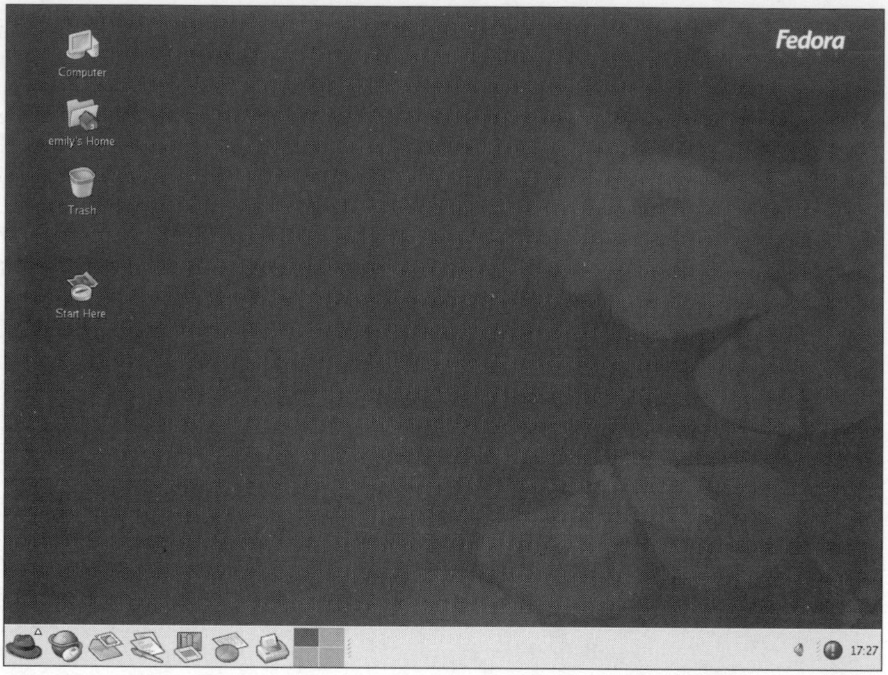

Figure 4-3: The initial GNOME GUI desktop after logging in.

The GNOME panel

The GNOME panel is a key feature of the GNOME desktop. The panel is a separate GNOME application. As Figure 4-4 shows, it provides a display area for menus and small panel applets. Each panel applet is a small program designed to work inside the panel. For example, the Clock applet on the panel's far right displays the current time.

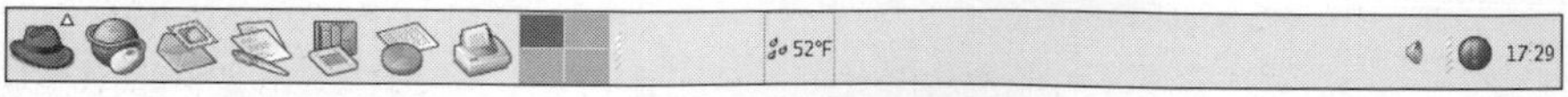

Figure 4-4: The GNOME panel.

The GNOME panel includes several other applets besides the Clock applet at the far right edge (the exact details depend on your Linux distribution):

✦ **The GNOME Pager applet:** Provides a virtual desktop that's larger than the physical dimensions of your system's screen. In Figure 4-4, the pager displays four pages in a small display area. Each page represents an area equal to the size of the display screen. To go to a specific page, click that page in the pager window. The GNOME Pager applet displays buttons for each window being displayed in the current virtual page.

- **Launcher applets:** The buttons to the right of the Main Menu button are launcher applets. Each of these applets displays a button with the icon of an application. Clicking a button starts (launches) that application. Try clicking each of these buttons to see what happens. The mouse and earth button launches the Mozilla Web browser, whereas clicking the pen and paper icon opens the OpenOffice.org Writer word processor. Move the mouse over a button and a small Help message appears with information about that button.
- **The GNOME Weather applet:** Displays the local weather. You don't see this applet until you start it. You can start it from the context menu that appears when you right-click in an empty area of the panel window.

The Main Menu button

In Figure 4-4, the leftmost edge of the panel shows a button sporting a red hat in Fedora Core or a stylized foot in other distributions — that's the Main Menu button, the most important part of the GNOME panel. Just like the Start button in Microsoft Windows, you can launch applications from the menu that pops up when you click the Main Menu button. Figure 4-5 shows a typical view of the Main Menu in GNOME.

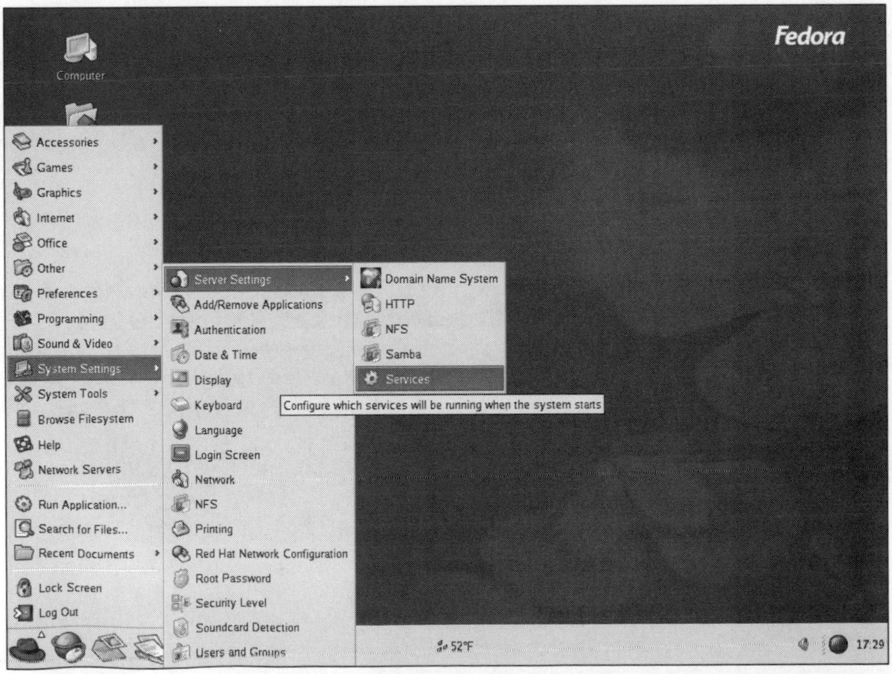

Figure 4-5: Click the Main Menu button and move the mouse pointer from menu to menu to start the program you want.

Typically, the Main Menu and its submenus list items that start an application. Some menu items have an arrow; move the mouse pointer on an item with an arrow, and another menu pops up. In Figure 4-5, the menu selection is Main Menu⇨System Settings⇨Server Settings⇨Services. Notice that when you point to a menu selection, a help balloon pops up with information about that selection.

TIP

You can start applets such as the Weather applet from the menu that appears when you right-click the GNOME panel. To start the Weather applet, right-click the panel and select Add to Panel⇨Accessories⇨Weather Report, as shown in Figure 4-6. In the Add to Panel menu, you find many more categories of applets you can try.

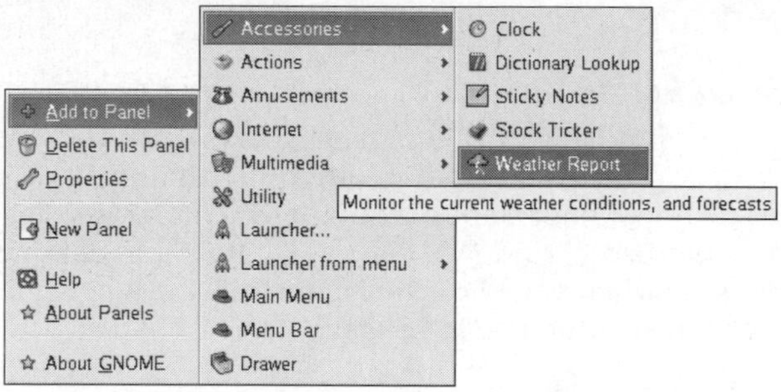

Figure 4-6: Right-click the panel and choose Add to Panel to see the available applets.

Explore all the items on the Main Menu to see all the tasks you can perform from this menu. In particular, move the mouse pointer over the Main Menu⇨Preferences item to see your options for changing the appearance of the desktop. For example, you can change the desktop's background from this menu, as shown in Figure 4-7.

Customizing the GNOME desktop

By now, you may be itching to do a bit of decorating. No one likes to stick to the plain blue GNOME desktop. After all, it's your desktop. You can set it up any way you want it. You can configure most aspects of the GNOME desktop's *look and feel* — the appearance and behavior — by choosing Main Menu⇨Preferences, and then choosing from among the various options.

To see how the desktop decorating business works in Fedora Core, start by choosing Main Menu⇨Preferences⇨Desktop Background; a dialog box appears, as shown in Figure 4-8.

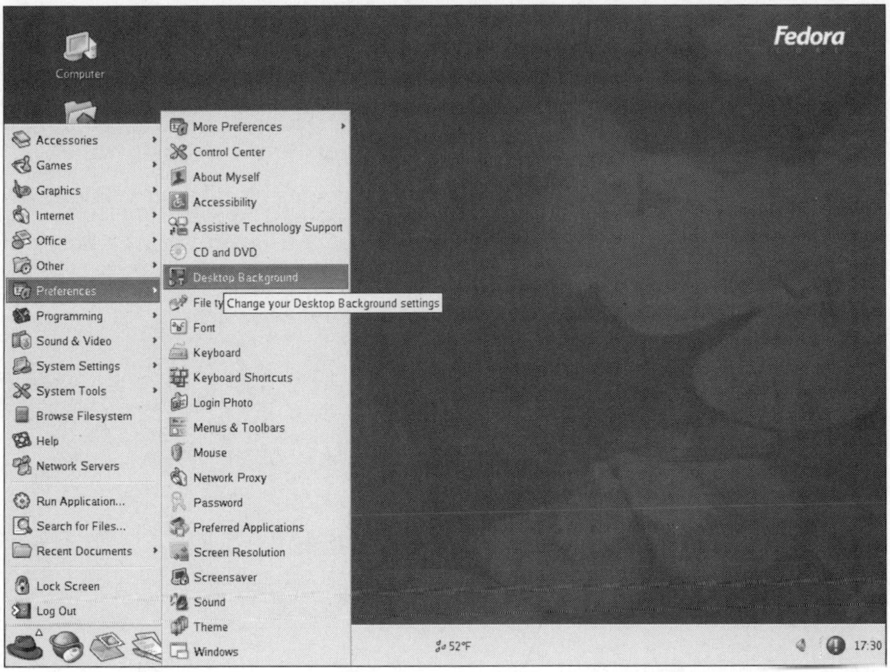

Figure 4-7: Options for customizing the desktop.

From this dialog box, you can select a background of a solid color, a color gradient, or a *wallpaper* (an image used as the background). A *color gradient* background starts with one color and gradually changes to another color. The gradient can be in the vertical direction (top to bottom) or horizontal (left to right).

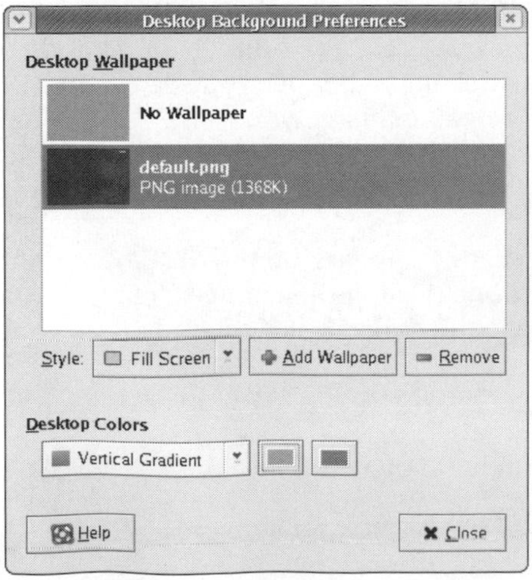

Figure 4-8: Changing the GNOME desktop's background in Fedora Core.

To select a horizontal color gradient, follow these steps:

1. **From the Desktop Colors drop-down list (refer to Figure 4-8), choose the Horizontal Gradient option.**
2. **Click the Left Color button next to the drop-down list.**

   A color selection dialog box comes up (shown in Figure 4-9) from which you can pick a color.

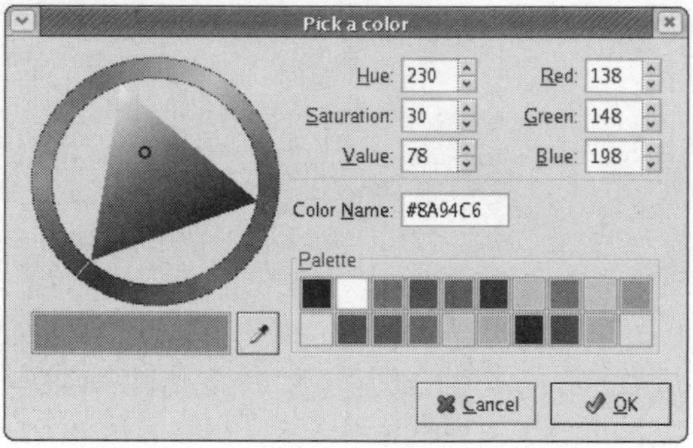

Figure 4-9: The Pick a Color dialog box.

3. **Repeat the same process to select the right color.**

After you complete these steps, the desktop shows the new background color.

If you want to use an image as wallpaper, click the Add Wallpaper button in the middle of the Desktop Background Preferences dialog box. The Add Wallpapers dialog box appears, from which you can select an image to use as wallpaper. By clicking the folder names in the Add Wallpapers dialog box, go to the `/usr/share/backgrounds/images` directory. That directory has the `default.png` file with the default wallpaper you see on the GNOME desktop. To change the wallpaper, select an image you want. You can select any *Joint Photographic Experts Group* (JPEG) or *Portable Network Graphics* (PNG) format image file as wallpaper. After selecting an image, click OK.

The new wallpaper immediately appears on the desktop, as shown in Figure 4-10. When you're done making the changes, click the Close button (refer to Figure 4-8) to close the dialog box and apply the changes.

Logging out of GNOME

To log out, choose Main Menu⇨Log Out. Click Yes when a dialog box asks whether you really want to log out.

Figure 4-10: The newly selected wallpaper.

KDE

KDE stands for the *K Desktop Environment*. The KDE project started in October 1996 with the intent to develop a common GUI for UNIX systems that use the X Window System. The first beta version of KDE was released a year later in October 1997. KDE version 1.0 was released in July 1998; KDE 2.0 on October 23, 2000; KDE 3.0 was released on April 3, 2002; and the latest version — KDE 3.3 — was released on August 19, 2004.

From the user's perspective, KDE provides a graphical desktop environment that includes a window manager, the Konqueror Web browser and file manager, a panel for starting applications, a help system, configuration tools, and many applications, including the OpenOffice.org office suite, image viewer, PostScript viewer, and mail and news programs.

From the developer's perspective, KDE has class libraries and object models for easy application development in C++. KDE is a large development project with many collaborators.

You can always find out the latest information about KDE by visiting the KDE home page at `www.kde.org`.

If your Linux system's default GUI is KDE, you get the KDE GUI as soon as you log in. Typically, you see an initial KDE desktop similar to the one shown in Figure 4-11. The initial KDE session includes a window showing a helpful tip.

You will find that KDE is very easy to use and is similar in many ways to the Windows GUI. You can start applications from a menu that's similar to the Start menu in Windows. As in Windows, you can place folders and applications directly on the KDE desktop.

KDE panel

The KDE panel appearing along the bottom edge of the screen is meant for starting applications. The most important component of the panel is the Main Menu button on the left-most side of the panel. That button is like the Start button in Windows. When you click the Main Menu button, a menu appears. From this menu, you can get to other menus by moving the mouse pointer over items that display a right-pointing arrow. For example, Figure 4-12 shows a typical menu selection for configuring various services.

You can start applications from this menu. That's why the KDE documentation calls the Main Menu button the *Application Starter* (of course, the KDE documentation refers to the button itself as the K button).

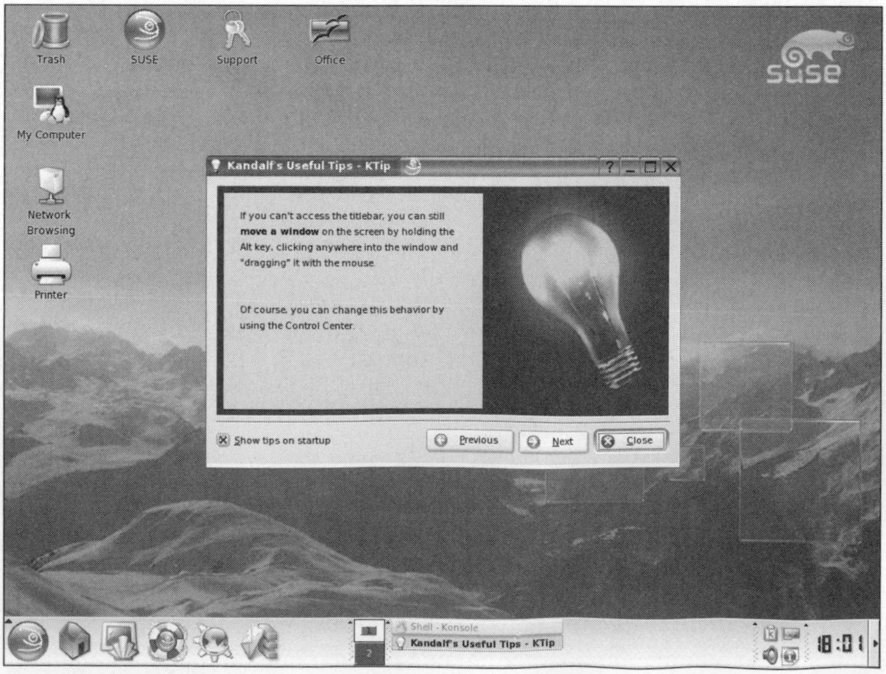

Figure 4-11: The initial KDE desktop for a typical user.

Figure 4-12: Click the Main Menu button and then move the mouse pointer from menu to menu to open the KDE menus.

Next to the Main Menu button, the panel includes many more buttons. If you don't know what a button does, simply move the mouse pointer over the button; a small pop-up window displays a brief message about that button.

Customizing the KDE desktop

KDE makes customizing the look and feel of the KDE desktop easy. Everything you have to decorate the desktop is in one place: the KDE Control Center. To start the KDE Control Center, choose Main Menu⇨Control Center.

When the KDE Control Center starts, it displays the main window with a list of items on the left side and some summary information about your system in the workspace to the right, as shown in Figure 4-13.

The KDE Control Center's left-hand side shows the items that you can customize with this program. The list is organized into categories such as Appearance & Themes, Desktop, Internet & Network, KDE Components, Peripherals, Security & Privacy, Sound & Multimedia, System Administration, and so on. Click an item to view the subcategories for that item. Click one of the subcategory items to change it. That item's configuration options then appear on the right side of the Control Center window.

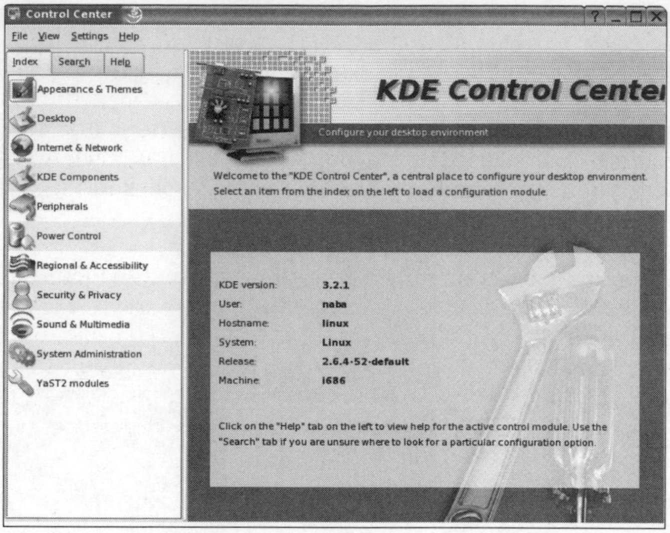

Figure 4-13: The initial window of the KDE Control Center.

To change the desktop's background, click Appearance & Themes, and then click Background. The right side of the Control Center (see Figure 4-14) shows the options for customizing the desktop's background.

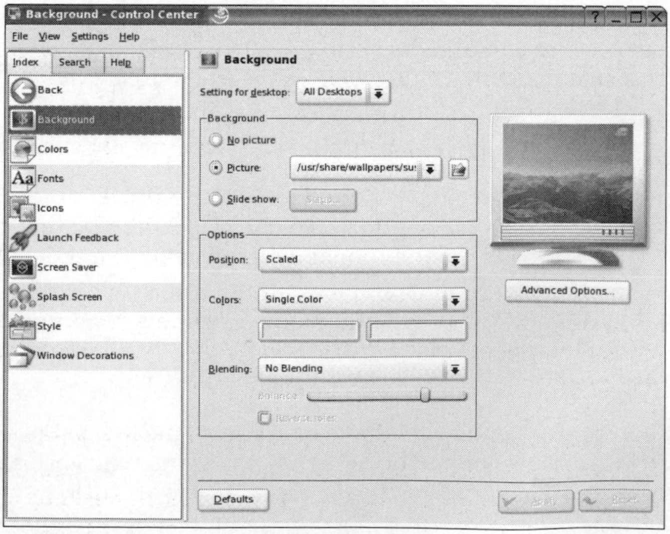

Figure 4-14: Changing the desktop background with KDE Control Center.

If you want to change the background of a specific desktop, click the Setting for Desktop drop-down list. From the list of desktops, you can select the desktop whose background you want to change.

For a colored background, select the No Picture radio button. From the Colors drop-down list, you can select either a single color background or a variety of color gradients (meaning the color changes gradually from one color to another) or a picture (an image used as a background). You can then pick the two colors by clicking the color buttons that appear under the Colors drop-down list. After making your selections, click Apply to try out the background. (If you don't like what you get, click Reset to revert back to the previous background.)

If you want to use a picture as background, select the Picture radio button and then click the folder icon next to that radio button. A dialog box comes up, showing the JPEG images in the `/usr/share/wallpapers` directory. You can select any one of these images or pick an image from another directory and click OK. Then click the Apply button in the KDE Control Center to apply this wallpaper to the desktop. If you don't like the appearance, click Reset.

Logging out of KDE

When you're done exploring KDE, log out. To log out of KDE, choose Main Menu⇨Logout. You can also right-click empty areas of the desktop and choose Logout from the context menu that appears.

Playing with the Shell

Linux is basically UNIX, and UNIX just doesn't feel like UNIX unless you can type cryptic commands in a text terminal. Although GNOME and KDE have done a lot to bring us into the world of *w*indows, *i*cons, *m*ouse, and *p*ointer (affectionately known as *WIMP* :-), sometimes you're stuck with nothing but a plain text screen with a prompt that looks something like this (when you log in as `naba`):

```
naba@linux:/etc>
```

You see the text screen most often when something is *wrong* with the X Window System, which is essentially the machinery that runs the windows and menus that you normally see. In those cases, you have to work with the shell and know some of the cryptic Linux commands.

You can prepare for unexpected encounters with the shell by trying out some Linux commands in a terminal window while you're in the GNOME or KDE GUI. After you get the hang of it, you might even keep a terminal window open, just so you can use one of those cryptic commands simply because it's faster than pointing and clicking. (Those two-letter commands do pack some punch!)

Starting the Bash shell

Simply put, the *shell* is the Linux *command interpreter* — a program that reads what you type, interprets that text as a command, and does what the command is supposed to do.

Before you start playing with the shell, open a terminal window. In either GNOME or KDE, the panel typically includes an icon that looks like a monitor. When you click that icon, what appears is a window with a prompt, like the one shown in Figure 4-15. That's a terminal window, and it works just like an old-fashioned terminal. A shell program is running and ready to accept any text that you type. You type text, press Enter, and something happens (depending on what you typed).

TIP

If the GNOME or KDE panel on your desktop does not seem to have an icon that starts a terminal or shell window, search through the Main Menu hierarchy and you should be able to find an item labeled "console" or "terminal." Selecting that item should then open up a terminal window.

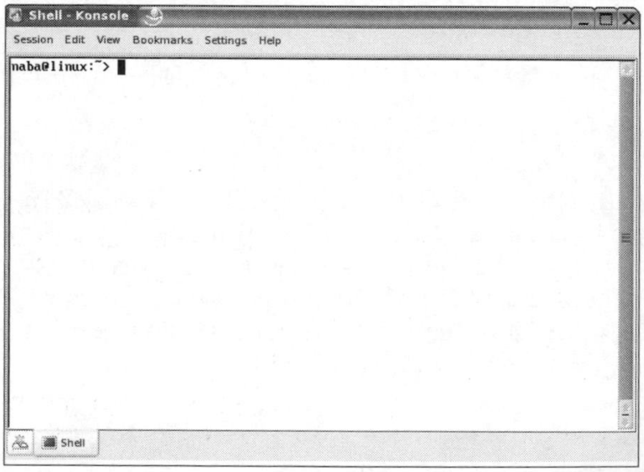

Figure 4-15: You can type Linux commands at the shell prompt in a terminal window.

The prompt that you see depends on the shell that runs in that terminal window. The default Linux shell is called *Bash*.

Bash understands a whole host of standard Linux commands, which you can use to look at files, go from one directory to another, see what programs are running (and who else is logged in), and a whole lot more.

In addition to the Linux commands, Bash can run any program stored in an executable file. Bash can also execute *shell scripts* — text files that contain Linux commands.

Understanding shell commands

Because a shell interprets what you type, knowing how the shell figures out the text that you enter is important. All shell commands have this general format:

```
command option1 option2 ... optionN
```

Such a single line of commands is commonly called a *command line*. On a command line, you enter a command followed by one or more optional parameters (or *arguments*). Such *command-line options* (or command-line arguments) help you specify what you want the command to do.

One basic rule is that you have to use a space or a tab to separate the command from the options. You also must separate options with a space or a tab. If you want to use an option that contains embedded spaces, you have to put that option inside quotation marks. For example, to search for two words of text in the password file, I enter the following `grep` command (`grep` is one of those cryptic commands used to search for text in files):

```
grep ftp /etc/passwd
```

When `grep` prints the line with those words, it looks like this:

```
ftp:x:40:49:FTP account:/srv/ftp:/bin/bash
```

If you created a user account in your name, go ahead and type the `grep` command with your name as an argument, but remember to enclose the name in quotes.

Trying a few Linux commands

While you have the terminal window open, try a few Linux commands just for fun. I guide you through some random examples to give you a feel for what you can do at the shell prompt.

To see how long the Linux PC has been up since you last powered it up, type the following. (***Note:*** I show the typed command in bold, followed by the output from that command.)

```
uptime
 21:19:01 up 29 days, 55 min,  3 users,  load average: 0.04,
   0.32, 0.38
```

The part `up 29 days, 55 min` tells you that this particular PC has been up for nearly a month. Hmmm . . . can Windows do that?

To see what version of Linux kernel your system is running, use the `uname` command like this:

```
uname -srv
```

This runs the `uname` command with three options: `-s`, `-r`, and `-v` (which can be combined as `-srv`, as this example shows). The `-s` option causes `uname` to print the name of the kernel, `-r` prints the kernel release number, and `-v` prints the kernel version number. The command generates the following output on one of my Linux systems:

```
Linux 2.6.8-1.541 #1 Wed Sep 1 18:01:20 EDT 2004
```

In this case, the system is running Linux kernel version 2.6.8.

To read a file, use the `more` command. Here's an example:

```
more /etc/passwd

root:x:0:0:root:/root:/bin/bash
daemon:x:1:1:daemon:/usr/sbin:/bin/sh
bin:x:2:2:bin:/bin:/bin/sh
sys:x:3:3:sys:/dev:/bin/sh
  ... lines deleted ...
```

To see a list of all the programs currently running on the system, use the `ps` command, like this:

```
ps ax
```

The `ps` command takes many options, and you can provide these options without the usual dash prefix. This example uses the `a` and `x` options. The `a` option lists all processes that you are running, and the `x` option displays all the rest of the processes. The net result is that `ps ax` prints a list of all processes running on the system, as shown in the following sample output:

```
  PID TTY      STAT   TIME COMMAND
    1 ?        S      0:00 init [2]
    2 ?        SN     0:00 [ksoftirqd/0]
    3 ?        S<     0:00 [events/0]
    4 ?        S<     0:00 [khelper]
   20 ?        S<     0:00 [kblockd/0]
   45 ?        S      0:00 [pdflush]
   46 ?        S      0:00 [pdflush]
   48 ?        S<     0:00 [aio/0]
   47 ?        S      0:00 [kswapd0]
  190 ?        S      0:00 [kseriod]
  306 ?        S      0:00 [kjournald]
```

```
 536 ?        S      0:00 [kjournald]
 720 ?        S      0:00 [khubd]
1970 ?        Ss     0:00 dhclient -e -pf
  /var/run/dhclient.eth0.pid -lf
  /var/run/dhclient.eth0.leases eth0
1974 ?        Ss     0:00 /sbin/portmap
2142 ?        Ss     0:00 /sbin/syslogd
2145 ?        Ss     0:00 /sbin/klogd
2153 ?        Ss     0:00 /usr/sbin/named -u bind
2163 ?        Ss     0:00 /usr/sbin/lwresd
 ... lines deleted ...
```

Amazing how many programs that can run on a system even when only you are logged in as a user, isn't it?

As you can guess, you can do everything from a shell prompt, but it does take some getting used to.

Shutting Down

When you're ready to shut down Linux, you must do so in an orderly manner. Even if you're the sole user of a Linux PC, several other programs are usually running in the background. Also, operating systems such as Linux try to optimize the way that they write data to the hard drive. Because hard drive access is relatively slow (compared with the time needed to access memory locations), data generally is held in memory and written to the hard drive in large chunks. Therefore, if you simply turn off the power, you run the risk that some files aren't updated properly.

Any user (you don't even have to be logged in) can shut down the system from the desktop or from the graphical login screen, although some distributions such as Debian prompt you for the `root` password. Choose Main Menu⇨Log Out. A Logout dialog box appears, providing the options for rebooting or halting the system or simply logging out. To shut down the system, simply select Shutdown, and click OK. The system then shuts down in an orderly manner.

If the logout menu does not have an option to shut down, first log out and then select Shutdown from the graphical login screen.

As the system shuts down, you see messages about processes being shut down. You may be surprised at how many processes there are, even when no one is explicitly running any programs on the system. If your system does not automatically power off on shutdown, you can manually turn off the power.

Note that shutting down or rebooting the system may *not* require `root` access. This is why it's important to make sure that physical access to the console is protected adequately so that anyone who wants to cannot simply walk up to the console and shut down your system.

Book II

Linux Desktops

The 5th Wave
By Rich Tennant
IF BOB DYLAN HAD PURSUED A CAREER IN COMPUTERS
©RICHTENNANT

"He's a whiz at developing applications, but thank goodness for email because I can't understand a word he says when he talks."

Contents at a Glance

Chapter 1: Introducing the GUI Desktops

In This Chapter

- **Discovering the common features of the GNOME and KDE GUIs**
- **Introducing Debian's KDE desktop**
- **Introducing Fedora Core's GNOME desktop**
- **Introducing the Knoppix desktop**
- **Introducing the SUSE desktop**
- **Introducing the Xandros desktop**

Linux distributions come with one of two popular graphical user interfaces (GUIs) — GNOME and KDE. GNOME and KDE are similar to Microsoft Windows, but they are unique in one respect. Unlike Microsoft Windows, you can pick your GUI in Linux. If you don't like GNOME, just log out and log back in with the KDE, the other GUI. Try doing that with Microsoft Windows!

GNOME and KDE were developed independently of Linux. In fact, GNOME and KDE run on other UNIX operating systems besides Linux. You also have the option to install other GUIs such as XFCE and Ximian Desktop 2 (XD2) in Linux. You can download and install Ximian Desktop 2 (XD2), a GUI desktop from Ximian, from `www.ximian.com/products/desktop/download.html`. You can download XFCE from `www.xfce.org`.

This chapter explores the major features of GNOME and KDE. You can best figure out these GUIs by simply starting to use them. By the way, you can try both GNOME and KDE, provided both are installed on your system.

Each Linux distribution typically installs one of the GUIs by default. The default GUI is GNOME in Fedora Core and KDE in Knoppix, SUSE, and Xandros. In Debian, you can install either GNOME or KDE. Each distribution also customizes GNOME or KDE to create a desktop that is unique to the distribution. For this reason, I also provide an overview of each distribution's desktop — GNOME with Fedora Core, and KDE with Debian, Knoppix, SUSE, and Xandros. Think of this as a brief introduction. You have to explore the desktops on your own because that's the best way to get used to the GUIs.

Getting to Know the Common Features of the GUIs

From a user's perspective, both GNOME and KDE probably seem similar because many features work similarly. Becoming familiar with these common features is helpful so that you can rely on them no matter which GUI you choose to use for your daily work.

For starters, the initial desktop for both GNOME and KDE looks like any other popular GUI, such as Microsoft Windows or the Apple desktop on a Mac. For example, Figure 1-1 and Figure 1-2, respectively, show typical GNOME and KDE desktops.

Both desktops (Figures 1-1 and 1-2) initially show icons for your computer, your home folder, and the trash can for deleted files. The other major feature of both GNOME and KDE desktops is the bar along the bottom, which is called the *panel*. The panel is similar to the Windows taskbar. It has buttons on the left (shortcuts to various programs) and a time display to the right. The middle part of the panel shows buttons for any applications you've started (or were automatically started for you).

Figure 1-1: A typical GNOME desktop.

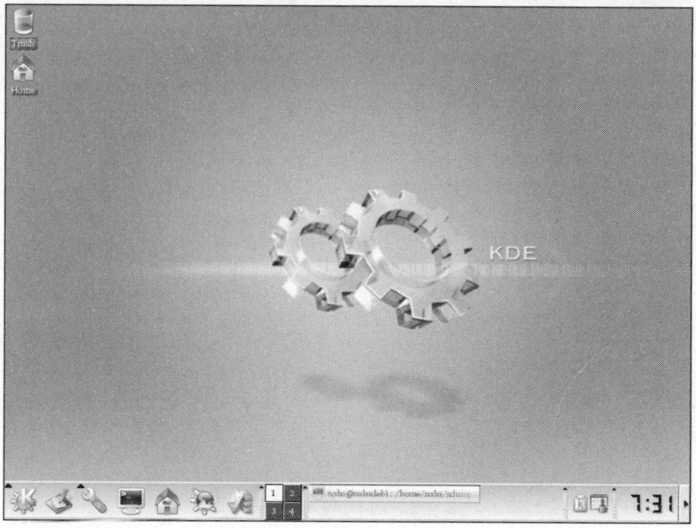

Figure 1-2: A typical KDE desktop.

TIP

Move the mouse over any icon on the panel and a small pop-up window displays the name of that icon. The pop-up window also gives a hint about what you can do with that icon.

Desktop context menus

Both GNOME and KDE desktops display a context menu when you right-click a clear area on the desktop. The exact contents of that menu depends on the desktop, but it typically offers menu options that enable you to perform the following types of tasks:

- Run a command.
- Open a terminal window where you can type Linux commands.
- Create a new folder.
- Configure the desktop background.
- Rearrange the icons on the desktop.

For example, Figures 1-3 and 1-4, respectively, show the desktop context menus in typical GNOME and KDE desktops. Desktop menu options with a right-pointing arrow have other menus that appear when you put the mouse pointer over the arrow.

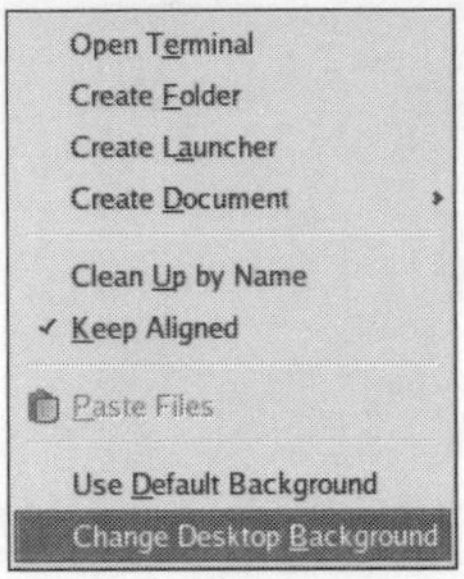

Figure 1-3: Typical right-click menu for a GNOME desktop.

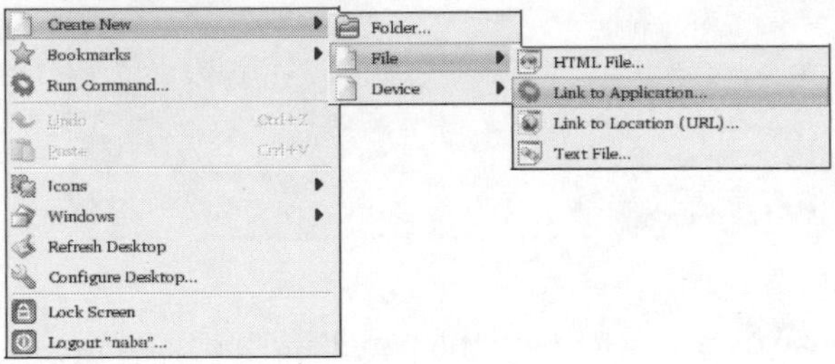

Figure 1-4: Typical right-click menu for a KDE desktop.

Icon context menus

Right-clicking any desktop icon in GNOME or KDE causes another menu to appear. (See Figures 1-5 and 1-6.) Many items on this context menu are the same no matter what icon you click — but right-clicking certain icons (for example, the Trash icon) produces a somewhat different menu. You can perform the following typical tasks from icon context menus:

✦ Open a folder in a file manager.

✦ Open a file with an application that you choose.

✦ Rename the icon.

✦ Move the icon to trash.

✦ View the properties of that icon.

For the Trash icon, the icon context menu typically provides an option to permanently delete the items in the trash. (You get a chance to say yes or no.)

TIP

I bet you see a pattern here. It's the right-click. No matter where you are in a GUI desktop, *always right-click before you pick*. You're bound to find something useful when you right-click!

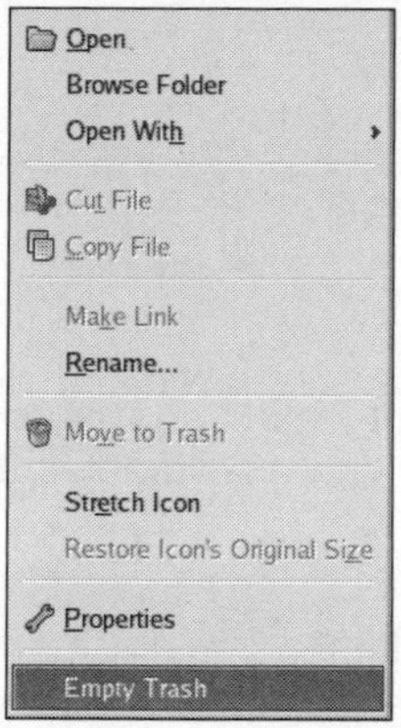

Figure 1-5: An icon context menu in GNOME.

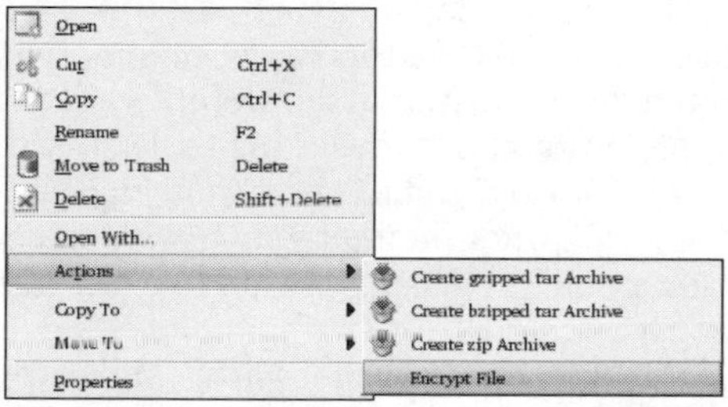

Figure 1-6: An icon context menu in KDE.

The panel

The panel is the long bar that stretches across the bottom of the desktop. Figures 1-7 and 1-8 show typical views of the GNOME and KDE panels, respectively.

The panel is a parking place for icons. Some icons start programs when you click them. Some show status (such as what programs are currently running), as well as information such as date and time.

Figure 1-7: A typical view of a GNOME panel.

Figure 1-8: A typical view of a KDE panel.

Starting at the left, the first icon (regardless of what it shows) is the Main Menu button — it's like the Start button in Microsoft Windows. Then come a few icons that start various programs.

By the way, if you move the mouse pointer on top of an icon, a small Help balloon pops up and gives you a helpful hint about the icon.

To the right of the leftmost set of icons, a workspace-switcher icon shows four rectangular areas, each representing a virtual desktop. The icon is variously known as Workspace Switcher, Desktop Pager, or simply Pager. You can click one of these rectangles to switch to a different virtual desktop. This feature is like having four separate virtual desktops to work with. To be honest, I end up using only one desktop, but I like knowing the others are there if I ever need them. On the other hand, if you're writing code and preparing a user's guide for a new program, you can use one desktop for all the coding work and a second desktop for writing the user's guide. You can, of course, switch from one desktop to the other with a single mouse click.

The area to the right of the Desktop Pager icon displays buttons for the programs you have started so far. This area is blank if you have not yet started any programs.

Other icons may be next to the Pager, but the date and time always appear at the far-right edge of the panel.

Now for a little bit of technical detail about these icons on the panel. The panel itself is a separate application; each icon is a button or a program called an *applet*. The applets are little applications (also called *plugins*). These panel applets can do things such as launching other programs or displaying the date and time. To run an applet, right-click an empty area of the panel and select the appropriate menu item to add an applet to the panel. After adding the applet, you can right-click the applet's icon to configure it or perform some task that the applet supports.

If you right-click any icon — or right-click anywhere on the panel — you get a context menu where you can do something relevant to that icon (such as move it or remove it entirely). You can also set some preferences and add more buttons and applets to the panel.

The Main Menu

The leftmost icon on the panel is the *Main Menu* button. That's where you typically find all the applications, organized into submenus. In this section, I provide some examples of the Main Menu and point out some interesting items. You can then do further exploration yourself.

Click the Main Menu button to bring up the first level menu. Then mouse over any menu item with an arrow to bring up the next level menu and so on. You can go through a menu hierarchy and make selections from the final menu. Figures 1-9 and 1-10, respectively, show the main menu hierarchies in typical GNOME and KDE desktops.

A word about the way I refer to a menu selection: I use the notation Main Menu⇨Utilities⇨More Programs⇨Personal Time Tracker to refer to the menu selection shown in Figure 1-10. Similarly, I say choose Main Menu⇨Preferences⇨More Preferences⇨Multimedia Systems Selector to refer to the menu sequence highlighted in Figure 1-9. You get the idea.

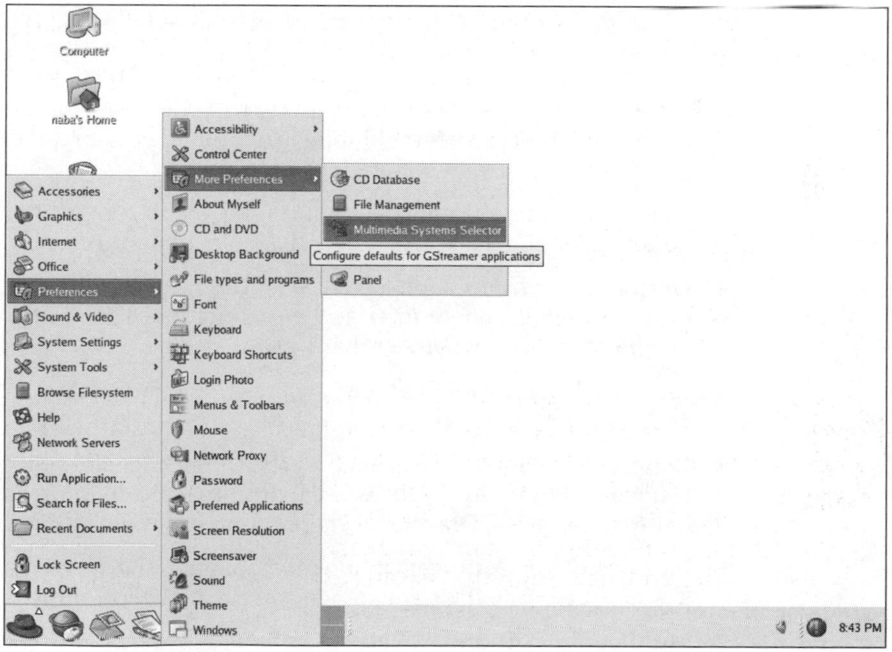

Figure 1-9: The main menu hierarchy in a typical GNOME desktop.

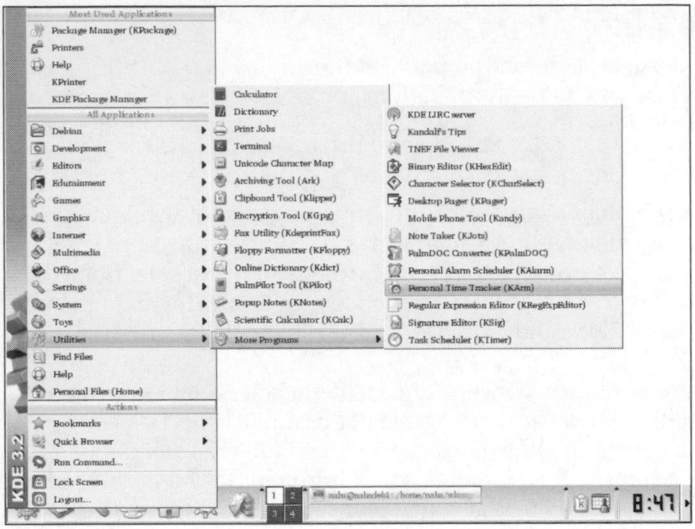

Figure 1-10: The main menu hierarchy in a typical KDE desktop.

In most desktops, the top-level main menu has the following types of menu categories:

- **Accessories** or **Utilities:** Lots of utility programs, such as a scientific calculator, character selector, floppy formatter, dictionary, Palm Pilot or Handspring sync, and so on.
- **Games:** A menu of what else, games (and a whole lot of them at that — Solitaire, Mahjongg, Mines, Reversi, and many more).
- **Graphics:** Programs such as the GIMP (an Adobe Photoshop-like program), a digital camera interface, a scanner interface, a screen capture program, and an Adobe Acrobat viewer.
- **Internet:** Internet applications, such as the Web browser, e-mail reader, and Instant Messenger.
- **Office:** Office applications such as the OpenOffice.org office suite (includes Writer word processor, Calc spreadsheet, Impress slide presentation program, Draw drawing program, and much more).
- **Preferences** or **Settings:** Options to configure many aspects of the system, including the appearance and the behavior of the desktop.
- **Multimedia** or **Sound & Video:** Multimedia applications such as CD player, sound mixer, sound recorder, and volume control.
- **System:** System administration tools for configuring your Linux system.

The Main Menu typically also has the a few menu items for some commonly performed tasks such as the following:

- ✦ Main Menu⇨Help displays online help.
- ✦ Main Menu⇨Run Command displays a dialog box where you can enter the name of a program to run and then click Run to start that program.
- ✦ Main Menu⇨Search for Files (or Find Files) runs a search tool from which you can search for files.
- ✦ Main Menu⇨Lock Screen starts the screen saver and locks the screen. When you want to return to the desktop, the system prompts you for your password.
- ✦ Main Menu⇨Logout logs you out. (You get a chance to confirm whether you really want to log out or not.)

The Main Menu in each distribution has different categories, but the menu organization is similar enough that you can usually find what you need.

Okay. That's all I'm telling you about the Main Menu. You'll use the Main Menu a lot as you use GNOME or KDE desktops. Even if it seems too much initially, it'll all become very familiar as you spend more time with Linux.

In the following sections, I provide an overview of specific desktops: Debian's KDE desktop, Fedora Core's GNOME desktop, Knoppix desktop, SUSE desktop, and Xandros desktop.

Introducing Debian's KDE Desktop

Debian's default KDE desktop has a simple look (see Figure 1-11) with just two icons — your home folder and the Trash icon — on the desktop.

In Figure 1-11, note the following major items in Debian's KDE desktop and what happens when you click on each:

- ✦ **Desktop icons:** The Home icon opens your home folder in a Konqueror File Manager window and the Trash icon represents a place where deleted items are stored until you empty the trash.
- ✦ **Main Menu:** Brings up the Main Menu from which you can select applications to run.
- ✦ **Show Desktop:** Shows the desktop by minimizing all windows.
- ✦ **Control Center Menu:** Brings up the Control Center Menu that provides access to various modules of the Control Center through which you can configure the system.

- **Terminal Window:** Runs Konsole, a program that provides a terminal window where you can type Linux commands.
- **Home Folder:** Opens your home directory in the Konqueror file manager.
- **Web Browser:** Runs the Konqueror Web browser.
- **KMail:** Runs the KMail mail client for KDE.
- **Desktop Pager:** Each square brings up a different desktop. This is similar to the Workspace Switcher in GNOME desktops.
- **Clipboard:** Shows what has been cut and what you can paste elsewhere.
- **KOrganizer:** Opens the personal organizer window showing the appointments for today's date.
- **Time:** Brings up a calendar showing the current date.

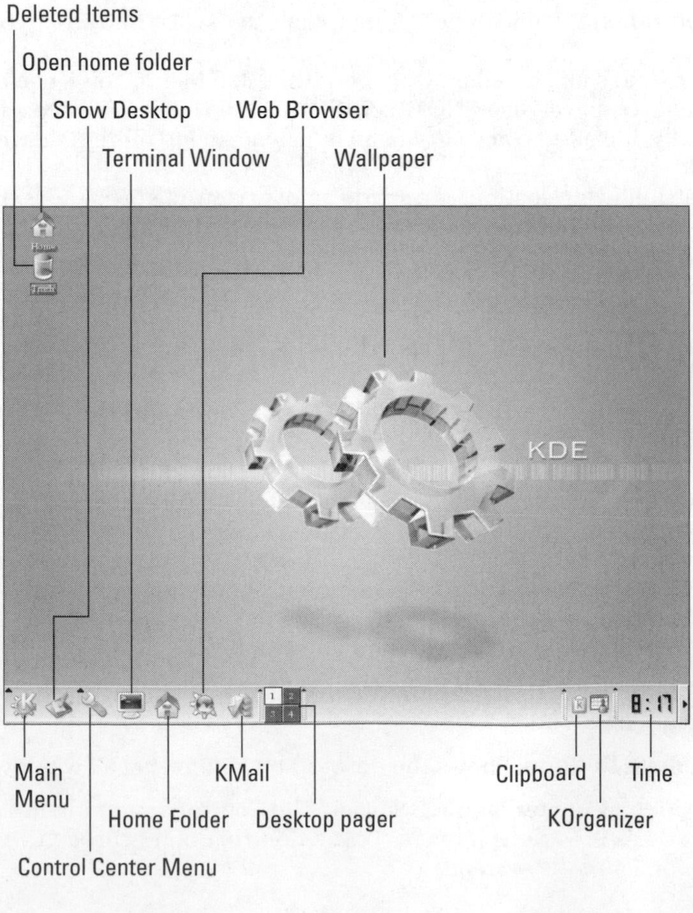

Figure 1-11: Debian's default KDE desktop.

Clicking Main Menu brings up the Main Menu, shown in Figure 1-12, that gives you access to most of the applications in Debian. Of course, the exact list of applications in various submenus depends on what you have installed, but Figure 1-12 gives you a view of a typical main menu in Debian. To browse the main menu, mouse over items that have a right arrow, and a submenu pops up with more items.

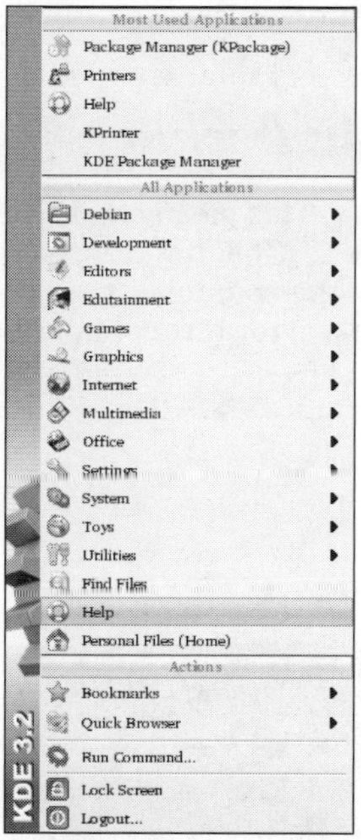

Figure 1-12: Start applications from the Main Menu in Debian's KDE desktop.

The Control Center Menu (see Figure 1-13) is the other menu that you can launch from the panel. Through the Control Center Menu, you can run the KDE Control Center or start individual modules of the Control Center for specific system configuration and administration tasks.

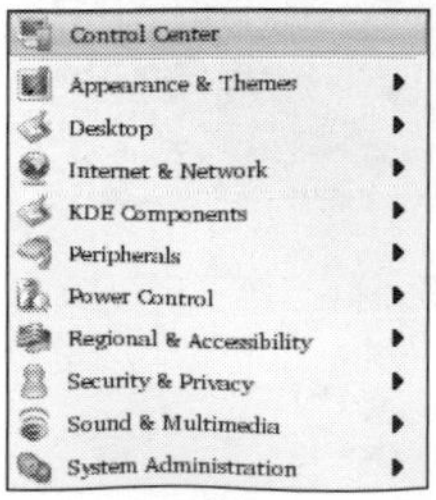

Figure 1-13: The Control Center Menu gives you access to the KDE Control Center.

To explore Debian's KDE desktop, try clicking the panel icons to start the applications. In particular, you can click the Home icon to open your home folder in the Konqueror file manager. After that window opens, you can explore other folders to get a feel for the file system.

You can also click the Main Menu and mouse over the items to see all the submenus to get an idea of the variety of applications that you can run in Debian. You can, of course, click an item to start a specific application and give each one a try.

Introducing Fedora Core's GNOME Desktop

GNOME is the default GUI for Fedora Core. This means that when you first log in at the GUI login screen, you get the GNOME desktop, as shown in Figure 1-14. The desktop shows icons for the computer, your home folder, trash, and a Start Here icon that you can use to start configuring the system.

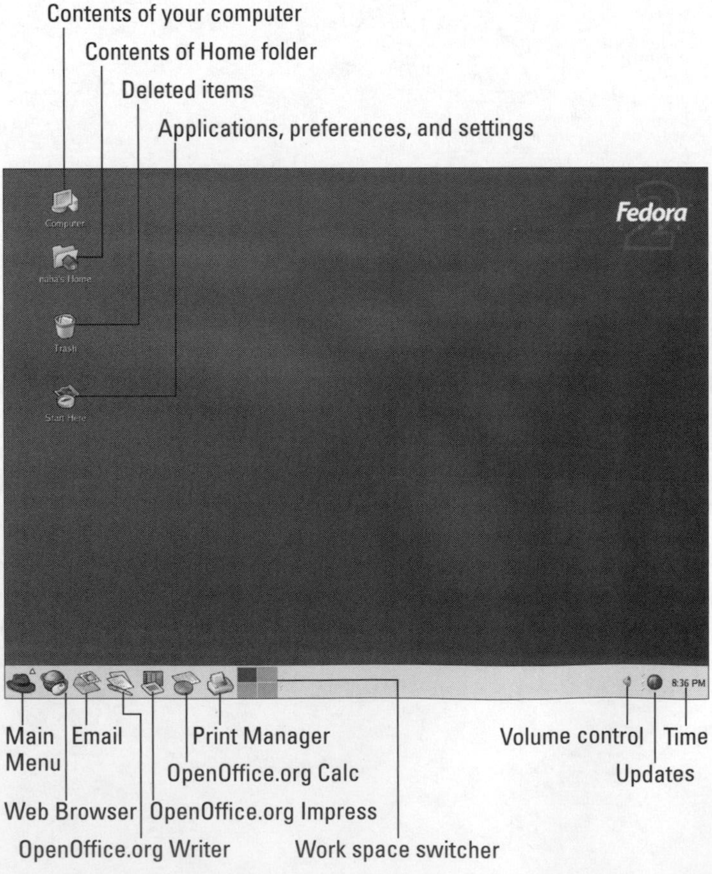

Figure 1-14: The GNOME desktop in Fedora Core.

The following list touches on the major parts of the GNOME desktop and gives a brief description of each part's purpose:

- **Desktop icons:** Double-click the Computer icon to view the contents of the computer and double-click the Home icon to open your home folder in a Nautilus File Manager window. The Trash icon holds deleted items. Double-click the Start Here icon to open a Nautilus window through which you can access the applications, preferences, and settings.
- **Main Menu:** Brings up the Main Menu from which you can select applications to run.
- **Web Browser:** Runs the Mozilla Web browser.
- **EMail:** Starts the Ximian Evolution e-mail and calendar software.
- **OpenOffice.org Writer:** Runs OpenOffice.org Writer, a Microsoft Word-like word processor.
- **OpenOffice.org Impress:** Runs the OpenOffice.org Impress slide-presentation program (which is similar to Microsoft PowerPoint).
- **OpenOffice.org Calc:** Runs the OpenOffice.org Calc, a Microsoft Excel-like spreadsheet program.
- **Print Manager:** Runs the Print Manager, which you can use to set up and monitor printers.
- **Workspace Switcher:** Each square brings up a different workspace. This has the same function as the Desktop Pager in KDE desktops.
- **Volume Control:** Shows a volume control bar that you can use to change the sound's volume by dragging a slider.
- **Updates:** Brings up the Red Hat Network window from which you can select updates to install.
- **Time:** Brings up a calendar showing the current date.

Click Main Menu (refer to Figure 1-14) to open the main menu and explore the categories. From the main menu, you can access nearly all applications and utilities in Fedora Core.

REMEMBER

Fedora Core's KDE desktop is configured to look very similar to its GNOME desktop. This makes it easy for Fedora Core users to switch between the two GUIs without having to relearn the menus and the location of icons on the panel.

Introducing the Knoppix Desktop

Knoppix does not require you to log in with a username. After you boot your PC from the Knoppix CD, you end up with the initial Knoppix desktop shown in Figure 1-15. Knoppix uses a customized version of KDE for its desktop, so you may notice similarities with other KDE-based desktops such as Debian, SUSE, and Xandros.

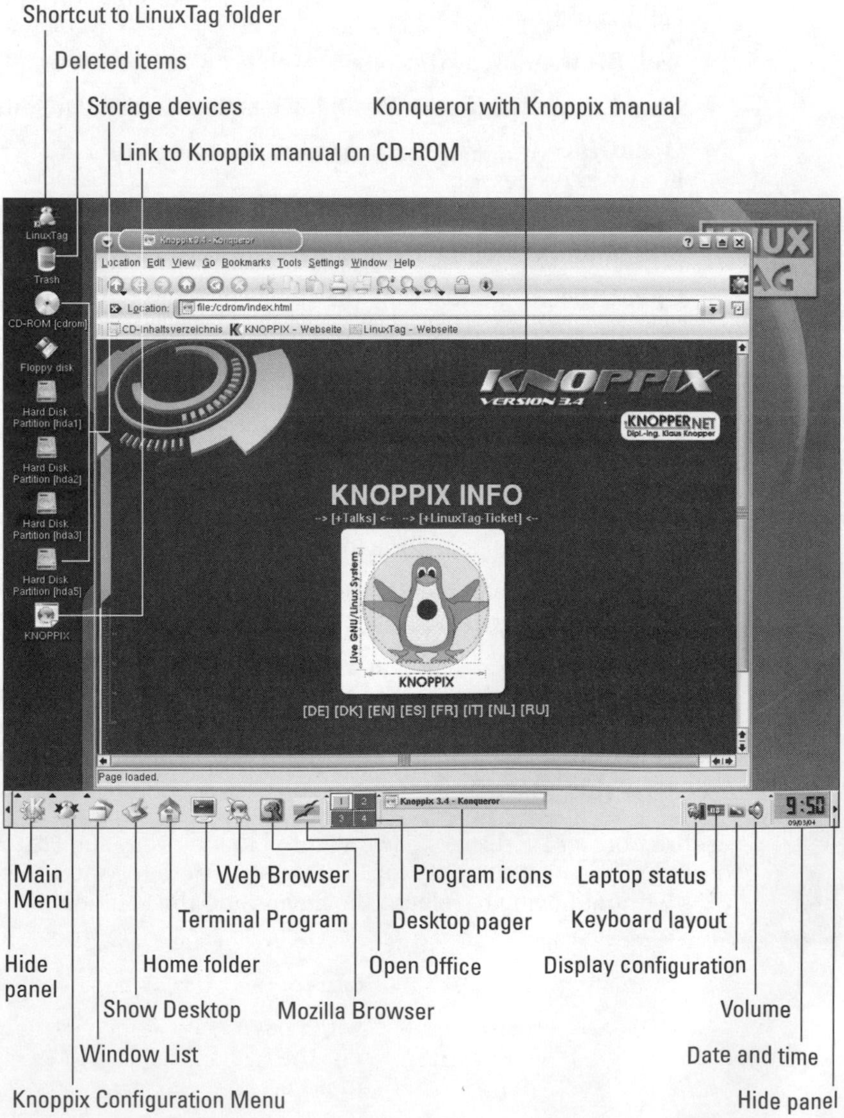

Figure 1-15: The Knoppix desktop is based on KDE.

Compared to some other distributions, Knoppix has a lot of desktop icons as well as items on the panel. This is primarily because Knoppix detects and adds desktop icons for all detected hard drive partitions, CD/DVD-ROM drives, and floppy drives.

In Figure 1-15, note the following major components of the Knoppix desktop:

- **Desktop icons:** Knoppix displays icons for all hard drive partitions, CD/DVD drives, and the floppy drive. Click to mount and open any of these storage devices and access their contents. Additionally, there is a Trash icon and shortcuts to some files, including the Knoppix manual (which Knoppix opens in a Konqueror window after it starts).
- **Hide Panel:** The two end-points of the panel serve as "hide panel" buttons, which means that if you click on these, the panel slides over and disappears. Click again and the panel reappears. You can hide the panel to create more room for other windows.
- **Main Menu:** Brings up the Main Menu (see Figure 1-16) from which you can select applications to run, lock the screen, get online help, or log out.
- **Knoppix Configuration Menu:** Brings up a menu that you can use to perform tasks such as configuring devices (printers, sound card), setting up a network, turning a few servers such as SSH and Samba on or off, and opening a `root` shell window where you can type commands as a superuser.
- **Window List:** Click to view the list of currently open windows and to arrange the windows on the desktop.
- **Show Desktop:** Shows the desktop by minimizing all windows.
- **Home Folder:** Opens your home directory in the Konqueror file manager.
- **Terminal Program:** Runs Konsole, a program that provides a terminal window where you can type Linux commands.
- **Web Browser:** Runs the Konqueror Web browser.
- **Mozilla Browser:** Runs the Mozilla Web browser.
- **Open Office:** Starts OpenOffice.org Writer, a Microsoft Word-like word processor. You can start other OpenOffice.org programs such as Impress, Calc, and Draw from the Main Menu.
- **Desktop Pager:** Each square brings up a different desktop.
- **Program Icons:** This area shows icons for the currently running programs.
- **Laptop Status:** Displays the status of the battery (appears only on laptops).
- **Keyboard Layout:** Click to switch between a number of keyboard layouts: U.S., German, and French (the flag on the icon indicates which country's layout the keyboard is currently using).

- **Display Configuration:** Click to change screen resolution or configure the display.
- **Volume:** Starts the KMix utility that enables you to change the volume as well as control other aspects of the sound card.
- **Date and Time:** Displays the current date and time. Click to bring up a calendar showing the current date.

Figure 1-16 shows the Knoppix Main Menu that appears when you click Main Menu on the panel. As in all desktops, the Main Menu is your first step to accessing the applications in Knoppix. For a single CD distribution, Knoppix packs a surprisingly large number of applications, as you can probably guess by looking at the application categories shown in the main menu in the Figure.

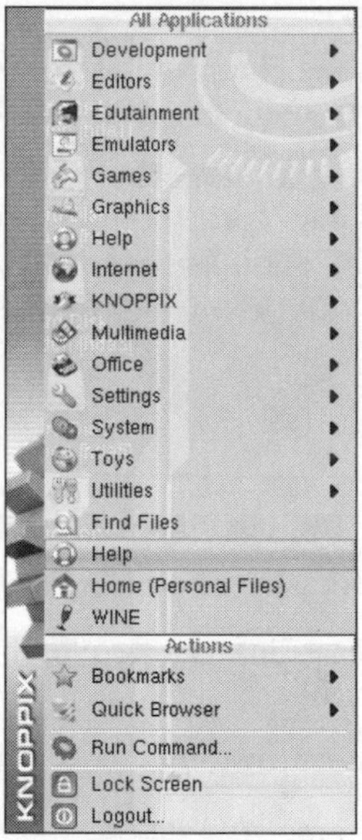

Figure 1-16: Start applications from the Knoppix Main Menu.

The Knoppix Configuration Menu, shown in Figure 1-17, is another important menu that you can launch from the panel. This menu enables you to configure devices, set up network connections, start servers, run some utility programs, and open a `root` shell — a terminal window where you can type Linux commands as `root` (the superuser).

Figure 1-17: Configure network connections and devices from the Knoppix Configuration Menu.

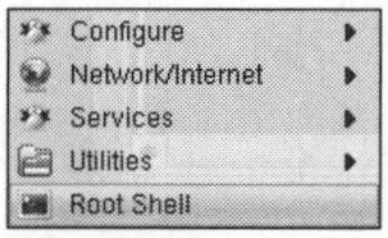

To explore the rest of Knoppix, start by clicking the panel icons to start applications such as the Web browser and OpenOffice.org Writer. One good place to start is the Home icon that opens your home directory in a Konqueror window. From that Konqueror window, you can explore the rest of the file system.

TIP

To mount and access files on any of the hard drive partitions detected by Knoppix, simply click on the icon on the desktop. Knoppix then mounts and shows that partition's contents in a Konqueror window. For example, Figure 1-18 shows the result of clicking on the Hard Disk Partition [hda2] icon on the desktop. That partition happens to be an NTFS partition with the Windows XP operating system on my laptop. As you can see in Figure 1-18, Knoppix can mount and open that partition so that I can access those files.

You can also click the Main Menu and explore the huge number of applications in Knoppix.

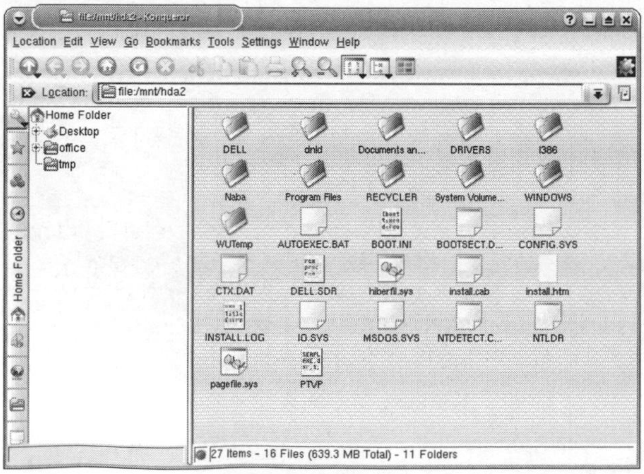

Figure 1-18: Configure network and devices from the Knoppix Configuration Menu.

Oh, the secret of how Knoppix packs so many applications on a single CD (with less than 700MB capacity) — Knoppix stores the files in a compressed format on the CD and then uncompresses them on the fly as they are needed. Impressive, isn't it?

Introducing the SUSE Desktop

SUSE Linux is a commercial product, and as such, it provides a customized desktop. SUSE automatically logs in the local user that you defined during installation and brings up the initial desktop, as shown in Figure 1-19.

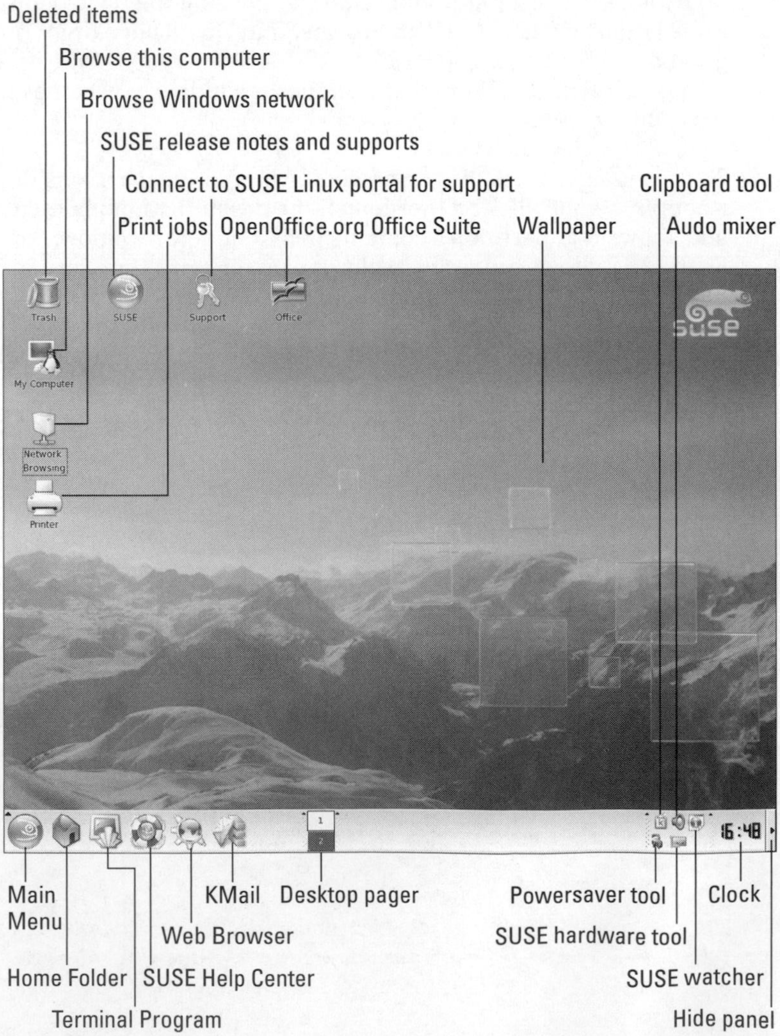

Figure 1-19: The initial SUSE desktop.

Follow along in Figure 1-19 as I point out some of the more noteworthy elements in the SUSE desktop:

- **Desktop icons:** SUSE displays the usual desktop icons — a My Computer icon for browsing the contents of the computer, a Trash icon, an icon for browsing the local Windows network, as well as icons for support, print manager, and OpenOffice.org office suite.
- **Main Menu:** Brings up the Main Menu (refer to Figure 1-16) from which you can start applications, lock the screen, get help, switch users, or log out.
- **Home Folder:** Opens your home directory in the Konqueror file manager.
- **Terminal Program:** Runs Konsole, a program that provides a terminal window where you can type Linux commands.
- **SUSE Help Center:** Starts the SUSE Help Center, where you can get help on various aspects of SUSE Linux.
- **Web Browser:** Runs the Konqueror Web browser.
- **KMail:** Starts the KMail mail client for KDE.
- **Desktop Pager:** Click on each square to bring up a different desktop.
- **Clipboard Tool:** Click to see what has been cut and what you can paste elsewhere.
- **Powersaver Tool:** Right-click to view a menu that you can use to start the YaST Power Management module that enables you to edit power-saver settings.
- **Audio Mixer:** Click to change the sound volume. Right-click to start the KAMix utility that enables you to change the volume as well as other aspects of the sound card.
- **SUSE Hardware Tool:** Click to view information about devices in the PC and configure them.
- **SUSE Watcher:** Click to open a window you can use to both check for online updates as well as start online updates.
- **Clock:** Displays the current time. Clicking brings up a calendar showing the current date.
- **Hide Panel:** The end-point of the panel serves as a "hide panel" button, which means that if you click this icon, the panel slides to the right and disappears. Click again and the panel reappears. You can hide the panel to create more room for other windows.

In addition to what you see on the SUSE desktop, you have many more choices in the main menu that appears when you click Main Menu on the panel. (See Figure 1-20.) Similar to Windows Start button, the Main Menu is where you start when you want to run an application.

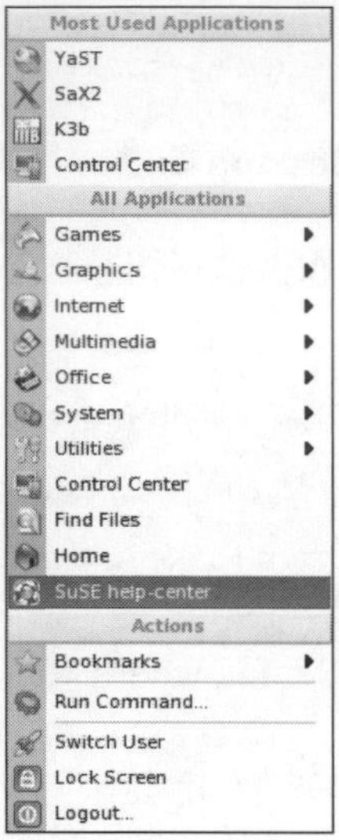

Figure 1-20: A typical Main Menu in SUSE.

The SUSE main menu (refer to Figure 1-20) has three broad categories — Most Used Applications shows the icons for applications you have used recently, All Applications organizes the applications that you can access, and Actions shows buttons for some common daily tasks such as locking the screen, running a command, or logging out. You should browse the All Applications category to familiarize yourself with what SUSE has to offer as a desktop operating system.

Introducing the Xandros Desktop

The official name of the commercial Xandros distribution is *Xandros Desktop OS,* so it's no surprise that Xandros comes with a well-designed desktop. On startup, Xandros automatically logs you in as a user (it uses the user account that you defined during installation), and you get the initial desktop, as shown in Figure 1-21.

Xandros is based on Debian, and it uses a customized version of KDE as its desktop. As Figure 1-21 illustrates, you should note the following key elements in the Xandros desktop:

✦ **Desktop icons:** The Xandros desktop displays a number of desktop icons — a Trash icon for deleted items, an icon for browsing your home folder, as well as icons for support, a link to the Xandros Quickstart guide, shortcuts to the StarOffice office suite and Mozilla Web browser, and an icon for connecting to Xandros Networks (which is how you can download and install updates and new applications in Xandros). You can double-click to open these icons. The result of double-clicking depends on the icon. For example, if you double-click the Xandros Quickstart Guide, the guide opens in a Mozilla Web browser window. On the other hand, double-clicking the StarOffice icon starts the word processor in StarOffice.

✦ **Main Menu:** Brings up the Main Menu (see Figure 1-22) from which you can start applications, run a command, get help, switch users, or log out.

✦ **Mozilla Web Browser:** Runs the Mozilla Web browser.

✦ **Mozilla Mail:** Starts the Mozilla Mail program for accessing your e-mail.

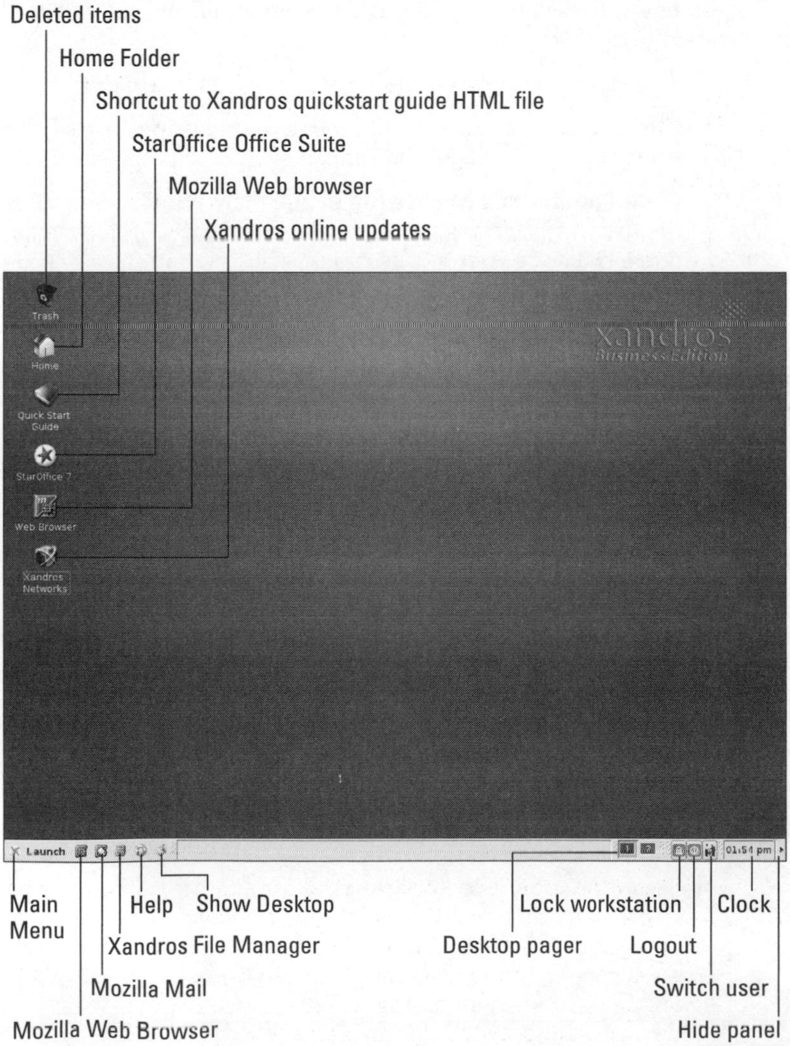

Figure 1-21: The initial Xandros desktop.

- **Xandros File Manager:** Starts the Xandros File Manager, which is similar to Windows Explorer in its layout and its ability to navigate local as well as remote file systems.
- **Help:** Click to open the Xandros Desktop Help Center window where you can get some help on Xandros and UNIX.
- **Show Desktop:** Click to hide all windows and show the desktop.
- **Desktop Pager:** Click on each square to bring up a different desktop.
- **Lock Workstation:** Click to lock the screen so that no one can access it. (You can access it again by entering your password.)
- **Logout:** Click to log out. (You have to confirm that you really want to log out.)
- **Switch User:** Click to switch to another user session.
- **Clock:** Displays the current time. Clicking brings up a Time and Date utility for setting date and time.
- **Hide Panel:** Click to hide the panel. (The panel slides to the right and disappears.) Click again to view the panel. By hiding the panel, you have more room for your applications' windows.

Xandros uses a streamlined main menu, shown in Figure 1-22, that appears when you click Main Menu on the panel. The menu has all applications organized into a single Applications category.

You can explore the main menu to find out more about the applications that come with Xandros. I provide an overview of the applications in Chapter 4 of this minibook.

TIP

Try out the Xandros File Manager by clicking the icon on the panel. From the Xandros File Manager, you can browse various folders in your system, as well as access any Windows shares on your local area network. You can do all the usual things — move or copy files by dragging them and double-click on files to open them. I found the Xandros File Manager to be a good starting point for my Xandros sessions.

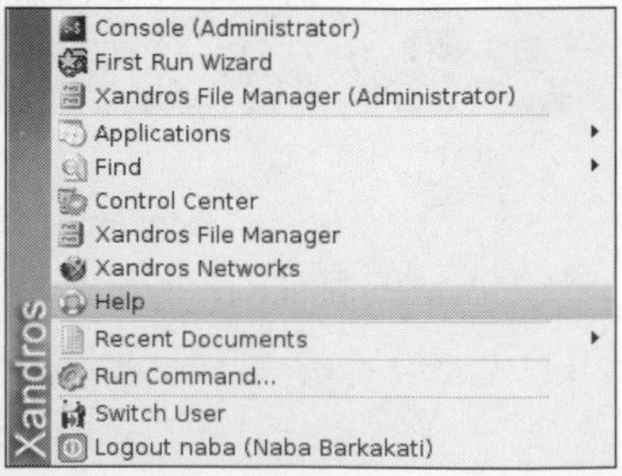

Figure 1-22: Xandros desktop provides a streamlined main menu.

Chapter 2: Commanding the Shell

In This Chapter

- **Opening terminal windows and virtual consoles**
- **Using the Bash shell**
- **Discovering some Linux commands**
- **Writing shell scripts**

Sometimes, things just don't work. What do you do if the GUI desktop stops responding to your mouse clicks? What if the GUI doesn't start at all? You can still tell your Linux system what to do, but you have to do it by typing commands into a text screen. In these situations, you work with the *shell* — the Linux command interpreter. I introduce the Bash shell (the default shell in most Linux distributions) in this chapter.

After you figure out how to work with the shell, you may even begin to like the simplicity and power of the Linux commands. And then, even if you're a GUI aficionado, someday soon you may find yourself firing up a terminal window and making the system sing and dance with two- or three-letter commands strung together by strange punctuation characters. (Hey, I can dream, can't I?)

Opening Terminal Windows and Virtual Consoles

First things first. If you're working in a GUI desktop such as GNOME or KDE, where do you type commands for the shell? Good question.

The easiest way to get to the shell is to open a *terminal* (also called *console*) window. The GNOME and KDE GUIs in most distributions include an icon (or a Main Menu option) to open a terminal window. Click that icon or select the menu option to get a terminal window. Now you can type commands to your heart's content.

If, for some reason, the GUI seems to be *hung* (you click and type but nothing happens), you can turn to the *virtual consoles*. (The *physical* console is the monitor-and-keyboard combination.) The idea of virtual consoles is to give you the ability to switch between several text consoles, even though you have only one physical console. Whether you are running a GUI or not, you can then use different text consoles to type different commands.

To get to the first virtual console from the GNOME or KDE desktop, press Ctrl+Alt+F1. Press Ctrl+Alt+F2 for the second virtual console, and so on. Each of these virtual consoles is a text screen where you can log in and type Linux commands to perform various tasks. When you're done, type **exit** to log out.

TIP

You can use up to six virtual consoles. In most distributions, the seventh one is used for the GUI desktop. To get back to the GUI desktop, press Ctrl+Alt+F7.

Using the Bash Shell

If you've used MS-DOS, you may be familiar with `COMMAND.COM`, the DOS command interpreter. That program displays the infamous `C:\>` prompt. In Windows, you can see this prompt if you open a command window. (To open a command window in Microsoft Windows, choose Start➪Run, type **command** in the text box, and then click OK.)

Linux comes with a command interpreter that resembles `COMMAND.COM` in DOS, but it can do a whole lot more. The Linux command interpreter is called a *shell.*

The default shell in many Linux distributions is Bash. When you open a terminal window or log in at a text console, the Bash shell is what prompts you for commands. Then, when you type a command, the shell executes your command. By the way, just as there are multiple GUIs (GNOME or KDE) for Linux, you have the choice of shells besides Bash. For example, the C Shell is an alternate shell that some people prefer. You can easily change your default shell by using the `chsh` command.

In addition to the standard Linux commands, Bash can execute any computer program. So you can type the name of an application (the name is usually more cryptic than what you see in GNOME or KDE menus) at the shell prompt, and the shell starts that application.

Understanding the syntax of shell commands

Because a shell interprets what you type, knowing how the shell processes the text you enter is important. All shell commands have this general format that starts with a command followed by options (some commands have no options):

```
command option1 option2 ... optionN
```

Such a single on-screen line giving a command is commonly referred to as a *command line*. On a command line, you enter a command, followed by zero or more options (or *arguments*). These strings of options — the *command-line options* (or command-line arguments) — modify the way the command works so that you can get it to do specific tasks.

The shell uses a blank space or a tab to distinguish between the command and options. Naturally, you help it by using a space or a tab to separate the command from the options and the options from one another.

An option can contain spaces — all you have to do is put that option inside quotation marks so that the spaces are included. For example, to search for my name in the password file, I enter the following `grep` command (`grep` is used for searching for text in files):

```
grep "Naba Barkakati" /etc/passwd
```

When `grep` prints the line with my name, it looks like this:

```
naba:x:1000:100:Naba Barkakati:/home/naba:/bin/bash
```

If you created a user account with your username, type the `grep` command with your username as an argument.

TECHNICAL STUFF

In the output from the `grep` command, you can see the name of the shell (`/bin/bash`) following the last colon (`:`).

The number of command-line options and their format, of course, depends on the actual command. Typically, these options look like `-X`, where `X` is a single character. For example, the `ls` command lists the contents of a directory. You can use the `-l` option to see more details. For example, here is a result of typing **ls -l** in a user's home directory:

```
total 1
drwxr-xr-x  2 naba users  48 2004-08-15 20:22 bin
drwx------  3 naba users 304 2004-08-15 20:26 Desktop
drwxr-xr-x  2 naba users  80 2004-08-15 20:22 Documents
drwx------  7 naba users 520 2004-09-04 17:07 Mail
drwxr-xr-x  5 naba users 416 2004-09-04 17:05 OpenOffice.org1.1
drwxr-xr-x  2 naba users  80 2004-08-15 20:22 public_html
drwxr-xr-x  2 naba users 784 2004-09-04 20:55 sdump
```

If a command is too long to fit on a single line, you can press the backslash key followed by Enter. Then, continue typing the command on the next line. For example, type the following command (press Enter after each line):

```
cat \
/etc/passwd
```

The `cat` command then displays the contents of the `/etc/passwd` file.

You can *concatenate* (that is, string together) several shorter commands on a single line. Just separate the commands by semicolons (`;`). For example, the following command

```
cd; ls -l; pwd
```

changes the current directory to your home directory, lists the contents of that directory, and then shows the name of that directory.

Combining shell commands

You can combine simple shell commands to create a more sophisticated command. For example, suppose that you want to find out whether a device file named `sbpcd` resides in your system's `/dev` directory because some documentation says you need that device file for a Sound Blaster Pro CD-ROM drive. You can use the `ls /dev` command to get a directory listing of the `/dev` directory, and then browse through it to see whether that listing contains `sbpcd`.

Unfortunately, the `/dev` directory has a great many entries, so you may find it hard to find any item that has `sbpcd` in its name. You can, however, combine the `ls` command with `grep` and come up with a command line that does exactly what you want. Here's that command line:

```
ls /dev | grep sbpcd
```

The shell sends the output of the `ls` command (the directory listing) to the `grep` command, which searches for the string `sbpcd`. That vertical bar (|) is known as a *pipe* because it acts as a conduit (think of a water pipe) between the two programs — the output of the first command is fed into the input of the second one.

Controlling command input and output

Most Linux commands have a common feature — they always read from the standard input (usually, the keyboard) and write to the standard output (usually, the screen). Error messages are sent to the standard error (usually to the screen as well). These three devices often are referred to as `stdin`, `stdout`, and `stderr`.

You can make a command get its input from a file and then send its output to another file. Just so you know, the highfalutin' term for this feature is *input and output redirection* or *I/O redirection*.

Getting command input from a file

If you want a command to read from a file, you can redirect the standard input to come from that file instead of from the keyboard. For example, type the following command:

```
sort < /etc/passwd
```

This command displays a sorted list of the lines in the `/etc/passwd` file. In this case, the less-than sign (<) redirects `stdin` so that the `sort` command reads its input from the `/etc/passwd` file.

Saving command output in a file

To save the output of a command in a file, redirect the standard output to a file. For example, type **cd** to change to your home directory and then type the following command:

```
grep typedef /usr/include/* > typedef.out
```

This command searches through all files in the `/usr/include` directory for the occurrence of the text `typedef` — and then saves the output in a file called `typedef.out`. The greater-than sign (>) redirects `stdout` to a file. This command also illustrates another feature of Bash. When you use an asterisk (*), Bash replaces the asterisk with a list of all filenames in the specified directory. Thus, `/usr/include/*` means *all the files in the `/usr/include` directory*.

If you want to append a command's output to the end of an existing file instead of saving the output in a new file, use two greater-than signs (>) like this:

```
command >> filename
```

Saving error messages in a file

Sometimes you type a command and it generates a whole lot of error messages that scroll by so fast you can't tell what's going on. One way to see all the error messages is to save the error messages in a file so that you can see what the heck happened. You can do that by redirecting `stderr` to a file.

For example, type the following command:

```
find / -name COPYING -print 2> finderr
```

This command looks throughout the file system for files named `COPYING`, but saves all the error messages in the `finderr` file. The number `2` followed by the greater-than sign (`2>`) redirects `stderr` to a file.

If you want to simply discard the error messages instead of saving them in a file, use `/dev/null` as the filename, like this:

```
find / -name COPYING -print 2> /dev/null
```

That `/dev/null` is a special file — often called the *bit bucket* and sometimes glorified as the *Great Bit Bucket in the Sky* — that simply discards whatever it receives. So now you know what they mean when you hear phrases such as, "Your mail probably ended up in the bit bucket."

Typing less with automatic command completion

Many commands take a filename as an argument. To view the contents of the `/etc/modprobe.conf` text file, for example, type the following command:

```
cat /etc/modprobe.conf
```

The `cat` command displays the `/etc/modprobe.conf` file. For any command that takes a filename as an argument, you can use a Bash feature to avoid having to type the whole filename. All you have to type is the bare minimum — just the first few characters — to uniquely identify the file in its directory.

To see an example, type **cat /etc/mod** but don't press Enter; press Tab instead. Bash automatically completes the filename, so the command becomes `cat /etc/modprobe.conf`. Now press Enter to run the command.

Whenever you type a filename, press Tab after the first few characters of the filename. Bash probably can complete the filename so that you don't have to type the entire name. If you don't enter enough characters to uniquely identify the file, Bash beeps. Just type a few more characters and press Tab again.

Going wild with asterisks and question marks

You can avoid typing long filenames another way. (After all, making less work for users is the idea of computers, isn't it?)

This particular trick involves using the asterisk (*) and question mark (?) and a few more tricks. These special characters are called *wildcards* because they match zero or more characters in a line of text.

If you know MS-DOS, you may have used commands such as `COPY *.* A:` to copy all files from the current directory to the A: drive. Bash accepts similar wildcards in filenames. As you'd expect, Bash provides many more wildcard options than the MS-DOS command interpreter does.

You can use three types of wildcards in Bash:

- The **asterisk (*)** character matches zero or more characters in a filename. That means * denotes all files in a directory.
- The **question mark (?)** matches any single character. If you type `test?`, that matches any five-character text that begins with `test`.
- A **set of characters in brackets** matches any single character from that set. The string `[aB]*`, for example, matches any filename that starts with `a` or `B`.

Wildcards are handy when you want to do something to a whole lot of files. For example, to copy all the files from the /mnt/cdrom directory to the current directory, type the following:

```
cp /mnt/cdrom/* .
```

Bash replaces the wildcard character * with the names of all the files in the /mnt/cdrom directory. The period at the end of the command represents the current directory.

You can use the asterisk with other parts of a filename to select a more specific group of files. Suppose you want to use the grep command to search for the text typedef struct in all files of the /usr/include directory that meet the following criteria:

- ✦ The filename starts with s.
- ✦ The filename ends with .h.

The wildcard specification s*.h denotes all filenames that meet these criteria. Thus you can perform the search with the following command:

```
grep "typedef struct" /usr/include/s*.h
```

The string contains a space that you want the grep command to find, so you have to enclose that string in quotation marks. That way, Bash does not try to interpret each word in that text as a separate command-line argument.

The question mark (?) matches a single character. Suppose that you have four files — image1.pcx, image2.pcx, image3.pcx, and image4.pcx — in the current directory. To copy these files to the /mnt/floppy directory, use the following command:

```
cp image?.pcx /mnt/floppy
```

Bash replaces the single question mark with any single character, and copies the four files to /mnt.

The third wildcard format — [...] — matches a single character from a specific set of characters enclosed in square brackets. You may want to combine this format with other wildcards to narrow down the matching filenames to a smaller set. To see a list of all filenames in the /etc/X11/xdm directory that start with x or X, type the following command:

```
ls /etc/X11/xdm/[xX]*
```

Repeating previously typed commands

To make repeating long commands easy for you, Bash stores up to 500 old commands as part of a *command history* (basically just a list of old commands). To see the command history, type **history**. Bash displays a numbered list of the old commands, including those that you entered during previous logins.

If the command list is too long, you can limit the number of old commands that you want to see. For example, to see only the ten most recent commands, type this command:

```
history 10
```

To repeat a command from the list that the `history` command shows, simply type an exclamation point (`!`), followed by that command's number. To repeat command number `3`, type **!3**.

You can repeat an old command without knowing its command number. Suppose you typed `more /usr/lib/X11/xdm/xdm-config` a few minutes ago, and now you want to look at that file again. To repeat the previous `more` command, type the following:

```
!more
```

Often, you may want to repeat the last command that you just typed, perhaps with a slight change. For example, you may have displayed the contents of the directory by using the `ls -l` command. To repeat that command, type two exclamation points as follows:

```
!!
```

Sometimes, you may want to repeat the previous command but add extra arguments to it. Suppose that `ls -l` shows too many files. Simply repeat that command, but pipe the output through the `more` command as follows:

```
!! | more
```

Bash replaces the two exclamation points with the previous command and then appends `| more` to that command.

TIP: Here's the easiest way to recall previous commands. Just press the up-arrow key and Bash keeps going backward through the history of commands you previously typed. To move forward in the command history, press the down-arrow key.

Discovering and Using Linux Commands

You type Linux commands at the shell prompt. By *Linux commands,* I mean some of the commands that the Bash shell understands as well as the command-line utilities that come with Linux. In this section, I introduce you to a few major categories of Linux commands.

I can't possibly cover every single Linux command in this chapter, but I want to give you a feel for the breadth of the commands by showing you a list of common Linux commands in Table 2-1. The table lists common Linux commands by category. Before you start memorizing any Linux commands, browse this table.

Table 2-1 Overview of Common Linux Commands

Command Name	*Action*
Getting Online Help	
`apropos`	Finds online manual pages for a specified keyword.
`info`	Displays online help information about a specified command.
`man`	Displays online help information.
`whatis`	Similar to `apropos`, but searches for complete words only.
Making Commands Easier	
`alias`	Defines an abbreviation for a long command.
`type`	Shows the type and location of a command.
`unalias`	Deletes an abbreviation defined using `alias`.
Managing Files and Directories	
`cd`	Changes the current directory.
`chmod`	Changes file permissions.
`chown`	Changes file owner and group.
`cp`	Copies files.
`ln`	Creates symbolic links to files and directories.
`ls`	Displays the contents of a directory.
`mkdir`	Creates a directory.
`mv`	Renames a file as well as moves a file from one directory to another.
`rm`	Deletes files.
`rmdir`	Deletes directories.
`pwd`	Displays the current directory.
`touch`	Updates a file's time stamp.

(continued)

Table 2-1 *(continued)*

Command Name	*Action*
Finding Files	
`find`	Finds files based on specified criteria such as name, size, and so on.
`locate`	Finds files using a periodically updated filename database (the database is created by the `updatedb` program).
`whereis`	Finds files based in the typical directories where executable (also known as *binary*) files are located.
`which`	Finds files in the directories listed in the PATH environment variable.
Processing Files	
`cat`	Displays a file on standard output (can be used to concatenate several files into one big file).
`cut`	Extracts specified sections from each line of text in a file.
`dd`	Copies blocks of data from one file to another (used to copy data from devices).
`diff`	Compares two text files and finds any differences.
`expand`	Converts all tabs into spaces.
`file`	Displays the type of data in a file.
`fold`	Wraps each line of text to fit a specified width.
`grep`	Searches for regular expressions within a text file.
`less`	Displays a text file, one page at a time (can go backward also).
`lpr`	Prints files.
`more`	Displays a text file, one page at a time (goes forward only).
`nl`	Numbers all nonblank lines in a text file and prints the lines to standard output.
`paste`	Concatenates corresponding lines from several files.
`patch`	Updates a text file using the differences between the original and revised copy of the file.
`sed`	Copies a file to standard output while applying specified editing commands.
`sort`	Sorts lines in a text file.
`split`	Breaks up a file into several smaller files with specified size.
`tac`	Reverses a file (last line first and so on).
`tail`	Displays the last few lines of a file.

Command Name	Action
tr	Substitutes one group of characters for another throughout a file.
uniq	Eliminates duplicate lines from a text file.
wc	Counts the number of lines, words, and characters in a text file.
zcat	Displays a compressed file (after decompressing).
zless	Displays a compressed file one page at a time (can go backward also).
zmore	Displays a compressed file one page at a time.
Archiving and Compressing Files	
compress	Compresses files.
cpio	Copies files to and from an archive.
gunzip	Decompresses files compressed with GNU ZIP (gzip).
gzip	Compresses files using GNU ZIP.
tar	Creates an archive of files in one or more directories (originally meant for archiving on tape).
uncompress	Decompresses files compressed with compress.
Managing Processes	
bg	Runs an interrupted process in the background.
fg	Runs a process in the foreground.
free	Displays the amount of free and used memory in the system.
halt	Shuts down Linux and halts the computer.
kill	Sends a signal to a process (usually used to terminate a process).
ldd	Displays the shared libraries needed to run a program.
nice	Runs a process with lower priority (referred to as nice mode).
ps	Displays a list of currently running processes.
printenv	Displays the current environment variables.
pstree	Similar to ps, but shows parent-child relationships clearly.
reboot	Stops Linux and then restarts the computer.
shutdown	Shuts down Linux.
top	Displays a list of most processor- and memory-intensive processes.
uname	Displays information about the system and the Linux kernel.

(continued)

Table 2-1 *(continued)*

Command Name	*Action*
Managing Users	
`chsh`	Changes the shell (command interpreter).
`groups`	Prints the list of groups that include a specified user.
`id`	Displays the user and group ID for a specified username.
`passwd`	Changes the password.
`su`	Starts a new shell as another user or `root` (when invoked without any argument).
Managing the File System	
`df`	Summarizes free and available space in all mounted storage devices.
`du`	Displays disk usage information.
`fdformat`	Formats a diskette.
`fdisk`	Partitions a hard drive.
`fsck`	Checks and repairs a file system.
`mkfs`	Creates a new file system.
`mknod`	Creates a device file.
`mkswap`	Creates a swap space for Linux in a file or a hard drive partition.
`mount`	Mounts a device (for example, the CD-ROM) on a directory in the file system.
`swapoff`	Deactivates a swap space.
`swapon`	Activates a swap space.
`sync`	Writes buffered (saved in memory) data to files.
`tty`	Displays the device name for the current terminal.
`umount`	Unmounts a device from the file system.
Working with Date and Time	
`cal`	Displays a calendar for a specified month or year.
`date`	Shows the current date and time or sets a new date and time.

Becoming root (superuser)

When you want to do anything that requires a high privilege level (for example, administering your system), you have to become `root`. Normally, you log in as a regular user with your everyday username. When you need the privileges of the superuser, though, use the following command to become `root`:

```
su -
```

That's su followed by the minus sign (or hyphen). The shell then prompts you for the root password. Type the password and press Enter.

Knoppix does not require you to enter any password to become root. After you type **su -** and press Enter, you will become root (the prompt will change to indicate the change). By the way, this is not as bad as it sounds because Knoppix is a Live CD distribution that you run directly from the CD-ROM, and the idea is to use Knoppix to try out Linux or fix some problems in an existing Linux installation.

After you're done with whatever you wanted to do as root (and you have the privilege to do anything as root), type **exit** to return to your normal username.

Instead of becoming root by using the su command, you can also type **sudo**, followed by the command that you want to run as root. If you are listed as an authorized user in the /etc/sudoers file, sudo executes the command as if you were logged in as root. Type **man sudoers** to read more about the /etc/sudoers file.

Managing processes

Every time the shell executes a command that you type, it starts a process. The shell itself is a process. So are any scripts or programs that the shell runs.

Use the ps ax command to see a list of processes. When you type **ps ax**, Bash shows you the current set of processes. Here are a few lines of output from the ps ax command (I also included the --cols 132 option to ensure that you can see each command in its entirety):

```
ps ax --cols 132
  PID TTY      STAT   TIME COMMAND
    1 ?        S      0:04 init [5]
    2 ?        SN     0:00 [ksoftirqd/0]
    3 ?        S<     0:00 [events/0]
    4 ?        S<     0:00 [kblockd/0]
    6 ?        S<     0:00 [khelper]
    5 ?        S      0:00 [kapmd]
    7 ?        S      0:00 [pdflush]
    8 ?        S      0:00 [pdflush]
   10 ?        S<     0:00 [aio/0]
    9 ?        S      0:00 [kswapd0]
  170 ?        S      0:00 [kseriod]
  541 ?        S<     0:00 [reiserfs/0]
  710 ?        S<     0:00 [kcopyd]
  745 ?        S      0:00 [kjournald]
 1461 ?        S      0:00 [khubd]
 1670 ?        Ss     0:00 /sbin/dhcpcd -H -D -N -t 999999 -h linux eth0
 1763 ?        Ss     0:00 /sbin/syslogd -a /var/lib/ntp/dev/log
... lines deleted ...
 4363 ?        S      0:00 sshd: naba@pts/1
 4364 pts/1    Ss     0:00 -bash
 4740 pts/1    R+     0:00 ps ax --cols 132
```

In this listing, the first column has the heading `PID` and shows a number for each process. PID stands for *process ID* (identification), which is a sequential number assigned by the Linux kernel. If you look through the output of the `ps ax` command, you see that the `init` command is the first process and that it has a PID or process number of 1. That's why `init` is referred to as the "mother of all processes."

The `COMMAND` column shows the command that created each process, and the `TIME` column shows the cumulative CPU time used by the process. The `STAT` column shows the state of a process — `S` means the process is sleeping and `R` means it's running. The symbols following the status letter have further meanings, such as < indicates a high-priority process and + means that the process is running in the foreground. The `TTY` column shows the terminal, if any, associated with the process.

The process ID or process number is useful when you have to forcibly stop an errant process. Look at the output of the `ps ax` command and note the `PID` of the offending process. Then, use the `kill` command with that process number. To stop process number 8550, for example, type the following command:

```
kill -9 8550
```

The `-9` option means send signal number 9 to the process. It just so happens that signal number 9 is the KILL signal, which causes the process to exit.

Working with date and time

You can use the `date` command to display the current date and time or set a new date and time. Type **date** at the shell prompt and you get a result similar to the following:

```
Sat Sep  4 21:38:08 EDT 2004
```

As you can see, the `date` command alone displays the current date and time.

To set the date, log in as `root` and then type **date** followed by the date and time in the `MMDDhhmmYYYY` format, where each character is a digit. For example, to set the date and time to December 31, 2005 and 9:30 p.m., you type

```
date 123121302005
```

The `MMDDhhmmYYYY` date and time format is similar to the 24-hour military clock, and has the following meaning:

- `MM` is a two-digit number for the month (01 through 12).
- `DD` is a two-digit number for the day of the month (01 through 31).

✦ hh is a two-digit hour in 24-hour format (00 is midnight and 23 is 11:00 p.m.).

✦ mm is a two-digit number for the minutes (00 through 59).

✦ YYYY is the four-digit year (such as 2005).

The other interesting date-related command is `cal`. If you type `cal` without any options, it prints a calendar for the current month. If you type `cal` followed by a number, `cal` treats the number as the year and prints the calendar for that year. To view the calendar for a specific month in a specific year, provide the month number (1 = January, 2 = February, and so on) followed by the year. Thus, to view the calendar for January 2005, type the following and you get the calendar for that month:

```
cal 1 2005
    January 2005
Su Mo Tu We Th Fr Sa
                   1
 2  3  4  5  6  7  8
 9 10 11 12 13 14 15
16 17 18 19 20 21 22
23 24 25 26 27 28 29
30 31
```


Processing files

You can search through a text file with `grep` and view a text file, a screen at a time, with `more`. For example, to search for my username in the `/etc/passwd` file, I use

```
grep naba /etc/passwd
```

To view the `/etc/inittab` file a screenful at a time, I type

```
more /etc/inittab
```

As each screen pauses, I press the spacebar to go to the next page.

Many more Linux commands work on files — mostly on text files, but some commands also work on any file. I describe a few of the file-processing tools next.

Counting words and lines in a text file

I am always curious about the size of files. For text files, the number of characters is basically the size of the file in bytes (because each character takes up a byte of storage space). What about words and the number of lines, though?

The Linux `wc` command comes to the rescue. The `wc` command displays the total number of characters, words, and lines in a text file. For example, type **wc /etc/inittab** and you see an output similar to the following:

```
  75     304    2341 /etc/inittab
```

In this case, `wc` reports that 75 lines, 304 words, and 2341 characters are in the `/etc/inittab` file. If you simply want to see the number of lines in a file, use the `-l` option and type **wc -l /etc/inittab**. The resulting output should be similar to the following:

```
75 /etc/inittab
```

As you can see, with the `-l` option, `wc` simply displays the line count.

If you don't specify a filename, the `wc` command expects input from the standard input. You can use the pipe feature of the shell to feed the output of another command to `wc`, which can be handy sometimes.

TIP

Suppose you want a rough count of the processes running on your system. You can get a list of all processes with the `ps ax` command, but instead of counting lines manually, just pipe the output of `ps` to `wc` and you get a rough count automatically:

```
ps ax | wc -l
76
```

Here the `ps` command produced 76 lines of output. Because the first line simply shows the headings for the tabular columns, you can estimate that about 75 processes are running on your system. (Of course, this count probably includes the processes used to run the `ps` and `wc` commands as well, but who's *really* counting?)

Sorting text files

You can sort the lines in a text file by using the `sort` command. To see how the `sort` command works, first type **more /etc/passwd** to see the current contents of the `/etc/passwd` file. Now type **sort /etc/passwd** to see the lines sorted alphabetically. If you want to sort a file and save the sorted version in another file, you have to use the Bash shell's output redirection feature like this:

```
sort /etc/passwd > ~/sorted.text
```

This command sorts the lines in the `/etc/passwd` file and saves the output in a file named `sorted.text` in your home directory.

Substituting or deleting characters from a file

Another interesting command is `tr` — it substitutes one group of characters for another (or deletes a selected character) throughout a file. Suppose that you occasionally have to use MS-DOS text files on your Linux system. Although you may expect to use a text file on any system without any problems, you find one catch: DOS uses a carriage return followed by a line feed to mark the end of each line, whereas Linux uses only a line feed.

TIP

On your Linux system, you can get rid of the extra carriage returns in the DOS text file by using the `tr` command with the `-d` option. Essentially, to convert the DOS text file `filename.dos` to a Linux text file named `filename.linux`, type the following:

```
tr -d '\015' < filename.dos > filename.linux
```

In this command, `'\015'` denotes the code for the carriage-return character in octal notation.

Splitting a file into several smaller files

The `split` command is handy for those times when you want to copy a file to a floppy disk, but the file is too large to fit on a single floppy. You can then use the `split` command to break up the file into multiple smaller files, each of which can fit on a floppy.

By default, `split` puts 1,000 lines into each file. The files are named by groups of letters such as `aa`, `ab`, `ac`, and so on. You can specify a prefix for the filenames. For example, to split a large file called `hugefile.tar` into smaller files that fit into several high-density 3.5-inch floppy disks, use `split` as follows:

```
split -b 1440k hugefile.tar part.
```

This command splits the `hugefile.tar` file into 1440K chunks so each one can fit onto a floppy disk. The command creates files named `part.aa`, `part.ab`, `part.ac`, and so on.

To combine the split files back into a single file, use the `cat` command as follows:

```
cat part.?? > hugefile.tar
```

In this case, the two question marks (`??`) match any two character extension in the filename. In other words, the filename `part.??` would match all filenames such as `part.12`, `part.aa`, `part.ab`, `part.2b`, and so on.

Writing Shell Scripts

If you have ever used MS-DOS, you may remember MS-DOS batch files. These are text files with MS-DOS commands. Similarly, shell scripts are also text files with a bunch of shell commands.

If you aren't a programmer, you may feel apprehensive about programming. But shell programming can be as simple as storing a few commands in a file. Right now, you might not be up to writing complex shell scripts, but you can certainly try out a simple shell script.

To try your hand at a little shell programming, type the following text at the shell prompt exactly as shown and then press Ctrl+D when you're done:

```
cd
cat > simple
#!/bin/sh
echo "This script's name is: $0"
echo Argument 1: $1
echo Argument 2: $2
```

The `cd` command changes the current directory to your home directory. Then the `cat` command displays whatever you type; in this case, I'm sending the output to a file named `simple`. After you press Ctrl+D, the `cat` command ends and you see the shell prompt again. What you have done is created a file named `simple` that contains the following shell script:

```
#!/bin/sh
echo "This script's name is: $0"
echo Argument 1: $1
echo Argument 2: $2
```

The first line causes Linux to run the Bash shell program (its name is `/bin/bash`). The shell then reads the rest of the lines in the script.

Just as most Linux commands accept command-line options, a Bash script also accepts command-line options. Inside the script, you can refer to the options as `$1`, `$2`, and so on. The special name `$0` refers to the name of the script itself.

To run this shell script, first you have to make the file executable (that is, turn it into a program) with the following command:

```
chmod +x simple
```

Now run the script with the following command:

```
./simple one two
```

```
This script's name is: ./simple
Argument 1: one
Argument 2: two
```

The ./ prefix to the script's name indicates that the `simple` file is in the current directory.

This script simply prints the script's name and the first two command-line options that the user types after the script's name.

Next, try running the script with a few arguments, as follows:

```
./simple "This is one argument" second-argument third
This script's name is: ./simple
Argument 1: This is one argument
Argument 2: second-argument
```


The shell treats the entire string within the double quotation marks as a single argument. Otherwise, the shell uses spaces as separators between arguments on the command line.

Most useful shell scripts are more complicated than this simple script, but this simple exercise gives you a rough idea of how to write shell scripts.

REMEMBER

Place Linux commands in a file and use the `chmod` command to make the file executable. *Voilà!* You have created a shell script!

Chapter 3: Navigating the Linux File System

In This Chapter

- **Understanding the Linux file system**
- **Navigating the file system with Linux commands**
- **Understanding file permissions**
- **Manipulating files and directories with Linux commands**

To use files and directories well, you need to understand the concept of a hierarchical file system. Even if you use the GUI file managers to access files and folders (folders are also called directories), you can benefit from a lay of the land of the file system.

In this chapter, I introduce you to the Linux file system, and you discover how to work with files and directories with several Linux commands.

Understanding the Linux File System

Like any other operating system, Linux organizes information in files and directories. Directories, in turn, hold the files. A *directory* is a special file that can contain other files and directories. Because a directory can contain other directories, this method of organizing files gives rise to a hierarchical structure. This hierarchical organization of files is called the *file system*.

The Linux file system gives you a unified view of all storage in your PC. The file system has a single root directory, indicated by a forward slash (/). Within the root directory is a hierarchy of files and directories. Parts of the file system can reside in different physical media, such as hard drive, floppy disk, and CD-ROM. Figure 3-1 illustrates the concept of the Linux file system (which is the same in any Linux system) and how it spans multiple physical devices.

If you're familiar with MS-DOS or Windows, you may find something missing in the Linux file system: You don't find drive letters in Linux. All disk drives and CD-ROM drives are part of a single file system.

In Linux, you can have long filenames (up to 256 characters), and filenames are case-sensitive. Often these filenames have multiple extensions, such as sample.tar.Z. UNIX filenames can take many forms, such as the following: index.html, Makefile, binutils_2.14.90.0.7-8_i386.deb, vsftpd-1.2.1-5.i386.rpm, .bash_profile, and httpd_src.tar.gz.

To locate a file, you need more than just the filename. You also need information about the directory hierarchy. The extended filename, showing the full hierarchy of directories leading to the file, is called the *pathname*. As the name implies, it's the path to the file through the maze of the file system. Figure 3-2 shows a typical pathname for a file in Linux.

As Figure 3-2 shows, the pathname has the following parts:

- ✦ The root directory, indicated by a forward slash (/) character.
- ✦ The directory hierarchy, with each directory name separated from the previous one by a forward slash (/) character. A / appears after the last directory name.
- ✦ The filename, with a name and one or more optional extensions. (A period appears before each extension.)

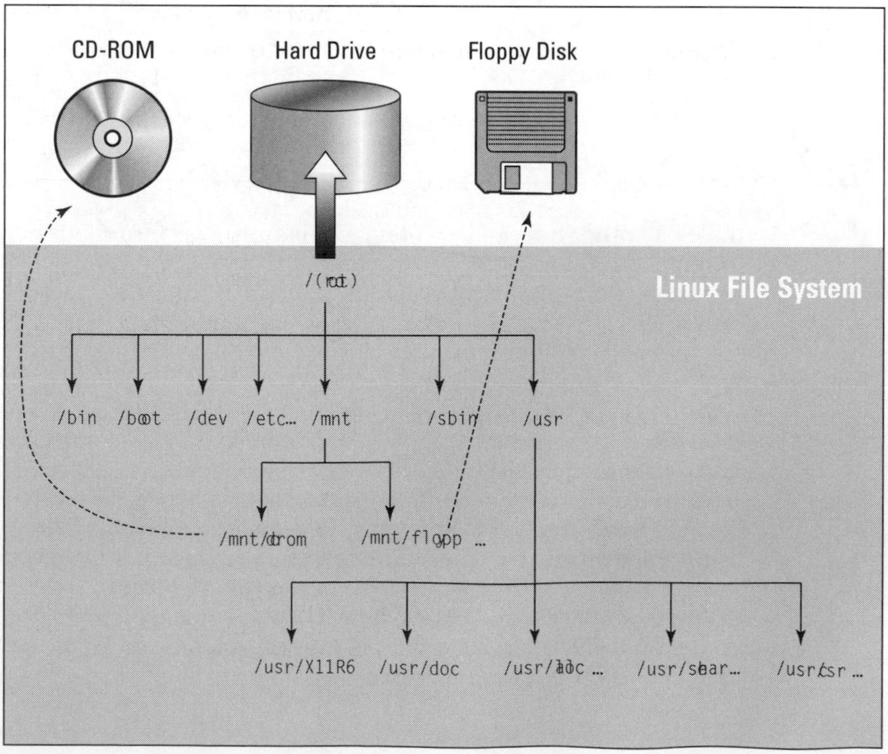

Figure 3-1: The Linux file system provides a unified view of storage that may span multiple storage devices.

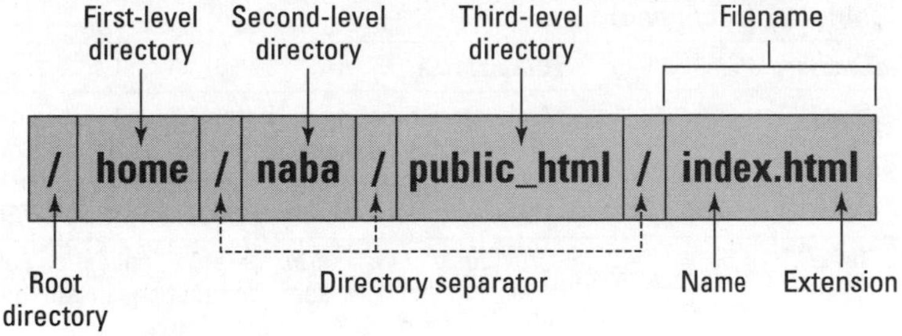

Figure 3-2: The pathname of a file shows the sequence of directories leading up to the file.

The Linux file system has a well-defined set of top-level directories, and some of these directories have specific purposes. Finding your way around the file system is easier if you know the purpose of these directories. You also become adept at guessing where to look for specific types of files when you face a new situation. Table 3-1 briefly describes the top-level directories in the Linux file system.

Table 3-1 Top-Level Directories in the Linux File System

Directory	*Description*
`/`	This root directory forms the base of the file system. All files and directories are contained logically in the root directory, regardless of their physical locations.
`/bin`	Contains the executable programs that are part of the Linux operating system. Many Linux commands, such as `cat`, `cp`, `ls`, `more`, and `tar`, are located in `/bin`.
`/boot`	Contains the Linux kernel and other files that the LILO and GRUB boot managers need. (The kernel and other files can be anywhere, but placing them in the `/boot` directory is customary.)
`/dev`	Contains special files that represent devices attached to the system.
`/etc`	Contains most system configuration files and the initialization scripts (in the `/etc/rc.d` subdirectory).
`/home`	Conventional location of the home directories of all users. User naba's home directory, for example, is `/home/naba`.
`/lib`	Contains library files for all programs stored in `/sbin` and `/bin` directories (including the loadable driver modules) needed to start Linux.
`/lost+found`	Directory for lost files. Every disk partition has a `lost+found` directory.

(continued)

Table 3-1 *(continued)*

Directory	*Description*
`/mnt`	A directory for temporarily mounted file systems, such as CD-ROM drives, floppy disks, and Zip drives. Contains the `/mnt/floppy` directory for mounting floppy disks and the `/mnt/cdrom` directory for mounting the CD-ROM drive.
`/opt`	Provides a storage area for large application software packages. For example, some distributions install the OpenOffice.org office suite in the `/opt` directory.
`/proc`	A special directory that contains various information about the processes running in the Linux system.
`/root`	The home directory for the `root` user.
`/sbin`	Contains executable files representing commands typically used for system administration tasks and used by the `root` user. Commands such as `halt` and `shutdown` reside in the `/sbin` directory.
`/selinux`	Contains information used by the Security Enhanced Linux (SELinux) kernel patch and utilities that provide a more secure access control system for Linux.
`/sys`	A special directory that contains information about the devices, as seen by the Linux kernel.
`/tmp`	A temporary directory that any user can use as a *scratch* directory, meaning that the contents of this directory are considered unimportant and usually are deleted every time the system boots.
`/usr`	Contains the subdirectories for many important programs, such as the X Window System (in the `/usr/X11R6` directory) and the online manual. (Table 3-2 shows some of the standard subdirectories in `/usr`.)
`/var`	Contains various system files (such as logs), as well as directories for holding other information, such as files for the Web server and anonymous FTP server.

The `/usr` and `/var` directories also contain a number of standard subdirectories. Table 3-2 lists the important subdirectories in `/usr`. Table 3-3 shows a similar breakdown for the `/var` directory.

Table 3-2 Important /usr Subdirectories

Subdirectory	*Description*
`/usr/X11R6`	Contains the X.org X11 (X Window System) software.
`/usr/bin`	Contains executable files for many more Linux commands, including utility programs that are commonly available in Linux but aren't part of the core Linux operating system.

Subdirectory	Description
/usr/games	Contains some old Linux games.
/usr/include	Contains the header files (files names ending in .h) for the C and C++ programming languages; also includes the X11 header files in the /usr/include/X11 directory and the Linux kernel header files in the /usr/include/linux directory.
/usr/lib	Contains the libraries for C and C++ programming languages; also contains many other libraries, such as database libraries, graphical toolkit libraries, and so on.
/usr/local	Contains local files. The /usr/local/bin directory, for example, is supposed to be the location for any executable program developed on your system.
/usr/sbin	Contains many administrative commands, such as commands for electronic mail and networking.
/usr/share	Contains shared data, such as default configuration files and images for many applications. For example, /usr/share/gnome contains various shared files for the GNOME desktop, and /usr/share/doc has the documentation files for many Linux applications (such as the Bash shell, the Sawfish window manager, and the GIMP image-processing program).
/usr/share/man	Contains the online manual (which you can read by using the man command).
/usr/src	Contains the source code for the Linux kernel (the core operating system).

Table 3-3 Important /var Subdirectories

Subdirectory	Description
/var/cache	Storage area for cached data for applications.
/var/lib	Contains information relating to the current state of applications.
/var/lock	Contains locked files to ensure that a resource is used by one application only.
/var/log	Contains log files organized into subdirectories. The syslogd server stores its log files in /var/log, with the exact content of the files depending on the syslogd configuration file /etc/syslog.conf. For example, /var/log/messages is the main system log file; /var/log/secure contains log messages from secure services (such as sshd and xinetd); and /var/log/maillog contains the log of mail messages.
/var/mail	Contains user mailbox files.
/var/opt	Contains variable data for packages stored in /opt directory.
/var/run	Contains data describing the system since it was booted.

(continued)

Table 3-3 (continued)

Subdirectory	*Description*
/var/spool	Contains data that's waiting for some kind of processing.
/var/tmp	Contains temporary files preserved between system reboots.
/var/yp	Contains Network Information Service (NIS) database files.

Using GUI File Managers

Both GNOME and KDE desktops come with GUI file managers that enable you to easily browse the file system and perform tasks such as copying or moving files. The GNOME file manager is called Nautilus and the KDE file manager is Konqueror. I briefly describe these GUI file managers in the following sections.

Using the Nautilus shell

The Nautilus file manager — more accurately called a *graphical shell* — comes with GNOME. Nautilus is intuitive to use — it's similar to the Windows Active Desktop. You can manage files and folders and also manage your system with Nautilus.

REMEMBER

The latest version of Nautilus has changed from what you may have known in previous versions of Red Hat Linux or Fedora Core. Nautilus now provides a new *Object Window* view in addition to the navigation window that you know from the past. When you double-click any object on the desktop, Nautilus opens an object window that shows that object's contents. If you want the older navigation window with its Web browser-like user interface, right-click a folder and choose Open⇨Browse Folder from the pop-up menu.

Viewing files and folders in object windows

When you double-click a file or a folder, Nautilus opens that object in what it calls an object window. Unlike the Nautilus windows of the past — windows that enabled you to navigate the directory hierarchy — the object window doesn't have any Back and Forward buttons, toolbars, or side panes. For example, double-click the Start Here icon on the left side of the GNOME desktop, and Nautilus opens an object window where it displays the contents of the Start Here object. If you then double-click an object inside that window, Nautilus opens another object window where that object's contents appear. Figure 3-3 shows the result of double-clicking some objects in Nautilus.

The Nautilus object window has a sparse user interface that has just the menu bar. You can perform various operations from the menu bar such as open an object using an application, create folders and documents, and close the object window.

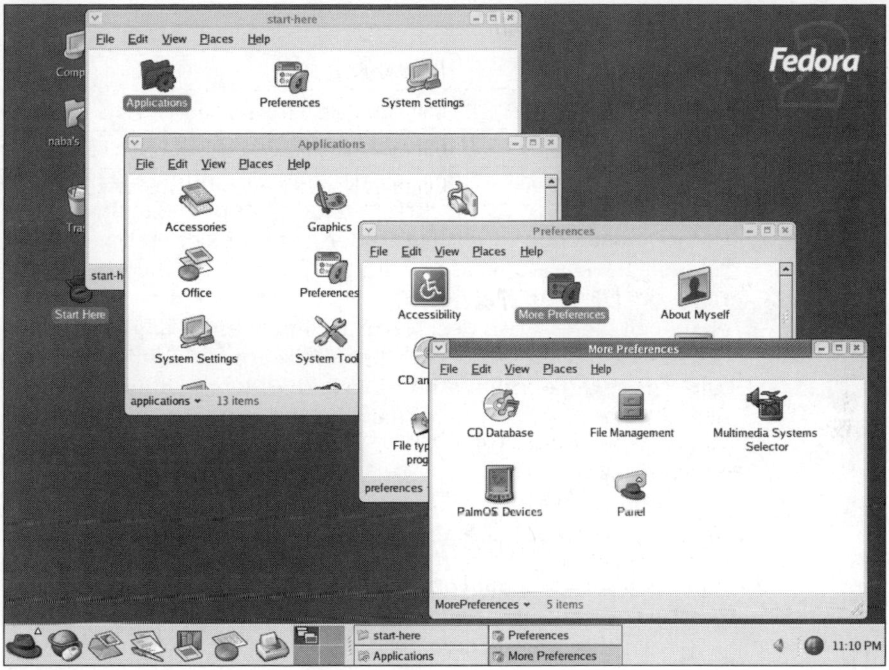

Figure 3-3: By default, Nautilus opens a new object window for each object.

Burning data CDs from Nautilus

If you have a CD recorder attached to your system (it can be a built-in ATAPI CD recorder or an external one attached to the USB port), you can use Nautilus to burn data CDs. From a Nautilus object window, you can access the CD Creator built into Nautilus. Just follow these simple steps:

1. **In any Nautilus object window, choose Places⇨CD Creator.**

   Nautilus opens a CD Creator object window.

   Note: If you don't have any Nautilus object windows open, just double-click the Computer icon on the desktop.

2. **From other Nautilus windows, drag and drop into the CD Creator window whatever files and folders you want to put on the CD.**

   To get to files on your computer, double-click the Computer icon to open it in Nautilus and find the files you want. Then drag and drop those file or folder icons into the CD Creator window.

3. **From the CD Creator window, choose File⇨Write to Disc.**

   Nautilus displays a dialog box where you can select the CD recorder, the write speed, and several other options, such as whether to eject the CD when done. You can also specify the CD title.

4. Click the Write button.

Nautilus burns the CD.

Browsing folders in a navigation window

If you prefer to use the familiar navigation window for browsing folders, you have to do a bit of extra work. Instead of double-clicking an icon, right-click the icon and choose Browse Folder from the context menu. Nautilus then opens a navigation window with the contents of the object represented by the icon. For example, double-click the Home Folder icon in the upper-left corner of the GNOME desktop. Nautilus opens a navigation window where it displays the contents of your home directory. (Think of a *directory* as a folder that can contain other files and folders.) Figure 3-4 shows a typical user's home directory in a Nautilus navigation window.

The navigation window is vertically divided into two parts. The left pane shows different views of the file system and other objects that you can browse with Nautilus. The right pane shows the files and folders in the currently selected folder in the left pane. Nautilus displays icons for files and folders. For image files, it shows a thumbnail of the image.

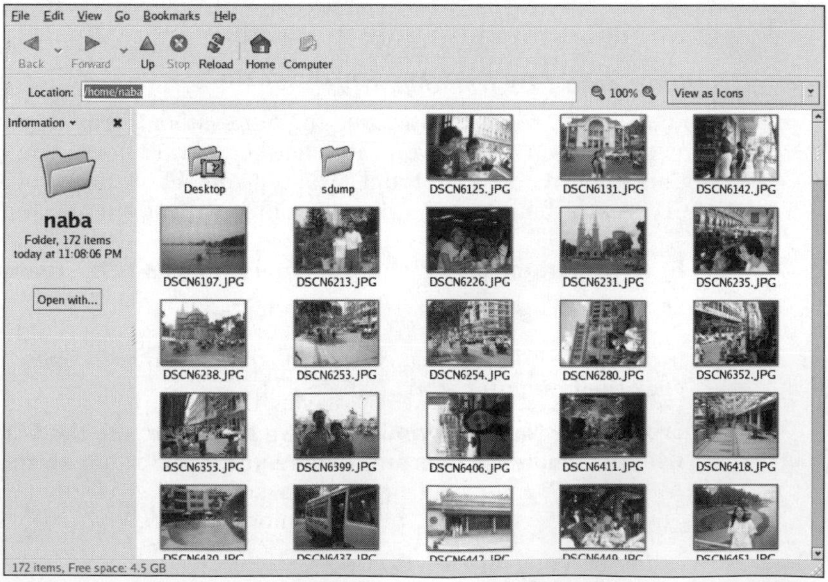

Figure 3-4: You can view files and folders in the Nautilus navigation window.

The navigation window's user interface is similar to that of a Web browser. The window's title bar shows the name of the currently selected folder. The Location text box along the top of the window shows the full name of the directory in Linuxspeak — for example, Figure 3-4 shows the contents of the `/home/naba` directory.

If you have used Windows Explorer, you can use the Nautilus navigation window in a similar manner. To view the contents of another directory, do the following:

1. **Select Tree from the Information drop-down menu (located in the left window).**

   A tree menu of directories appears in that window. Initially the tree shows your home folder and the file system's root directory as a `FileSystem` folder.

2. **Click the right arrow next to the `FileSystem` folder; in the resulting tree view, locate the directory you want to browse.**

   For example, to look at the `/etc` directory, click the right arrow next to the `etc` directory. Nautilus displays the subdirectories in `/etc` and changes the right arrow to a down arrow. `X11` is one of the subdirectories in `/etc` that you view in the next step.

3. **To view the contents of the `X11` subdirectory, click `X11`.**

   The window on the right now shows the contents of the `/etc/X11` directory.

Nautilus displays the contents of the selected directory by using different types of icons. Each directory appears as a folder with the name of the directory shown underneath the folder icon. Ordinary files, such as `xorg.conf`, appear as a sheet of paper. The `X` file is a link to an executable file. The `prefdm` file is another executable file.

The Nautilus navigation window has the usual menu bar and a toolbar. Notice the View as Icons button in Figure 3-4 on the right side of the toolbar. This button shows that Nautilus is displaying the directory contents with large icons. Click the button, and a drop-down list appears. Select View as List from the list, and Nautilus displays the contents by using smaller icons in a list format, along with detailed information, such as the size of each file or directory and the time when each was last modified, as shown in Figure 3-5.

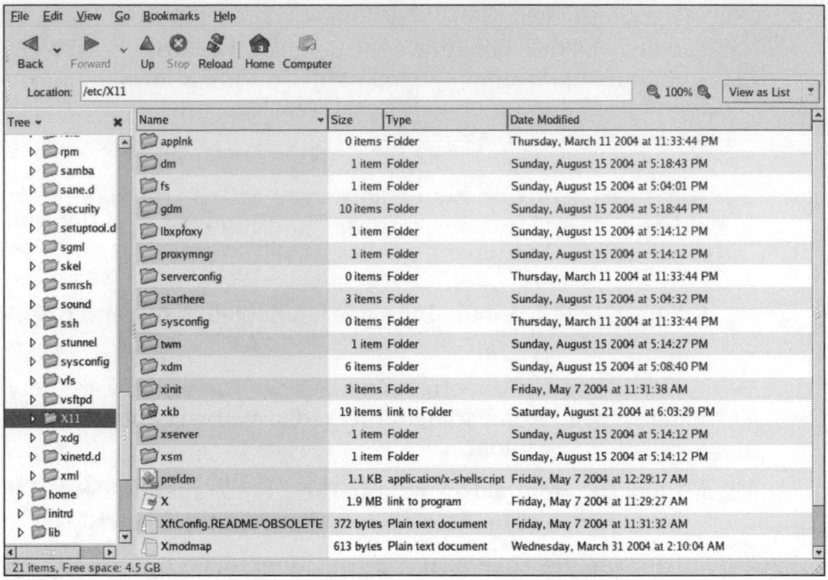

Figure 3-5: The Nautilus navigation window with a list view of the /etc/X11 directory.

If you click any of the column headings — Name, Size, Type, or Date Modified — along the top of the list view, Nautilus sorts the list according to that column. For example, go ahead and click the Date Modified column heading. Nautilus now displays the list of files and directories sorted according to the time of their last modification. Clicking the Name column heading sorts the files and folders alphabetically.

Not only can you move around different folders by using the Nautilus navigation window, you can also do things such as move a file from one folder to another or delete a file. I don't outline each step — the steps are intuitive and similar to what you do in any GUI, such as Windows or Mac. Here are some of the things you can do in Nautilus:

- To move a file to a different folder, drag and drop the file's icon on the folder where you want the file.
- To copy a file to a new location, select the file's icon and choose Edit⇨Copy File from the Nautilus menu. You can also right-click the file's icon and choose Copy File from the context menu. Then move to the folder where you want to copy the file and choose Edit⇨Paste Files.
- To delete a file or directory, right-click the icon, and choose Move to Trash from the context menu. (You can do this only if you have permission to delete the file.) To permanently delete the file, right-click the Trash icon on the desktop and choose Empty Trash from the context menu. Of course, do this only if you really want to delete the file. Once you Empty Trash, you are never going to see the file again. If you have to

retrieve a file from the trash, double-click the Trash icon and then drag the file's icon back to the folder where you want to save it. You can retrieve a file from the trash until you empty it.

- To rename a file or a directory, right-click the icon and choose Rename from the context menu. Then you can type the new name (or edit the name) in the text box that appears.
- To create a new folder, right-click an empty area of the window on the right and choose Create Folder from the context menu. After the new folder icon appears, you can rename it by right-clicking the icon and choosing Rename from the context menu. If you don't have permission to create a folder, that menu item is grayed out.

Using Konqueror

Konqueror is a file manager and Web browser that comes with KDE. It's intuitive to use — somewhat similar to the Windows Active Desktop. You can manage files and folders (and also view Web pages) with Konqueror.

Viewing files and folders

When you double-click a folder icon on the desktop, Konqueror starts automatically. For example, double-click the Home icon in the upper-left corner of the KDE desktop. Konqueror runs and displays the contents of your home directory (think of a *directory* as a folder that can contain other files and folders). Figure 3-6 shows a typical user's home directory in Konqueror.

If you've used Windows Explorer, you can use Konqueror in a similar manner.

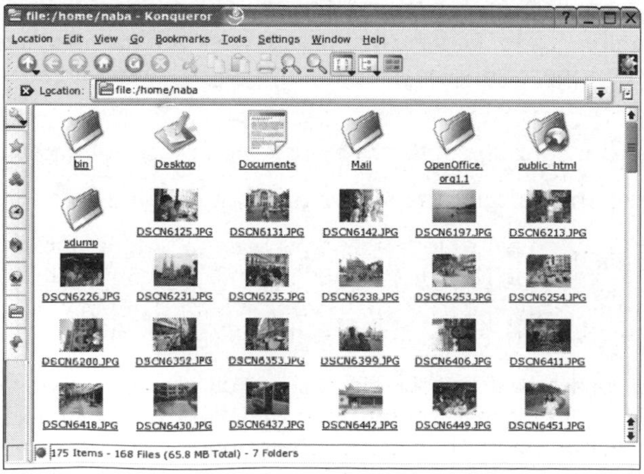

Figure 3-6: You can view files and folders in Konqueror.

The Konqueror window is vertically divided into three parts:

- ✦ A narrow left pane shows icons you can click to perform various tasks in Konqueror.
- ✦ A wider middle pane (that can be toggled on or off) shows a tree view of the current folder.
- ✦ The widest pane (at the right) uses icons to show the files and folders in the current folder.

Konqueror uses different types of icons for different files and shows a preview of each file's contents. For image files, the preview is a thumbnail version of the image.

The Konqueror window's title bar shows the name of the currently selected directory. The Location text box (along the top of the window) shows the full name of the directory — in this case, Figure 3-6 shows the contents of the `/home/naba` directory.

Use the leftmost vertical row of buttons to select other things to browse. When you click one of these buttons, the middle pane displays a tree menu of items that you can browse. For example, to browse other parts of the file system, do the following:

1. **From the leftmost vertical column of icons in the Konqueror window (refer to Figure 3-6), click the Root Folder icon (the second icon from the bottom).**

   A tree menu of directories appears in the middle pane.

2. **In the tree view, locate the folder that you want to browse.**

   For example, to look at the `etc` folder, click the plus sign next to the `etc` folder. Konqueror displays the other folders and changes the plus sign to a minus sign.

3. **To view the contents of the `X11` subdirectory, scroll down and click `X11`.**

   The pane on the right now shows the contents of the `/etc/X11` directory.

Konqueror displays the contents of a folder using different types of icons. Each directory appears as a folder, with the name of the directory shown underneath the folder icon. Ordinary files appear as a sheet of paper.

The Konqueror window has the usual menu bar and a toolbar. You can view the files and folders in other formats as well. For example, choose View➪View Mode➪Detailed List View to see the folder's contents with smaller icons in a list format (see Figure 3-7), along with detailed information (such as the size of each file or directory, and at what time each was last modified).

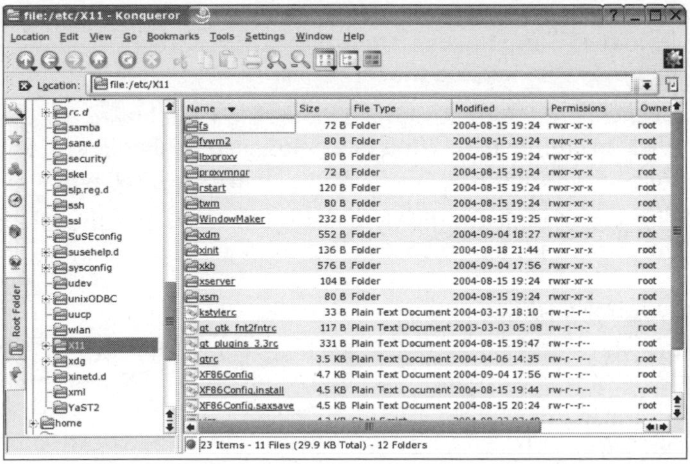

Figure 3-7: Konqueror shows a detailed list view of the `/etc/X11` directory.

If you click any of the column headings — Name, Size, File Type, or Modified, to name a few — along the top of the list view, Konqueror sorts the list according to that column. For example, if you click the Modified column heading, Konqueror displays the list of files and folders sorted according to the time of last modification. Clicking the Name column heading sorts the files and directories alphabetically by name.

Not only can you move around different folders by using Konqueror, you can also do things such as move a file from one folder to another or delete a file. I don't outline each step because the steps are intuitive and similar to what you do in any GUI (such as Windows or the Mac interface). Here are some things you can do in Konqueror:

- **View a text file:** Click the filename, and Konqueror runs the KWrite word processor, displaying the file in a new window.
- **Copy or move a file to a different folder:** Drag and drop the file's icon on the folder where you want the file to go. A menu pops up and asks you whether you want to copy, move, or simply link the file to that directory.
- **Delete a file or directory:** Right-click the icon and choose Move to Trash from the context menu. To permanently delete the file, right-click the Trash icon on the desktop and choose Empty Trash from the context menu. Of course, do this only if you really want to delete the file. When you Empty Trash, the deleted files are really gone forever. If you want to recover a file from the trash, double-click the Trash icon on the desktop and from that window drag and drop the file icon into the folder where you want to save the file. When asked whether you want to copy or move, select Move. You can recover files from the trash until the moment you empty the trash.

- **Rename a file or a directory:** Right-click the icon and choose Rename from the context menu. Then you can type the new name (or edit the old name) in the text box that appears.
- **Create a new folder:** Choose View⇨View Mode⇨Icon View. Then right-click an empty area of the rightmost pane and choose Create New⇨Directory from the context menu. Then type the name of the new directory and click OK. (If you don't have permission to create a directory, you get an error message.)

Viewing Web pages

Konqueror is much more than a file manager. With it, you can view a Web page as easily as you can view a folder. Just type a Web address in the Location text box and see what happens. For example, Figure 3-8 shows the Konqueror window after I type `www.irs.gov` in the Location text box on the toolbar and press Enter.

Konqueror displays the Web site in the pane on the right. The left pane still shows whatever it was displaying earlier.

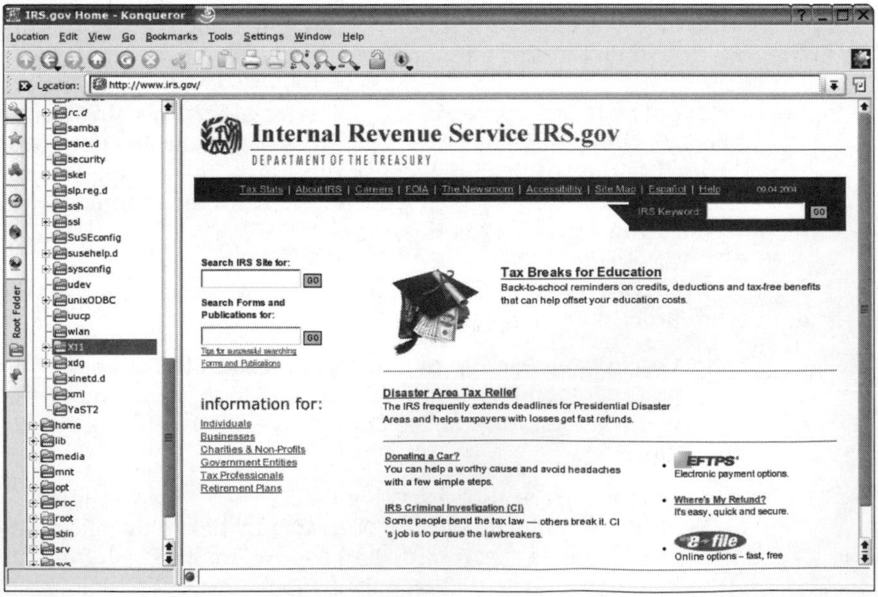

Figure 3-8: Konqueror can browse the Web as well.

Navigating the File System with Linux Commands

Although GUI file managers such as Nautilus (in GNOME) or Konqueror (in KDE) are easy to use, you can use them only if you have a working GUI desktop. Sometimes, you may not have a graphical environment to run a graphical file manager. For example, you may be logged in through a text terminal, or X may not be working on your system. In those situations, you have to rely on Linux commands to work with files and directories. Of course, you can always use Linux commands, even in the graphical environment — all you have to do is open a terminal window and type the Linux commands.

In the sections that follow, I briefly show some Linux commands for moving around the Linux file system.

Commands for directory navigation

In Linux, when you log in as `root`, your home directory is `/root`. For other users, the home directory is usually in the `/home` directory. My home directory (when I log in as `naba`) is `/home/naba`. This information is stored in the `/etc/passwd` file. By default, only you have permission to save files in your home directory, and only you can create subdirectories in your home directory to further organize your files.

Linux supports the concept of a current directory, which is the directory on which all file and directory commands operate. After you log in, for example, your current directory is the home directory. To see the current directory, type the `pwd` command.

To change the current directory, use the `cd` command. To change the current directory to `/usr/lib`, type the following:

```
cd /usr/lib
```

Then, to change the directory to the `cups` subdirectory in `/usr/lib`, type this command:

```
cd cups
```

Now, if you use the `pwd` command, that command shows `/usr/lib/cups` as the current directory.

These two examples show that you can refer to a directory's name in two ways:

- An **absolute pathname** (such as `/usr/lib`) that specifies the exact directory in the directory tree
- A **relative directory name** (such as `cups`, which represents the `cups` subdirectory of the current directory, whatever that may be)

If you type `cd cups` in `/usr/lib`, the current directory changes to `/usr/lib/cups`. However, if I type the same command in `/home/naba`, the shell tries to change the current directory to `/home/naba/cups`.

Use the `cd` command without any arguments to change the current directory back to your home directory. No matter where you are, typing **cd** at the shell prompt brings you back home!

By the way, the tilde character (~) refers to your home directory. Thus the command `cd ~` also changes the current directory to your home directory. You can also refer to another user's home directory by appending that user's name to the tilde. Thus, `cd ~superman` changes the current directory to the home directory of `superman`.

Wait, there's more. A single dot (`.`) and two dots (`..`) — often cleverly referred to as *dot-dot* — also have special meanings. A single dot (`.`) indicates the current directory, whereas two dots (`..`) indicate the parent directory. For example, if the current directory is `/usr/share`, you go one level up to `/usr` by typing

```
cd ..
```

Commands for directory listings and permissions

You can get a directory listing by using the `ls` command. By default, the `ls` command — without any options — displays the contents of the current directory in a compact, multicolumn format. For example, type the next two commands to see the contents of the `/etc/X11` directory:

```
cd /etc/X11
ls
```

The output looks like this (on the console, you see some items in different colors):

```
X             Xsession.options          fonts      serverconfig xserver
XF86Config-4  Xwrapper.config           gdm        starthere    xsm
Xresources    app-defaults              rgb.txt    sysconfig
Xsession      cursors                   rstart     xinit
Xsession.d    default-display-manager   rxvt.menu  xkb
```

From this listing (without the colors), you cannot tell whether an entry is a file or a directory. To tell the directories and files apart, use the `-F` option with `ls` like this:

```
ls -F
```

This time, the output gives you some more clues about the file types:

```
X@             Xsession.options           fonts/     serverconfig/  xserver/
XF86Config-4   Xwrapper.config            gdm@       starthere/     xsm/
Xresources/    app-defaults/              rgb.txt    sysconfig/
Xsession*      cursors/                   rstart/    xinit/
Xsession.d/    default-display-manager    rxvt.menu  xkb/
```

The output from `ls -F` shows the directory names with a slash (/) appended to them. Plain filenames appear as is. The *at sign* (@) appended to a file's name (for example, notice the file named `X`) indicates that this file is a link to another file. (In other words, this filename simply refers to another file; it's a shortcut.) An asterisk (*) is appended to executable files. (`Xsession`, for example, is an executable file.) The shell can run any executable file.

You can see even more detailed information about the files and directories with the `-l` option:

```
ls -l
```

For the `/etc/X11` directory, a typical output from `ls -l` looks like the following:

```
total 104
lrwxrwxrwx   1 root root    20 Aug 22 15:15 X -> /usr/bin/X11/XFree86
-rw-r--r--   1 root root  3126 Aug 22 15:15 XF86Config-4
drwxr-xr-x   2 root root  4096 Aug 22 15:13 Xresources
-rwxr-xr-x   1 root root  3322 May 29 03:57 Xsession
drwxr-xr-x   2 root root  4096 Sep  5 10:44 Xsession.d
-rw-r--r--   1 root root   217 May 29 03:57 Xsession.options
-rw-------   1 root root   771 Aug 22 15:15 Xwrapper.config
drwxr-xr-x   2 root root  4096 Aug 22 15:15 app-defaults
... lines deleted ...
```

This listing shows considerable information about every directory entry — each of which can be a file or another directory. Looking at a line from the right column to the left, you see that the rightmost column shows the name of the directory entry. The date and time before the name show when the last modifications to that file were made. To the left of the date and time is the size of the file in bytes.

The file's group and owner appear to the left of the column that shows the file size. The next number to the left indicates the number of links to the file. (A *link* is like a shortcut in Windows.) Finally, the leftmost column shows the file's permission settings, which determine who can read, write, or execute the file.

The first letter of the leftmost column has a special meaning, as the following list shows:

- ✦ If the first letter is `l`, the file is a *symbolic link* (a shortcut) to another file.
- ✦ If the first letter is `d`, the file is a directory.
- ✦ If the first letter is a dash (`-`), the file is normal.
- ✦ If the first letter is `b`, the file represents a block device, such as a disk drive.
- ✦ If the first letter is `c`, the file represents a character device, such as a serial port or a terminal.

After that first letter, the leftmost column shows a sequence of nine characters, which appear as `rwxrwxrwx` when each letter is present. Each letter indicates a specific permission. A hyphen (`-`) in place of a letter indicates no permission for a specific operation on the file. Think of these nine letters as three groups of three letters (`rwx`), interpreted as follows:

- ✦ The leftmost group of `rwx` controls the *read*, *write*, and *execute* permission of the file's owner. In other words, if you see `rwx` in this position, the file's owner can read (`r`), write (`w`), and execute (`x`) the file. A hyphen in the place of a letter indicates no permission. Thus the string `rw-` means the owner has read and write permission but no execute permission. Although executable programs (including shell programs) typically have execute permission, directories treat execute permission as equivalent to *use* permission — a user must have execute permission on a directory before he or she can open and read the contents of the directory.
- ✦ The middle three `rwx` letters control the read, write, and execute permission of any user belonging to that file's group.
- ✦ The rightmost group of `rwx` letters controls the read, write, and execute permission of all other users (collectively referred to as *the world*).

Thus, a file with the permission setting `rwx------` is accessible only to the file's owner, whereas the permission setting `rwxr--r--` makes the file readable by the world.

An interesting feature of the `ls` command is that it doesn't list any file whose name begins with a period. To see these files, you must use the `ls` command with the `-a` option, as follows:

```
ls -a
```

Try this command in your home directory (and then compare the result with what you see when you don't use the `-a` option):

1. **Type** cd **to change to your home directory.**
2. **Type** ls -F **to see the files and directories in your home directory.**
3. **Type** ls -aF **to see everything, including the hidden files.**

TIP

Most Linux commands take single-character options, each with a minus sign (think of this sign as a hyphen) as a prefix. When you want to use several options, type a hyphen and *concatenate* (string together) the option letters, one after another. Thus, `ls -al` is equivalent to `ls -a -l` as well as `ls -l -a`.

Commands for changing permissions and ownerships

You may need to change a file's permission settings to protect it from others. Use the `chmod` command to change the permission settings of a file or a directory.

To use `chmod` effectively, you have to specify the permission settings. A good way is to concatenate letters from the columns of Table 3-4 in the order shown (Who/Action/Permission).

Note: You use only the single character from each column — the text in parentheses is for explanation only.

Table 3-4 Letter Codes for File Permissions

Who	*Action*	*Permission*
u (user)	+ (add)	r (read)
g (group)	- (remove)	w (write)
o (others)	= (assign)	x (execute)
a (all)	s (set user ID)	

For example, to give everyone read access to all files in a directory, pick `a` (for *all*) from the first column, + (for *add*) from the second column, and `r` (for *read*) from the third column to come up with the permission setting `a+r`. Then use the whole set of options with `chmod`, like this:

```
chmod a+r *.
```

On the other hand, to permit everyone to execute one specific file, type

```
chmod a+x filename
```

Suppose you have a file named `mystuff` that you want to protect. You can make it accessible to no one but you if you type the following commands, in this order:

```
chmod a-rwx mystuff
chmod u+rw mystuff
```

The first command turns off all permissions for everyone, and the second command turns *on* the read and write permissions for the owner (you). Type **ls -l** to verify that the change took place. (You see a permission setting of `-rw-------`.) Here's a sample output from `ls -l`:

```
drwxr-xr-x  2 naba naba   4096 Sep  5 22:18 sdump
```

Note: The third and fourth fields show `naba naba`. These two fields show the file's user and group ownership. In this case, the name of the user is `naba` and the name of the group is also `naba`.

Sometimes you have to change a file's user or group ownership for everything to work correctly. For example, suppose you are instructed (by a manual, what else?) to create a directory named `cups` and give it the ownership of user ID `lp` and group ID `sys`. How do you it?

Well, you can log in as `root` and create the `cups` directory with the command `mkdir`:

```
mkdir cups
```

If you check the file's details with the `ls -l` command, you see that the user and group ownership is `root root`.

To change the owner, use the `chown` command. For example, to change the ownership of the `cups` directory to user ID `lp` and group `ID` sys, type

```
chown lp.sys cups
```

Commands for working with files

To copy files from one directory to another, use the `cp` command. For example, to copy the file `/usr/X11R6/lib/X11/xinit/Xclients` to the `Xclients.sample` file in the current directory (such as your home directory), type the following:

```
cp /usr/X11R6/lib/X11/xinit/xinitrc xinitrc.sample
```

If you want to copy a file to the current directory but retain the original name, use a period (.) as the second argument of the cp command. Thus, the following command copies the Xresources file from the /etc/X11 directory to the current directory (denoted by a single period):

```
cp /etc/X11/Xresources .
```

The cp command makes a new copy of a file and leaves the original intact.

TIP

If you want to copy the entire contents of a directory — including all subdirectories and their contents — to another directory, use the command cp -ar *sourcedir destdir*. (This command copies everything in *sourcedir* directory to *destdir*.) For example, to copy all files from the /etc/X11 directory to the current directory, type the following command:

```
cp -ar /etc/X11 .
```

TIP

To move a file to a new location, use the mv command. The original copy is gone, and a new copy appears at the destination. You can use mv to rename a file. If you want to change the name of today.list to old.list, use the mv command, as follows:

```
mv today.list old.list
```

On the other hand, if you want to move the today.list file to a subdirectory named saved, use this command:

```
mv today.list saved
```

An interesting feature of mv is that you can use it to move entire directories — with all their subdirectories and files — to a new location. If you have a directory named data that contains many files and subdirectories, you can move that entire directory structure to old_data by using the following command:

```
mv data old_data
```

To delete files, use the rm command. For example, to delete a file named old.list, type the following command:

```
rm old.list
```

WARNING!

Be careful with the rm command — especially when you log in as root. You can inadvertently delete important files with rm.

Commands for working with directories

To organize files in your home directory, you have to create new directories. Use the `mkdir` command to create a directory. For example, to create a directory named `images` in the current directory, type the following:

```
mkdir images
```

After you create the directory, you can use the `cd images` command to change to that directory.

TIP

You can create an entire directory tree by using the `-p` option with the `mkdir` command. For example, suppose your system has a `/usr/src` directory and you want to create the directory tree `/usr/src/book/java/examples/applets`. To create this directory hierarchy, type the following command:

```
mkdir -p /usr/src/book/java/examples/applets
```

REMEMBER

When you no longer need a directory, use the `rmdir` command to delete it.

You can delete a directory only when the directory is empty.

To remove an empty directory tree, you can use the `-p` option, like this:

```
rmdir -p /usr/src/book/java/examples/applets
```

This command removes the empty parent directories of `applets`. The command stops when it encounters a directory that's not empty.

Commands for finding files

The `find` command is very useful for locating files (and directories) that meet your search criteria.

When I began using UNIX many years ago (Berkeley UNIX in the early 1980s), I was confounded by the `find` command. I stayed with one basic syntax of `find` for a long time before graduating to more complex forms. The basic syntax that I discovered first was for finding a file anywhere in the file system. Here's how it goes: Suppose you want to find any file or directory with a name that starts with `gnome`. Type the following `find` command to find these files:

```
find / -name "gnome*" -print
```

If you're not logged in as root, you may get a bunch of error messages. If these error messages annoy you, just modify the command as follows and the error messages are history (or, as UNIX aficionados say, "Send 'em to the bit bucket"):

```
find / -name "gnome*" -print 2> /dev/null
```

This command tells find to start looking at the root directory (/), to look for filenames that match gnome*, and to display the full pathname of any matching file. The last part (2> /dev/null) simply sends the error messages to a special file that's the equivalent of simply ignoring them.

You can use variations of this simple form of find to locate a file in any directory (as well as any subdirectories contained in the directory). If you forget where in your home directory you've stored all files named report* (names that start with report), you can search for the files by using the following command:

```
find ~ -name "report*" -print
```

When you become comfortable with this syntax of find, you can use other options of find. For example, to find only specific types of files (such as directories), use the type option. The following command displays all top-level directory names in your Linux system:

```
find / -type d -maxdepth 1 -print
```

You probably don't have to use the complex forms of find in a typical Linux system — but if you ever need to, you can look up the rest of the find options by using the following command:

```
man find
```

An easy way to find all files that match a name is to use the locate command that searches a periodically updated database of files on your system. For example, here's a typical output I get when I type **locate Xresources** on a Debian system:

```
/etc/X11/Xresources
/etc/X11/Xresources/xbase-clients
/etc/X11/Xresources/xfree86-common
```

The locate command isn't installed by default in SUSE Linux. To install it, select Main Menu➪System➪YaST from the SUSE desktop to start the YaST2 Control Center. Click Software in the left-hand side of the window and then click Install/Remove Software in the right-hand side of the window. In the YaST software installation window, search for locate. Then select the package from the search results and click Accept to install it.

Commands for mounting and unmounting

Suppose you want to access the files on this book's companion DVD-ROM when you are logged in at a text console (with no GUI to help you). To do so, you have to first mount the DVD-ROM drive's file system on a specific directory in the Linux file system.

Start by looking at the `/etc/fstab` file for clues to the name of the CD-ROM device. For example, some Linux distributions use the device name `/dev/cdrom` to refer to CD/DVD-ROM drives, whereas others may use device names such as `/dev/hdc`, `/dev/cdroms/cdrom0`, or `/dev/cdrecorder` (for a DVD/CD-R drive). The entry in `/etc/fstab` file also tells you the directory where that distribution expects the CD/DVD to be mounted. Some distributions use `/mnt/cdrom` as the mount point, whereas others use `/mnt/cdrom0`, `/media/cdrom0`, or `/media/cdrecorder`.

Log in as `root` (or type **su -** to become `root`), insert the DVD-ROM in the DVD drive, and then type the following command:

```
mount /dev/hdc /media/cdrom0
```

This command mounts the file system on the device named `/dev/hdc` (An IDE DVD/CD-ROM drive) on the `/media/cdrom0` directory (which is also called the *mount point*) in the Linux file system.

After the `mount` command successfully completes its task, you can access the files on the DVD-ROM by referring to the `/media/cdrom0` directory as the top-level directory of the disc. In other words, to see the contents of the DVD-ROM, type

```
ls -F /media/cdrom0
```

When you're done using the DVD-ROM — and before you eject it from the drive — you have to unmount the disc drive with the following `umount` command:

```
umount /dev/hdc
```

You can mount devices on any empty directory on the file system. However, each distribution has customary locations with directories meant for mounting devices. For example, some distributions use directories in `/mnt` whereas others use the `/media` directory for the mount points.

Commands for checking disk-space usage

I want to tell you about two commands — df and du — that you can use to check the disk-space usage on your system. These commands are simple to use. The df command shows you a summary of disk-space usage for all mounted devices, as shown in this example:

```
df
Filesystem           1K-blocks      Used Available Use% Mounted on
/dev/hda10             5766924   2491424   2982552  46% /
tmpfs                   124624         0    124624   0% /dev/shm
/dev/hda6                42469     10497     29706  27% /boot
/dev/hdc                714214    714214         0 100% /media/cdrom0
```


The output is a table that lists the device, the total kilobytes of storage, how much is in use, how much is available, the percentage being used, and the mount point.

TIP

To see the output of df in a more human-readable format, type df -h. Here is the output of the df -h command:

```
Filesystem            Size  Used Avail Use% Mounted on
/dev/hda10            5.5G  2.4G  2.9G  46% /
tmpfs                 122M     0  122M   0% /dev/shm
/dev/hda6              42M   11M   30M  27% /boot
/dev/hdc              698M  698M     0 100% /media/cdrom0
```

If you compare this output with the output of plain df (see previous listing), you see that df -h prints the sizes with terms like M for megabytes and G for gigabytes. These are clearly easier to understand than 1K-blocks.

The other command — du — is useful for finding out how much space a directory takes up. For example, type **du /etc/X11** to view the contents of all the directories in the /etc/X11 directory. (This directory contains X Window System configuration files.) You end up with the following:

```
12      /etc/X11/Xresources
36      /etc/X11/Xsession.d
272     /etc/X11/app-defaults
20      /etc/X11/cursors
12      /etc/X11/xinit
... lines deleted ...
12      /etc/X11/fonts/misc
8       /etc/X11/fonts/100dpi
8       /etc/X11/fonts/75dpi
8       /etc/X11/fonts/Speedo
8       /etc/X11/fonts/Type1
48      /etc/X11/fonts
2896    /etc/X11
```

Each directory name is preceded by a number — which tells you the number of kilobytes of disk space used by that directory. Thus the `/etc/X11` directory, as a whole, uses 2896KB (or about 2.9MB) disk space. If you simply want the total disk space used by a directory (including all the files and subdirectories contained in that directory), use the `-s` option, as follows:

```
du -s /etc/X11
2896    /etc/X11
```

The `-s` option causes `du` to print just the summary information for the entire directory.

TIP

Just as `df -h` prints the disk-space information in megabytes and gigabytes, you can use the `du -h` command to view the output of `du` in more human-readable form. For example, here's how I combine it with the `-s` option to see the space that I'm using in my home directory (`/home/naba`):

```
du -sh /home/naba
645M    /home/naba
```

Chapter 4: Introducing Linux Applications

In This Chapter

- Taking stock of typical Linux applications
- Trying out the office applications
- Setting up databases
- Playing with multimedia
- Working with images

Each Linux distribution comes with a whole lot of applications. All you have to do is look at the menus in the GUI desktops to see what I mean. Often more than one application of the same type exists. Most distributions come with the OpenOffice.org office application suite with a word processor, spreadsheet, presentation software, and more. You find many choices for CD players and multimedia players, not to mention the games, utility programs, and useful tools, such as a scanner and digital camera applications. Some commercial distributions come with commercial office suites such as StarOffice from Sun Microsystems.

When it comes to playing multimedia — audio and video in various formats such as MP3, MPEG, QuickTime, freely available Linux distributions rarely come with the appropriate decoders because of licensing restrictions on some of these decoders. Commercial distributions such as Xandros and SUSE usually come with some of these decoders.

I give you an overview of some of these Linux applications. After you know about these applications, you can explore them further and use them when you need them.

Taking Stock of Linux Applications

Table 4-1 shows a sampling of major Linux applications, organized by category. For the major applications, I also show a relevant Web site where you can get more information about that application. This list is by no means comprehensive. Each Linux distribution comes with many more applications and utilities than the ones I show in this table.

If your system has both GNOME and KDE installed, most of these applications are already available from either GUI desktop.

In later sections of this chapter, I briefly introduce some of the applications from Table 4-1, selecting one or two from each category. I describe the Internet applications in Book IV.

Table 4-1 A Sampling of Linux Applications

Application	*Description*
Office Applications	
OpenOffice.org	Free open-source office suite (compatible with Microsoft Office) that includes the *Writer* word-processor, *Calc* spreadsheet, *Impress* presentation application, *Draw* drawing program, and *Math* equation editor (`www.openoffice.org`)
StarOffice	Commercial office suite from which OpenOffice.org was derived (`www.sun.com/staroffice`)
CrossOver Office	Commercial office suite that enables you to install and run Microsoft Office software on Linux (`www.codeweavers.com/products/office`)
AbiWord	A free word processing program similar to Microsoft Word (`www.abisource.com`)
Dia	Drawing program, designed to be like the Windows application called Visio (`www.gnome.org/gnome-office/dia.shtml`)
Office Tools	
GNOME Calculator	Simple calculator for GNOME
KCalc	Calculator for KDE
KOrganizer	Calendar and scheduling program for KDE (`korganizer.kde.org`)
Aspell	Text-mode spell checker (`aspell.sourceforge.net`)
Dictionary	Graphical client for the `dict.org` dictionary server so you can look up words
Text Editors	
Emacs	Well-known text editor with both text and graphical interfaces (`www.gnu.org/software/emacs`)
KWrite	Text editor for KDE
Kate	Advanced text editor for KDE
Vim	Text editor with text-mode interface and compatible with the well-known UNIX editor `vi` (`www.vim.org`)

Application	*Description*
Database	
PostgreSQL	A sophisticated object-relational database-management system that supports Structured Query Language (SQL) (`www.postgresql.org`)
MySQL	A popular relational database-management system that supports SQL (`www.mysql.com`)
Rekall	A commercially-available database front-end for KDE that can access a number of databases, including PostgeSQL, MySQL, and IBM DB2 (`www.thekompany.com/products/rekall`)
Multimedia	
GNOME CD Player	Audio CD player (needs a working sound card)
KsCD	Audio CD player from KDE (needs a working sound card)
Rhythmbox	A multimedia audio player that can play several different sound formats (`rhythmbox.sourceforge.net`) — including MP3 files if you download a plugin for the purpose
XMMS	X Multimedia System — a multimedia audio player that can play many different sound formats (`www.xmms.org`) — including MP3 files (for some distributions, you have to download a plugin to play MP3)
Xine	A free multimedia player that can play CDs, DVDs, and video CDs (VCDs) and also decode multimedia files such as AVI, MOV, WMV, and MP3 (`xinehq.de`)
Kaffeine	A KDE media player that is based on Xine, so Kaffeine's capabilities are similar to those of Xine (`kaffeine.sourceforge.net`)
Cdrdao	A command-line application that can burn audio or data CD-Rs in disk-at-once (DAO) mode based on the descriptions of the CD's content in a text file (`cdrdao.sourceforge.net`)
Cdrecord	A command-line application that can burn audio and data CD-Rs as well as DVD-Rs (`www.fokus.gmd.de/research/cc/glone/employees/joerg.schilling/private/cdrecord.html`)
Growisofs	A command-line application that uses the `mkisofs` command to append data to a ISO 9660 file system that's used in CD-Rs and DVD-Rs (`fy.chalmers.se/~appro/linux/DVD+RW`)
X-CD-Roast	GUI front-end for `cdrecord` and `cdrdao` that makes burning data and audio CD-Rs easy (`www.xcdroast.org`)

(continued)

Table 4-1 *(continued)*

Application	*Description*
K3b	KDE-based GUI front-end for `cdrecord`, `cdrdao`, and `growisofs` for burning CD-Rs and DVD-Rs (`k3b.sourceforge.net`)
Gtkam	GUI front-end for the gPhoto2 (`gphoto.sourceforge.net`) command-line application that provides access to nearly 400 digital cameras (`gphoto.sourceforge.net/proj/gtkam`)
Digikam	A digital camera and photo management application that supports all the digital cameras supported by gPhoto2 (`digikam.sourceforge.net`)
Graphics and Imaging	
The GIMP	The GNU Image Manipulation Program, an application suitable for tasks such as photo retouching, image composition, and image authoring (`www.gimp.org`)
Gqview	Powerful image viewer (`gqview.sourceforge.net`)
Kfax	Fax viewer for KDE
Kview	Simple image viewer for KDE
GGV	Gnome Ghostview (GGV) is a PostScript document viewer (`www.gnu.org/directory/print/misc/ggv.html`)
Xpdf	Adobe PDF document viewer (`www.foolabs.com/xpdf`)
Xsane	Graphical front-end for accessing scanners with the SANE (Scanner Access Now Easy) library (`www.xsane.org`)
Ksnapshot	Screen-capture program
Kooka	A scanner program for KDE that uses the SANE library (`www.kde.org/apps/kooka`)
xscanimage	Graphical front-end for controlling a scanner
Internet	
Novell Evolution (formerly Ximian Evolution)	Personal information management application that integrates e-mail, calendar, contact management, and online task lists (`www.novell.com/products/evolution`)
GFTP	Graphical FTP client for downloading files from the Internet
Gaim	GNOME Instant Messenger client (`gaim.sourceforge.net`)

Application	Description
Kopete	KDE Instant Messenger client (`kopete.kde.org`)
Mozilla	Well-known open-source Web browser that started with source code from Netscape (`www.mozilla.org`)
Epiphany	A Mozilla-based open-source Web browser for GNOME (`www.gnome.org/projects/epiphany`)
Lynx	Text-mode Web browser (`lynx.browser.org`)
XChat	Internet Relay Chat (IRC) client (`www.xchat.org`)
Konqueror	Web browser and file manager in KDE (`www.konqueror.org`)
KMail	E-mail client for KDE (`kmail.kde.org`)

Not all Linux distributions come with all the applications shown in Table 4-1, although you can often download and install all these applications in any distribution. Table 4-2 lists the default availability of major applications in each of this book's Linux distributions — Debian GNU/Linux, Fedora Core, Knoppix, SUSE, and Xandros. A check mark indicates that the application is available by default.

You typically must select specific groups of applications to install as you install a Linux distribution. The exact list of applications on your Linux system depend on the choices you make during the installation.

It's very easy to install missing applications in Debian as long as you have a broadband (cable or DSL) connection to the Internet. For example, to see whether the k3b CD/DVD burner exists for Debian, I type **apt-cache search k3b**. I get the following output:

```
k3b - A sophisticated KDE cd burning application
k3b-i18n - Internationalized (i18n) files for k3b
k3blibs - The KDE cd burning application library - runtime files
k3blibs-dev - The KDE cd burning application library - development files
```

Next, I type **apt-get install k3b** and a few moments later I have k3b installed on my Debian system. This ease of installing (or upgrading) software is why Debian users swear by `apt-get` (even though it's a command-line tool).

Table 4-2 Default Availability of Some Applications

Application	Debian	Fedora	Knoppix	SUSE	Xandros
Calculator - Gcalctool		✓			
Calculator - KCalc	✓		✓	✓	✓
CD/DVD burning - K3b			✓	✓	

(continued)

Table 4-2 *(continued)*

Application	*Debian*	*Fedora*	*Knoppix*	*SUSE*	*Xandros*
CD player - GNOME	✓	✓			
CD player - KsCD	✓		✓	✓	✓
Database - PostgreSQL	✓	✓		✓	
Database - MySQL	✓		✓		✓
Database - Rekall				✓	
Dictionary - GNOME dictionary		✓			
Dictionary - KDict	✓				
Digital camera tool - Gtkam		✓	✓		
Digital camera tool - Digikam				✓	✓
Drawing program - Dia	✓	✓			
E-mail - KMail	✓		✓	✓	
E-mail - Novell Evolution	✓	✓			
File manager - Konqueror	✓		✓	✓	✓
File manager - Nautilus (integrated CD writer)	✓	✓			
File manager - Xandros File Manager (integrated CD writer)					✓
Image processing - ImageMagick	✓	✓	✓		
Image processing - The GIMP	✓	✓	✓	✓	✓
Instant messenger - Gaim		✓	✓		
Instant messenger - Kopete				✓	✓
Internet Relay Chat - XChat		✓	✓		
Music player - RealPlayer				✓	✓
Music player - Rhythmbox	✓	✓*			
Music player - XMMS	✓		✓	✓	✓
Office suite - CrossOver Office for Microsoft Office					✓
Office suite - OpenOffice.org	✓	✓	✓	✓	✓
Office suite - StarOffice					✓
PDF viewer - Acrobat Reader				✓	✓
PDF viewer - gpdf		✓			
PDF viewer - xpdf			✓		
Personal organizer - KOrganizer	✓		✓	✓	✓
PostScript viewer - GNOME Ghostview (GGV)	✓	✓			

Application	Debian	Fedora	Knoppix	SUSE	Xandros
PostScript/PDF viewer - KGhostview	✓		✓	✓	
Scanner - Kooka					✓
Scanner - xsane				✓	
Scanner - xscanimage			✓		
Screen capture - ksnapshot	✓		✓	✓	✓
Sound recorder - GNOME sound recorder	✓	✓			
Sound recorder - KDE sound recorder (Krecord)				✓	✓
Spellcheck - aspell	✓	✓			
Web browser - Epiphany	✓				
Web browser - Konqueror	✓		✓	✓	
Web browser - Lynx text-mode browser			✓	✓	
Web browser - Mozilla	✓	✓	✓		✓
Word processor - AbiWord	✓				
Video player - xine	✓				✓
Video player - Kaffeine				✓	

** Requires additional plugin*

Office Applications and Tools

Word processor, spreadsheet, presentation software, calendar, calculator — these are some of the staples of the office. Most Linux distributions come with the OpenOffice.org (often shortened as *OO.o* or *Ooo*) suite of office applications and tools. You can try all of them one by one and see which one takes your fancy. Each application is fairly intuitive to use. Even though some nuances of the user interface may be new to you, you'll become comfortable with it after using it a few times. I briefly introduce a few of the following applications in this section:

- **OpenOffice.org Office Suite:** A Microsoft Office-like office suite with the Writer word processor; Calc spreadsheet program; Impress presentation program; Draw drawing and illustration application; and Math, a mathematical formula editor
- **KOrganizer:** A calendar in KDE
- **Calculators:** A GNOME calculator and KDE calculator

- **aspell:** A spelling checker
- **And more:** Commercially available office applications for Linux

OpenOffice.org Office Suite

OpenOffice.org is an office suite developed by the OpenOffice.org project (`www.openoffice.org`). OpenOffice.org is similar to major office suites such as Microsoft Office. It's main components are the Writer word processor, Calc spreadsheet, and Impress presentation program.

You can easily start OpenOffice.org — either the overall suite or each individual application — from most GUI desktops by clicking a panel icon or by selecting from the Main Menu. For example, in SUSE, you can click a desktop icon to open the initial window of the OpenOffice.org suite. You can create new OpenOffice documents or open existing documents (which can be Microsoft Office files as well) from the main window of the OpenOffice.org.

I briefly introduce Writer, Calc, and Impress in the following sections.

Writer

Choosing File⇨New⇨Text Document from any OpenOffice.org window starts OpenOffice.org Writer with a blank document in its main window. Using Writer is simple — it's similar to other word processors such as Microsoft Word. For example, you can type text into the blank document, format text, and save text when done.

You can also open documents that you have prepared with Microsoft Word on a Windows machine. Figure 4-1 shows a Microsoft Word document being opened in OpenOffice.org Writer.

When you save a document, by default Writer saves it in OpenOffice.org 1.0 Text Document format in a file with the `.sxw` extension.

TIP: If you need to share OpenOffice.org Writer documents with Microsoft Word, you can save the documents in one of several formats, including Microsoft Word 97/2000/XP, Microsoft Word 95, Microsoft Word 6.0, and Rich Text Format (`.rtf`). Microsoft Word can open `.rtf` files.

I don't explain how to use Writer because it's simple and intuitive to use. If you need it, online help is available. Choose Help⇨Contents from the Writer menu. This brings up the OpenOffice.org Help window with help information on Writer. You can then click the links to view specific help information.

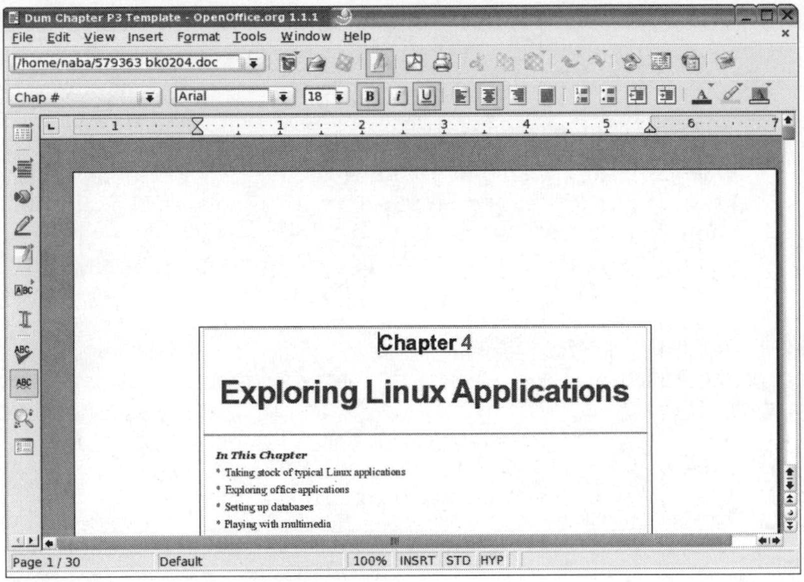

Figure 4-1: You can prepare documents in OpenOffice.org Writer.

Calc

Calc is the spreadsheet program in the OpenOffice.org application suite. To start Calc, choose File⇨New⇨Spreadsheet from any OpenOffice.org window. Calc displays its main window, which looks similar to Windows-based spreadsheets, such as Microsoft Excel. (In fact, Calc can read and write Microsoft Excel format spreadsheet files.)

Use Calc in the same way you use Microsoft Excel. You can type entries in cells, use formulas, and format the cells (for example, you can specify the type of value and the number of digits after the decimal point). Figure 4-2 shows a typical spreadsheet in Calc.

When preparing the spreadsheet, use formulas that you normally use in Microsoft Excel. For example, use the formula SUM(D2:D6) to add up the entries from cell D2 to D6. To set cell D2 as the product of the entries A2 and C2, type **=A2*C2** in cell D2. To find out more about the functions available in OpenOffice.org Calc, choose Help⇨Contents from the menu. This opens the OpenOffice.org Help window, from which you can browse the functions by category and click a function to read more about it.

To save the spreadsheet, choose File⇨Save As. A dialog box appears, from which you can specify the file format, the directory location, and the name of the file. OpenOffice.org Calc can save the file in several formats, including Microsoft Excel 97/2000/XP, Microsoft Excel 95, Microsoft Excel 5.0, as well as text file with comma separated values (CSV).

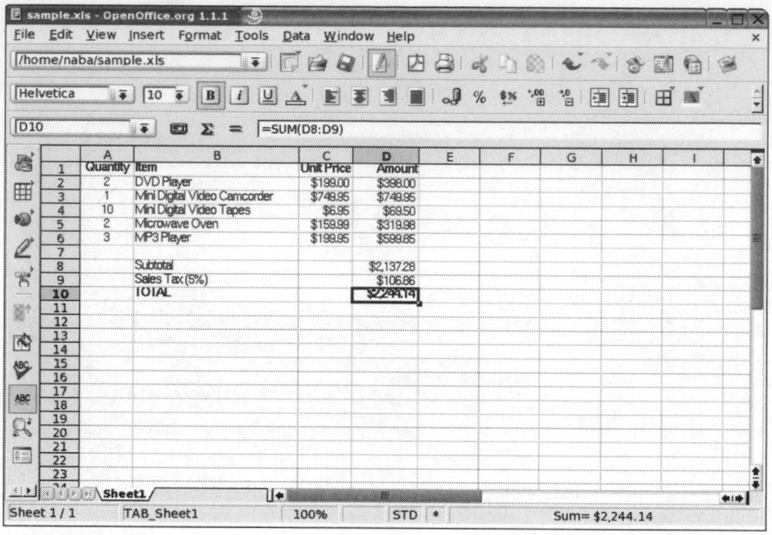

Figure 4-2: Prepare your spreadsheets with OpenOffice.org Calc.

TIP

If you want to exchange files with Microsoft Excel, save the spreadsheet in Microsoft Excel format (choose an appropriate version of Excel). Then you can transfer that file to a Windows system and open it in Microsoft Excel.

Impress

Impress is similar to Microsoft PowerPoint. You can prepare briefing packages (slide presentations) with Impress. To run Impress, choose File⇨New⇨Presentation from any OpenOffice.org window.

When you first start it, Impress prompts you for the presentation style and template. To begin working, select the type of document (paper or screen presentation) and any template you want to use. The template provides a style for the presentation package that you want to prepare. You can also choose to open an existing document.

The Impress window in Figure 4-3 shows the first slide. The exact appearance depends on the document type and template that you select. You can begin adding text and other graphic objects, such as images, text, and lines, to the slide.

To insert a new slide, choose Insert Slide from the floating menu. A gallery of slide layouts appear in a dialog box. Click the style of slide you want in the dialog box. You can then add text and graphic to that new slide.

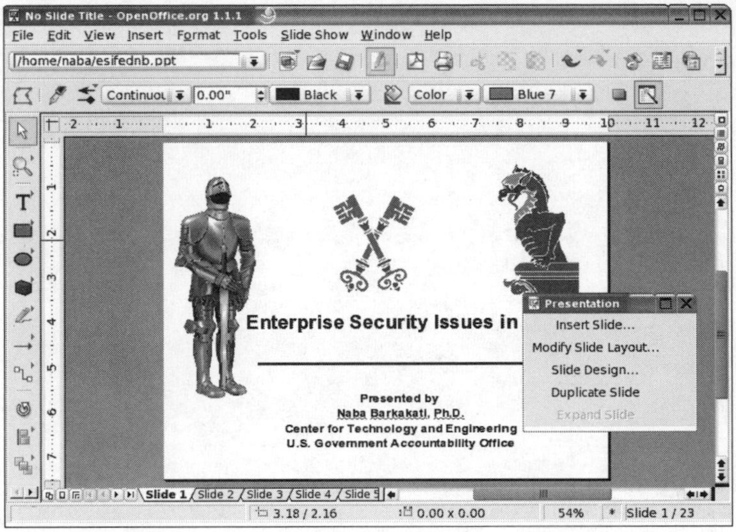

Figure 4-3: You can prepare briefing packages in OpenOffice.org Impress.

To save a presentation, choose File➪Save. For new documents, you have to provide a filename and select the directory where you want to save the file.

TIP

If you want to share the slides with someone who uses Microsoft PowerPoint, save the presentation in Microsoft PowerPoint 97/2000/XP format.

Calendars

KDE comes with KOrganizer — a calendar program. You can start it from panel icons or the main menu. (The exact location of the menu entry depends on the Linux distribution.) The KOrganizer program displays a window from which you can click a date to set or view that day's schedule. Figure 4-4 shows a typical calendar.

You can go to a different month or year by clicking the arrows next to the month and the year. To add a to-do item for a specific date, select the date from the calendar, click the To-do item's text box, and type the description of the task.

To add appointments for a specific time, double-click the time and type a brief description of the appointment in the dialog box that appears. Click OK when done. After you finish adding events and appointments, choose File➪Save to save the calendar. The first time you save the calendar, you have to provide a name for the file.

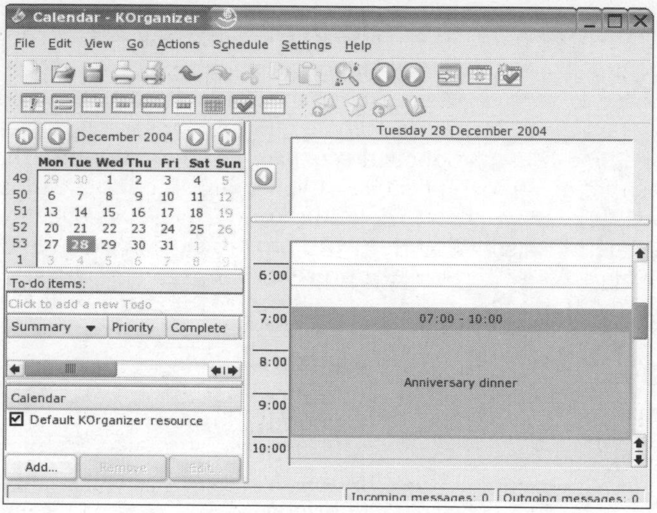

Figure 4-4: Store your appointments and view your calendar in KOrganizer.

Calculators

You have a choice of the GNOME calculator or the KDE calculator. Both are scientific calculators, and you can do the typical scientific calculations, such as square root and inverse, as well as trigonometric functions, such as sine, cosine, and tangent.

To use the calculator, look for it in the Utilities or Accessories category of the main menu. Figure 4-5 shows the KDE calculator in SUSE.

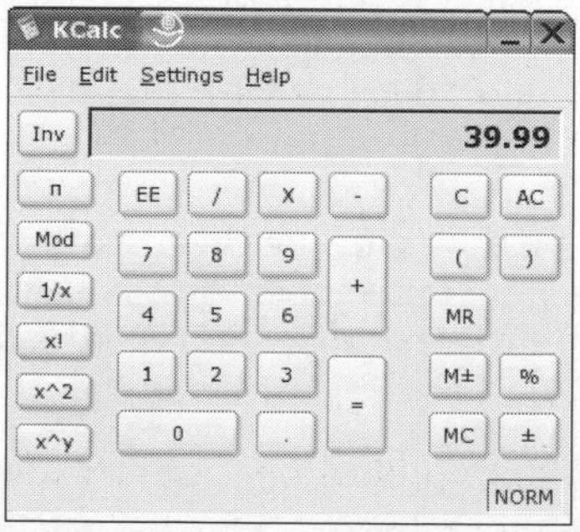

Figure 4-5: Do your calculations in the KDE calculator.

You can display additional buttons by selecting options from the Settings menu. For example, choose Settings➪Trigonometric Buttons to show buttons that enable you to perform trigonometric calculations with the calculator.

Commercially available office applications for Linux

Because office applications are important to many businesses as well as individuals, I briefly mention some of the commercial office applications available for Linux. These commercial offerings include Applixware Office and StarOffice. These products do cost some money, but the cost is usually less than that of Microsoft Office — the leading office application suite for Windows. (In case you don't know, Microsoft Office is a collection of several applications: Microsoft Word for word processing, Microsoft Excel for spreadsheets, Microsoft PowerPoint for presentation graphics, and Microsoft Access for databases.)

Another commercial product for Linux is CrossOver Office from CodeWeavers. With CrossOver Office, you can run your existing Microsoft Office applications such as Word, Excel, and PowerPoint under Linux and the X Window System.

REMEMBER

This book's companion DVD-ROM doesn't include any of these commercial office applications for Linux, but I briefly describe them in the next few sections. You can visit each vendor's Web site for more about the products.

Applixware Office

`www.vistasource.com/products`

Applixware Office is an office application suite for all Linux distributions. In April 2000, Applix, Inc., formed a separate group — VistaSource, Inc. — that focuses solely on Linux applications.

Like other office suites, Applixware Office includes Words (for word processing), Spreadsheets (for spreadsheets), Graphics, and Presents (for presentational graphics). In addition, it also has Mail (an e-mail interface) and Data (an interactive relational database-browsing tool). Applixware Office can read and write documents in Microsoft Office and Corel WordPerfect formats, as well as in several other file formats.

StarOffice

`www.sun.com/staroffice`

StarOffice is another commercial office applications suite; it was created by StarDivision of Hamburg, Germany, and was recently purchased by Sun Microsystems. StarOffice is a cross-platform solution — it runs on Linux, Windows 95/98/Me/NT/2000/XP, Sun Solaris SPARC, and Sun Solaris x86. Also, StarOffice is available in several languages: English, French, German, Spanish, Italian, and Swedish.

StarOffice is unique in that it combines all its components into a common desktop from which you can open new documents, drag and drop documents from one application to another, and access the Internet. Here's what StarOffice 7 includes:

- StarOffice Writer for word processing (Microsoft Word–compatible)
- StarOffice Calc for spreadsheets (Microsoft Excel–compatible)
- StarOffice Impress for presentations (Microsoft PowerPoint–compatible)
- StarOffice Draw for vector graphics drawing
- StarOffice Base for data management

In October 2000, Sun released the source code of StarOffice under open-source licenses. OpenOffice.org, an open-source project that Sun supports, released the OpenOffice.org 1.0 office productivity suite in May 2002. Current Linux distributions come with OpenOffice.org 1.1.1 or later versions. To find out more about OpenOffice.org, visit `www.openoffice.org`.

Xandros comes with StarOffice 7. Look for the desktop icon that you can click to start StarOffice. Xandros also includes OpenOffice.org.

CrossOver Office

`www.codeweavers.com/products/office`

Chances are better than good that you have Windows and Microsoft Office installed on your PC. When you decide to run Linux on the PC, you can continue to run most Microsoft Office applications from the GNOME or KDE desktop. The convenience of running Microsoft Office in Linux comes from a commercial product called CrossOver Office.

CrossOver Office, from CodeWeavers, is a software package that enables you to install your Microsoft Office applications (all versions of Office, including Office 97, Office 2000, and Office XP) in Linux. You don't need Microsoft Windows to run the Office applications in CrossOver Office. You simply install CrossOver Office and then install Microsoft Office (as well as many other Windows applications) from the CD-ROM. After you install Microsoft Office, the Office applications are available directly from GNOME or KDE desktop.

CrossOver Office uses Wine — an open-source implementation of the Windows Win32 and Win16 application programming interfaces (APIs) using the X Window System and designed to run in UNIX and Linux systems. Wine includes the Wine loader and WineLib. Wine loader can load and run Windows applications. WineLib is used for compiling and linking Windows applications in Linux. Wine is available free of charge from `www.winehq.com`.

CodeWeavers created CrossOver Office by using a customized version of Wine to make sure that the Microsoft Office applications (especially Microsoft Word, Excel, and PowerPoint) run properly on Wine. CodeWeavers charges a nominal amount for CrossOver Office — the list price for the CrossOver Office Standard Download version is $39.95 for a single copy — but all code changes and improvements to Wine are returned to the Wine project. Thus, the Wine open-source project benefits from the sale of CrossOver Office.

DISTRIBUTION SPECIFIC

Xandros comes with CrossOver Office. You have to run the CrossOver Office setup and then install Microsoft Office from the original CD before you can start using Microsoft Office applications. During installation, you have to enter the product key for Microsoft Office, just as you would on a Windows installation.

aspell spelling checker

The aspell utility is an interactive spelling checker. You can use it to check the spelling of words in a text file. To do so, simply type the following command in a terminal window:

```
aspell check filename
```

If you want to try out aspell, type some notes and save them in a text file named `notes.txt`. (The filename can be anything, but I use this filename in this section.) To run the spelling checker on that file, type the following command in a terminal window:

```
aspell check notes.txt
This note describes the *concensus* reached during the August
   16 meeting.
1) consensus                                6) consensual
2) con census                               7) consciences
3) con-census                               8) incenses
4) condenses                                9) consensus's
5) concerns                                 0) consensuses
i) Ignore                                   I) Ignore all
r) Replace                                  R) Replace all
a) Add                                      x) Exit
?
```

Everything from the second line on is what aspell displays. When aspell finds a misspelled word (any word that doesn't appear in its dictionary), it displays the sentence with the misspelled word (`concensus`) and highlights that word by enclosing it in a pair of asterisks. Below that sentence, aspell lists possible corrections, numbering them sequentially from 1. In this case, aspell lists `consensus` — the correct choice — as the first correction for `concensus`.

After the sentence, aspell displays a list of 16 options — 10 numbered 0 through 9, 6 of which are labeled with single letters i, r, a, I, R, and x — followed by a question mark prompt. You have to press one of the numbers or letters from the list shown in the output to indicate what you want aspell to do. The numbered options show 10 possible replacement words for the misspelled word. Here are the meanings of the letter options:

- Space means accept the word this time.
- `i` means ignore the misspelled word.
- `I` means ignore all occurrences of the word.
- `r` means replace this occurrence (after pressing `r`, you have to type a replacement word).
- `R` means replace all occurrences (after pressing `R`, you have to type a replacement word).
- `a` means accept the word and add it to the your private dictionary.
- `x` means save the rest of the file and exit, ignoring misspellings.

These options are case sensitive. Make sure you don't have Caps Lock engaged.

Databases

Linux distributions typically come with one of two common relational databases — PostgreSQL and MySQL.

PostgreSQL (pronounced *Post Gres Que Ell*), is a powerful and popular *relational database* (the type of database that works as a collection of connected tables). You can use the Structured Query Language (SQL) to work with the database. PostgreSQL is developed by a team of developers and distributed under the BSD (Berkeley System Development) open-source license. The license places no restrictions on how the PostgreSQL source code may be used. To keep up with the latest PostgreSQL developments, visit `www.PostgreSQL.org`.

MySQL, pronounced *My Ess Que Ell,* is another popular relational database. You can use SQL to work with MySQL databases. A Swedish company called MySQL AB develops MySQL (`www.mysql.com`).

I briefly show you how to use MySQL on Xandros. By the way, if you don't see MySQL in Debian, log in as `root` and type **apt-get install mysql-admin mysql-client mysql-common mysql-server** in a terminal window.

To use MySQL, you have to first log in as `root` and start the database server with the following command:

```
/etc/init.d/mysqld start
```

The database server `mysqld` is a *daemon* (a background process that runs continuously) that accepts database queries from the MySQL monitor.

Now you have to design a database, create that database in MySQL, and load it with the data.

Reviewing the steps to build the database

Use this basic sequence of steps to build a database:

1. Design the database.

   This involves defining the tables and attributes that will be used to store the information.

2. Create an empty database.

   Before you can add tables, database systems require you to build an empty database.

3. Create the tables in the database.

   In this step, you define the tables by using the `CREATE TABLE` statement of SQL.

4. Load the tables with any fixed data.

   For example, if you had a table of manufacturer names or publisher names (in the case of books), you'd want to load that table with information that's already known.

5. Back up the initial database.

   This step is necessary to ensure that you can create the database from scratch, if necessary.

6. Load data into tables.

   You may either load data from an earlier dump of the database or interactively through forms.

7. Use the database by querying it.

   Make queries, update records, or insert new records using SQL commands.

To illustrate how to create and load a database, I set up a simple book catalog database as an example.

Designing the database

For my book catalog example, I don't follow all the steps of database building. For the example, the database design step is going to be trivial because my book catalog database will include a single table. The attributes of the table are as follows:

- Book's title with up to 50 characters
- Name of first author with up to 20 characters
- Name of second author (if any) with up to 20 characters
- Name of publisher with up to 30 characters
- Page count as a number
- Year published as a number (such as 2005)
- International Standard Book Number (ISBN), as a 10-character text (such as 0764579363)

I store the ISBN without the dashes that are embedded in a typical ISBN. I also use the ISBN as the primary key of the table because ISBN is a worldwide identification system for books. That means each book entry must have a unique ISBN because all books have unique ISBNs.

Creating an empty database

To create the empty database in MySQL, use the `mysqladmin` program. For example, to create an empty database named `books`, I type the following command:

```
mysqladmin create books
```

You have to log in as `root` to run the `mysqladmin` program. As the name suggests, `mysqladmin` is the database administration program for MySQL.

In addition to creating a database, you can use `mysqladmin` to remove a database, shutdown the database server, or check the MySQL version. For example, to see the version information, type the following command:

```
mysqladmin version
```

Using the MySQL monitor

After you create the empty database, all of your interactions with the database are through the `mysql` program — the MySQL monitor that acts as a client to the database server. You need to run `mysql` with the name of a database as argument. The mysql program then prompts you for input. Here is an example where I type the first line and the rest is the output from the mysql program:

```
mysql books

Reading table information for completion of table and column names
You can turn off this feature to get a quicker startup with -A

Welcome to the MySQL monitor.  Commands end with ; or \g.
Your MySQL connection id is 10 to server version: 3.23.49

Type 'help;' or '\h' for help. Type '\c' to clear the buffer.

mysql>
```


When creating tables or loading data into tables, a typical approach is to place the SQL statements (along with mysql commands such as \g) in a file and then run mysql with the standard input directed from that file. For example, suppose a file named sample.sql contains some SQL commands that you want to try out on a database named books. Then, you should run mysql with the following command:

```
mysql books < sample.sql
```

I use mysql in this manner to create a database table.

Defining a table

To create a table named books, I edited a text file named makedb.sql and placed the following line in that file:

```
#
# Table structure for table 'books'
#
CREATE TABLE books (
  isbn CHAR(10) NOT NULL PRIMARY KEY,
  title CHAR(50),
  author1 CHAR(20),
  author2 CHAR(20),
  pubname CHAR(30),
  pubyear INT,
  pagecount INT
) \g
```

CREATE TABLE books is an SQL statement to create the table named books. The \g at the end of the statement is a mysql command. The attributes of the table appear in the lines enclosed in parentheses.

If a table contains fixed data, you can also include other SQL statements (such as INSERT INTO) to load the data into the table right after the table is created.

To execute the SQL statements in the makedb.sql file in order to create the books table, I run mysql as follows:

```
mysql books < makedb.sql
```

Now the books database should have a table named books. (Okay, maybe I should have named them differently, but it seemed convenient to call them by the same name). I can now begin loading data into the table.

Loading data into a table

One way to load data into the table is to prepare SQL statements in another file and then run mysql with that file as input. For example, suppose I want to add the following book information into the books table:

```
isbn = '156884798X'
title = 'Linux SECRETS'
author1 = 'Naba Barkakati'
author2 = NULL
pubname = 'IDG Books Worldwide'
pubyear = 1996
pagecount = 900
```

Then, the following MySQL statement loads this information into the books table:

```
INSERT INTO books VALUES
( '156884798X', 'Linux SECRETS', 'Naba Barkakati', NULL,
'IDG Books Worldwide', 1996, 900) \g
```

On the other hand, suppose you had the various fields available in a different order — an order different from the one you defined by using the CREATE TABLE statement. In that case, you can use a different form of the INSERT INTO command to add the row in the correct order, as shown in the following example:

```
INSERT INTO books (pubyear, author1, author2, title,
    pagecount, pubname, isbn) values
(1996, 'Naba Barkakati', NULL, 'Linux SECRETS', 900, 'IDG
    Books Worldwide', '156884798X')\g
```

Essentially, you have to specify the list of attributes as well as the values and make sure that the order of the attributes matches that of the values.

If I save all the INSERT INTO commands in a file named additems.sql, I can load the database from the mysql command line by using the source command like this (type **mysql books** to start the SQL client):

```
mysql> source additems.sql
```

Querying the database

You can query the database interactively through the `mysql` monitor. You do have to know SQL to do this. For example, to query the books database, I start the SQL client with the command:

```
mysql books
```

Then I would type SQL commands at the `mysql>` prompt to look up items from the database. When done, I type **quit** to exit the `mysql` program. Here's an example (I typed all of this in a terminal window):

```
mysql> select title from books where pubyear < 2005 \g
+-------------------------------------+
| title                               |
+-------------------------------------+
| Linux SECRETS                       |
| Linux All-in-One Desk Ref For Dummies|
+-------------------------------------+
2 rows in set (0.09 sec)
mysql> quit
Bye
```


Multimedia Applications

Most Linux distributions include quite a few multimedia applications — mostly multimedia audio players and CD players, but also applications for using digital cameras and burning CD-ROMs. To play some other multimedia files (such as MPEG video), you may have to download and install additional software in your Linux system. Here's a quick sketch of a few typical multimedia tasks and the applications you can use to perform these tasks:

- **Using digital cameras:** Use the Digital Camera tool to download photos from your digital camera in Linux (or simply access the camera as a USB mass storage device).
- **Playing audio CDs:** Use one of many audio CD players that come with Linux.
- **Playing sound files:** Use Rhythmbox or XMMS multimedia audio players. (You have to download some additional software to play MP3 files with Rhythmbox or XMMS.) You can also download other players from the Internet.
- **Burning a CD:** Use a CD burner such as K3b to burn audio and data CDs.

Using a digital camera

Most Linux distributions come with a digital-camera application that you can use to download pictures from digital cameras. For example, SUSE and Xandros come with Digikam, which works with many different makes and models of digital cameras. Depending on the model, the cameras can connect to the serial port or the Universal Serial Bus (USB) port.

To use Digikam with your digital camera, follow these steps:

1. **Connect your digital camera to the serial port or USB port (whichever interface the camera supports) and turn on the camera.**
2. **Start Digikam.**

   Look for it in the Main Menu under graphics or images.
3. **From the Digikam menu, choose Settings⇨Configure Digikam.**

   A configuration dialog box appears.
4. **Click the Cameras tab in the dialog box and click Auto Detect.**

   If your camera is supported and the camera is configured to be in PTP (Picture Transfer Protocol) mode, the camera is detected. If not, you can get the photos from your camera by using an alternate method that I describe after these steps.
5. **Select your camera model from the Camera menu.**

   A new window appears and, after a short while, displays the photos in the camera.
6. **Click the thumbnails to select the images you want to download; then choose Camera⇨Download to download the images.**

   Digikam then downloads the images. You can save the file in a folder and edit the photos in The GIMP or your favorite photo editor.

TIP: Don't despair if Digikam doesn't recognize your digital camera. You can still access the digital camera's storage media (compact flash card, for example) as a USB mass storage device, provided your camera supports USB Mass Storage. To access the images on your USB digital camera, use the following steps. (I tested these steps on SUSE Linux, but they should work on most Linux distributions.)

1. **Read the camera manual and use the menu options of the camera to set the USB mode to Mass Storage.**

   If the camera doesn't support USB Mass Storage, you cannot use this procedure to access the photos. If the camera supports the Picture Transfer Protocol mode, you can use Digikam to download the pictures.

2. **Connect your digital camera to the USB port by using the cable that came with the camera, and then turn on the camera.**

   This causes Linux to detect the camera and open the contents of the camera in a file manager window (see Figure 4-6).

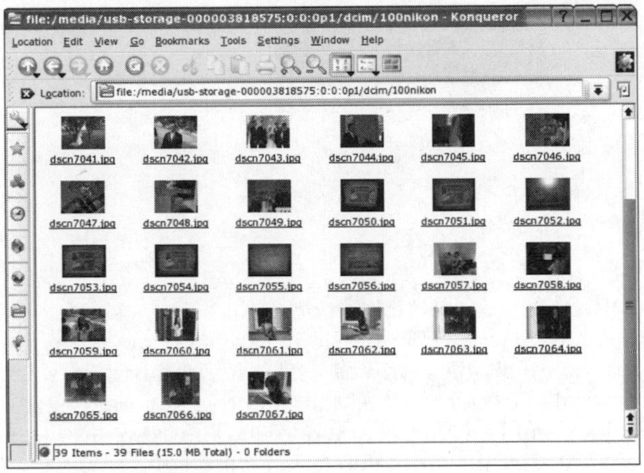

Figure 4-6: You can access your camera as a USB mass storage device.

3. **Click to select photos and copy them to your hard drive by dragging and dropping them into a selected folder.**
4. **Turn off the camera and disconnect the USB cable from the PC.**

Who needs a digital camera tool when you can access the camera just like any other storage device!

Playing audio CDs

All Linux distributions come with either the GNOME or KDE CD player applications. To play an audio CD, you need a sound card, and that sound card must be configured to work in Linux.

In some distributions, you can insert an audio CD into the drive, and a dialog box appears and asks whether you want to play the CD with the CD player. For example, Figure 4-7 shows the KDE CD Player (KsCD) playing a track from an audio CD in SUSE Linux.

The KDE CD Player displays the title of the CD and the name of the current track. The CD Player gets the song titles from `freedb.org` — a free open-source CD database on the Internet (`freedb.freedb.org` at port 888). You need an active Internet connection for the CD Player to download song information from the CD database. After the CD Player downloads information about a particular CD, it caches that information in a local database for future use. The CD Player user interface is intuitive, and you can figure it out easily. One nice feature is that you can select a track by title.

Figure 4-7: Play audio CDs with the KDE CD Player.

Playing sound files

You can use Rhythmbox or XMMS to open and play a sound file. Rhythmbox is liked by users with large MP3 music libraries because Rhythmbox can help organize the music files. You can start Rhythmbox by selecting the music player application from the Main Menu in several distributions, including Debian and Fedora Core. When you first start Rhythmbox, it displays an assistant that prompts you (see Figure 4-8) for the location of your music files so that Rhythmbox can manage your music library.

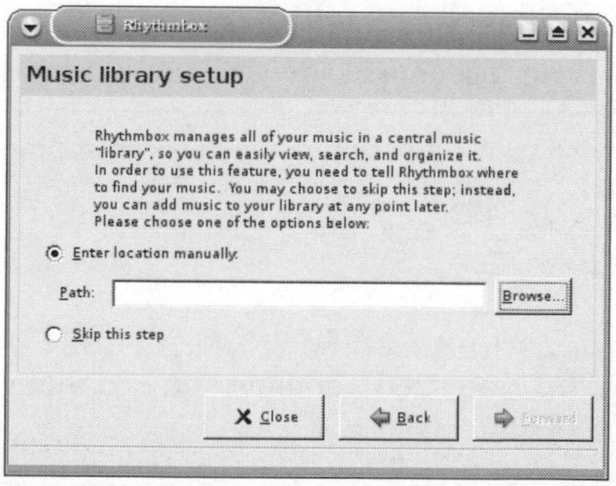

Figure 4-8: Rhythmbox can manage your music library.

After you identify the locations of music files, Rhythmbox starts and displays the library in an organized manner. You can then select music and play it, as shown in Figure 4-9. (Here you see Rhythmbox running on Debian.)

XMMS is another music player that can play many types of sound files, including Ogg Vorbis, FLAC (Free Lossless Audio Codec, an audio file format that is similar to MP3), and Windows WAV.

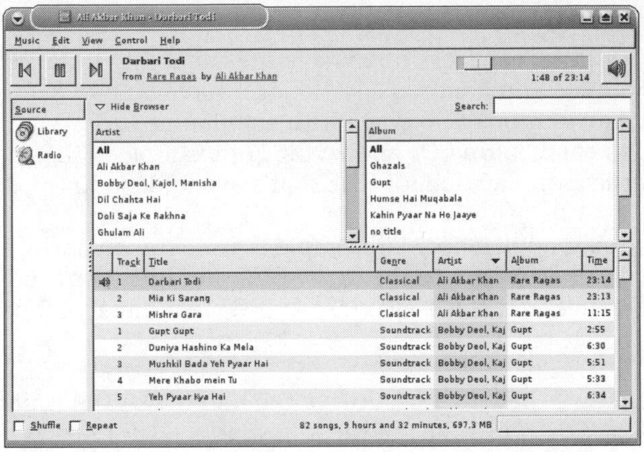

Figure 4-9: You can play music from your library in Rhythmbox.

You can start XMMS by selecting the audio player application from the Main Menu (look under Multimedia or Sound & Video). After XMMS starts, you can open a sound file (such as an MP3 file) by choosing Window Menu⇨Play File or by pressing L. Then select one or more music files from the Load File dialog box. Click the Play button, and XMMS starts playing the sound file. Figure 4-10 shows the XMMS window (in SUSE Linux) when it's playing a sound file.

Figure 4-10: You can play many different types of sound files in XMMS.

DISTRIBUTION SPECIFIC

In some free Linux distributions, you may not be able to play MP3 files because the MP3 decoder is not included. However, MP3 playing works fine in Debian, Knoppix, SUSE, and Xandros. Because of legal reasons, the versions of Rhythmbox and XMMS in Fedora Core don't include the code needed to play MP3 files, so you have to somehow translate MP3s into a supported format, such as WAV, before you can play them. You can, however, download the source code for Rhythmbox and XMMS and build the applications with MP3 support. You can also use the Ogg Vorbis format for compressed audio files because Ogg Vorbis is a patent- and royalty-free format.

Burning a CD

Nowadays, GUI file managers often have the capability to burn CDs. For example, Nautilus and Xandros File Manager have built-in features to burn CDs. Linux distributions also come with standalone GUI programs that enable you to easily burn CDs and DVDs. For example, K3b is a popular CD/DVD burning application for KDE that's available in Knoppix and SUSE.

Most CD burning applications are simple to use. You basically gather up the files that you want to burn to the CD or DVD and then start the burning process. Of course, for this to work, your PC must have a CD or DVD burner installed.

Figure 4-11 shows the initial window of the K3b CD/DVD burning application in SUSE Linux. The upper part of the K3b window is for browsing the file system to select what you want to burn onto a CD or DVD. The upper-left corner shows the CD writer device installed; in this example, it's a DVD/CD-RW drive so that the drive can read DVDs and CDs, but burn CDs only.

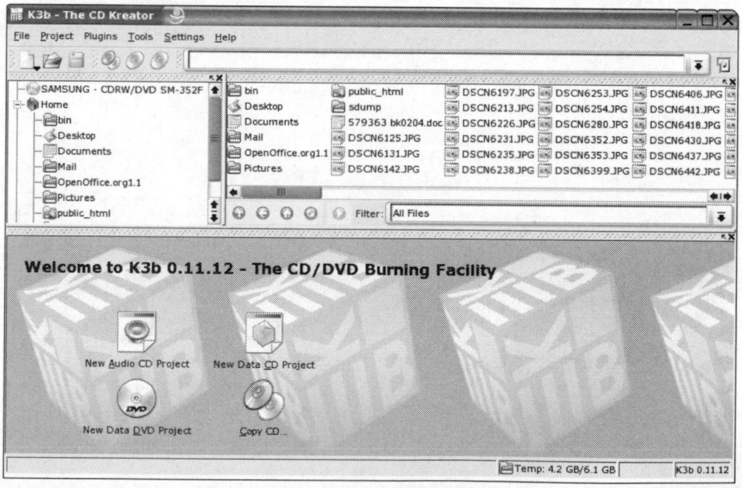

Figure 4-11: You can burn CDs and DVDs with the K3b application.

To burn a CD, you start with one of the projects shown in the lower part of the K3b window — New Audio CD Project, for example, or New Data DVD Project. Then you have to add files and, finally, burn the project to the CD or DVD by choosing Project➪Burn or pressing Ctrl+B. For an audio CD, you can drag and drop MP3 files as well as audio tracks.

K3b needs the external command-line programs `cdrecord` and `cdrdao` to burn CDs. K3b also needs the `growisofs` program to burn DVDs.

If you get an error about missing `cdrdao` in Debian, make sure that your Debian system is connected to the Internet and then type **apt-get install cdrdao** to install it.

Graphics and Imaging

You can use graphics and imaging applications to work with images and graphics (line drawings and shapes). I discuss two applications:

- **The GIMP (GNU Image Manipulation Program)** is a program for viewing and performing image-manipulation tasks, such as photo retouching, image composition, and image creation.
- **Gnome Ghostview (GGV)** is a graphical application capable of displaying PostScript files.

The GIMP

The GIMP is an image-manipulation program written by Peter Mattis and Spencer Kimball and released under the GNU General Public License (GPL). Most Linux distributions come with this program, although you may have to specifically select a package to install it. The GIMP is comparable to other image-manipulation programs, such as Adobe Photoshop and Corel PHOTO-PAINT.

To try out The GIMP, look for it under the Graphics category in the Main Menu. When you start it, The GIMP displays a window with copyright and license information. Click the Continue button to proceed with the installation. The next screen shows the directories to be created when you proceed with a personal installation of The GIMP.

The GIMP installation involves creating a directory in your home directory and placing a number of files in that directory. This directory essentially holds information about any changes to user preferences you may make to The GIMP. Go ahead and click the Continue button at the bottom of the window. The GIMP creates the necessary directories, copies the necessary files to those directories, and guides you through a series of dialog boxes to complete the installation.

After the installation is done, click the Continue button. From now on, you don't see the installation window anymore; you have to deal with installation only when you run The GIMP for the first time.

The GIMP then loads any *plugins* — external modules that enhance its functionality. It displays a startup window that shows a message about each plugin as it loads. After finishing the startup, The GIMP displays a tip of the day in a window. You can browse the tips and click the Close button to close the Tip window. At the same time, The GIMP displays a number of windows, as shown in Figure 4-12.

Figure 4-12: Touch up your photos with The GIMP.

These windows include a main toolbox window titled The GIMP, a Tool Options window, a Brush Selection window, and a Layers, Channels, Paths window. Of these, the main toolbox window is the most important — in fact, you can close the other windows and work by using the menus and buttons in the toolbox.

The toolbox has three menus on the menu bar:

- **The File menu** has options to create a new image, open an existing image, save and print an image, mail an image, and quit The GIMP.
- **The Xtns menu** gives you access to numerous extensions to The GIMP. The exact content of the Xtns menu depends on which extensions are installed on your system.
- **The Help menu** is where you can get help and view tips. For example, choose Help⇨Help to bring up The GIMP Help Browser with online information about The GIMP.

To open an image file in The GIMP, choose File⇨Open. The Load Image dialog box comes up, which you can then use to select an image file. You can change directories and select the image file that you want to open. The GIMP can read all common image-file formats, such as GIF, JPEG, TIFF, PCX, BMP,

PNG, and PostScript. After you select the file and click OK, The GIMP loads the image into a new window. (Refer to Figure 4-12 to see an image after it's loaded in The GIMP, along with all the other The GIMP windows.)

The toolbox also has many buttons that represent the tools you use to edit the image and apply special effects. You can get pop-up help on each tool button by placing the mouse pointer on the button. You can select a tool by clicking the tool button, and you can apply that tool's effects to the image.

For your convenience, The GIMP displays a pop-up menu when you right-click the image window. The pop-up menu has most of the options from the File and Xtns menus in the toolbox. You can then select specific actions from these menus.

You can do much more than just load and view images with The GIMP, but a complete discussion of all its features is beyond the scope of this book. If you want to try the other features of The GIMP, consult The GIMP User Manual (GUM), available online at `manual.gimp.org`. You can also choose Xtns⇨Web Browser⇨GIMP.ORG⇨Documentation to access the online documentation for The GIMP. (Of course, you need an Internet connection for this command to work.)

Visit The GIMP home page at `www.gimp.org` to find the latest news about The GIMP and links to other resources.

Gnome Ghostview

Gnome Ghostview is a graphical application ideal for viewing and printing PostScript or PDF documents. For a long document, you can view and print selected pages. You can also view the document at various levels of magnification by zooming in or out.

To run Gnome Ghostview in Fedora Core, choose Main Menu⇨Graphics⇨ PostScript Viewer from GUI desktop. The Gnome Ghostview application window appears. In addition to the menu bar and toolbar along the top edge, a vertical divide splits the main display area of the window into two parts.

To load and view a PostScript document in Gnome Ghostview, choose File⇨Open, or click the Open icon on the toolbar. Gnome Ghostview displays a File-Selection dialog box. Use this dialog box to navigate the file system and select a PostScript file. You can select one of the PostScript files that come with Ghostscript. For example, open the file `tiger.ps` in the `/usr/share/ghostscript/7.07/examples` directory. (If your system has a version of Ghostscript later than 7.07, you have to use the new version number in place of 7.07.)

To open the selected file, click the Open File button in the File-Selection dialog box. Gnome Ghostview opens the selected file, processes its contents, and displays the output in its window, as shown in Figure 4-13.

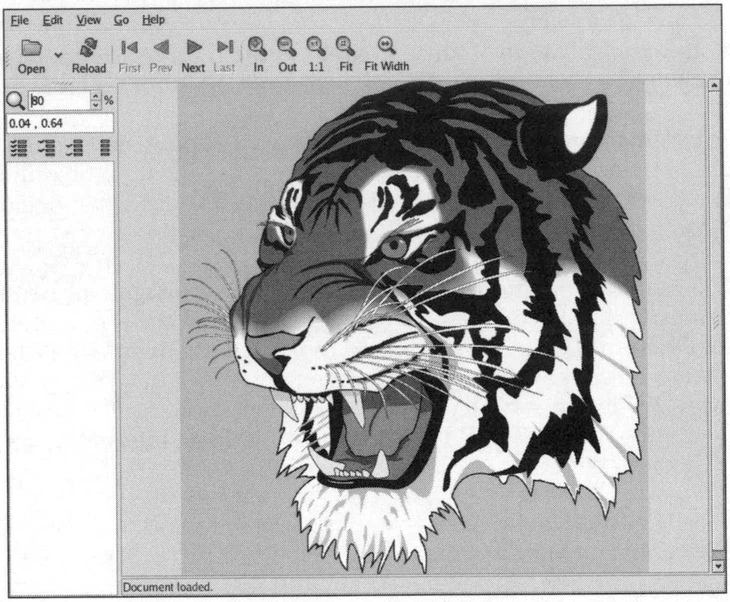

Figure 4-13: You can view PostScript files in Gnome Ghostview.

Gnome Ghostview is useful for viewing various kinds of documents that come in PostScript format. (These files typically have the `.ps` extension in their names.) You can also open PDF files — which typically have `.pdf` extensions — in Gnome Ghostview.

Chapter 5: Using Text Editors

In This Chapter

- **Using GUI text editors**
- **Working with the `ed` text editor**
- **Getting to know the `vi` text editor**

In Linux, most system-configuration files are text files. If you write any shell scripts or other computer programs, they're text files too. Sometimes you have to edit these files by using programs designed for that purpose: *text editors*. For example, you may need to edit files such as `/etc/hosts`, `/etc/resolv.conf`, `/etc/X11/XF86Config`, `/etc/apt/sources.list`, and many more.

In this chapter, I introduce you to a few text editors — both the GUI editors and text-mode editors.

Using GUI Text Editors

Each of the GUI desktops — GNOME and KDE — comes with GUI text editors (text editors that have graphical user interfaces).

To use a GUI text editor, look in the Main Menu and search for text editors in an appropriate category. For example, in Fedora Core, choose Main Menu➪Accessories➪Text Editor from the GNOME desktop. In Debian, choose Main Menu➪Editors➪Advanced Text Editor. After you have a text editor up and running, you can open a file by clicking the Open button on the toolbar, which brings up the Open File dialog box. You can then change directories and select the file to edit by clicking the OK button.

The GNOME text editor then loads the file in its window. You can open more than one file at a time and move among them as you edit the files. Figure 5-1 shows a typical editing session with the editor.

In this case, the editor has three files — `hosts`, `fstab`, and `inittab` (all from the `/etc` directory) — open for editing. The filenames appear as tabs below the toolbar of the editor's window. You can switch among the files by clicking the tabs.

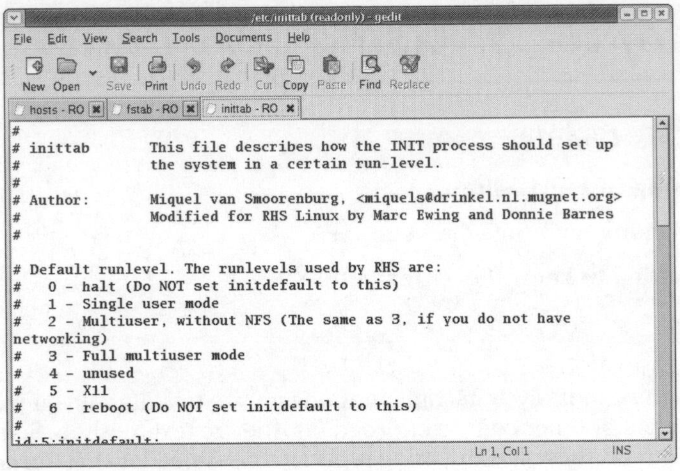

Figure 5-1: You can use the GNOME text editor to edit text files.

If you open a file for which you have only read permission, the text `RO-` is appended to the filename to indicate that the file is read-only. In Figure 5-1, all the files are opened read-only because here I'm logged in as a normal user and I'm opening system files that only the `root` can modify.

The rest of the text-editing steps are intuitive. To enter new text, click to position the cursor and then begin typing. You can select text, copy, cut, and paste by using the buttons on the toolbar above the text-editing area.

From the KDE desktop, you can start the KDE advanced text editor (Kate) by choosing Main Menu⇨Editors⇨Advanced Text Editor. To open a text file, choose File⇨Open. Kate displays a dialog box. From this dialog box, you can go to the directory of your choice, select the file to open, and click OK. Kate then opens the file and displays its contents in the window. You can then edit the file.

Text Editing with ed and vi

GUI text editors enable you to edit text files using the mouse and keyboard much the same way as you use any word processor. Text-mode editors are a complete different beast — you work using only the keyboard and you have to type cryptic commands to perform editing tasks such as cutting and pasting text or entering and deleting text. Linux comes with two text-mode text editors:

- `ed`, a line-oriented text editor
- `vi`, a full-screen text editor that supports the command set of an earlier editor named `ex`

The ed and vi editors are cryptic compared to the graphical text editors. However, you should still get to know the basic editing commands of ed and vi because sometimes these two may be the only editors available. For example, if Linux refuses to boot from the hard drive, you may have to boot from a floppy disk. In that case, you have to edit system files with the ed editor because that editor is small enough to fit on the floppy. I walk you through the basic text-editing commands of ed and vi — they're not that hard.

Using ed

Typically, you have to use ed only when you boot a minimal version of Linux (for example, from a floppy you've set up as a boot disk), and the system doesn't support full-screen mode. In all other situations, you can use the vi editor that works in full-screen text mode.

When you use ed, you work in command mode or text-input mode:

- **Command mode** is what you get by default. In this mode, anything that you type is interpreted as a command. The ed text editor has a simple command set where each command consists of one or more characters.
- **Text-input mode** is for typing text. You can enter input mode with the commands a (append), c (change), or i (insert). After entering lines of text, you can leave input mode by entering a period (.) on a line by itself.

To practice editing a file, copy the /etc/fstab file to your home directory by issuing the following commands:

```
cd
cp /etc/fstab .
```

Now you have a file named fstab in your home directory. Type **ed -p: fstab** to begin editing a file in ed. The editor responds thusly:

```
526
:
```

This example uses the -p option to set the prompt to the colon character (:) and opens the fstab file (in the current directory, which is your home directory) for editing. The ed editor opens the file, reports the number of characters in the file (526), displays the prompt (:), and waits for a command.

TIP

When you're editing with ed, make sure you that always turn on a prompt character (use the -p option). Without the prompt, distinguishing whether ed is in input mode or command mode is difficult.

After ed opens a file for editing, the current line is the last line of the file. To see the current line number (the current line is the line to which ed applies your command), use the .= command like this:

```
:.=
9
```

This output tells you that the fstab file has nine lines. (Your system's /etc/fstab file may have a different number of lines, in which case ed shows a different number.)

You can use the 1,$p command to see all lines in a file, as the following example shows:

```
:1,$p
# /etc/fstab: static file system information.
#
# <file system> <mount point>   <type>  <options>       <dump>  <pass>
proc            /proc           proc    defaults        0       0
/dev/hda10      /               ext3    defaults,errors=remount-ro 0       1
/dev/hda6       /boot           ext3    defaults        0       2
/dev/hda8       none            swap    sw              0       0
/dev/hdc        /media/cdrom0   iso9660 ro,user,noauto  0       0
/dev/fd0        /media/floppy0  auto    rw,user,noauto  0       0
:
```

To go to a specific line, type the line number:

```
:7
```

The editor responds by displaying that line:

```
/dev/hda8       none            swap    sw              0       0
:
```

Suppose you want to delete the line that contains cdrom. To search for a string, type a slash (/) followed by the string that you want to locate:

```
:/cdrom
/dev/hdc        /media/cdrom0   iso9660 ro,user,noauto  0       0
:
```

The editor locates the line that contains the string and then displays it. That line becomes the current line.

To delete the current line, use the d command as follows:

```
:d
:
```

To replace a string with another, use the `s` command. To replace `cdrom` with the string `cd`, for example, use this command:

```
:s/cdrom/cd/
:
```

To insert a line in front of the current line, use the `i` command:

```
:i
    (type the line you want to insert)
.   (type a single period to indicate you're done)
:
```


You can enter as many lines as you want. After the last line, enter a period (.) on a line by itself. That period marks the end of text-input mode, and the editor switches to command mode. In this case, you can tell that `ed` switches to command mode because you see the prompt (:).

When you're happy with the changes, you can write them to the file with the `w` command. If you want to save the changes and exit, type **wq** to perform both steps at the same time:

```
:wq
531
```

The `ed` editor saves the changes in the file, displays the number of saved characters, and exits. If you want to quit the editor without saving any changes, use the `Q` command.

These examples give you an idea of how to use `ed` commands to perform the basic tasks of editing a text file. Table 5-1 lists some of the commonly used `ed` commands.

Table 5-1 Commonly Used ed Commands

Command	*Does the Following*
`!command`	Executes a shell command. (For example, `!pwd` shows the current directory.)
`$`	Goes to the last line in the buffer.
`%`	Applies a command that follows to all lines in the buffer. (For example, `%p` prints all lines.)
`+`	Goes to the next line.
`+n`	Goes to the *n*th next line (where *n* is a number you designate).
`,`	Applies a command that follows to all lines in the buffer. (For example, `,p` prints all lines.) Similar to `%`.

(continued)

Table 5-1 (continued)

Command	*Does the Following*
`-`	Goes to the preceding line.
`-n`	Goes to the *n*th previous line (where *n* is a number you designate).
`.`	Refers to the current line in the buffer.
`/text/`	Searches forward for the specified text.
`;`	Refers to a range of lines; current through last line in the buffer.
`=`	Prints the line number.
`?text?`	Searches backward for the specified text.
`^`	Goes to the preceding line; see also the `-` command.
`^n`	Goes to the *n*th previous line (where *n* is a number you designate); see also the `-n` command.
`a`	Appends after the current line.
`c`	Changes the specified lines.
`d`	Deletes the specified lines.
`i`	Inserts text before the current line.
`n`	Goes to line number *n*.
Press Enter	Displays the next line and makes that line current.
`q`	Quits the editor.
`Q`	Quits the editor without saving changes.
`r file`	Reads and inserts the contents of the file after the current line.
`s/old/new/`	Replaces an old string with a new one.
`u`	Undoes the last command.
`W file`	Appends the contents of the buffer to the end of the specified file.
`w file`	Saves the buffer in the specified file. (If no file is named, it saves in the default file — the file whose contents `ed` is currently editing.)

Using vi

The `vi` editor is a full-screen text editor, so you can view several lines at the same time. Most UNIX systems, including Linux, come with `vi`. Therefore, if you know the basic features of `vi`, you can edit text files on almost any UNIX system.

When `vi` edits a file, it reads the file into a *buffer* — a block of memory — so you can change the text in the buffer. The `vi` editor also uses temporary files during editing, but the original file isn't altered until you save the changes.

To start the editor, type **vi** and follow it with the name of the file you want to edit, like this:

```
vi /etc/fstab
```

The `vi` editor then loads the file into memory and displays the first few lines in a text screen and positions the cursor on the first line, as shown in Figure 5-2.

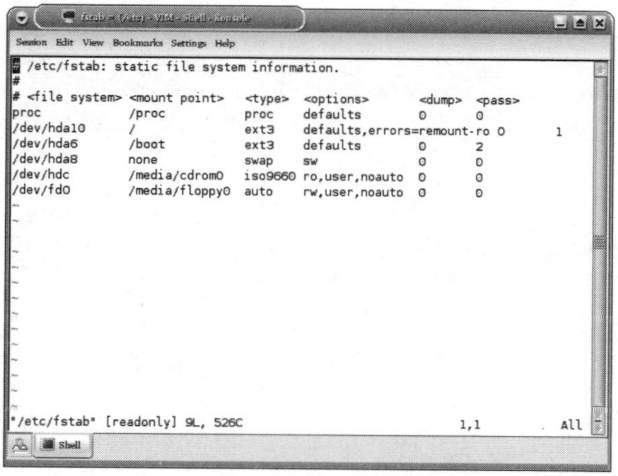

Figure 5-2: You can edit text files with the vi full-screen text editor.

The last line shows the pathname of the file as well as the number of lines (9) and the number of characters (526) in the file. In this case, the text `[readonly]` appears after the filename because I'm opening the `/etc/fstab` file while I am logged in as a normal user (which means I don't have permission to modify the file). Later, the last line in the `vi` display functions as a command-entry area. The rest of the lines display the file. If the file contains fewer lines than the screen, `vi` displays the empty lines with a tilde (~) in the first column.

The current line is marked by the cursor, which appears as a small black rectangle. The cursor appears on top of a character.

When using `vi`, you work in one of three modes:

- **Visual-command mode** is what you get by default. In this mode, anything that you type is interpreted as a command that applies to the line containing the cursor. The `vi` commands are similar to the `ed` commands.
- **Colon-command mode** is for reading or writing files, setting `vi` options, and quitting `vi`. All colon commands start with a colon (`:`). When you enter the colon, `vi` positions the cursor on the last line and waits for you to type a command. The command takes effect when you press Enter.

- **Text-input mode** is for typing text. You can enter input mode with the command `a` (insert after cursor), `A` (append at end of line), or `i` (insert after cursor). After entering lines of text, you have to press Esc to leave input mode and re-enter visual-command mode.

One problem with all these modes is that you cannot easily tell the current mode that `vi` is in. You may begin typing only to realize that `vi` is not in input mode, which can be frustrating.

If you want to make sure that `vi` is in command mode, just press Esc a few times. (Pressing Esc more than once doesn't hurt.)

To view online help in `vi`, type **:help** while in colon-command mode. When you're done with help, type **:q** to exit the Help screen and return to the file you're editing.

The `vi` editor initially positions the cursor on the first character of the first line — and one of the handiest things you can know is how to move the cursor around. To get a bit of practice, try the commands shown in Table 5-2.

Table 5-2 Cursor Movement Commands in vi

Key	*Does the Following*
↓	Moves the cursor one line down.
↑	Moves the cursor one line up.
←	Moves the cursor one character to the left.
→	Moves the cursor one character to the right.
W	Moves the cursor one word forward.
B	Moves the cursor one word backward.
Ctrl+D	Moves down half a screen.
Ctrl+U	Scrolls up half a screen.

You can go to a specific line number at any time by using the handy colon command. To go to line 6, for example, type the following and then press Enter:

```
:6
```

When you type the colon, `vi` displays the colon on the last line of the screen. From then on, `vi` uses any text you type as a command. You have to press Enter to submit the command to `vi`. In colon-command mode, `vi` accepts all commands that the `ed` editor accepts — and then some.

To search for a string, first type a slash (/). The `vi` editor displays the slash on the last line of the screen. Type the search string and then press Enter. The `vi` editor locates the string and positions the cursor at the beginning of that string. Thus, to locate the string `cdrom` in the file `/etc/fstab`, type

```
/cdrom
```

To delete the line that contains the cursor, type **dd** (two lowercase *ds*). The `vi` editor deletes that line of text and makes the next line the current one.

To begin entering text in front of the cursor, type **i** (a lowercase *i* all by itself). The `vi` editor switches to text-input mode. Now you can enter text. When you finish entering text, press Esc to return to visual-command mode.

After you finish editing the file, you can save the changes in the file with the `:w` command. To quit the editor without saving any changes, use the `:q!` command. If you want to save the changes and exit, you can type **:wq** to perform both steps at the same time. The `vi` editor saves the changes in the file and exits. You can also save the changes and exit the editor by pressing Shift+ZZ (hold Shift down and press Z twice).

`vi` accepts a large number of commands in addition to the commands I mention above. Table 5-3 lists some commonly used `vi` commands, organized by task.

Table 5-3 Commonly Used vi Commands

Command	*Does the Following*
Insert Text	
`a`	Inserts text after the cursor.
`A`	Inserts text at the end of the current line.
`I`	Inserts text at the beginning of the current line.
`i`	Inserts text before the cursor.
Delete Text	
`D`	Deletes up to the end of the current line.
`dd`	Deletes the current line.
`dw`	Deletes from the cursor to the end of the following word.
`x`	Deletes the character on which the cursor rests.
Change Text	
`C`	Changes up to the end of the current line.
`cc`	Changes the current line.

(continued)

Table 5-3 *(continued)*

Command	*Does the Following*
`rx`	Replaces the character under the cursor with *x* (where *x* is any character).
`J`	Joins the current line with the next one.
Move Cursor	
`h` or ←	Moves one character to the left.
`j` or ↓	Moves one line down.
`k` or ↑	Moves one line up.
`L`	Moves to the end of the screen.
`l` or →	Moves one character to the right.
`w`	Moves to the beginning of the following word.
Scroll Text	
Ctrl+D	Scrolls forward by half a screen.
Ctrl+U	Scrolls backward by half a screen.
Refresh Screen	
Ctrl+L	Redraws screen.
Cut and Paste Text	
`yy`	Yanks (copies) current line into an unnamed buffer.
`P`	Puts the yanked line above the current line.
`p`	Puts the yanked line below the current line.
Colon Commands	
`:!`*`command`*	Executes a shell command.
`:q`	Quits the editor.
`:q!`	Quits without saving changes.
`:r` *`filename`*	Reads the file and inserts it after the current line.
`:w` *`filename`*	Writes a buffer to the file.
`:wq`	Saves changes and exits.
Search Text	
/string	Searches forward for a string.
?string	Searches backward for a string.
Miscellaneous	
`u`	Undoes the last command.
Esc	Ends input mode and enters visual-command mode.
`U`	Undoes recent changes to the current line.

Book III

Networking

The 5th Wave By Rich Tennant

Contents at a Glance

Chapter 1: Connecting to the Internet

In This Chapter

- **Understanding the Internet**
- **Deciding how to connect to the Internet**
- **Connecting to the Internet with DSL**
- **Connecting to the Internet with cable modem**
- **Setting up a dialup PPP link**

The Internet is quickly becoming a lifeline for most people. Seems like a lot of folks can't get through a day without it (and I know I could not write this book without it). Sometimes, I wonder how we ever managed without the Internet. Given the prevalence and popularity of the Internet, it's a pretty safe bet for me to assume that you want to connect your Linux system to the Internet. In this chapter, I show you how to connect to the Internet in several different ways — depending on whether you have a DSL, cable modem, or dialup network connection.

Two of the options for connecting to the Internet — DSL and cable modem — involve connecting a special modem to an Ethernet card on your Linux system. In these cases, you have to set up Ethernet networking on your Linux system. (I explain networking in Chapter 2 of this minibook.) In this chapter, I show you in detail how to set up a DSL or a cable modem connection.

I also show you the other option — dialup networking — that involves dialing up an Internet Service Provider (ISP) from your Linux system.

Understanding the Internet

How you view the Internet depends on your perspective. Common folks see the Internet in terms of the services they use. For example, as a user, you might think of the Internet as an information-exchange medium with features such as

- **E-mail:** Send e-mail to any other user on the Internet, using addresses such as `mom@home.net`.

- **Web:** Download and view documents from millions of servers throughout the Internet.
- **Newsgroups:** Read newsgroups and post news items to newsgroups with names such as `comp.os.linux.networking` or `comp.os.linux.setup`.
- **Information sharing:** Download software, music files, videos, and so on. Reciprocally, you may provide files that users on other systems can download.
- **Remote access:** Log on to another computer on the Internet, assuming that you have access to that remote computer.

The techies say that the Internet is a worldwide *network of networks*. The term *internet* (without capitalization) is a shortened form of *internetworking* — the interconnection of networks. The Internet Protocol (IP) was designed with the idea of connecting many separate networks.

In terms of physical connections, the Internet is similar to a network of highways and roads. This similarity is what has prompted the popular press to dub the Internet "the Information Superhighway." Just as the network of highways and roads includes some interstate highways, many state roads, and many more residential streets, the Internet has some very high-capacity networks (for example, a 10 Gbps backbone can handle 10 billion bits per second) and a large number of lower-capacity networks ranging from 56 Kbps dialup connections to 45 Mbps T3 links. (*Kbps* is thousand-bits-per-second, and *Mbps* is million-bits-per-second.) The high-capacity network is the backbone of the Internet.

In terms of management, the Internet is not run by a single organization, nor is it managed by any central computer. You can view the physical Internet as a "network of networks" managed collectively by thousands of cooperating organizations. Yes, a collection of networks managed by *thousands* of organizations — sounds amazing, but it works!

Deciding How to Connect to the Internet

So you want to connect to the Internet, but you don't know how? Let me count the ways. Nowadays you have three popular options for connecting homes and small offices to the Internet (of course, huge corporations and governments have many other ways to connect):

- **Digital Subscriber Line (DSL):** Your local telephone company, as well as other telecommunications companies, may offer DSL. DSL provides a way to send high-speed digital data over a regular phone line. Typically, DSL offers data transfer rates of between 128 Kbps and 1.5 Mbps. You can download from the Internet at much higher rates than when you send data from your PC to the Internet *(upload).* One caveat with DSL is that your home must be between 12,000 and 15,000 feet from your local central office (the phone company facility where your phone lines end up). The distance limitation varies from provider to provider. In the United States, you can check out the distance limits for many providers at `www.dslreports.com/distance`.

- **Cable modem:** If the cable television company in your area offers Internet access over cable, you can use that service to hook up your Linux system to the Internet. Typically, cable modems offer higher data-transfer rates than DSL — for about the same cost. Downloading data from the Internet via cable modem is much faster than sending data from your PC to the Internet. You can expect routine download speeds of 1.5 Mbps and upload speeds of around 128 Kbps, but sometimes you may get even higher speeds than these.
- **Dialup networking:** A dialup connection is what most folks were using before DSL and cable modems came along. You hook up your PC to a modem that's connected to the phone line. Then you dial up an ISP to connect to the Internet. That's why it's called *dialup networking* — establishing a network connection between your Linux PC and another network (the Internet) through a dialup modem. In this case, the maximum data-transfer rate is 56 Kbps.

DSL and cable modem services connect you to the Internet and also act as your Internet Service Provider (ISP); in addition to improved speed, what you're paying for is an IP address and your e-mail accounts. If you use a dialup modem to connect to the Internet, first you have to connect to the phone line (for which you pay the phone company) and then select and pay a separate ISP — which gives you a phone number to dial and all the other necessary goodies (such as an IP address and e-mail accounts).

Table 1-1 summarizes all these options. You can consult that table and select the type of connection that's available to you and that best suits your needs.

Table 1-1 Comparison of Dialup, DSL, and Cable

Feature	*Dialup*	*DSL*	*Cable*
Equipment	Modem	DSL modem, Ethernet card	Cable modem, Ethernet card
Also requires	Phone service and an Internet Service Provider (ISP)	Phone service and location within 12,000 to 15,000 feet of central office	Cable TV connection
Connection type	Dial to connect	Always on, dedicated	Always on, shared

(continued)

Table 1-1 *(continued)*

Feature	*Dialup*	*DSL*	*Cable*
Typical speed	56 Kbps maximum	640 Kbps download, 128 Kbps upload (higher speeds cost more)	1.5 Mbps down load, 128 Kbps upload
One-time costs (estimate)	None	Install = $100-200; Equipment = $200-300 (may be leased and may require activation cost)	Install = $100-200; Equipment = $60-100 (may be leased)
Typical monthly cost (2004)	Phone charges = $20/month; ISP charges = $15-30/ month	$50/month; may require monthly modem lease	$50/month; may require monthly modem lease

Note: *Costs vary by region and provider. Costs shown are typical ones for U.S. metropolitan areas.*

Connecting with DSL

DSL stands for *Digital Subscriber Line.* DSL uses your existing phone line to send digital data in addition to the normal analog voice signals (*analog* means continuously varying, whereas digital data is represented by 1s and 0s). The phone line goes from your home to a central office, where the line connects to the phone company's network — by the way, the connection from your home to the central office is called the *local loop.* When you sign up for DSL service, the phone company hooks up your phone line to some special equipment at the central office. That equipment can separate the digital data from voice. From then on, your phone line can carry digital data that is then directly sent to an Internet connection at the central office.

How DSL works

A special box called a *DSL modem* takes care of sending digital data from your PC to the phone company's central office over your phone line. Your PC can connect to the Internet with the same phone line that you use for your normal telephone calls — you can make voice calls even as the line is being used for DSL. Figure 1-1 shows a typical DSL connection to the Internet.

Your PC talks to the DSL modem through an Ethernet connection, which means that you need an Ethernet card in your Linux system.

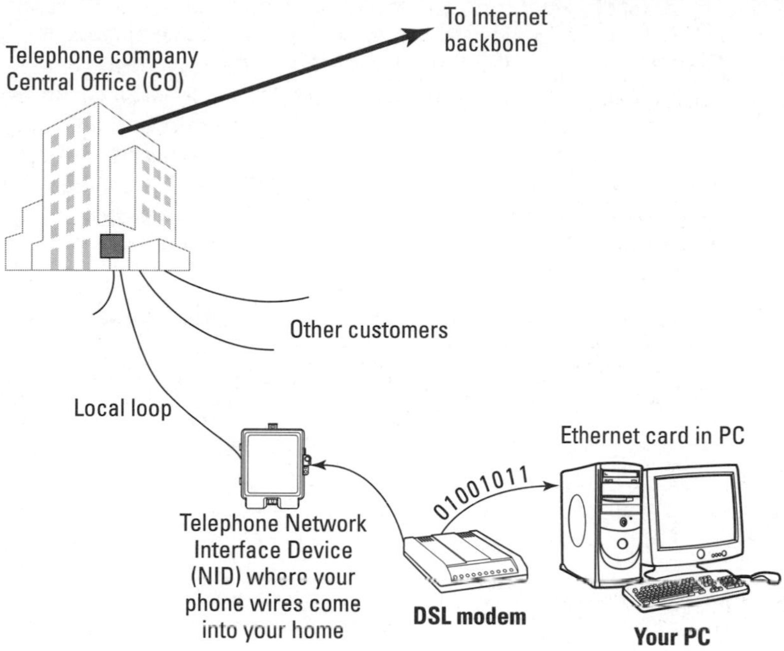

Figure 1-1: DSL provides high-speed connection to the Internet over a regular phone line.

Your PC sends digital data over the Ethernet connection to the DSL modem. The DSL modem sends the digital data at different frequencies than those used by the analog voice signals. The voice signals occupy a small portion of all the frequencies that the phone line can carry. DSL uses the higher frequencies to transfer digital data, so both voice and data can travel on the same phone line.

The distance between your home and the central office — the *loop length* — is a factor in DSL's performance. Unfortunately, the phone line can reliably carry the DSL signals over only a limited distance — typically three miles or less, which means that you can get DSL service only if your home (or office) is located within about three miles of your phone company's central office. Your phone company can tell you whether your location can get DSL or not. Often, it has a Web site where you can type in your phone number and get a response about DSL availability. For example, try `www.dslavailability.com` for U.S. locations.

DSL alphabet soup: ADSL, IDSL, SDSL

I have been using the term *DSL* as if there were only one kind of DSL. As you may imagine, nothing is ever that simple. There are in fact three variants of DSL, each with different features. Take a look:

- **ADSL:** *Asymmetric DSL,* the most common form of DSL, has much higher download speeds (from the Internet to your PC) than upload speeds (from your PC to the Internet). ADSL can have download speeds of up to 8 Mbps and upload speeds of up to 1 Mbps. ADSL works best when your location is within about 2½ miles (12,000 feet) of your central office. ADSL service is priced according to the download and upload speeds you want. A popular form of ADSL, called G.lite, is specifically designed to work on the same line you use for voice calls. G.lite has a maximum download speed of 1.5 Mbps and maximum upload speed of 512 Kbps.
- **IDSL:** *ISDN DSL* (ISDN is an older technology called *Integrated Services Digital Network*) is a special type of DSL that works at distances of up to five miles between your phone and the central office. The downside is that IDSL only offers *downstream* (from the Internet to your PC) and *upstream* (from your PC to the Internet) speeds of up to 144 Kbps.
- **SDSL:** *Symmetric DSL* provides equal download and upload speeds of up to 1.5 Mbps. SDSL is priced according to the speed you want, with the higher speeds costing more. The closer your location is to the phone company central office, the faster the connection you can get.

TECHNICAL STUFF

DSL speeds are typically specified by two numbers separated by a slash, such as this: 1500/384. The numbers refer to data-transfer speeds in kilobits per second (that is, thousands-of-bits per second, abbreviated Kbps). The first number is the download speed, the second the upload. Thus, 1500/384 means you can expect to download from the Internet at a maximum rate of 1,500 Kbps (or 1.5 Mbps) and upload to the Internet at 384 Kbps. If your phone line's condition is not perfect, you may not get these maximum rates — both ADSL and SDSL adjust the speeds to suit existing line conditions.

The price of DSL service depends on which variant — ADSL, IDSL, or SDSL — you select. For most home users, the primary choice is ADSL (or, more accurately, the G.lite form of ADSL) with transfer speed ratings of 1500/128.

Typical DSL setup

To get DSL for your home or business, you have to contact a DSL provider. In addition to your phone company, you can find many other DSL providers. No matter who provides the DSL service, some work has to be done at your central office — the place where your phone lines connect to the rest of the phone network. The work involves connecting your phone line to equipment that can work with the DSL modem at your home or office. The central office equipment and the DSL modem at your location can then do whatever magic is needed to send and receive digital data over your phone line.

Because of the need to set up your line at the central office, it takes some time after you place an order to get your line ready for DSL.

The first step for you is to check out the DSL providers that provide service and see if you can actually get the service. Because DSL can work only over certain distances — typically less than 2.5 miles — between your location and the central office, you have to check to see if you are within that distance limit. Contact your phone company to verify. You may be able to check this availability on the Web. Try typing into Google (`www.google.com`) the words **DSL, availability** and then your local phone company's name. The search results will probably include a Web site where you can type in your phone number to find out if DSL is available for your home or office.

If DSL is available, you can look for the types of service — ADSL versus SDSL — and the pricing. The price depends on the download and upload speeds you want. Sometimes, phone companies offer a simple residential DSL (basically the G.lite form of ADSL) with a 1500/128 speed rating — meaning you can download at up to 1,500 Kbps and upload at 128 Kbps. Of course, these are the *maximums,* and your mileage may vary.

After selecting the type of DSL service and provider you want, you can place an order and have the provider install the necessary equipment at your home or office. Figure 1-2 shows a sample connection diagram for typical residential DSL service.

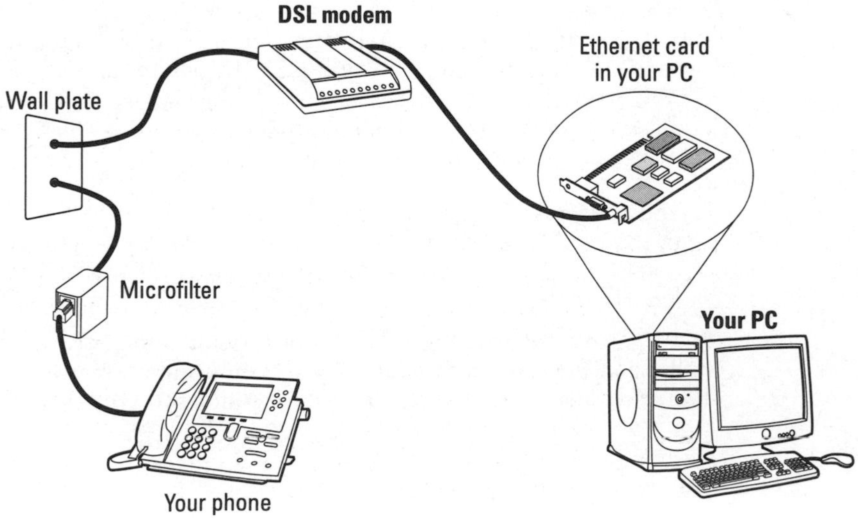

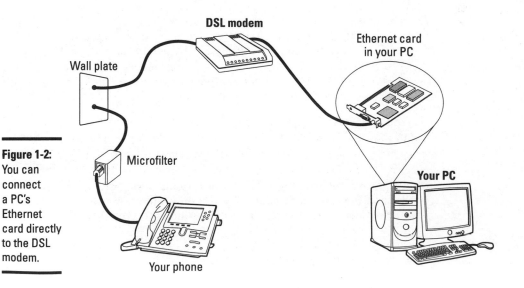

Figure 1-2: You can connect a PC's Ethernet card directly to the DSL modem.

Here are some key points to note in Figure 1-2:

- Connect your DSL modem's data connection to the phone jack on a wall plate.
- Connect the DSL modem's Ethernet connection to the Ethernet card on your PC.
- When you connect other telephones or fax machines on the same phone line, install a *microfilter* between the wall plate and each of these devices.

Because the same phone line carries both voice signals and DSL data, you need the microfilter to protect the DSL data from possible interference. You can buy them at electronics stores or from the DSL provider.

WARNING!

When you connect your Linux PC to the Internet using DSL, the connection is always on, which means a greater potential for outsiders to break into the PC.

TIP

You can protect your Linux system from intruders and, as an added bonus, share the high-speed connection with other PCs in a local area network (LAN) by using a router that can perform Network Address Translation (NAT). Such a *NAT router* translates multiple private Internet Protocol (IP) addresses from an internal LAN into a single public IP address, which allows all the internal PCs to access the Internet. The NAT router acts as a gateway between your LAN and the Internet, and it isolates your LAN from the Internet — this makes it harder for intruders to reach the systems on your LAN.

If you also want to set up a local area network, you need an Ethernet hub to connect the other PCs to the network. Figure 1-3 shows a typical setup that connects a LAN to the Internet through a NAT router and a DSL modem.

Here are the points to note when setting up a connection like the one shown in Figure 1-3:

- You need a NAT router with two 10BaseT Ethernet ports (the 10BaseT port looks like a large phone jack, also known as an *RJ-45 jack*). Typically, one Ethernet port is labeled *Internet* (or *External* or *WAN* for *wide area network*) and the other one is labeled *Local* or *LAN* (for *local area network*).
- You also need an Ethernet hub. For a small home network, you can buy a 4- or 8-port Ethernet hub. Basically, you want a hub with as many ports as the number of PCs you intend to connect to your local area network.
- Connect the Ethernet port of the DSL modem to the Internet port of the NAT router, using a 10BaseT Ethernet cable. (These look like phone wires with bigger RJ-45 jacks and are often labeled *Category 5* or *Cat 5* wire.)
- Connect the Local Ethernet port of the NAT router to one of the ports on the Ethernet hub, using a 10BaseT Ethernet cable.
- Now connect each of the PCs to the Ethernet hub. (Of course, to do so, you must first have an Ethernet card installed and configured in each PC.)

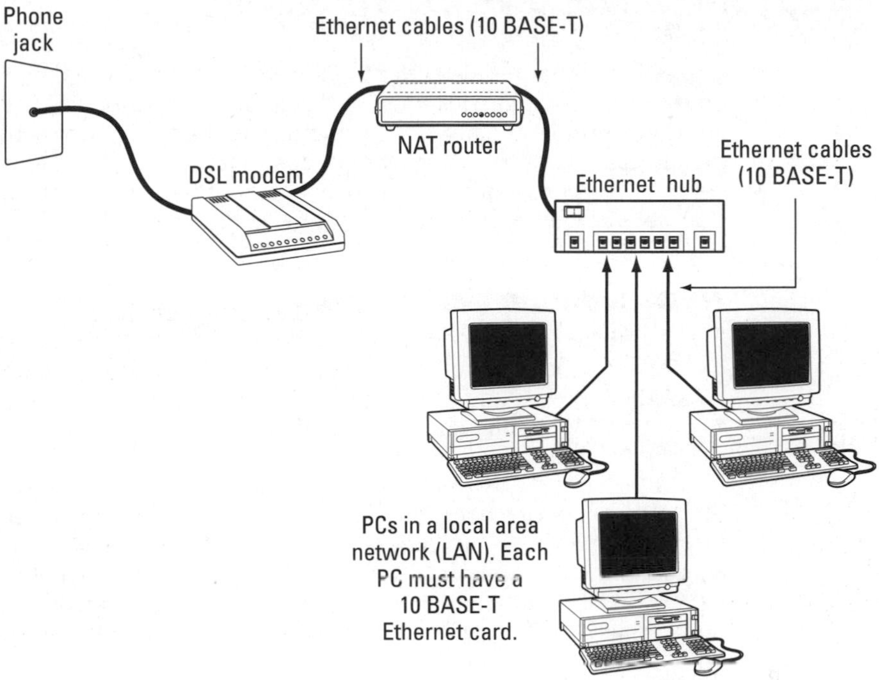

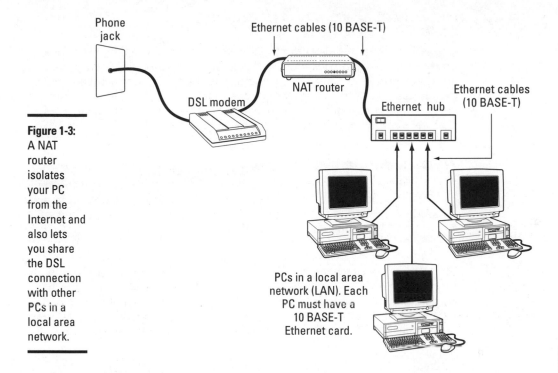

Figure 1-3: A NAT router isolates your PC from the Internet and also lets you share the DSL connection with other PCs in a local area network.

TIP

You can also buy a NAT router with a built-in 4- or 8-port Ethernet hub. With such a combined router-hub, you need only one box to set up a LAN and connect it to the Internet via a DSL modem. These boxes are typically sold under the name Cable/DSL router because they work with both DSL and a cable modem.

Consult Chapter 2 of this minibook for information on how to configure networking on the Linux system so that your system can access the Internet.

REMEMBER

DSL providers typically use a protocol known as PPP over Ethernet (PPPoE) to establish a connection between your PC and the equipment at the provider's central office. PPPoE requires you to provide a username and password to establish the network connection over Ethernet. To set up your system for a PPPoE DSL connection, all you have to do is run a utility program that configures the system for PPPoE. You can find the utility by searching in the Main Menu in the GUI desktop.

DISTRIBUTION SPECIFIC

In Fedora Core, you can set up a PPPoE DSL connection by choosing Main Menu➪System Tools➪Internet Configuration Wizard and clicking *xDSL connection* from the list. Then go through the successive screens and provide the requested information, such as login name and password.

Connecting with a Cable Modem

Cable TV companies also offer high-speed Internet access over the same coaxial cable that carries television signals to your home. After the cable company installs the necessary equipment at its facility to send and receive digital data over the coaxial cables, customers can sign up for cable Internet service. You can then get high-speed Internet access over the same cable that delivers cable TV signals to your home.

How cable modem works

A box called a *cable modem* is at the heart of Internet access over the cable TV network. (See Figure 1-4.) The cable modem takes digital data from your PC's Ethernet card and puts it in an unused block of frequency. (Think of it as another TV channel, but instead of pictures and sound, this channel carries digital data.)

The cable modem places *upstream data* — data that's being sent from your PC to the Internet — in a different channel than the *downstream* data that's coming from the Internet to your PC. By design, the speed of downstream data transfers is much higher than that of upstream transfers. The assumption is that people download far more stuff from the Internet than they upload. (Probably true for most of us.)

The coaxial cable that carries all those hundreds of cable TV channels to your home is a very capable signal carrier. In particular, the coaxial cable can carry signals covering a huge range of frequencies — hundreds of megahertz (MHz). Each TV channel requires 6 MHz — and the coaxial cable can carry hundreds of such channels. The cable modem places the upstream data in a small frequency band and expects to receive the downstream data in a whole other frequency band.

At the other end of your cable connection to the Internet is the *Cable Modem Termination System* (CMTS) — also known as the *head end* — that your cable company installs at its central facility. (Refer to Figure 1-4.) The CMTS connects the cable TV network to the Internet. It also extracts the upstream digital data sent by your cable modem (and by those of your neighbors as well), and sends all of it to the Internet. The CMTS also puts digital data into the upstream channels so that your cable modem can extract that data and provide it to your PC via the Ethernet card.

Cable modems can receive downstream data at the rate of about 30 Mbps and send data upstream at around 3 Mbps. However, all the cable modems in a neighborhood share the same downstream capacity. Each cable modem filters out — separates — the data it needs from the stream of data that the CMTS sends out. Cable modems follow a modem standard called DOCSIS, which stands for Data Over Cable Service Interface. You can buy any DOCSIS-compliant modem and use it with your cable Internet service; all you have to do is call the cable company and give them the modem's identifying information so that the CMTS can recognize and initialize the modem.

REMEMBER

In practice, with a cable modem you can get downstream transfer rates of around 1.5 Mbps and upstream rates of 128 Kbps. These are maximum rates, and your transfer rate is typically lower, depending on how many users in your neighborhood are using cable modems at the same time.

TIP

If you want to check your downstream transfer speed, go to `bandwidthplace.com/speedtest` and click the link to start the test. For my cable modem connection (for example), the tests reported a downstream transfer rate of about 1.4 Mbps.

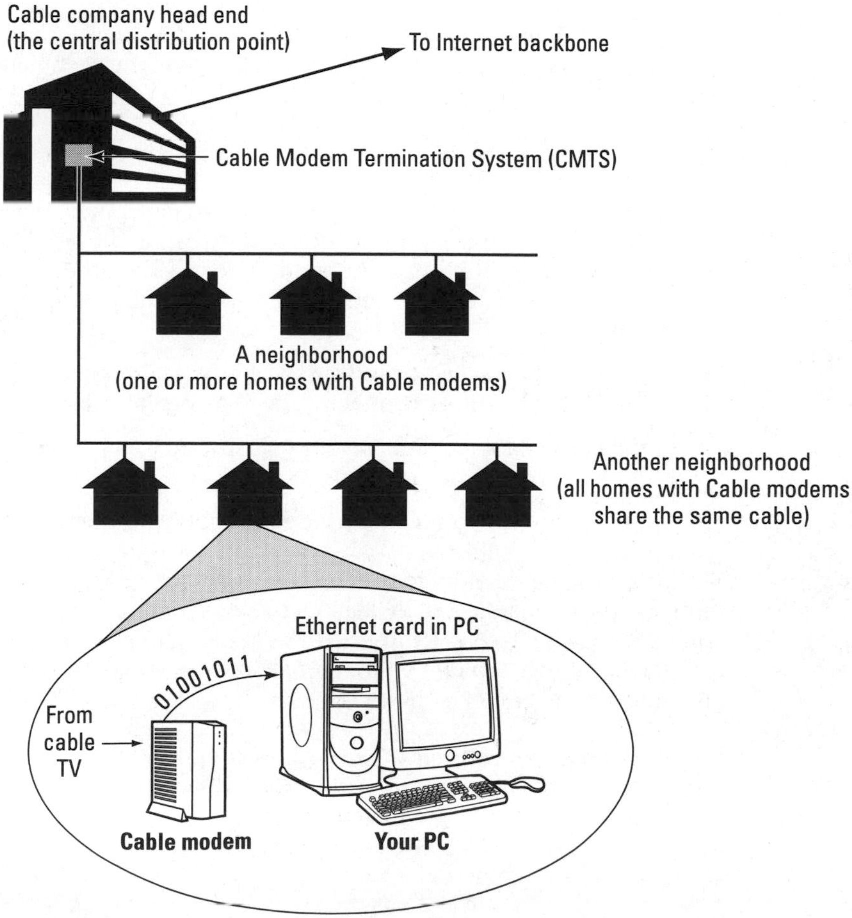

Figure 1-4: Cable modems provide high-speed Internet access over the cable TV network.

Typical cable modem setup

To set up cable modem access, your cable TV provider must offer high-speed Internet access. If the service is available, you can call to sign up. The cable companies often have promotional offers such as no installation fee or a reduced rate for three months. Look for these offers. If you are lucky, a local cable company may have a promotion going on just when you want to sign up.

The installation is typically done by a technician, who splits your incoming cable into two — one side goes to the TV and the other to the cable modem. The technician provides information about the cable modem to the cable company's head end for set up at its end. When all that is done, you can plug in your PC's Ethernet card to the cable modem and you're all set to enjoy high-speed Internet access. Figure 1-5 shows a typical cable-modem hookup.

The cable modem connects to an Ethernet card in your PC. If you don't have an Ethernet card in your PC, the cable company technician often provides one.

Here are some key points to note about the cable modem setup in Figure 1-5:

- Split the incoming cable TV signal into two parts by using a two-way splitter. (The cable company technician installs the splitter.) By the way, the two-way splitter needs to be rated for 1 GHz; otherwise, it may not let the frequencies that contain the downstream data from the Internet pass through.
- Connect one of the video outputs from the splitter to your cable modem's F-type video connector using a coaxial cable.
- Connect the cable modem's 10BaseT Ethernet connection to the Ethernet card on your PC.
- Connect your TV to the other video output from the two-way splitter.

WARNING! When you use cable modem to directly connect your Linux PC to the Internet, the connection is always on, so you have more of a chance that someone may try to break into the PC. Linux includes the `iptables` packet filtering capability, which you may want to use to protect your PC from unwanted Internet connections.

DISTRIBUTION SPECIFIC: In Fedora Core, you can set the firewall setting to High Security. To configure the firewall settings in Fedora Core, choose Main Menu➪System Settings➪Security Level from the GUI desktop.

TIP

To isolate your Linux PC or local area network from the public Internet, you may want to add a NAT router between your PC and the cable modem. One of the NAT router's network interfaces connects to the Internet, and the other connects to your LAN; the router then acts as a gateway between your LAN and the Internet. As an added bonus, you can even share a cable modem connection with all the PCs in your own local area network (LAN) by adding an Ethernet hub. Better yet, buy a combination NAT-router-and-hub so you have only one box do the whole job. By the way, the NAT router/hubs are typically sold under the name *Cable/DSL router* because they work with both DSL and cable modem.

The NAT router translates private IP addresses into a public IP address. When connected through a NAT router, any PC in the internal LAN can access the Internet as if it had its own unique IP address. Result: You can share a single Internet connection among many PCs. (An ideal solution for an entire family of Net surfers!)

Figure 1-6 shows a typical setup with a cable modem connection being shared by a number of PCs in a LAN.

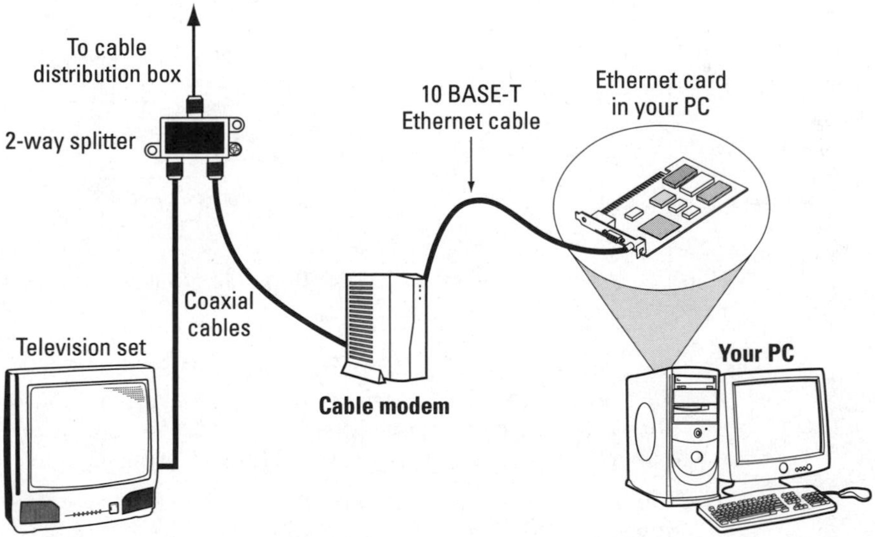

Figure 1-5: The cable TV signal is split between the TV and the cable modem.

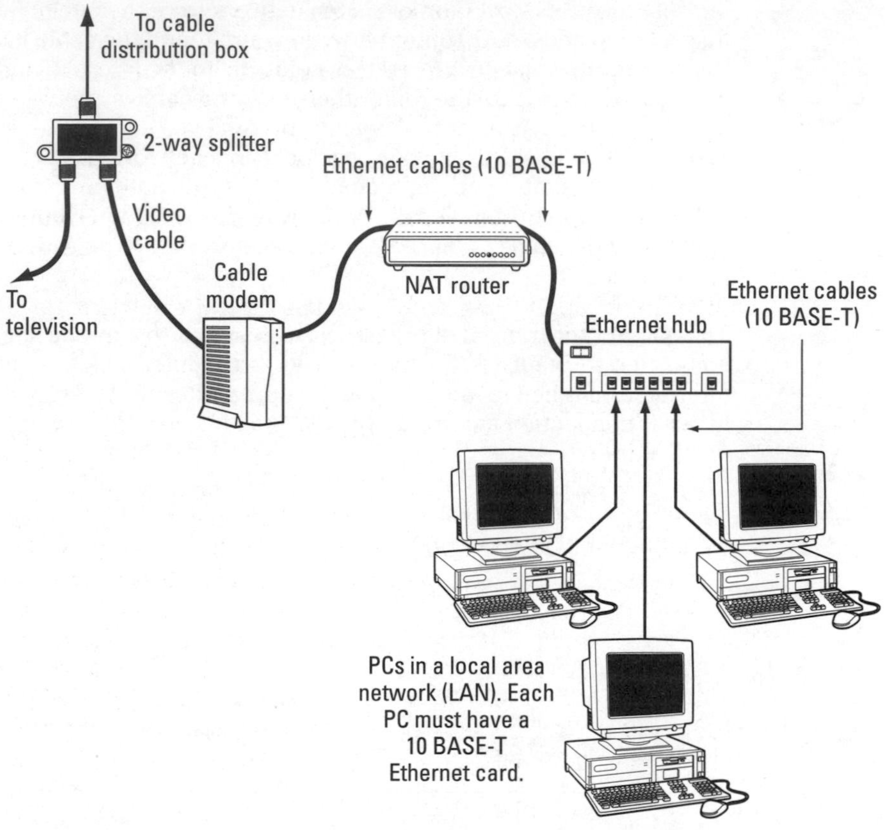

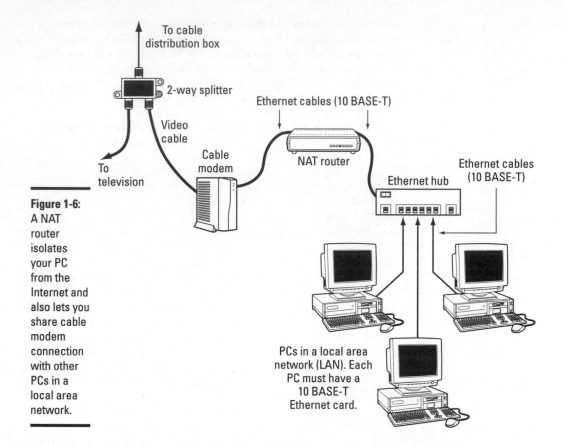

Figure 1-6: A NAT router isolates your PC from the Internet and also lets you share cable modem connection with other PCs in a local area network.

Here are the points to note when setting up a connection like the one shown in Figure 1-6:

✦ You need a Cable/DSL NAT router with two 10BaseT Ethernet ports (the 10BaseT port — also known as an *RJ-45 jack,* which looks like a large phone jack). Typically, one Ethernet port is labeled *Internet* (or *External* or *WAN* for *wide area network*), and the other one is labeled *Local.*

✦ If you plan to set up a LAN, you also need an Ethernet hub. For a small home network, you can buy a 4- or 8-port Ethernet hub. Basically, you want a hub with as many ports as the number of PCs you intend to connect to your local area network.

✦ Consider buying a single box that acts as both a NAT router and a hub with a number of Ethernet ports.

✦ Connect the video cable to the video input port of the cable modem.

- Connect the Ethernet port of the cable modem to the Internet port of the NAT router using a 10BaseT Ethernet cable. (These look like phone wires except that the Ethernet cables have bigger RJ-45 jacks and are often labeled Category 5 or Cat 5 wire.)
- Connect the Local Ethernet port of the NAT router to one of the ports on the Ethernet hub using a 10BaseT Ethernet cable.
- Now connect each of the PCs to the Ethernet hub. Of course, each PC must have an Ethernet card.

In Chapter 2 of this minibook, I explain how to configure the PCs in such a LAN so that they can all access the Internet through the router.

Setting Up Dialup Networking

Dialup networking refers to connecting a PC to a remote network through a dialup modem. If you are ancient enough to remember the days of dialing up with Procomm or some serial communications software, realize that there is a significant difference between dialup networking and the old days of serial communication. Both approaches use a modem to dial up a remote computer and to establish a communication path, but the serial-communication software makes your computer behave like a dumb terminal connected to the remote computer. The serial-communication software exclusively uses dialup connection. You cannot run another copy of the communication software and use the same modem connection, for example.

In dialup networking, both your PC and the remote system run network-protocol (called TCP/IP) software. When your PC dials up and sets up a communication path, the network protocols exchange data packets over that dialup connection. The neat part is that any number of applications can use the same dialup connection to send and receive data packets. So your PC becomes a part of the network to which the remote computer belongs. (If the remote computer is not on a network, dialup networking creates a network that consists of the remote computer and your PC.)

In Chapter 2 of this minibook, I describe TCP/IP protocol some more, but I have to use the term as well as a few concepts such as *Internet Protocol* (IP) address and *Domain Name Service* (DNS) when describing how to set up dialup networking.

Setting up a TCP/IP network over a dialup link involves specifying the protocol — the convention — for packaging a data packet over the communication link. *Point-to-Point Protocol* (PPP) is such a protocol for establishing a TCP/IP connection over any point-to-point link, including dialup phone lines. Linux supports PPP, and it comes with the configuration tools you can use to set up PPP so that your system can establish a PPP connection with your ISP.

Here's what you have to do to set up dialup networking in Linux:

1. Install an internal or external modem in your PC. If your PC did not already come with an internal modem, you can buy an external modem and connect it to the PC's serial or USB port.
2. Connect the modem to the phone line, and power up the modem.
3. Get an account with an ISP. Every ISP provides you a phone number to dial, a username, and a password. Additionally, the ISP gives you the full names of servers for e-mail and news. Typically, your system automatically gets an IP address.
4. Run a GUI tool (if available) to set up a PPP connection. If you cannot find a GUI tool, type **wvdialconf /etc/wvdial.conf** at the shell prompt. The `wvdialconf` program automatically detects the modem and sets up the configuration file `/etc/wvdial.conf`. Now use a text editor to edit the file `/etc/wvdial.conf` and enter the ISP's phone number as well as the username and password of your Internet account with the ISP. (You can guess where to enter these items, just look for the fields labeled Username, Password, and Phone.)
5. Use a GUI tool (if available) to activate the PPP connection to connect to the Internet. If there is no GUI tool, log in as `root` and type **wvdial** to establish the PPP connection.

I briefly go over these steps in the following sections.

Connecting the modem

Modem is a contraction of modulator/demodulator — a device that converts digital signals (strings of 1s and 0s) into continuously varying analog signals that transmit over telephone lines and radio waves. Thus, the modem is the intermediary between the digital world of the PC and the analog world of telephones. Figure 1-7 illustrates the concept of a modem.

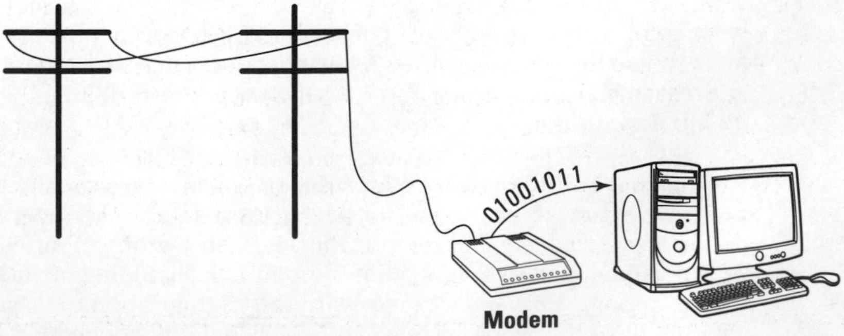

Figure 1-7: A modem bridges the digital world of PCs and the analog world of telephones.

Inside the PC, 1s and 0s are represented with voltage levels, but signals carried over telephone lines are usually tones of different frequencies. The modem sits between the PC and the telephone lines and makes data communication possible over the phone lines. The modem converts information back and forth between the voltage/no voltage representation of digital circuits and different frequency tones that are appropriate for transmission over phone lines.

Before you can dial out using an external modem, you have to make sure that the modem is properly connected to one of the serial or USB ports of your PC.

If you have an external modem, make sure that your modem is properly connected to the power supply and that the modem is connected to the telephone line. Buy the right type of cable to connect the modem to the PC. You need a straight-through serial cable to connect the modem to the PC. The connectors at the ends of the cable depend on the type of serial connector on your PC. The modem end of the cable needs a male 25-pin connector. The PC end of the cable often is a female 9-pin connector. You can buy modem cables at most computer stores. Often, you can find 9-pin-female-to-25-pin-male modem cables sold under the label *AT Modem Cable.* Connect USB modems by using a USB cable.

TIP

If your PC has an internal modem, all you have to do is connect the phone line to the phone jack at the back of the internal modem card. If it's a WinModem, you still connect the phone line, but you also have to do a bit of research on the Internet and download a driver that makes the WinModem

WinModems: They do *only* Windows

A quick word of caution about the *WinModems* that come with many new PCs and laptops. WinModems are software-based internal modems — totally different from the traditional hardware modems. Also known as *Windows modems* or *software modems* (*softmodem* for short), they work only with special driver software (which in turn works only with Microsoft Windows). With WinModems and Linux, you're pretty much on your own — but you can find some useful guidance online at the Linux WinModem Support home page at `www.linmodems.org`. For example, I found out that the WinModem in my laptop uses a Conexant chipset and that a Linux driver is available from `www.linuxant.com/drivers/hsf/full/downloads.php`. I could then download a version appropriate for my distribution — the Web site offered both Debian package (DPKG) and RPM format files. By the way, the free version of the driver from Conexant is limited to 14.4 Kbps only. To go up to 56 Kbps, you have to get the full version for a modest price of around $15 (U.S. dollars). The free version, however, is good for testing to make sure that the driver works with your softmodem. By the way, you can locate Linux drivers for many other WinModems by checking the `www.linmodems.org` Web site.

work in Linux. After you install a working Linux driver for a WinModem, it works just like the older serial port modems. See the sidebar, "WinModems: They *only* do Windows," for more information.

Setting up and activating a PPP connection

Most ISPs provide PPP dialup access to the Internet through one or more systems that the ISP maintains. If you sign up for such a service, the ISP provides you the information that you need to make a PPP connection to the ISP's system. Typically, this information includes the following:

- The phone number to dial to connect to the remote system.
- The username and password that you must use to log in to the remote system.
- The names of the ISP's mail and news servers.
- The IP address for your PPP connection. Your ISP does not provide this address if the IP address is assigned dynamically (which means the IP address may change every time that your system establishes a connection).
- IP addresses of the ISP's *Domain Name Servers* (DNS). The ISP does not provide these addresses if it assigns the IP address dynamically.

Of this information, the first two items are what you need to set up a PPP connection. The exact steps for setting up and using a PPP connection depend on the distribution. For distributions with a GUI Internet connection tool, you can easily figure out where to enter your ISP account information — the phone number, username, and password. I point out distribution-specific approaches for configuring PPP next.

Debian does not have a GUI tool to set up a PPP connection. Instead, you should use the command-line utilities `wvdialconf` and `wvdial`. If `wvdial` is not installed on your system, type **apt-get install wvdial** to install it. Then type **wvdialconf /etc/wvdial.conf** to set up the configuration file. Edit the file to add on appropriate lines — the ISP's phone number and your ISP account's username and password, to be precise. Then you can type **wvdial** to establish a PPP connection.

In Fedora Core, choose Main Menu⇨System Tools⇨Internet Configuration Wizard from the GNOME desktop. Select the Modem Connection option from the first dialog box (see Figure 1-8) and continue with the configuration.

In SUSE, choose Main Menu⇨System⇨YaST to open the YaST control center window. Click Network Devices on the left-hand side of the window and then click Modem on the right-hand side. (See Figure 1-9.) YaST detects the modem and displays a window with information about the modem. You can then configure the detected modem for a PPP connection. You can either select your ISP from a list or enter the ISP's name as well as an access phone number and the ISP account's username and password.

After you set up the modem in SUSE, the KInternet tool should start and a plug icon should appear in the panel, as shown in Figure 1-10. You can then click the KInternet tool's icon to activate the PPP connection. If the connection does not seem to come up, right-click the KInternet icon, select View Log, and look for clues about any problems.

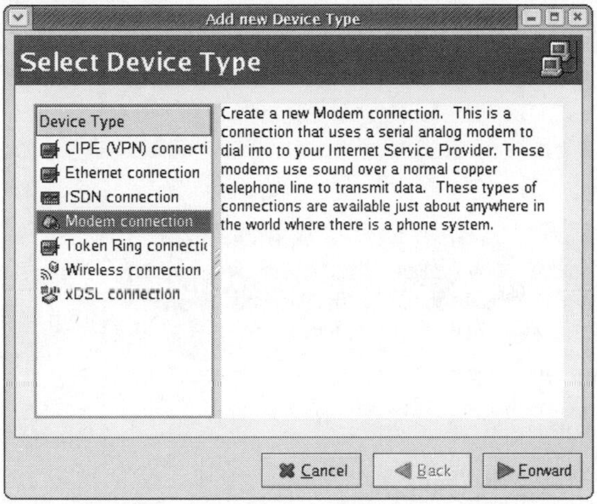

Figure 1-8: In Fedora Core, configure the PPP connection from this dialog box.

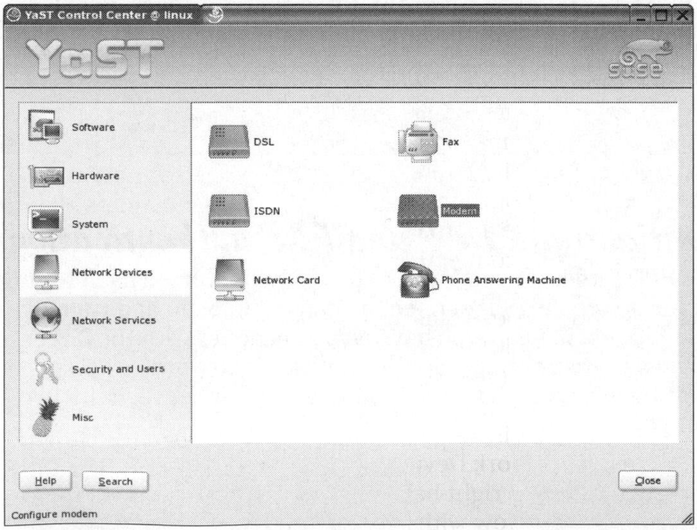

Figure 1-9: In SUSE, configure the modem from YaST.

In Xandros, select Main Menu➪Applications➪Internet➪Connection Wizard. The Connection Wizard dialog box appears (see Figure 1-11). Select the Dialup Modem (PPP) option in the dialog box and then continue with the PPP setup process.

Figure 1-10: In SUSE, click the KInternet tool to activate a PPP connection.

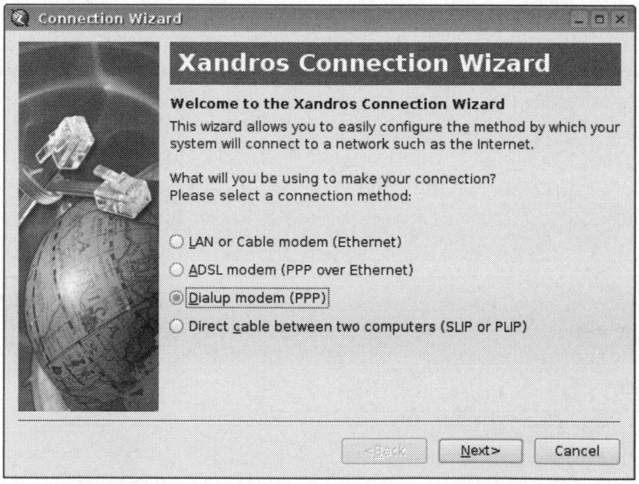

Figure 1-11: In Xandros, configure the dialup PPP connection from this dialog box.

Configuring CHAP and PAP authentication

The PPP server on your system has to authenticate itself to the ISP's PPP server before the PPP connection can get fully up and running. *Authentication* requires proving that you have a valid account with the ISP, essentially providing a username and a *secret* (that is, a password). PPP specifies two ways of exchanging the authentication information between the two ends of the connection:

✦ **Challenge Handshake Authentication Protocol (CHAP)** requires the remote end to send a randomly generated challenge string along with the remote server's name. The local system looks up the secret, using the server's name; then it sends back a response that includes its name and a value that combines the secret and the challenge, using a one-way hash function. The remote system then checks that value against its own calculation of the expected hash value. If the values match, the authentication succeeds; otherwise, the remote system terminates the connection. In this case, the name and secret are stored in the `/etc/ppp/chap-secrets` file. Note that the remote system can repeat the CHAP authentication any time while the PPP link is up.

✦ **Password Authentication Protocol (PAP)** is like the normal login process. When using PAP, the local system repeatedly sends a username (name) and password (secret) until the remote system acknowledges the authentication or ends the connection. The name and secret are stored in the `/etc/ppp/pap-secrets` file. Note that the username and password are sent in the clear (that is, unencrypted).

The Linux PPP server supports both types of authentication. For both PAP and CHAP, the information that the PPP server needs is a name and a secret — a username-password pair. This authentication information is stored in the following configuration files:

✦ `/etc/ppp/chap-secrets` stores the information for CHAP. Here's what a typical `chap-secrets` file looks like:

```
# Secrets for authentication using CHAP
# client     server     secret          IP addresses
"naba"         *       "mypassword"
```

✦ `/etc/ppp/pap-secrets` stores the information for PAP. Here's a typical `pap-secrets` file:

```
# Secrets for authentication using PAP
# client     server     secret          IP addresses
"naba"         *       "mypassword"
```

As you can see, the formats of the entries are the same for both `chap-secrets` and `pap-secrets`. Four fields are in each line, in the following order:

✦ `client`: This field contains the name that is used during authentication. You get this name from the ISP.

✦ `server`: This field contains the name of the remote system to which you are authenticating the local system. If you don't know the server's name, put an asterisk to indicate any server.

- `secret`: This field is the secret that your system's PPP server has to send to the remote system to authenticate itself. You receive this password from the ISP.
- `IP addresses`: This optional field can contain a list of the IP addresses that the local system may use when connecting to the specified server. Typically, this field is left blank because the local system usually gets a dynamic IP address from the server and (therefore) doesn't know what IP address it uses.

Chapter 2: Setting Up a Local Area Network

In This Chapter

- **Understanding TCP/IP networks**
- **Setting up an Ethernet LAN**
- **Configuring TCP/IP networking**
- **Connecting your LAN to the Internet**

Linux comes with built-in support for Transmission Control Protocol/Internet Protocol (TCP/IP) networking, as do most modern operating systems from Windows to Mac OS. You can have TCP/IP networking over many different physical interfaces, such as Ethernet cards, serial ports, and parallel ports.

Typically, you use an Ethernet network for your local area network (LAN) — at your office or even your home (if you happen to have several systems at home). To connect to remote systems over a modem, you use TCP/IP networking over Point-to-Point Protocol (PPP).

This chapter describes how to set up an Ethernet network. Even if you have a single PC, you may need to set up an Ethernet network interface so that you can connect your PC to high-speed Internet access that uses a DSL or cable modem. (I cover DSL and cable modems in Chapter 1 of this minibook.)

Understanding TCP/IP

You can understand TCP/IP networking best if you think in terms of a layered model with four layers. Think of each layer as responsible for performing a particular task. The layered model describes the flow of data between the physical connection to the network and the end-user application. Figure 2-1 shows the four-layer network model for TCP/IP.

In this four-layer model, information always moves from one layer to the next. For example, when an application sends data to another application, the data goes through the layers in this order: Application⇨Transport⇨Network⇨Physical. At the receiving end, the data goes up from Physical⇨Network⇨Transport⇨Application.

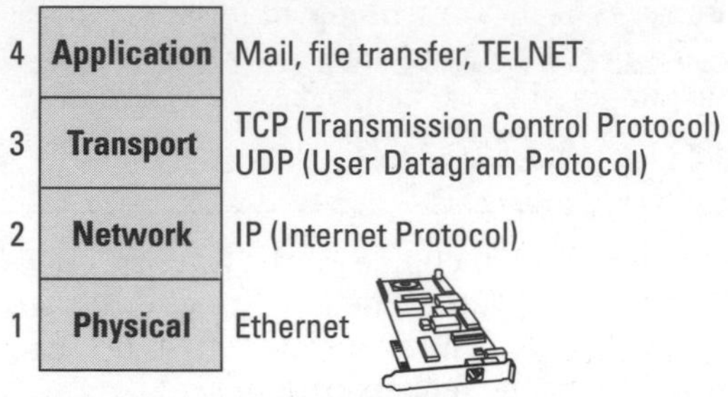

Figure 2-1: You can understand TCP/IP using the four-layer network model.

Each layer has its own set of *protocols* — conventions — for handling and formatting the data. If you think of sending data as something akin to sending letters through the postal service, a typical protocol is a preferred sequence of actions for a task such as addressing an envelope (first the name, then the street address, and then city, state, and ZIP or other postal code).

Here's what each of the four layers does, top to bottom:

- **Application:** Runs the applications that users use, such as e-mail readers, file transfers, and Web browsers. Application-level protocols are Simple Mail Transfer Protocol (SMTP) and Post Office Protocol (POP) for e-mail; HyperText Transfer Protocol (HTTP) for the Web; and File Transfer Protocol (FTP) for file transfers. Application-level protocols also have a *port number* that you can think of as an identifier for a specific application. For example, port 80 is associated with HTTP or the Web server.
- **Transport:** Sends data from one application to another. The two most important protocols in this layer are Transmission Control Protocol (TCP) and User Datagram Protocol (UDP). TCP guarantees delivery of data; UDP just sends the data without ensuring that it actually reaches the destination.
- **Network:** This layer is responsible for getting data packets from one *network* to another. If the networks are far apart, the data packets are routed from one network to the next until they reach their destination. The primary protocol in this layer is the Internet Protocol (IP).
- **Physical:** Refers to the physical networking hardware (such as an Ethernet card or token ring card) that carries the data packets in a network.

The beauty of the layered model is that each layer takes care of only its specific task, leaving the rest to the other layers. The layers can mix and match — you can have TCP/IP network over any type of physical network medium, from Ethernet to radio waves (in a wireless network). The software is modular as well because each layer can be implemented in different modules. For example, typically the Transport and Network layers already exist as part of the operating system, and any application can make use of these layers.

TCP/IP and the Internet

TCP/IP has become the protocol of choice on the Internet — *the* "network of networks" that evolved from ARPAnet. The U.S. Government's Advanced Research Projects Agency (ARPA) initiated research in the 1970s on a new way of sending information, using packets of data sent over a network. The result was ARPAnet: a national network of linked computers. Subsequently, ARPA acquired a Defense prefix and became DARPA. Under the auspices of DARPA, the TCP/IP protocols emerged as a popular collection of protocols for *internetworking* — communication among networks.

TCP/IP has flourished because the protocol is open. That means the technical descriptions of the protocol appear in public documents, so anyone can implement TCP/IP on specific hardware and software.

TCP/IP also made great inroads because stable, working software was available. Instead of a paper description of network architecture and protocols, the TCP/IP protocols *started out* as working software — and who can argue with what's already working? These days (as a result), TCP/IP rules the Internet.

Next-generation IP (IPv6)

When the 4-byte IP address was created, the number of available addresses seemed adequate. Now, however, the 4-byte addresses are running out. The Internet Engineering Task Force (IETF) recognized the potential for running out of IP addresses in 1991 and began work on the next-generation IP addressing scheme. They called it IPng (for Internet Protocol Next Generation) and intended that it will eventually replace the old 4-byte addressing scheme (called IPv4, for IP Version 4).

Several alternative addressing schemes for IPng were proposed and debated. The final contender, with a 128-bit (16-byte) address, was dubbed IPv6 (for IP Version 6). On September 18, 1995, the IETF declared the core set of IPv6 addressing protocols to be an IETF Proposed Standard.

IPv6 is designed to be an evolutionary step from IPv4. The proposed standard provides direct interoperability between hosts using the older IPv4 addresses and any new IPv6 hosts. The idea is that users can upgrade their systems to use IPv6 when they want and that network operators are free to upgrade their network hardware to use IPv6 without affecting current users of IPv4. Sample implementations of IPv6 are being developed for many operating systems, including Linux. For more information about IPv6 in Linux, consult the Linux IPv6 FAQ/HOWTO at `www.linuxhq.com/IPv6/`.

The IPv6 128-bit addressing scheme allows for 340,282,366,920,938,463,463,374,607,431,768,211,456 unique hosts! That should last us for a while!

IP addresses

When you have many computers on a network, you need a way to identify each one uniquely. In TCP/IP networking, the address of a computer is the IP address. Because TCP/IP deals with internetworking, the address is based on the concepts of a network address and a host address. You may think of the idea of a network address and a host address as having to provide two addresses to identify a computer uniquely:

- **Network address** indicates the network on which the computer is located.
- **Host address** indicates a specific computer on that network.

The network and host addresses together constitute an *IP address,* and it's a 4-byte (32-bit) value. The convention is to write each byte as a decimal value and to put a dot (.) after each number. Thus, you see network addresses such as 132.250.112.52. This way of writing IP addresses is known as *dotted-decimal* or *dotted-quad* notation.

In decimal notation, a byte (which has 8 bits) can have a value between 0 and 255. Thus, a valid IP address can use only the numbers between 0 and 255 in the dotted-decimal notation.

Internet services and port numbers

The TCP/IP protocol suite has become the *lingua franca* of the Internet because many standard services are available on any system that supports TCP/IP. These services make the Internet tick by facilitating the transfer of mail, news, and Web pages. These services go by well-known names such as the following:

- **DHCP** (Dynamic Host Configuration Protocol) is for dynamically configuring TCP/IP network parameters on a computer. DHCP is primarily used to assign dynamic IP addresses and other networking information (such as name server, default gateway, and domain names) needed to configure TCP/IP networks. The DHCP server listens on port 67.
- **FTP** (File Transfer Protocol) is used to transfer files between computers on the Internet. FTP uses two ports — data is transferred on port 20, and control information is exchanged on port 21.
- **HTTP** (HyperText Transfer Protocol) is a protocol for sending documents from one system to another. HTTP is the underlying protocol of the Web. By default, the Web server and client communicate on port 80.
- **SMTP** (Simple Mail Transfer Protocol) is for exchanging e-mail messages between systems. SMTP uses port 25 for information exchange.
- **NNTP** (Network News Transfer Protocol) is for distribution of news articles in a store-and-forward fashion across the Internet. NNTP uses port 119.

- **SSH** (Secure Shell) is a protocol for secure remote login and other secure network services over an insecure network. SSH uses port 22.
- **TELNET** is used when a user on one system logs in to another system on the Internet. (The user must provide a valid user ID and password to log in to the remote system.) TELNET uses port 23 by default, but the TELNET client can connect to any port.
- **SNMP** (Simple Network Management Protocol) is for managing all types of network devices on the Internet. Like FTP, SNMP uses two ports: 161 and 162.
- **TFTP** (Trivial File Transfer Protocol) is for transferring files from one system to another (typically used by X terminals and diskless workstations to download boot files from another host on the network). TFTP data transfer takes place on port 69.
- **NFS** (Network File System) is for sharing files among computers. NFS uses Sun's Remote Procedure Call (RPC) facility, which exchanges information through port 111.

A well-known port is associated with each of these services. The TCP protocol uses each such port to locate a service on any system. (A *server process* — a special computer program running on a system — provides each service.)

Setting Up an Ethernet LAN

Ethernet is a standard way to move packets of data between two or more computers connected to a single hub. (You can create larger networks by connecting multiple Ethernet segments with gateways.) To set up an Ethernet local area network (LAN), you need an Ethernet card for each PC. Linux supports a wide variety of Ethernet cards for the PC.

Ethernet is a good choice for the physical data-transport mechanism for the following reasons:

- Ethernet is a proven technology that has been in use since the early 1980s.
- Ethernet provides good data-transfer rates: Typically 10 million bits per second (10 Mbps), although 100-Mbps Ethernet and Gigabit Ethernet (1,000 Mbps) are now available.
- Ethernet hardware is often built into the PC or can be installed at a relatively low cost. (PC Ethernet cards cost about $10–$20 U.S.)
- With wireless Ethernet, you can easily connect laptop PCs to your Ethernet LAN without having to run wires all over the place. (Go to Chapter 3 of this minibook for more information on wireless Ethernet.)

How Ethernet works

So what makes Ethernet tick? In essence, it's the same thing that makes playground recess work: taking turns.

In an Ethernet network, all systems in a segment are connected to the same wire. Because a single wire is used, a protocol is used for sending and receiving data because only one data packet can exist on the cable at any time. An Ethernet LAN uses a data-transmission protocol known as *Carrier-Sense Multiple Access/Collision Detection* (CSMA/CD) to share the single transmission cable among all the computers. Ethernet cards in the computers follow the CSMA/CD protocol to transmit and receive Ethernet packets.

The idea behind the CSMA/CD protocol is similar to the way in which you have a conversation at a party. You listen for a pause (that's sensing the carrier) and talk when no one else is speaking. If you and another person begin talking at the same time, both of you realize the problem (that's collision detection) and pause for a moment; then one of you starts speaking again. As you know from experience, everything works out.

In an Ethernet LAN, each Ethernet card checks the cable for signals — that's the carrier-sense part. If the signal level is low, the Ethernet card sends its packets on the cable; the packet contains information about the sender and the intended recipient. All Ethernet cards on the LAN listen to the signal, and the recipient receives the packet. If two cards send out a packet simultaneously, the signal level in the cable rises above a threshold, and the cards know a collision has occurred. (Two packets have been sent out at the same time.) Both cards wait for a random amount of time before sending their packets again.

Ethernet was invented in the early 1970s at the Xerox Palo Alto Research Center (PARC) by Robert M. Metcalfe. In the 1980s, Ethernet was standardized by the cooperative effort of three companies: Digital Equipment Corporation (DEC), Intel, and Xerox. Using the first initials of the company names, that Ethernet standard became known as the DIX standard. Later, the DIX standard was included in the 802-series standards developed by the Institute of Electrical and Electronics Engineers (IEEE). The final Ethernet specification is formally known as IEEE 802.3 CSMA/CD, but people continue to call it *Ethernet.*

Ethernet sends data in *packets* (discrete chunks also known as *frames*). You don't have to hassle much with the innards of Ethernet packets, except to note the 6-byte source and destination addresses. Each Ethernet controller has a unique 6-byte (48-bit) address at the Physical layer; every packet must have one.

Ethernet cables

Any time you hear experts talking about Ethernet, you're also going to hear some bewildering terms used for the cables that carry the data. Here's a quick rundown.

The original Ethernet standard used a thick coaxial cable, nearly half an inch in diameter. This wiring is called *thickwire* or *thick Ethernet* although the IEEE 802.3 standard calls it 10Base5. That designation means several things: The data-transmission rate is 10 megabits per second (10 Mbps); the transmission is *baseband* (which simply means that the cable's signal-carrying capacity is devoted to transmitting Ethernet packets only), and the total length of the cable can be no more than 500 meters. Thickwire was expensive, and the cable was rather unwieldy. Unless you're a technology history buff, you don't have to care one whit about 10Base5 cables.

Nowadays, two other forms of Ethernet cabling are more popular. The first alternative to thick Ethernet cable is *thinwire,* or 10Base2, which uses a thin, flexible coaxial cable. A thinwire Ethernet segment can be, at most, 185 meters long. The other, more recent, alternative is Ethernet over unshielded twisted-pair cable (UTP), known as 10BaseT. The Electronic Industries Association/Telecommunications Industries Association (EIA/TIA) defines the following five categories of shielded and unshielded twisted-pair cables:

- **Category 1 (Cat 1):** Traditional telephone cable.
- **Category 2 (Cat 2):** Cable certified for data transmissions up to 4 Mbps.
- **Category 3 (Cat 3):** Cable that can carry signals up to a frequency of 16 MHz. Cat 3 is the most common type of wiring in old corporate networks and it normally contains four pairs of wire.
- **Category 4 (Cat 4):** Cable that can carry signals up to a frequency of 20 MHz. Cat 4 wires are not that common.
- **Category 5 (Cat 5):** Cable that can carry signals up to a frequency of 100 MHz. Cat 5 cables normally have four pairs of copper wire. Cat 5 UTP is the most popular cable used in new installations today.

To set up a 10BaseT Ethernet network, you need an Ethernet hub — a hardware box with RJ-45 jacks. (These look like big telephone jacks.) You build the network by running twisted-pair wires (usually, Category 5, or Cat5, cables) from each PC's Ethernet card to this hub. You can get a 4-port 10BaseT hub for about $20 U.S. Figure 2-2 shows a typical small 10BaseT Ethernet LAN that you may set up at a small office or your home.

When you install any of the Linux distributions from this book's companion DVD-ROM on a PC connected with an Ethernet card, the Linux kernel automatically detects the Ethernet card and installs the appropriate drivers. The installer also lets you set up TCP/IP networking.

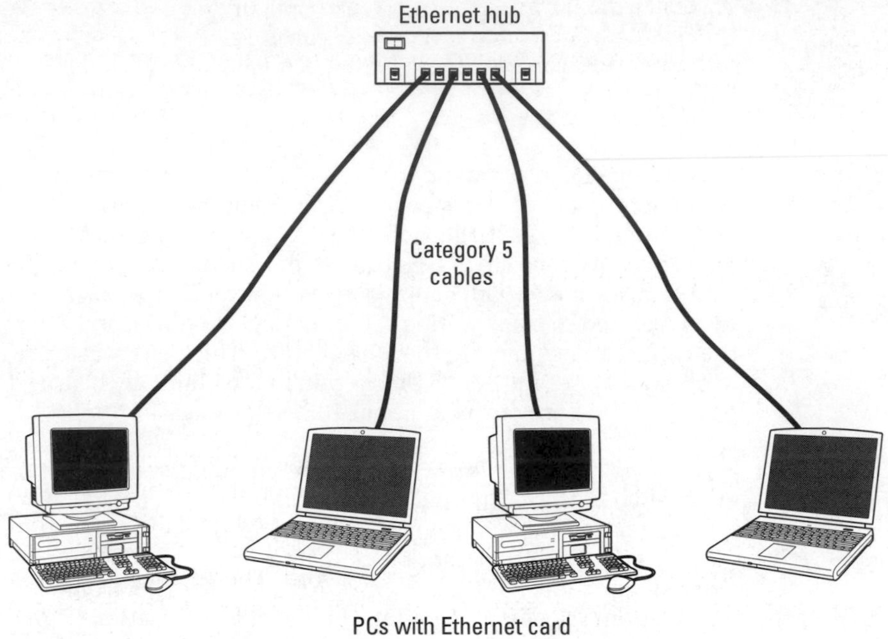

Figure 2-2: You can use an Ethernet hub to set up a 10BaseT Ethernet LAN.

TIP

The Linux kernel loads the driver for the Ethernet card every time it boots. To verify that the Ethernet driver is loaded, type the following command in a terminal window:

```
dmesg | grep eth0
```

On one of my PCs, I get the following output when I type that command:

```
eth0: RealTek RTL8139 at 0xd016c000, 00:0c:76:f4:38:b3, IRQ 11
eth0:  Identified 8139 chip type 'RTL-8101'
eth0: link up, 100Mbps, full-duplex, lpa 0x45E1
eth0: no IPv6 routers present
```

You should see something similar, showing the name of your Ethernet card and other related information.

Configuring TCP/IP Networking

When you set up TCP/IP networking during Linux installation, the installation program prepares all appropriate configuration files using the information you provide. This means that you typically never have to manually configure the network. However, most Linux distributions come with GUI tools to configure the network devices, just in case something needs changing.

In Debian, the network interfaces are configured in the text file `/etc/network/interfaces`. For example, here is a typical `/etc/network/interfaces` file with a network card configured using DHCP:

```
# The loopback network interface
auto lo
iface lo inet loopback

# The primary network interface
auto eth0
iface eth0 inet dhcp
```

Then you can activate the network interfaces by logging in as `root` and typing **ifup eth0**. To deactivate the Ethernet connection, type **ifdown eth0**. A bit cryptic, but not that hard.

Fedora Core comes with the graphical network configuration tool that you can use to add a new network interface or alter information such as name servers and host names. To start the GUI network configuration tool, choose Main Menu⇨System Settings⇨Network. If you are not logged in as `root`, you're prompted for the `root` password. The network configuration tool displays a tabbed dialog box, as shown in Figure 2-3. You can then configure your network through the four tabs that appear along the top of the dialog box. After configuring the network card, you can select the device and click the Activate button to turn the Ethernet on.

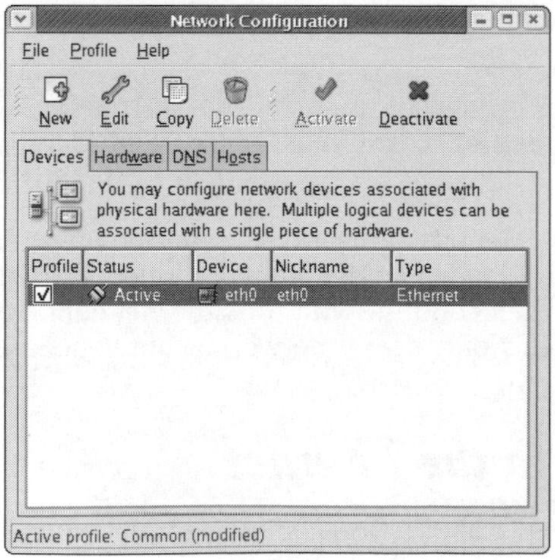

Figure 2-3: In Fedora Core, configure the Ethernet network with this network configuration tool.

In most cases, you can set the network card so that it can automatically obtain an IP address (which is the case when the Ethernet card is connected to DSL or cable modem) by using the DHCP. If your network does not have a DHCP server (which is typically built into routers), you have to specify an IP address for the network card. If you are running a private network, you may use IP addresses in the 192.168.0.0 to 192.168.255.255 range. (Other ranges of addresses are reserved for private networks, but this range suffices for most needs.)

In SUSE, choose Main Menu⇨System⇨YaST to open the YaST Control Center. Then select Network Devices on the left-hand side of the window and Network card on the right-hand side. YaST then brings up a window (as shown in Figure 2-4) with information about the already configured network card and any new network cards that it detects. You can then configure any new network card.

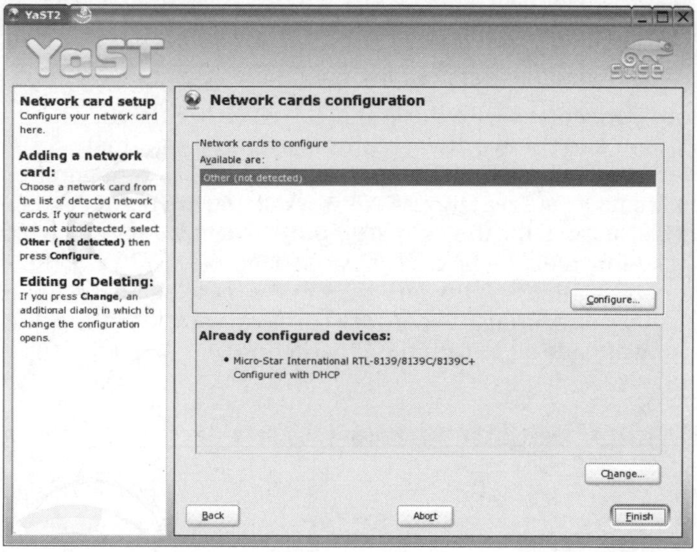

Figure 2-4: In SUSE, configure the Ethernet network with YaST.

In Xandros, choose Main Menu⇨Applications⇨Internet⇨Connection Wizard. In the Connection Wizard dialog box that appears, select LAN or Cable Modem (Ethernet) and then continue with the Ethernet configuration. Of course, you need to do this only if your network is not yet configured.

Connecting Your LAN to the Internet

If you have a LAN with several PCs, you can connect the entire LAN to the Internet by using DSL or cable modem. Basically, you can share the high-speed DSL or cable modem connection with all the PCs in the LAN.

In Chapter 1 of this minibook, I explain how to set up a DSL or cable modem. In this section, I briefly explain how to connect a LAN to the Internet so that all the PCs can access the Internet.

The most convenient way to connect a LAN to the Internet via DSL or cable modem is to buy a hardware device called DSL/Cable Modem NAT Router with a 4- or 8-port Ethernet hub. NAT stands for *Network Address Translation,* and the NAT router can translate many private IP addresses into a single externally known IP address. The Ethernet hub part appears to you as a number of RJ-45 Ethernet ports where you can connect the PCs to set up a LAN. In other words, you need only one extra box besides the DSL or cable modem.

Figure 2-5 shows how you might connect your LAN to the Internet through a NAT router with a built-in Ethernet hub. Of course, you need a DSL or cable modem hookup for this scenario to work (and you have to sign up with the phone company for DSL service or with the cable provider for cable Internet service).

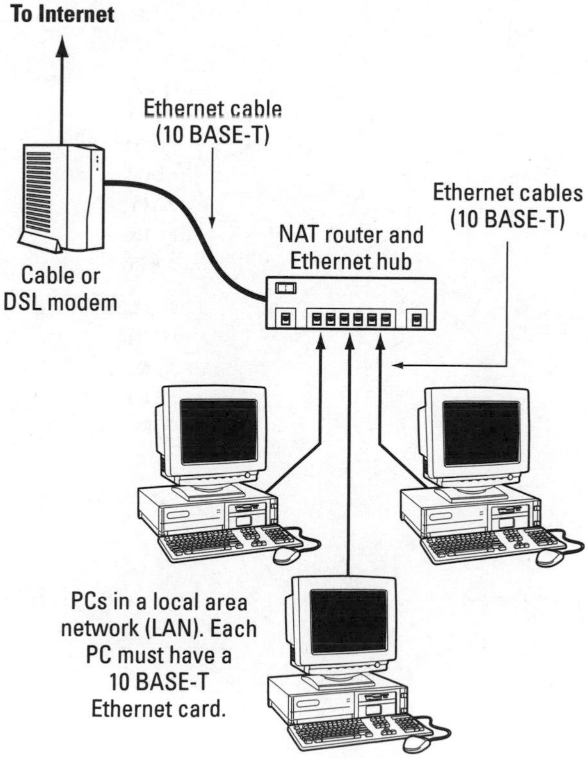

Figure 2-5: Connect your LAN to the Internet through a NAT router with a built-in Ethernet hub.

When you connect a LAN to the Internet, the NAT router acts as a gateway for your LAN. The NAT router also dynamically provides IP addresses to the PCs in your LAN. Therefore, on each PC, you have to set up the networking options to obtain the IP address dynamically.

Your LAN can mix and match all kinds of computers: Some may be running Linux, and some may be running Microsoft Windows or any other operating system that supports TCP/IP. When configuring the network settings, remember to select the option that enables Linux to automatically obtain IP address settings and DNS information with DHCP.

Chapter 3: Adding a Wireless Ethernet LAN

In This Chapter

- **Understanding wireless Ethernet networks**
- **Setting up the wireless hardware**
- **Configuring the wireless network**

If you have laptop computers on your LAN — or if you don't want to run a rat's nest of wires to connect a PC to the LAN — you have the option of using a wireless Ethernet network. In a typical scenario, you have a cable modem or DSL connection to the Internet, and you want to connect one or more laptops with wireless network cards to access the Internet through the cable or DSL modem. This chapter shows you how to set up wireless networking for connecting to an Ethernet LAN and accessing the Internet.

Understanding Wireless Ethernet Networks

You've probably heard about Wi-Fi. Wi-Fi stands for *Wireless Fidelity* network — a short-range wireless network similar to the wired Ethernet networks. A number of standards from an organization known as IEEE (the Institute of Electrical and Electronics Engineers) defines the technical details of how Wi-Fi networks work. Manufacturers use these standards to build the components that you can buy to set up a wireless network, also known as WLAN for short.

Until mid-2003, two popular IEEE standards — 802.11a and 802.11b — were for wireless Ethernet networks. These two standards were finalized in 1999. A third standard — 802.11g — was finalized by the IEEE in the summer of 2003. All these standards specify how the wireless Ethernet network works at the Physical layer. You don't have to fret all the details of all those standards to set up a wireless network, but knowing some pertinent details is good so that you can buy the right kind of equipment for your wireless network.

The three wireless Ethernet standards have the following key characteristics:

- **802.11b:** Operates in the 2.4 GHz radio band (2.4 GHz to 2.4835 GHz) in up to three non-overlapping frequency bands or channels. Supports a maximum bit rate of 11 Mbps per channel. One disadvantage of 802.11b is that the 2.4 GHz frequency band is crowded — many devices (such as microwave ovens, cordless phones, medical and scientific equipment, as well as Bluetooth devices), all work within the 2.4 GHz frequency band. Nevertheless, 802.11b is very popular in corporate and home networks.

- **802.11a:** Operates in the 5 GHz radio band (5.725 GHz to 5.850 GHz) in up to eight non-overlapping channels. Supports a maximum bit rate of 54 Mbps per channel. The 5 GHz band is not as crowded as the 2.4 GHz band, but the 5 GHz band is not approved for use in Europe. Products conforming to 802.11a standard are available on the market, and wireless access points are designed to handle both 802.11a and 802.11b connections.
- **802.11g:** Supports up to 54 Mbps data rate in the 2.4 GHz band. (The same band that 802.11b uses.) 802.11g achieves the higher bit rate by using a technology called *OFDM* (orthogonal frequency-division multiplexing), which is also used by 802.11a. Although 802.11g was only recently finalized, equipment that complies with it is already on the market. That's because 802.11.g has generated excitement by working in the same band as 802.11b but promising much higher data rates and by being backward-compatible with 802.11b devices. Vendors currently offer access points that can support both the 802.11b and 802.11g connection standards.

TIP

If you are buying a new wireless access point, get an 802.11g one. An 802.11g access point can also communicate with older (and slower) 802.11b devices.

The maximum data throughput that a user actually sees is much less because all users of that radio channel share the capacity of the channel. Also, the data transfer rate decreases as the distance between the user's PC and the wireless access point increases.

REMEMBER

To find out more about wireless Ethernet, visit `www.wi-fi.org`, the home page of the Wi-Fi Alliance, which is the nonprofit international association formed in 1999 to certify interoperability of wireless LAN products based on IEEE 802.11 standards.

Understanding infrastructure and ad hoc modes

The 802.11 standard defines two modes of operation for wireless Ethernet networks: infrastructure and ad hoc. *Ad hoc mode* is simply two or more wireless Ethernet cards communicating with each other without an access point.

Infrastructure mode refers to the approach in which all the wireless Ethernet cards communicate with each other and with the wired LAN through an access point. For the discussions in this chapter, I assume that you set your wireless Ethernet card to infrastructure mode. In the configuration files, this mode is referred to as *Managed mode.*

Understanding Wired Equivalent Privacy (WEP)

The 802.11 standard includes Wired Equivalent Privacy (WEP) for protecting wireless communications from eavesdropping. WEP relies on a 40-bit or 104-bit secret key that is shared between a *mobile station* (such as a laptop with a wireless Ethernet card) and an *access point* (also called a *base station*). The secret key is used to encrypt data packets before they transmit and an integrity check performs to ensure that packets are not modified in transit. The 802.11 standard does not explain how the shared key is established. In practice, most wireless LANs use a single key that is shared between all mobile stations and access points. Such an approach, however, does not scale up very well to an environment such as a college campus because the keys are shared with all users — and you know how it is if you share a "secret" with hundreds of people. That's why WEP is typically not used on large wireless networks such as the ones at universities. In such wireless networks, you have to use other security approaches such as SSH (Secure Shell) to log in to remote systems. WEP, however, is good to use on your home wireless network.

WEP has its weaknesses, but it's better than nothing. You can use it in smaller wireless LANs where sharing the same key among all wireless stations is not an onerous task.

Work is underway to provide better security than WEP for wireless networks. The soon-to-be-finalized 802.11i standard uses public key encryption with digital certificates — along with an authentication, authorization, and accounting done on a RADIUS (Remote Authentication Dial-In User Service) server — to provide better security for wireless Ethernet networks.

While the 802.11i standard is in progress, the Wi-Fi Alliance — a multivendor consortium that supports Wi-Fi — has developed an interim specification called Wi-Fi Protected Access (WPA) that's a precursor to 802.11i. WPA replaces the existing WEP standard and improves security by making some changes. For example, unlike WEP (which uses fixed keys), the WPA standard uses Temporal Key-Integrity Protocol (TKIP), which generates new keys for every 10K of data transmitted over the network. TKIP makes WPA more difficult to break. You may want to consider wireless products that support WPA while waiting for products that implement 802.11i.

Setting Up the Wireless Hardware

To set up the wireless connection, you need a wireless access point and a wireless network card in each PC. You can also set up an ad hoc wireless network among two or more PCs with wireless network cards, but that is a standalone wireless LAN among those PCs only. In this section, I focus on the scenario in which you want to set up a wireless connection to an established LAN that has a wired Internet connection through a cable modem or DSL.

Is the WEP stream cipher good enough?

WEP uses the RC4 encryption algorithm, which is known as a *stream cipher.* Such an algorithm works by taking a short secret key and generating an infinite stream of *pseudorandom bits.* Before sending the data, the sending station performs an *exclusive-OR operation* between the pseudorandom bits and the bits representing the data packet, which results in a 1 when two bits are different and 0 if they are the same. The receiver has a copy of the same secret key, and generates an identical stream of pseudorandom bits — and performs an identical exclusive-OR operation between this pseudorandom stream and the received bits. Doing so regenerates the original, unencrypted data packet.

Such a method of stream cipher has a few problems. If a bit is flipped (from a 0 to 1 or vice versa) in the encrypted data stream, the corresponding bit is flipped in the decrypted output, which can help an attacker derive the encryption key. Also, an eavesdropper who intercepts two encoded messages *that were encoded with the same stream* can generate the exclusive-OR of the original messages. That knowledge is enough to mount attacks that can eventually break the encryption.

To counter these weaknesses, WEP uses some defenses:

- **Integrity Check (IC) field:** To make sure that data packets are not modified in transit, WEP uses an Integrity Check field in each packet.
- **Initialization vector (IV):** To avoid encrypting two messages with the same key stream, WEP uses a 24-bit initialization vector (IV) that augments the shared secret key to produce a different RC4 key for each packet. The IV itself is also included in the packet.

Experts say that both these defenses are poorly implemented, making WEP ineffective. IC and IV have two main problems:

- The Integrity Check field is implemented by using a checksum algorithm called 32-bit cyclic redundancy code (CRC-32); that checksum *is then included as part of the data packet.* Unfortunately, an attacker can flip arbitrary bits in an encrypted message and correctly adjust the checksum so that the resulting message appears valid.
- The 24-bit IV is sent in the clear (unencrypted). There are only 2^{24} possible initialization vectors (no big challenge for a fast machine), and they have to be reused after running through all of them. In other words, after sending 2^{24}, or 16,777,216 packets, the IV is repeated. The number may sound like a lot, but consider the case of a busy access point that sends 1,500-byte packets at a rate of 11 Mbps. Each packet has 8 × 1,500 = 12,000 bits. That means each second the access point sends 11,000,000/12,000 = 916 packets. At that rate, the access point sends 16,777,216 packets in 16,777,216/916 = 18,315 seconds or 5 hours. That means the IV is reused after 5 hours, and the time may be less than that because many messages are smaller than 1,500 bytes. Thus an attacker has ample opportunities to collect two encrypted messages encrypted with the same key stream — and perform *statistical attacks* (which amount to trying the possible "combinations" really fast) to decrypt the message.

In addition to the wireless access point, you also need a cable modem or DSL connection to the Internet, along with a NAT router/hub, as described in the previous chapters of this minibook. Figure 3-1 shows a typical setup for wireless Internet access through an existing cable modem or DSL connection.

As Figure 3-1 shows, the LAN has both wired and wireless PCs. In this example, either a cable or DSL modem connects the LAN to the Internet through a NAT router/hub. Laptops with wireless network cards connect to the LAN through a wireless access point attached to one of the RJ-45 ports on the hub. To connect desktop PCs to this wireless network, you can use a USB wireless network card (which connects to a USB port).

If you have not yet purchased a NAT router/hub for your cable or DSL connection, consider buying a router/hub that has a built-in wireless access point.

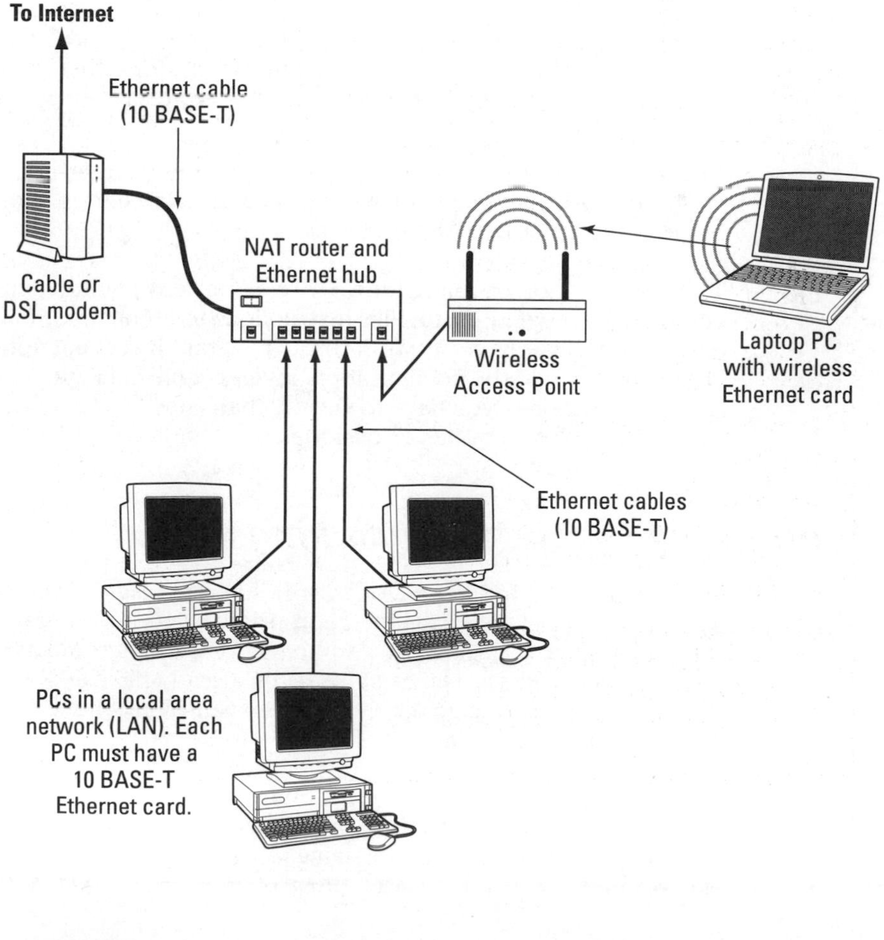

Figure 3-1: Typical connection of a mixed wired and wireless Ethernet LAN to the Internet.

Configuring the wireless access point

Configuring the wireless access point involves the following tasks:

- ✦ Setting a name for the wireless network. (The technical term is ESSID.)
- ✦ Setting the frequency or channel on which the wireless access point communicates with the wireless network cards. The access point and the cards must use the same channel.
- ✦ Deciding whether to use encryption.
- ✦ If encryption is to be used, setting the number of bits in the encryption key and the value of the encryption key. For the encryption key, 24 bits are internal to the access point; you specify only the remaining bits. Thus, for 64-bit encryption, you have to specify a 40-bit key, which comes to 10 hexadecimal digits. (A *hexadecimal digit* is an integer from 0–9 or a letter from A–F.) For a 128-bit encryption key, you specify 104 bits, or 26 hexadecimal digits.
- ✦ Setting the access method that wireless network cards must use when connecting to the access point. You can opt for either open access or shared key. The open-access method is typical (even when using encryption).
- ✦ Setting the wireless access point to operate in infrastructure (managed) mode (because that's the way you connect wireless network cards to an existing Ethernet LAN).

The exact method of configuring a wireless access point depends on make and model; the vendor provides instructions to configure the wireless access point. You typically work through a graphical client application on a Windows PC to do the configuration. If you enable encryption, make note of the encryption key; you have to specify that same key for each wireless network card on your laptops or desktops.

Configuring Wireless Networking

On your Linux laptop, the PCMCIA or PC Card manager recognizes the wireless network card and loads the appropriate driver for the card. Linux treats the wireless network card like another Ethernet device and assigns it a device name such as `eth0` or `eth1`. If you already have an Ethernet card in the laptop, that card gets the `eth0` device name, and the wireless PC Card becomes the `eth1` device.

You do have to configure certain parameters to enable the wireless network card to communicate with the wireless access point. For example, you have to specify the wireless network name assigned to the access point — and the encryption settings must match those on the access point. You can usually configure everything using a graphical network configuration tool that's available for your Linux distribution — just select the Wireless Network option and fill in the requested information.

For example, in Fedora Core, choose Main Menu⇨System Settings⇨Network from the GUI desktop. Then add a wireless device. You can then select the wireless device and get to a window where you can configure the wireless connection. (See Figure 3-2.) In particular, set the Mode to Managed, specify the name of the wireless network (the one you want to connect to), and set the encryption key, if any. You can set the option for getting the IP address to DHCP (a protocol for obtaining network configuration parameters, including IP addresses from a server on the network). When everything is done and you return to the Network Configuration tool's main window, select the new wireless device and click the Activate button. If all goes well, the wireless network should be up and running after a few moments.

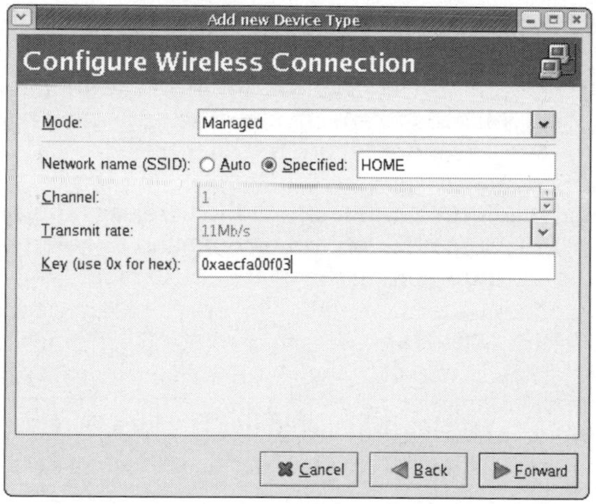

Figure 3-2: In Fedora Core, configure the wireless connection from this window.

In Fedora Core, the Network Configuration tool saves your wireless network settings in a text file whose name depends on the wireless network device name. If the wireless network device name is `eth0`, the configuration is stored in the text file `/etc/sysconfig/network-scripts/ifcfg-eth0`. If the wireless device name is `eth1`, the file is `/etc/sysconfig/network-scripts/ifcfg-eth1`. This configuration file contains various settings for the wireless network card. Table 3-1 explains the meaning of the settings. Here is a slightly edited version of the `/etc/sysconfig/network-scripts/ifcfg-eth1` file from my laptop PC running Fedora Core:

```
IPV6INIT=no
USERCTL=no
PEERDNS=yes
TYPE=Wireless
```

```
DEVICE=eth1
HWADDR=00:02:2d:8c:f9:c4
BOOTPROTO=dhcp
ONBOOT=no
DHCP_HOSTNAME=
NAME=
ESSID='HOME'
CHANNEL=6
MODE=Managed
RATE=auto
```

In Fedora Core, the encryption key is stored separately. For a wireless Ethernet card whose device name is `eth1`, the encryption key is stored in the `/etc/sysconfig/network-scripts/keys-eth1` file. For example, here is what this file contains for my example:

```
KEY=AECFA00F03
```

Note that the key has 10 hexadecimal digits for a 40-bit key (for example, `1fdf-3fde-fe`) or 26 hexadecimal digits for a 104-bit key. The keys are, in fact, 64-bit and 128-bit, but the encryption algorithm automatically generates 24 bits of the key, so you need to specify only the remaining bits. Needless to say, the longer the key, the more secure the encryption.

If you ever manually edit the parameters in the wireless Ethernet configuration file in Fedora Core, type the following command to reactivate the wireless network interface after editing the configuration file:

```
/etc/init.d/pcmcia restart
```

Table 3-1 Settings in Configuration File for a Wireless Ethernet Network Interface in Fedora Core

This Parameter	*Means the Following*
`BOOTPROTO`	The name of the protocol used to get the IP address for the interface. It's either `dhcp` or `bootp` for an Ethernet interface.
`CHANNEL`	Channel number (between 1 and 14 in United States and Canada). Must be the same as that set for the wireless access point. In Managed mode, you don't need to specify the channel.
`DEVICE`	The device name for the wireless Ethernet network interface (`eth0` for the first interface, `eth1` for second, and so on).
`ESSID`	Extended Service Set (ESS) Identifier, also known as the wireless network name. It is case sensitive and must be the same as the name specified for the wireless access point. Provide the name within single quotes (for example, 'HOME').

This Parameter	*Means the Following*
`HWADDR`	The hardware address (also called the MAC address) of the wireless network card (six pairs of colon-separated hexadecimal numbers; for example, 00:02:2d:8c:f9:c4). The wireless card's device driver automatically detects this address.
`IPV6INIT`	When set to `yes`, this parameter initializes IPv6 configuration for the wireless interface. Set it to `no` if you are not using IPv6.
`MODE`	The mode of operation of the wireless network card. Set to `Managed` for a typical network that connects through a wireless access point.
`NAME`	A nickname for your wireless network. If you don't specify it, the host name is used as the nickname.
`ONBOOT`	Set to `yes` to activate the wireless interface at boot time; otherwise, set to `no`.
`PEERDNS`	Set to `yes` to enable the interface to modify your system's `/etc/resolv.conf` file to use the DNS servers obtained from the DHCP server (the same server that provides the IP address for the interface). If you set this parameter to `no`, the `/etc/resolv.conf` file is left unchanged.
`RATE`	Bit rate for the wireless connection (set to one of the following options: `1M`, `2M`, `5.5M`, `11M`, or `auto`). The M means Mbps or a million bits per second. Set to `auto` to use the maximum possible transmission rate.
`TYPE`	Set to `Wireless` for wireless network interface.
`USERCTL`	When set to `yes`, a non-`root` user can control the device. Set it to `no` so that only `root` can control the device.

In SUSE Linux, use YaST to configure the wireless network. SUSE stores the wireless configuration parameters in a file whose name begins with `ifcfg-eth`, followed by the unique hardware address of the wireless Ethernet card. The configuration file is stored in the `/etc/sysconfig/network` directory. Here is a typical list of wireless configuration parameters from a configuration file in SUSE Linux:

```
WIRELESS='yes'
WIRELESS_MODE='Managed'
WIRELESS_ESSID='HOME'
WIRELESS_NICK=''
WIRELESS_CHANNEL='6'
WIRELESS_RATE='auto'
WIRELESS_KEY='0123-4567-89'
```

To check the status of the wireless network interface, type the following command:

```
iwconfig
```

Here's a typical output from a Fedora Core laptop with a wireless Ethernet PC card (the output should be similar in other Linux distributions):

```
lo        no wireless extensions.

eth0      no wireless extensions.

eth1      IEEE 802.11-DS  ESSID:"HOME"  Nickname:"localhost.localdomain"
          Mode:Managed  Frequency:2.437GHz  Access Point: 00:30:AB:06:2E:5D
          Bit Rate=11Mb/s   Tx-Power=15 dBm   Sensitivity:1/0
          Retry limit:4   RTS thr:off   Fragment thr:off
          Encryption key:AECF-A00F-03
          Power Management:off
          Link Quality:66/0  Signal level:-27 dBm  Noise level:-93 dBm
          Rx invalid nwid:0  Rx invalid crypt:0  Rx invalid frag:0
          Tx excessive retries:0  Invalid misc:0   Missed beacon:0
```

Here, the `eth1` interface refers to the wireless network card. I edited the encryption key and some other parameters to hide those details, but the sample output shows you what you'd typically see when the wireless link is working.

Chapter 4: Managing the Network

In This Chapter

- **Learning the TCP/IP configuration files**
- **Checking TCP/IP networks**
- **Configuring networks at boot time**

Like almost everything else in Linux, TCP/IP setup is a matter of preparing numerous configuration files (text files you can edit with any text editor). Most of these configuration files are in the `/etc` directory. The Linux installer tries to be helpful by hiding the details of the TCP/IP configuration files. Nevertheless, if you know the names of the files and their purposes, editing the files manually, if necessary, is easier.

Discovering the TCP/IP Configuration Files

You can configure TCP/IP networking when you install Linux. However, if you want to effectively manage the network, you need to become familiar with the TCP/IP configuration files so that you can edit the files, if necessary. (For example, if you want to check whether the name servers are specified correctly, you have to know about the `/etc/resolv.conf` file, which stores the IP addresses of name servers.)

Table 4-1 summarizes the basic TCP/IP configuration files. I describe these configuration files in the next few sections.

Table 4-1 Basic TCP/IP Network Configuration Files

This File	*Contains the Following*
`/etc/hosts`	IP addresses and host names for your local network as well as any other systems that you access often
`/etc/networks`	Names and IP addresses of networks
`/etc/host.conf`	Instructions on how to translate host names into IP addresses
`/etc/resolv.conf`	IP addresses of name servers
`/etc/hosts.allow`	Instructions on which systems can access Internet services on your system
`/etc/hosts.deny`	Instructions on which systems must be denied access to Internet services on your system
`/etc/nsswitch.conf`	Instructions on how to translate host names into IP addresses

/etc/hosts

The /etc/hosts text file contains a list of IP addresses and host names for your local network. In the absence of a name server, any network program on your system consults this file to determine the IP address that corresponds to a host name. Think of /etc/hosts as the local phone directory where you can look up the IP address (instead of a phone number) for a local host.

Here is the /etc/hosts file from a system, showing the IP addresses and names of other hosts on a typical LAN:

```
127.0.0.1       localhost        localhost.localdomain
# Other hosts on the LAN
192.168.0.100   lnbp933
192.168.0.50    lnbp600
192.168.0.200   lnbp200
192.168.0.233   lnbp233
192.168.0.40    lnbp400
```

As the example shows, each line in the file starts with an IP address, followed by the host name for that IP address. (You can have more than one host name for any given IP address.)

/etc/networks

/etc/networks is another text file that contains the names and IP addresses of networks. These network names are commonly used in the routing command (/sbin/route) to specify a network by name instead of by its IP address.

Don't be alarmed if your Linux PC does not have the /etc/networks file. Your TCP/IP network works fine without this file. In fact, the Linux installer does not create a /etc/networks file.

/etc/host.conf

Linux uses a special *library* (that is, a collection of computer code) called the *resolver library* to obtain the IP address that corresponds to a host name. The /etc/host.conf file specifies how names are resolved (that is, how the name gets converted to a numeric IP address). A typical /etc/host.conf file might contain the following lines:

```
order hosts, bind
multi on
```

The entries in the /etc/host.conf file tell the resolver library what services to use (and in which order) to resolve names.

The `order` option indicates the order of services. The sample entry tells the resolver library to first consult the `/etc/hosts` file and then check the name server to resolve a name.

Use the `multi` option to indicate whether or not a host in the `/etc/hosts` file can have multiple IP addresses. Hosts that have more than one IP address are called *multihomed* because the presence of multiple IP addresses implies that the host has several network interfaces. (In effect, the host "lives" in several networks simultaneously.)

/etc/resolv.conf

The `/etc/resolv.conf` file is another text file used by the *resolver* — the library that determines the IP address for a host name. Here is a sample `/etc/resolv.conf` file:

```
nameserver 192.168.0.1 # dhcp: eth0
search nrockv01.md.comcast.net
```

The `nameserver` line provides the IP addresses of name servers for your domain. If you have multiple name servers, list them on separate lines. They are queried in the order in which they appear in the file.

The `search` line tells the resolver how to search for a host name. For example, when trying to locate a host name `myhost`, the `search` directive in the example causes the resolver to try `myhost.nrockv01.md.comcast.net` first, then `myhost.md.comcast.net`, and finally `myhost.comcast.net`.

If you do not have a name server for your network, you can safely ignore this file. TCP/IP still works, even though you may not be able to refer to hosts by name (other than those listed in the `/etc/hosts` file).

/etc/hosts.allow

The `/etc/hosts.allow` file specifies which hosts are allowed to use the Internet services (such as TELNET and FTP) running on your system. This file is consulted before certain Internet services start. The services start only if the entries in the `hosts.allow` file imply that the requesting host is allowed to use the services.

The entries in `/etc/hosts.allow` are in the form of a *`servername:IP address`* format, where *`server`* refers to the name of the program providing a specific Internet service, and *`IP address`* identifies the host allowed to use that service. For example, if you want all hosts in your local network (which has the network address 192.168.0.0) to access the TELNET service (provided by the `in.telnetd` program), add the following line in the `/etc/hosts.allow` file:

```
in.telnetd:192.168.0.
```

If you want to let all local hosts have access to all Internet services, you can use the `ALL` keyword and rewrite the line as follows:

```
ALL:192.168.0.
```

Finally, to open all Internet services to all hosts, you can replace the IP address with `ALL`, as follows:

```
ALL:ALL
```

You can also use host names in place of IP addresses.

TIP: To find out the detailed syntax of the entries in the `/etc/hosts.allow` file, type **man hosts.allow** at the shell prompt in a terminal window.

/etc/hosts.deny

This file is just the opposite of `/etc/hosts.allow` whereas `hosts.allow` specifies which hosts may access Internet services (such as TELNET and TFTP) on your system, the `hosts.deny` file identifies the hosts that must be denied services. The `/etc/hosts.deny` file is consulted if no rules are in the `/etc/hosts.allow` file that apply to the requesting host. Service is denied if the `hosts.deny` file has a rule that applies to the host.

The entries in `/etc/hosts.deny` file have the same format as those in the `/etc/hosts.allow` file; they are in the form of a *`server:IP address`* format, where *`server`* refers to the name of the program providing a specific Internet service and *`IP address`* identifies the host that must not be allowed to use that service.

If you already set up entries in the `/etc/hosts.allow` file to allow access to specific hosts, you can place the following line in `/etc/hosts.deny` to deny all other hosts access to any service on your system:

```
ALL:ALL
```

TIP: To find out the detailed syntax of the entries in the `/etc/hosts.deny` file, type **man hosts.deny** at the shell prompt in a terminal window.

/etc/nsswitch.conf

This file, known as the *name service switch* (NSS) file, specifies how services such as the resolver library, NIS, NIS+, and local configuration files (such as `/etc/hosts` and `/etc/shadow`) interact.

NIS and NIS+ are *network information services* — another type of name-lookup service. Newer versions of the Linux kernel use the `/etc/nsswitch.conf` file to determine what takes precedence: a local configuration file, a service such as DNS (Domain Name Service), or NIS.

As an example, the following `hosts` entry in the `/etc/nsswitch.conf` file says that the resolver library first tries the `/etc/hosts` file, and then tries NIS+, and finally tries DNS:

```
hosts:      files nisplus dns
```

TIP

You can find out more about the `/etc/nsswitch.conf` file by typing **man nsswitch.conf** in a terminal window.

Checking Out TCP/IP Networks

After you configure Ethernet and TCP/IP (whether during Linux installation or by running a network configuration tool or command later on), you can use various networking applications without much problem. On the off chance that you do run into trouble, Linux includes several tools to help you monitor and diagnose problems.

Checking the network interfaces

Use the `/sbin/ifconfig` command to view the currently configured network interfaces. The `ifconfig` command is used to configure a network interface (that is, to associate an IP address with a network device). If you run `ifconfig` without any command-line arguments, the command displays information about current network interfaces. The following is a typical invocation of `ifconfig` and the resulting output:

```
/sbin/ifconfig
eth0      Link encap:Ethernet  HWaddr 00:08:74:E5:C1:60
          inet addr:192.168.0.6  Bcast:192.168.0.255  Mask:255.255.255.0
          inet6 addr: fe80::208:74ff:fee5:c160/64 Scope:Link
          UP BROADCAST RUNNING MULTICAST  MTU:1500  Metric:1
          RX packets:93700 errors:0 dropped:0 overruns:1 frame:0
          TX packets:74097 errors:0 dropped:0 overruns:0 carrier:0
          collisions:0 txqueuelen:1000
          RX bytes:33574333 (32.0 Mb)  TX bytes:8832457 (8.4 Mb)
          Interrupt:10 Base address:0x3000

eth1      Link encap:Ethernet  HWaddr 00:02:2D:8C:F8:C5
          inet addr:192.168.0.8  Bcast:192.168.0.255  Mask:255.255.255.0
          inet6 addr: fe80::202:2dff:fe8c:f8c5/64 Scope:Link
          UP BROADCAST RUNNING MULTICAST  MTU:1500  Metric:1
          RX packets:3403 errors:0 dropped:0 overruns:0 frame:0
          TX packets:22 errors:1 dropped:0 overruns:0 carrier:0
          collisions:0 txqueuelen:1000
          RX bytes:254990 (249.0 Kb)  TX bytes:3120 (3.0 Kb)
          Interrupt:3 Base address:0x100
```

```
lo        Link encap:Local Loopback
          inet addr:127.0.0.1  Mask:255.0.0.0
          inet6 addr: ::1/128 Scope:Host
          UP LOOPBACK RUNNING  MTU:16436  Metric:1
          RX packets:3255 errors:0 dropped:0 overruns:0 frame:0
          TX packets:3255 errors:0 dropped:0 overruns:0 carrier:0
          collisions:0 txqueuelen:0
          RX bytes:2686647 (2.5 Mb)  TX bytes:2686647 (2.5 Mb)
```

This output shows that three network interfaces — the loopback interface (`lo`) and two Ethernet cards (`eth0` and `eth1`) — are currently active on this system. For each interface, you can see the IP address, as well as statistics on packets delivered and sent. If the Linux system has a dialup PPP link up and running, you also see an item for the `ppp0` interface in the output.

Checking the IP routing table

The other network configuration command, `/sbin/route`, also provides status information when it is run without any command-line argument. If you're having trouble checking a connection to another host (that you specify with an IP address), check the IP routing table to see whether a default gateway is specified. Then check the gateway's routing table to ensure that paths to an outside network appear in that routing table.

A typical output from the `/sbin/route` command looks like the following:

```
/sbin/route
Kernel IP routing table
Destination     Gateway         Genmask         Flags Metric Ref    Use Iface
192.168.0.0     *               255.255.255.0   U     0      0        0 eth0
192.168.0.0     *               255.255.255.0   U     0      0        0 eth1
169.254.0.0     *               255.255.0.0     U     0      0        0 eth1
127.0.0.0       *               255.0.0.0       U     0      0        0 lo
default         192.168.0.1     0.0.0.0         UG    0      0        0 eth0
```

As this routing table shows, the local network uses the `eth0` and `eth1` Ethernet interfaces, and the default gateway is the `eth0` Ethernet interface. The default gateway is a routing device that handles packets addressed to any network other than the one in which the Linux system resides. In this example, packets addressed to any network address other than those beginning with 192.168.0 are sent to the gateway — 192.168.0.1. The gateway forwards those packets to other networks (assuming, of course, that the gateway is connected to another network, preferably the Internet).

Checking connectivity to a host

To check for a network connection to a specific host, use the `ping` command. `ping` is a widely used TCP/IP tool that uses a series of Internet Control Message Protocol (ICMP, pronounced *eye-comp*) messages. ICMP provides for an Echo message to which every host responds. Using the ICMP messages and replies, `ping` can determine whether or not the other system is alive and can compute the round-trip delay in communicating with that system.

The following example shows how I run `ping` to see whether a system on my network is alive:

```
ping 192.168.0.1
```

Here is what this command displays on my home network:

```
PING 192.168.0.1 (192.168.0.1) 56(84) bytes of data.
64 bytes from 192.168.0.1: icmp_seq=1 ttl=63 time=0.256 ms
64 bytes from 192.168.0.1: icmp_seq=2 ttl=63 time=0.267 ms
64 bytes from 192.168.0.1: icmp_seq=3 ttl=63 time=0.272 ms
64 bytes from 192.168.0.1: icmp_seq=4 ttl=63 time=0.267 ms
64 bytes from 192.168.0.1: icmp_seq=5 ttl=63 time=0.275 ms

--- 192.168.0.1 ping statistics ---
5 packets transmitted, 5 received, 0% packet loss, time 3999ms
rtt min/avg/max/mdev = 0.256/0.267/0.275/0.016 ms
```

In Linux, `ping` continues to run until you press Ctrl+C to stop it; then it displays summary statistics showing the typical time it takes to send a packet between the two systems. On some systems, `ping` simply reports that a remote host is alive. However, you can still get the timing information by using appropriate command-line arguments.

Checking network status

To check the status of the network, use the `netstat` command. This command displays the status of network connections of various types (such as TCP and UDP connections). You can view the status of the interfaces quickly with `netstat -i`, as follows:

```
netstat -i
Kernel Interface table
Iface  MTU Met   RX-OK RX-ERR RX-DRP RX-OVR    TX-OK TX-ERR TX-DRP TX-OVR Flg
eth0  1500   0   94237      0      0      1    74889      0      0      0 BMRU
eth1  1500   0    3942      0      0      0       24      1      0      0 BMRU
lo   16436   0    3255      0      0      0     3255      0      0      0 LRU
```

In this case, the output shows the current status of the loopback and Ethernet interfaces. Table 4-2 describes the meanings of the columns.

Table 4-2 Meaning of Columns in the Kernel Interface Table

Column	*Meaning*
`Iface`	Name of the interface.
`MTU`	Maximum Transfer Unit — the maximum number of bytes that a packet can contain.
`RX-OK`, `TX-OK`	Number of error-free packets received (`RX`) or transmitted (`TX`).
`RX-ERR`, `TX-ERR`	Number of packets with errors.

(continued)

Table 4-2 (continued)

Column	*Meaning*
`RX-DRP, TX-DRP`	Number of dropped packets.
`RX-OVR, TX-OVR`	Number of packets lost due to overflow.
`Flg`	`A` = receive multicast; `B` = broadcast allowed; `D` = debugging turned on; `L` = loopback interface (notice the flag on `lo`), `M` = all packets received, `N` = trailers avoided; `O` = no ARP on this interface; `P` = point-to-point interface; `R` = interface is running; and `U` = interface is up.

Another useful form of `netstat` option is `-t`, which shows all active TCP connections. Following is a typical result of typing **netstat -t** on one Linux PC:

```
Active Internet connections (w/o servers)
Proto Recv-Q Send-Q Local Address           Foreign Address         State
tcp        0      0 localhost:2654          localhost:1024          ESTABLISHED
tcp        0      0 localhost:1024          localhost:2654          ESTABLISHED
tcp        0      0 LNBNECXAN.nrockv01.:ssh 192.168.0.6:1577        ESTABLISHED
```

In this case, the output columns show the protocol (`Proto`); the number of bytes in the Receive and Transmit queues (`Recv-Q`, `Send-Q`); the local TCP port in `hostname:service` format (`Local Address`); the remote port (`Foreign Address`); and the state of the connection.

Type **netstat -ta** to see all TCP connections — both active and the ones your Linux system is listening to (with no connection established yet). For example, here's a typical output from the `netstat -ta` command:

```
Active Internet connections (servers and established)
Proto Recv-Q Send-Q Local Address           Foreign Address         State
tcp        0      0 LNBNECXAN.nrockv01.:427 *:*                     LISTEN
tcp        0      0 localhost:427           *:*                     LISTEN
tcp        0      0 *:netbios-ssn           *:*                     LISTEN
tcp        0      0 *:sunrpc                *:*                     LISTEN
tcp        0      0 *:ftp                   *:*                     LISTEN
tcp        0      0 *:ssh                   *:*                     LISTEN
tcp        0      0 *:ipp                   *:*                     LISTEN
tcp        0      0 *:microsoft-ds          *:*                     LISTEN
tcp        0      0 *:2654                  *:*                     LISTEN
tcp        0      0 *:639                   *:*                     LISTEN
tcp        0      0 localhost:2654          localhost:1024          ESTABLISHED
tcp        0      0 localhost:1024          localhost:2654          ESTABLISHED
tcp        0      1 LNBNECXAN.nrockv01:1037 192.168.0.6:auth        SYN_SENT
tcp        0      0 LNBNECXAN.nrockv01.:ftp 192.168.0.6:1593        ESTABLISHED
tcp        0    132 LNBNECXAN.nrockv01.:ssh 192.168.0.6:1577        ESTABLISHED
```

Sniffing network packets

Sniffing network packets — sounds like something illegal, doesn't it? Nothing like that. *Sniffing* simply refers to viewing the TCP/IP network data packets. The concept is to capture all the network packets so that you can examine them later.

TIP

If you feel like sniffing TCP/IP packets, you can use `tcpdump`, a command-line utility that comes with Linux. As its name implies, it "dumps" (prints) the headers of TCP/IP network packets.

To use `tcpdump`, log in as `root` and type the `tcpdump` command in a terminal window. Typically, you want to save the output in a file and examine that file later. Otherwise, `tcpdump` starts spewing out results that just flash by on the window. For example, to capture 1,000 packets in a file named `tdout` and attempt to convert the IP addresses to names, type the following command:

```
tcpdump -a -c 1000 > tdout
```

After capturing 1,000 packets, `tcpdump` quits. Then you can examine the output file, `tdout`. It's a text file, so you can simply open it in a text editor or type **more tdout** to view the captured packets.

Just to whet your curiosity, here are some lines from a typical output from `tcpdump`:

```
20:05:57.723621 arp who-has 192.168.0.1 tell LNBNECXAN.nrockv01.md.comcast.net
20:05:57.723843 arp reply 192.168.0.1 is-at 0:9:5b:44:78:fc
20:06:01.733633 LNBNECXAN.nrockv01.md.comcast.net.1038 > 192.168.0.6.auth: S
    536321100:536321100(0) win 5840 <mss 1460,sackOK,timestamp 7030060
    0,nop,wscale 0> (DF)
20:06:02.737022 LNBNECXAN.nrockv01.md.comcast.net.ftp > 192.168.0.6.1596: P 1:72
    (71) ack 1 win 5840 (DF)
20:06:02.935335 192.168.0.6.1596 > LNBNECXAN.nrockv01.md.comcast.net.ftp: . ack
    72 win 65464 (DF)
20:06:05.462481 192.168.0.6.1596 > LNBNECXAN.nrockv01.md.comcast.net.ftp: P 1:12
    (11) ack 72 win 65464 (DF)
20:06:05.462595 LNBNECXAN.nrockv01.md.comcast.net.ftp > 192.168.0.6.1596: . ack
    12 win 5840 (DF)
20:06:05.465344 LNBNECXAN.nrockv01.md.comcast.net.ftp > 192.168.0.6.1596: P
    72:105(33) ack 12 win 5840 (DF)
... lines deleted...
```

The output does offer some clues to what's going on — each line shows information about one network packet. Each line starts with a timestamp, followed by details of the packet, information such as where it originates and where it is going. I don't try to explain the details here, but you can type **man tcpdump** to find out more about some of the details (and, more importantly, see what other ways you can use `tcpdump`).

If tcpdump is not installed in Debian, type **apt-get install tcpdump** to install it.

You can use another packet sniffer called Ethereal in Linux. To find out more about Ethereal, visit www.ethereal.com.

Configuring Networks at Boot Time

It makes sense to start your network automatically every time you boot the system. For that to happen, various startup scripts must contain appropriate commands. You don't have to do anything special other than configure your network (either during installation or by using the Network Configuration tool at a later time). If the network balks at startup, however, you can troubleshoot by checking the files I mention in this section.

In Debian and Xandros, the /etc/network/interfaces file describes the network interfaces available in your system and the /sbin/ifup command activates the interfaces when you boot the system. Here is the content of a typical /etc/network/interfaces file from a Debian system:

```
# This file describes the network interfaces available on your system
# and how to activate them. For more information, see interfaces(5).

# The loopback network interface
auto lo
iface lo inet loopback

# The primary network interface
auto eth0
iface eth0 inet dhcp
```

The auto eth0 line indicates that the Ethernet interface can be brought up at initialization by the command ifup -a invoked by a system startup script. The line ifup eth0 inet dhcp identifies the Ethernet as a TCP/IP network interface that is configured by Dynamic Host Configuration Protocol (DHCP).

In Fedora Core, the network-activation script uses a set of text files in the /etc/sysconfig directory to activate the network interfaces. For example, the script checks the variables defined in the /etc/sysconfig/network file to decide whether to activate the network. In /etc/sysconfig/network, you see a line with the NETWORKING variable as follows:

```
NETWORKING=yes
```

The network activates only if the NETWORKING variable is set to yes. A number of scripts in the /etc/sysconfig/network-scripts directory activate specific network interfaces. For example, the configuration file for activating the

Ethernet interface `eth0`, is the file `/etc/sysconfig/network-scripts/ifcfg-eth0`. Here is what a typical `/etc/sysconfig/network-scripts/ifcfg-eth0` file contains:

```
DEVICE=eth0
BOOTPROTO=dhcp
ONBOOT=yes
TYPE=Ethernet
```

The `DEVICE` line provides the network device name. The `BOOTPROTO` variable is set to `dhcp`, indicating that the IP address is obtained dynamically by using DHCP. The `ONBOOT` variable states whether this network interface activates when Linux boots. If your PC has an Ethernet card and you want to activate the `eth0` interface at boot time, `ONBOOT` must be set to `yes`. Of course, the configuration file `ifcfg-eth0` in the `/etc/sysconfig/network-scripts` directory works only if your PC has an Ethernet card and the Linux kernel has detected and loaded the specific driver for that card.

DISTRIBUTION SPECIFIC

In SUSE, the network information is kept in the `/etc/sysconfig/network` directory in files whose names begin with `ifcfg`. For Ethernet interfaces, the configuration filename begins with `ifcfg-eth`. Here are the key lines in a typical Ethernet configuration file:

```
BOOTPROTO='dhcp'
STARTMODE='onboot'
```

The `BOOTPROTO='dhcp'` line indicates that the interface is set up using DHCP, and `STARTMODE='onboot'` means that the interface is initialized when the system boots.

Book IV

Internet

"I'm setting preferences—do you want Oriental or Persian carpets in the living room?"

Contents at a Glance

Chapter 1: E-Mailing and IMing in Linux

In This Chapter

- **Understanding electronic mail**
- **Taking stock of mail readers and IM (Instant Messaging) clients**
- **Introducing Ximian Evolution**
- **Introducing Mozilla Mail**
- **Introducing KMail**
- **Instant messaging with Gaim and Kopete**

Electronic mail (e-mail) is a mainstay of the Internet. E-mail is great because you can exchange messages and documents with anyone on the Internet. One of the most common ways people use the Internet is to keep in touch with friends, acquaintances, loved ones, and strangers through e-mail. You can send a message to a friend thousands of miles away and get a reply within a couple of minutes. Essentially, you can send messages anywhere in the world from an Internet host, and that message typically makes its way to its destination within minutes — something you cannot do with paper mail (also known as *snail mail,* and appropriately so).

I love e-mail because I can communicate without having to play the game of "phone tag," in which two people can leave a seemingly infinite number of telephone messages for each other without ever successfully making contact. When I send an e-mail message, it waits in the recipient's mailbox to be read at the recipient's convenience. I guess I like the converse even better — when people send me e-mail, I can read and reply at *my* convenience.

Linux comes with several mail clients — also called mail readers — that can download mail from your Internet Service Provider (ISP). You can also read and send e-mail using these mail clients. In this chapter, I mention several mail clients available in Linux and briefly introduce you to a few of them. And when you know one, you can easily use any of the mail readers.

There is yet another type of "keeping in touch" that's more in line with today's teenagers. I'm talking about *IM* — instant messaging. IM is basically one-to-one chat, and Linux includes IM clients for AOL Instant Messenger (or AIM), as well as other instant messaging protocols such as Jabber, ICQ, MSN Messenger, Yahoo!, Gadu-Gadu, IRC (Internet Relay Chat), and SMS (Short Message Service or text messaging). I briefly describe a few IM clients in this chapter.

Understanding Electronic Mail

E-mail messages are addressed to a username at a host (*host* is just a fancy name for an online computer). That means if John Doe logs in with the *username* `jdoe`, e-mail to him is addressed to `jdoe`. The only other piece of information needed to identify the recipient uniquely is the fully qualified *domain name* of the recipient's system. Thus, if John Doe's system is named `someplace.com`, his complete e-mail address becomes `jdoe@someplace.com`. Given that address, anyone on the Internet can send e-mail to John Doe.

How MUA and MTA work

The two types of mail software are as follows:

- **Mail-user agent (MUA)** is the fancy name for a mail reader — a client that you use to read your mail messages, write replies, and compose new messages. Typically, the mail-user agent retrieves messages from the mail server by using the POP3 or IMAP4 protocol. POP3 is the *Post Office Protocol Version 3*, and IMAP4 is the *Internet Message Access Protocol Version 4*. Linux comes with mail-user agents such as Balsa, Mozilla Mail, KMail, and Ximian Evolution.
- **Mail-transport agent (MTA)** is the fancy name for a mail server that actually sends and receives mail-message text. The exact method used for mail transport depends on the underlying network. In TCP/IP networks, the mail-transport agent delivers mail using the *Simple Mail Transfer Protocol* (SMTP). Linux includes sendmail, a powerful and popular mail-transport agent for TCP/IP networks.

Figure 1-1 shows how the MUAs and MTAs work with one another when Alice sends an e-mail message to Bob. (In case you didn't know, using *Alice* and *Bob* to explain e-mail and cryptography is customary — just pick up any book on cryptography and you'll see what I mean.) And you may already know this, but the Internet is always diagrammed as a cloud — the boundaries of the Internet are so fuzzy that a cloud seems just right to represent it (or is it because no one knows where it starts and where it ends?).

The scenario in Figure 1-1 is typical of most people. Alice and Bob both connect to the Internet through an ISP and get and send their e-mail through their ISPs. When Alice types a message and sends it, her mail-user agent (MUA) sends the message to her ISP's mail-transfer agent (MTA) using the Simple Mail Transfer Protocol (SMTP). The sending MTA then sends that message to the receiving MTA — Bob's ISP's MTA — using SMTP. When Bob connects to the Internet, his MUA downloads the message from his ISP's MTA using the POP3 (or IMAP4) protocol. That's the way mail moves around the Internet — from sending MUA to sending MTA to receiving MTA to receiving MUA.

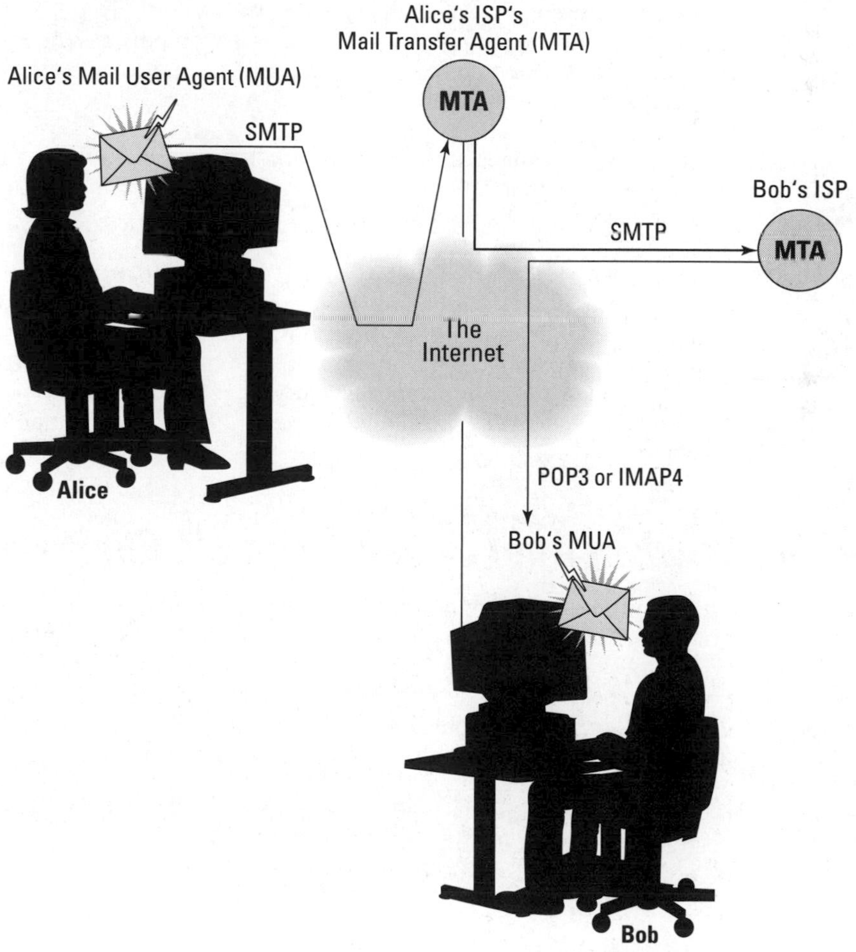

Figure 1-1: How Alice sends e-mail to Bob (or all about MUAs and MTAs).

Mail message enhancements

Mail messages used to be plain text (and most still are), but many messages today have much more than text. Two typical new features of today's mail are

- **Attachments:** Many messages today include attached files, which can be anything from documents to images. The recipient can save the attachment on disk or open it directly from the mail reader. Unfortunately, attachments are one way hackers try to get viruses and worms into your PC. (If it's any consolation, most Windows-based viruses and worms do not work in Linux.)
- **HTML messages:** Mail messages can be in *HTML* (HyperText Markup Language), the language used to lay out Web pages. When you read an HTML message on a capable mail reader, the message appears in its full glory with nice fonts and embedded graphics.

While HTML messages are nice, they don't appear right when you use a text-based mail reader. In a text mail reader, HTML messages appear as a bunch of gobbledygook (which is just the HTML code).

If you have an ISP account, all you need is a *mail client* to access your e-mail. In this case, your e-mail resides on your ISP's server and the mail reader downloads mail when you run it. You have to do some setup before you can start reading mail from your ISP's mail server. The setup essentially requires you to enter information that you get from your ISP — the mail server's name, server type (POP3, for example), your username, and your password.

Taking Stock of Mail Readers and IM Clients in Linux

Time was when most mail readers were text programs, but times have changed. Now mail readers are graphical applications capable of displaying HTML messages and handling attachments with ease. They are easy to use; if you can work with one, it's a pretty sure bet that you can use any of the graphical mail readers out there. (Linux comes with several mail readers; feel free to try a few out to see which one fits your needs best.)

IM (instant messaging) is a more recent phenomenon, but Linux tries to stay on top of things, so it comes with two IM clients that can work with various IM protocols. Table 1-1 gives you an overview of the major mail readers and IM clients in Linux.

Table 1-1 Linux Mail Readers and IM Clients

Software	*Description*
Kmail	The KDE e-mail client that supports both POP3 and IMAP4
Mozilla Mail	A mail client as well as a newsreader, part of the Mozilla open-source Web browser (open-source incarnation of Netscape Communicator)
Ximian Evolution	A *personal information manager* (PIM) that includes e-mail, calendar, contact management, and an online task list
Gaim	An IM client for GNOME that supports a number of instant-messaging protocols such as AIM, ICQ, Yahoo!, MSN, Gadu-Gadu, and Jabber
Kopete	An IM client for KDE that supports a number of messaging protocols such as Jabber, ICQ, AIM, MSN, Yahoo!, IRC, Gadu-Gadu, and SMS

If you don't see a specific mail or IM client in your distribution, chances are that you can easily download and install it from the Internet.

E-Mailing in Linux

Each Linux distribution's GUI desktop has one or two default e-mail clients. GNOME desktops typically offer Ximian Evolution, whereas KDE desktops go with KMail. Both GNOME and KDE desktops often come with Mozilla as the Web browser and Mozilla includes a mail client as well.

Debian includes KMail and Ximian Evolution. Fedora Core offers Ximian Evolution as its default mail client. SUSE uses KMail as the default mail reader, and Xandros provides Mozilla Mail. In Debian, you can easily install the mail and news component of Mozilla and then use Mozilla Mail.

In the following sections, I briefly introduce you to Ximian Evolution, Mozilla Mail, and KMail. All mail clients are intuitive to use, so you don't need much more than an introduction to start using them effectively.

Introducing Ximian Evolution

I have heard so much about Ximian Evolution that I want to start with it. What better way than to just jump right in!

In Fedora Core, you can start Evolution by selecting Main Menu⇨Internet⇨Evolution Email from the GNOME or KDE desktop. (In Debian, I had to select Main Menu⇨Debian⇨Apps⇨Net⇨Evolution.)

When you start Evolution for the first time, the Evolution Setup Assistant window appears, as shown in Figure 1-2.

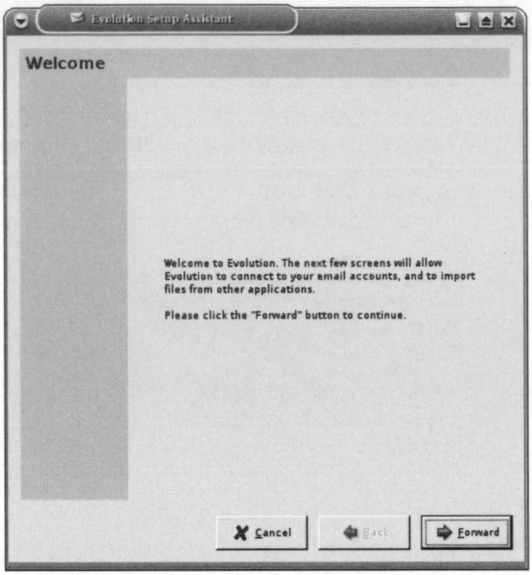

Figure 1-2: The Evolution Setup Assistant guides you through the initial setup.

Click Forward in the Welcome screen and the Setup Assistant guides you through the following steps:

1. **Enter your name and e-mail address in the Identity screen and click the Forward button.**

   For example, if your e-mail address is `jdoe@someplace.com`, that's what you enter.

2. **Set up the options for receiving e-mail and click Forward.**

   Select the type of mail download protocol — POP or IMAP. Then provide the name of the mail server (for example, `mail.comcast.net`). You are prompted for the password when Evolution connects to the mail server for the first time.

3. **Provide further information about receiving e-mail — how often to check for mail and whether to leave messages on the server — and then click Forward.**

   Typically, you want to download the messages and delete them from the server (otherwise the ISP complains when your mail piles up).

4. **Set up the following options for sending e-mail and click Forward when you're done:**

   - Select the server type as SMTP.
   - Enter the name of the server, such as `smtp.comcast.net`.

- If the server requires you to log in, select the Server Requires Authentication check box.
- Enter your username — the same username you use to log in to your ISP's mail server. (Often, you don't have to log in to send mail; you only log in when receiving — downloading — mail messages.)

5. **Indicate whether you want this e-mail account to be your default account, and, if you want, give this e-mail account a descriptive name; click Forward.**
6. **Set your time zone by clicking a map; click Forward.**
7. **Click Apply to complete the Evolution setup.**

After you complete the setup, Evolution opens its main window, as shown in Figure 1-3.

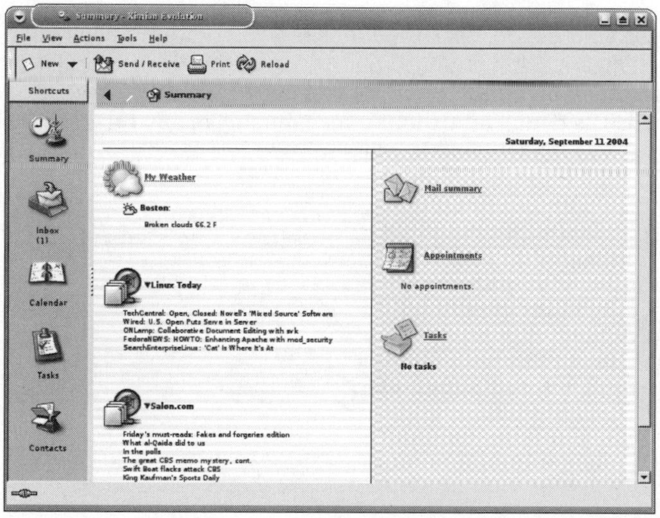

Figure 1-3: Evolution takes care of mail, calendar, contact management, and to-do lists.

The main display area is vertically divided into two windows: a narrow window on the left (containing a number of shortcut icons), and a bigger window that's further divided into two. In the right-hand window, Evolution displays information relevant to the currently selected shortcut icon. Initially, the Summary icon is selected by default.

You can click the icons in the lower-left area to switch to different views. Table 1-2 describes what happens when you click each of the five shortcut icons in Evolution's Shortcuts window.

Table 1-2	Shortcut Icons in Ximian Evolution
Name of Icon	*What It Does*
Summary	Displays a summary of mail, appointments, and tasks.
Inbox	Switches to mail display, where you can read mail and send mail.
Calendar	Opens your calendar, where you can look up and add appointments.
Tasks	Shows your task ("to do") list, where you can add new tasks and check what's due when.
Contacts	Opens your contact list, where you can add new contacts or look up someone from your current list.

As the icons listed in Table 1-2 show, Ximian Evolution has all the necessary components of a PIM — e-mail, calendar, task list, and contacts.

To access your e-mail, click the Inbox icon. Evolution opens your Inbox, as shown in Figure 1-4. If you turn on the feature to automatically check for mail every so often, Evolution prompts you for your mail password and downloads your mail. The e-mail Inbox looks very much like any other mail reader's inbox, such as the Outlook Express Inbox.

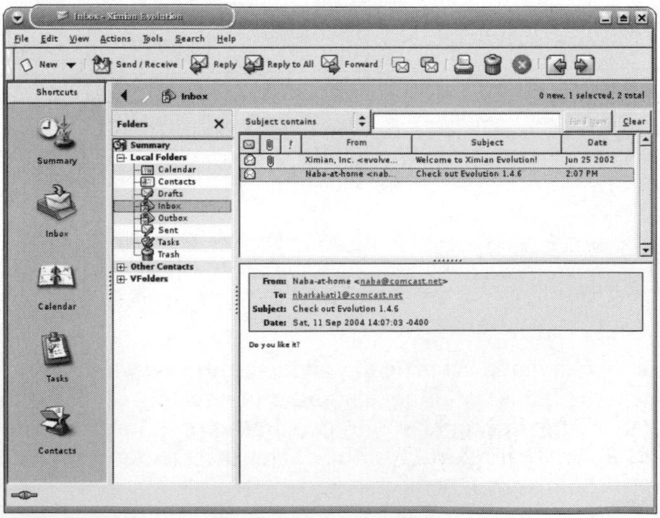

Figure 1-4: Read your e-mail in the Evolution Inbox.

To read a message, click the message in the upper window of the Inbox and the message text appears in the lower window.

To reply to the current message, click the Reply button on the toolbar. A message composition window pops up. You can write your reply and then click the Send button on the toolbar to send the reply. Simple, isn't it?

To send a new e-mail, click the New Message button on the Evolution toolbar. A new message composition window appears; you can type your message in that window, and when you're finished composing the message, click Send.

Ximian Evolution comes with extensive online help. Choose Help⇨Contents from the Evolution menu and *A User's Guide to Ximian Evolution* appears in a window. You can then read the user's guide in that window.

Introducing Mozilla Mail

Mozilla Mail is the mail and newsreader that comes with Mozilla — the open source successor to Netscape Communicator. Mozilla is a Web browser that also includes a mail and newsreader. Mozilla is available on every Linux distribution.

To use Mozilla Mail, start by running the Mozilla Web browser. You can typically click an icon on the panel. Otherwise, look for the Web browser in the Main Menu under the Internet category. Some distributions provide a menu choice for directly accessing Mozilla Mail (instead of having to start it from the Mozilla Web browser window).

Some distributions do not install Mozilla's mail and news component by default. You can, however, install these components easily. For example, in Debian, type **su -** and enter the `root` password in a terminal window and then type **apt-get install mozilla-mailnews** to install the mail and news component of Mozilla. After you install this component, you can access Mozilla Mail from the Mozilla Web browser.

To access the Mozilla Mail e-mail and newsreader from the Mozilla Web browser, choose Window⇨Mail and Newsgroups. Mozilla Mail runs, starts the Account Wizard (shown in Figure 1-5), and prompts you for information about your e-mail account.

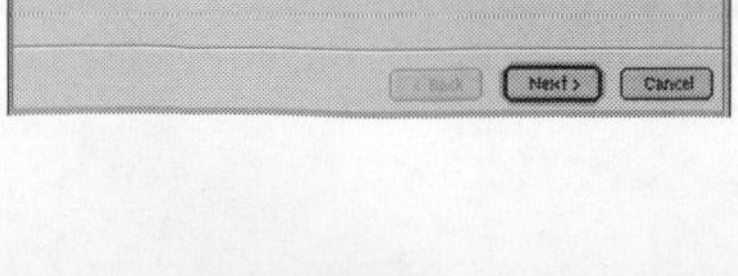

Figure 1-5: Enter your e-mail account information in Mozilla Mail's Account Wizard.

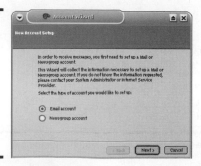

Select the Email Account radio button and click Next. The Account Wizard then takes you through the following steps:

1. **Enter your identity information — your name and your full e-mail address, such as** `jdoe@someplace.com` **— and then click Next.**
2. **Provide information about your ISP's mail server — the protocol type (POP or IMAP) as well as the incoming and outgoing server names — and click Next.**

   The incoming server is the POP or IMAP server, whereas the outgoing server is the one through which you send mail out. (It's the SMTP server.)
3. **Enter the username that your ISP has given you; click Next.**
4. **Enter a name that you want to use to identify this account and click Next.**

   This name is just for Mozilla Mail, so you can pick anything you want, such as "My home account."

   The Account Wizard then displays a summary of the information you entered.
5. **Verify the information; if it's correct, click Finish. Otherwise, click Back and fix the errors.**

After you set up the e-mail account, Mozilla Mail's main window appears and shows you the contents of your Inbox. Soon a dialog box pops up and asks you for your e-mail password. Mozilla Mail needs your password to download your e-mail messages from your ISP. Enter your password and click OK.

Mozilla Mail downloads your messages and displays them in a familiar format. To read a message, click that message, and the full text appears in the lower window, as shown in Figure 1-6.

Mozilla Mail is intuitive to use. Most of the time, you can click the toolbar buttons to do most anything you want to do with the e-mail messages. Here's what each toolbar button does:

- **Get Msgs:** Downloads messages from your e-mail accounts. (You can set up as many as you want.)
- **Compose:** Opens a window where you can compose and send a message.
- **Reply:** Opens a window where you can send back a reply to the person who sent you the message you are reading now.
- **Reply All:** Opens a window for sending a reply to everyone who was on the addressee list of the message you are reading now.
- **Forward:** Brings up the current message in a window so that you can forward it to someone else.
- **Next:** Shows the next unread message.

✦ **Junk:** Marks the selected messages as junk. (You can mark selected messages as junk and select Tools⇨Junk Mail Controls to block similar messages.)

✦ **Delete:** Deletes the selected message.

If you use any GUI mail reader — from Microsoft Outlook Express to Novell GroupWise — you find a similar set of toolbar buttons. In the following sections, I describe how to perform a few common e-mail-related tasks.

Figure 1-6: You can read and send e-mail messages from Mozilla Mail.

Managing your Inbox

Mozilla Mail downloads your incoming mail and stores it in the Inbox folder. You can see the folders organized along the narrow window on the left-hand side. (Refer to Figure 1-6.) Each e-mail account you have set up has a set of folders. You have the following folders by default:

✦ **Inbox:** Holds all your incoming messages for this e-mail account.

✦ **Drafts:** Contains the messages that you save as a draft. (Click the Save button on the message composition window to save something as a draft.)

✦ **Templates:** Contains the messages you save as templates.

✦ **Sent:** Holds all the messages you send.

✦ **Trash:** Contains the messages you delete. (To empty the Trash folder, choose File⇨Empty Trash from the Mozilla Mail menu.)

You can create other folders to better organize your mail. To create a folder, do the following:

1. **Choose File⇨New⇨Folder.**

   The New Folder dialog box appears.

2. **Fill in the folder name and select where you want to put the folder; then click OK.**

   The new folder appears in the left window of Mozilla Mail. You can then drag and drop messages into the folder.

When you select a folder from the left window, Mozilla Mail displays the contents of that folder in the upper window on the right-hand side. The list is normally sorted by date, with the latest messages shown at the end of the list. If you want to sort the list any other way — say, by sender or by subject — simply click that column heading and Mozilla Mail sorts the list according to that column.

Composing and sending messages

To send an e-mail message, you either write a new message or reply to a message you are reading. The general steps for sending an e-mail message are as follows:

1. **To reply to a message, click the Reply or Reply All button on the toolbar as you are reading the message. To write a new message, click the Compose button on the toolbar. To forward a message, click the Forward button.**

   A message composition window appears, as shown in Figure 1-7.

2. **In the message composition window, fill in the subject line and type your message.**

   The message can include images as well as links to Web sites. To insert any of these items, choose Insert⇨Image or Insert⇨Link from the menu.

3. **If you're creating a new message or forwarding a message, type the e-mail addresses of the recipients.**

   To select addressees from the Address Book, click the Address button on the toolbar. Your Address Book opens, from which you can select the addressees.

4. **When you're done composing the message, click the Send button.**

   Mozilla Mail asks whether you want to send the message in HTML format or plain text or both.

5. **Select a format and then click Send to send the message.**

   If you inserted images and Web links and you know the recipient can read HTML mail, be sure to select HTML format; otherwise, choose plain text.

Figure 1-7: Compose your message and then enter the e-mail addresses of the recipients.

If you want to complete a message later, click Save in the message composition window and then close the window. Mozilla Mail saves the message in the Drafts folder. When you're ready to work on that message again, go to the Drafts folder and then double-click the saved message to open it.

Introducing KMail

KMail is a mail reader for KDE. When you first run KMail, you get its main window, but you cannot start using it to send and receive e-mail until you have configured the mail accounts in KMail.

You can use KMail as your mail client in SUSE and Debian's KDE desktop.

To configure KMail, select Settings⇨Configure KMail. In the Configure KMail window (see Figure 1-8), click Network on the left side of the window and then set up the information about your e-mail accounts. KMail uses this information to send and receive mail.

For outgoing mail, click the Add button on the Sending tab (see Figure 1-8) and then select the mail transport agent. Typically, for an ISP-provided mail account, you should select SMTP and enter the mail server's name (for example, `smtp.comcast.net`) that your ISP provided you.

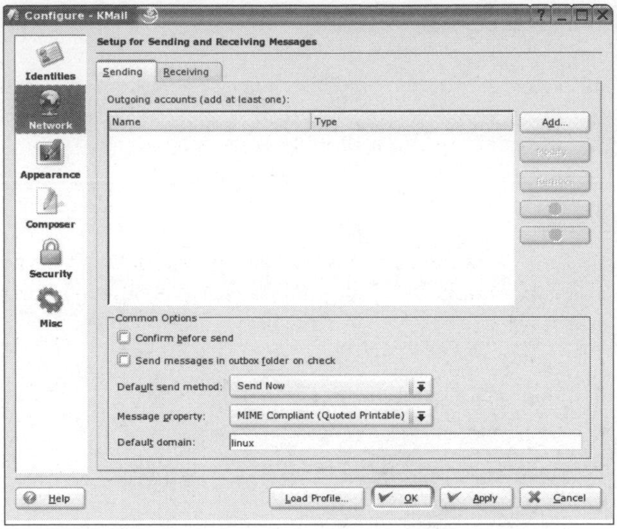

Figure 1-8: Configure e-mail accounts in the Configure KMail window.

To set up the incoming mail information, click Add on the Receiving tab, and then select the mail protocol such as POP3 or IMAP. Your ISP would have told you what protocol to use. (Typically, it's POP3 or IMAP.) Then enter the mail server's name (for example, `mail.comcast.net`) as well as the username and password of your ISP account.

After the e-mail account information is set up, you can start using KMail. The user interface is intuitive, as shown in Figure 1-9. KMail periodically checks and downloads messages from your incoming mail accounts. You can view messages as they arrive in your Inbox.

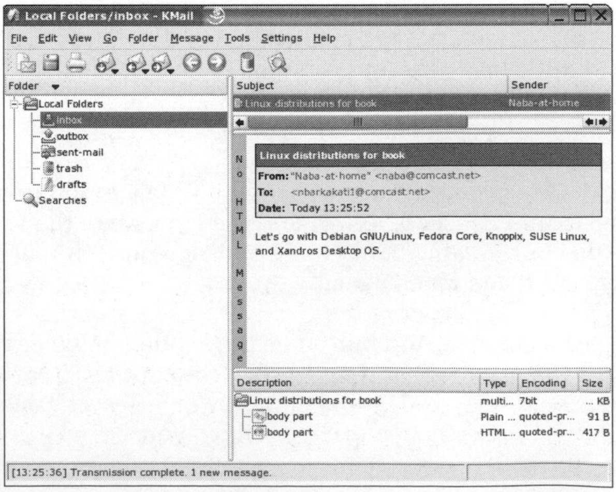

Figure 1-9: Read and manage your e-mail in KMail.

Instant Messaging in Linux

There are two major IM clients in Linux. In GNOME desktops, you can use Gaim, whereas Kopete is designed to work well on KDE desktops. I briefly describe both IM clients in the following sections.

Using Gaim

You can use Gaim to keep in touch with all of your contacts on many different IM services such as AIM, ICQ, Yahoo!, MSN, Gadu-Gadu, and Jabber. If you use any of the IM services, you'll be right at home with Gaim.

In Fedora Core, start Gaim by choosing Main Menu⇨Internet⇨Messaging Client from the GNOME desktop. You can start Gaim in a similar manner from GNOME desktops in other distributions. The initial Gaim window appears together with an Accounts window, as shown in Figure 1-10.

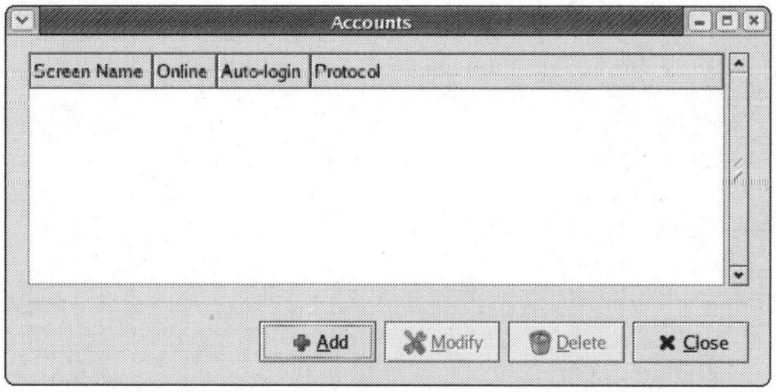

Figure 1-10: Manage all of your IM accounts in this window.

Start by setting up your messaging accounts in the Accounts window. Click the Add button, and then fill in the requested information in the Add Account window, as shown in Figure 1-11. You have to select the protocol for your IM service. For example, the protocol for AIM is AIM/ICQ. Other protocol choices include Gadu-Gadu, Jabber, MSN, and Yahoo!, among others.

After you enter account information, the Accounts window shows all currently defined accounts. You can then select an account from the Gaim main window and click Sign On, as shown in Figure 1-12.

After Gaim logs you in, it opens the standard Buddy List window. (See Figure 1-13.)

To add buddies, select Buddies⇨Add Buddy. In the Add Buddy window that appears, enter the screen name of the buddy and click Add. To create a new group, choose Buddies⇨Add Group. Type the name of the new group in the Add Group window that appears and then click Add.

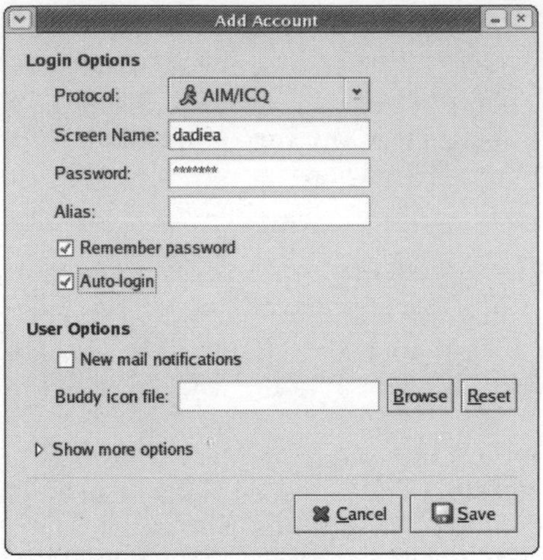

Figure 1-11: Enter information about each IM account.

Figure 1-12: Sign on to AIM with Gaim.

Figure 1-13: A buddy list window in Gaim.

If any of your buddies are online, their names show up in the Buddy List window. To send a message to a buddy, double-click the name and a message window pops up. If someone sends you a message, a message window pops up with the message and you can begin conversing in that window.

Using Kopete

Kopete — the KDE IM client — enables you to connect to many messaging services including AIM, IRC, MSN Messenger, Yahoo!, Gadu-Gadu, and SMS.

In Debian, you can run Kopete by selecting Main Menu⇨Internet⇨Instant Messenger. In SUSE, select Main Menu⇨Internet⇨Chat to start Kopete. In Xandros, start Kopete by choosing Main Menu⇨Applications⇨Internet⇨ Instant Messaging.

When you first run Kopete, you get the Configure Kopete window (see Figure 1-14), where you can enter information about your IM and other messaging service accounts.

For example, to add your AIM account information, click New and then answer and respond to the prompts from the Account Wizard. The first step is to select your messaging service. (See Figure 1-15.)

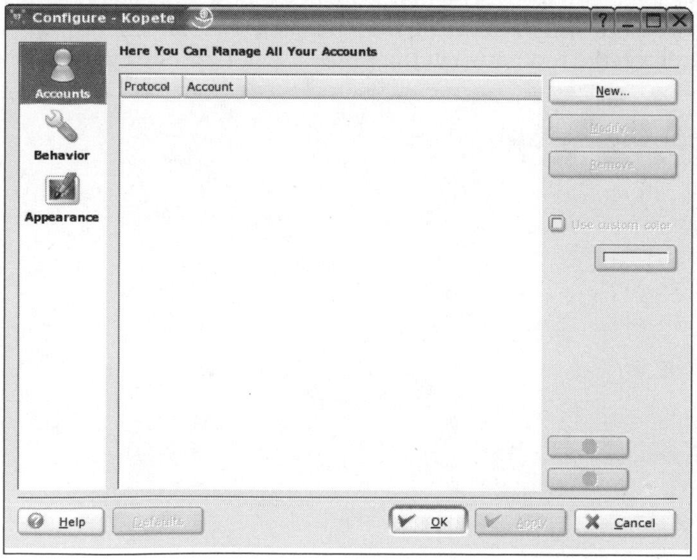

Figure 1-14: Enter information about your messaging accounts in this window.

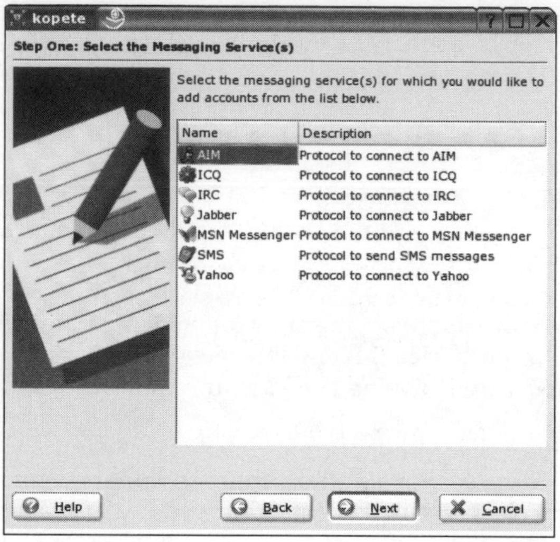

Figure 1-15: Select your messaging service in this window.

Select the appropriate messaging service, such as AIM if you use AOL's instant messaging service. Then provide the AIM screen name and the password.

After you have set up your messaging service accounts, the Account Wizard closes and you get the regular Kopete window. To sign on with your messaging services and begin using Kopete, click the Connect button — the leftmost button on the toolbar — in the Kopete window. (See Figure 1-16.)

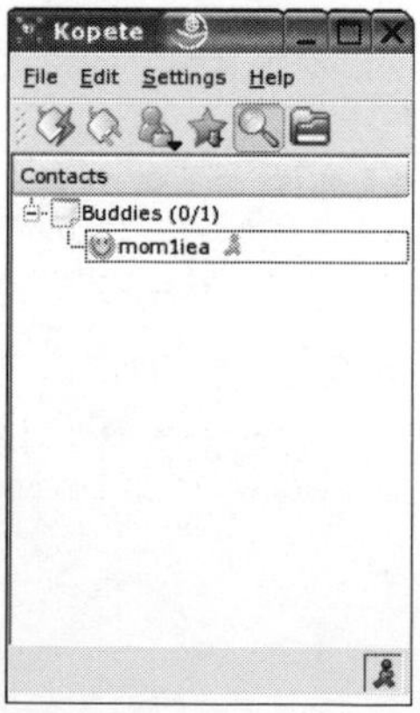

Figure 1-16: Viewing a buddy list in Kopete.

Click the magnifying-glass icon to see your buddies. You see a solid smiley face icon for buddies who are online. Click an online buddy to start chatting. Select File⇨Add Contact to add more contacts.

Well, if you know AIM, you know what to do: Have fun IMing with Kopete!

Chapter 2: Browsing the Web

In This Chapter

- Discovering the World Wide Web
- Understanding a URL
- Checking out Web servers and Web browsers
- Taking stock of Web browsers for Linux
- Web browsing with Mozilla
- Introducing Epiphany and Firefox

I suspect you already know about the Web, but did you know that the Web (or more formally, the World Wide Web), made the Internet what it is today? The Internet has been around for quite a while, but it did not reach the masses until the Web came along in 1993.

Before the Web came along, you had to use arcane UNIX commands to download and use files, which was simply too complicated for most of us. With the Web, however, anyone can enjoy the benefits of the Internet by using a *Web browser* — a graphical application that downloads and displays Web documents. A click of the mouse is all you need to go from reading a document from your company Web site to downloading a video clip from across the country.

In this chapter, I briefly describe the Web and introduce Mozilla — the primary Web browser (and, for that matter, mail and newsreader, too) in most Linux distributions. I also briefly discuss how you can create your own Web pages.

KDE desktops often use Konqueror as the Web browser, but after you have used one Web browser, you can easily use any other Web browser.

Discovering the World Wide Web

If you have used a file server at work, you know the convenience of sharing files. You can use the word processor on your desktop to get to any document on the shared server.

Now imagine a word processor that enables you to open and view a document that resides on any computer on the Internet. You can view the document in its full glory, with formatted text and graphics. If the document makes a reference to another document (possibly residing on yet another computer), you can open that linked document by clicking the reference. That kind of easy access to distributed documents is essentially what the World Wide Web provides.

Of course, the documents have to be in a standard format, so that any computer (with the appropriate Web browser software) can access and interpret the document. And a standard protocol is necessary for transferring Web documents from one system to another.

The standard Web document format is *HyperText Markup Language* (HTML), and the standard protocol for exchanging Web documents is *HyperText Transfer Protocol* (HTTP). HTML documents are text files and don't depend on any specific operating system, so they work on any system from Windows and Mac to any type of UNIX and Linux.

A *Web server* is software that provides HTML documents to any client that makes the appropriate HTTP requests. A *Web browser* is the client software that actually downloads an HTML document from a Web server and displays the contents graphically.

Like a giant spider's web

The World Wide Web is the combination of the Web servers and the HTML documents that the servers offer. When you look at the Web in this way, the Web is like a giant book whose pages are scattered throughout the Internet. You use a Web browser running on your computer to view the pages — the pages are connected like a giant spider's web, with the documents everywhere, as illustrated in Figure 2-1.

Imagine that the Web pages — HTML documents — are linked by network connections that resemble a giant spider's web, so you can see why the Web is called "the Web." The "World Wide" part comes from the fact that the Web pages are scattered around the world.

Links and URLs

Like the pages of real books, Web pages contain text and graphics. Unlike real books, however, Web pages can include multimedia, such as video clips, sound, and links to other Web pages that can actually take you to those Web pages.

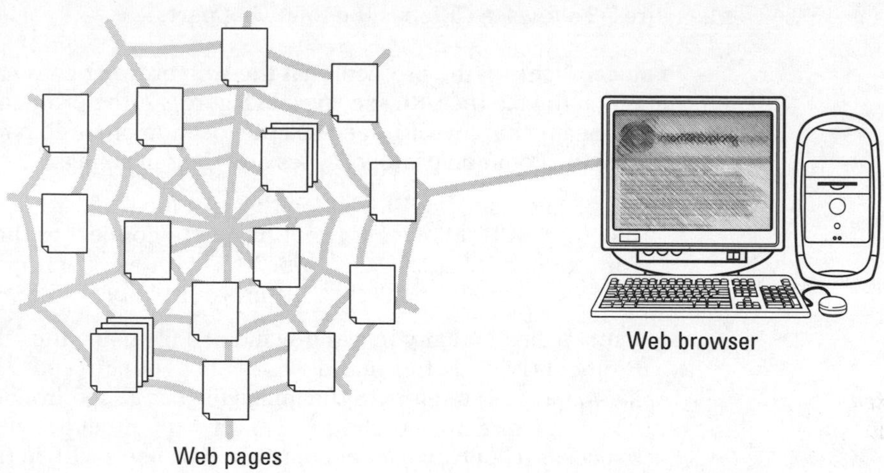

Figure 2-1: The Web is like billions of pages, scattered across the network, that you can read from your computer by using a Web browser.

The *links* in a Web page are references to other Web pages that you can follow to go from one page to another. The Web browser typically displays these links as underlined text (in a different color) or as images. Each link is like an instruction to you — something like, "For more information, please consult Chapter 4," that you might find in a real book. In a Web page, all you have to do is click the link; the Web browser brings up the referenced page, even though that document may actually reside on a far-away computer somewhere on the Internet.

The links in a Web page are referred to as *hypertext links* because when you click a link, the Web browser jumps to the Web page referenced by that link.

This arrangement brings up a question. In a real book, you might ask the reader to go to a specific chapter or page in the book. How does a hypertext link indicate the location of the referenced Web page? In the World Wide Web, each Web page has a special name, called a *Uniform Resource Locator* (URL). A URL uniquely specifies the location of a file on a computer. Figure 2-2 shows the parts of a URL.

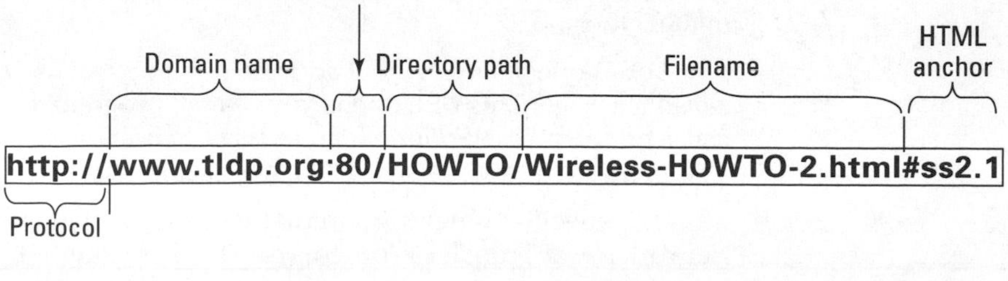

Figure 2-2: The parts of a Uniform Resource Locator (URL).

As Figure 2-2 shows, a URL has the following parts:

✦ **Protocol:** Name of the protocol that the Web browser uses to access the data from the file the URL specifies. In Figure 2-2, the protocol is `http://`, which means that the URL specifies the location of a Web page. Here are some of the common protocol types and their meanings:

  - `file://` means the URL is pointing to a local file. You can use this URL to view HTML files without having to connect to the Internet. For example, `file:///var/www/html/index.html` opens the file `/var/www/html/index.html` from your Linux system.
  - `ftp://` means that you can download a file using the File Transfer Protocol (FTP). For example, `ftp://ftp.purdue.edu/pub/uns/NASA/nasa.jpg` refers to the image file `nasa.jpg` from the `/pub/uns/NASA` directory of the FTP server `ftp.purdue.edu`. If you want to access a specific user account via FTP, use a URL in the following form:

    ```
    ftp://username:password@ftp.somesite.com/
    ```

    with the username and password embedded in the URL. (Note that the password is in plain text and not secure.)
  - `http://` means that the file is downloaded using the HyperText Transfer Protocol (HTTP). This protocol is the well-known format of URLs for all Web sites, such as `http://fedora.redhat.com` for the Fedora Project's home page. If the URL does not have a filename, the Web server sends a default HTML file named `index.html`. (That's the default filename for the popular UNIX-based Apache Web servers; Microsoft Windows Web servers use a different default filename.)
  - `https://` specifies that the file is accessed through a Secure Sockets Layer (SSL) connection — a protocol designed by Netscape Communications for encrypted data transfers across the Internet. This form of URL is typically used when the Web browser sends sensitive information (such as credit card number, username, and password) to a Web server. For example, a URL such as

    ```
    https://some.site.com/secure/takeorder.html
    ```

    may display an HTML form that requests credit card information and other personal information (such as name, address, and phone number).
  - `mailto://` specifies an e-mail address that you can use to send an e-mail message. This URL opens your e-mail program, from which you can send the message. For example, `mailto:webmaster@someplace.com` refers to the Webmaster at the host `someplace.com`.
  - `news://` specifies a newsgroup that you can read by means of the Network News Transfer Protocol (NNTP). For example,

    ```
    news://news.md.comcast.giganews.com/comp.os.linux.setup
    ```

accesses the comp.os.linux.setup newsgroup at the news server news.md.comcast.giganews.com. If you have a default news server configured for the Web browser, you can omit the news server's name and use the URL news:comp.os.linux.setup to access the newsgroup.

- **Domain name:** Contains the fully qualified domain name of the computer that has the file this URL specifies. You can also provide an IP address in this field. The domain name is not case sensitive.
- **Port:** Port number that is being used by the protocol listed in the first part of the URL. This part of the URL is optional; all protocols have default ports. The default port for HTTP, for example, is 80. If a site configures the Web server to listen to a different port, the URL has to include the port number.
- **Directory path:** Directory path of the file being referred to in the URL. For Web pages, this field is the directory path of the HTML file. The directory path is case sensitive.
- **Filename:** Name of the file. For Web pages, the filename typically ends with .htm or .html. If you omit the filename, the Web server returns a default file (often named index.html). The filename is case sensitive.
- **HTML anchor:** Optional part of the URL that makes the Web browser jump to a specific location in the file. If this part starts with a question mark (?) instead of a hash mark (#), the browser takes the text following the question mark to be a query. The Web server returns information based on such queries.

Web servers and Web browsers

The Web server serves up the Web pages, and the Web browser downloads them and displays them to the user. That's pretty much the story with these two cooperating software packages that make the Web work.

In a typical scenario, the user sits in front of a computer that's connected to the Internet and runs a Web browser. When the user clicks a link or types a URL into the Web browser, the browser connects to the Web server and requests a document from the server. The Web server sends the document (usually in HTML format) and ends the connection. The Web browser interprets and displays the HTML document with text, graphics, and multimedia (if applicable). Figure 2-3 illustrates this typical scenario of a user browsing the Web.

The Web browser's connection to the Web server ends after the server sends the document. When the user browses through the downloaded document and clicks another hypertext link, the Web browser again connects to the Web server named in the hypertext link, downloads the document, ends the connection, and displays the new document. That's how the user can move from one document to another with ease.

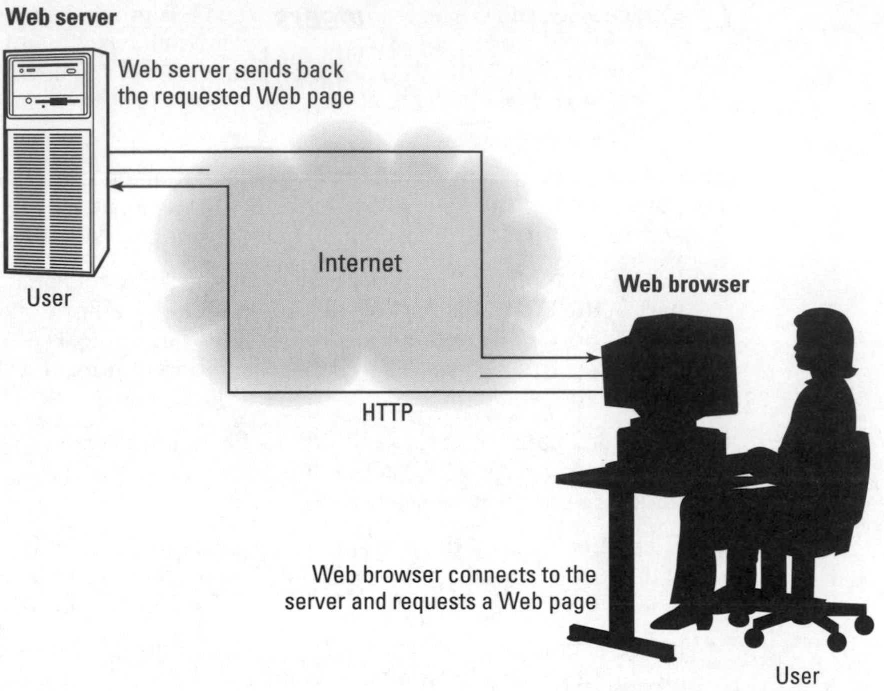

Figure 2-3: The Web browser requests documents and the Web server sends them.

A Web browser can do more than simply "talk" HTTP with the Web server — in fact, Web browsers can also download documents using FTP and many have integrated mail and newsreaders as well.

Web Browsing in Linux

Web browsing is fun because so many of today's Web pages are so full of graphics and multimedia. Then there's the element of surprise — you can click a link and end up at unexpected Web pages. Links are the most curious (and useful) aspect of the Web. You can start at a page that shows today's weather, and a click later, you can be reading this week's issue of *Time* magazine.

To browse the Web, all you need is a Web browser and an Internet connection. I assume that you've already taken care of the Internet connection (see Book III, Chapter 1 if you haven't yet set up your Internet connection), so all you need to know are the Web browsers in Linux.

Checking out Web browsers for Linux

Many Linux distributions come with the Mozilla Web browser. Mozilla is an open source version of the venerable Netscape Communicator.

Several other Web browsers are available for Linux. I briefly mention the other browsers, but I focus on Mozilla in the rest of the discussions. Here are the major Web browsers for Linux:

- **Mozilla:** The reincarnation of that old workhorse — Netscape Communicator — only better. Includes mail and a newsreader. The Web browser is called the Mozilla Navigator, or simply Navigator (just as it was in Netscape Communicator).
- **Epiphany:** The GNOME Web browser that uses parts of the Mozilla code to draw the Web pages, but has a simpler user interface than Mozilla. If Epiphany is not installed, you can download it from `www.gnome.org/projects/epiphany`.
- **Firefox:** Mozilla's next-generation browser that blocks pop-up ads, provides tabs for easily viewing multiple Web pages in a single window, and includes a set of privacy tools. You can download Firefox from `www.mozilla.org/download.html`.
- **Konqueror:** The KDE Web browser that also doubles as a file manager and a universal viewer.

In addition to these, many other applications are capable of downloading and displaying Web pages.

DISTRIBUTION SPECIFIC

Mozilla may not be installed by default on SUSE, but you can easily use YaST to search for `mozilla` and then install it. You can install Mozilla Firefox the same way in SUSE. In Debian, you can install Firefox by typing **apt-get install mozilla-firefox** in a terminal window.

Learning Mozilla's user interface

You can typically start Mozilla by clicking an icon on the panel or by selecting it from the Main Menu.

When Mozilla starts, it displays a browser window with a default home page. (The main Web page on a Web server is known as the *home page.*) You can configure Mozilla to use a different Web page as the default home page.

Figure 2-4 shows a Web page from a U.S. government Web site (`www.gao.gov`), as well as the main elements of the Mozilla browser window.

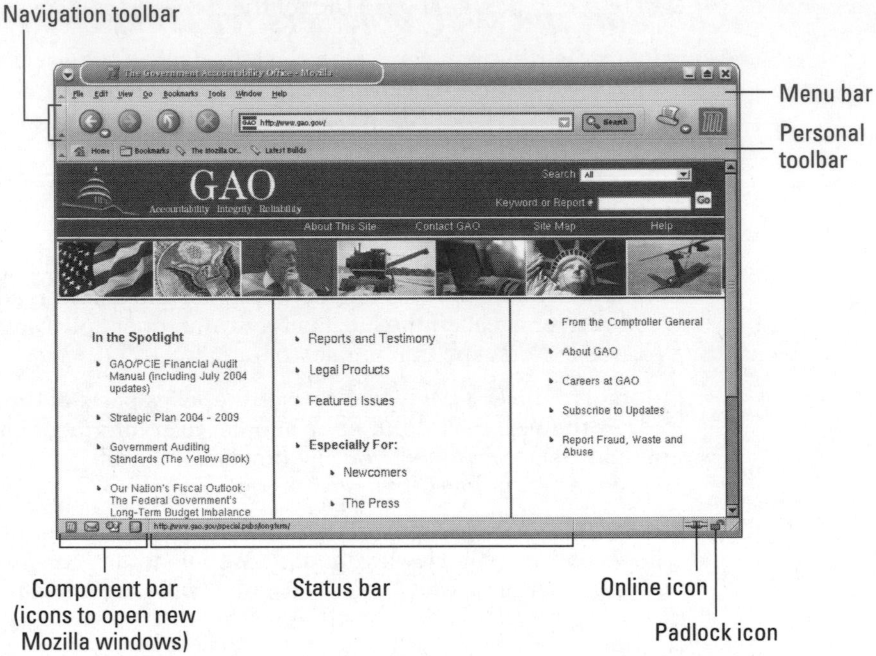

Figure 2-4: The Mozilla Web browser in action.

The Mozilla Web browser includes lots of features in its user interface, but you can master it easily. You can turn off some of the items that make it look busy. You can also start with just the basics to get going with Mozilla and then gradually expand to areas that you haven't yet explored.

Mozilla toolbars

Starting from the top of the window, you see a menu bar with the standard menus (File, Edit, and so forth), followed by the two toolbars — the Navigation toolbar and the Personal toolbar. The area underneath the Personal toolbar is where the current Web page appears.

Here's what you can do with the buttons on the Navigation toolbar that appears just below the menu bar, from left to right:

- **Back:** Move to the previous Web page.
- **Forward:** Move to the page from which you may have gone backward.
- **Reload:** Reload the current Web page.
- **Stop:** Stop loading the current page.

- **Location text box:** Show the URL of the current Web page. (Type a URL in this box to view that Web page.)
- **Search:** Takes you to the Google Web Search page (`www.google.com`).
- **Print:** Print the current Web page. (You can also preview how the page will appear when printed.)
- **Mozilla icon:** Go to the Mozilla.org Web site (`www.mozilla.org`).

Immediately below the Navigation toolbar comes the Personal toolbar with the Home and Bookmarks buttons. These two buttons serve the following purposes:

- **Home:** Takes you to the home page.
- **Bookmarks:** Displays a menu from which you can bookmark the current page as well as manage your bookmarks.

Mozilla includes a number of other links and a folder, named Bookmarks, on the Personal toolbar. You can save links by dragging and dropping them into the Bookmarks folder on the Personal toolbar.

Status bar

You can think of the bar along the bottom edge of the Mozilla window as the status bar because the middle part of that area displays status information as Mozilla loads a Web page.

The left side of the status bar includes a component bar, which displays a few small icons. If you want a hint about what any of these icons do, simply mouse over the button, and Mozilla displays a small balloon help message. You can click these icons to open other Mozilla windows to perform various tasks.

TECHNICAL STUFF

In the right corner of Mozilla's status bar, to the right of the status message, you see two icons. The icon on the left indicates that you're online; if you click it, Mozilla goes offline. The rightmost icon is a security padlock. Mozilla supports a secure version of HTTP that uses a protocol called *Secure Sockets Layer* (SSL) to transfer encrypted data between the browser and the Web server. When Mozilla connects to a Web server that supports secure HTTP, the security padlock appears locked. Otherwise the security padlock is open, signifying an insecure connection. The URL for secure HTTP transfers begins with `https://` instead of the usual `http://`. (Note the extra `s` in `https`.)

TIP

Mozilla displays status messages in the middle portion of the status bar. You can watch the messages in this area to see what's going on. If you mouse over a link on the Web page, the status bar displays the URL for that link.

Mozilla menus

I haven't mentioned the Mozilla menus much. That's because you can usually get by without having to go to them. Nevertheless, taking a quick look through the Mozilla menus is worthwhile so you know what each one offers. Table 2-1 gives you an overview of the Mozilla menus.

Table 2-1 Mozilla Menus

This Menu	*Enables You to Do the Following*
File	Open a file or Web location, close the browser, send a Web page or link by e-mail, edit a Web page, print the current page, and quit Mozilla.
Edit	Copy and paste selections, find text in the current page, and edit your preferences.
View	Show or hide various toolbars, reload the current page, make the text larger or smaller, view the HTML code for the page, and view information about the page.
Go	Go backward and forward in the list of pages you have visited, or jump to other recently visited Web pages.
Bookmarks	Bookmark a page, manage the bookmarks, and add links to the Personal toolbar folder. (These then appear in the Personal toolbar.)
Tools	Search the Web and manage various aspects of the Web page, such as image loading, cookies, and stored passwords.
Window	Open other Mozilla windows, such as Mozilla Mail, Navigator, Address Book, and Composer.
Help	Get online help on Mozilla.

Changing your home page

Your *home page* is the page that Mozilla loads when you start it. By default, Mozilla loads a file from your system's hard drive. Changing the home page is easy.

First locate the page on the Web that you want to be the home page. You can get to that page any way you want. You can search with a search engine to find the page you want, you can type in the URL in the Location text box, or you may even accidentally end up on a page that you want to make your home page. It doesn't matter.

When you're viewing the Web page that you want to make your home page in Mozilla, choose Edit⇨Preferences from the Mozilla menu. The Preferences dialog box appears, as shown in Figure 2-5.

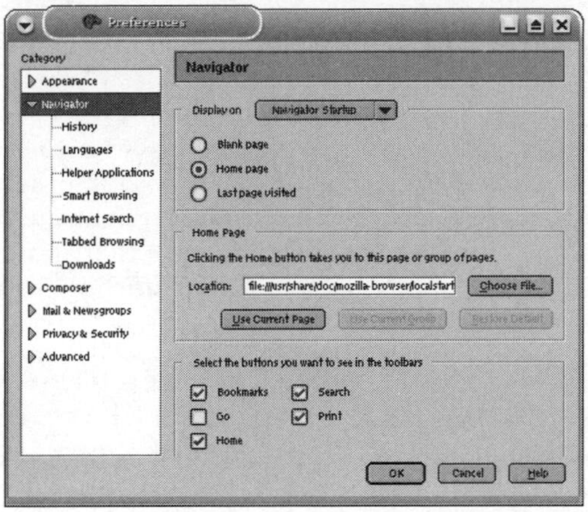

Figure 2-5: Click the Use Current Page button to make the current Web page your home page.

On the right side of Figure 2-5, notice that the Home Page radio button is selected. This option means that Mozilla Navigator displays the home page when you start it up. Then you see the URL for the home page, and underneath the address is a Use Current Page button. Click that button to make the current page your home page.

REMEMBER

You can set a lot of other options using the Preferences window. Although I am not explaining all the options, you can click around to explore everything that you can do from this window. For example, you can click the Choose File button to select a file on your local system as the home page.

Surfing the Net with Mozilla

Where you go from the Mozilla home page depends on you. All you have to do is click and see where you end up. Move your mouse around. You know when you are on a link because the mouse pointer changes to a hand with an extended index finger. Click the link, and Mozilla downloads the Web page referenced by that link.

How you use the Web depends on what you want to do. When you first get started, you may explore a lot — browsing through Web sites and following links without any specific goal in mind; what you may call Web window-shopping.

The other, more purposeful, use of the Web is to find specific information from the Net. For example, you might want to locate all the Web sites that contain documents with a specified keyword. For such searches, you can use one of many Web search tools available on the Net. Mozilla's Search button takes you to the Google Web Search page (`www.google.com`).

A third type of use is a visit to a specific site with a known URL. For example, when reading about a specific topic in this book, you may come across a specific URL. In that case, you want to go directly to that Web page.

If you want to surf the Net with Mozilla, all you need is a starting Web page — then you can click whatever catches your fancy. For example, select the text in the Location text box in Mozilla's Navigation toolbar, type **www.yahoo.com**, and then press Enter. You get to the Yahoo! home page that shows the Yahoo! Web directory — organized by subject. There's your starting point. All you have to do is click and you're on your way!

Introducing Epiphany and Firefox

Epiphany is the GNOME Web browser (you can run it in both GNOME and KDE desktops) with a simple user interface. You can download Epiphany and get more information from `www.gnome.org/projects/epiphany`.

Debian's KDE desktop includes the Epiphany Web browser. To start Epiphany in Debian, select Main Menu⇨Debian⇨Apps⇨Net⇨Epiphany Web Browser. In SUSE, select Main Menu⇨System⇨YaST to start YaST, select Software and then Install/Remove Software. In the YaST2 window that appears, enter **mozilla** — the name of the Mozilla package — in the search field and press Enter. You should then see `epiphany` in the results list. Select it and click Accept to install it.

Figure 2-6 shows the initial Epiphany window showing a U.S. government Web site.

If you compare Figure 2-6 with the Mozilla window in Figure 2-4, you can probably see that the Epiphany window is simpler, with just the navigation toolbar and the text entry area where you can type a new URL. Epiphany supports tabs. You can press Ctrl+T (or select File⇨New Tab) to open a new tab where you can view a new Web page.

Firefox is the next-generation Web browser from Mozilla and, like Mozilla, Firefox is available for many different operating systems, including Linux. You can download it from `www.mozilla.org/download.html`.

In Debian, it's easy to install Firefox. Make sure that your Debian system is connected to the Internet. Type **su -** in a terminal window and enter the `root` password, and then type **apt-get install mozilla-firefox**. After you install Firefox, start it by selecting Main Menu⇨Internet⇨Mozilla Firefox. Figure 2-7 shows the Mozilla Firefox window showing a U.S. government Web site.

Firefox has a user interface that's similar to Mozilla. Like Epiphany, Firefox also supports tabbed browsing, which means that you can open a new tab (by pressing Ctrl+T) and view a Web page in that tab. That way, you can view multiple Web pages in a single window.

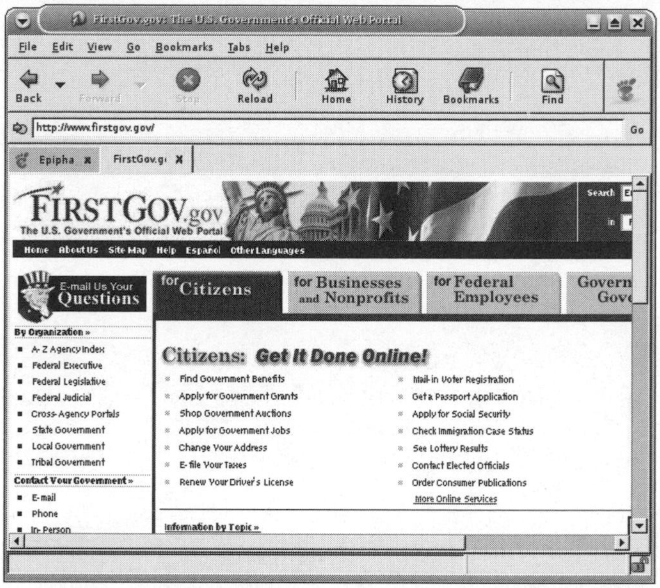

Figure 2-6: Epiphany Web browser window with a typical Web page.

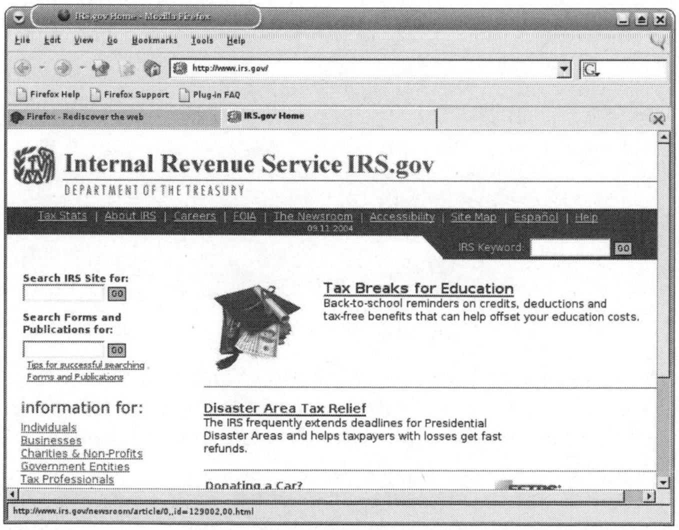

Figure 2-7: Mozilla Firefox displaying a U.S. government Web site.

Chapter 3: Reading Newsgroups

In This Chapter

- Understanding newsgroups
- Reading newsgroups from your ISP using Mozilla Mail, KNode, and Pan
- Reading and searching newsgroups at some Web sites

Internet newsgroups are like the bulletin board systems (BBSs) of the pre-Web age or the forums offered on online systems such as AOL and MSN. Essentially, newsgroups provide a distributed conferencing system that spans the globe. You can post articles — essentially e-mail messages to a whole group of people — and respond to articles others have posted.

Think of an Internet newsgroup as a gathering place — a virtual meeting place where you can ask questions and discuss various issues (and best of all, everything you discuss gets archived for posterity).

To participate in newsgroups, you need access to a news server — your Internet Service Provider (ISP) can give you this access. You also need a newsreader. Luckily, Linux comes with software that you can use to read newsgroups. In this chapter, I introduce you to newsgroups and show you how to read newsgroups with a few of the newsreaders. I also briefly explain how you can read and search newsgroups for free from a few Web sites.

Understanding Newsgroups

Newsgroups originated in Usenet — a store-and-forward messaging network that was widely used for exchanging e-mail and news items. Usenet works like a telegraph in that news and mail are relayed from one system to another. In Usenet, the systems are not on any network; the systems simply dial up one another and use the UNIX-to-UNIX Copy Protocol (UUCP) to transfer text messages.

Although it's a very loosely connected collection of computers, Usenet works well and continues to be used because very little expense is involved in connecting to it. All you need is a modem and a site willing to store and forward your mail and news. You have to set up UUCP on your system, but you don't need a sustained network connection; just a few phone calls are all you need to keep the e-mail and news flowing. The downside of Usenet is that you cannot use TCP/IP services such as the Web, TELNET, or FTP with UUCP.

From their Usenet origins, the newsgroups have now migrated to the Internet (even though the newsgroups are still called *Usenet newsgroups*). Instead of UUCP, the Network News Transfer Protocol (NNTP) now transports the news.

Although (for most of the online world) the news transport protocol has changed from UUCP to NNTP, the store-and-forward concept of news transfer remains. Thus, if you want to get news on your Linux system, you have to find a news server from which your system can download news. Typically, you can use your ISP's news server.

Newsgroup hierarchy

The Internet newsgroups are organized in a hierarchy for ease of maintenance as well as ease of use. The newsgroup names help keep things straight by showing the hierarchy.

Admittedly, these newsgroup names are written in Internet-speak, which can seem rather obscure at first. But the language is pretty easy to pick up after a little bit of explanation. For example, a typical newsgroup name looks like this:

```
comp.os.linux.announce
```

This name says that `comp.os.linux.announce` is a newsgroup for announcements (`announce`) about the Linux operating system (`os.linux`) and that these subjects fall under the broad category of computers (`comp`).

As you can see, the format of a newsgroup name is a sequence of words separated by periods. These words denote the hierarchy of the newsgroup. Figure 3-1 illustrates the concept of hierarchical organization of newsgroups.

To understand the newsgroup hierarchy, compare the newsgroup name with the path name of a file (for example, `/usr/lib/X11/xinit/Xclients`) in Linux. Just as a file's path name shows the directory hierarchy of the file, the newsgroup name shows the newsgroup hierarchy. In filenames, a slash (`/`) separates the names of directories; in a newsgroup's name, a period (`.`) separates the different levels in the newsgroup hierarchy.

In a newsgroup name, the first word represents the newsgroup *category*. The `comp.os.linux.announce` newsgroup, for example, is in the `comp` category, whereas `alt.books.technical` is in the `alt` category.

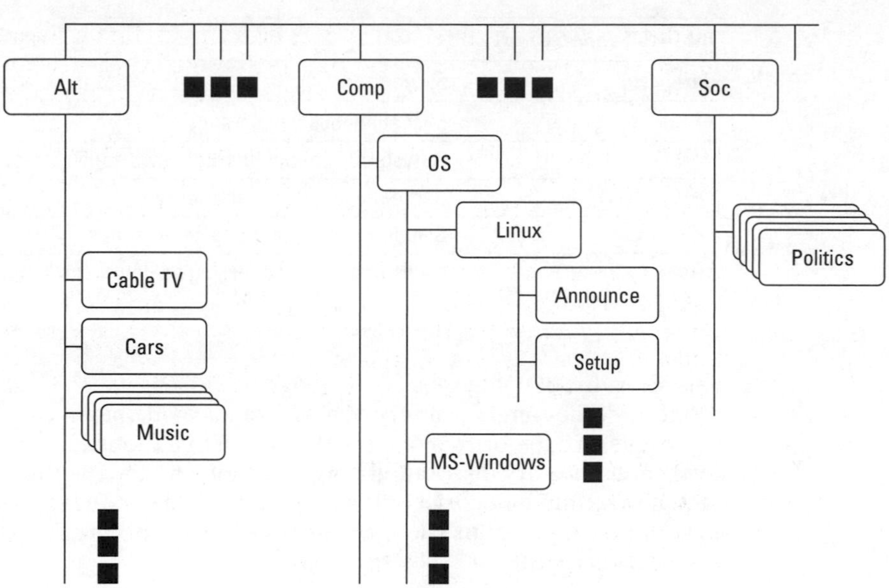

Figure 3-1: Newsgroups are organized in a hierarchy with many top-level categories.

Top-level newsgroup categories

Table 3-1 lists some of the major newsgroup categories. You find a wide variety of newsgroups covering subjects ranging from politics to computers. The Linux-related newsgroups are in the `comp.os.linux` hierarchy.

Table 3-1 Some Major Newsgroup Categories

Category	*Subject*
`alt`	"Alternative" newsgroups (not subject to any rules), which run the gamut from the mundane to the bizarre
`bionet`	Biology newsgroups
`bit`	Bitnet newsgroups
`biz`	Business newsgroups
`clari`	Clarinet news service (daily news)
`comp`	Computer hardware and software newsgroups (includes operating systems such as Linux and Microsoft Windows)
`ieee`	Newsgroups for the Institute of Electrical and Electronics Engineers (IEEE)
`k12`	Newsgroups devoted to elementary and secondary education
`linux`	Newsgroups devoted to Linux (includes a `linux.redhat` hierarchy)

(continued)

Table 3-1 *(continued)*

Category	*Subject*
`misc`	Miscellaneous newsgroups
`news`	Newsgroups about Internet news administration
`rec`	Recreational and art newsgroups
`sci`	Science and engineering newsgroups
`soc`	Newsgroups for discussing social issues and various cultures
`talk`	Discussions of current issues (think "talk radio")

This short list of categories is deceptive because it doesn't really tell you about the wide-ranging variety of newsgroups available in each category. The top-level categories alone number close to a thousand, but many top-level categories are distributed only in specific regions of the world. Because each newsgroup category contains several levels of subcategories, the overall count of newsgroups can be close to 60,000 or 70,000! The `comp` category alone has more than 500 newsgroups.

Unfortunately, many newsgroups are flooded with spam, just like your e-mail inbox only worse because anyone can post anything on a newsgroup. There are some newsgroups, called *moderated newsgroups*, that offer some relief. Anyone who wants to post on a moderated newsgroup must first submit the article to a moderator — a human being — who can then decide whether to post the article or reject it. You can reduce the spam overload by browsing moderated newsgroups whenever possible.

TIP: To browse newsgroup categories and get a feel for the breadth of topics covered by the newsgroups, visit the Free Usenet Newsgroup News Web site at `newsone.net`.

Linux-related newsgroups

Typically, you have to narrow your choice of newsgroups according to your interests. If you're interested in Linux, for example, you can pick one or more of these newsgroups:

- `comp.os.linux.admin`: Information about Linux system administration.
- `comp.os.linux.advocacy`: Discussions about promoting Linux.
- `comp.os.linux.announce`: Important announcements about Linux. This newsgroup is moderated, which means you must mail the article to a moderator, who then posts it to the newsgroup if the article is appropriate for the newsgroup. (This method keeps the riff-raff from clogging up the newsgroup with marketing pitches.)

- comp.os.linux.answers: Questions and answers about Linux. All the Linux HOWTOs are posted in this moderated newsgroup.
- comp.os.linux.development: Current Linux development work.
- comp.os.linux.development.apps: Linux application development.
- comp.os.linux.development.system: Linux operating system development.
- comp.os.linux.hardware: Discussions about Linux and various types of hardware.
- comp.os.linux.help: Help with various aspects of Linux.
- comp.os.linux.misc: Miscellaneous Linux-related topics.
- comp.os.linux.networking: Networking under Linux.
- comp.os.linux.redhat: Red Hat Linux-related topics.
- comp.os.linux.setup: Linux setup and installation.
- comp.os.linux.x: Discussions about setting up and running the X Window System under Linux.
- linux.debian: Moderated newsgroup about Debian GNU/Linux.
- linux.debian.news: Moderated newsgroup for news items about Debian GNU/Linux.
- linux.redhat: Discussions about Red Hat Linux.

TIP

You have to be selective about what newsgroups you read because keeping up with all the news is impossible, even in a specific area such as Linux. When you first install and set up Linux, you might read newsgroups such as comp.os.linux.help, comp.os.linux.setup, comp.os.linux.hardware, and comp.os.linux.x (especially if you run X). After you have Linux up and running, you may want to find out about only new things happening in Linux. For such information, read the comp.os.linux.announce newsgroup.

Reading Newsgroups from Your ISP

If you sign up with an ISP for Internet access, it can provide you with access to a news server. Such Internet news servers communicate by using the Network News Transfer Protocol (NNTP). You can use an NNTP-capable newsreader, such as Pan, to access the news server and read selected newsgroups. You can also read news by using the newsreader that comes with the Mozilla Web browser. Using a newsreader is the easiest way to access news from your ISP's news server.

My discussion of reading newsgroups assumes that you obtained access to a news server from your ISP. The ISP provides you the name of the news server and any username and password needed to set up your news account on the newsreader you use.

To read news, you need a *newsreader* — a program that enables you to select a newsgroup and view the items in that newsgroup. You also have to understand the newsgroup hierarchy and naming conventions (which I describe in the "Newsgroup hierarchy" section, earlier in this chapter). Now I show you how to read news from a news server.

If you don't have access to newsgroups through your ISP, you can try using one of the many public news servers that are out there. For a list of public news servers, visit NewzBot at `www.newzbot.com`. At this Web site, you can search for news servers that carry specific newsgroups.

Taking stock of newsreaders

You can use one of several software packages that enable you to download and read newsgroups in Linux. Here are a few major newsreaders:

- **Mozilla Mail:** Mozilla's mail and news component includes the ability to download news from an NNTP server. You can read newsgroups and post items to newsgroups. Xandros uses Mozilla Mail for mail and news.
- **KNode:** A newsreader for KDE that you can download from `knode.sourceforge.net`. Debian and SUSE use KNode as the newsreader.
- **Pan:** A GUI newsreader that, according to the developer's Web site (`pan.rebelbase.com`), " . . . attempts to be pleasing to both new and experienced users." You can download Pan for various Linux distributions from `pan.rebelbase.com/download`.

If you don't find any newsreader in your Linux system, you can download and install any of these newsreaders easily in any of the Linux distributions. Often, you can locate the download site by a simple search at a search engine — just search for the word "download" and the name of the newsreader.

Reading newsgroups with Mozilla Mail

You can browse newsgroups and post articles from Mozilla Mail, one of the components of Mozilla.

In some distributions such as Xandros, the Main Menu has options to start Mozilla Mail directly. In others, you can first start Mozilla (either from the panel or by selecting a menu option from the Main Menu) and then select Windows⇨Mail & Newsgroups from the Mozilla menu. In many Linux distributions, the mail and news component of Mozilla may not be installed. In that case, you have to download and install the Mozilla mail and news component or use another newsreader.

When you're starting to read newsgroups for the first time, follow these steps to set up the news account:

1. **Choose Edit⇨Mail & Newsgroups Account Settings from the Mozilla Mail menu.**

   A dialog box appears.

2. **Click Add Account.**

   The Account Wizard appears, as shown in Figure 3-2.

Figure 3-2: Mozilla's Account Wizard guides you through the newsgroup account setup.

3. **Select the Newsgroup Account radio button (see Figure 3-2) and click Next.**
4. **In the new screen that appears, fill in your identity information — name and e-mail address — and click Next to move to the next screen.**
5. **Enter your news server name and click Next.**
6. **Enter a descriptive name of the newsgroup account and click Next.**
7. **Click Finish to complete the newsgroup account setup.**

The new newsgroup account now appears in the list of accounts on the left side of the Mozilla Mail window. Click the newsgroup account name, and the right side of the window shows the options for the newsgroup account.

Click the Subscribe to Newsgroups link. Mozilla Mail starts to download the list of newsgroups from the news server.

REMEMBER

If your ISP's news server requires a username and password, you're prompted for that information. After that, Mozilla Mail downloads the list of newsgroups and displays them in the Subscribe dialog box. (You can enter a search string in a text box to narrow the list.) When you find the newsgroups you want, click the check box to subscribe to these newsgroups, as shown in Figure 3-3. Then click OK to close the dialog box.

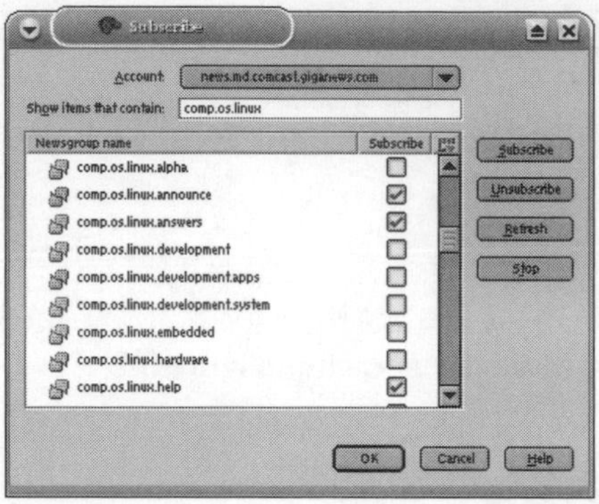

Figure 3-3: Indicate which newsgroups you want to subscribe to in this dialog box.

After you subscribe to newsgroups, these newsgroups appear under the newsgroup account name in the left side of the Mozilla Mail window. You can then read a newsgroup using these steps:

1. **Click a newsgroup name (for example, `comp.os.linux.announce`).**

   If your news server requires a username and password, a dialog box prompts you for this information. Then another dialog box asks you how many message headers you want to download.

2. **Specify the number of headers (for example, 500) you want and then click Download to proceed.**

   Mozilla Mail downloads the headers from the newsgroup and displays a list in the upper-right area of the window.

3. **From the list of headers, click an item to read that article, as shown in Figure 3-4.**

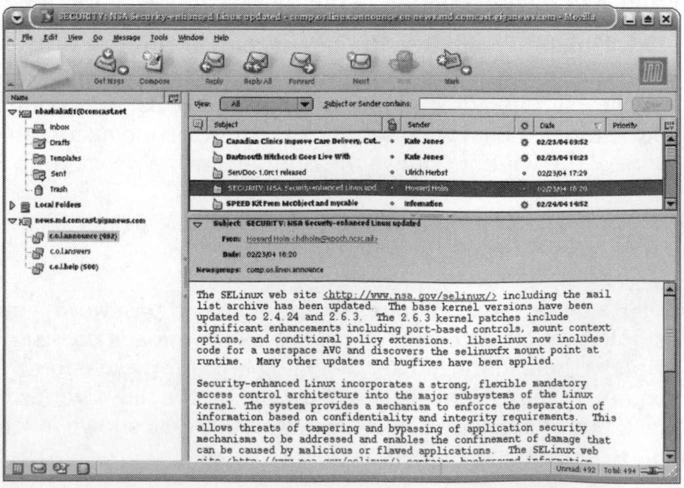

Figure 3-4: Click an article to read it in the lower-right part of the window.

To select other subscribed newsgroups, simply click the newsgroup's name in the left side of the window.

Newsgroup subscriptions

Unlike magazines or newspapers, newsgroups don't require that you subscribe to them; you can read any available newsgroup on the news server. The news server's administrator may decide to exclude certain newsgroups, however; if they aren't included, you cannot read them.

The only thing that can be called "subscribing" is when you indicate the newsgroups you routinely want to read. The news server does not receive any of this subscription information — the information is used only by the newsreader to determine what to download from the news server.

Posting news

You can use any newsreader to post a news article (a new item or a reply to an old posting) to one or more newsgroups. The exact command for posting a news item depends on the newsreader. For example, in the Mozilla Mail newsreader, you follow these steps to post an article:

1. **Click the Reply button on the toolbar to post a follow-up to a news item you're reading. To post a new news article, click the Compose button.**

   A window appears where you can compose the message.

2. **Type the names of the newsgroups, just as you would type the addresses of recipients when sending e-mail; then enter the subject and your message.**

   For this test posting, type `ignore` as the subject line and enter `misc.test` as the name of the newsgroup.

   Otherwise, any site that receives your article replies by mail to tell you the article has reached the site; that's in keeping with the purpose of the `misc.test` newsgroup.

3. **After you finish composing the message, click Send on the toolbar.**

   Mozilla Mail sends the message to the news server, which in turn sends it to other news servers, and soon it's all over the world!

4. **To verify that the test message reaches the newsgroup, choose File⇨Subscribe; then subscribe to the `misc.test` newsgroup (that's where you recently posted the new article). Look at the latest article (or one of the most recent ones) in `misc.test`; it should be the article you recently posted.**

If you post an article and read the newsgroup immediately, you see the new article, but that does not mean the article has reached other sites on the Internet. After all, your posting shows up on your news server immediately because that's where you posted the article. Because of the store-and-forward model of news distribution, the news article gradually propagates from your news server to others around the world.

The `misc.test` newsgroup provides a way to see whether or not your news posting is really getting around. If you post to that newsgroup and don't include the word *ignore* in the subject, news servers acknowledge receipt of the article by sending an e-mail message to the address listed in the Reply To field of the article's header.

Using KNode

Debian and SUSE use KNode as its default newsreader. In Debian, select Main Menu⇨Internet⇨News Reader to start KNode. In SUSE, select Main Menu⇨Internet⇨Usenet News Reader.

When KNode runs for the first time, it brings up the Configure KNode dialog box, shown in Figure 3-5, through which you can configure everything needed to read newsgroups and post items to newsgroups.

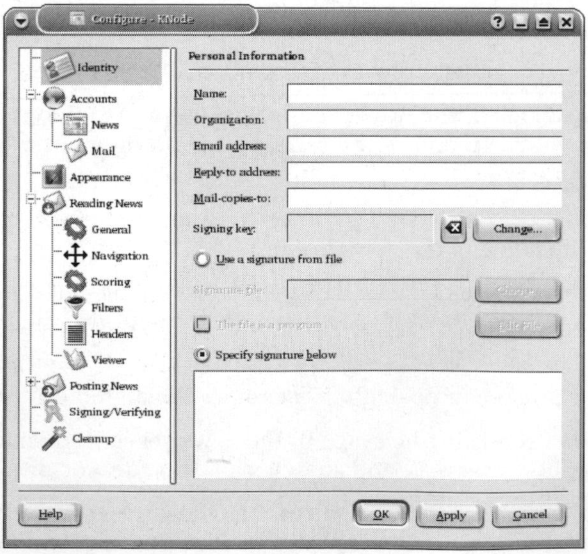

Figure 3-5: Configure KNode from this dialog box.

The left-hand side of the dialog box shows all the items that you can configure, and the right-hand side is where you enter the information for the item that you have currently selected on the left-hand side.

When the Configure KNode dialog box first opens, it prompts for your personal information. Enter your identification information such as name, e-mail address, and organization — this information is used when you post a new item to a newsgroup.

Then, click the plus sign next to Accounts in the left-hand side. (Refer to Figure 3-5.) Then click News to set up information about the news server from which you will be reading news. Click New in the Newsgroup servers window to bring up a dialog box (see Figure 3-6) where you can enter the information about the news server. Your ISP should have provided you with the information needed to access the news server. If the news server requires a login name and a password, you must enter that information as well.

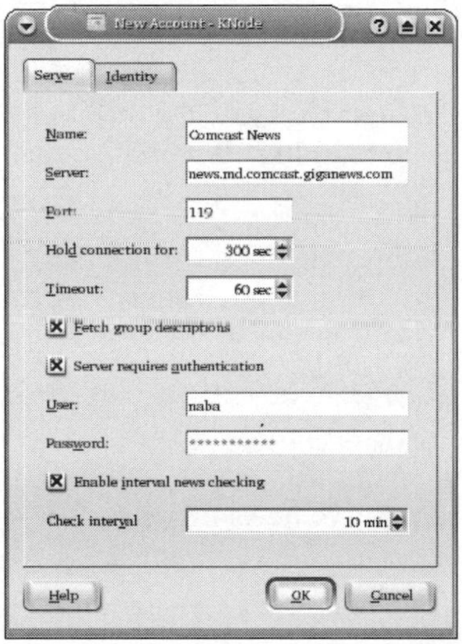

Figure 3-6: Enter information about the news server in this dialog box.

After you set up the news account, the KNode window shows the name of the news server in its left-hand side, as shown in Figure 3-7. Right-click on the server's name and select Subscribe to Newsgroups from the pop-up menu. A dialog box appears where you can subscribe to selected newsgroups (such as `comp.os.linux.announce`).

Figure 3-7 shows a typical view of the KNode window while reading an article from one of the subscribed newsgroups. The KNode user interface is similar to many other mail and newsreaders, including Mozilla Mail.

Using Pan

Pan is a GUI newsreader that you can run on any Linux GUI. Pan may not be installed in your Linux distribution, but you can download it from `pan.rebelbase.com/download`.

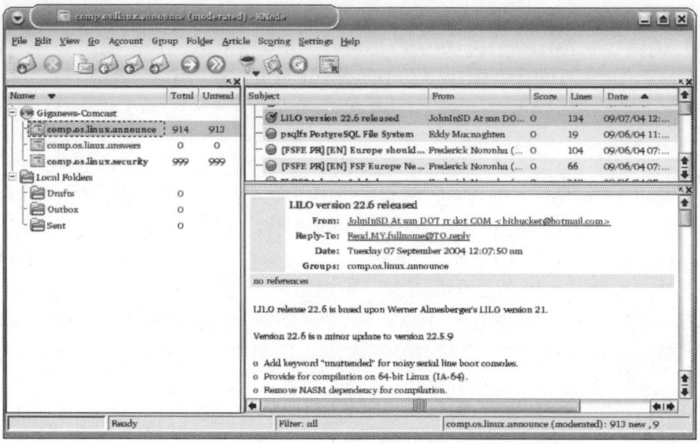

Figure 3-7: Read news items from newsgroups in KNode.

In Debian, it's simple to install Pan. Just type **su -** in a terminal window, enter the `root` password, and then type **apt-get install pan**. If you get some errors, try typing **apt-get update** followed by **apt-get upgrade**.

When you first run Pan, the Pan Setup Wizard starts and prompts you for information. Enter identifying information about yourself — your name and e-mail address. Next, Pan Setup Wizard prompts for information about the news server, as shown in Figure 3-8.

You also have to indicate which mail server Pan should use. Specify the SMTP server that you use to send mail through your ISP account. Pan uses the mail server when you want to reply to news items.

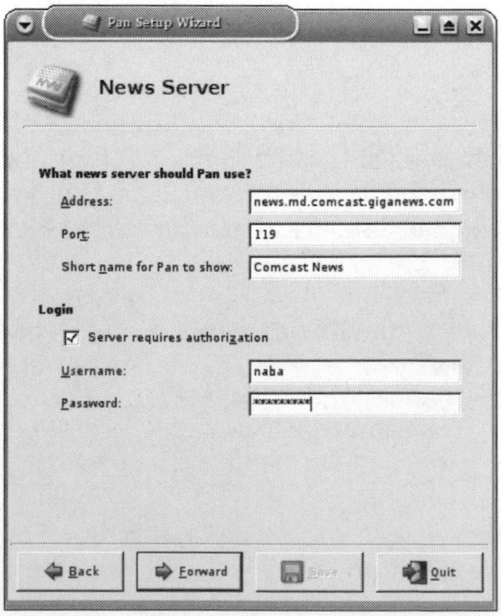

Figure 3-8: Enter information about the news server in this window in Pan Setup Wizard.

Click Save after providing all the setup information. The Pan window appears, and a dialog box asks if you want to download a list of groups. Click Yes.

Pan downloads the list of newsgroups and displays it in the left-hand side of its main window, as shown in Figure 3-9. An easy way to get to your desired newsgroup is to enter the first part of the newsgroup name (for example, `comp.news.linux`) in the Find box in the toolbar and press Enter. Pan displays the newsgroups that contain the text you entered.

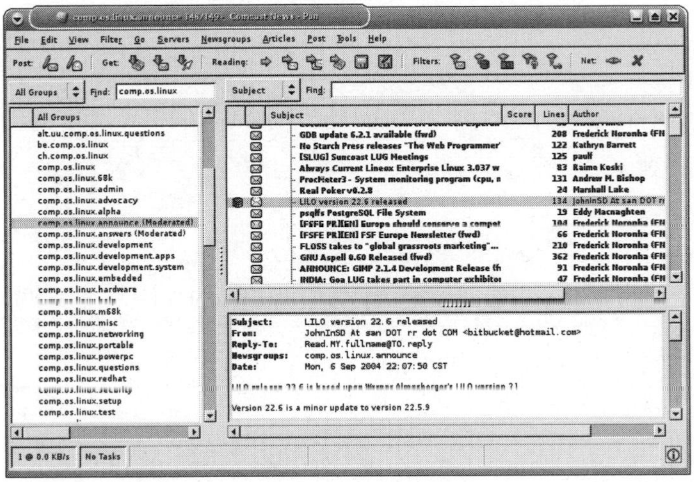

Figure 3-9: Reading a news item in Pan.

You can then click a newsgroup to download the headers from that group. Pan displays the headers in the upper-right side of the window. You can click a header and Pan displays the contents of that news item in the lower-right part of the window. (Refer to Figure 3-9.)

Reading and Searching Newsgroups at Web Sites

If you don't have access to newsgroups through your ISP, you can still read newsgroups and post articles to newsgroups at a number of Web sites. Some of them archive old news articles and provide good search capabilities, so you can search these for articles related to some question you may have.

The best part about reading newsgroups through a Web site is that you don't even need access to a news server and you can read news from your Web browser.

Table 3-2 lists Web sites that offer free access to Usenet newsgroups. Some sites offer Usenet newsgroup service for a fee. I don't list them here, but you can search for them with Google (`www.google.com`) — type the search words **usenet newsgroup access** to get a list of all Web sites that offer newsgroup access (including the ones that charge a fee).

Table 3-2 Web Sites with Free Access to Usenet Newsgroups

Web Site	*URL*
Google Groups	`groups.google.com`
News2Web	`www.news2web.com`
InterBulletin	`news.interbulletin.com`
Usenet Replayer	`www.usenet-replayer.com`
Mailgate	`www.mailgate.org`

One of the best places to read newsgroups, post articles, and search old newsgroup archives is Google Groups — Google's Usenet discussion forums — on the Web at `groups.google.com`. At that Web site, you can select a newsgroup to browse and you can post replies to articles posted on various newsgroups.

The best part of Google Groups is the search capability. You already know how good Google's Web search is; you get that same comprehensive search capability to locate newsgroup postings that relate to your search words. To search newsgroups, fill in the search form at `groups.google.com` and press Enter.

To browse newsgroups in Google Groups, ignore the search box and look at the list of high-level newsgroup categories such as `alt`, `comp`, and `soc`. Click the category, and you can gradually drill down to specific newsgroups. When viewing an article in Google Groups, you can click a link that enables you to post a follow-up to that article.

Chapter 4: Using FTP

In This Chapter

- **Using the GNOME FTP client**
- **Using the Mozilla Web browser as an FTP client**
- **Getting to know the FTP commands**

Just as the name implies, *File Transfer Protocol* (FTP) is used to transfer files between computers. For example, if your Internet Service Provider (ISP) gives you space for a personal Web site, you may have already used FTP to upload the files making up the Web site. Using an FTP client on your computer, you log in to your ISP account, provide your password, and then copy the files from your home system to the ISP's server.

You can also use FTP to download other files anonymously, such as open-source software from other computers on the Internet — in which case, you don't need an account on the remote system to download files. You can simply log in using the word `anonymous` as the username and provide your e-mail address as the password. (In fact, your Web browser can do this on your behalf, so you may not even know this process is happening.) This type of anonymous FTP is great for distributing files to anyone who wants them. For example, a hardware vendor might use anonymous FTP to provide updated device drivers to anyone who needs them.

Linux comes with several FTP clients, both command-line ones and GUI ones. In this chapter, I introduce you to a few GUI FTP clients and, for the command-line FTP client, describe the commands you use to work with remote directories.

Using Graphical FTP Clients

You can use one of the following GUI FTP clients in Linux:

- gFTP — a graphical FTP client for GNOME (`gftp.seul.org`)
- KBear — a graphical FTP client for KDE (`kbear.sourceforge.net`)
- Mozilla Web browser for anonymous FTP downloads

For uploading files, you may want to use gFTP because you typically have to provide a username and password for such transfers. Web browsers work fine for anonymous downloads, which is how you typically download software from the Internet.

I briefly describe all three GUI FTP clients in the next two sections.

Using gFTP

GNOME comes with gFTP, a graphical FTP client. gFTP is not installed by default, but you can download it from `gftp.seul.org` and install it easily. In some distributions, it may be in a package already and all you have to do is install that package.

In Debian, type **su -** in a terminal window and enter the `root` password, then type **apt-get install gftp**.

In Fedora Core, install gFTP from the companion DVD. Log in as `root`, insert the DVD into the DVD drive, and type **mount /mnt/cdrom** in a terminal window. (You may have to change `cdrom` to `cdrom1`, if the DVD drive is the second CD/DVD drive on your system.) Then type **cd /mnt/cdrom/Fedora/RPMS**, followed by **rpm -ivh gftp***.

In Fedora Core, start gFTP by selecting Main Menu⇨Internet⇨gFTP. In other distributions, you should be able to find it in the Main Menu. The gFTP window appears, as shown in Figure 4-1.

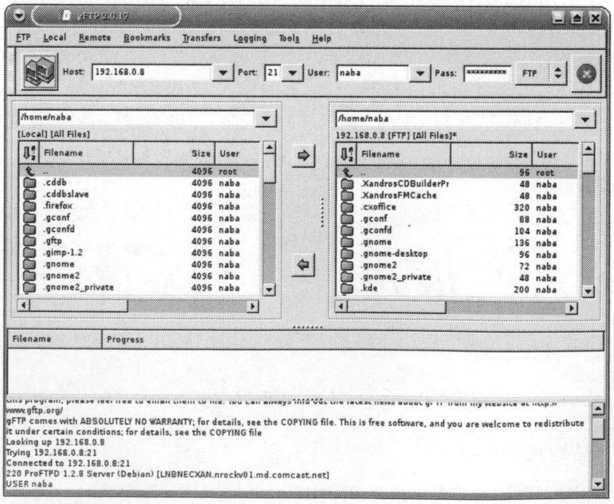

Figure 4-1: The gFTP window just after opening a connection to an FTP server.

The gFTP window has a menu bar with menus for performing various tasks. Just below the menu bar is a toolbar with a number of buttons and text fields. Here you can type the name or IP address of the remote host, the username, and the password needed to log in to the remote host. Figure 4-1 shows the gFTP window after you fill in this information and establish a connection with the remote host by clicking the button with the icon showing two computers (the leftmost one on the toolbar).

To upload or download files using gFTP, follow these steps:

1. **Fill in the host name or the IP address of the remote system in the Host field.**

   If you have used that host before, you can select it from the drop-down list that appears when you click the downward-pointing arrow next to the Host field.

2. **Provide the username in the User field and the password in the Pass field, and then click the button with the icon showing two computers (to the left of the Host field).**

   This operation causes gFTP to connect to your chosen host and to log in with the username and password you provided. The lower part of the gFTP window shows the FTP protocol messages exchanged between the two systems.

3. **Observe this area for any indication of error messages.**

   The directory listing of the remote system appears in the right half of the gFTP window. The left half shows the current local directory.

4. **To upload one or more files from the current system to the remote system, select the files in the list on the left, and then click the right-arrow button.**

5. **To download files from the remote system, select the filenames in the list on the right, and then click the left-arrow button.**

6. **When you're done transferring files, choose FTP⇨Quit from the menu.**

As these steps show, transferring files with a GUI FTP client, such as gFTP, is a simple task.

Believe it or not, gFTP isn't for FTP transfers alone. It can also transfer files using the HTTP protocol and secure file transfers using the Secure Shell (SSH) protocol.

Introducing KBear

KBear is a GUI FTP client for KDE. You find it in the Main Menu (in the Internet category) on KDE desktops such as the one in Debian. When you first start KDE, it runs the KBear Wizard that enables you to configure KBear. This configuration step mostly involves the layout of the KBear window, so you can just accept the defaults.

When the main KBear window appears, it displays your home folder in a view similar to that in Windows Explorer. To connect to an FTP server, choose FTP⇨Quick Connect. A dialog box (see Figure 4-2) prompts you for the hostname of the FTP server as well as the username and password.

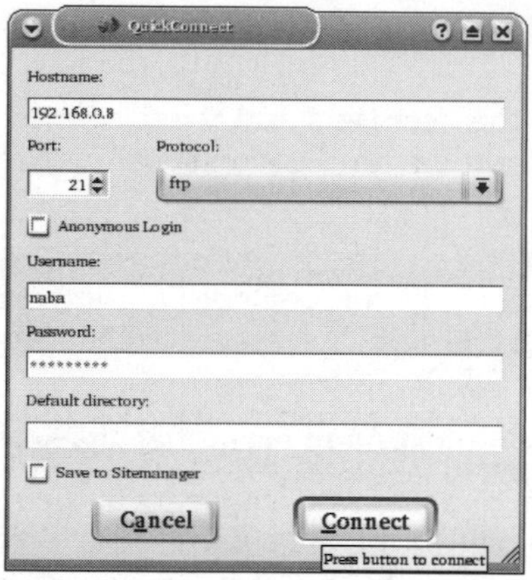

Figure 4-2: Enter information about the remote FTP server and click Connect.

After entering the requested information, click Connect. KBear establishes a connection to the remote FTP server. In the KBear main window, shown in Figure 4-3, you see both the local and remote directories side by side.

You can now transfer files by dragging them from one system's folder and dropping them on the other system's folder, so FTP transfers become just normal drag-and-drop file copying.

When you are done using KBear, select FTP⇨Quit or click the power off button (the leftmost one) on the toolbar.

Using a Web browser as an FTP client

Any Web browser can act as an FTP client, but such programs are best for anonymous FTP downloads, where the Web browser can log in using the anonymous username and any password.

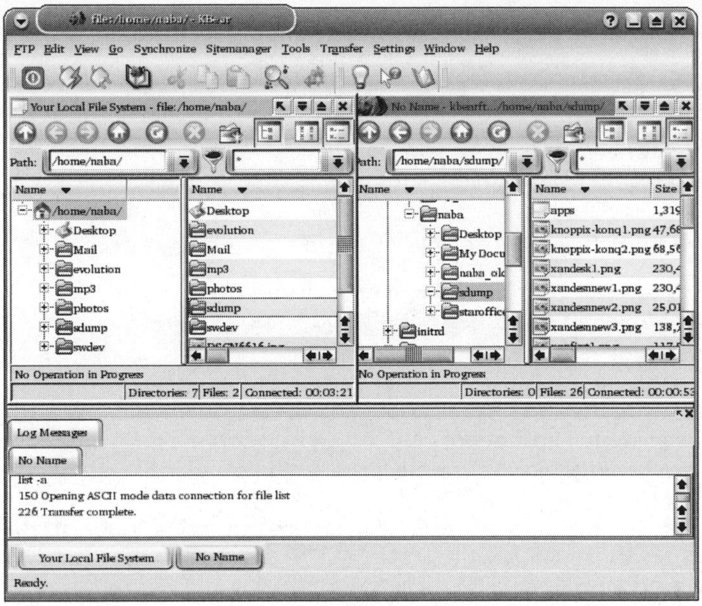

Figure 4-3: The KBear window shows the local directory and the remote FTP server's directory side by side.

For example, you can use the Mozilla Web browser as an FTP client. All you have to know is how to write the URL so that the Web browser can tell that you want to download a file using FTP. The syntax of the FTP URL is like this:

```
ftp://hostname/pathname
```

The first part (`ftp://`) indicates that you want an FTP transfer. The `hostname` part is the name of the FTP server (the name often starts with an `ftp` — for example, `ftp.netscape.com`). The *`pathname`* is the full directory path and filename of the file that you want to download.

If you simply provide the hostname for the FTP server, the Web browser displays the contents of the anonymous FTP directory. If you want to access anonymous FTP on your Linux system, start Mozilla (click the Mozilla icon on the GNOME panel), and then type the following line in the Location text box:

```
ftp://localhost/
```

Then press Enter. Mozilla shows the contents of the anonymous FTP directory on your Linux system. Figure 4-4 shows a typical appearance of an anonymous FTP directory in Mozilla. You can click folders to see their contents and download any files. Although I am showing how you can access your local system by using Mozilla's FTP capabilities, the purpose of FTP is (of course) to download files from other systems to your system.

Figure 4-4: You can use Mozilla to download files from anonymous FTP servers.

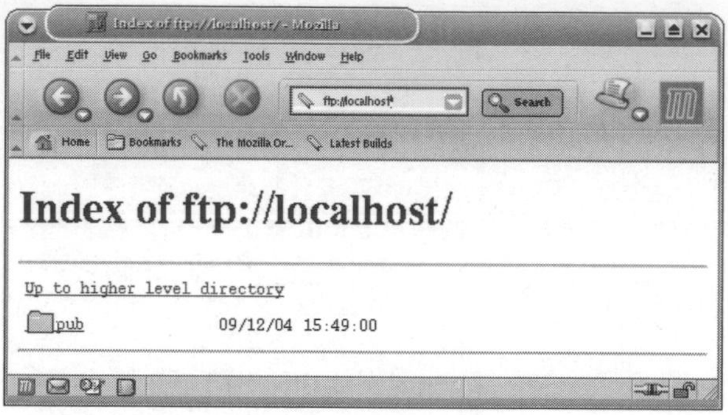

When you use the `ftp://localhost/` URL, you won't get a response from your system if you're not running an FTP server or if you have set up your firewall so that no FTP connections are allowed.

In Debian and Fedora Core, log in as `root` and type **/etc/init.d/vsftpd start** (in a terminal window) to start the FTP server. In SUSE, the `xinetd` super server controls the FTP server `vsftpd`. The `/etc/xinetd.d/vsftpd` configuration file specifies how `vsftpd` is started. See Book VII, Chapter 1 for more information about `xinetd` configuration files.

The same approach of accessing anonymous FTP sites works if you type the hostname of some other anonymous FTP server. For example, try typing the following URL:

```
ftp://ftp.netscape.com/
```

You get the directory of the `ftp.netscape.com` server.

Using the Command-Line FTP Client

Knowing how to use FTP from the command line is a good idea — just in case. For example, your GUI desktop may not be working, and in order to fix the problem, you may have to download some files. If you know how to use the command-line FTP client, you can download the files and take care of the problem. It's not that hard, and the command-line FTP client is available in all Linux distributions.

The best way to figure out the command-line FTP client is to try it out. The command is called `ftp`, and you can try out the `ftp` commands from your Linux system. You don't even need an Internet connection because you can use the `ftp` command to connect to your own system — I show you how.

Note that the exact output from the `ftp` command might be different because some distributions, such as Debian, use a text-mode version of gFTP as the command-line FTP client.

In the following sample FTP session, I use the command-line FTP client to log in using my username (`naba`) and browse the directories on one of my Linux systems. When you try a similar operation, replace the name with your username and provide your password. Here's the listing illustrating interaction with a typical command-line FTP client (my comments appear in italics):

```
ftp localhost
Connected to localhost (127.0.0.1).
220 (vsFTPd 2.0.1)
Name (localhost:naba):      (I press Enter.)
331 Please specify the password.
Password:           (I type my password.)
230 Login successful.
Remote system type is UNIX.
Using binary mode to transfer files.
ftp> help           (I type help to see a list of FTP commands.)
Commands may be abbreviated.  Commands are:

!              debug          mdir           sendport       site
$              dir            mget           put            size
account        disconnect     mkdir          pwd            status
append         exit           mls            quit           struct
ascii          form           mode           quote          system
bell           get            modtime        recv           sunique
binary         glob           mput           reget          tenex
bye            hash           newer          rstatus        tick
case           help           nmap           rhelp          trace
cd             idle           nlist          rename         type
cdup           image          ntrans         reset          user
chmod          lcd            open           restart        umask
close          ls             prompt         rmdir          verbose
cr             macdef         passive        runique        ?
delete         mdelete        proxy          send
ftp> help mget    (I can get help on a specific command.)
mget            get multiple files
ftp> cd /var/ftp (This changes directory to /var/ftp.)
250 Directory successfully changed.
ftp> ls   (This command lists the contents of the directory.)
227 Entering Passive Mode (127,0,0,1,38,142)
150 Here comes the directory listing.
drwxr-xr-x    2 0        0            4096 Feb 21 21:42 pub
226 Directory send OK.
ftp> bye            (This command ends the session.)
221 Goodbye.
```

As the listing shows, you can start the command-line FTP client by typing the command `ftp hostname`, where *hostname* is the name of the system you want to access. When the FTP client establishes a connection with the FTP server at the remote system, the FTP server prompts you for a username and password. After you supply the information, the FTP client displays the `ftp>` prompt, and you can begin typing commands to perform specific tasks. If you can't remember a specific FTP command, type **help** to view a list of them. You can get additional help for a specific command by typing **help *command***, where *command* is what you want help on.

Many FTP commands are similar to the Linux commands for navigating the file system. For example, `cd` changes directory, `pwd` prints the name of the current working directory, and `ls` lists the contents of the current directory. Two other common commands are `get` and `put` — `get` is what downloads a file from the remote system to your system, and `put` uploads (sends) a file from your system to the remote host.

Table 4-1 describes some commonly used FTP commands. You don't have to type the entire FTP command. For a long command, you only have to type the first few characters — enough to identify the command uniquely. For example, to delete a file, you can type **dele** and to change the file transfer mode to binary, you can type **bin**.

TIP: When downloading files from the Internet, you almost always want to transfer the files in binary mode because the software is usually archived and compressed in a binary form. (Its files aren't plain text files.) So always use the `binary` command to set the mode to binary. Then use the `get` command to download the files.

TIP: When transferring multiple files with similar names (such as `image1.jpg`, `image2.jpg`, and so on), type **prompt** to turn off prompting. (Otherwise the FTP client will ask you after each file transfer whether you want to transfer the next file.) Then type **mget** followed by the filename with wildcard. For example, to download all files with name starting with `image` and the `.jpg` extension, type **mget image*.jpg**.

Table 4-1 Commonly Used FTP Commands

Command	*Description*
`!`	Executes a shell command on the local system. For example, `!ls` lists the contents of the current directory on the local system.
`?`	Displays a list of commands (same as `help`).
`append`	Appends a local file to a remote file.
`ascii`	Sets the file-transfer type to ASCII (or plain text). This command is the default file-transfer type.
`binary`	Sets the file-transfer type to binary.

Command	*Description*
`bye`	Ends the FTP session with the remote FTP server and quits the FTP client.
`cd`	Changes the directory on the remote system. For example, `cd /pub/Linux` changes the remote directory to `/pub/Linux`.
`chmod`	Changes the permission settings of a remote file. For example, `chmod 644 index.html` changes the permission settings of the `index.html` file on the remote system.
`close`	Ends the FTP session with the FTP server and returns to the FTP client's prompt.
`delete`	Deletes a remote file. For example, `delete bigimage.jpg` deletes that file on the remote system.
`dir`	Lists the contents of the current directory on the remote system.
`disconnect`	Ends the FTP session and returns to the FTP client's prompt. (This command is the same as `close`.)
`get`	Downloads a remote file. For example, `get junk.tar.gz junk.tgz` downloads the file `junk.tar.gz` from the remote system and saves it as the file `junk.tgz` on the local system.
`hash`	Turns on or off the hash-mark (#) printing that shows the progress of file transfer. When this feature is turned on, a hash mark prints on-screen for every 1,024 bytes transferred from the remote system. (It's the command-line version of a progress bar.)
`help`	Displays a list of commands.
`image`	Same as `binary`.
`lcd`	Changes the current directory on the local system. For example, `lcd /var/ftp/pub` changes the current local directory to `/var/ftp/pub`.
`ls`	Lists the contents of the current remote directory.
`mdelete`	Deletes multiple files on a remote system. For example, `mdelete *.jpg` deletes all remote files with names ending in `.jpg` in the current directory.
`mdir`	Lists multiple remote files and saves the listing in a specified local file. For example, `mdir /usr/share/doc/w* wlist` saves the listing in the local file named `wlist`.
`mget`	Downloads multiple files. For example, `mget *.jpg` downloads all files with names ending in `.jpg`. If the prompt is turned on, the FTP client asks for confirmation before downloading each file.
`mkdir`	Creates a directory on the remote system. `mkdir images` creates a directory named `images` in the current directory on the remote system.
`mls`	Same as `mdir`.
`mput`	Uploads multiple files. For example, `mput *.jpg` sends all files with names ending in `.jpg` to the remote system. If the prompt is turned on, the FTP client asks for confirmation before sending each file.

(continued)

Table 4-1 *(continued)*

Command	*Description*
`open`	Opens a connection to the FTP server on the specified host. For example, `open ftp.netscape.com` connects to the FTP server on the host `ftp.netscape.com`.
`prompt`	Turns the prompt on or off. When the prompt is on, the FTP client prompts you for confirmation before downloading or uploading each file during a multiple-file transfer.
`put`	Sends a file to the remote system. For example, `put index.html` sends the `index.html` file from the local system to the remote system.
`pwd`	Displays the full pathname of the current directory on the remote system. When you log in as a user, the initial current working directory is your home directory.
`quit`	Same as `bye`.
`recv`	Same as `get`.
`rename`	Renames a file on the remote system. For example, `rename old.html new.html` renames the file `old.html` to `new.html` on the remote system.
`rmdir`	Deletes a directory on the remote system. For example, `rmdir images` deletes the `images` directory in the current directory of the remote system.
`send`	Same as `put`.
`size`	Shows the size of a remote file. For example, `size bigfile.tar.gz` shows the size of that remote file.
`status`	Shows the current status of the FTP client.
`user`	Sends new user information to the FTP server. For example, `user naba` sends the username `naba`; the FTP server then prompts for the password for that username.

Book V

Administration

The 5th Wave — By Rich Tennant

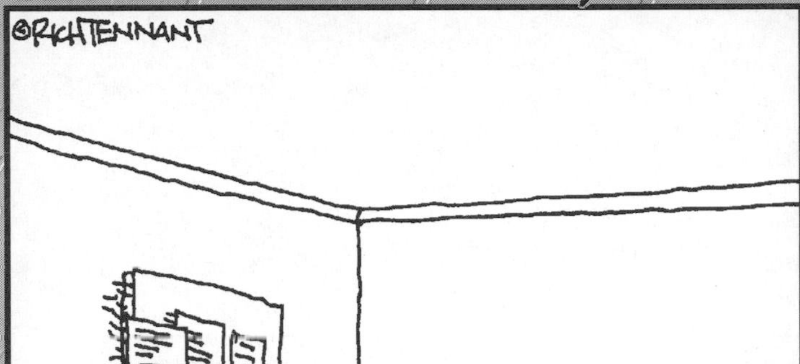

"Think of our relationship as a version of Red Hat Linux – I will not share a directory on the love-branch of your life."

Contents at a Glance

Chapter 1: Learning Basic System Administration

In This Chapter

- **Introducing the GUI `sysadmin` tools**
- **Becoming `root`**
- **Understanding the system startup process**
- **Taking stock of the system configuration files**
- **Viewing system information through the `/proc` file system**
- **Monitoring system performance**
- **Managing devices**
- **Scheduling jobs**

System administration or *sysadmin* refers to whatever has to be done to keep a computer system up and running; the *system administrator* (also called the *sysadmin*) is whoever is in charge of taking care of these tasks.

If you're running Linux at home or in a small office, you're most likely the system administrator for your systems. Or maybe you're the system administrator for a whole LAN full of Linux systems. No matter. In this chapter, I introduce you to basic system administration procedures and show you how to perform some common tasks.

Each Linux distribution comes with quite a few graphical tools for performing specific system administration tasks. I introduce you to some of these GUI tools in this chapter and describe some of them in greater detail in the other chapters of this minibook.

Taking Stock of System Administration Tasks

So what *are* system administration tasks? My off-the-cuff reply is *anything you have to do to keep the system running well.* More accurately, though, a system administrator's duties include the following:

- **Adding and removing user accounts.** You have to add new user accounts and remove unnecessary user accounts. If a user forgets the password, you have to change the password.
- **Managing the printing system.** You have to turn the print queue on or off, check the print queue's status, and delete print jobs if necessary.
- **Installing, configuring, and upgrading the operating system and various utilities.** You have to install or upgrade parts of the Linux operating system and other software that are part of the operating system.
- **Installing new software.** You have to install software that comes in various package formats such as RPM or DEB. You also have to download and unpack software that comes in source-code form — and then build executable programs from the source code.
- **Managing hardware.** Sometimes, you have to add new hardware and install drivers so the devices work properly.
- **Making backups.** You have to back up files, either in a Zip drive or on tape (if you have a tape drive).
- **Mounting and unmounting file systems.** When you want to access the files on a CD-ROM, for example, you have to mount that CD-ROM's file system on one of the directories in your Linux file system. You also have to mount floppy disks, in both Linux format and DOS format.
- **Automating tasks.** You have to schedule Linux tasks to take place automatically (at specific times) or periodically (at regular intervals).
- **Monitoring the system's performance.** You may want to keep an eye on system performance to see where the processor is spending most of its time, and to see the amount of free and used memory in the system.
- **Starting and shutting down the system.** Although starting the system typically involves nothing more than powering up the PC, you do have to take some care when you want to shut down your Linux system. If your system is set up for a graphical login screen, you can perform the shutdown operation by selecting a menu item from the login screen. Otherwise, use the `shutdown` command to stop all programs before turning off your PC's power switch.
- **Monitoring network status.** If you have a network presence (whether a LAN, a DSL line, or cable modem connection), you may want to check the status of various network interfaces and make sure your network connection is up and running.
- **Setting up host and network security.** You have to make sure that system files are protected and that your system can defend itself against attacks over the network.
- **Monitoring security.** You have to keep an eye on any intrusions, usually by checking the log files.

That's a long list of tasks! I don't cover all of them in this chapter, but the rest of the minibook describes most of these tasks. Here, I focus on some of the basics by introducing you to some GUI tools, explaining how to become `root` (the superuser), describing the system configuration files, and showing you how to monitor system performance, manage devices, and set up periodic jobs.

Introducing Some GUI Sysadmin Tools

Each Linux distribution comes with GUI tools for performing system administration tasks. The GUI tools prompt you for input and then run the necessary Linux commands to perform the task. In the following sections, I briefly introduce the GUI sysadmin tools in Debian, Fedora Core, SUSE, and Xandros.

GUI sysadmin tools in Debian

Debian does not have too many GUI tools for performing sysadmin tasks. You can, however, use some of the KDE GUI tools to take care of some sysadmin chores. Table 1-1 lists some common tasks and the menu selection you use to start the GUI tool that enables you to perform that task.

Table 1-1 Performing Sysadmin Tasks with GUI Tools in Debian

To Do This	*Select the Following the KDE Desktop*
Add or remove software	Main Menu⇨System⇨Package Manager
Change password	Main Menu⇨Settings⇨Change Password
Configure KDE desktop	Main Menu⇨Settings⇨Control Center
Find files	Main Menu⇨Find Files
Format floppy	Main Menu⇨Utilities⇨Floppy Formatter
Manage printers	Main Menu⇨System⇨Printers
Manage user accounts	Main Menu⇨System⇨User Manager
Monitor system performance	Main Menu⇨System⇨System Monitor
Schedule a task	Main Menu⇨System⇨Task Scheduler
View system logs	Main Menu⇨System⇨System Log

GUI sysadmin tools in Fedora Core

Fedora Core comes with a set of GUI system configuration tools that can ease the burden of performing typical sysadmin chores. Table 1-2 briefly summarizes the menu selections you use to start a GUI tool for a specific task.

Table 1-2 Starting GUI Sysadmin Tools in Fedora Core

To Configure or Manage This	*Start GUI Tool by Selecting This*
Date and time	Main Menu➪System Settings➪Date&Time
Disks and DVD/CD-ROM	Main Menu➪System Tools➪Disk Management
Display settings	Main Menu➪System Settings➪Display
Firewall settings	Main Menu➪System Settings➪Security Level
Hardware	Main Menu➪System Tools➪Hardware Browser
Internet connection	Main Menu➪System Tools➪Internet Configuration Wizard
Network	Main Menu➪System Settings➪Network
Preferences such as desktop and password	Main Menu➪Preferences
Printer	Main Menu➪System Settings➪Printing
`root` password	Main Menu➪System Settings➪Root Password
Servers	Main Menu➪System Settings➪Server Settings
Software	Main Menu➪System Settings➪Add/Remove Application
System logs	Main Menu➪System Tools➪System Logs
System performance	Main Menu➪System Tools➪System Monitor
User accounts	Main Menu➪System Settings➪Users and Groups

GUI sysadmin tools in Knoppix

Knoppix is a Live CD distribution that you can use either to try out Linux or as a tool to fix problems in an existing Linux system. As such, Knoppix comes with several GUI tools that you can use for system administration tasks. Table 1-3 summarizes some of the GUI tools in Knoppix.

Table 1-3 Using GUI tools for Sysadmin Tasks in Knoppix

To Do This	*Select This from the Knoppix GUI Desktop*
Configure desktop	Main Menu➪Settings➪Desktop Settings Wizard
Configure KDE	Main Menu➪Settings➪Control Center
Configure network	Main Menu➪KNOPPIX➪Network/Internet➪Network card configuration
Configure printer	Main Menu➪KNOPPIX➪Configure➪Configure printer(s)
Find Files	Main Menu➪Find Files

To Do This	*Select This from the Knoppix GUI Desktop*
Manage disk partitions (for troubleshooting existing Linux installations)	Main Menu➪System➪QTParted
Open a terminal window with `root` permission	Main Menu➪KNOPPIX➪Root Shell
Start Samba Server	Main Menu➪KNOPPIX➪Services➪Start Samba Server
Start SSH server	Main Menu➪KNOPPIX➪Services➪Start SSH Server

GUI sysadmin tools in SUSE

In SUSE, select Main Menu➪System➪YaST to start your system administration tasks in the YaST Control Center. Figure 1-1 shows the YaST Control Center window.

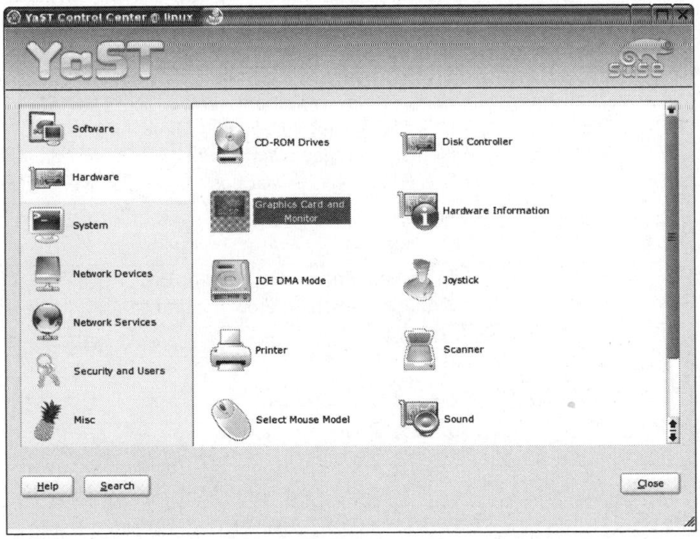

Figure 1-1: YaST Control Center is your starting point for many sysadmin tasks in SUSE.

The left side of the YaST Control Center shows icons for the categories of tasks you can perform. The right-hand side shows icons for specific tasks in the currently selected category. When you click an icon in the right-hand side of the YaST Control Center, a new YaST window appears and enables you to perform that task.

Table 1-4 summarizes the tasks for each of the category icons you see in the left side of the YaST Control Center. As you can see from the entries in the second column of Table 1-4, YaST Control Center is truly one-stop shopping for all of your sysadmin chores.

Table 1-4 Tasks by Category in the YaST Control Center

This Category	*Enables You to Configure/Manage the Following*
Software	Online Update; Install and Remove Software; Change Source of Installation; Installation into Directory; Patch CD Update; System Update
Hardware	CD-ROM Drives; Disk Controllers; Graphics Card and Monitor; Hardware Information; IDE DMA Mode; Joystick; Printer; Scanner; Select Mouse Model; Sound; TV Card
System	`/etc/sysconfig` Editor; Boot Loader Configuration; Choose Language; Create a Boot, Rescue, or Module Floppy; Date and Time; LVM; Partitioner; Power Management; Powertweak Configuration; Profile Manager; Restore System; Runlevel Editor; Select Keyboard Layout; System Backup
Network Devices	DSL; Fax; ISDN; Modem; Network Card; Phone Answering Machine
Network Services	DHCP Server; DNS Server; DNS Host and Name; HTTP Server; Host Names; Kerberos Client; LDAP Client; Mail Transfer Agent; NFS Client; NFS Server; NIS Client; NIS Server; NTP Client; Network Services (inetd); Proxy; Remote Administration; Routing; SLP Browser; Samba Client; Samba Server; TFTP Server
Security and Users	Edit and create groups; Edit and create users; Firewall; Security settings
Misc	Autoinstallation; Load Vendor Driver CD; Post a Support Query; View Start-up Log; View System Log

GUI sysadmin tools in Xandros

Xandros is designed to be a desktop operating system, and as such, everything is easily accessible from the desktop. For most sysadmin tasks, you start at the Xandros Control Center — select Main Menu⇨Control Center to get there. (Figure 1-2 shows you what you find when you do get there.)

As you can see, the left-hand side of the window shows a tree menu of task categories. You can click the plus sign next to a category to view the subcategories. When you click a specific task, the right-hand side of the window displays the GUI through which you can perform that task.

For some tasks, such as mounting file systems or adding printers, you can open the Xandros File Manager as a system administrator by selecting Main Menu⇨Applications⇨System⇨Administrator Tools⇨Xandros File Manager (Administrator). Figure 1-3 shows the Xandros File Manager window from which you can perform some sysadmin tasks.

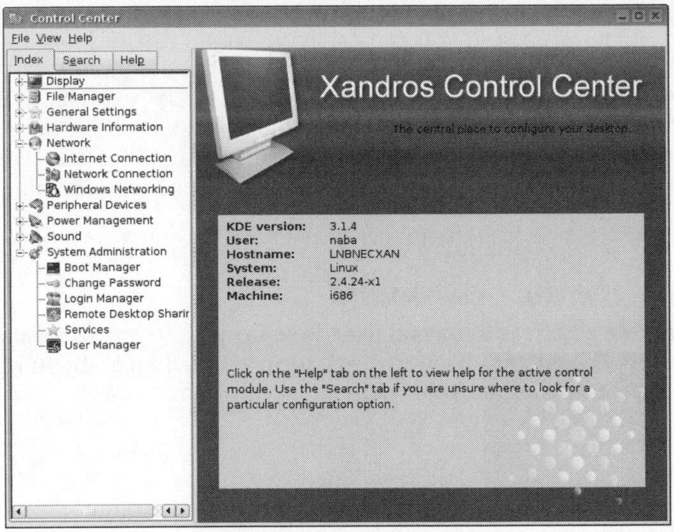

Figure 1-2: You can perform many sysadmin tasks from the Xandros Control Center.

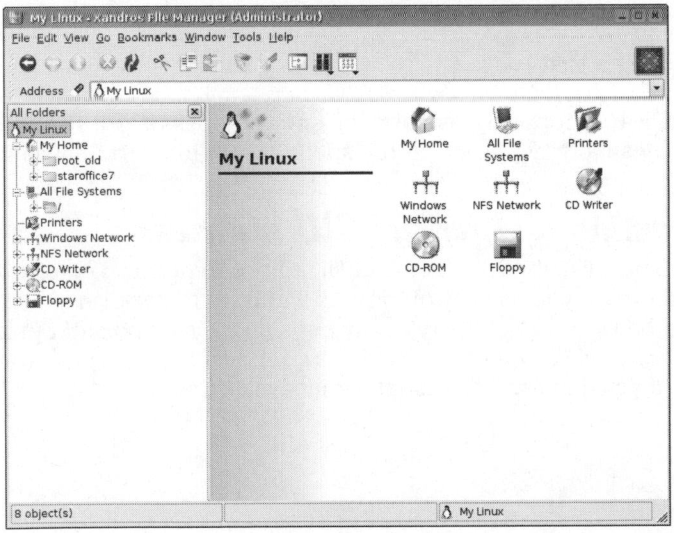

Figure 1-3: For some sysadmin tasks, use the Xandros File Manager.

How to Become root

You have to log in as `root` to perform the system administration tasks. The `root` user is the superuser and the only account with all the privileges needed to do anything in the system.

Common wisdom says you should *not* normally log in as `root`. When you're `root`, one misstep, and you can easily delete all the files — especially when you're typing commands. Take, for example, the command `rm *.html` that you may type to delete all files that have the `.html` extension. What if you accidentally press the spacebar after the asterisk (*)? The shell takes the command to be `rm * .html` and — because `*` matches any filename — deletes everything in the current directory. Seems implausible until it happens to you!

Using the su - command

If you're logged in as a normal user, how do you do any system administration chores? Well, you become `root` for the time being. If you're working at a terminal window or console, type

```
su -
```

Then enter the `root` password in response to the prompt. From this point on, you're `root`. Do whatever you have to do. To return to your usual self, type

```
exit
```

That's it! It's that easy.

By the way, Knoppix does not have any `root` password, so you can become `root` by simply typing **su -** at the shell prompt in a terminal window.

Becoming root for the GUI utilities

Most Linux distributions include GUI utilities to perform system administration chores. If you use any of these GUI utilities to perform a task that requires you to be `root`, the utility typically pops up a dialog box that prompts you for the `root` password, as shown in Figure 1-4. Just type the password and press Enter. If you don't want to use the utility, click Cancel.

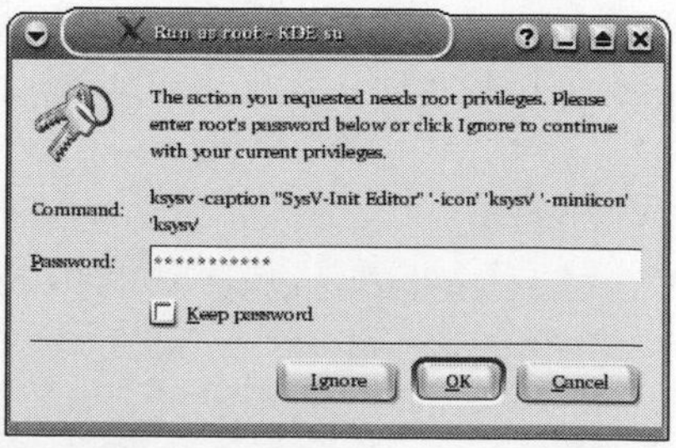

Figure 1-4: Type the `root` password and press Enter to gain `root` privileges.

Recovering from a forgotten root password

To perform system administration tasks, you have to know the `root` password. What happens if you forget the `root` password? Not to worry: Just reboot the PC and you can reset the `root` password by following these steps:

1. **Reboot the PC (select Reboot as you log out of the GUI screen) or power up as usual.**

   Soon you see the graphical GRUB boot loader screen that shows the names of the operating systems you can boot. If your system runs the LILO boot loader, press Ctrl+X and at the `boot:` prompt, type **linux single** and press Enter. Then proceed to step 4.

2. **If you have more than one operating system installed, use the arrow key to select Linux as your operating system. Then press the A key.**

   GRUB prompts you for commands to add to its default boot command.

3. **Press the spacebar, type the following, and then press Enter:**

   ```
   single
   ```

   Linux starts up as usual but runs in a single-user mode that does not require you to log in. After Linux starts, you see the following command-line prompt that ends with a hash mark (#), similar to the following:

   ```
   sh-2.05b#
   ```

4. **Type the `passwd` command to change the `root` password as follows:**

   ```
   sh-2.05b# passwd
   Changing password for user root.
   New password:
   ```

5. **Type the new `root` password that you want to use (it doesn't appear on-screen) and then press Enter.**

   Linux asks for the password again, like this:

   ```
   Retype new password:
   ```

6. **Type the password again, and press Enter.**

   If you enter the same password both times, the `passwd` command changes the `root` password.

7. **Now type** reboot **to reboot the PC.**

   After Linux starts, it displays the familiar login screen. Now you can log in as `root` with the new password.

Make sure that your Linux PC is *physically* secure. As these steps show, anyone who can physically access your Linux PC can simply reboot, set a new `root` password, and do whatever he or she wants with the system. Another way to protect against resetting the password is to set a GRUB password, which causes GRUB to require a valid password before it boots Linux. Of course, you must then remember to enter the GRUB password every time you boot your system!

Understanding How Linux Boots

Knowing the sequence in which Linux starts processes as it boots is important. You can use this knowledge to start and stop services, such as the Web server and Network File System (NFS). The next few sections provide you with an overview of how Linux boots and starts the initial set of processes. These sections also familiarize you with the shell scripts that start various services on a Linux system.

Understanding the init process

When Linux boots, it loads and runs the core operating system program from the hard drive. The core operating system is designed to run other programs. A process named `init` starts the initial set of processes on your Linux system.

To see the processes currently running on the system, type

```
ps ax | more
```

You get an output listing that starts off like this:

```
  PID TTY      STAT   TIME COMMAND
    1 ?        S      0:22 init [2]
```

The first column, with the heading `PID`, shows a number for each process. PID stands for *process ID* (identification) — a sequential number assigned by the Linux kernel. The first entry in the process list, with a *process ID* (PID) of 1, is the `init` process. It's the first process, and it starts all other processes in your Linux system. That's why `init` is sometimes referred to as the "mother of all processes."

What the `init` process starts depends on the following:

- The *run level,* an identifier that identifies a system configuration in which only a selected group of processes can exist.
- The contents of the `/etc/inittab` file, a text file that specifies which processes to start at different run levels.

- A number of shell scripts that are executed at specific run levels. (The scripts are located in the /etc/init.d directory and a number of subdirectories in /etc — these subdirectories have names that begin with rc.)

Most Linux distributions use seven run levels — 0 through 6. The meaning of the run levels differ from one distribution to another. Table 1-5 shows the meanings of the run levels and points out some of the actions specific to Fedora Core, Debian, SUSE, and Xandros.

Table 1-5 Run Levels in Linux

Run Level	*Meaning*
0	Shuts down the system
1	Runs in single-user standalone mode (no one else can log in; you work at the text console)
2	Runs in multiuser mode (Debian and Xandros use run level 2 as the default run level)
3	Runs in full multiuser mode (used for text-mode login in Fedora Core and SUSE)
4	Runs in full multiuser mode (unused in Fedora Core and SUSE)
5	Runs in full multiuser mode (used as the default run level with graphical login in Fedora Core and SUSE)
6	Reboots the system

The current run level, together with the contents of the /etc/inittab file, controls which processes init starts in Linux. The default run level is 2 in Debian and Xandros. In Fedora Core and SUSE, run level 3 is used for text-mode login screens and 5 for the graphical login screen. You can change the default run level by editing a line in the /etc/inittab file.

To check the current run level, type the following command in a terminal window:

```
/sbin/runlevel
```

In Debian, the runlevel command prints an output like this:

```
N 2
```

The first character of the output shows the previous run level (N means no previous run level), and the second character shows the current run level (2). In this case, the system started at run level 2. If you are in a GUI desktop in Fedora Core, the runlevel command should show 5 as the current run level.

Examining the /etc/inittab file

The `/etc/inittab` file is the key to understanding the processes that `init` starts at various run levels. You can look at the contents of the file by using the `more` command, as follows:

```
more /etc/inittab
```

To see the contents of the `/etc/inittab` file with the `more` command, you don't have to log in as `root`.

To interpret the contents of the `/etc/inittab` file, follow these steps:

1. **Look for the line that looks like this:**

   ```
   id:2:initdefault:
   ```

   That line shows the default run level. In this case, it's 2.

2. **Find all the lines that specify what `init` runs at run level 2. Look for a line that has a 2 between the first two colons (:). Here is a relevant line in Debian:**

   ```
   l2:2:wait:/etc/init.d/rc 2
   ```

   This line specifies that `init` executes the file `/etc/init.d/rc` with 2 as an argument.

If you look at the file `/etc/init.d/rc` in a Debian system, you find it's a shell script. You can study this file to see how it starts various processes for run levels 1 through 5.

Each entry in the `/etc/inittab` file tells `init` what to do at one or more run levels — you simply list all run levels at which the process runs. Each `inittab` entry has four fields — separated by colons — in the following format:

id:*runlevels*:*action*:*process*

Table 1-6 shows what each of these fields means.

Table 1-6 Meaning of the Fields in Each inittab Entry

Field	*Meaning*
`id`	A unique one- or two-character identifier. The `init` process uses this field internally. You can use any identifier you want, as long as you don't use the same identifier on more than one line.

Field	*Meaning*
`runlevels`	A sequence of zero or more characters, each denoting a run level. For example, if the `runlevels` field is 12345, that entry applies to each of the run levels 1 through 5. This field is ignored if the `action` field is set to `sysinit`, `boot`, or `bootwait`.
`action`	Tells the `init` process what to do with that entry. If this field is `initdefault`, for example, `init` interprets the `runlevels` field as the default run level. If this field is set to `wait`, `init` starts the program or script specified in the `process` field and waits until that process exits.
`process`	Name of the script or program that `init` starts. Of course, some settings of the action field require no `process` field. For example, when the `action` field is `initdefault`, there is no need for a `process` field.

Trying a new run level with the init command

To try a new run level, you don't have to change the default run level in the `/etc/inittab` file. If you log in as `root`, you can change the run level (and, consequently, the processes that run in Linux) by typing **init** followed by the run level.

For example, to put the system in single-user mode, type the following:

```
init 1
```

Thus, if you want to try run level 3 without changing the default run level in `/etc/inittab` file, enter the following command at the shell prompt:

```
init 3
```

The system ends all current processes and enters run level 3. By default, the `init` command waits 20 seconds before stopping all current processes and starting the new processes for run level 3.

TIP

To switch to run level 3 immediately, type the command **init -t0 3**. The number after the `-t` option indicates the number of seconds `init` waits before changing the run level.

You can also use the `telinit` command, which is simply a symbolic link (a shortcut) to `init`. If you make changes to the `/etc/inittab` file and want `init` to reload its configuration file, use the command `telinit q`.

Understanding the Linux startup scripts

The `init` process runs a number of scripts at system startup. In the following discussions, I use a Debian system as an example, but the basic sequence is similar in other distributions — only the names and locations of the scripts may vary.

If you look at the `/etc/inittab` file in a Debian system, you find the following lines near the beginning of the file:

```
# Boot-time system configuration/initialization script.
si::sysinit:/etc/init.d/rcS
```

The first line is a comment line. The second line causes `init` to run the `/etc/init.d/rcS` script — the first Linux startup script that `init` runs in a Debian system. The `rcS` script performs many initialization tasks, such as mounting the file systems, setting the clock, configuring the keyboard layout, starting the network, and loading many other driver modules. The `rcS` script performs these initialization tasks by calling many other scripts and reading configuration files located in the `/etc/rcS.d` directory.

After executing the `/etc/init.d/rcS` script, the `init` process runs the `/etc/init.d/rc` script with the run level as argument. For example, for run level 2, the following line in `/etc/inittab` specifies what `init` executes:

```
l2:2:wait:/etc/init.d/rc 2
```

This example says `init` executes the command `/etc/init.d/rc 2` and waits until that command completes.

The `/etc/init.d/rc` script is somewhat complicated. Here's how it works:

- It executes scripts in a directory corresponding to the run level. For example, for run level 2, the `/etc/init.d/rc` script runs the scripts in the `/etc/rc2.d` directory.
- In the directory that corresponds with the run level, `/etc/init.d/rc` looks for all files that begin with a `K` and executes each of them with the `stop` argument. This argument kills any currently running processes. Then it locates all files that begin with an `S` and executes each file with a `start` argument. This argument starts the processes needed for the specified run level.

To see what gets executed at run level 2, type the following command:

```
ls -l /etc/rc2.d
```

In the resulting listing, the K scripts — the files whose names begin with K — stop (or "kill") servers, whereas the S scripts start servers. The /etc/init.d/rc script executes these files in exactly the order in which they appear in the directory listing.

Manually starting and stopping servers

In Linux, the server startup scripts reside in the /etc/init.d directory. You can manually invoke scripts in this directory to start, stop, or restart specific processes — usually servers. For example, to stop the FTP server (the server program is called vsftpd), type the following command:

```
/etc/init.d/vsftpd stop
```

If vsftpd is already running and you want to restart it, type the following command:

```
/etc/init.d/vsftpd restart
```

You can enhance your system administration skills by familiarizing yourself with the scripts in the /etc/init.d directory. To see its listing, type the following command:

```
ls /etc/init.d
```

The script names give you some clue about which server the script can start and stop. For example, the samba script starts and stops the processes required for Samba Windows networking services. At your leisure, you may want to study some of these scripts to see what each one does. You don't have to understand all the shell programming; the comments help you discover the purpose of each script.

Automatically starting servers at system startup

You want some servers to start automatically every time you boot the system. The exact commands to configure the servers varies from one distribution to another.

In Fedora Core and SUSE, use the chkconfig command to set up a server to start whenever the system boots into a specific run level. For example, if you start the SSH server, you want the sshd server to start whenever the system starts. You can make that happen by using the chkconfig command. To set sshd to start whenever the system boots into run level 3, 4, or 5, you type the following command (while logged in as root):

```
chkconfig --level 345 sshd on
```

In Fedora Core and SUSE, you can also use the `chkconfig` command to check which servers are turned on or off. For example, to see the complete list of all servers for all run levels, type the following command:

```
chkconfig --list
```

In Debian and Xandros, you can use the `update-rc.d` command to enable a server to start automatically at system startup. For example, to set `sshd` to start automatically at the default run levels, type **update-rc.d sshd defaults** in a terminal window while logged in as `root`. You can also specify the exact run levels and the sequence number (the order in which each server starts). To find out more about the `update-rc.d` command, type **man update-rc.d** in a terminal window.

Taking Stock of Linux System Configuration Files

Linux includes a host of configuration files. All these files share text files that you can edit with any text editor. To edit these configuration files, you must log in as `root`. I don't discuss the files individually, but I show a selection of the configuration files in Table 1-7, along with a brief description of each. This listing gives you an idea of what types of configuration files a system administrator has to work with. In many cases, Linux includes GUI utility programs to set up many of these configuration files.

Table 1-7 Some Linux Configuration Files

Configuration File	*Description*
`/boot/grub`	Location of files for the GRUB boot loader
`/boot/grub/menu.lst`	Configuration file for the boot menu that GRUB displays before it boots your system
`/boot/System.map`	Map of the Linux kernel (maps kernel addresses into names of functions and variables)
`/boot/vmlinuz`	The Linux kernel (the operating system's core)
`/etc/apache2/httpd.conf`	Configuration file for the Apache Web server (Debian)
`/etc/apt/sources.list`	Configuration file that lists the sources — FTP or Web sites or CD-ROM — from which the Advanced Packaging Tool (APT) obtains packages (Debian and Xandros)
`/etc/at.allow`	Usernames of users allowed to use the `at` command to schedule jobs for later execution
`/etc/at.deny`	Usernames of users forbidden to use the `at` command

Configuration File	Description
/etc/bashrc	System-wide functions and aliases for the BASH shell (Fedora Core)
/etc/bash.bashrc	System-wide functions and aliases for the BASH shell (Debian, SUSE, and Xandros)
/etc/cups/cupsd.conf	Printer configuration file for the Common UNIX Printing System (CUPS) scheduler
/etc/fonts	Directory with font configuration files (in particular, you can put local font configuration settings in the file /etc/fonts/local.conf)
/etc/fstab	Information about file systems available for mounting and where each file system is to be mounted
/etc/group	Information about groups
/etc/grub.conf	The configuration for the GRUB boot loader in Fedora Core and SUSE
/etc/hosts	List of IP numbers and their corresponding host-names
/etc/hosts.allow	Hosts allowed to access Internet services on this system
/etc/hosts.deny	Hosts forbidden to access Internet services on this system
/etc/httpd/conf/httpd.conf	Configuration file for the Apache Web server (Fedora Core)
/etc/init.d	Directory with scripts to start and stop various servers
/etc/inittab	Configuration file used by the init process that starts all the other processes
/etc/issue	File containing a message to be printed before displaying the text-mode login prompt (usually the distribution name and the version number)
/etc/lilo.conf	The configuration for the Linux Loader (LILO) — one of the boot loaders that can load the operating system from disk (present only if you use the LILO boot loader)
/etc/login.defs	Default information for creating user accounts, used by the useradd command
/etc/modprobe.conf	Configuration file for loadable kernel modules, used by the modprobe command (Fedora Core and SUSE)
/etc/modules.conf	Configuration file for loadable modules (Debian and Xandros)
/etc/mtab	Information about currently mounted file systems

(continued)

Table 1-7 *(continued)*

Configuration File	*Description*
/etc/passwd	Information about all user accounts (actual passwords are stored in /etc/shadow)
/etc/profile	System-wide environment and startup file for the BASH shell
/etc/profile.d	Directory containing script files (with names that end in .sh) that the /etc/profile script executes
/etc/init.d/rcS	Linux initialization script in Debian, SUSE, and Xandros
/etc/rc.d/rc.sysinit	Linux initialization script in Fedora Core
/etc/shadow	Secure file with encrypted passwords for all user accounts (can be read only by root)
/etc/shells	List of all the shells on the system that the user can use
/etc/skel	Directory that holds initial versions of files such as .bash_profile that copy to a new user's home directory
/etc/sysconfig	Linux configuration files (Fedora Core and SUSE)
/etc/sysctl.conf	Configuration file with kernel parameters that are read in and set by sysctl at system startup
/etc/termcap	Database of terminal capabilities and options (Fedora Core and SUSE)
/etc/udev	Directory containing configuration files for udev — the program that provides the ability to dynamically name hot-pluggable devices and create device files in the /dev directory
/etc/X11	Directory with configuration files for the X Window System (X11) and various display managers such as gdm and xdm
/etc/X11/XF86Config or /etc/X11/XF86Config-4	Configuration file for XFree86 X11 (Debian, SUSE, and Xandros)
/etc/X11/xorg.xonf	Configuration file for X.org X11 — the X Window System (Fedora Core)
/etc/xinetd.conf	Configuration for the xinetd daemon that starts a number of Internet services on demand
/etc/yum.conf	Configuration for the yum package updater and installer (Fedora Core)
/var/log/apache2	Web-server access and error logs (Debian)
/var/log/cron	Log file with messages from the cron process that runs scheduled jobs

Configuration File	Description
/var/log/boot.msg	File with boot messages (SUSE)
/var/log/dmesg	File with boot messages (Debian, Fedora Core, and Xandros)
/var/log/httpd	Web server access and error logs (Fedora Core)
/var/log/messages	System log

Monitoring System Performance

When you're the system administrator, you must keep an eye on how well your Linux system is performing. You can monitor the overall performance of your system by looking at information such as

- ✦ Central Processing Unit (CPU) usage
- ✦ Physical memory usage
- ✦ Virtual memory (swap-space) usage
- ✦ Hard drive usage

Linux comes with a number of utilities that you can use to monitor one or more of these performance parameters. Here I introduce a few of these utilities and show you how to understand the information presented by these utilities.

Using the top utility

To view the top CPU processes — the ones that are using most of the CPU time — you can use the text mode `top` utility. To start that utility, type **top** in a terminal window (or text console). The `top` utility then displays a text screen listing the current processes, arranged in the order of CPU usage, along with various other information, such as memory and swap-space usage. Figure 1-5 shows a typical output from the `top` utility.

TIP

The `top` utility updates the display every 5 seconds. If you keep `top` running in a window, you can continually monitor the status of your Linux system. To quit `top`, press Q or Ctrl+C or close the terminal window.

The first five lines of the output screen (refer to Figure 1-5) provide summary information about the system. Here is what these five lines show:

- ✦ The first line shows the current time, how long the system has been up, how many users are logged in, and three *load averages* — the average number of processes ready to run during the last 1, 5, and 15 minutes.

- The second line lists the total number of processes and the status of these processes.
- The third line shows CPU usage — what percentage of CPU time is used by user processes, what percentage by system (kernel) processes, and during what percentage of time the CPU is idle.
- The fourth line shows how the physical memory is being used — the total amount, how much is used, how much is free, and how much is allocated to buffers (for reading from the hard drive, for example).
- The fifth line shows how the virtual memory (or swap space) is being used — the total amount of swap space, how much is used, how much is free, and how much is being cached.

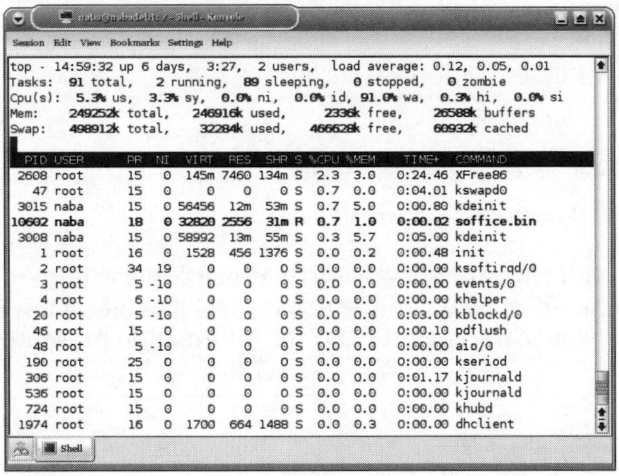

Figure 1-5: You can see the top CPU processes by using the `top` utility.

The table that appears below the summary information (refer to Figure 1-5) lists information about the current processes, arranged in decreasing order by amount of CPU time used. Table 1-8 summarizes the meanings of the column headings in the table that `top` displays.

Table 1-8 Meanings of Column Headings in top Utility's Output

Heading	*Meaning*
`PID`	The process ID of the process
`USER`	Username under which the process is running
`PR`	Priority of the process

Heading	Meaning
NI	*Nice value* of the process — the value ranges from -20 (highest priority) to 19 (lowest priority) and the default is 0 (the *nice value* represents the relative priority of the process, the higher the value the lower the priority and the nicer the process — because it yields to other processes)
VIRT	The total amount of virtual memory used by the process, in kilobytes
RES	Total physical memory used by a task (typically shown in kilobytes, but an m suffix indicates megabytes)
SHR	Amount of shared memory used by process
S	State of the process (S for sleeping, D for uninterruptible sleep, R for running, Z for *zombies* — processes that should be dead, but are still running — or T for stopped)
%CPU	Percentage of CPU time used since last screen update
%MEM	Percentage of physical memory used by the process
TIME+	Total CPU time the process has used since it started
COMMAND	Shortened form of the command that started the process

Using the uptime command

You can use the `uptime` command to get a summary of the system's state. Just type the command like this:

```
uptime
```

It displays output similar to the following:

```
15:03:21 up 32 days, 57 min, 3 users, load average: 0.13, 0.23, 0.27
```

This output shows the current time, how long the system has been up, the number of users, and (finally) the three load averages — the average number of processes that were ready to run in the past 1, 5, and 15 minutes. Load averages greater than 1 imply that many processes are competing for CPU time simultaneously.

The load averages give you an indication of how busy the system is.

Using the vmstat utility

You can get summary information about the overall system usage with the `vmstat` utility. To view system usage information averaged over 5-second intervals, type the following command (the second argument indicates the total number of lines of output `vmstat` displays):

```
vmstat 5 8
```

You see output similar to the following listing:

```
procs -----------memory---------- ---swap-- -----io---- --system-- ----cpu----
 r  b   swpd   free   buff  cache   si   so    bi    bo   in    cs us sy id wa
 0  0  31324   4016  18568 136004    1    1    17    16    8   110 33  4 61  1
 0  1  31324   2520  15348 139692    0    0  7798   199 1157   377  8  8  6 78
 1  0  31324   1584  12936 141480    0   19  5784   105 1099   437 12  5  0 82
 2  0  31324   1928  13004 137136    7    0  1586   138 1104   561 43  6  0 51
 3  1  31324   1484  13148 132064    0    0  1260    51 1080   427 50  5  0 46
 0  0  31324   1804  13240 127976    0    0  1126    46 1082   782 19  5 47 30
 0  0  31324   1900  13240 127976    0    0     0     0 1010   211  3  1 96  0
 0  0  31324   1916  13248 127976    0    0     0    10 1015   224  3  2 95  0
```

The first line of output shows the averages since the last reboot. After that, `vmstat` displays the 5-second average data seven more times, covering the next 35 seconds. The tabular output is grouped as six categories of information, indicated by the fields in the first line of output. The second line shows further details for each of the six major fields. You can interpret these fields using Table 1-9.

Table 1-9 Meaning of Fields in the vmstat Utility's Output

Field Name	*Description*
`procs`	Number of processes and their types: `r` = processes waiting to run; `b` = processes in uninterruptible sleep; `w` = processes swapped out, but ready to run
`memory`	Information about physical memory and swap-space usage (all numbers in kilobytes): `swpd` = virtual memory used; `free` = free physical memory; `buff` = memory used as buffers; `cache` = virtual memory that's cached
`swap`	Amount of swapping (the numbers are in kilobytes per second): `si` = amount of memory swapped in from disk; `so` = amount of memory swapped to disk
`io`	Information about input and output (the numbers are in blocks per second where the block size depends on the disk device): `bi` = rate of blocks sent to disk; `bo` = rate of blocks received from disk

Field Name	Description
`system`	Information about the system: `in` = number of interrupts per second (including clock interrupts); `cs` = number of context switches per second — how many times the kernel changed which process was running
`cpu`	Percentages of CPU time used: `us` = percentage of CPU time used by user processes; `sy` = percentage of CPU time used by system processes; `id` = percentage of time CPU is idle; `wa` = time spent waiting for input or output (I/O)

TECHNICAL STUFF

In the `vmstat` utility's output, high values in the `si` and `so` fields indicate too much swapping. (*Swapping* refers to the copying of information between physical memory and the virtual memory on the hard drive.) High numbers in the `bi` and `bo` fields indicate too much disk activity.

Checking disk performance and disk usage

Linux comes with the `/sbin/hdparm` program that you can use to control IDE or ATAPI hard drives that are common on most PCs. One feature of the `hdparm` program is that you can use the `-t` option to determine the rate at which data is read from the disk into a buffer in memory. For example, here's the result of the command on my system:

```
/sbin/hdparm -t /dev/hda

/dev/hda:
 Timing buffered disk reads:  64 MB in  3.04 seconds = 21.05 MB/sec
```

The command requires the IDE drive's device name (`/dev/hda`) as an argument. If you have an IDE hard drive, you can try this command to see how fast data is read from your system's disk drive.

To display the space available in the currently mounted file systems, use the `df` command. If you want a more human-readable output from `df`, type the following command:

```
df -h
```

Here's a typical output from this command:

```
Filesystem            Size  Used Avail Use% Mounted on
/dev/hda5             7.1G  3.9G  2.9G  59% /
/dev/hda3              99M   18M   77M  19% /boot
none                  125M     0  125M   0% /dev/shm
/dev/scd0             3.8G  3.8G     0 100% /mnt/cdrom1
```

As this example shows, the -h option causes the df command to show the sizes in gigabytes (G) and megabytes (M).

To check the disk space being used by a specific directory, use the du command — you can specify the -h option to view the output in kilobytes (k) and megabytes (M), as shown in the following example:

```
du -h /var/log
```

Here's a typical output of that command:

```
152K    /var/log/cups
4.0K    /var/log/vbox
4.0K    /var/log/httpd
508K    /var/log/gdm
4.0K    /var/log/samba
8.0K    /var/log/mail
4.0K    /var/log/news/OLD
8.0K    /var/log/news
4.0K    /var/log/squid
2.2M    /var/log
```

The du command displays the disk space used by each directory and the last line shows the total disk space used by that directory. If you want to see only the total space used by a directory, use the -s option, like this:

```
du -sh /home
89M     /home
```

Viewing System Information via the /proc File System

Your Linux system has a special file system called the /proc file system. You can find out many things about your system from this file system. In fact, you can even change kernel parameters through the /proc file system (just by writing to a file in that file system), thereby modifying the system's behavior.

The /proc file system isn't a real directory on the hard drive but a collection of data structures in memory, managed by the Linux kernel, that appears to you as a set of directories and files. The purpose of /proc (also called the *process file system*) is to give you access to information about the Linux kernel as well as to help you find out about all processes currently running on your system.

You can access the /proc file system just as you access any other directory, but you have to know the meaning of various files to interpret the information. Typically, you can use the cat or more commands to view the contents of a file in /proc; the file's contents provide information about some aspect of the system.

As with any directory, start by looking at a detailed directory listing of `/proc`. To do so, log in as `root` and type **ls -l /proc** in a terminal window. In the output, the first set of directories (indicated by the letter `d` at the beginning of the line) represents the processes currently running on your system. Each directory that corresponds to a process has the process ID (a number) as its name.

WARNING!

Notice also a very large file named `/proc/kcore`; that file represents the *entire* physical memory of your system. Although `/proc/kcore` appears in the listing as a huge file, no single physical file is occupying that much space on your hard drive — so don't try to remove the file to reclaim disk space.

Several files and directories in `/proc` contain interesting information about your Linux PC. The `/proc/cpuinfo` file, for example, lists the key characteristics of your system, such as processor type and floating-point processor information. You can view the processor information by typing **cat /proc/cpuinfo**. For example, here's what I get when I type **cat /proc/cpuinfo** on my system:

```
processor       : 0
vendor_id       : GenuineIntel
cpu family      : 15
model           : 3
model name      : Intel(R) Celeron(R) CPU 2.53GHz
stepping        : 3
cpu MHz         : 2533.129
cache size      : 256 KB
fdiv_bug        : no
hlt_bug         : no
f00f_bug        : no
coma_bug        : no
fpu             : yes
fpu_exception   : yes
cpuid level     : 5
wp              : yes
flags           : fpu vme de pse tsc msr pae mce cx8 apic sep
   mtrr pge mca cmov pat pse36 clflush dts acpi mmx fxsr sse
   sse2 ss ht tm pbe pni monitor ds_cpl cid
bogomips        : 4997.12
```

This output is from a 2.5 GHZ Celeron system. The listing shows many interesting characteristics of the processor. Notice the line that starts with `fdiv_bug`. Remember the infamous Pentium floating-point-division bug? The bug is in an instruction called `fdiv` (for *floating-point division*). Thus, the `fdiv_bug` line indicates whether this particular Pentium has the bug. (Fortunately, my PC's processor does not.)

The last line in the `/proc/cpuinfo` file shows the BogoMips for the processor, as computed by the Linux kernel when it boots. BogoMips is something that Linux uses internally to time-delay loops.

Table 1-10 summarizes some of the files in the /proc file system that provide information about your Linux system. You can view some of these files on your system to see what they contain, but note that not all files shown in Table 1-10 are present on your system. The specific contents of the /proc file system depends on the kernel configuration and the driver modules that are loaded (which, in turn, depend on your PC's hardware configuration).

TIP

You can navigate the /proc file system just as you'd work with any other directories and files in Linux. Use the more or cat commands to view the contents of a file.

Table 1-10 Some Files and Directories in /proc

Filename	*Content*
/proc/acpi	Information about Advanced Configuration & Power Interface (ACPI) — an industry-standard interface for configuration and power management on laptops, desktops, and servers
/proc/bus	Directory with bus-specific information for each bus type, such as PCI
/proc/cmdline	The command line used to start the Linux kernel (for example, ro root=LABEL=/ rhgb)
/proc/cpuinfo	Information about the CPU (the microprocessor)
/proc/devices	Available block and character devices in your system
/proc/dma	Information about DMA (direct memory access) channels that are being used
/proc/driver/rtc	Information about the PC's real-time clock (RTC)
/proc/filesystems	List of supported file systems
/proc/ide	Directory containing information about IDE devices
/proc/interrupts	Information about interrupt request (IRQ) numbers and how they are being used
/proc/ioports	Information about input/output (I/O) port addresses and how they are being used
/proc/kcore	Image of the physical memory
/proc/kmsg	Kernel messages
/proc/loadavg	Load average (average number of processes waiting to run in the last 1, 5, and 15 minutes)
/proc/locks	Current kernel locks (used to ensure that multiple processes don't write to a file at the same time)
/proc/meminfo	Information about physical memory and swap-space usage
/proc/misc	Miscellaneous information
/proc/modules	List of loaded driver modules
/proc/mounts	List of mounted file systems

Filename	Content
`/proc/net`	Directory with many subdirectories that contain information about networking
`/proc/partitions`	List of partitions known to the Linux kernel
`/proc/pci`	Information about PCI devices found on the system
`/proc/scsi`	Directory with information about SCSI devices found on the system (present only if you have a SCSI device)
`/proc/stat`	Overall statistics about the system
`/proc/swaps`	Information about the swap space and how much is used
`/proc/sys`	Directory with information about the system; you can change kernel parameters by writing to files in this directory (using this method to tune system performance requires expertise to do properly)
`/proc/uptime`	Information about how long the system has been up
`/proc/version`	Kernel version number

Understanding Linux Devices

Linux treats all devices as files and uses a device just as it uses a file — opens it, writes data to it, reads data from it, and closes it when done. This ability to treat every device as a file comes through the use of device drivers. A *device driver* is a special program that controls a particular type of hardware. When the kernel writes data to the device, the device driver does whatever is appropriate for that device. For example, when the kernel writes data to the floppy drive, the floppy device driver puts that data onto the physical medium of the floppy disk. On the other hand, if the kernel writes data to the parallel port device, the parallel port driver sends the data to the printer connected to the parallel port.

Thus the device driver isolates the device-specific code from the rest of the kernel and makes a device look like a file. Any application can access a device by opening the file specific to that device. Figure 1-6 illustrates this concept of a Linux device driver.

Device files

As Figure 1-6 shows, applications can access a device as if it were a file. These files are special files called *device files,* and they appear in the `/dev` directory in the Linux file system.

If you use the `ls` command to look at the list of files in the `/dev` directory, you see several thousand files. These files do not mean that your system has several thousand devices. The `/dev` directory has files for all possible types of devices — that's why the number of device files is so large.

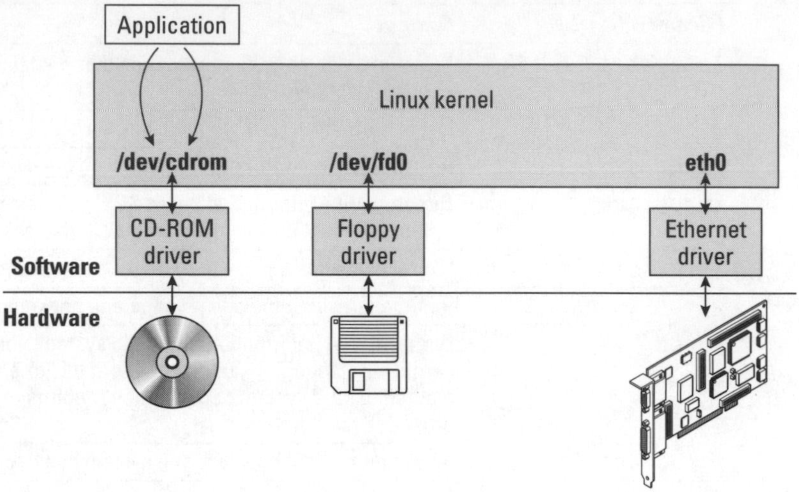

Figure 1-6: An application can access a device through a special file that, in turn, uses a device driver.

So how does the kernel know which device driver to use when an application opens a specific device file? The answer is in two numbers called the *major* and *minor device numbers*. Each device file is mapped to a specific device driver through these numbers.

To see an example of the major and minor device numbers, type the following command in a terminal window:

```
ls -l /dev/hda
```

You see a line of output similar to the following:

```
brw-rw----   1 root   disk    3,  0 Jul 23 14:50 /dev/hda
```

In this line, the major and minor device numbers appear just before the date. In this case, the major device number is 3 and the minor device number is 0. The kernel selects the device driver for this device file by using the major device number.

You don't really have to know much about the device files and the device numbers, except to be aware of their existence.

In case you are curious, all the major and minor numbers for devices are assigned according to device type. The Linux Assigned Names And Numbers Authority (LANANA) assigns these numbers. You can see the current device list at `www.lanana.org/docs/device-list/devices.txt`.

Block devices

The first letter in the listing of a device file also provides an important clue. For the /dev/hda device, the first letter is a b, which indicates that /dev/hda is a *block device* — one that can accept or provide data in chunks (typically 512 bytes or 1KB). By the way, /dev/hda refers to the first IDE hard drive on your system (the C: drive in Windows). Hard drives, floppy drives, and CD-ROM drives are all examples of block devices.

Character devices

If the first letter in the listing of a device file is a c, the device is a *character device* — one that can receive and send data one character (one byte) at a time. For example, the serial port and parallel ports are character devices. To see the specific listing of a character device, type the following command in a terminal window:

```
ls -l /dev/ttyS0
```

The listing of this device is similar to the following:

```
crw-rw----   1 root   uucp    4, 64 Jul 23 14:50 /dev/ttyS0
```

Notice that the very first letter is a c because /dev/ttyS0 — the first serial port — is a character device.

Network devices

Network devices that enable your system to interact with a network — for example, Ethernet and dialup *point-to-point protocol* (PPP) connections — are somewhat special because they need no file to correspond to the device. Instead, the kernel uses a special name for the device. For example, the Ethernet devices are named eth0 for the first Ethernet card, eth1 for the second one, and so on. PPP connections are named ppp0, ppp1, and so on.

Because network devices aren't mapped to device files, no files corresponding to these devices are in the /dev directory.

Persistent device naming with udev

Linux kernel 2.6 introduces a new approach for handling devices, based on the following features:

✦ **sysfs:** Kernel 2.6 provides the sysfs file system that is mounted on the /sys directory of the file system. The sysfs file system shows all the devices in the system as well as lots of information about each device. The information includes location of the device on the bus, attributes such as name and serial number, and the major and minor numbers of the device.

- /sbin/hotplug: This program is called whenever a device is added or removed. It can then do whatever is necessary to handle the device.
- /sbin/udev: This program takes care of dynamically named devices based on device characteristics such as serial number, device number on a bus, or a user-assigned name based on a set of rules that are set through the text file /etc/udev/udev.rules.

REMEMBER

The udev program's configuration file is /etc/udev/udev.conf. Based on settings in that configuration file, udev creates device nodes automatically in the directory specified by the udev_root parameter. For example, to manage the device nodes in the /dev directory, udev_root should be defined in /etc/udev/udev.conf as follows:

```
udev_root="/dev/"
```

Managing Loadable Driver Modules

To use any device, the Linux kernel must contain the driver. If the driver code is linked into the kernel as a *monolithic* program (a program that's in the form of a single large file), adding a new driver means rebuilding the kernel with the new driver code. Rebuilding the kernel means you have to reboot the PC with the new kernel before you can use the new device driver. Luckily, the Linux kernel uses a modular design that does away with rebooting hassles. Linux device drivers can be created in the form of modules that the kernel can load and unload without having to restart the PC.

REMEMBER

Driver modules are one type of a broader category of software modules called Loadable Kernel Modules. Other types of kernel modules include code that can support new types of file systems, modules for network protocols, and modules that interpret different formats of executable files.

Loading and unloading modules

You can manage the loadable device driver modules by using a set of commands. You have to log in as root to use some of these commands. In Table 1-11, I summarize a few of the commonly used module commands.

Table 1-11 Commands to Manage Kernel Modules

This Command	*Does the Following*
insmod	Inserts a module into the kernel
rmmod	Removes a module from the kernel
depmod	Determines interdependencies between modules

This Command	Does the Following
ksyms	Displays a list of symbols along with the name of the module that defined the symbol
lsmod	Lists all currently loaded modules
modinfo	Displays information about a kernel module
modprobe	Inserts or removes a module or a set of modules intelligently (for example, if module A requires B, then modprobe automatically loads B when asked to load A)

If you have to use any of these commands, log in as root or type **su -** in a terminal window to become root.

To see what modules are currently loaded, type

```
lsmod
```

You see a long list of modules that depends on the types of devices installed on your system.

The list displayed by lsmod includes all types of Linux kernel modules, not just device drivers. For example, you typically find two modules — jbd, and ext3 — that are all part of the EXT3 file system (the latest file system for Linux).

Besides lsmod, one commonly used module command is modprobe. Use modprobe whenever you need to manually load or remove one or more modules. The best thing about modprobe is that you don't need to worry if a module requires other modules to work. The modprobe command automatically loads any other module needed by a module. On one of my systems, for example, I manually load the sound driver with the command

```
modprobe snd-card-0
```

This command causes modprobe to load everything needed to make sound work.

You can use modprobe with the -r option to remove modules. For example, to remove the sound modules, I use the following command:

```
modprobe -r snd-card-0
```

This command gets rid of all the modules that the modprobe snd-card-0 command had loaded.

Using the /etc/modprobe.conf file

How does the `modprobe` command know that it needs to load the `snd-intel8x0` driver module when I use a module name `snd-card-0`? The answer is in the `/etc/modprobe.conf` configuration file. That file contains a line that tells `modprobe` what it should load when it sees the module name `snd-card-0`.

To view the contents of `/etc/modprobe.conf`, type

```
cat /etc/modprobe.conf
```

On one of my Fedora Core PCs running Linux 2.6, the `/etc/modprobe.conf` file contains the following lines:

```
alias eth0 3c59x
alias snd-card-0 snd-intel8x0
alias usb-controller uhci-hcd
```

Each line that begins with the keyword `alias` defines a standard name for an actual driver module. For example, the first line defines `3c59x` as the actual driver name for the alias `eth0`, which stands for the first Ethernet card. Similarly, the third line defines `snd-intel8x0` as the module to load when I use the name `snd-card-0`.

The `modprobe` command consults the `/etc/modprobe.conf` file to convert an alias to the real name of a driver module as well as for other tasks, such as obtaining parameters for driver modules. For example, you can insert lines that begin with the `options` keyword to provide values of parameters that a driver may need.

For example, to set the debug level parameter for the Ethernet driver to 5 (this parameter generates lots of information in `/var/log/messages`), I add the following line to the `/etc/modprobe.conf` file:

```
options 3c59x debug=5
```

This line specifies `5` as the value of the parameter named `debug` in the `3c59x` module.

If you want to know the names of the parameters that a module accepts, use the `modinfo` command. For example, to view information about the `3c59x` driver module, I type

```
modinfo 3c59x | more
```

From the resulting output, I can tell that `debug` is the name of the parameter for setting the debug level.

Unfortunately, the information shown by the `modinfo` command can be somewhat cryptic. The only saving grace is that you may not have to do much more than use a graphical utility to configure the device, and the utility takes care of adding whatever is needed to configuration files, such as `/etc/modprobe.conf`.

Scheduling Jobs in Linux

As a system administrator, you may have to run some programs automatically at regular intervals or execute one or more commands at a specified time in the future. Your Linux system includes the facilities to schedule jobs to run at any future date or time you want. You can also set up the system to perform a task periodically or just once. Here are some typical tasks you can perform by scheduling jobs on your Linux system:

- Back up the files in the middle of the night.
- Download large files in the early morning when the system isn't busy.
- Send yourself messages as reminders of meetings.
- Analyze system logs periodically and look for any abnormal activities.

You can set up these jobs by using the `at` command or the `crontab` facility of Linux. In the next few sections, I introduce these job-scheduling features of Linux.

Scheduling one-time jobs

If you want to run one or more commands at a later time, you can use the `at` command. The `atd` *daemon* — a program designed to process jobs submitted using `at` — runs your commands at the specified time and mails the output to you.

Before you try the `at` command, you need to know that the following configuration files control which users can schedule tasks using the `at` command:

- `/etc/at.allow` contains the names of the users who may submit jobs using the `at` command.
- `/etc/at.deny` contains the names of users not allowed to submit jobs using the `at` command.

If these files aren't present, or if you find an empty `/etc/at.deny` file, any user can submit jobs by using the `at` command. The default in Linux is an empty `/etc/at.deny` file; with this default in place, anyone can use the `at` command. If you don't want some users to use `at`, simply list their usernames in the `/etc/at.deny` file.

To use `at` to schedule a one-time job for execution at a later time, follow these steps:

1. **Run the `at` command with the date or time when you want your commands executed.**

   When you press Enter, the `at>` prompt appears, as follows:

   ```
   at 21:30
   at>
   ```

   This method is the simplest way to indicate the time when you want to execute one or more commands — simply specify the time in a 24-hour format. In this case, you want to execute the commands at 9:30 p.m. tonight (or tomorrow, if it's already past 9:30 p.m.). You can, however, specify the execution time in many different ways. (See Table 1-12 for examples.)

2. **At the `at>` prompt, type the commands you want to execute as if typing at the shell prompt; after each command, press Enter and continue with the next command. When you finish entering the commands you want to execute, press Ctrl+D to indicate the end.**

   Here is an example showing how to execute the `ps` command at a future time:

   ```
   at> ps
   at> <EOT>
   job 1 at 2004-12-28 21:30
   ```

   After you press Ctrl+D, the `at` command responds with a job number and the date and time when the job will execute.

Table 1-12 Formats for the Time of Execution with the at Command

Command	*When the Job Will Run*
`at now`	Immediately
`at now + 15 minutes`	15 minutes from the current time
`at now + 4 hours`	4 hours from the current time
`at now + 7 days`	7 days from the current time
`at noon`	At noontime today (or tomorrow, if already past noon)
`at now next hour`	Exactly 60 minutes from now
`at now next day`	At the same time tomorrow
`at 17:00 tomorrow`	At 5:00 p.m. tomorrow
`at 4:45pm`	At 4:45 p.m. today (or tomorrow, if it's already past 4:45 p.m.)
`at 3:00 Dec 28, 2004`	At 3:00 a.m. on December 28, 2004

After you enter one or more jobs, you can view the current list of scheduled jobs with the `atq` command:

```
atq
```

The output looks similar to the following:

```
4       2004-12-28 03:00 a root
5       2004-10-26 21:57 a root
6       2004-10-26 16:45 a root
```

The first field on each line shows the job number — the same number that the `at` command displays when you submit the job. The next field shows the year, month, day, and time of execution. The last field shows the jobs pending in the queue named `a`.

If you want to cancel a job, use the `atrm` command to remove that job from the queue. When removing a job with the `atrm` command, refer to the job by its number, as follows:

```
atrm 4
```

This command deletes job 4 scheduled for 3:00 a.m. December 28, 2004.

TIP

When a job executes, the output is mailed to you. Type **mail** at a terminal window to read your mail and to view the output from your jobs.

Scheduling recurring jobs

Although `at` is good for running commands at a specific time, it's not useful for running a program automatically at repeated intervals. You have to use `crontab` to schedule such recurring jobs — for example, if you want to back up your files to tape at midnight every evening.

You schedule recurring jobs by placing job information in a file with a specific format and submitting this file with the `crontab` command. The `cron` daemon — `crond` — checks the job information every minute and executes the recurring jobs at the specified times. Because the `cron` daemon processes recurring jobs, such jobs are also referred to as *`cron` jobs*.

Any output from a `cron` job is mailed to the user who submits the job. (In the submitted job-information file, you can specify a different recipient for the mailed output.)

Two configuration files control who can schedule `cron` jobs using `crontab`:

- /etc/cron.allow contains the names of the users who may submit jobs using the crontab command.
- /etc/cron.deny contains the names of users not allowed to submit jobs using the crontab command.

If the /etc/cron.allow file exists, only users listed in this file can schedule cron jobs. If only the /etc/cron.deny file exists, users listed in this file cannot schedule cron jobs. If neither file exists, the default Linux setup enables any user to submit cron jobs.

To submit a cron job, follow these steps:

1. **Prepare a shell script (or an executable program in any programming language) that can perform the recurring task you want to perform.**

   You can skip this step if you want to execute an existing program periodically.

2. **Prepare a text file with information about the times when you want the shell script or program (from Step 1) to execute, and then submit this file by using** crontab**.**

   You can submit several recurring jobs with a single file. Each line with timing information about a job has a standard format with six fields — the first five specify when the job runs, and the sixth and subsequent fields constitute the actual command that runs. For example, here is a line that executes the myjob shell script in a user's home directory at five minutes past midnight each day:

   ```
   5 0 * * * $HOME/myjob
   ```

   Table 1-13 shows the meaning of the first five fields. ***Note:*** An asterisk (*) means all possible values for that field. Also, an entry in any of the first five fields can be a single number, a comma-separated list of numbers, a pair of numbers separated by a dash (indicating a range of numbers), or an asterisk.

3. **Suppose the text file** jobinfo **(in the current directory) contains the job information. Submit this information to** crontab **with the following command:**

   ```
   crontab jobinfo
   ```

That's it! You are set with the cron job. From now on, the cron job runs at regular intervals (as specified in the job information file), and you receive mail messages with the output from the job.

To verify that the job is indeed scheduled, type the following command:

```
crontab -l
```

The output of the `crontab -l` command shows the `cron` jobs currently installed in your name. To remove your `cron` jobs, type **crontab -r**.

Table 1-13 Format for the Time of Execution in crontab Files

Field Number	*Meaning of Field*	*Acceptable Range of Values**
1	Minute	0–59
2	Hour of the day	0–23
3	Day of the month	0–31
4	Month	1–12 (1 means January, 2 means February, and so on) or the names of months using the first three letters (Jan, Feb, Mar, Apr, May, Jun, Jul, Aug, Sep, Oct, Nov, Dec)
5	Day of the week	0–6 (0 means Sunday, 1 means Monday, and so on) or the three-letter abbreviations of weekdays (Sun, Mon, Tue, Wed, Thu, Fri, Sat)

** An asterisk in a field means all possible values for that field. For example, if an asterisk is in the third field, the job is executed every day.*

If you log in as `root`, you can also set up, examine, and remove `cron` jobs for any user. To set up `cron` jobs for a user, use this command:

```
crontab -u username filename
```

Here, *`username`* is the user for whom you install the `cron` jobs, and *`filename`* is the file that contains information about the jobs.

Use the following form of `crontab` command to view the `cron` jobs for a user:

```
crontab -u username -l
```

To remove a user's `cron` jobs, use the following command:

```
crontab -u username -r
```

Note: The `cron` daemon also executes the `cron` jobs listed in the system-wide `cron`-job file `/etc/crontab`. Here's a typical `/etc/crontab` file from a Linux system (type **cat /etc/crontab** to view the file):

```
SHELL=/bin/bash
PATH=/sbin:/bin:/usr/sbin:/usr/bin
MAILTO=root
HOME=/
```

```
# run-parts
01 * * * * root run-parts /etc/cron.hourly
02 4 * * * root run-parts /etc/cron.daily
22 4 * * 0 root run-parts /etc/cron.weekly
42 4 1 * * root run-parts /etc/cron.monthly
```

The first four lines set up several environment variables for the jobs listed in this file. The `MAILTO` environment variable specifies the user who receives the mail message with the output from the `cron` jobs in this file.

The line that begins with a # is a comment line. The four lines following the `run-parts` comment execute the `run-parts` shell script (located in the `/usr/bin` directory) at various times with the name of a specific directory as argument. Each of the arguments to `run-parts` — `/etc/cron.hourly`, `/etc/cron.daily`, `/etc/cron.weekly`, and `/etc/cron.monthly` — are directories. Essentially, `run-parts` executes all scripts located in the directory that you provide as an argument.

Table 1-14 lists the directories where to locate these scripts and when they execute. You have to look at the scripts in these directories to know what executes at these periodic intervals.

Table 1-14 Script Directories for cron Jobs

Directory Name	*Contents*
`/etc/cron.hourly`	Scripts execute every hour.
`/etc/cron.daily`	Scripts execute each day.
`/etc/cron.weekly`	Scripts execute weekly.
`/etc/cron.monthly`	Scripts execute once each month.

Chapter 2: Managing Users and Groups

In This Chapter

- Adding user accounts
- Understanding the password file
- Managing groups
- Exploring the user environment
- Changing user and group ownerships of files and directories

Linux is a multiuser system, so it has many user accounts. Even if you are the only user on your system, many servers require a unique username and group name. Take, for example, the FTP server. It runs under the username `ftp`. A whole host of system users are not for people, but just for running specific programs.

Also, users can belong to one or more groups. Typically, each username has a corresponding private group name. By default, each user belongs to that corresponding private group. However, you can define other groups for the purpose of providing access to specific files and directories based on group membership.

User and group ownerships of files are a way to make sure that only the right people (or the right process) can access the right files and directories. Managing the user and group accounts is a typical system administration job. It's not that hard to do this part of the job, given the tools that come with Linux. I show you how in this chapter.

Adding User Accounts

You get the chance to add user accounts when you boot your system for the first time after installing Linux. The `root` account is the only one that you must set up during installation. If you didn't add other user accounts when you start the system for the first time, you can do so later on, using a GUI user account manager or the `useradd` command to add new users on your system.

Creating other user accounts besides `root` is a good idea. Even if you're the only user of the system, logging in as a less privileged user is good practice because that way you can't damage any important system files inadvertently. If necessary, you can type **su -** to log in as `root` and then perform any system administration tasks.

Using a GUI User Manager to add user accounts

Most Linux distributions come with a GUI tool to manage user accounts. You can use that GUI tool to add new user accounts. The basic steps, regardless of the specific GUI tool, involves the following:

1. The tool displays a list of current user accounts and has an Add button for adding new users.
2. Click the Add button to bring up a dialog box that prompts you for information about the new user account.
3. Enter the requested information — the username, the password (enter twice), and the full name of the user.
4. Click the button to create a new account and the GUI tool takes care of adding the new user account.

For example, in SUSE, select the Security and Users category from the YaST Control Center's left side and then click the Edit and Create Users icon in the right-hand side of the window. YaST then brings up the User and Group Administration pane, shown in Figure 2-1, where you can define new user accounts.

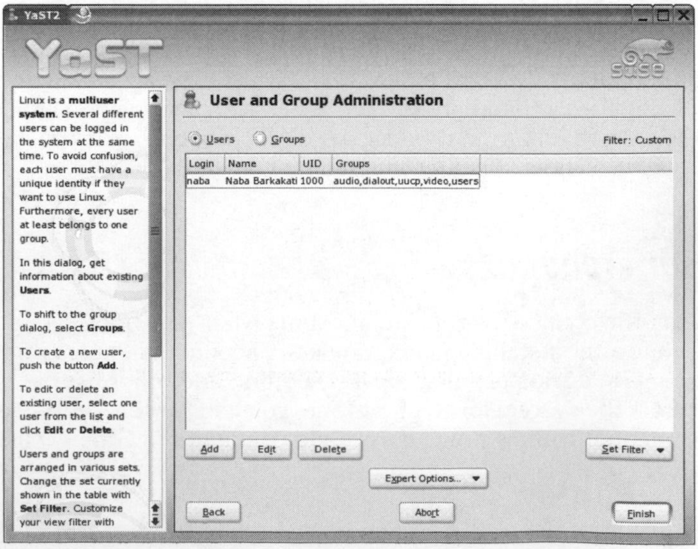

Figure 2-1: In SUSE, you can manage user accounts and groups from YaST.

Notice that the pane has two radio buttons: Users and Groups (as shown in Figure 2-1). Selecting the Users radio button displays the current list of users from the /etc/passwd file. Selecting the Groups radio button lists the names of groups from the /etc/group. Initially, the User and Group Administration tool filters out any system users and groups. However, you can view the system users by clicking Set Filter and selecting System Users from the drop-down menu. (*System users* refer to user accounts that are not assigned to human users, rather these user accounts are used to run various services.)

You can add new users and groups or edit existing users and groups from the pane shown in Figure 2-1.

To add a new user account, click the Add button and enter the information requested in the Add a New Local User window, as shown in Figure 2-2.

Fill in the requested information in the window (refer to Figure 2-2), and click the Create button. The new user now appears in the list of users in the User and Group Administration pane.

You can add more user accounts, if you like. When you are done, click the Finish button in the User and Group Administration pane (refer to Figure 2-1) to create the new user accounts.

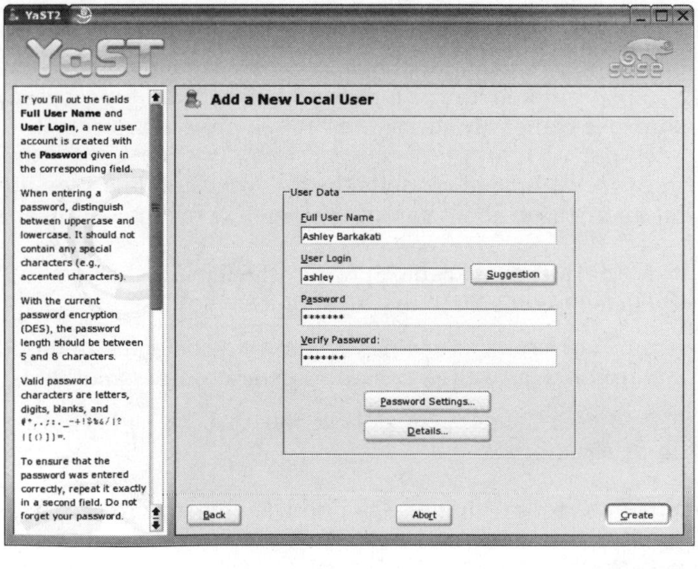

Figure 2-2: Create a new user account by filling in the information in this YaST window.

By default, YaST places all local users in a group named users. Sometimes you want a user to be in other groups as well, so that the user can access the files owned by that group. Adding a user to another group is easy. For example, suppose I want to add the username `naba` to the group called `wheel`. I simply type the following command in a terminal window:

```
usermod -G wheel naba
```

To remove a user account in SUSE, click the username in the list of user accounts (refer to Figure 2-1). Then click the Delete button.

Using commands to manage user accounts

If you're working from a text console, you can create a new user account by using the `useradd` command. Follow these steps to add an account for a new user:

1. **Log in as `root`.**

   If you're not already logged in as `root`, type **su -** to become `root`.

2. **Type the following `useradd` command with the `-c` option to create the account:**

   ```
   /usr/sbin/useradd -c "Ashley Barkakati" ashley
   ```

3. **Set the password by using the `passwd` command, as follows:**

   ```
   passwd ashley
   ```

   You're prompted for the password twice. If you type a password that someone can easily guess, the `passwd` program rejects it.

The `useradd` command consults the following configuration files to obtain default information about various parameters for the new user account:

- `/etc/default/useradd`: Specifies the default shell (`/bin/bash`) and the default home directory location (`/home`).
- `/etc/login.defs`: Provides system-wide defaults for automatic group and user IDs, as well as password-expiration parameters.
- `/etc/skel`: Contains the default files that `useradd` creates in the user's home directory.

Examine these files with the `cat` or `more` commands to see what they contain.

You can delete a user account by using the `userdel` command. Simply type **/usr/sbin/userdel *username*** at the command prompt to delete a user's account. To wipe out that user's home directory as well, type **/usr/sbin/userdel -r *username***.

To modify any information in a user account, use the `usermod` command. For example, if I want my username, `naba`, to have `root` as the primary group, I type the following:

```
usermod -g root naba
```

TIP

To find out more about the `useradd`, `userdel`, and `usermod` commands, type **man useradd**, **man userdel**, or **man usermod** in a terminal window.

Understanding the /etc/passwd File

The `/etc/passwd` file is a list of all user accounts. It's a text file and any user can read it — no special privileges needed. Each line in `/etc/passwd` has seven fields, separated by colons (`:`).

Here is a typical entry from the `/etc/passwd` file:

```
naba:x:500:10:Naba Barkakati:/home/naba:/bin/bash
```

Figure 2-3 explains the meaning of the seven fields in this entry.

Figure 2-3: This typical `/etc/passwd` entry illustrates the meaning of the various fields.

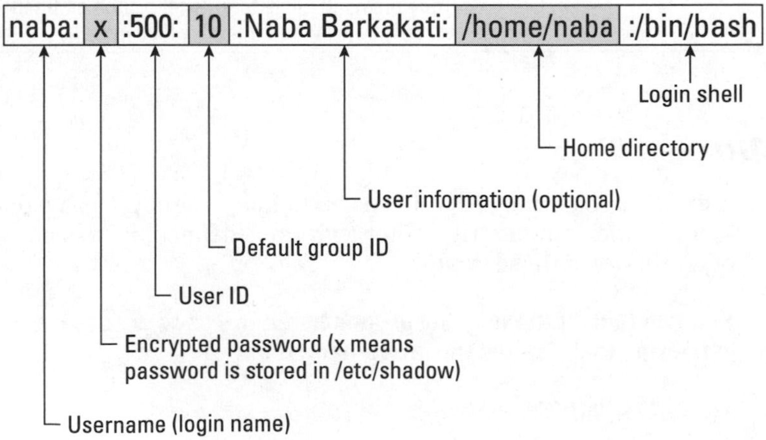

As the example shows, the format of each line in `/etc/passwd` looks like this:

```
username:password:UID:GID:GECOS:homedir:shell
```

Table 2-1 explains the meaning of the seven fields in each /etc/passwd entry.

Table 2-1 Meaning of the Fields in /etc/passwd File

This Field	*Contains*
username	An alphanumeric username, usually eight characters long and unique (Linux allows usernames to be longer than eight characters, but some other operating systems do not)
password	When present, a 13-character encrypted password (an empty field means that no password is required to access the account, an x means the password is stored in the /etc/shadow file, which is more secure)
UID	A unique number that serves as the user identifier (root has a UID of 0 and usually the UIDs between 1 to 100 are reserved for non-human users such as servers; keeping the UID less than 32,767 is best)
GID	The default group ID of the group to which the user belongs (GID 0 is for group root, other groups are defined in /etc/group and users can be and usually are in more than one group at a time)
GECOS	Optional personal information about the user (the finger command uses this field and GECOS stands for General Electric Comprehensive Operating System, a long-forgotten operating system that's immortalized by the name of this field in /etc/passwd)
homedir	The name of the user's home directory
shell	The command interpreter (shell), such as Bash (/bin/bash), that executes when this user logs in

Managing Groups

A group is something to which users belong. A group has a name and an identification number (ID). After a group is defined, users can belong to one or more of these groups.

You can find all the existing groups listed in /etc/group. For example, here is the line that defines the group named wheel:

```
wheel:x:10:root,naba
```

As this example shows, each line in /etc/group has the following format, with four fields separated by colons:

```
groupname:password:GID:membership
```

Table 2-2 explains the meaning of the four fields in a group definition.

Table 2-2 Meaning of Fields in /etc/group File

Field Name	*Meaning*
groupname	The name of the group (for example, `wheel`)
password	The group password (an `x` means that the password is stored in the `/etc/shadow` file)
GID	The numerical group ID (for example, 10)
membership	A comma-separated list of usernames that belong to this group (for example, `root,naba`)

If you want to create a new group, you can simply use the `groupadd` command. For example, to add a new group called `class` with an automatically selected group ID, just type the following command in a terminal window (you have to be logged in as `root`):

```
groupadd class
```

Then you can add users to this group with the `usermod` command. For example, to add the users `naba` and `ashley` to the group named `class`, I type the following commands:

```
usermod -G class naba
usermod -G class ashley
```

That's it. Now I check `/etc/group` to find that it contains the following definition of `class`:

```
class:x:502:naba,ashley
```

It's that simple!

If you want to remove a group, use the `groupdel` command. For example, to remove group named `class`, type

```
groupdel class
```

Exploring the User Environment

When you log in as a user, you get a set of environment variables that control many aspects of what you see and do on your Linux system. If you want to see your current environment, go ahead and type the following command in a terminal window:

```
env
```

(By the way, the printenv command also displays the environment, but env is shorter.)

The env command prints a long list of lines. That whole collection of lines is the current environment, and each line defines an environment variable. For example, the env command displays this typical line:

```
HOSTNAME=localhost.localdomain
```

This line defines the environment variable HOSTNAME, and it's defined as localhost.localdomain.

An *environment variable* is nothing more than a name associated with a string. For example, the environment variable named PATH is typically defined as follows for a normal user:

```
PATH=/usr/local/bin:/bin:/usr/bin:/usr/X11R6/bin
```

The string to the right of the equal sign is the value of the PATH environment variable. By convention, the PATH environment variable is a sequence of directory names, each name separated from the preceding one by a colon (:).

Each environment variable has a specific purpose. For example, when the shell has to search for a file, it simply searches the directories listed in the PATH environment variable. The shell searches the directories in PATH in the order of their appearance. Therefore, if two programs have the same name, the shell executes the one it finds first.

In a fashion similar to the shell's use of the PATH environment variable, an editor such as vi uses the value of the TERM environment variable to figure out how to display the file you are editing with vi. To see the current setting of TERM, type the following command at the shell prompt:

```
echo $TERM
```

If you type this command in a terminal window, the output is as follows:

```
xterm
```

To define an environment variable in Bash, use the following syntax:

```
export NAME=Value
```

Here, *NAME* denotes the name of the environment variable, and *Value* is the string representing its value. Therefore, you set TERM to the value xterm by using the following command:

```
export TERM=xterm
```

TIP

After you define an environment variable, you can change its value by simply specifying the new value with the syntax `NAME=new-value`. For example, to change the definition of `TERM` to `vt100`, type **TERM=vt100** at the shell prompt.

With an environment variable such as `PATH`, you typically want to append a new directory name to the existing definition, rather than define the `PATH` from scratch. For example, if you download and install the Java 2 Development Kit (available from `java.sun.com/j2se/1.5.0/download.jsp`), you have to add the location of the Java binaries to `PATH`. Here's how you accomplish that task:

```
export PATH=$PATH:/usr/java/jdk1.5.0/bin
```

This command appends the string `:/usr/java/jdk1.5.0/bin` to the current definition of the `PATH` environment variable. The net effect is to add `/usr/java/jdk1.5.0/bin` to the list of directories in `PATH`.

Note: You also can write this `export` command as follows:

```
export PATH=${PATH}:/usr/java/jdk1.5.0/bin
```

After you type that command, you can access programs in the `/usr/java/jdk1.5.0/bin` directory such as `javac`, the Java compiler that converts Java source code into a form that the Java interpreter can execute.

`PATH` and `TERM` are only two of a handful of common environment variables. Table 2-3 lists some of the environment variables for a typical Linux user.

Table 2-3 Typical Environment Variables in Linux

Environment Variable	*Contents*
`DISPLAY`	The name of the display on which the X Window System displays output (typically set to :0.0)
`HOME`	Your home directory
`HOSTNAME`	The host name of your system
`LOGNAME`	Your login name
`MAIL`	The location of your mail directory
`PATH`	The list of directories in which the shell looks for programs
`SHELL`	Your shell (`SHELL=/bin/bash` for Bash)
`TERM`	The type of terminal

Changing User and Group Ownership of Files

In Linux, each file or directory has two types of owners — a user and a group. In other words, a user and group own each file and directory. The user and group ownerships can control who can access a file or directory.

To view the owner of a file or directory, use the `ls -l` command to see the detailed listing of a directory. For example, here's a typical file's information:

```
-rw-rw-r--  1 naba   naba    40909 Aug 16 20:37 composer.txt
```

In this example, the first set of characters shows the file's permission setting — who can read, write, or execute the file. The third and fourth fields (in this example, `naba naba`) indicate the user and group owner of the file. Each user has a private group that has the same name as the username. So most files' user and group ownership appear to show the username twice.

As a system administrator, you may decide to change the group ownership of a file to a common group. For example, suppose you want to change the group ownership of the `composer.txt` file to the `class` group. To do that, log in as `root` and type the following command:

```
chgrp class composer.txt
```

This `chgrp` command changes the group ownership of `composer.txt` to `class`. After I tried this, I typed **ls -l** again to verify the ownership, and here's what I got:

```
-rw-rw-r--  1 naba   class   40909 Aug 16 20:37 composer.txt
```

You can use the `chown` command to change the user owner. The command has the following format:

```
chown username filename
```

For example, to change the user ownership of a file named `sample.jpg` to `naba`, I type

```
chown naba sample.jpg
```

In fact, `chown` can change both the user and group owner at the same time. For example, to change the user owner to `naba` and the group owner to `class`, I type

```
chown naba.class composer.txt
```

In other words, you simply append the group name to the username with a period in between, and use that as the name of the owner.

Chapter 3: Managing File Systems

In This Chapter

- **Navigating the Linux file system**
- **Sharing files with NFS**
- **Backing up and restoring files**
- **Mounting the NTFS file system**
- **Accessing MS-DOS files**

A *file system* refers to the organization of files and directories. As a system administrator, you have to perform certain operations to manage file systems on various storage media. For example, you have to know how to *mount* — add a file system on a storage medium by attaching it to the overall Linux file system. You also have to back up important data and restore files from a backup. Other file system operations include sharing files with the *Network File System* (NFS) and accessing MS-DOS files. In this chapter, I show you how to perform all the file system management tasks.

Exploring the Linux File System

The files and directories in your PC store information in an organized manner, just like paper filing systems. When you store information on paper, you typically put several pages in a folder and then store the folder in a file cabinet. If you have many folders, you probably have some sort of filing system. For example, you may label each folder's tab and then arrange them alphabetically in the file cabinet. You probably have several file cabinets, each with lots of drawers, which, in turn, contain folders full of pages.

Operating systems such as Linux organize information in your computer in a manner similar to your paper filing system. Linux uses a file system to organize all information in your computer. Of course, the storage medium isn't a metal file cabinet and paper. Instead, Linux stores information on devices such as hard drives, floppy disk drives, and CD-ROM drives.

To draw an analogy between your computer's file system and a paper filing system, think of a disk drive as the file cabinet. The drawers in the file cabinet correspond to the directories in the file system. The folders in each drawer are also directories — because a directory in a computer file system can contain other directories. You can think of files as the pages inside the folder — and that's where the actual information is stored. Figure 3-1 illustrates the analogy between a file cabinet and the Linux file system.

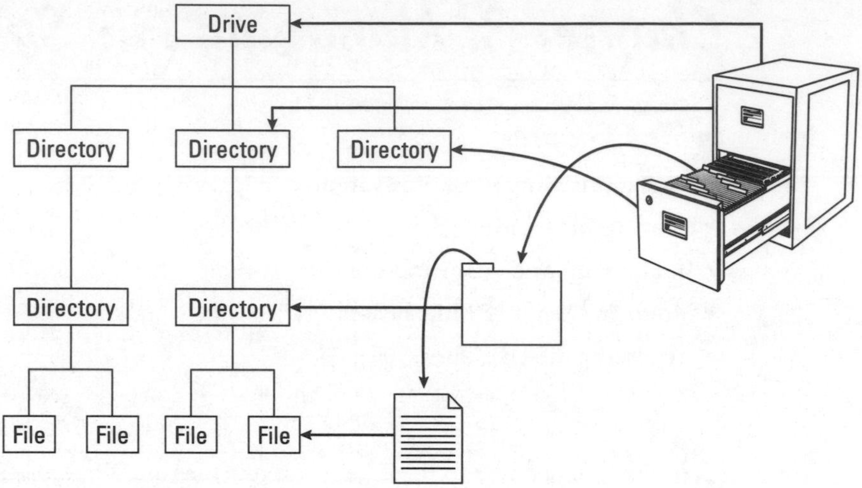

Figure 3-1: It's a bit of a stretch, but you can think of the Linux file system as similar to a filing cabinet.

The Linux file system has a *hierarchical* structure — directories can contain other directories, which in turn contain individual files.

Everything in your Linux system is organized in files and directories in the file system. To access and use documents and programs on your system, you have to be familiar with the file system.

Understanding the file-system hierarchy

The Linux file system is organized like a tree, with a *root directory* from which all other directories branch out. When you write a complete pathname, the root directory is represented by a single slash (/). Then there is a hierarchy of files and directories. Parts of the file system can be in different physical drives or different hard drive partitions.

Linux uses a standard directory hierarchy. Figure 3-2 shows the standard parts of the Linux file system. Of course, you can create new directories anywhere in this structure.

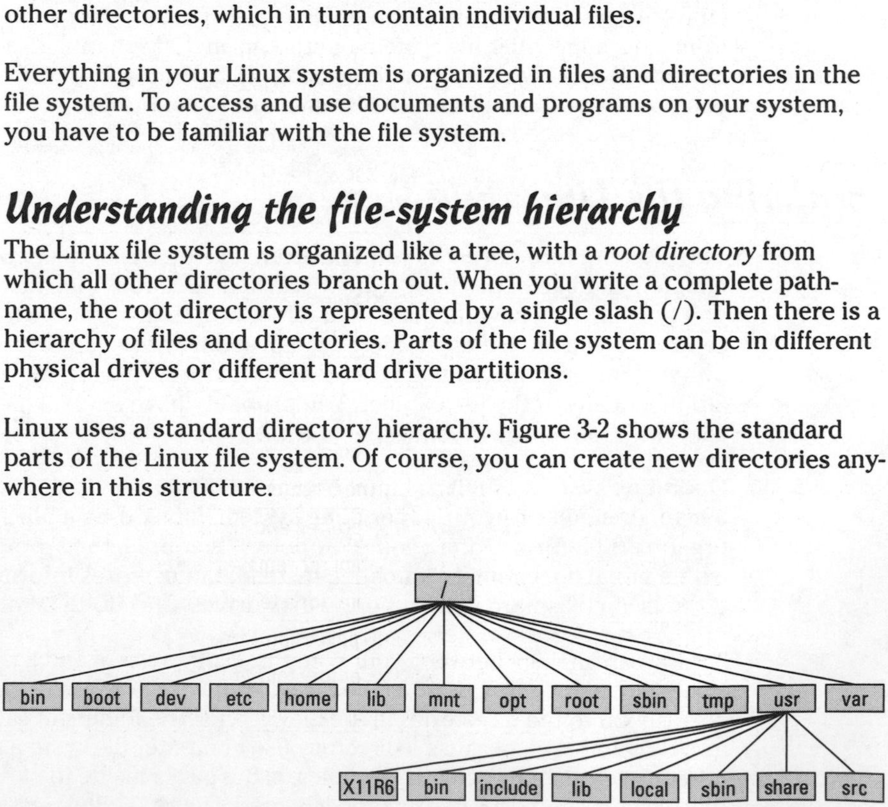

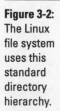

Figure 3-2: The Linux file system uses this standard directory hierarchy.

Write the name of any file or directory by concatenating the names of directories that identify where that file or directory is and using the forward slash (/) as a separator. For example, in Figure 3-2, the `usr` directory at the top level is written as `/usr` because the root directory (/) contains `usr`. On the other hand, the `X11R6` directory is inside the `usr` directory, which is inside the root directory (/). Therefore, the `X11R6` directory is uniquely identified by the name `/usr/X11R6`. This type of full name is called a *pathname* because the name identifies the path you take from the root directory to reach a file. Thus, `/usr/X11R6` is a pathname.

The Filesystem Hierarchy Standard (FHS) specifies the organization of files and directories in UNIX-like operating systems such as Linux. FHS defines a standard set of directories and their intended use. The FHS, if faithfully adopted by all Linux distributions, should help improve the interoperability of applications, system administration tools, development tools, and scripts across all Linux distributions. FHS even helps the system documentation as well as books like this one because the same description of the file system applies to all Linux distributions. Version 2.3 of FHS was announced on January 29, 2004. FHS 2.3 is part of the Linux Standard Base version 2.0 (LSB 2.0), which was released on August 30, 2004. LSB 2.0 (see `www.linuxbase.org`) is a set of binary standards aimed at reducing variations among the Linux distributions and promoting portability of applications. To find out more about FHS, check out the FHS home page at `www.pathname.com/fhs`.

Each of the standard directories in the Linux file system has a specific purpose. Table 3-1 summarizes these directories.

Table 3-1 Standard Directories in Linux File System

Directory	*Used to Store*
`/bin`	Executable files for user commands (for use by all users)
`/boot`	Files needed by the boot loader to load the Linux kernel
`/dev`	Device files
`/etc`	Host-specific system configuration files
`/home`	User home directories
`/lib`	Shared libraries and kernel modules
`/media`	Mount point for removable media
`/mnt`	Mount point for a temporarily mounted file system
`/opt`	Add-on application software packages
`/root`	Home directory for the `root` user
`/sbin`	Utilities for system administration

(continued)

Table 3-1 *(continued)*

Directory	*Used to Store*
`/srv`	Data for services (such as Web and FTP) offered by this system
`/tmp`	Temporary files
The `/usr` Hierarchy	**Secondary Directory Hierarchy**
`/usr/X11R6`	X Window System, Version 11 Release 6
`/usr/bin`	Most user commands
`/usr/include`	Directory for included files used in developing Linux applications
`/usr/lib`	Libraries used by software packages and for programming
`/usr/libexec`	Libraries for applications
`/usr/local`	Any local software
`/usr/sbin`	Nonessential system administrator utilities
`/usr/share`	Shared data that does not depend on the system architecture (whether the system is an Intel PC or a Sun SPARC workstation)
`/usr/src`	Source code
The `/var` Hierarchy	**Variable Data**
`/var/cache`	Cached data for applications
`/var/lib`	Information relating to the current state of applications
`/var/lock`	Lock files to ensure that a resource is used by one application only
`/var/log`	Log files organized into subdirectories
`/var/mail`	User mailbox files
`/var/opt`	Variable data for packages stored in the `/opt` directory
`/var/run`	Data describing the system since it was booted
`/var/spool`	Data that's waiting for some kind of processing
`/var/tmp`	Temporary files preserved between system reboots
`/var/yp`	Network Information Service (NIS) database files

Mounting a device on the file system

The storage devices that you use in Linux contain Linux file systems. Each device has its own local file system consisting of a hierarchy of directories. Before you can access the files on a device, you have to attach the device's directory hierarchy to the tree that represents the overall Linux file system.

Mounting is the operation you perform to cause the file system on a physical storage device (a hard drive partition or a CD-ROM) to appear as part of the Linux file system. Figure 3-3 illustrates the concept of mounting.

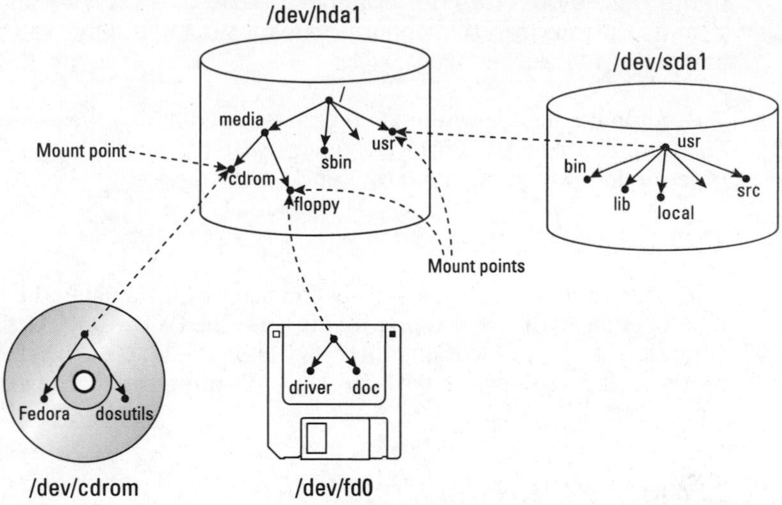

Figure 3-3: You have to mount a device on the Linux file system before accessing it.

Figure 3-3 shows each device with a name that begins with `/dev`. For example, `/dev/cdrom` is the first DVD/CD-ROM drive and `/dev/fd0` is the floppy drive. These physical devices are mounted at specific mount points on the Linux file system. For example, the DVD/CD-ROM drive, `/dev/cdrom`, is mounted on `/media/cdrom` in the file system. After mounting the CD-ROM in this way, the `Fedora` directory on a CD-ROM or DVD-ROM appears as `/media/cdrom/Fedora` in the Linux file system.

You can use the `mount` command to manually mount a device on the Linux file system at a specified directory. That directory is the *mount point*. For example, to mount the DVD/CD-ROM drive at `/media/cdrom` directory, you type the following command (after logging in as `root`):

```
mount /dev/cdrom /media/cdrom
```

The `mount` command reports an error if the DVD/CD-ROM device is mounted already or if no CD or DVD media is in the drive. Otherwise, the `mount` operation succeeds, and you can access the DVD or CD's contents through the `/media/cdrom` directory.

You can use any directory as the mount point. If you mount a device on a nonempty directory, however, you cannot access the files in that directory until you unmount the device by using the `umount` command. Therefore, always use an empty directory as the mount point.

Debian and Fedora Core define `/media/cdrom` directory as the mount point for mounting DVDs and CDs and `/media/floppy` for mounting floppies. Knoppix comes with the `/mnt/cdrom` directory for mounting DVDs or CDs and `/mnt/floppy` for mounting floppy drives. SUSE also uses mount points in the /media directory (for example, /media/cdrecorder and /mnt/floppy). In Xandros, the mount points for CD and floppy are /mnt/cdrom0 and /mnt/fd0, respectively.

To unmount a device when you no longer need it, use the umount command. For example, for a DVD/CD-ROM device with the device name /dev/cdrom, type the following command to unmount the device:

```
umount /dev/cdrom
```

The umount command succeeds as long as no one is using the DVD/CD-ROM. If you get an error when trying to unmount the DVD/CD-ROM, check to see whether the current working directory is on the DVD or CD. If you're currently working in one of the DVD/CD-ROM's directories, that also qualifies as a use of the DVD/CD-ROM.

Examining the /etc/fstab file

The mount command has the following general format:

```
mount device-name mount-point
```

However, you can mount by specifying only the CD-ROM device name or the mount-point name, provided there is an entry in the /etc/fstab file for the CD-ROM mount point. That entry specifies the CD-ROM device name and the file system type. That's why you can mount the CD-ROM with a shorter mount command.

For example, in Debian, you can mount the CD-ROM by typing one of the following commands:

```
mount /dev/cdrom
mount /media/cdrom
```

The /etc/fstab file is a *configuration file* — a text file containing information that the mount and umount commands use. Each line in the /etc/fstab file provides information about a device and its mount point in the Linux file system. Essentially, the /etc/fstab file associates various mount points within the file system with specific devices, which enables the mount command to work from the command line with only the mount point or the device as argument.

Here is a /etc/fstab file from a SUSE system (the file has a similar format in other Linux distributions):

```
/dev/hda11       /                  reiserfs acl,user_xattr       1 1
/dev/hda7        /boot              ext3     acl,user_xattr       1 2
/dev/hda6        /data1             auto     noauto,user          0 0
/dev/hda9        /data2             auto     noauto,user          0 0
/dev/hda10       /data3             auto     noauto,user          0 0
/dev/hda5        /data4             auto     noauto,user          0 0
/dev/hda2        /windows/C         ntfs
    ro,users,gid=users,umask=0002,nls=utf8 0 0
/dev/hda8        swap               swap     pri=42               0 0
devpts           /dev/pts           devpts   mode=0620,gid=5      0 0
proc             /proc              proc     defaults             0 0
usbfs            /proc/bus/usb      usbfs    noauto               0 0
sysfs            /sys               sysfs    noauto               0 0
/dev/cdrecorder  /media/cdrecorder subfs
    fs=cdfss,ro,procuid,nosuid,nodev,exec,iocharset=utf8 0 0
/dev/fd0         /media/floppy      subfs
    fs=floppyfss,procuid,nodev,nosuid,sync 0 0
```

The first field on each line shows a device name, such as a hard drive partition. The second field is the mount point, and the third field indicates the type of file system on the device. You can ignore the last three fields for now.

This /etc/fstab file shows that the /dev/hda8 device functions as a swap device for virtual memory, which is why both the mount point and the file system type are set to swap.

The Linux operating system uses the contents of the /etc/fstab file to mount various file systems automatically. During Linux startup, the init process executes a shell script that runs the mount -a command. That command reads the /etc/fstab file and mounts all listed file systems (except those with the noauto option). The third field on each line of /etc/fstab specifies the type of file system on that device and the fourth field shows a comma-separated list of options that the mount command uses when mounting that device on the file system. Typically, you find the defaults option in this field. The defaults option implies — among other things — that the device mounts at boot time; that only the root user can mount the device; and that the device mounts for both reading and writing. If the options include noauto, the device doesn't mount automatically as the system boots.

In Fedora Core, you often find the kudzu option in the fourth field of /etc/fstab entries. The kudzu option indicates that the line was added to the fstab file by the kudzu hardware-detection utility — kudzu runs the updfstab command to add an entry in the /etc/fstab file for each removable drive it detects. You typically find that the entries for DVD/CD-ROM drives (/dev/cdrom and /dev/cdrom1) and floppy drive (dev/fd0) have the kudzu option in the fourth field. On a PC with an IDE Zip drive, for instance, the /etc/fstab file has another entry set up by kudzu that associates the /mnt/zip mount point with the Zip drive device (/dev/hdd4), as follows:

```
/dev/hdd4  /mnt/zip    auto  noauto,owner,kudzu   0 0
```

Sharing Files with NFS

Sharing files through the Network File System (NFS) is simple and involves two basic steps:

- ✦ On the NFS server, export one or more directories by listing them in the `/etc/exports` file and by running the `/usr/sbin/exportfs` command. In addition, you must run the NFS server.
- ✦ On each client system, use the `mount` command to mount the directories the server has exported.

How you start the NFS server depends on the Linux distribution. In Debian, you can type **invoke-rc.d nfs-kernel-server start** and **invoke-rc.d nfs-common start** to start the NFS server. In Fedora Core, type **service nfs start**. In SUSE, you can use YaST Control Center (Main Menu➪System➪YaST) to start the NFS server. (It's in the Network Services category.) In Xandros, you can start the NFS server from the Xandros Control Center (Main Menu➪Control Center) or you can type **invoke-rc.d nfs-user-server start** in a terminal window.

The only problem in using NFS is that each client system must support it. Most PCs don't come with NFS — that means you have to buy NFS software separately if you want to share files by using NFS. If, however, all systems on your LAN run Linux (or other variants of UNIX with built-in NFS support), using NFS makes sense.

NFS has security vulnerabilities. Therefore, do not set up NFS on systems directly connected to the Internet.

In the upcoming section, I walk you through an NFS setup, using an example of two Linux PCs on a LAN.

Exporting a file system with NFS

Start with the server system that *exports* — makes available to the client systems — the contents of a directory. On the server, you must run the NFS service and also designate one or more file systems to be exported, or made available, to the client systems.

To export a file system, you have to add an appropriate entry to the `/etc/exports` file. For example, suppose you want to export the `/home` directory and you want to enable the host named LNBP75 to mount this file system for read-and-write operations. (You can use a host's IP address in place of the host name.) You can do so by adding the following entry to the `/etc/exports` file:

```
/home LNBP75(rw)
```

If you use the IP address of a host, the entry might look like this:

```
/home 192.168.0.2(rw)
```

This specifies that 192.168.0.2 is the IP address of the host that's allowed full access to the `/home` directory.

After adding the entry in the `/etc/exports` file, start the NFS server using a method appropriate for your Linux distribution. For example, in Fedora Core, I log in as `root` and type the following command in a terminal window:

```
service nfs start
```

When the NFS service is up, the server side of NFS is ready. Now you can try to mount the exported file system from a client system and access the exported file system.

TIP: If you ever make any changes to the exported file systems listed in the `/etc/exports` file, remember to restart the NFS service. For example, in Fedora Core, I type **service nfs restart** in a terminal window. In Xandros, I type **invoke-rc.d nfs-user-server restart**.

Mounting an NFS file system

To access an exported NFS file system on a client system, you have to mount that file system on a mount point — which is, in practical terms, nothing more than a local directory. For example, suppose you want to access the `/home` directory exported from the server named `LNBP200` at the local directory `/mnt/lnbp200` on the client system. To do so, follow these steps:

1. **Log in as `root`, and then create the directory with the following command:**

   ```
   mkdir /mnt/lnbp200
   ```

2. **Type the following command to perform the `mount` operation:**

   ```
   mount lnbp200:/home/public /mnt/lnbp200
   ```

   If you only know the IP address of the server, replace the host name (in this case, `lnbp200`) with the IP address.

3. **Change the directory to `/mnt/lnbp200` with the command `cd /mnt/lnbp200`.**

   Now you can view and access exported files from this directory.

To confirm that the NFS file system is indeed mounted, log in as `root` on the client system and type **mount** in a terminal window. You see a line similar to the following one about the NFS file system:

```
lnbp200:/home/public on /mnt/lnbp200 type nfs (rw,addr=192.168.1.200)
```

Backing Up and Restoring Files

Backing up and restoring files is a crucial system administration task. If something happens to your system's hard drive, you have to rely on the backups to recover important files. Here I present some backup strategies, describe several backup media, and explain how to back up and restore files by using the *tape archiver* (`tar`) program that comes with Linux. Also, you find out how to perform incremental and automatic backups on tapes.

If you have a CD burner, you can also back up files by recording them on a CD-R. Consult Book II, Chapter 4 for information on what application you can use to burn a data CD.

Selecting a backup strategy and media

Your Linux system's hard drive contains everything needed to keep the system running — as well as other files (such as documents and databases) that keep your business running. You have to back up these files so you can recover quickly and bring the system back to normal in case the hard drive crashes. Typically, you have to follow a strict regimen of regular backups because you can never tell when the hard drive may fail or the file system may get corrupted. To implement such a regimen, first decide which files you want to back up, how often, and what backup storage media to use. This process is what I mean by selecting a backup strategy and backup media.

Your choice of backup strategy and backup media depends on your assessment of the risk of business disruption due to hard drive failure. Depending on how you use your Linux system, a disk failure may or may not have much impact on you.

For example, if you use your Linux system as a learning tool (to find out more about Linux or programming), all you may need are backup copies of some system files required to configure Linux. In this case, your backup strategy can be to save important system configuration files on one or more floppies every time you change any system configuration.

On the other hand, if you use your Linux system as an office server that provides shared file storage for many users, the risk of business disruption due to disk failure is much higher. In this case, you have to back up all the files every week and back up any new or changed files every day. You can perform these backups in an automated manner (where you can use the job-scheduling features that I describe in Chapter 1 of this minibook). Also, you probably need a backup storage medium that can store large amounts (many gigabytes) of data. In other words, for high-risk situations, your backup strategy is more elaborate and requires additional equipment (such as a tape drive).

Your choice of backup media depends on the amount of data you have to back up. For a small amount of data (such as system configuration files), you can use floppy disks or USB flash drives as the backup media. If your PC has a Zip drive, you can use Zip disks as backup media; these are good for backing up a single-user directory. To back up entire servers, use a tape drive, typically a 4mm or 8mm tape drive that connects to a SCSI controller. Such tape drives can store several gigabytes of data per tape, and you can use them to back up an entire file system on a single tape.

When backing up files to these media, you have to refer to the backup device by name. Table 3-2 lists device names for some common backup devices.

Table 3-2 Device Names for Common Backup Devices

Backup Device	*Linux Device Name*
Floppy disk	`/dev/fd0`
IDE Zip drive	`/dev/hdc4` or `/dev/hdd4`
SCSI Zip drive	`/dev/sda` (assuming it's the first SCSI drive; otherwise, the device name depends on the SCSI ID)
SCSI tape drive	`/dev/st0` or `/dev/nst0` (the `n` prefix means that the tape isn't rewound after files copy to the tape)

Commercial backup utilities for Linux

In the next section, I explain how to back up and restore files using the tape archiver (`tar`) program that comes with Linux. Although you can manage backups with `tar`, a number of commercial backup utilities come with graphical user interfaces and other features to simplify backups. Here are some well-known commercial backup utilities for Linux:

- **BRU:** A backup and restore utility from The TOLIS Group, Inc. (`www.tolisgroup.com`)
- **LONE-TAR:** Tape-backup software package from Lone Star Software Corporation (`www.cactus.com`)
- **Arkeia:** Backup and recovery software for heterogeneous networks from Arkeia (`www.knox-software.com`)

- **CTAR:** Backup and recovery software for UNIX systems from UniTrends Software Corporation (`www.unitrends.com`)
- **BrightStor ARCserve Backup for Linux:** Data-protection technology for Linux systems from Computer Associates (`www3.ca.com/Solutions/Product.asp?ID=3370`)

Using the tape archiver — tar

You can use the `tar` command to archive files to a device, such as a floppy disk or tape. The `tar` program creates an archive file that can contain other directories and files and (optionally) compress the archive for efficient storage. The archive is then written to a specified device or another file. In fact, many software packages are distributed in the form of a compressed `tar` file.

The command syntax of the `tar` program is as follows:

```
tar options destination source
```

Here, *`options`* are usually specified by a sequence of single letters, with each letter specifying what `tar` will do. The *`destination`* is the device name of the backup device. And *`source`* is a list of file or directory names denoting the files to back up.

Backing up and restoring a single-volume archive

For example, suppose you want to back up the contents of the `/etc/X11` directory on a floppy disk. Log in as `root`, place a disk in the floppy drive, and type the following command:

```
tar zcvf /dev/fd0 /etc/X11
```

The `tar` program displays a list of filenames as each file copies to the compressed `tar` archive on the floppy disk. In this case, the options are `zcvf`, the destination is `/dev/fd0` (the floppy disk), and the source is the `/etc/X11` directory (which implies all its subdirectories and their contents). You can use a similar `tar` command to back up files to a tape — simply replace `/dev/fd0` with the tape device — such as `/dev/st0` for a SCSI tape drive.

Table 3-3 defines a few common `tar` options.

Table 3-3 Common tar Options

Option	*Does the Following*
`c`	Creates a new archive
`f`	Specifies the name of the archive file or device on the next field in the command line

Option	Does the Following
`M`	Specifies a multivolume archive (the next section describes multivolume archives)
`t`	Lists the contents of the archive
`v`	Displays verbose messages
`x`	Extracts files from the archive
`z`	Compresses the `tar` archive using `gzip`

To view the contents of the `tar` archive you create on the floppy disk, type the following command:

```
tar ztf /dev/fd0
```

You see a list of the filenames (each begins with `/etc/X11`) indicating what's in the backup. In this `tar` command, the `t` option lists the contents of the `tar` archive.

To extract the files from a `tar` backup, follow these steps while logged in as `root`:

1. **Change the directory to `/tmp` by typing this command:**

   ```
   cd /tmp
   ```

   TIP

   This step is where you can practice extracting the files from the `tar` backup. For a real backup, change the directory to an appropriate location (typically, you type **cd /**).

2. **Type the following command:**

   ```
   tar zxvf /dev/fd0
   ```

   This `tar` command uses the `x` option to extract the files from the archive stored on `/dev/fd0` (the floppy disk).

Now if you check the contents of the `/tmp` directory, you notice that the `tar` command creates an `etc/X11` directory tree in `/tmp` and restores all the files from the `tar` archive into that directory. The `tar` command strips off the leading / from the filenames in the archive and restores the files in the current directory. If you want to restore the `/etc/X11` directory from the archive on the floppy, use this command:

```
tar zxvf /dev/fd0 -C /
```

The `/` at the end of the command denotes the directory where you want to restore the backup files.

You can use the `tar` command to create, view, and restore an archive. You can store the archive in a file or in any device you specify with a device name.

Backing up and restoring a multivolume archive

Sometimes the capacity of a single storage medium is less than the total storage space needed to store the archive. In this case, you can use the `M` option for a multivolume archive — meaning the archive can span multiple tapes or floppies. Note, however, that you cannot create a compressed, multivolume archive. That means you have to drop the `z` option. To see how multivolume archives work, log in as `root`, place one disk in the floppy drive, and type the following `tar` command:

```
tar cvfM /dev/fd0 /usr/share/doc/ghostscript*
```

Note: The `M` option is in the option letters; it tells `tar` to create a multivolume archive. The `tar` command prompts you for a second floppy when the first one is filled. Take out the first floppy, and then insert another floppy when you see the following prompt:

```
Prepare volume #2 for '/dev/fd0' and hit return:
```

When you press Enter, the `tar` program continues with the second floppy. In this example, you need only two floppies to store the archive; for larger archives, the `tar` program continues to prompt for floppies in case more floppies are needed.

To restore from this multivolume archive, type **cd /tmp** to change the directory to `/tmp` (I use the `/tmp` directory for illustrative purposes here, but you have to use a real directory when you restore files from archive). Then type

```
tar xvfM /dev/fd0
```

The `tar` program prompts you to feed the floppies as necessary.

TIP

Use the `du -s` command to determine the amount of storage you need for archiving a directory. For example, here's how you can get the total size of the `/etc` directory in kilobytes:

```
du -s /etc
35724   /etc
```

The resulting output shows that the `/etc` directory requires at least 35,724K of storage space to back up.

Backing up on tapes

Although backing up on tapes is as simple as using the right device name in the `tar` command, you do have to know some nuances of the tape device to use it well. When you use `tar` to back up to the device named `/dev/st0` (the first SCSI tape drive), the tape device automatically rewinds the tape after the `tar` program finishes copying the archive to the tape. The `/dev/st0` device is called a rewinding tape device because it rewinds tapes by default.

If your tape can hold several gigabytes of data, you may want to write several `tar` archives — one after another — to the same tape (otherwise much of the tape may be left empty). If you plan to do so, your tape device can't rewind the tape after the `tar` program finishes. To help you with scenarios like this one, several Linux tape devices are nonrewinding. The nonrewinding SCSI tape device is called `/dev/nst0`. Use this device name if you want to write one archive after another on a tape.

TIP

After each archive, the nonrewinding tape device writes an *end-of-file* (EOF) marker to separate one archive from the next. Use the `mt` command to control the tape — you can move from one marker to the next or rewind the tape. For example, after you finish writing several archives to a tape using the `/dev/nst0` device name, you can force the tape to rewind with the following command:

```
mt -f /dev/nst0 rewind
```

After rewinding the tape, you can use the following command to extract files from the first archive to the current disk directory:

```
tar xvf /dev/nst0
```

After that, you must move past the EOF marker to the next archive. To do so, use the following `mt` command:

```
mt -f /dev/nst0 fsf 1
```

This positions the tape at the beginning of the next archive. Now use the `tar xvf` command again to read this archive.

REMEMBER

If you save multiple archives on a tape, you have to keep track of the archives yourself. The order of the archives can be hard to remember, so you may be better off simply saving one archive per tape.

Performing incremental backups

Suppose you use `tar` to back up your system's hard drive on a tape. Because such a full backup can take quite some time, you don't want to repeat this task every night. (Besides, only a small number of files may have changed during the day.) To locate the files that need backing up, you can use the `find` command to list all files that have changed in the past 24 hours:

```
find / -mtime -1 -type f -print
```

This command prints a list of files that have changed within the last day. The `-mtime -1` option means you want the files that were last modified less than one day ago. You can now combine this `find` command with the `tar` command to back up only those files that have changed within the last day:

```
tar cvf /dev/st0 `find / -mtime -1 -type f -print`
```

When you place a command between single back quotes, the shell executes that command and places the output at that point in the command line. The net result is that the `tar` program saves only the changed files in the archive. What this process gives you is an *incremental backup* of only the files that have changed since the previous day.

Performing automated backups

In Chapter 1 of this minibook, I show you how to use `crontab` to set up recurring jobs (called *cron jobs*). The Linux system performs these tasks at regular intervals. Backing up your system is a good use of the `crontab` facility. Suppose your backup strategy is as follows:

- Every Sunday at 1:15 a.m., your system backs up the entire hard drive on the tape.
- Monday through Saturday, your system performs an incremental backup at 3:10 a.m. by saving only those files that have changed during the past 24 hours.

To set up this automated backup schedule, log in as `root` and type the following lines in a file named `backups` (this example assumes that you use a SCSI tape drive):

```
15 1 * * 0 tar zcvf /dev/st0 /
10 3 * * 1-6 tar zcvf /dev/st0 `find / -mtime -1 -type f -print`
```

Next, submit this job schedule by using the following `crontab` command:

```
crontab backups
```

Now you are set for an automated backup. All you need to do is to place a new tape in the tape drive everyday. Remember to also give each tape an appropriate label.

Accessing a DOS/Windows File System

If you have Microsoft Windows 95/98/Me installed on your hard drive, you've probably already mounted the DOS/Windows partition under Linux. If not, you can easily mount DOS/Windows partitions in Linux. Mounting makes the DOS/Windows directory hierarchy appear as part of the Linux file system.

Mounting a DOS/Windows disk partition

To mount a DOS/Windows hard drive partition or floppy in Linux, use the `mount` command but include the option `-t vfat` to indicate the file system type as DOS. For example, if your DOS partition happens to be the first partition on your *IDE* (Integrated Drive Electronics) drive and you want to mount it on `/dosc`, use the following `mount` command:

```
mount -t vfat /dev/hda1 /dosc
```

The `-t vfat` part of the `mount` command specifies that the device you mount — `/dev/hda1` — has an MS-DOS file system. Figure 3-4 illustrates the effect of this `mount` command.

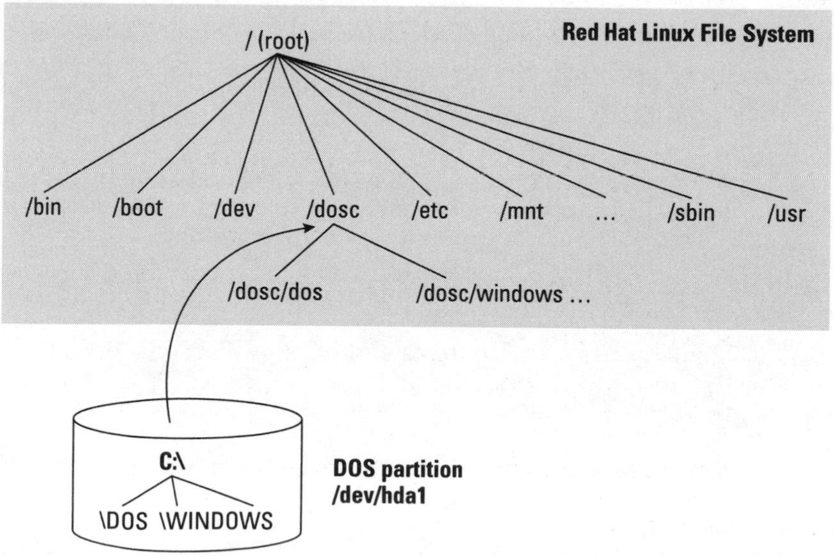

Figure 3-4: Here's how you mount a DOS partition on the `/dosc` directory.

Figure 3-4 shows how directories in your DOS partition map to the Linux file system. What was the C:\DOS directory under DOS becomes /dosc/dos under Linux. Similarly, C:\WINDOWS now is /dosc/windows. You probably can see the pattern. To convert a DOS filename to Linux (when you mount the DOS partition on /dosc), perform the following steps:

1. **Change the DOS names to lowercase.**
2. **Change C:\ to /dosc/.**
3. **Change all backslashes (\) to slashes (/).**

Mounting DOS floppy disks

Just as you mount a DOS hard drive partition on the Linux file system, you can also mount a DOS floppy disk. You must log in as root to mount a floppy, but you can follow the steps I show in the latter part of this section to set up your system so that any user can mount a DOS floppy disk. You also have to know the device name for the floppy drive. By default, Linux defines the following two generic floppy device names:

- /dev/fd0 is the A drive (the first floppy drive)
- /dev/fd1 is the B drive (the second floppy drive, if you have one)

As for the mount point, you can use any empty directory in the file system as the mount point, but the Linux system comes with a directory, /media/floppy, specifically for mounting a floppy disk.

To mount a DOS floppy disk on the /media/floppy directory, put the floppy in the drive and type the following command:

```
mount -t vfat /dev/fd0 /media/floppy
```

After you mount the floppy, you can copy files to and from the floppy by using the Linux copy command (cp). To copy the file gnome1.pcx from the current directory to the floppy, type the following:

```
cp gnome1.pcx /media/floppy
```

Similarly, to see the contents of the floppy disk, type the following:

```
ls /media/floppy
```

If you want to remove the floppy disk from the drive, first *unmount* the floppy drive. Unmounting removes the association between the floppy disk's file system and the mount point on the Linux file system. Use the umount command to unmount the floppy disk like this:

```
umount /dev/fd0
```

You can set up your Linux system so that any user can mount a DOS floppy. To enable any user to mount a DOS floppy in the A drive on the `/a` directory, for example, perform the following steps:

1. **Log in as `root`.**
2. **Create the `/a` directory (the mount point) by typing the following command in a terminal window:**

   ```
   mkdir /a
   ```

3. **Edit the `/etc/fstab` file in a text editor (such as `vi` or emacs) by inserting the following line, and then save the file and quit the editor:**

   ```
   /dev/fd0     /a     vfat     noauto,user       0 0
   ```

   The first field in that line is the device name of the floppy drive (`/dev/fd0`); the second field is the mount directory (`/a`); and the third field shows the type of file system (`vfat`). The `user` option (which appears next to `noauto`) is what enables all users to mount DOS floppy disks.

4. **Log out and then log back in as a normal user.**
5. **To confirm that you can mount a DOS floppy as a normal user and not just as `root`, insert a DOS floppy in the A drive and type the following command:**

   ```
   mount /a
   ```

   The `mount` operation succeeds, and you see a listing of the DOS floppy when you type the command **ls /a**.

6. **To unmount the DOS floppy, type** umount /a.

Mounting an NTFS partition

Nowadays, most PCs come with Windows XP or Windows 2000 preinstalled on the hard drive. Both Windows XP and 2000, as well as Windows NT, typically use the NT File System (NTFS). Linux supports read-only access to NTFS partitions and many distributions come with the `ntfs.ko` kernel module that's needed to access an NTFS partition.

If you have installed Linux on a Windows XP system and want to access files on the NTFS partition but your distribution does not include the `ntfs.ko` module, you can build the kernel after enabling an NTFS module during the kernel configuration step. (See Chapter 5 of this minibook for detailed instructions on configuring, building, and installing the kernel.)

After rebuilding and booting from the new kernel, log in as `root`, and then type the following command to create a mount point for the NTFS partition (in this case, I am creating a mount point in the `/mnt` directory):

```
mkdir /mnt/xp
```

Now, you can mount the NTFS partition with the following command:

```
mount /dev/hda2 /mnt/xp -t ntfs -r -o umask=0222
```

REMEMBER

Replace `/dev/hda2` with the device name for the NTFS partition on your system. On most PCs that come with Windows XP preinstalled, the NTFS partition is the second one (`/dev/hda2`) — the first partition (`/dev/hda1`) is usually a hidden partition used to hold files used for Windows XP installation.

Using mtools

One way to access the MS-DOS file system is to first mount the DOS hard drive or floppy disk by using the `mount` command and then use regular Linux commands, such as `ls` and `cp`, to work with the mounted DOS file system. This approach of mounting a DOS file system is fine for hard drives. Linux can mount the DOS partition automatically at startup, and you can access the DOS directories on the hard drive at any time.

If you want a quick directory listing of a DOS floppy disk, however, mounting can soon become quite tedious. First, you have to mount the floppy drive. Then you must use the `ls` command. Finally, you must use the `umount` command before ejecting the floppy out of the drive.

This situation is where the `mtools` package comes to the rescue. The `mtools` package implements most common DOS commands; the commands use the same names as in DOS except that you add an `m` prefix to each command. Thus the command for getting a directory listing is `mdir`, and `mcopy` copies files. The best part of `mtools` is the fact that you don't have to mount the floppy disk to use the `mtools` commands.

TECHNICAL STUFF

Because the `mtools` commands write to and read from the physical device (floppy disk), you must log in as `root` to perform these commands. If you want any user to access the `mtools` commands, you must alter the permission settings for the floppy drive devices. Use the following command to permit anyone to read from and write to the first floppy drive:

```
chmod o+rw /dev/fd0
```

Trying mtools

To try out `mtools`, follow these steps:

1. **Place an MS-DOS floppy disk in your system's A drive.**
2. **Type** `mdir`.

   You see the directory of the floppy disk (in the standard DOS directory-listing format).

Typically, you use the `mtools` utilities to access the floppy disks. The default configuration file, `/etc/mtools.conf`, is set up to access the floppy drive as the A drive. Although you can edit that file to define C and D drives for your DOS hard drive partitions, you can access the hard drive partitions as well by using the Linux `mount` command to mount them. Because you can mount the hard drive partitions automatically at startup, accessing them through the Linux commands is normally just as easy.

Understanding the /etc/mtools.conf file

The `mtools` package works with the default setup, but if you get any errors, check the `/etc/mtools.conf` file. That file contains the definitions of the drives (such as A, B, and C) that the `mtools` utilities see. Following are a few lines from a typical `/etc/mtools.conf` file:

```
drive a: file="/dev/fd0" exclusive mformat_only
drive b: file="/dev/fd1" exclusive mformat_only

# First SCSI hard disk partition
#drive c: file="/dev/sda1"

# First IDE hard disk partition on a Windows 98 PC
drive c: file="/dev/hda1"

# Internal IDE Zip drive
drive e: file="/dev/hdd4" exclusive
```

The pound sign (#) indicates the start of a comment. Each line defines a drive letter, the associated Linux device name, and some keywords that indicate how to access the device. In this example, the first two lines define drives A and B. The third noncomment line defines drive C as the first partition on the first IDE drive (`/dev/hda1`). If you have other DOS drives (D, for example), you can add another line that defines drive D as the appropriate disk partition.

If your system's A drive is a high-density, 3.5-inch drive, you don't need to change anything in the default `/etc/mtools.conf` file to access the floppy drive. If you also want to access any DOS partition in the hard drive, uncomment and edit an appropriate line for the C drive.

You also can access Iomega Zip drives through `mtools`. Simply specify a drive letter and the appropriate device's filename. For built-in IDE (ATAPI) Zip drives, try `/dev/hdd4` as the device file and add the following line in the `/etc/mtools.conf` file:

```
drive e: file="/dev/hdd4"
```

After that, you can use `mtools` commands to access the Zip drive (refer to it as the E drive). For example, to see the directory listing, place the Zip disk in the Zip drive and type:

```
mdir e:
```

Learning the mtools commands

The `mtools` package is a collection of utilities. So far, I have been using `mdir` — the `mtools` counterpart of the `DIR` command in DOS. The other `mtools` commands are fairly easy to use.

If you know MS-DOS commands, using the `mtools` commands is easy. Type the DOS command in lowercase letters, and remember to add `m` in front of each command. Because the Linux commands and filenames are case sensitive, you must use all lowercase letters as you type `mtools` commands.

Table 3-4 summarizes the commands available in `mtools`.

Table 3-4	**The mtools Commands**	
mtools Utility	***MS-DOS Command (If Any)***	***The mtools Utility Does the Following***
`mattrib`	`ATTRIB`	Changes MS-DOS file-attribute flags
`mbadblocks`		Tests a floppy disk and marks the bad blocks in the file allocation table (FAT)
`mcd`	`CD`	Changes an MS-DOS directory
`mcopy`	`COPY`	Copies files between MS-DOS and Linux
`mdel`	`DEL` or `ERASE`	Deletes an MS-DOS file
`mdeltree`	`DELTREE`	Recursively deletes an MS-DOS directory
`mdir`	`DIR`	Displays an MS-DOS directory listing
`mdu`		Lists space that a directory and its contents occupy

mtools Utility	MS-DOS Command (If Any)	The mtools Utility Does the Following
mformat	FORMAT	Places an MS-DOS file system on a low-level-formatted floppy disk (Use fdformat to low-level format a floppy disk in Linux.)
minfo		Gets information about an MS-DOS file system
mkmanifest		Makes a list of short name equivalents
mlabel	LABEL	Initializes an MS-DOS volume label
mmd	MD or MKDIR	Creates an MS-DOS directory
mmove		Moves or renames an MS-DOS file or subdirectory
mmount		Mounts an MS-DOS disk
mpartition		Creates an MS-DOS file system as a partition
mrd	RD or RMDIR	Deletes an MS-DOS directory
mren	REN or RENAME	Renames an existing MS-DOS file
mshowfat		Shows FAT entries for an MS-DOS file
mtoolstest		Tests and displays the current mtools configuration
mtype	TYPE	Displays the contents of an MS-DOS file
mwrite	COPY	Copies a Linux file to MS-DOS
mzip		Performs certain operations on SCSI Zip disks

You can use the mtools commands just as you use the corresponding DOS commands. The mdir command, for example, works the same as the DIR command in DOS. The same goes for all the other mtools commands shown in Table 3-4.

You can use wildcard characters (such as *) with mtools commands, but you must remember that the Linux shell is the first program to see your command. If you don't want the shell to expand the wildcard character all over the place, use quotation marks around filenames that contain any wildcard characters. For example, to copy all *.txt files from the A drive to your current directory, use the following command:

```
mcopy "a:*.txt" .
```

If you omit the quotation marks, the shell tries to expand the string a:*.txt with filenames from the current Linux directory. It also tries to copy those files (if any) from the DOS floppy disk.

On the other hand, if you want to copy files from the Linux directory to the DOS floppy disk, you do want the shell to expand any wildcard characters. To copy all `*.jpg` files from the current Linux directory to the DOS floppy disk, for example, use `mcopy` like this:

```
mcopy *.jpg a:
```

With the `mtools` utilities, you can use the backslash character (\) as the directory separator, just as you do in DOS. However, when you type a filename that contains the backslash character, you must enclose the name in double quotation marks (" "). For example, here's a command that copies a file from a subdirectory on the A drive to the current Linux directory:

```
mcopy "a:\test\sample.dat" .
```

Chapter 4: Installing and Updating Applications

In This Chapter

- **Working with RPM files with the `rpm` command**
- **Working with DEB files with `dpkg`, `dselect`, and APT**
- **Building applications from source files**
- **Updating Linux applications online**

Most software packages for Linux are distributed in one of two special file formats — *Red Hat Package Manager* (RPM) files or Debian (DEB) files, which is why you have to know how to install or remove software packages that come in the form of RPM or DEB files. Luckily for you, this is the chapter where I show you how to work with RPM and DEB files.

You can install RPM and DEB files in all Linux distributions, but each distribution has its favored distribution format. Fedora Core, with its Red Hat Linux heritage, favors RPM files, whereas most Debian-based distributions use DEB files for distributing software. (To prove there's an exception to every rule, SUSE Linux is Debian-based, but SUSE uses RPM files for its software packages.)

Many other open-source software packages come in source-code form, usually in compressed archives. You have to unpack, build, and install the software to use it. I describe the steps you typically follow when downloading, building, and installing source-based software packages.

Finally, I briefly describe how to update your Linux system online. As you'll find out, each distribution has its own tools for online updates.

Working with RPM Files

Red Hat Package Manager (RPM) is a system for packaging all the necessary files for a software product in a single file — called an *RPM file* or simply an *RPM*. In fact, the entire Fedora Core and SUSE distributions are a whole lot of RPMs. The best way to work with RPMs is through the RPM commands. You have to type these commands at the shell prompt in a terminal window or a text console.

In Fedora Core, the RPM commands are suitable only if you have to install only a handful of RPM files. To install large number of RPM files, you should select Main Menu➪System Settings➪Add/Remove Applications from the desktop. If you are installing RPM files from a CD or DVD, first mount the CD/DVD and then type **system-cdinstall-helper /mnt/cdrom**. (If your CD/DVD is mounted at some other directory, replace `/mnt/cdrom` with that directory name.) That should bring up a Package Management window from which you can select and install groups of packages.

Using the RPM commands

When you install an RPM-based distribution such as Fedora Core, the installer uses the `rpm` command to unpack the packages (RPM files) and to copy the contents to your hard drive.

You don't have to understand the internal structure of an RPM file, but you need to know how to use the `rpm` command to work with RPM files. Here are some of the things you can do with the `rpm` command:

- Find out the version numbers and other information about the RPMs installed on your system.
- Install a new software package from an RPM. For example, you may install a package you skipped during the initial installation. You can do that with the `rpm` command.
- Remove (uninstall) unneeded software you previously installed from an RPM. You may uninstall a package to reclaim the disk space, if you find that you rarely (or never) use the package.
- Upgrade an older version of an RPM with a new one. For example, in Fedora Core, you may upgrade after you download a new version of a package from Fedora Core download sites (listed online at `fedora.redhat.com/download/mirrors.html`). You must upgrade an RPM to benefit from the fixes in the new version.
- Verify that an RPM is in working order. You can verify a package to check that all necessary files are in the correct locations.

As you can see, the `rpm` command is versatile — it can do a lot of different things, depending on the options you use.

If you ever forget the `rpm` options, type the following command to see a list:

```
rpm --help | more
```

The number of `rpm` options will amaze you!

Understanding RPM filenames

An RPM contains a number of files, but it appears as a single file on your Fedora Core system. By convention, the RPM filenames have a specific format. A typical RPM filename looks like this:

```
OpenOffice_org-1.1.1-20.i586.rpm
```

This filename has the following parts, the first three of which are separated by dashes (-):

- **Package name:** `OpenOffice_org`
- **Version number:** `1.1.1`
- **Release number:** `20`
- **Architecture:** `i586` (this package is for Intel 80586 or Pentium-compatible processors)

Usually, the package name is descriptive enough for you to guess what the RPM may contain. The version number is the same as that of the software package's current version number (even when it's distributed in some other form, such as a `tar` file). Developers assign the release number to keep track of changes. The architecture is `i386` or `noarch` for the RPMs you want to install on a PC with an Intel x86-compatible processor.

Querying RPMs

As it installs packages, the `rpm` command builds a database of installed RPMs. You can use the `rpm -q` command to query this database to find out information about packages installed on your system.

For example, to find out the version number of the Linux kernel installed on your system, type the following `rpm -q` command:

```
rpm -q cups
```

You see a response similar to the following:

```
cups-1.1.20-103
```

The response is the name of the RPM for the kernel. (This version is the executable version of the kernel, not the source files.) The name is the same as the RPM filename, except that the last part — `.i386.rpm` — isn't shown. In this case, the version part of the RPM tells you that you have `cups` (the Common UNIX Printing System) version 1.1.20 installed.

You can see a list of all installed RPMs by using the following command:

```
rpm -qa
```

You see a long list of RPMs scroll by your screen. To view the list one screen at a time, type

```
rpm -qa | more
```

If you want to search for a specific package, feed the output of `rpm -qa` to the `grep` command. For example, to see all packages with `kernel` in their names, type

```
rpm -qa | grep kernel
```

The result depends on what parts of the kernel RPMs are installed on a system.

You can query much more than a package's version number with the `rpm -q` command. By adding single-letter options, you can find out other useful information. For example, try the following command to see the files in the `cups` package:

```
rpm -ql cups
```

Here are a few more useful forms of the `rpm -q` commands to query information about a package (to use any of these `rpm -q` commands, type the command, followed by the package name):

- `rpm -qc`: Lists all configuration files in a package.
- `rpm -qd`: Lists all documentation files in a package. These are usually the online manual pages (also known as *man pages*).
- `rpm -qf`: Displays the name of the package (if any) to which a specified file belongs.
- `rpm -qi`: Displays detailed information about a package, including version number, size, installation date, and a brief description.
- `rpm -ql`: Lists all the files in a package. For some packages, you see a very long list.
- `rpm -qs`: Lists the state of all files in a package (the state of a file can be one of the following: normal, not installed, or replaced).

These rpm commands provide information about installed packages only. If you want to find information about an uninstalled RPM file, add the letter *p* to the command-line option of each command. For example, to view the list of files in the RPM file named rdist-6.1.5-792.i586.rpm, go to the directory where that file is located and then type the following command:

```
rpm -qpl rdist-*.rpm
```

Of course, this command works only if the current directory *contains* that RPM file.

Two handy rpm -q commands enable you to find out which RPM file provides a specific file and which RPMs need a specified package. To find out the name of the RPM that provides a file, use the following command:

```
rpm -q --whatprovides filename
```

For example, to see which RPM provides the file /etc/vsftpd.conf, type

```
rpm -q --whatprovides /etc/vsftpd.conf
```

RPM then prints the name of the package that provides the file, like this:

```
vsftpd-1.2.1-69
```

If you provide the name of a package instead of a filename, RPM displays the name of the RPM package that contains the specified package.

On the other hand, to find the names of RPMs that need a specific package, use the following command:

```
rpm -q --whatrequires packagename
```

For example, to see which packages need the openssl package, type

```
rpm -q --whatrequires openssl
```

The output from this command shows all the RPM packages that need the openssl package.

Installing an RPM

To install an RPM, use the rpm -i command. You have to provide the name of the RPM file as the argument. If you want to view the progress of the RPM installation, use rpm -ivh. A series of hash marks (#) displays as the package is unpacked.

For example, to install the kernel-source RPM (which contains the source files for the Linux operating system) for Fedora Core from the companion DVD-ROM, I insert the DVD and after it's mounted, I type the following commands:

```
cd /mnt/cdrom/Fedora/RPMS
rpm -ivh kernel-source*
```

You don't have to type the full RPM filename — you can use a few characters from the beginning of the name followed by an asterisk (*). Make sure you type enough of the name to identify the RPM file uniquely.

If you try to install an RPM that's already installed, the rpm -i command displays an error message. For example, here is what happens when I type the following command to install the man package on my system:

```
rpm -i man-2*
```

I get the following error message from the rpm -i command:

```
package man-2.4.1-209 is already installed
```

To force the rpm command to install a package even if errors are present, just add --force to the rpm -i command, like this:

```
rpm -i --force man-1*
```

Removing an RPM

You may want to remove — uninstall — a package if you realize you don't really need the software. For example, if you have installed the X Window System development package but discover you're not interested in writing X applications, you can easily remove the package by using the rpm -e command.

You have to know the name of the package before you can remove it. One good way to find the name is to use rpm -qa in conjunction with grep to search for the appropriate RPM file.

For example, to remove the package named qt3-devel, type

```
rpm -e qt3-devel
```

To remove an RPM, you don't need the full RPM filename; all you need is the package name — the first part of the filename up to the dash (-) before the version number.

The rpm -e command does not remove a package that other packages need.

Upgrading an RPM

Use the `rpm -U` command to upgrade an RPM. You must provide the name of the RPM file that contains the new software. For example, if I have version 1.1.19 of `cups` (printing system) installed on my system but I want to upgrade to version 1.1.20, I download the RPM file `cups-1.1.20-103.i586.rpm` from a repository and use the following command:

```
rpm -U cups-1.1.20-103.i586.rpm
```

The `rpm` command performs the upgrade by removing the old version of the `cups` package and installing the new RPM.

TIP

Whenever possible, upgrade rather than remove the old package and install a new one. Upgrading automatically saves your old configuration files, which saves you the hassle of reconfiguring the software after a fresh installation.

WARNING!

When you're upgrading the `kernel` packages that contain a ready-to-run Linux kernel, install it by using the `rpm -i` command (instead of the `rpm -U` command). That way, you won't overwrite the current kernel.

Verifying an RPM

You may not do so often, but if you suspect that a software package isn't properly installed, use the `rpm -V` command to verify it. For example, to verify the kernel package, type the following:

```
rpm -V kernel
```

This command causes `rpm` to compare the size and other attributes of each file in the package against those of the original files. If everything verifies correctly, the `rpm -V` command does not print anything. If it finds any discrepancies, you see a report of them. For example, I have modified the configuration files for the Apache `httpd` Web server. Here is what I type to verify the `httpd` package:

```
rpm -V httpd
```

Here's the result I get:

```
S.5....T c /etc/httpd/conf/httpd.conf
```

In this case, the output from `rpm -V` tells me that a configuration file has changed. Each line of this command's output has three parts:

- The line starts with eight characters: Each character indicates the type of discrepancy found. For example, `S` means the size is different, and `T` means the time of last modification is different. Table 4-1 shows each character and its meaning. A period means that that specific attribute matches the original.

- For configuration files, a c appears next; otherwise, this field is blank. That's how you can tell whether or not a file is a configuration file. Typically, you don't worry if a configuration file has changed; you probably made the changes yourself.
- The last part of the line is the full pathname of the file. From this part, you can tell exactly where the file is located.

Table 4-1 Characters Used in RPM Verification Reports

Character	*Meaning*
S	Size has changed
M	Permissions and file type are different
5	Checksum computed with the MD5 algorithm is different
D	Device type is different
L	Symbolic link is different
U	File's user is different
G	File's group is different
T	File's modification time is different

Working with DEB Files

Debian packages with `.deb` file extensions store executable files together with configuration files, online documentation, and other information. You can unpack and manipulate these DEB files using the Debian utility `dpkg`, which is a command-line program that takes many options. A text-mode, menu-driven program called `dselect` is also available for you to manage the packages without having to type `dpkg` commands.

TIP

You typically use a higher-level utility called APT (Advanced Packaging Tool) to work with packages in Debian. For example, instead of downloading a DEB file and installing it with the `dpkg` command, you can simply use the `apt-get` command to install the package. The `apt-get` command can even download the package from an online Debian repository and then install it on your system. The `dpkg` command is still useful when you want to look at the contents of a DEB file that you have manually downloaded from a repository or that might be in the APT cache directory (`/var/cache/apt/archives` in Debian).

I introduce you to `dpkg`, `dselect`, and APT in the following sections.

Understanding DEB filenames

A typical DEB package has a filename of the following form:

```
vsftpd_2.0.1-1_i386.deb
```

The filename has three parts separated by underscores (_):

- **Package name:** `vsftpd`
- **Version and Revision:** `2.0.1-1` (version has two parts separated by a dash — the first part is the package maintainer's version number, the second part is the Debian revision number)
- **Architecture:** `i386` (the package is for Intel x386 compatible systems)

The filename has a `.deb` extension, which indicates that this is a DEB file.

Using the dpkg command

To get a feel for the `dpkg` command, type **dpkg --help | more**. The output shows the large number of options that `dpkg` accepts. You can also type **man dpkg** to read the online man page for `dpkg`.

You can use `dpkg` to perform a whole lot of operations on packages, but you have to work at a shell prompt in a terminal window or a text console. The format of a dpkg command is

```
dpkg [options] action package
```

with zero or more *`options`*, an *`action`* indicating what `dpkg` has to do, and the name of a *`package`*, a DEB file, or a directory (depends on the *`action`* argument). Sometimes the `dpkg` command does not need any name of package or file, just an *`action`*.

Here are some examples of actions you can perform with `dpkg`:

- **Install** a package from a DEB file with the command `dpkg -i` *`packagefile`* where *`packagefile`* is the name of the DEB file (for example, `vsftpd-*.deb`).
- **Remove** a package but retain the configuration files with the command `dpkg -r` *`packagename`* where *`packagename`* is the name of the package (for example, `vsftpd`)
- **Configure** a package with the command `dpkg --configure` *`packagename`* where *`packagename`* is the name of a package (for example, `vsftpd`)

- **Purge** — remove everything including the configuration files — with the command dpkg -P *packagename* where *packagename* is the name of a package (for example, vsftpd)
- **Audit** packages (and find the ones that are partially installed on your system) with the command dpkg -C (does not need any file or package name)
- **List contents** of a DEB file with the command dpkg -c *packagefile* where *packagefile* is the name of the DEB file (for example, vsftpd-*.deb)
- **View information** about a DEB file with the command dpkg -I *packagefile* where *packagefile* is the name of the DEB file (for example, vsftpd-*.deb)
- **List packages matching pattern** with the command dpkg -l *pattern* where *pattern* is the package name pattern, usually with wildcard characters, that you want to match (for example, kernel*)
- **Find packages that contain file** with the command dpkg -S *pattern* where *pattern* is the filename pattern, usually with wildcard characters, that the package contains (for example, stdio*)
- **List files installed from a package** with the command dpkg -L *packagename* where *packagename* is the name of a package (for example, vsftpd)

You can try these commands out on a Debian system or any system that uses DEB packages. For example, to look for all packages matching names that begin with mozilla, type **dpkg -l mozilla*** in a terminal window. Here is the relevant portion of this command's output on my Debian system:

```
||/ Name           Version        Description
+++-==============-==============-============================================
ii  mozilla-browse 1.6-5          Mozilla Web Browser - core and browser
ii  mozilla-firefo 0.8-12         lightweight web browser based on Mozilla
ii  mozilla-mailne 1.6-5          Mozilla Web Browser - mail and news support
ii  mozilla-psm    1.6-5          Mozilla Web Browser - Personal Security Mana
un  mozilla-xft    <none>         (no description available)
```

The ii in the first column indicates that the package is installed; un means the package is not installed.

Another common use of dpkg -l is to list all packages and use grep to find lines that match a search string. For example, to find anything containing kernel, type **dpkg -l | grep kernel**. If the package names (in the second column of the dpkg -l output) are truncated, adjust the width of the output lines with a command like this:

```
COLUMNS=132 dpkg -l | grep kernel
```

I find the `dpkg -S` command a handy way to locate which package provided a specific file in the system. For example, if I want to figure out what package includes the `/etc/host.conf` file, I type **dpkg -S /etc/host.conf** and the output shows that the `base-files` package contains `/etc/host.conf`:

```
base-files: /etc/host.conf
```

Introducing dselect

The `dselect` is meant to be a front-end to the `dpkg` utility. To try out `dselect`, log in as `root` and type **dselect** in a terminal window (or a text console). When `dselect` starts, you get `dselect`'s text-mode menu (as shown in Figure 4-1).

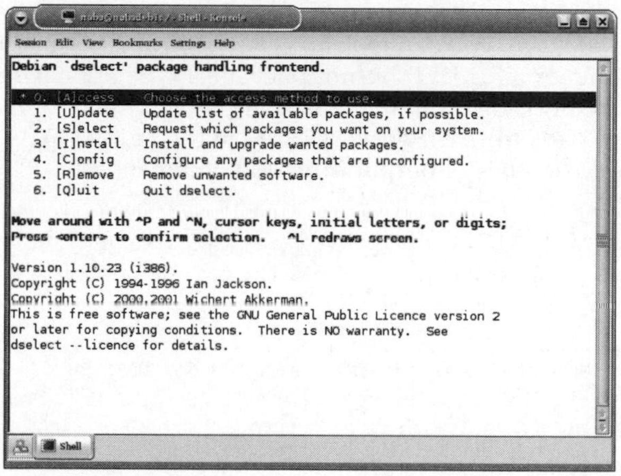

Figure 4-1: You can use `dselect` to manage packages in Debian.

I won't describe `dselect` in detail, but here are some of the tasks you can perform from the `dselect` main menu:

- Specify an access method — how to find the DEB packages.
- Update the list of available packages.
- View the status of installed and available packages.
- Select packages and manage dependencies among packages.
- Install new packages or upgrade to existing ones to newer versions.
- Configure packages that are not yet configured.
- Remove packages.

One common sequence in `dselect` is to update the list of available packages and then upgrade all packages for which updates are available. You can, of course, perform that same task with a simple APT command as well.

Using APT to manage DEB packages

APT stands for Advanced Packaging Tool, and it's truly an advanced utility for keeping your Debian system up to date. You can use a number of APT utilities to manage DEB packages. The two commonly used commands are `apt-get` and `apt-cache`.

To install a package with `apt-get`, simply type **apt-get install *packagename*** where ***packagename*** is the name of the package that you want to install. For example, to install the `vsftpd` package, type **apt-get install vsftpd**.

Removing a package is equally simple. Type **apt-get remove *packagename*** where ***packagename*** is the name of the package you want to remove.

If you want to find the name of a package and you know some terms associated with the package, you can look for it with the `apt-cache` utility. For example, to look for a CD/DVD burner package, I type **apt-cache search burn | more** to search through the APT's package cache (list of Debian packages that APT downloads from the servers listed in the `/etc/apt/sources.list` file). Here are some lines of output from that command:

```
arson - KDE frontend for burning CDs
bootcd-dvdplus - bootcd extension to use DVD+ media
burn - Command line Data-CD, Audio-CD, ISO-CD, Copy-CD writing tool
caca-utils - text mode graphics utilities
cdcontrol - A parallel burner that allow you to write to one or more CD-Writers
at once
cdlabelgen - generates front cards and tray cards for CDs
cdrtoaster - Tcl/Tk front-end for burning cdrom
cdw - Tool for burning CD's - console version
cdw-common - Tool for burning CD's - common files
cpuburn - a collection of programs to put heavy load on CPU
cwcdr - Chez Wam CD Ripper
dvd+rw-tools - DVD+-RW/R tools
dvdbackup - Tool to rip DVD's from the command line
gcdw - Tool for burning CD's - graphical version
gcombust - GTK+ based CD mastering and burning program
... lines deleted ...
```

The output shows several potential CD/DVD burning programs that I could install. To discover more about any of the packages, I type **apt-cache show *packagename*** where ***packagename*** is the name of the package for which I want information. For example, to find out more about the `dvd+rw-tools` package, I type **apt-cache show dvd+rw-tools** and the output shows me a description of the package. I can then install the package with `apt-get install`.

TIP

To search for a keyword that appears in the package's name only, use the `--names-only` option like this: **apt-cache search --names-only *keyword*** where ***keyword*** is something that appears in the package's name. For example, if I want to find packages that contain `selinux` in their names, I type **apt-cache search --names-only selinux**.

TIP: Run `apt-get clean` periodically to clean out the local repository (in the `/var/cache/apt/archives` directory) of DEB files that have already been installed. You can free up some disk space by removing these DEB files.

Building Software Packages from Source Files

Many open-source software packages are distributed in source-code form, without executable binaries. Before you can use such software, you have to build the executable binary files by compiling, and you have to follow some instructions to install the package. In this section, I show you how to build software packages from source files.

Downloading and unpacking the software

Open-source software source files are typically distributed in compressed `tar` archives. These archives are created by the `tar` program and compressed with the `gzip` program. The distribution is in the form of a single large file with the `.tar.gz` or `.tar.Z` extension — often referred to as a *compressed tarball*. If you want the software, you have to download the compressed tarball and unpack it.

Download the compressed `tar` file by using anonymous FTP or through your Web browser. Typically, this process involves no effort on your part beyond clicking a link and saving the file in an appropriate directory on your system.

To try your hand at downloading and building a software package, you can practice on the X Multimedia System (XMMS) — a graphical X application for playing MP3 and other multimedia files. XMMS is bundled with Fedora Core and already installed on your system. However, you do no harm in downloading and rebuilding the XMMS package again.

Download the source files for XMMS from `www.xmms.org/download.php`. The files are packed in the form of a compressed `tar` archive. Click the `http` link for the source files, and then save them in the `/usr/local/src` directory in your Linux system. (Be sure to log in as `root`; otherwise you cannot save in the `/usr/local/src` directory.)

After downloading the compressed `tar` file, examine the contents with the following `tar` command:

```
tar ztf xmms*.gz | more
```

You see a listing similar to the following:

```
xmms-1.2.10/
xmms-1.2.10/intl/
xmms-1.2.10/intl/ChangeLog
```

```
xmms-1.2.10/intl/Makefile.in
xmms-1.2.10/intl/config.charset
xmms-1.2.10/intl/locale.alias
xmms-1.2.10/intl/ref-add.sin
xmms-1.2.10/intl/ref-del.sin
xmms-1.2.10/intl/gmo.h
xmms-1.2.10/intl/gettextP.h
xmms-1.2.10/intl/hash-string.h
xmms-1.2.10/intl/loadinfo.h
... rest of the output not shown ...
```

The output of this `tar` command shows you what's in the archive and gives you an idea of the directories that are created after you unpack the archive. In this case, a directory named `xmms-1.2.10` is created in the current directory, which, in my case, is `/usr/local/src`. From the listing, you also figure out the programming language used to write the package. If you see `.c` and `.h` files, the source files are in the C programming language used to write many open-source software packages.

To extract the contents of the compressed `tar` archive, type the following `tar` command:

```
tar zxvf xmms*.gz
```

You again see the long list of files as they extract from the archive and copy to the appropriate directories on your hard drive.

Now you're ready to build the software.

Building the software from source files

After you unpack the compressed `tar` archive, all source files are in a directory whose name is usually that of the software package with a version-number suffix. For example, the XMMS version 1.2.10 source files extract to the `xmms-1.2.10` directory. To start building the software, change directories with the following command:

```
cd xmms*
```

You don't have to type the entire name — the shell can expand the directory name and change to the `xmms-1.2.10` directory.

Nearly all software packages come with some sort of `README` or `INSTALL` file — a text file that tells you how to build and install the package. XMMS is no exception; it comes with a `README` file you can peruse by typing **more README**. An `INSTALL` file contains instructions for building and installing XMMS.

Most open-source software packages, including XMMS, also come with a file named `COPYING`. This file contains the full text of the *GNU General Public License* (GPL), which spells out the conditions under which you can use and redistribute the software. If you're not familiar with the GNU GPL, read this file and show the license to your legal counsel for a full interpretation and an assessment of applicability to your business.

To build the software package, follow the instructions in the `README` or `INSTALL` file. For the XMMS package, the `README` file lists some of the prerequisites (such as libraries) and tells you what commands to type to build and install the package. In the case of XMMS, the instructions tell you to use the following steps:

1. **Type** ./configure **to run a shell script that checks your system configuration and creates a file named** `Makefile` **— a file the** `make` **command uses to build and install the package. (You can type** ./configure --help **to see a list of options that** `configure` **accepts.)**

   If you get any errors about missing packages, you have to install those missing packages. Use your distribution's software installation tools to add the missing packages. For example, in Debian use the `apt-get install` command. In Fedora Core, select Main Menu➪System Settings➪Add/Remove Applications. In SUSE, use the YaST GUI tool.

2. **Type** make **to build the software.**

   This step compiles the source files in all the subdirectories. (Compiling source code converts each source file into an object file — a file containing binary instructions that your PC's processor can understand.)

3. **Type** make install **to install the software.**

   This step copies libraries and executable binary files to appropriate directories on your system.

Although these steps are specific to XMMS, most other packages follow these steps — `configure`, `make`, and `install`. The `configure` shell script guesses system-dependent variables and creates a `Makefile` with commands needed to build and install the software.

Usually, you don't have to do anything but type the commands to build the software, but you must install the software-development tools on your system. In Fedora Core, you must install the Development Tools and the GNOME Software Development packages. In Debian, to build and run XMMS, you must also install the X Software Development package because it's an X application.

After you have installed XMMS, try running it from the GNOME or KDE desktop by typing **xmms** in a terminal window. From the XMMS window, press **L** to get the Load File dialog box and select an MP3 file to play. Your PC must have a sound card, and the sound card must be configured correctly for XMMS to work.

XMMS already comes with Fedora Core, but that version does not include the plugin needed to play MP3 files. After you build the new version of XMMS, you should be able to play MP3 files.

To summarize, here's an overview of the steps you follow to download, unpack, build, and install a typical software package:

1. Use a Web browser to download the source code, usually in the form of a `.tar.gz` file, from the anonymous FTP site or Web site.
2. Unpack the file with a `tar zxvf` *`filename`* command.
3. Change the directory to the new subdirectory where the software is unpacked, with a command such as `cd` *`software_dir`*.
4. Read any `README` or `INSTALL` files to get a handle on any specific instructions you must follow to build and install the software.
5. The details of building the software may differ slightly from one software package to another, but typically you type the following commands to build and install the software:

   ```
   ./configure
   make
   make install
   ```

6. Read any other documentation that comes with the software to find out how to use the software and whether you must configure the software further before using it.

Installing SRPMS

If you have the source CDs for Fedora Core (you can download the source CD images from one of the sites listed at `fedora.redhat.com/download/mirrors.html`), you can install the source files and build various applications directly from the source files. Fedora Core source-code files also come in RPMs, just as the executable binary files, and these source-code RPM files are generally known as SRPMS (for *source RPMs*).

To install a specific source RPM and build the application, follow these steps:

1. **Mount the DVD-ROM by typing** mount /mnt/cdrom **or waiting for the GNOME desktop to mount the DVD.**

2. **Typically, source RPMs are in the SRPMS directory. Change to that directory by typing the following command:**

   ```
   cd /mnt/cdrom/SRPMS
   ```

3. **Install the source RPM file by using the `rpm -i` command. For example, to install the Web server (`httpd`) source, type**

   ```
   rpm -ivh httpd*.src.rpm
   ```

   The files install in the `/usr/src/redhat/SOURCES` directory. A spec file with a `.spec` extension is placed in the `/usr/src/redhat/SPECS` directory. The *spec file* describes the software and also contains information used to build and install the software.

4. **Use the `rpmbuild` command with the spec file to build the software. You perform different tasks from unpacking the source files to building and installing the binaries by using different options with the `rpmbuild` command. For example, to process the entire spec file, type:**

   ```
   rpmbuild -ba packagename.spec
   ```

   Here *`packagename`* is the name of the SRPM. This command typically builds the software and installs the binary files.

Updating Linux Applications Online

Each of the Linux distributions — Debian, Fedora Core, SUSE, and Xandros — come with utilities that enable you to update the software online. In the following sections, I provide an overview of the update methods in Debian, Fedora Core, SUSE, and Xandros.

WARNING!

You need a fast Internet connection (such as a DSL or cable modem) to easily update your Linux applications or download new software packages. Make sure that your Internet connection is up and running before you attempt to update your Linux system online.

DISTRIBUTION SPECIFIC

Keeping Debian updated with APT

The best way to keep your Debian system updated is to use APT. More specifically, you use the `apt-get` command-line utility with appropriate options.

In a nutshell, assuming the APT sources were configured during Debian installation, you can keep the current collection of software updated with the following two commands, typed in that order:

```
apt-get update
apt-get upgrade
```

The `apt-get update` command checks the current list of packages against the ones available from the locations specified in `/etc/apt/sources.list` file and gathers information about new versions of installed packages.

The `apt-get upgrade` command actually installs any available new versions of the packages installed in your Debian system. You must perform `apt-get upgrade` to install any available upgrades.

To install new packages in Debian, use `apt-cache search` to find the package name in APT's package cache and then use `apt-get install` to install the package.

Updating Fedora Core Applications

Fedora Core comes with Up2date — a graphical Update Agent that can download any new RPM files your system requires and install those files for you. Up2date is also known as the Red Hat Update Agent because Red Hat developed it for its Red Hat Network through which Red Hat provides services to its commercial customers.

To update Fedora Core software packages using Up2date, follow these steps:

1. **Log in as `root`, and choose Main Menu⇨System Tools⇨Red Hat Network. You can also type** up2date **in a terminal window.**

   The Red Hat Update Agent starts, and, if you're using Up2date for the first time, a dialog box prompts you to install a public key in your GPG key ring. (*GPG* refers to GNU Privacy Guard or GnuPG, a program for encrypting, decrypting, and signing e-mail and other data using the OpenPGP Internet standard.) That public GPG key verifies that the package developer has securely signed the package that Up2date has downloaded. If prompted to do so, click Yes to install the public key.

2. **Up2date displays a window with a welcome message. Click the Forward button to proceed.**

3. **Up2date displays a list of what it calls channels — repositories from where the agent downloads package headers. Click Forward to continue.**

   By default, the Update Agent uses a channel that works with Yum — a command-line package updater/installer that I describe in the next section. The channels are identified in the text configuration file `/etc/sysconfig/rhn/sources`. Besides Yum, the Up2date can also access repositories meant for APT — the Advanced Packaging Tool used in Debian.

   After you click Forward, Up2date figures out what needs to be updated and retrieves a list of all headers from the specified channel.

4. **After Up2date downloads the headers, it displays a list of packages. You can then scroll through the list and pick the packages you want to update; click the box to the left of a package's name to select it. Click Forward to continue.**

   Up2date then checks for any package dependencies and begins downloading the packages. Progress bars show the status of the download.

5. **After the download finishes, click the Forward button to proceed with the installation.**

6. **Up2date displays progress bars as it installs each package update. Click the Forward button when the installation is complete.**

   Up2date displays a message about the package(s) it installs successfully.

7. **Click the Finish button to exit Up2date.**

In Fedora Core, you can also use the Yellow dog Updater, Modified (Yum) — a command-line utility for updating as well as installing and removing RPM packages. Yum downloads RPM package headers from a specified Web site and then uses the `rpm` utility to figure out any interdependencies among packages and what needs to be installed on your system. Then it downloads and uses `rpm` to install the necessary packages. Yum downloads just the headers to do its job and the headers are much smaller in size than the complete RPM packages. Yum is much faster than the alternative, where you manually download the complete RPM packages using the `rpm` command.

Typically, you keep your system up to date with the graphical Update Agent because it's easy to use. However, knowing how to run Yum from the command line is good, just in case you have problems with the Update Agent.

TIP

You can read more about Yum and keep up with Yum news by visiting the Yum Web page at `linux.duke.edu/projects/yum`.

The command line for Yum has the following syntax:

```
yum [options] command [packagenames]
```

options is a list of Yum options, *command* specifies what you want Yum to do, and *packagenames* are the names of a packages on which Yum performs that action. You must provide the *command*, but the *options* and *packagenames* are optional. That's why I show them in square brackets in the syntax. Table 4-2 summarizes the Yum commands and Table 4-3 lists some common Yum options.

Table 4-2 Yum Commands

Command	*What Yum Does for This Command*
`check-update`	Checks for available updates for your system.
`clean`	Cleans up the cache directory.
`info`	Displays summary information about the specified packages.
`install`	Installs latest versions of specified packages, making sure that all dependencies are satisfied.
`list`	Lists information about available packages.
`provides`	Provides information on which package provides a file.
`remove`	Removes specified packages as well as any packages that depend on the packages being removed.
`search`	Finds packages whose header contains what you specify as the package name.
`update`	Updates specified packages, making sure that all dependencies are satisfied.

Table 4-3 Some Common Yum Options

Option	*Causes Yum to Do the Following*
`--download-only`	Downloads the packages, but does not install them.
`--exclude=`*pkgname*	Excludes the specified package. (You can use this option more than once on the command line.)
`--help`	Displays a help message and quits.
`--installroot=`*path*	Uses the specified path name as the directory under which all packages are installed.
`-y`	Assumes that your answer to any question is yes.

If you simply want Yum to update your system, just type the following (you have to be logged in as `root`):

```
yum update
```

Yum consults its configuration file, `/etc/yum.conf`, and does everything needed to update the packages installed on your system.

You can specify package names to update only some packages. For example, to update the kernel and `xorg-x11` packages, use the following Yum command:

```
yum update kernel* xorg-x11*
```

This command updates all packages whose names begin with `kernel` and `xorg-x11`.

You may use the options to further instruct Yum what to do. For example, if you want to download the updated packages, but not install them, type

```
yum --download-only update
```

Another typical option is `--exclude`, which enables you to exclude one or more packages from the update process. Suppose you want to update everything except the GNOME packages (whose names begin with `gnome`) and the `rhythmbox` package. Then you type the following Yum command:

```
yum --exclude=gnome* --exclude=rhythmbox upd
```

Updating SUSE online

SUSE comes with YOU — YaST Online Update — for online software updates. To access YOU, select Main Menu➪System➪YaST and from the YaST Control Center's Software category, click Online Update. This brings up the YaST Online Update window, as shown in Figure 4-2.

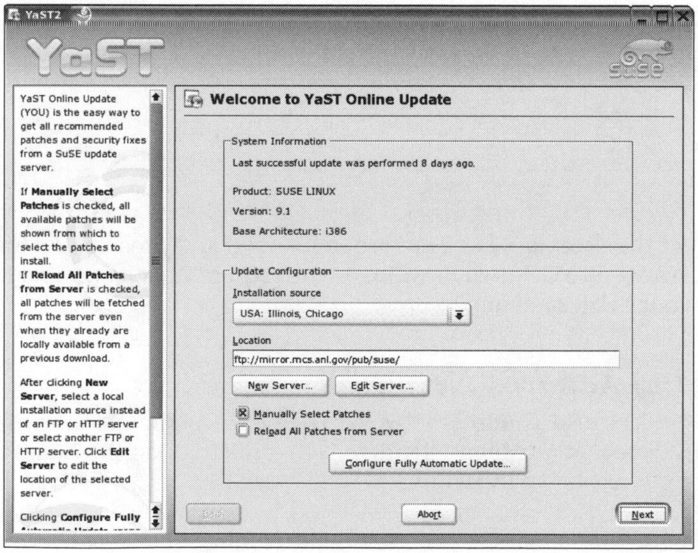

Figure 4-2: You can keep your SUSE system updated with YaST Online Update.

To set up YOU automatic updates, click the Configure Fully Automatic Update button. You can then specify a time of the day when you want YOU to download any available patches and install them. If you want, you can specify that YOU only download the patches and not install them.

To update your SUSE system online, select the installation source and click Next. (Refer to Figure 4-2.) YOU then downloads the list of patches and displays them, as shown in Figure 4-3.

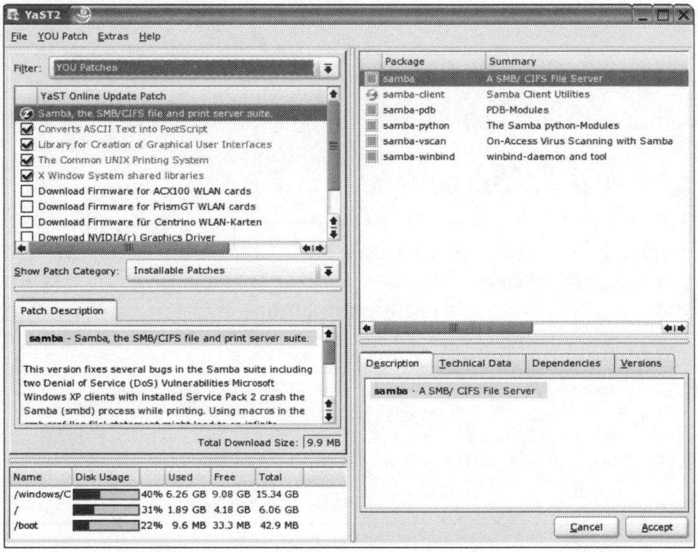

Figure 4-3: Select YOU patches and click Accept to install them.

Select the patches (some are recommended and preselected for you) and click Accept. YOU then downloads the required packages and installs them on your SUSE system.

Using Xandros Networks

In Xandros, use Xandros Networks to update applications or install new ones. Select Main Menu⇨Xandros Networks to open the Xandros Networks window, as shown in Figure 4-4.

To install the latest updates from Xandros, select File⇨Install All Latest Updates from Xandros or click the Update button (to the left of the key in the toolbar at the top of Figure 4-4). Xandros Networks then downloads information about the available updates and shows a summary (see Figure 4-5) of the packages to be downloaded and the disk space needed to install them.

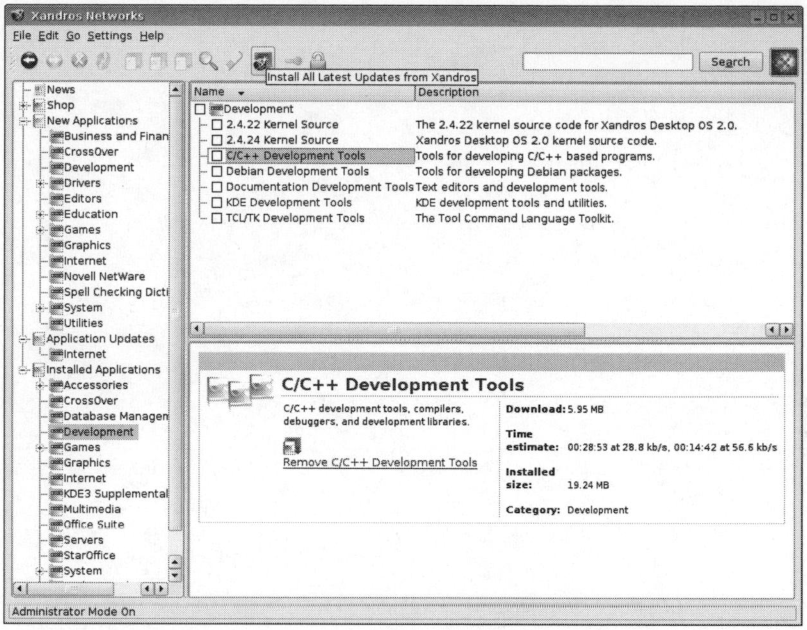

Figure 4-4: Use Xandros Networks to update or install software in Xandros.

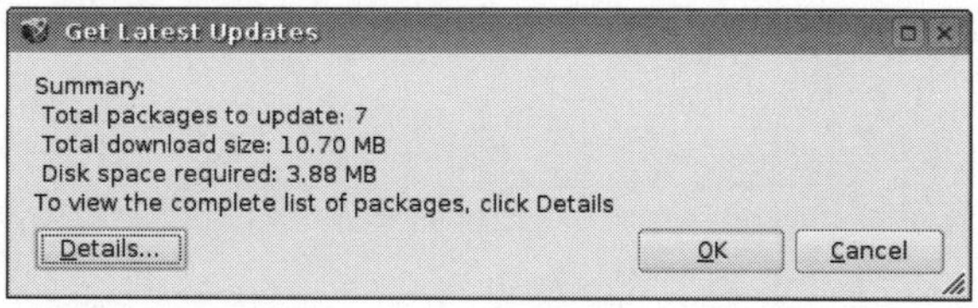

Figure 4-5: Xandros Networks displays summary information about updates.

Click Ok. Xandros Networks then downloads the software updates and installs them.

Behind the scenes, Xandros Networks uses Debian's `apt-get` command to download and install the software updates.

The Xandros Networks window also offers options to install new software. You can even shop for new applications through Xandros Networks. If you have RPM or DEB files to install, you can do so in Xandros Networks by selecting File⇨Install RPM File or File⇨Install DEB File.

Chapter 5: Customizing the Linux Kernel

In This Chapter

- **Configuring the kernel**
- **Building a new kernel and any modules**
- **Installing the modules**
- **Building and installing a new initial RAM disk file**
- **Installing the kernel and setting up GRUB**

One reason why Linux is so exciting is that many programmers are constantly improving it. Some programmers, for example, write drivers that add support for new hardware, such as a new sound card or a new networking card. All these innovations come to you in the form of new versions of the Linux kernel.

Although you don't have to upgrade or modify the Linux operating system — the kernel — every time a new version is available, sometimes you have to upgrade simply because the new version corrects some problems or supports your hardware better. On the other hand, if an earlier kernel version has everything you need, you don't have to rush out and upgrade.

Sometimes, you may want to rebuild the kernel even when it has no fixes or enhancements. The Linux kernel on the companion DVD-ROM is generic and uses modules to support all types of hardware. You may want to build a new kernel that *links in* — incorporates into the kernel's binary file — the drivers for only the devices installed on your system. In particular, if you have a SCSI hard drive, you may want to create a kernel that supports your SCSI adapter. Depending on your needs, you may also want to change some of the kernel-configuration options, such as creating a kernel that's specific for your processor (instead of a generic Intel 386 processor).

In this chapter, I explain how to rebuild and install a new Linux kernel.

Rebuilding the Kernel

Rebuilding the kernel refers to creating a new binary file for the core Linux operating system. This binary file is the one that runs when Linux boots.

You may wonder why you would ever want to rebuild the kernel. Well, here are a few reasons:

- After you initially install Linux, you may want to create a new kernel that includes support for only the hardware installed on your system. In particular, if you have a SCSI adapter, you may want to create a kernel that links in the SCSI driver. The kernel on the companion DVD-ROM includes the SCSI driver as an external module that the kernel loads at startup.
- If you have a system with hardware for which only experimental support is available, you have to rebuild the kernel to include that support into the operating system.
- You may want to recompile the kernel and generate code that works well on your specific Pentium processor (instead of the generic 386 processor code that comes in most Linux distributions).

To rebuild the Linux kernel, you need the kernel source files. The kernel source files are not normally installed. Use your distribution's software installation tool to install the kernel source package. For example, in Fedora Core, you can install the kernel source RPM file (the filename begins with `kernel-source`) from the DVD's `Fedora/RPMS` directory. (If the DVD is mounted on `/media/cdrom`, then the RPM is in the `/media/cdrom/Fedora/RPMS` directory.) In SUSE, use YaST to install the kernel sources — to find it, use the search feature in YaST's software installation window.

After installing the kernel source package, the source files appear in the `/usr/src/linux-`*`VERSION`* directory, where *`VERSION`* is the version number of the kernel. Thus, for kernel version 2.6.5-7.108, the source files are in the `/usr/src/linux-2.6.5-7.108` directory. Some distributions set up `/usr/src/linux` as a symbolic link (shortcut) to the version-specific directory containing the source files for the Linux kernel.

In Debian, the kernel sources are installed in the `/usr/src/kernel-source-`*`VERSION`* directory, where *`VERSION`* is the kernel version. Therefore, for kernel version 2.6.8, the sources are in `/usr/src/kernel-source-2.6.8`. To change to the kernel source directory in Debian, type **cd /usr/src/kernel-source***.

Building the kernel involves the following phases:

- Configuring the kernel
- Building the kernel
- Building and installing the modules
- Building a new initial RAM disk (`initrd`) file
- Installing the kernel and setting up GRUB

I explain these phases in the next few sections, but first you need to know the difference between linking in a driver versus building a driver as a loadable module.

Creating a monolithic versus a modular kernel

You have two options for the device drivers needed to support various hardware devices in Linux:

- **Link in support:** You can link the drivers for all hardware on your system into the kernel. The size of the kernel grows as device-driver code incorporates into the kernel. A kernel that links in all necessary code is called a *monolithic kernel* because it's one big file.
- **Use modules:** You can create the device drivers in the form of loadable kernel modules. A *module* is a block of code that the kernel can load after it starts running. A typical use of modules is to add support for a device without having to rebuild the kernel for each new device. Modules don't have to be device drivers; they can also add new functionality to the kernel. A kernel that uses modules is called a *modular kernel.*

You don't have to create a fully monolithic or fully modular kernel. In fact, linking some support directly into the kernel but building infrequently used device drivers in the form of modules is common practice. For a Linux distribution, including a mostly modular kernel makes sense, along with a large number of modules that can support many different types of hardware. Then the Linux installer configures the system to load only modules needed to support the hardware installed in a user's system.

TIP

When you create a custom kernel for your hardware configuration, you may want to link all required device drivers into the kernel. You can still keep the size of such a monolithic kernel under control because you link in device drivers only for the exact set of hardware installed on your system.

Configuring the kernel

The first phase in rebuilding a kernel is to configure it. To configure the kernel, log in as `root`. Then change the kernel source directory by using the `cd` command as follows:

```
cd /usr/src/linux*
```

To configure the kernel, you have to indicate which features and device drivers you want to include in your Linux kernel. In essence, you build your very own version of the Linux kernel with just the features you want.

Linux provides several ways for you to configure the kernel:

- Type **make menuconfig** to enter the kernel-configuration parameters through a text-based interface similar to the one the Linux installation program uses.
- Type **make xconfig** to use an X Window System-based configuration program to configure the kernel. You have to run X to use this configuration program with a graphical interface.
- Type **make config** to use a shell script that prompts you for each configuration option one by one. You can use this configuration program from the Linux command prompt. When you use this option, you undergo a long question-and-answer process to specify the configuration parameters. For each question, respond with a *y* to link support into the kernel, *m* to build a module, and *n* to skip the support for that specific device.
- Type **make oldconfig** to use a shell script to reconfigure the kernel after upgrading the sources. This configuration script keeps the existing options and prompts you only for new or changed options.

The `make menuconfig`, `make xconfig`, `make config`, and `make oldconfig` commands achieve the same end result — each stores your choices in a text file named `.config` located in the `/usr/src/linux*` directory. Because the filename starts with a period, you don't see it when you use the `ls` command alone to list the directory. Instead, type **ls -a** to see the `.config` file in the directory listing.

REMEMBER

The kernel-configuration step merely captures your choices in the `.config` file. (In fact, the `.config` file does not exist until you configure the kernel once.) The kernel file does not change until you compile the kernel with the `make` command. That means you can go through the kernel-configuration option as many times as you want. If you want to start over with default settings, type the following command before you start configuring the kernel:

```
make mrproper
```

TIP

For an overview of the kernel configuration build steps that you can perform with the `make` command, type the following in a terminal window (after you type **cd /usr/src/linux*** to change the current directory to the correct location):

```
make help | more
```

Before starting to reconfigure the kernel, take a look at a typical `.config` file. For example, here are some lines of output when I type **more .config** on a Linux system (after I configure the kernel):

```
#
# Automatically generated make config: don't edit
#
CONFIG_X86=y
CONFIG_MMU=y
CONFIG_UID16=y
CONFIG_GENERIC_ISA_DMA=y

#
# Code maturity level options
#
CONFIG_EXPERIMENTAL=y
CONFIG_CLEAN_COMPILE=y
CONFIG_BROKEN_ON_SMP=y

#
# General setup
#
CONFIG_SWAP=y
CONFIG_SYSVIPC=y
(rest of the file not shown)
```

Essentially, each configuration option has a name, and each one is assigned a value. The name begins with CONFIG_ followed by a word that identifies the option. Each selected option has a value of y (to link in support for that feature) or m (to use a module for that feature). Lines beginning with # are comments. Comment lines list features not selected.

I describe the configuration process through the make config command. Although this approach is somewhat tedious because it walks you through each option one by one, it is ideal as a learning tool. As you step through the groups of configuration options, I provide notes explaining what most of the options mean. You can then configure the kernel using whichever configuration tool (make xconfig, make menuconfig, make config, or make oldconfig) you like most.

As you configure the kernel with the make config command, you have to select how to include support for specific devices. Typically, for each configuration option, you have to respond with one of the following choices:

- **y** to link support into the kernel
- **m** to use a module
- **n** to skip the support for that specific device or feature
- **?** to get help on that kernel-configuration option

If a device does not have a modular device driver, you won't see the m option. For some configuration options, you may have to pick a number from a list.

Starting the kernel configuration

To start configuring the kernel, log in as `root`, change to the directory with the Linux kernel's source (type **cd /usr/src/linux*** or **cd /usr/src/kernel-source***, depending on your distribution) and type **make menuconfig** in a terminal window. The configuration tool then displays the first prompt:

```
*
* Linux Kernel Configuration
*
*
* Code maturity level options
*
Prompt for development and/or incomplete code/drivers (EXPERIMENTAL) [Y/n/?]
```

Press Enter to accept the default Yes answer. This causes the configuration process to show all experimental device drivers.

The possible answers to each prompt appear in square brackets with the default answer in uppercase. Thus, `[Y/n/?]` means the default answer is Yes, and two other possible answers are `n` and `?`. To accept the default, press Enter. For help on this option, press **?**. If you have questions about any option, press **?** and carefully read the help text before you decide what to do. You can use this general guideline to make your choices. In the following sections, I explain only selected groups of kernel configuration options.

General setup options

This group of options enables you to indicate if you want to enable support for general features such as System V Inter Process Communication (IPC), process accounting based on BSD (Berkeley Software Distribution) UNIX, and hot-pluggable devices. You can press Enter to accept the default choices.

Loadable module support

This group of options asks you about support for loadable modules. A loadable module is a block of code that the Linux kernel can load and execute as if it were a part of the operating system.

```
*
* Loadable module support
*
Enable loadable module support (MODULES) [Y/n/?]
  Module unloading (MODULE_UNLOAD) [Y/n/?]
    Forced module unloading (MODULE_FORCE_UNLOAD) [Y/n/?]
  Module versioning support (EXPERIMENTAL) (MODVERSIONS) [Y/n/?]
  Automatic kernel module loading (KMOD) [Y/n/?]
```

You want to include support for modules, so answer Yes to the first question and accept the default for the next two questions. If modules have version information, the module is checked for compatibility with the current kernel version. Because it is easy to unload a module that does not work, I tend to answer No to this option. However, you may safely accept the default and press Enter. The last question asks whether or not you want the kernel to be capable of loading required modules. You should answer Yes to this option.

Processor type and features

This set of options is for setting the subarchitecture type, the processor family, and support for specific processor-related features:

```
*
* Processor type and features
*
Subarchitecture Type
> 1. PC-compatible (X86_PC)
  2. AMD Elan (X86_ELAN)
  3. Voyager (NCR) (X86_VOYAGER)
  4. NUMAQ (IBM/Sequent) (X86_NUMAQ)
  5. SGI 320/540 (Visual Workstation) (X86_VISWS)
choice[1-5]:
```

The Subarchitecture Type options enable you to select from different types of fundamental system designs that make use of the Intel x86 processor family but that may differ fundamentally from the well-known PC-compatible machines. Prior to version 2.6, the Linux kernel made an implicit assumption that the system's architecture was based on the old IBM PC-AT family. Starting with kernel version 2.6, you can build the kernel for other types of Intel x86-based architectures such as SGI Visual Workstation and multiprocessor systems with non-uniform memory access (NUMA). You probably can select the default PC-compatible subarchitecture, but the other options are available if you have to build the kernel for a different type of x86-based system.

The next set of options prompt you for the processor family:

```
Processor family
> 1. 386 (M386)
  2. 486 (M486)
  3. 586/K5/5x86/6x86/6x86MX (M586)
  4. Pentium-Classic (M586TSC)
  5. Pentium-MMX (M586MMX)
  6. Pentium-Pro (M686)
  7. Pentium-II/Celeron(pre-Coppermine) (MPENTIUMII)
  8. Pentium-III/Celeron(Coppermine)/Pentium-III Xeon (MPENTIUMIII)
  9. Pentium M (MPENTIUMM)
  10. Pentium-4/Celeron(P4-based)/Pentium-4 M/Xeon (MPENTIUM4)
  11. K6/K6-II/K6-III (MK6)
  12. Athlon/Duron/K7 (MK7)
  13. Opteron/Athlon64/Hammer/K8 (MK8)
  14. Crusoe (MCRUSOE)
  15. Winchip-C6 (MWINCHIPC6)
  16. Winchip-2 (MWINCHIP2)
  17. Winchip-2A/Winchip-3 (MWINCHIP3D)
  18. CyrixIII/VIA-C3 (MCYRIXIII)
  19. VIA C3-2 (Nehemiah) (MVIAC3_2)
choice[1-19]:
```

If you select 386, the compiled kernel can run on any other processor (such as a 486 or any type of Pentium). However, if you're creating a kernel specifically for your system's processor, select your processor type from the list.

Subsequent options prompt you for a host of other processor-related options, which you can leave in their default settings.

Power management options

This set of options deals with managing the system's power and includes advanced configuration and power interface (ACPI), advanced power management (APM) BIOS support, and CPU frequency scaling. You can simply accept the default settings for these options. If you don't understand what an option means, press **?** to get help on that option.

Bus options

These options ask you about supporting specific buses: PCI, ISA, EISA, MCA, and PCMCIA. The Industry Standard Architecture (ISA) bus was once the most widely used bus (until the PCI bus came along); this bus was used in the original IBM PC-AT. The Micro Channel Architecture (MCA) bus is IBM's proprietary bus, which first appeared in the PS/2 PCs. IBM designed this bus as a high-speed bus, but its proprietary nature kept it from being widely used in PCs. The Extended Industry Standard Architecture (EISA) bus came about as an alternative to the MCA bus, with performance comparable to that of the MCA. The EISA bus is not widely used because the EISA bus peripheral cards are more expensive than their ISA bus counterparts. The Peripheral Component Interconnect (PCI) bus is the latest high-performance bus; the current crop of PCs use the PCI bus, but also offer ISA bus slots so that you can continue to use ISA cards.

PCMCIA stands for Personal Computer Memory Card International Association, a nonprofit organization that standardized the interface for adding memory cards to laptop computers. Although originally conceived for memory cards, PCMCIA devices became popular for a wide variety of add-ons for laptops. The PCMCIA devices are called PC cards and the term CardBus refers to the electrical specification of PC cards.

Typically, you want to build in support for PCI and ISA and build modules for PCMCIA support. You can also add support for the PCI hot plug if your system supports adding or removing PCI cards while the system is powered up and running.

Executable file formats

Turn on the support for Executable and Linkable Format (ELF), which is the standard format for executables and libraries in Linux. Prior to ELF, the format for executables was called a.out (based on the default name of the executable generated by the C compiler). In kernel version 2.6, you can build a module to support the old a.out format.

Device drivers

This category of options provides support for file systems resident on memory technology devices, such as flash memory and random access memory. These file systems are often used in embedded devices. This category includes a number of options for building kernel modules to support various memory devices. There is no harm in building the modules because they are not loaded if your computer doesn't have the appropriate memory device.

Parallel port support

These options are important if you use any devices such as printers or parallel port Zip drives connected to the parallel port of your PC. Answer `m` to the Parallel port support and PC-style hardware options so that the drivers are built as modules.

Plug-and-Play support

These options ask if you want to enable Plug-and-Play (PnP) support in the kernel. If you enable PnP support, the kernel automatically configures PnP devices (just as Windows does). Enable these two options.

Block devices

Block devices (such as disk drives) transfer data in chunks (as opposed to keyboards, which transfer data one character at a time). This set of options involves the floppy and IDE (Integrated Drive Electronics) devices connected to the PC's parallel port as well as other block devices.

```
*
* Block devices
*
Normal floppy disk support (BLK_DEV_FD) [M/n/y/?]
PS/2 ESDI hard disk support (BLK_DEV_PS2) [M/n/y/?]
XT hard disk support (BLK_DEV_XD) [M/n/y/?]
Parallel port IDE device support (PARIDE) [M/n/?]
```

The first question asks if you want floppy drive support. Because most PCs do have a floppy drive, your answer generally is Yes. You should press Enter to accept the default for the third question if you have external CD-ROM or disk devices that connect through your PC's parallel port. Some IDE devices use a parallel port IDE adapter — that's what the `PARIDE` in the `CONFIG_PARIDE` option refers to.

The next set of options is for various parallel IDE drivers. You may want to build in support for parallel port IDE devices through loadable modules. That way, the modules are there if you need them, but the kernel doesn't get bloated with extra code.

Next comes another set of options for block devices. The `CONFIG_BLK_DEV_LOOP` option is for a loopback device. Enabling the loopback device lets the Linux kernel manipulate an entire file system image stored in a single large file. This option is useful if you want to mount a CD or DVD image (for example, a Linux ISO file) and check it out before actually burning the CD or DVD.

The multiple devices driver (`CONFIG_BLK_DEV_MD` option) allows Linux to combine several hard drive partitions into a single, logical device. This option supports RAID (Redundant Array of Independent Disks) devices. The RAM disk support allows the kernel to use a portion of your system's memory as a disk capable of storing a file system. Typically, a RAM disk functions only during system startup when the hard drive may not be available yet. The RAM disk is essential if you are booting a SCSI disk and you haven't compiled the SCSI drivers into the kernel.

ATA/ATAPI/MFM/RLL support

The next set of questions involves IDE devices, such as hard drives and ATAPI CD-ROM drives.

```
*
* ATA/ATAPI/MFM/RLL support
*
ATA/ATAPI/MFM/RLL support (IDE) [M/n/y/?]
  Enhanced IDE/MFM/RLL disk/cdrom/tape/floppy support (BLK_DEV_IDE) [M/n/?]
```

When you're configuring an operating system, you have to expect a fair share of acronyms — this one has four acronyms: ATA, ATAPI, MFM, and RLL. All these relate to hard drives or the interface that links disk drives to the PC. Here's what they mean:

- **ATA** stands for *AT Attachment* and refers to the PC-AT style interface that connects hard drives and CD-ROM drives to the PC's motherboard.
- **ATAPI** stands for *AT Attachment Packet Interface* and refers to the original PC hard drives that integrate the disk controller onto the hard drive itself. This interface used to be called *Integrated Drive Electronics* or IDE. You typically see the terms IDE, ATA, and ATAPI used interchangeably.
- **MFM** stands for *Modified Frequency Modulation,* the way data was encoded on older hard drives. These hard drives can work over an IDE interface.
- **RLL** stands for *Run Length Limited,* an old technique for storing data on a hard drive from the early days of the PC. RLL disks can work over an IDE interface.

The first question asks if you want the kernel to support IDE devices. The second question asks if you want to use the full-featured IDE device that can control up to ten IDE interfaces. Because each IDE interface can have a master and a slave device, this enables Linux to access a total of up to 20 IDE devices, such as disks or CD-ROM drives. You can press Enter to accept the default choices of module for both of these options.

The next set of options concerns various IDE drivers. You can accept the default answers for these options. Note that `IDE/ATAPI FLOPPY` refers to IDE floppy drives, such as the Iomega Zip drive or the Imation Superdisk LS-120 drive. The questions about CMD640 and RZ1000 bug fixes refer to some known problems with specific chipsets used in IDE interfaces.

SCSI device support

This set of options has to do with SCSI devices. SCSI stands for *Small Computer Systems Interface* — a type of interface through which you can connect multiple devices (such as hard drives and scanners) to the PC. This set of options has to do with SCSI devices. If your system has a SCSI adapter, you should start by answering Yes to the `CONFIG_SCSI` option. After that, you have to answer questions about the types of devices (disk, tape, CD-ROM) connected to the SCSI adapter. Finally, you must enable support for the specific SCSI adapter model on your system.

IEEE 1394 (FireWire) support

The next set of options is for enabling IEEE 1394 support, either as a module or linked into the kernel. IEEE 1394 is a high-speed serial bus for connecting peripherals to PCs. Apple calls this bus FireWire; Sony calls it i.Link. IEEE 1394 is similar to USB, but it can transfer data at rates up to 400Mbps, which is more than 30 times the data rate of the older USB version 1.1. (Note that USB 2.0 is much faster; it can transfer data at rates of up to 480Mbps.) Because of its high data-transfer rates, IEEE 1394 is ideal for connecting high-speed peripherals such as digital audio and video devices and external hard drives to the PC.

Currently, Linux supports IEEE 1394 chipsets that are compatible with Texas Instruments PCILynx/PCILynx2 and OHCI chipsets. If your PC has an IEEE 1394 adapter, you can build the necessary drivers through these options.

```
*
* IEEE 1394 (FireWire) support
*
IEEE 1394 (FireWire) support (IEEE1394) [M/n/y/?]
```

REMEMBER

To find out more about using IEEE 1394 peripherals in Linux, visit the Web site of the IEEE 1394 for Linux project at `www.linux1394.org`.

I2O device support

Pronounced *eye-two-oh,* I2O refers to Intelligent Input/Output — a new device driver architecture independent of the operating system and the controlled device. I2O functions by logically separating the part responsible for managing the device from the part that contains operating system-specific details. (It's called the I2O Split Driver model.) The two parts of an I2O driver are the OS Services Module (OSM), which works with the operating system, and the Hardware Device Module (HDM) that interfaces with the particular device the driver manages. The OSM and HDM communicate by passing messages to each other.

Linux comes with some I2O drivers for SCSI and PCI devices. You can build the I2O drivers through the following configuration options:

```
*
* I2O device support
*
I2O support (I2O) [M/n/y/?]
  I2O Configuration support (I2O_CONFIG) [M/n/?]
  I2O Block OSM (I2O_BLOCK) [M/n/?]
  I2O SCSI OSM (I2O_SCSI) [M/n/?]
  I2O /proc support (I2O_PROC) [M/n/?]
```

Networking support

This set of options deals with networking. How you set these options depends on how you want to use your Linux system in a network. Always say Yes to the TCP/IP Networking option because the X Window System uses TCP/IP networking (even if your PC isn't on any network). You can also enable experimental support for IPv6 — the next-generation Internet Protocol.

Answer Yes to the Network packet filtering option if you want to use your Linux system as a firewall — an intermediary system that controls information flowing between a local area network (LAN) and the Internet.

Other categories in the Networking Support options include wireless LAN, Ethernet (10/100Mpbs as well as Gigabit), ATM (Asynchronous Transfer Mode), Token ring, ARCnet, AppleTalk, wide area network (WAN), PCMCIA network devices, amateur radio, infrared, and Bluetooth.

The infrared support is for infrared communication using the protocols specified by the Infrared Data Association (IrDA). IrDA communication is used by many laptops and personal digital assistants (PDAs), such as Palm and Handspring.

Bluetooth is a low-power, short-range wireless technology for connecting devices on the 2.4 GHz frequency band. Devices that use Bluetooth can usually connect when they are within 10 meters of one another. To find out more about Bluetooth, visit `www.bluetooth.com`. Linux supports Bluetooth through a core driver and several other modules. You can answer `y` to enable Bluetooth support and then select other options specific to your Bluetooth device.

ISDN subsystem

This set of options enables you to include support for *ISDN* (Integrated Services Digital Network) — a digital telephone line that you can use to connect the Linux system to the Internet. These ISDN-related options include the configuration of specific ISDN adapters.

Build the ISDN driver only if your PC has an ISDN card. If you anticipate adding an ISDN card and purchase ISDN service from the phone company, you can build the driver as a module.

Telephony support

With the right hardware and software, the Telephony Support options enable you to use the Linux system for making phone calls over the Internet (also known as *voiceover IP* or *VoIP*). You can choose to build driver modules for telephony support if you have a telephony card, such as the Internet PhoneJACK or Internet LineJACK manufactured by Quicknet Technologies, Inc. If you don't have a telephony card, you can safely leave these options turned off.

Character devices

These options deal with configuring character devices, which include devices connected to the serial and parallel ports. These options also include configuration of multiport serial interface cards that enable you to connect multiple terminals or other devices to your Linux system.

Other subcategories of character devices include

- **Mice:** You can include support for bus mice in this option category.
- **Watchdog cards:** You can enable support for special watchdog cards that can monitor the PC's status (including the temperature, for instance) and reboot the PC when necessary. This option can be helpful if you want to have a networked PC automatically reboot after it hangs up for whatever reason.
- `Ftape` **or the floppy-tape device driver:** If you have a tape drive connected to your floppy controller, you can configure it through this category of options.
- **PCMCIA character devices:** These options are for configuring PC card serial adapters that are meant for laptop PCs.

Watchdog timer

These configuration options enable you to turn on support for the watchdog timer. Essentially, this causes the kernel to create a special file; failure to open the file and write to it every minute causes the system to reboot. Some watchdog boards can monitor the PC's status (including the temperature). You can also enable support for specific watchdog cards from this set of options.

If you want access to the PC's nonvolatile (battery-backed) memory — NVRAM — in the real-time clock, answer Yes to the `CONFIG_NVRAM` option. You can get access to the real-time clock by enabling the `CONFIG_RTC` configuration option.

Floppy tape drive

If you have a tape drive connected to your floppy controller, answer `y` or `m` to the next option, and select the other parameters appropriately (or accept the default choices):

```
*
* Ftape, the floppy tape device driver
*
Ftape (QIC-80/Travan) support (FTAPE) [M/n/y/?]
  Zftape, the VFS interface (ZFTAPE) [M/n/?]
    Default block size (ZFT_DFLT_BLK_SZ) [10240]
```

You can also enable several parameters related to floppy tape drives.

Advanced graphics support

The next set of options configures support for advanced video cards that can perform hardware-accelerated, 3-D graphics. You can enable the first option to build the AGP (Accelerated Graphics Port) driver and can answer Yes to the option for your specific chipset.

```
/dev/agpgart (AGP Support) (AGP) [M/n/y/?]
  ALI chipset support (AGP_ALI) [M/n/?]
  ATI chipset support (AGP_ATI) [M/n/?]
  AMD Irongate, 761, and 762 chipset support (AGP_AMD) [M/n/?]
  AMD Opteron/Athlon64 on-CPU GART support (AGP_AMD64) [M/n/?]
  Intel 440LX/BX/GX, I8xx and E7x05 chipset support (AGP_INTEL) [M/n/?]
  Intel i865 chipset support (AGP_INTEL_MCH) [M/n/?]
  NVIDIA nForce/nForce2 chipset support (AGP_NVIDIA) [M/n/?]
... lines not shown ...
```

Next, you have to configure a set of options for the Direct Rendering Manager (DRM) — a device-independent driver that supports the XFree86 Direct Rendering Infrastructure (DRI). DRI is meant for direct access to 3-D graphics hardware in advanced graphics cards, such as 3Dfx Banshee and Voodoo3+. To find out more about DRI, use the Web browser to visit the URL `dri.sourceforge.net`.

If you have a 3-D graphics card, you can answer Yes to `CONFIG_DRM` and build the module for the graphics card in your system. If you do not have one of the listed graphics cards, you should answer No to these options.

I2C Support

I2C — pronounced *eye-squared-see* — is a protocol Philips has developed for communication over a pair of wires at rates between 10 and 100 kHz. System Management Bus (SMBus) is a subset of the I2C protocol. Many modern motherboards have an SMBus meant for connecting devices such as EEPROM (electrically erasable programmable read only memory) and chips for hardware monitoring. Linux supports the I2C and SMBus protocols. You need this support for video for Linux. If you have any hardware sensors or video equipment that needs I2C support, answer `m` (for module) to the I2C Support option and answer `m` for the specific driver for your hardware.

Multimedia devices

This category of options configures support for multimedia devices such as video cameras, television tuners, and FM radio cards.

Frame buffer

Through these options you can enable support for frame-buffer devices. A frame buffer is an abstraction for the graphics hardware so that the kernel and other software can produce graphical output without having to rely on the low-level details (such as hardware registers) of a video card. Frame buffer support is available for many video cards.

Sound

Use this set of options to configure sound card support. If you have a sound card installed, start by answering `m` to the Sound Card Support option. After that, answer `m` for Advanced Linux Sound Architecture (ALSA) and the sound devices. You can always build the sound modules for all types of sound cards. That way, the modules needed for your system's sound card are available when needed.

USB support

Use this category of options to configure support for the Universal Serial Bus (USB) — a serial bus that comes built into most new PCs. USB version 1.1 supports data-transfer rates as high as 12 Mbps — 12 million bits per second or 1.5MB per second — compared with 115 Kbps or the 0.115 Mbps transfer rate of a standard serial port (such as COM1). You can daisy chain up to 127 devices on a USB bus. The bus also provides power to the devices, and you can attach or remove devices while the PC is running — a capability commonly referred to as *hot swapping* or *hotplugging*. USB version 2.0 (or USB 2.0

or USB2, for short) ups the data-transfer ante to 480 Mbps, slightly faster than the competing IEEE 1394 (FireWire) bus.

USB can replace the functionality of the PC's serial and parallel ports, as well as the keyboard and mouse ports. Nowadays, many PC peripherals — such as the mouse, keyboard, printer, scanner, modem, digital camera, and so on — are designed to connect to the PC through a USB port.

If your PC has a USB port, answer `m` to the Support for USB option (so that a module is built). Then you have to answer `m` to the UHCI or OHCI option, depending on the type of USB interface — UHCI (Intel) or OHCI (Compaq and others) — your PC has. To determine the type of USB interface, type **lspci** in a terminal window and look for the USB controller's make and model in the output. If the controller is by Intel, use the UHCI driver.

For USB 2.0 support, you can answer `m` to the EHCI HCD (that's host controller device) option.

After you select the UHCI or OHCI interface support, you have to build the driver modules for specific USB devices on your system.

File systems

Through this category of options, you can turn on support for specific types of file systems. You'd be amazed by the many different file systems that the Linux kernel can support. (Table 5-1 lists just some of them) You typically build a kernel with support for the core Linux file systems (ext2 and ext3), CD-ROM file system (ISO 9660 and Joliet), and DOS/Windows file systems (MSDOS, FAT, and VFAT). For sharing files with Windows 2000/XP systems, you also build the module for CIFS.

Table 5-1 Some File Systems Supported by the Linux Kernel

File System	*Description*
Apple Macintosh	The Macintosh HFS file system (Linux can read and write Macintosh-formatted floppy disks and hard drives).
CIFS	The Common Internet File System (CIFS) — a successor to the Server Message Block (SMB) protocol — is the new file system for Windows servers such as Windows 2000, Windows XP, and Samba.
Coda	An advanced network file system that is similar to NFS but that better supports disconnected operation (for example, laptops) and is a better security model.
Ext2	The second extended file system — the current standard file system for Linux.

File System	*Description*
Ext3	Ext2 file system with support for journaling — a facility that allows quick recovery of the disk after a crash.
FAT	Refers to any File Allocation Table (FAT)-based file system (including MS-DOS and Windows 95 VFAT file systems).
HPFS	The OS/2 HPFS file system (Linux can only read HPFS files).
ISO 9660	The standard ISO 9660 file system used on CD-ROMs. (This system is also known as the High Sierra File System and is referred to as `hsfs` on some UNIX workstations.)
Joliet	Microsoft's Joliet extension for the ISO 9660 CD-ROM file system, which allows for long filenames in Unicode format. (Unicode is the new 16-bit character code that can encode the characters of almost all languages of the world.)
MSDOS	The MS-DOS file system.
NFS	Network File System for sharing files and directories from other systems on a network.
NTFS	NT file system (NTFS) — the file system used by Microsoft Windows NT and XP (Linux can only read NTFS disks).
`/proc`	A virtual file system through which you can get information about the kernel. The `/proc` file system does not exist on the disk; files are created when you access them.
ReiserFS	An efficient file system that stores both filenames and files in a balanced tree and uses journaling.
SMB	File system that uses the Server Message Block (SMB) protocol to access shared directories from networked PCs running Windows 95/98/NT/2000.
System V	File system used by SCO, Xenix, and Coherent variants of UNIX for Intel PCs.
UDF	A new file system used on some CD-ROMs and DVDs (for example, UDF file system is used on rewritable CDs written in packet mode or written by UDF utilities such as DirectCD).
UFS	File system used by the BSD (Berkeley Software Distribution) variants of UNIX (such as SunOS, FreeBSD, NetBSD, and NeXTstep).
VFAT	Windows 95/98/NT/2000 file systems with long filenames.

Partition types

Linux can read and manipulate disk partitions created by many different systems. These options enable you to include support for specific partition types:

```
*
* Partition Types
*
Advanced partition selection (PARTITION_ADVANCED) [Y/n/?]
  Acorn partition support (ACORN_PARTITION) [Y/n/?]
    Cumana partition support (ACORN_PARTITION_CUMANA) [Y/n/?]
... lines not shown ...
```

Native language support

This set of configuration options requires you to select a native language character set. The Microsoft FAT file systems use these character sets to store and display filenames in one of several languages. The character sets are stored in files called DOS codepages. You have to include the appropriate codepages so that the Linux kernel can read and write filenames correctly in any DOS partitions on the hard drive. Note that the codepages apply only to filenames; they have nothing to do with the actual contents of files.

You can include support for as many codepages as you want. Simply answer Yes to the codepages for your selection of languages.

Kernel hacking

This set of options enables you to debug the kernel and use the SysRq key (equivalent to pressing Alt+PrintScreen) to get important status information right after a system crash. This information is useful if you are a Linux developer who expects to debug the kernel. Most users answer No (because most users run a stable version of the kernel and do not expect to fix kernel errors) to disable these options.

Security options

Through these options, you can include support for the Security Enhanced Linux (SELinux), which was developed by the National Security Agency (NSA) — a U.S. government agency. SELinux comes with Linux, but you can turn it off during booting by providing `selinux=0` as a boot option. For more information on SELinux, visit `www.nsa.gov/selinux`.

Cryptography support

This set of options are for enabling cryptography support in the kernel. You can enable support, as the default selections of the following options show:

```
*
* Cryptographic options
*
Cryptographic API (CRYPTO) [Y/?] y
  HMAC support (CRYPTO_HMAC) [Y/?] y
  Null algorithms (CRYPTO_NULL) [M/n/y/?]
```

```
   MD4 digest algorithm (CRYPTO_MD4) [M/n/y/?]
   MD5 digest algorithm (CRYPTO_MD5) [Y/m/?]
   SHA1 digest algorithm (CRYPTO_SHA1) [M/y/?]
   SHA256 digest algorithm (CRYPTO_SHA256) [M/n/y/?]
... lines not shown ...
```

Building the Kernel and the Modules

After configuring the kernel options, you have to build the kernel. This part can take a while. Depending on your system, making a new kernel can take anywhere from a few minutes to over an hour.

Type the following on a single line to initiate the process:

```
make
```

The `make` command creates the new kernel as well as any modules that you have specified through the configuration step.

REMEMBER

As the kernel is built, you see a lot of messages on-screen. When it's all over, a new kernel in the form of a compressed file named `bzImage` is in the `arch/i386/boot` subdirectory of where the kernel sources are located.

To use the new kernel, you have to copy the kernel file and the `System.map` file to the `/boot` directory under a specific name and edit the GRUB menu to set up GRUB — the boot loader. Before you proceed with the kernel installation, however, you have to install the modules and build a new initial RAM disk.

Installing the Modules

If you select any modules during the kernel configuration, the kernel building step also builds the modules. All you have to do is install them. Perform this task with the following commands:

```
cd /usr/src/linux*
make modules_install
```

The `make modules_install` command copies all the modules to a new subdirectory in the `/lib/modules` directory. The subdirectory name should be the same as the kernel version number.

Now you can install the kernel and make it available for GRUB to boot.

Creating the Initial RAM Disk File

The new kernel needs a new initial RAM disk file that you can create by using the `mkinitrd` command. Usually, the initial RAM disk image is stored in a file whose name begins with `initrd`. As you might have guessed, `initrd` is shorthand for initial RAM disk, and the `mkinitrd` command is so named because it makes an `initrd` file.

The `mkinitrd` program is in the `/sbin` directory, and you have to log in as `root` and use a command line of the following form to create the `initrd` file:

```
/sbin/mkinitrd /boot/initrd-filename.img  module-directory
```

The `initrd` file has to be in the `/boot` directory where the kernel is also located. You can use any filename for *`initrd-filename`*. The *`module-directory`* is the name of the directory in `/lib/modules` where the module files for the new kernel are located. The `make modules_install` step places the modules in a directory whose name is the kernel version number. For example, if your kernel version (as reported by the `uname -r` command) is 2.6.8, the *`module-directory`*, after the `make modules_install` step, is `2.6.8`.

Another common practice is to use an `initrd` filename created by appending the module directory name to the `initrd-` prefix. Thus, for module directory `2.6.8`, the `initrd` file would be `initrd-2.6.8.img`.

To create the initial RAM disk image for the newly built kernel, type the following command:

```
/sbin/mkinitrd /boot/2.6.8.img 2.6.8
```

This command creates the file `initrd-2.6.8.img` in the `/boot` directory. You have to refer to this `initrd` file in the GRUB menu file (`/etc/grub.conf`) in Fedora Core and `/boot/grub/menu.lst` in Debian and SUSE).

Installing the New Kernel and Setting Up GRUB

Most Linux distributions use GRUB to load the Linux kernel from the disk. You have to add the new kernel to the GRUB menu so that GRUB can display it as an option that you can boot.

DISTRIBUTION SPECIFIC

In Debian and SUSE, the GRUB menu is the `/boot/grub/menu.lst` file. In Fedora Core, the GRUB menu is specified by the `/etc/grub.conf` file. You should edit the file that applies to your distribution.

Here is a typical GRUB menu file of my systems:

```
default         0
# Set a timeout, in seconds, before automatically booting the default entry
# (normally the first entry defined).
timeout         5
# Debian GNU/Linux
title           Debian GNU/Linux, kernel 2.6.7-1-386
root            (hd0,2)
kernel          /vmlinuz-2.6.7-1-386 root=/dev/hda10 ro acpi=off
initrd          /initrd.img-2.6.7-1-386
savedefault
boot
# Windows XP
title           Windows XP
root            (hd0,1)
savedefault
makeactive
chainloader     +1
```

Here's what some of the lines in the GRUB menu file mean (the lines that begin with # are comments):

✦ `default 0`: Specifies the first boot entry as the default one that GRUB boots. If this line is set to 1, GRUB boots the second entry (2 means the third entry, 3 is the fourth, and so on).

✦ `timeout 5`: Causes GRUB to boot the default entry automatically after waiting for 5 seconds. If other boot entries are in the file, the user may select another one from a boot menu that GRUB displays.

✦ The lines starting with `title` constitute the first boot entry (the next entry begins with another `title` line) — and this entry defines a specific kernel file GRUB can boot. You can make GRUB boot another kernel by adding a similar section to the configuration file. Here's the meaning of the lines in this boot entry:

  • `root (hd0,2)`: Sets the `root` device to the third partition of the first hard drive. This partition is where the Linux kernel is installed on this particular system.

  • `kernel /vmlinuz-2.6.7-1-386 root=/dev/hda10 ro acpi=off`: Identifies the kernel that GRUB loads if the user selects this boot entry. In this case, the kernel file is `/vmlinuz-2.6.7-1-386`, which is located in the `root` device. In a Linux system, that partition is typically mounted on the `/boot` directory. In other words, GRUB loads the kernel file `/boot/vmlinuz-2.6.7-1-386`. The items following the kernel name are options provided to the kernel. For example, the `root` option identifies the partition containing the root filesystem (/).

  • `initrd /initrd.img-2.6.7-1-386`: Specifies a file that contains an initial RAM disk (`initrd`) image that serves as a file system before the disks are available. The Linux kernel uses the RAM disk — a block of memory used as a disk — to get started; then it loads other driver modules and begins using the hard drive.

- The lines starting with `title Windows XP` are the second boot entry and refer to the Windows XP operating system that happens to be on this system. The text next to the title line appears in the GRUB menu from which the user selects which operating system to boot.

To configure GRUB to boot the new Linux kernel (the one you just built), follow these steps:

1. **Copy the new kernel binary to the `/boot` directory.**

   The new, compressed kernel file is in the `arch/i386/boot` subdirectory of where the kernel source resides. The kernel filename is usually `bzImage`. I simply copy that file to the `/boot` directory with the same name.

   If the kernel filename is `vmlinux`, make sure you use `vmlinux` instead of `bzImage`. You can change the kernel filename in `/boot` to anything you want, as long as you use the same filename when referring to the kernel in the GRUB menu file in Step 3.

2. **Copy the new `System.map` file from the kernel source directory to the `/boot` directory.**

3. **Use your favorite text editor to edit the GRUB menu file to add the following lines in the file:**

   ```
   title New Linux kernel (2.6.8)
           root (hd0,2)
           kernel /bzImage root=/dev/hda10 ro
           initrd /initrd-2.6.8.img
   ```

   On your system, make sure that the `root` line is correct — instead of `(hd0,2)`, list the correct disk partition that's mounted on `/boot`. Also, use the correct filename for the kernel image file (for example, `/vmlinux` if the kernel file is so named).

   Note: The `initrd` line refers to the `initrd` file that you created in an earlier step.

4. **Save the GRUB menu file and exit the editor.**

Now you're ready to reboot the system and try out the new kernel.

Rebooting the System

After you finish configuring GRUB, you can restart the system. While you're still logged in as `root`, type the following command to reboot the system:

```
reboot
```

When you see the GRUB screen, select the name you assigned to the new kernel in the GRUB menu file.

After the system reboots, you see the familiar graphical login screen. To see proof that you're indeed running the new kernel, log in as a user, open a terminal window, and type **uname -srv**. This command shows you the kernel version, as well as the date and time when this kernel was built. If you upgraded the kernel source, you see the version number for the new kernel. If you have simply rebuilt the kernel for the same old kernel version, the date and time matches the time when you rebuilt the kernel. That's your proof that the system is running the new kernel.

TIP

If the system hangs (nothing seems to happen — you don't see any output on-screen or any disk activity), you may have skipped a step during the kernel rebuild. You can power the PC off and on to reboot. This time, select the name of the old working kernel at the GRUB screen.

Book VI

Security

The 5th Wave By Rich Tennant

"We take network security very seriously here."

Contents at a Glance

Chapter 1: Introducing Linux Security

In This Chapter

- Establishing a security policy and framework
- Understanding host security issues
- Understanding network security issues
- Translating computer security terminology
- Keeping up with security news and updates

In this chapter, I explain why you need to worry about security and give you a high-level view of how to get a handle on security. I explain the idea of an overall security framework and explain the two key aspects of security — host security and network security. I end this chapter by introducing you to the terminology used in discussing computer security.

Why Worry about Security?

In today's networked world, you have to worry about your Linux system's security. For a standalone system, or a system used in an isolated local area network (LAN), you have to focus on protecting the system from the users and the users from one another. In other words, you don't want a user to modify or delete system files, whether intentionally or unintentionally. Also, you don't want a user destroying another user's files.

If your Linux system is connected to the Internet, you have to secure the system from unwanted accesses over the Internet. These intruders — or *crackers,* as they are commonly known — typically impersonate a user, steal or destroy information, and even deny you access to your own system (known as a *Denial of Service* or *DoS* attack).

By its very nature, an Internet connection makes your system accessible to any other system on the Internet. After all, the Internet connects a huge number of networks across the globe. In fact, the client/server architecture of Internet services, such as HTTP (Web) and FTP, rely on the wide-open network access the Internet provides. Unfortunately, the easy accessibility to Internet services running on your system also means that anyone on the Net can easily access your system.

If you operate an Internet host that provides information to others, you certainly want everyone to access your system's Internet services, such as FTP and Web servers. However, these servers often have vulnerabilities that crackers may exploit in order to cause harm to your system. You need to know about the potential security risks of Internet services — and the precautions you can take to minimize the risk of someone exploiting the weaknesses of your FTP or Web server.

You also want to protect your company's internal network from outsiders, even though your goal is to provide information to the outside world through a Web or FTP server. You can protect your internal network by setting up an Internet *firewall* — a controlled access point to the internal network — and placing the Web and FTP servers on a host outside the firewall.

Establishing a Security Framework

The first step in securing your Linux system is to set up a *security policy* — a set of guidelines that state what you enable users (as well as visitors over the Internet) to do on your Linux system. The level of security you establish depends on how you use the Linux system — and on how much is at risk if someone gains unauthorized access to your system.

If you're a system administrator for one or more Linux systems at an organization, you probably want to involve company management, as well as the users, in setting up the security policy. Obviously, you cannot create a draconian policy that blocks all access. (That would prevent anyone from effectively working on the system.) On the other hand, if the users are creating or using data valuable to the organization, you have to set up a policy that protects the data from disclosure to outsiders. In other words, the security policy should strike a balance between the users' needs and the need to protect the system.

For a standalone Linux system, or a home system that you occasionally connect to the Internet, the security policy can be just a listing of the Internet services that you want to run on the system and the user accounts that you plan to set up on the system. For any larger organization, you probably have one or more Linux systems on a LAN connected to the Internet — preferably through a firewall. (To reiterate, a *firewall* is a device that controls the flow of Internet Protocol — IP — packets between the LAN and the Internet.) In such cases, thinking of computer security across the entire organization systematically is best. Figure 1-1 shows the key elements of an organization-wide framework for computer security.

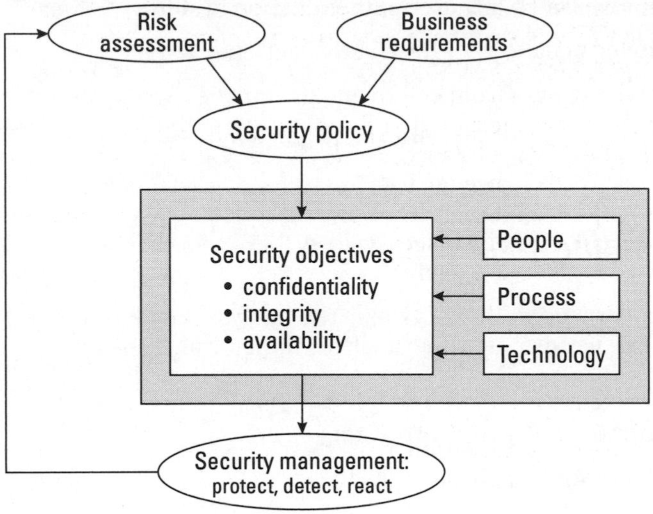

Figure 1-1: Start with an organization-wide framework for computer security.

The security framework outlined in Figure 1-1 includes:

- Determining the business requirements for security
- Performing risk assessments
- Establishing a security policy
- Implementing a cyber security solution that includes people, process, and technology to mitigate identified security risks
- Continuously monitoring and managing security

In the following sections, I discuss some of the key elements of the security framework.

Determining business requirements for security

The business requirements identify the security needs of the business — the computer resources and information you have to protect (including any requirements imposed by applicable laws, such as the requirement to protect the privacy of some types of data). Typical security requirements may include items such as the following:

- Enabling access to information by authorized users
- Implementing business rules that specify who has access to what information

- Employing a strong user-authentication system
- Denying malicious or destructive actions on data
- Protecting data from end to end as it moves across networks
- Implementing all security and privacy requirements that applicable laws impose

Performing risk analysis

Risk analysis is all about identifying and assessing risks — potential events that can harm your Linux system. The analysis involves determining the following and performing some analysis to determine the priority of handling the risks:

- **Threats:** What you're protecting against
- **Vulnerabilities:** Weaknesses that may be exploited by threats (these are the risks)
- **Probability:** The likelihood that a threat will exploit the vulnerability
- **Impact:** The effect of exploiting a specific vulnerability
- **Mitigation:** What to do to reduce vulnerabilities

Typical threats

Before I further describe risk analysis, here are some typical threats to your Linux system:

- **Denial of Service:** The computer and network are tied up so legitimate users cannot make use of the systems. For businesses, Denial of Service can mean a loss of revenue.
- **Unauthorized access:** Use of the computer and network by someone who isn't an authorized user. The unauthorized user can steal information or maliciously corrupt or destroy data. Some businesses may be hurt by the negative publicity from the mere act of an unauthorized user gaining access to the system, even if data shows no sign of explicit damage.
- **Disclosure of information to the public:** The unauthorized release of information to the public. For example, the disclosure of a password file enables potential attackers to figure out username and password combinations for accessing a system. Exposure of other sensitive information, such as financial and medical data, may be a potential liability for a business.

Typical vulnerabilities

The threats to your system and network come from exploitation of vulnerabilities in your organization's resources — both computer and people. Some common vulnerabilities are the following:

- People's foibles (divulging passwords, losing security cards, and so on)
- Internal network connections (routers, switches)
- Interconnection points (gateways — routers and firewalls — between the Internet and the internal network)
- Third-party network providers (ISPs, long-distance carriers) with looser security
- Operating system security holes (potential holes in Internet servers, such as those associated with `sendmail`, `named`, `bind`, and so on)
- Application security holes (known security holes in specific applications)

The 1-2-3 of risk analysis (probability and impact)

To perform risk analysis, assign a numeric value to the probability and impact of each potential vulnerability. To develop a workable risk analysis, do the following for each vulnerability or risk:

1. Assign subjective ratings of Low, Medium, and High for the probability. As the ratings suggest, Low probability means a lesser chance that the vulnerability will be exploited; High probability means a greater chance.
2. Assign similar ratings to impact. What you consider impact is up to you. If the exploitation of a vulnerability will affect your business greatly, assign it a High impact.
3. Assign a numeric value to the three levels — Low = 1, Medium = 2, and High = 3 — for both probability and impact.
4. Multiply the probability by the impact — you can think of this product as the risk level. Then make a decision to develop protections for vulnerabilities that exceed a specific threshold for the product of probability and impact. For example, you may choose to handle all vulnerabilities with a probability-times-impact of greater than 6.

If you want to characterize the probability and impact with finer gradations, pick a scale of 1 through 5 (for example) instead of 1 through 3, and follow the same steps as before.

Establishing a security policy

Using risk analysis and any business requirements that you may have to address (regardless of risk level) as a foundation, you can craft a security policy for the organization. Such a security policy typically addresses high-level objectives such as ensuring the confidentiality, integrity, and availability of data and systems.

The security policy typically addresses the following areas:

- **Authentication:** What method is used to ensure that a user is the real user? Who gets access to the system? What is the minimum length and complexity of passwords? How often do users change passwords? How long can a user be idle before that user is logged out automatically?
- **Authorization:** What can different classes of users do on the system? Who can have the `root` password?
- **Data protection:** What data must be protected? Who has access to the data? Is encryption necessary for some data?
- **Internet access:** What are the restrictions on users (from the LAN) accessing the Internet? What Internet services (such as Web, Internet Relay Chat, and so on) can users access? Are incoming e-mails and attachments scanned for viruses? Is there a network firewall? Are virtual private networks (VPNs) used to connect private networks across the Internet?
- **Internet services:** What Internet services are allowed on each Linux system? Are there any file servers? Mail servers? Web servers? What services run on each type of server? What services, if any, run on Linux systems used as desktop workstations?
- **Security audits:** Who tests whether the security is adequate? How often is the security tested? How are problems found during security testing handled?
- **Incident handling:** What are the procedures for handling any computer security incidents? Who must be informed? What information must be gathered to help with the investigation of incidents?
- **Responsibilities:** Who is responsible for maintaining security? Who monitors log files and audit trails for signs of unauthorized access? Who maintains the security policy?

Implementing security solutions (mitigation)

After you analyze the risks — vulnerabilities — and develop a security policy, you have to select the mitigation approach: how to protect against specific vulnerabilities. This is where you develop an overall security solution based on security policy, business requirements, and available technology — a solution that makes use of people, process, and technology and includes the following:

- ✦ Services (authentication, access control, encryption)
- ✦ Mechanisms (username/password, firewalls)
- ✦ Objects (hardware, software)

Because it is impossible to protect computer systems from all attacks, solutions identified through the risk management process must support three integral concepts of a holistic security program: protection, detection, and reaction:

- ✦ *Protection* provides countermeasures such as policies, procedures, and technical solutions to defend against attacks on the assets being protected.
- ✦ *Detection* monitors for potential breakdowns in the protective measures that could result in security breaches.
- ✦ *Reaction* or *Response,* which often requires human involvement, responds to detected breaches to thwart attacks before damage can be done.

Because absolute protection from attacks is impossible to achieve, a security program that does not incorporate detection and reaction is incomplete.

Managing security

In addition to implementing security solutions, you have to install security management that continually monitors, detects, and responds to any security incidents.

The combination of the risk analysis, security policy, security solutions, and security management provides the overall security framework. Such a framework helps establish a common level of understanding of security concerns — and a common basis for the design and implementation of security solutions.

Securing Linux

After you define a security policy, you can proceed to secure the system according to the policy. The exact steps depend on what you want to do with the system — whether it's a server or a workstation and how many users must access the system.

To secure the Linux system, you have to handle two broad categories of security issues:

- **Host security issues** that relate to securing the operating system and the files and directories on the system
- **Network security issues** that refer to the threat of attacks over the network connection

Understanding the host security issues

Here are some high-level guidelines to address host security (I cover some of these topics in detail in Chapter 2 of this minibook):

- When installing Linux, select only the package groups that you need for your system. Don't install unnecessary software. For example, if your system is used as a workstation, you don't have to install most of the servers (Web server, news server, and so on).
- Create initial user accounts and make sure that all passwords are strong enough that password-cracking programs can't "guess" them. Linux includes tools to enforce strong passwords.
- Set file ownerships and permissions to protect important files and directories.
- If available, enable mandatory access control capabilities provided by Security Enhanced Linux (SELinux). Linux kernel 2.6 supports SELinux.
- Use the GNU Privacy Guard (GnuPG) to encrypt or decrypt files with sensitive information and to authenticate files that you download from the Internet. GnuPG comes with Linux and you can use the `gpg` command to perform the tasks such as encrypting or decrypting a file and digitally signing a file. (See Chapter 2 of this minibook for an explanation of digital signatures).
- Use file-integrity checking tools, such as Tripwire, to monitor any changes to crucial system files and directories. The open source version of Tripwire (which is somewhat old) is available from `www.tripwire.org`. Visit `www.tripwire.com` for the commercial version.
- Periodically check various log files for signs of any break-ins or attempted break-ins. These log files are in the `/var/log` directory of your system.
- Install security updates as soon as they become available. These security updates fix known vulnerabilities in Linux.

Understanding network security issues

The issue of security comes up as soon as you connect your organization's internal network to the Internet. You need to think of security even if you connect a single computer to the Internet, but security concerns are more pressing when an entire internal network is opened to the world.

If you're an experienced system administrator, you already know that the cost of managing an Internet presence doesn't worry corporate management; their main concern is security. To get your management's backing for the Web site, you have to lay out a plan to keep the corporate network secure from intruders.

You may think that you can avoid jeopardizing the internal network by connecting only the external servers, such as Web and FTP servers, to the Internet. However, employing this simplistic approach isn't wise. It's like deciding not to drive because you may have an accident. Not having a network connection between your Web server and your internal network also has the following drawbacks:

- ✦ You cannot use network file transfers, such as FTP, to copy documents and data from your internal network to the Web server.
- ✦ Users on the internal network cannot access the corporate Web server.
- ✦ Users on the internal network don't have access to Web servers on the Internet. Such a restriction makes a valuable resource — the Web — inaccessible to the users in your organization.

A practical solution to this problem is to set up an Internet firewall and to put the Web server on a highly secured host outside the firewall.

In addition to using a firewall, here are some of the other steps to take to address network security (I explain these further in Chapter 3 of this minibook):

- ✦ Enable only those Internet services you need on a system. In particular, don't enable services that are not properly configured.
- ✦ Use Secure Shell (`ssh`) for remote logins. Don't use the `r` commands, such as `rlogin` and `rsh`.
- ✦ Secure any Internet services, such as FTP or TELNET, that you want to run on your system. You can use the TCP wrapper access control files — `/etc/hosts.allow` and `/etc/hosts.deny` — to secure some of these services. (See Chapter 3 of this minibook for more on the TCP wrapper).
- ✦ Promptly fix any known vulnerabilities of Internet services that you choose to run. Typically, you can download and install the latest security updates from your Linux distribution's online update sites.

Delving Into Computer Security Terminology

Computer books, magazine articles, and experts on computer security use a number of terms with unique meanings. You need to know these terms to understand discussions about computer security (and to communicate effectively with security vendors). Table 1-1 describes some of the commonly used computer security terms.

Table 1-1 Commonly Used Computer Security Terminology

Term	*Description*
Application gateway	A proxy service that acts as a gateway for application-level protocols, such as FTP, HTTP, NNTP, and SSH.
Authentication	The process of confirming that a user is indeed who he or she claims to be. The typical authentication method is a challenge-response method wherein the user enters a username and secret password to confirm his or her identity.
Backdoor	A security weakness a cracker places on a host in order to bypass security features.
Bastion host	A highly secured computer that serves as an organization's main point of presence on the Internet. A bastion host typically resides on the perimeter network, but a dual-homed host (with one network interface connected to the Internet and the other to the internal network) is also a bastion host.
Buffer overflow	A security flaw in a program that enables a cracker to send an excessive amount of data to that program and to overwrite parts of the running program with code in the data being sent. The result is that the cracker can execute arbitrary code on the system and possibly gain access to the system as a privileged user. The new `exec-shield` feature of the Linux kernel protects against buffer overflows.
Certificate	An electronic document that identifies an entity (such as an individual, an organization, or a computer) and associates a public key with that identity. A certificate contains the certificate holder's name, a serial number, expiration date, a copy of the certificate holder's public key, and the digital signature of the Certificate Authority so a recipient can verify that the certificate is real.
Certificate Authority (CA)	An organization that validates identities and issues certificates.
Cracker	A person who breaks into (or attempts to break into) a host, often with malicious intent.
Confidentiality	Of data, a state of being accessible to no one but you (usually achieved by encryption).
Decryption	The process of transforming encrypted information into its original, intelligible form.

Term	Description
Denial of Service (DoS)	An attack that uses so many of the resources on your computer and network that legitimate users cannot access and use the system. From a single source, the attack overwhelms the target computer with messages and blocks legitimate traffic. It can prevent one system from being able to exchange data with other systems or prevent the system from using the Internet.
Distributed Denial of Service (DDoS)	A variant of the denial-of-service attack that uses a coordinated attack from a distributed system of computers rather than a single source. It often makes use of worms to spread to multiple computers that can then attack the target.
Digital signature	A one-way MD5 or SHA-1 hash of a message encrypted with the private key of the message originator, used to verify the integrity of a message and ensure nonrepudiation.
DMZ	Another name for the perimeter network. (DMZ originally stood for *demilitarized zone*, the buffer zone separating the warring North and South in Korea and Vietnam.)
Dual-homed host	A computer with two network interfaces (think of each network as a home).
Encryption	The process of transforming information so it's unintelligible to anyone but the intended recipient. The transformation is done by a mathematical operation between a key and the information.
Exploit tools	Publicly available and sophisticated tools that intruders of various skill levels can use to determine vulnerabilities and gain entry into targeted systems.
Firewall	A controlled-access gateway between an organization's internal network and the Internet. A dual-homed host can be configured as a firewall.
Hash	The result when a mathematical function converts a message into a fixed-size numeric value known as a *message digest* (or *hash*). The MD5 algorithm, for example, produces a 128-bit message digest; the Secure Hash Algorithm-1 (SHA-1) generates a 160-bit message digest. The hash of a message is encrypted with the private key of the sender to produce the digital signature.
Host	A computer on a network that is configured to offer services to other computers on the network.
Integrity	Of received data, a state of being the same as originally sent (that is, unaltered in transit).

(continued)

Book VI
Chapter 1

Introducing Linux Security

Table 1-1 ***(continued)***

Term	*Description*
IPSec (IP Security Protocol)	A security protocol for the Network layer of the OSI Networking Model, designed to provide cryptographic security services for IP packets. IPSec provides encryption-based authentication, integrity, access control, and confidentiality. (Visit `www.ietf.org/html.charters/ipsec-charter.html` for the list of RFCs related to IPSec.)
IP spoofing	An attack in which a cracker figures out the IP address of a trusted host and then sends packets that appear to come from the trusted host. The attacker can send packets but cannot see responses. However, the attacker can predict the sequence of packets and essentially send commands that set up a backdoor for future break-ins.
Logic bombs	A form of sabotage in which a programmer inserts code that causes the program to perform a destructive action when some triggering event occurs, such as terminating the programmer's employment.
Nonrepudiation	A security feature that prevents the sender of data from being able to deny ever having sent the data.
Packet	A collection of bytes, assembled according to a specific protocol, that serves as the basic unit of communication on a network. On TCP/IP networks, for example, the packet may be referred to as an *IP packet* or a *TCP/IP packet.*
Packet filtering	Selective blocking of packets according to type of packet (as specified by the source and destination IP address or port).
Perimeter network	A network between the Internet and the protected internal network. The perimeter network (also known as DMZ) is where the bastion host resides.
Port scanning	A method of discovering which ports are open (in other words, which Internet services are enabled) on a system, performed by sending connection requests to the ports, one by one. This procedure is usually a precursor to further attacks.
Proxy server	A server on the bastion host that enables internal clients to access external servers (and enables external clients to access servers inside the protected network). There are proxy servers for various Internet services, such as FTP and HTTP.
Public-key cryptography	An encryption method that uses a pair of keys — a private key and a public key — to encrypt and decrypt the information. Anything encrypted with the public key is decrypted only with the corresponding private key, and vice versa.

Term	*Description*
Public-Key Infrastructure (PKI)	A set of standards and services that enables the use of public-key cryptography and certificates in a networked environment. PKI facilitates tasks, such as issuing, renewing, and revoking certificates, and generating and distributing public- and private-key pairs.
Screening router	An Internet router that filters packets.
Setuid program	A program that runs with the permissions of the owner regardless of who runs the program. For example, if `root` owns a setuid program, that program has `root` privileges regardless of who started the program. Crackers often exploit vulnerabilities in setuid programs to gain privileged access to a system.
Sniffer	Synonymous with packet sniffer — a program that intercepts routed data and examines each packet in search of specified information, such as passwords transmitted in clear text.
Symmetric-key encryption	An encryption method wherein the same key is used to encrypt and decrypt the information.
Spyware	Any software that covertly gathers user information through the user's Internet connection and usually transmits that information in the background to someone else. Spyware can also gather information about e-mail addresses and even passwords and credit card numbers. Spyware is similar to a Trojan horse in that users are tricked into installing spyware when they install something else.
Threat	An event or activity, deliberate or unintentional, with the potential for causing harm to a system or network.
Trojan Horse	A program that masquerades as a benign program, but in fact is a backdoor used for attacking a system. Attackers often install a collection of Trojan Horse programs that enable the attacker to freely access the system with `root` privileges, yet hide that fact from the system administrator. Such collections of Trojan Horse programs are called *rootkits*.
Virus	A self-replicating program that spreads from one computer to another by attaching itself to other programs.
Vulnerability	A flaw or weakness that may cause harm to a system or network.
War-dialing	Simple programs that dial consecutive phone numbers looking for modems.
War-driving	A method of gaining entry into wireless computer networks using a laptop, antennas, and a wireless network card that involves patrolling locations to gain unauthorized access.
Worm	A self-replicating program that copies itself from one computer to another over a network.

Keeping Up with Security News and Updates

To keep up with the latest security alerts, you may want to visit one or more of the following sites on a daily basis:

- CERT Coordination Center (CERT/CC) at `www.cert.org`
- Computer Incident Advisory Capability (CIAC) at `www.ciac.org/ciac`
- United States Computer Emergency Readiness Team (US-CERT) at `www.us-cert.gov`

If you have access to Internet newsgroups, you can periodically browse the following:

- `comp.security.announce`: A moderated newsgroup that includes announcements from CERT about security.
- `comp.security.linux`: A newsgroup that includes discussions of Linux security issues.
- `comp.security.unix`: A newsgroup that includes discussions of UNIX security issues, including items related to Linux.

If you prefer to receive regular security updates through e-mail, you can also sign up for (subscribe to) various mailing lists:

- **FOCUS-LINUX:** Fill out the form at `www.securityfocus.com/subscribe` to subscribe to this mailing list focused on Linux security issues.
- **US-CERT National Cyber Alert System:** Follow the directions at `www.us-cert.gov` to subscribe to this mailing list. The Cyber Alert System features four categories of security information through its mailing lists:
  - Technical Cyber Security Alerts provide technical information about vulnerabilities in various common software products.
  - Cyber Security Alerts are sent when vulnerabilities affect the general public. They outline the steps and actions that non-technical home and corporate computer users can take to protect themselves from attacks.
  - Cyber Security Bulletins are bi-weekly summaries of security issues and new vulnerabilities along with patches, workarounds, and other actions that users can take to help reduce the risk.
  - Cyber Security Tips offer advice on common security issues for non-technical computer users.

DISTRIBUTION SPECIFIC

Finally, check your distribution's Web site for updates that may fix any known security problems with that distribution. In Debian, you can update the system with the commands `apt-get update` followed by `apt-get upgrade`. For Fedora Core, the Web site is `fedora.redhat.com/download/updates.html`. In SUSE, use YaST Online Update to keep your system up to date. In Xandros, obtain the latest updates from Xandros Networks.

Chapter 2: Securing a Linux Host

In This Chapter

- **Securing passwords**
- **Protecting files and directories**
- **Encrypting and signing files with GnuPG**
- **Monitoring system security**

Host is the techie term for your Linux system — especially when you use it to provide services on a network. But the term makes sense even when you think of the computer by itself; it's the host for everything that runs on it — the operating system and all the applications. A key aspect of computer security is to secure the host.

In this chapter, I take you through a few key steps to follow in securing your Linux host. These steps include installing operating system updates, protecting passwords, protecting the files and directories, using encryption if necessary, and monitoring the security of the system. You can monitor host security by examining log files for any suspicious activities and by using the Tripwire tool (a great third-party tool for detecting changes to system files) to see whether anyone has messed with important files on your system.

Securing Passwords

Historically, UNIX passwords are stored in the `/etc/passwd` file, which any user can read. For example, a typical old-style `/etc/passwd` file entry for the `root` user looks like this:

```
root:t6Z7NWDK1K8sU:0:0:root:/root:/bin/bash
```

The fields are separated by colons (`:`), and the second field contains the password in encrypted form. To check whether a password is valid, the login program encrypts the plain-text password the user enters and compares the password with the contents of the `/etc/passwd` file. If there is a match, the user is allowed to log in.

Password-cracking programs work just like the login program, except that these programs pick one word at a time from a dictionary, encrypt the word, and compare the encrypted word with the encrypted passwords in the

/etc/passwd file for a match. To crack the passwords, the intruder needs the /etc/passwd file. Often, crackers use weaknesses of various Internet servers (such as mail and FTP) to get a copy of the /etc/passwd file.

Several improvements have made passwords more secure in Linux. These include shadow passwords and pluggable authentication modules — described in the next two sections — and you can install these easily as you install Linux. During Linux installation, you typically get a chance to configure the authentication. If you enable MD5 password and enable shadow passwords, you automatically enable more secure passwords in Linux.

Shadow passwords

Obviously, leaving passwords lying around where anyone can get at them — even if they're encrypted — is bad security. So instead of storing passwords in the /etc/passwd file (which any user can read), Linux now stores them in a shadow password file, /etc/shadow. Only the superuser (root) can read this file. For example, here is the entry for root in the new-style /etc/passwd file:

```
root:x:0:0:root:/root:/bin/bash
```

In this case, note that the second field contains an x instead of an encrypted password. The x is the *shadow password*; the actual encrypted password is now stored in the /etc/shadow file where the entry for root is like this:

```
root:$1$AAAni/yN$uESHbzUpy9Cgfoo1Bf0tS0:11077:0:99999:7:-1:-1:134540356
```

The format of the /etc/shadow entries with colon-separated fields resembles the entries in the /etc/passwd file, but the meanings of most of the fields differ. The first field is still the username, and the second one is the encrypted password.

The remaining fields in each /etc/shadow entry control when the password expires. You don't have to interpret or change these entries in the /etc/shadow file. Instead, use the chage command to change the password-expiration information. For starters, you can check a user's password-expiration information by using the chage command with the -l option, as follows (in this case, you have to be logged in as root):

```
chage -l root
```

This command displays expiration information, including how long the password lasts and how often you can change the password.

If you want to ensure that the user is forced to change a password every 90 days, you can use the -M option to set the maximum number of days that a password stays valid. For example, to make sure that user naba is prompted to change the password in 90 days, I log in as root and type the following command:

```
chage -M 90 naba
```

You can use the command for each user account to ensure that all passwords expire when appropriate, and that all users must pick new passwords.

Pluggable authentication modules (PAMs)

In addition to improving the password file's security by using shadow passwords, Linux also improves the actual encryption of the passwords stored in the /etc/shadow file, using the MD5 message-digest algorithm described in RFC 1321 (www.ietf.org/rfc/rfc1321.txt or www.cis.ohio-state.edu/cgi-bin/rfc/rfc1321.html). MD5 reduces a message of any length to a 128-bit message digest (or *fingerprint*) of a document so that you can digitally sign it by encrypting it with your private key. MD5 works quite well for password encryption, too.

Another advantage of MD5 over older-style password encryption is that the older passwords were limited to a maximum of eight characters; new passwords (encrypted with MD5) can be much longer. Longer passwords are harder to guess, even if the /etc/shadow file falls into the wrong hands.

You can tell that MD5 encryption is in effect in the /etc/shadow file. The encrypted passwords are longer and they all sport the 1 prefix, as in the second field of the following sample entry:

```
root:$1$AAAni/yN$uESHbzUpy9Cgfoo1Bf0tS0:11077:0:99999:7:-1:-1:134540356
```

An add-in program module called a *pluggable authentication module* (PAM) performs the actual MD5 encryption. Linux PAMs provide a flexible method for authenticating users. By setting the PAMs' configuration files, you can change your authentication method on the fly, without having to actually modify vital programs (such as login and passwd) that verify a user's identity.

Linux uses PAM capabilities extensively. The PAMs reside in many different modules (about which more momentarily); their configuration files are in the /etc/pam.d directory of your system. Check out the contents of this directory on your system by typing the following command:

```
ls /etc/pam.d
```

Each configuration file in this directory specifies how users are authenticated for a specific utility.

Protecting Files and Directories

One important aspect of securing the host is to protect important system files — and the directories that contain these files. You can protect the files through the file ownership and through the permission settings that control who can read, write, or (in case of executable programs) execute the file.

The default Linux file security is controlled through the following settings for each file or directory:

- User ownership
- Group ownership
- Read, write, execute permissions for the owner
- Read, write, execute permissions for the group
- Read, write, execute permissions for others (everyone else)

Viewing ownerships and permissions

You can see these settings for a file when you look at the detailed listing with the `ls -l` command. For example, type the following command to see the detailed listing of the `/etc/inittab` file:

```
ls -l /etc/inittab
```

The resulting listing looks something like this:

```
-rw-r--r--  1 root root 1666 Feb 16 07:57 /etc/inittab
```

The first set of characters describes the file permissions for user, group, and others. The third and fourth fields show the user and group that own this file. In this case, both user and group names are the same: `root`.

Changing file ownerships

You can set the user and group ownerships with the `chown` command. For example, if the file `/dev/hda` should be owned by the user `root` and the group `disk`, then you type the following command as `root` to set up this ownership:

```
chown root.disk /dev/hda
```

To change the group ownership alone, use the `chgrp` command. For example, here's how you can change the group ownership of a file from whatever it was earlier to the group named `accounting`:

```
chgrp accounting ledger.out
```

Changing file permissions

Use the chmod command to set the file permissions. To use chmod effectively, you have to specify the permission settings. One way is to *concatenate* one or more letters from each column of Table 2-1, in the order shown (Who/Action/Permission).

Table 2-1 File Permission Codes

Who	*Action*	*Permission*
u user	+ add	r read
g group	- remove	w write
o others	= assign	x execute
a all	s set user ID	

To give everyone read and write access to all files in a directory, type **chmod a+rw ***. On the other hand, to permit everyone to execute a specific file, type **chmod a+x *filename***.

Another way to specify a permission setting is to use a three-digit sequence of numbers. In a detailed listing, the read, write, and execute permission settings for the user, group, and others appear as the sequence

```
rwxrwxrwx
```

with dashes in place of letters for disallowed operations. Think of rwxrwxrwx as three occurrences of the string rwx. Now assign the values r=4, w=2, and x=1. To get the value of the sequence rwx, simply add the values of r, w, and x. Thus, rwx = 7. Using this formula, you can assign a three-digit value to any permission setting. For example, if the user can read and write the file but everyone else can only read the file, the permission setting is rw-r--r-- (that's how it appears in the listing), and the value is 644. Thus, if you want all files in a directory to be readable by everyone but writable only by the user, use the following command:

```
chmod 644 *
```

Setting default permission

What permission setting does a file get when you (or a program) create a new file? The answer is in what is known as the user file-creation mask that you can see and set using the umask command.

Type **umask**, and it prints out a number showing the current file-creation mask. The default setting is different for the root user and other normal users. For the root user, the mask is set to 022, whereas the mask for normal users is 002. To see the effect of this file-creation mask and to interpret the meaning of the mask, follow these steps:

1. **Log in as `root` and type the following command:**

   ```
   touch junkfile
   ```

   This command creates a file named `junkfile` with nothing in it.

2. **Type** ls -l junkfile **to see that file's permissions.**

   You see a line similar to the following:

   ```
   -rw-r--r--  1 root   root      0 Aug 24 10:56 junkfile
   ```

   Interpret the numerical value of the permission setting by converting each three-letter permission in the first field (excluding the very first letter) into a number between 0 and 7. For each letter that's present, the first letter gets a value of 4, second letter is 2, and the third is 1. For example, `rw-` translates to 4+2+0 (because the third letter is missing) or 6. Similarly, `r--` is 4+0+0 = 4. Thus the permission string `-rw-r--r--` becomes 644.

3. **Subtract the numerical permission setting from 666 and what you get is the `umask` setting.**

   In this case, 666 – 644 results in an `umask` of 022.

Thus, an `umask` of 022 results in a default permission setting of 666 – 022 = 644. When you rewrite 644 in terms of a permission string, it becomes `rw-r--r--`.

To set a new `umask`, type **umask** followed by the numerical value of the mask. Here is how you go about it:

1. **Figure out what permission settings you want for new files.**

   For example, if you want new files that can be read and written only by the owner and by nobody else, the permission setting looks like this:

   ```
   rw-------
   ```

2. **Convert the permissions into a numerical value by using the conversion method that assigns 4 to the first field, 2 to the second, and 1 to the third.**

   Thus, for files that are readable and writable only by their owner, the permission setting is 600.

3. **Subtract the desired permission setting from 666 to get the value of the mask.**

   For a permission setting of 600, the mask becomes 666 – 600 = 066.

4. **Use the `umask` command to set the file-creation mask:**

   ```
   umask 066
   ```

A default umask of 022 is good for system security because it translates to files that have read and write permission for the owner and read permissions for everyone else. The bottom line is that you don't want a default umask that results in files that are writable by the whole wide world.

Checking for set user ID permission

Another permission setting can be a security hazard. This permission setting, called the set user ID (or setuid for short), applies to executable files. When the setuid permission is enabled, the file executes under the user ID of the file's owner. In other words, if an executable program is owned by root and the setuid permission is set, no matter who executes that program, it runs as if root is executing it. This permission means that the program can do a lot more (for example, read all files, create new files, and delete files) than what a normal user program can do. Another risk is that if a setuid program file has some security hole, crackers can do a lot more damage through such programs than through other vulnerabilities.

You can find all setuid programs with a simple find command:

```
find / -type f -perm +4000 -print
```

You see a list of files such as the following:

```
/usr/bin/chage
/usr/bin/gpasswd
/usr/bin/chfn
/usr/bin/chsh
/usr/bin/newgrp
/usr/bin/passwd
/usr/bin/at
/usr/bin/rcp
/usr/bin/rlogin
/usr/bin/rsh
/usr/bin/sudo
/usr/bin/crontab
... lines deleted ...
```

Many of the programs have the setuid permission because they need it, but check the complete list and make sure that there are no strange setuid programs (for example, setuid programs in a user's home directory).

If you want to see how these permissions are listed by the ls command, type **ls -l /usr/bin/passwd** and you see the permission settings:

```
-r-s--x--x    1 root     root        16128 Jun  5 23:03 /usr/bin/passwd
```

The s in the owner's permission setting (r-s) tells you that the setuid permission is set.

Encrypting and Signing Files with GnuPG

Linux comes with the *GNU Privacy Guard* (GnuPG or, simply GPG) encryption and authentication utility. With GPG, you can create your public- and private-key pair, encrypt files using your key, and also digitally sign a message to authenticate that it's really from you. If you send a digitally signed message to someone who has your public key, the recipient can verify that it was you who signed the message.

Understanding public-key encryption

The basic idea behind public-key encryption is to use a pair of keys — one private and the other public — that are related but can't be used to guess one from the other. Anything encrypted with the private key can be decrypted only with the corresponding public key, and vice versa. The public key is for distribution to other people while you keep the private key in a safe place.

You can use public-key encryption to communicate securely with others; Figure 2-1 illustrates the basic idea. Suppose Alice wants to send secure messages to Bob. Each of them generates public key and private key pairs, after which they exchange their public keys. Then, when Alice wants to send a message to Bob, she simply encrypts the message using Bob's public key and sends the encrypted message to him. Now the message is secure from any eavesdropping because only Bob's private key can decrypt the message — and only Bob has that key. When Bob receives the message, he uses his private key to decrypt the message and read it.

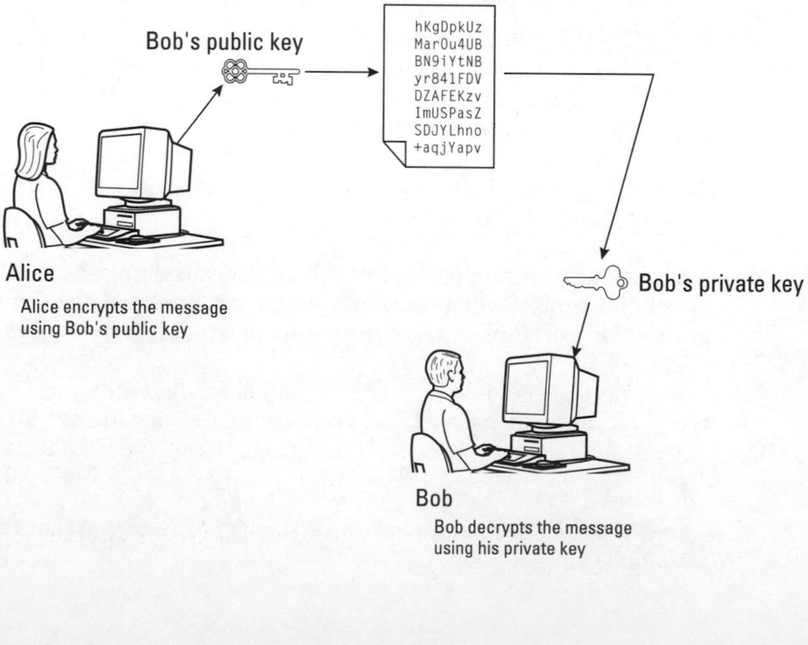

Figure 2-1: Bob and Alice can communicate securely with public-key encryption.

At this point, you need to stop and think and say, "Wait a minute! How does Bob know the message really came from Alice? What if someone else uses Bob's public key and sends a message as if it came from Alice?" This situation is where digital signatures come in.

Understanding digital signatures

The purpose of digital or electronic signatures is the same as pen-and-ink signatures, but how you sign digitally is completely different. Unlike pen-and-ink signatures, your digital signature depends on the message you're signing. The first step in creating a digital signature is to apply a mathematical function on the message and reduce it to a fixed-size message digest (also called a *hash* or a *fingerprint*). No matter how big your message is, the message digest is always around 128 or 160 bits, depending on the hashing function.

The next step is to apply public-key encryption. Simply encrypt the message digest with your private key, and you get the digital signature for the message. Typically, the digital signature is appended to the end of the message, and *voilà* — you get an electronically signed message.

What good does the digital signature do? Well, anyone who wants to verify that the message is indeed signed by you takes your public key and decrypts the digital signature. What that person gets is the message digest (the encrypted hash) of the message. Then he or she applies the same hash function to the message and compares the computed hash with the decrypted value. If the two match, then no one has tampered with the message. Because your public key was used to verify the signature, the message must have been signed with the private key known only to you. So the message must be from you!

In the theoretical scenario of Alice sending private messages to Bob, Alice can digitally sign her message to make sure that Bob can tell that the message is really from her. Figure 2-2 illustrates the use of digital signatures along with normal public-key encryption.

Here's how Alice sends her private message to Bob with the assurance that Bob can really tell it's from her:

1. Alice uses software to compute the message digest of the message and then encrypts the digest by using her private key. This is her digital signature for the message.
2. Alice encrypts the message (again, using some convenient software *and* Bob's public key).
3. She sends both the encrypted message and the digital signature to Bob.
4. Bob decrypts the message using his private key.
5. Bob decrypts the digital signature using Alice's public key. This gives him the message digest.

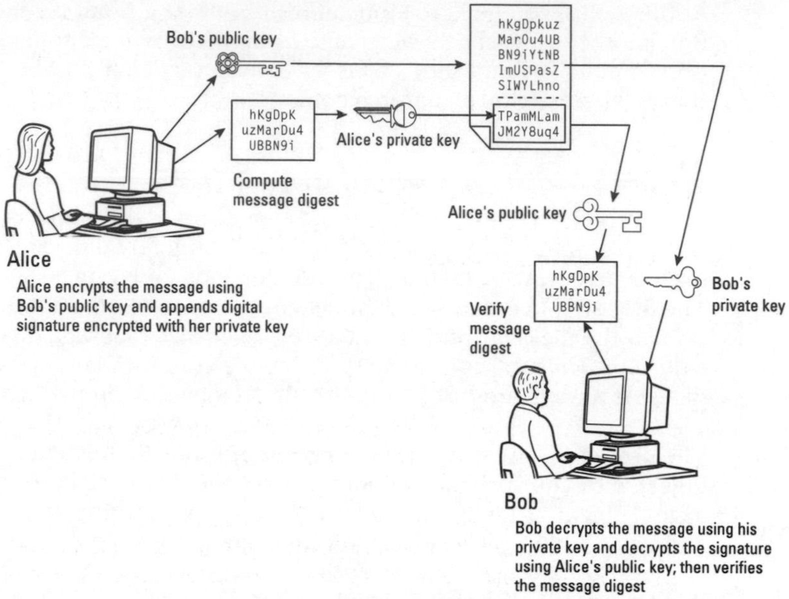

Figure 2-2: Alice can digitally sign her message so that Bob can tell it's really from her.

6. Bob computes the message digest of the message and compares it with what he got by decrypting the digital signature.
7. If the two message digests match, Bob can be sure that the message really came from Alice.

Using GPG

GPG includes the tools you need to use public key encryption and digital signatures. What you use is the `gpg` command. You can figure out how to use GPG gradually as you begin using encryption. I show you some of the typical tasks you may perform with GPG.

Generating the key pair

The steps for generating the key pairs go like this:

1. **Type** gpg --gen-key **command.**

   If you're using `gpg` for the first time, it creates a `.gnupg` directory in your home directory and a file named `gpg.conf` in that directory. Then GPG asks what kind of keys you want:

   ```
   Please select what kind of key you want:
      (1) DSA and ElGamal (default)
      (2) DSA (sign only)
      (4) RSA (sign only)
   Your selection?
   ```

2. **Press Enter for the default choice because it's good enough.**

   GPG then prompts you for the key size (the number of bits).

3. **Press Enter again to accept the default value of 1,024 bits.**

   GPG asks you when the keys expire. The default is to never expire.

4. **If the default is what you want (and why not?), press Enter.**
5. **When GPG asks if you really want the keys to never expire, press the Y key to confirm.**

   GPG prompts you for your name, your e-mail address, and finally a comment so that the key pair is associated with your name.

6. **Type each piece of requested information and press Enter.**
7. **When GPG gives you a chance to change the information or confirm it as is, confirm by typing** o **and pressing Enter.**

   GPG next prompts you for a passphrase that protects your private key.

8. **Type a long phrase that includes lower- and uppercase letters, numbers, and punctuation marks — the longer the better — and then press Enter.**

   Be careful to pick a passphrase that you can easily remember.

   GPG generates the keys. It may ask you to perform some work on the PC so that the random number generator can generate enough random numbers for the key-generation process.

Exchanging keys

To communicate with others, you have to give them your public key. You also have to get public keys from those who may send you a message (or someone who might sign a file and you want to verify the signature). GPG keeps the public keys in your key ring. (The *key ring* is simply the public keys stored in a file, but it sounds nice to call it a key ring because everybody has a key ring out in the real world and these are keys of a sort, right?) To list the keys in your key ring, type

```
gpg --list-keys
```

To send your public key to someone or place it on a Web site, you have to export the key to a file. The best way is to put the key in what GPG documentation calls an *ASCII-armored* format with a command like this:

```
gpg --armor --export naba@comcast.net > nabakey.asc
```

This command saves my public key in an ASCII-armored format (it basically looks like garbled text) in the file named `nabakey.asc`. Of course, you replace the e-mail address with your e-mail address (the one you used when you created the key) and the output filename to something different.

After you export the public key to a file, you can mail that file to others or place it on a Web site for use by others.

When you import a key from someone else, you typically get it in an ASCII-armored format as well. For example, if I have a `us-cert@us-cert.gov` GPG public key in a file named `uscertkey.asc`, I import it into my key ring with the following command:

```
gpg --import uscertkey.asc
```

Use the `gpg --list-keys` command to verify that the key is in your key ring. For example, here's what I see when I type **gpg --list-keys** on my system:

```
/home/naba/.gnupg/pubring.gpg
------------------------------
pub  1024D/397F3C69 2004-09-21 Naba Barkakati (author) <naba@comcast.net>
sub  1024g/AE72AD66 2004-09-21

pub  2048R/F0E187D0 2004-09-08 US-CERT Operations Key <us-cert@us-cert.gov>
```

The next step is to check the fingerprint of the new key. I type the following command to get the fingerprint of the US-CERT key:

```
gpg --fingerprint us-cert@us-cert.gov
```

GPG prints the fingerprint:

```
pub  2048R/F0E187D0 2004-09-08 US-CERT Operations Key <us-cert@us-cert.gov>
     Key fingerprint = 049F E3BA 240B 4CF1 3A76  06DC 1868 49EC F0E1 87D0
```

At this point, you need to verify the key fingerprint with someone at the US-CERT organization. For a large organization such as US-CERT, you can verify the fingerprint from the US-CERT Web page (`www.us-cert.gov/pgp/encryptmail.html`). I checked and the fingerprint matches what appears at the US-CERT Web site.

If you think the key fingerprint is good, you can sign the key and validate it. Here's the command you use to sign the key:

```
gpg --sign-key us-cert@us-cert.gov
```

GPG displays a message and prompts you on the level of key verification you have performed.

```
gpg: checking the trustdb
gpg: checking at depth 0 signed=0 ot(-/q/n/m/f/u)=0/0/0/0/0/1
pub  2048R/F0E187D0  created: 2004-09-08 expires: 2005-10-01 trust: -/-
(1). US-CERT Operations Key <us-cert@us-cert.gov>


pub  2048R/F0E187D0  created: 2004-09-08 expires: 2005-10-01 trust: -/-
 Primary key fingerprint: 049F E3BA 240B 4CF1 3A76  06DC 1868 49EC F0E1 87D0

     US-CERT Operations Key <us-cert@us-cert.gov>

This key is due to expire on 2005-10-01.
Do you want your signature to expire at the same time? (Y/n)
How carefully have you verified the key you are about to sign actually belongs
to the person named above?  If you don't know what to answer, enter "0".

   (0) I will not answer. (default)
   (1) I have not checked at all.
   (2) I have done casual checking.
   (3) I have done very careful checking.

Your selection? (enter '?' for more information):
```


After you answer and press Enter, GPG asks for confirmation and then prompts you for your passphrase. After that, GPG signs the key.

WARNING!

Because the key verification and signing is a potential weak link in GPG, be careful about what keys you sign. By signing a key, you basically say that you trust the key to be from that person or organization.

Signing a file

You may find signing files useful if you send out a file to someone and want to assure the recipient that no one tampered with the file and that you did in fact send the file. GPG makes signing a file very easy. You can compress and sign a file named `message` with the following command:

```
gpg -o message.sig -s message
```

To verify the signature, type

```
gpg --verify message.sig
```

To get back the original document, simply type

```
gpg -o message --decrypt message.sig
```

Sometimes you don't care about keeping a message secret, but you simply want to sign it to indicate that the message is from you. In such a case, you can generate and append a clear-text signature with the following command:

```
gpg -o message.asc --clearsign message
```

This command basically appends a clear-text signature to the text message. Here's a typical clear-text signature block:

```
-----BEGIN PGP SIGNATURE-----
Version: GnuPG v1.2.4 (GNU/Linux)

iD8DBQFAfdhOH/butdGSkSMRAo5VAJsFGSlwA3z6PQJwXZVSDCVMjphZFACeIYfB
YSZSM86EedATw/Hexeqa6TM=
=vyUl
-----END PGP SIGNATURE-----
```

When a message has a clear-text signature appended, you can use GPG to verify the signature with the following command:

```
gpg --verify message.asc
```

The last line of the output says that it's good signature.

Encrypting and decrypting documents

To encrypt a message meant for a recipient, you can use the `--encrypt` (or `-e`) GPG command. Here's how you might encrypt a message for US-CERT using its GPG key:

```
gpg -o message.gpg -e -r us-cert@us-cert.gov message
```

The message is encrypted using the US-CERT public key (without any signature, but you can add the signature with an `-s` command).

When US-CERT receives the `message.gpg` file, the recipient has to decrypt it using US-CERT's private key. Here's the command someone at US-CERT can use:

```
gpg -o message --decrypt message.gpg
```

GPG then prompts for the passphrase to unlock the US-CERT private key and then decrypts the message and saves the output in the file named `message`.

If you simply want to encrypt a file and no one else has to decrypt the file, you can use GPG to perform what is called *symmetric encryption*. In this case, you provide a passphrase to encrypt the file with the following GPG command:

```
gpg -o secret.gpg -c somefile
```

GPG prompts you for the passphrase and asks you to repeat the passphrase (to make sure that you didn't mistype anything). Then GPG encrypts the file using a key generated from the passphrase.

To decrypt a file encrypted with a symmetric key, type

```
gpg -o myfile --decrypt secret.gpg
```

GPG prompts you for the passphrase. If you enter the correct passphrase, GPG decrypts the file and saves the output (in this example) in the file named `myfile`.

Monitoring System Security

Even if you secure your system, you have to monitor the log files periodically for signs of intrusion. You may want to install the Tripwire software, a great tool for detecting any changes made to the system files so that you can monitor the integrity of critical system files and directories. Your Linux system probably does not come with the Tripwire package. To use Tripwire, you have to download it from `www.tripwire.org/downloads/index.php`. You should know that you have to download the source tarball (a compressed archive of source files) and then build Tripwire. (Book V, Chapter 4 provides more information on how to build software packages from source files.) After you build and install Tripwire, you can configure it to monitor any changes to specified system files and directories on your system.

DISTRIBUTION SPECIFIC

In Debian, type **apt-get install tripwire** to download and install Tripwire.

Periodically examine the log files in the `/var/log` directory and its subdirectories. Many Linux applications, including some servers, write log information using the logging capabilities of `syslogd`. On Linux systems, the log files written by `syslogd` reside in the `/var/log` directory. Make sure that only the `root` user can read and write these files.

REMEMBER

The `syslogd` configuration file is `/etc/syslog.conf`. The default configuration of `syslogd` generates the necessary log files; however, if you want to examine and understand the configuration file, type **man syslog.conf** for more information.

Chapter 3: Improving Network Security

In This Chapter

- Securing Internet services
- Using Secure Shell (SSH) for secure remote logins
- Setting up simple firewalls
- Enabling packet filtering on your Linux system

To secure your Linux system, you have to pay attention to both host security and network security. The distinction between the two types of security is somewhat arbitrary because securing the network involves fixing up things on the host that relate to what Internet services your system offers. In this chapter, I explain how you can secure the Internet services (mostly by not offering unnecessary services), how you can use a firewall to stop unwanted network packets from reaching your network, and how to use Secure Shell for secure remote logins.

Securing Internet Services

For an Internet-connected Linux system (or even one on a TCP/IP LAN that's not connected to the Internet), a significant threat is the possibility that someone could use one of many Internet services to gain access to your system. Each service — such as mail, Web, or FTP — requires running a server program that responds to client requests arriving over the TCP/IP network. Some of these server programs have weaknesses that can allow an outsider to log in to your system — maybe with `root` privileges. Luckily, Linux comes with some facilities that you can use to make the Internet services more secure.

Potential intruders can employ a *port-scanning tool* — a program that attempts to establish a TCP/IP connection at a port and to look for a response — to check which Internet servers are running on your system. Then, to gain access to your system, the intruders can potentially exploit any known weaknesses of one or more services.

Turning off standalone services

To provide Internet services such as Web, mail, and FTP, your Linux system has to run server programs that listen to incoming TCP/IP network requests. Some of these servers are started when your system boots, and they run all the time. Such servers are called *standalone servers*. The Web server and mail server are examples of standalone servers.

Another server, called `xinetd`, starts other servers that are configured to work under `xinetd`. Some Linux systems use the `inetd` server, instead of `xinetd` to start other servers.

Some servers can be configured to run standalone or under a super server such as `xinetd`. For example, the `vsftpd` FTP server can be configured to run standalone or to run under the control of `xinetd`.

In Debian and Xandros, use the `update-rc.d` command to turn off standalone servers. To get a clue about the available services, type **ls /etc/init.d** and look at all the script files designed to turn services on or off. You have to use these filenames when you want to turn a service on or off. For example, to turn off Samba service, type **update-rc.d -f samba remove**. If the service was already running, type **invoke-rc.d samba stop** to stop the service. You can use the `invoke-rc.d` command to stop any service in a similar manner.

In Fedora Core and SUSE, you can turn the standalone servers on or off by using the `chkconfig` command. You can get the names of the service scripts by typing **ls /etc/init.d**. Then you can turn off a service (for example, Samba) by typing **chkconfig --del samba**. (In Fedora Core, the Samba service script is named `smb`, so you have to type **chkconfig --del smb**.) If the service was already running, type **/etc/init.d/samba stop** to stop the service. You can run scripts from the `/etc/init.d` directory with the `stop` argument to stop any service in a similar manner.

Configuring the Internet super server

In addition to standalone servers such as a Web server or mail server, there are other servers — `inetd` or `xinetd` — that you have to configure separately. These servers are called *Internet super servers* because they can start other servers on demand.

Type **ps ax | grep inetd** to see which Internet super server — `inetd` or `xinetd` — your system runs.

The `inetd` server is configured through the `/etc/inetd.conf` file. You can disable a service by locating the appropriate line in that file and commenting it out by placing a hash mark (#) at the beginning of the line. After saving the configuration file, type **/etc/init.d/inetd restart** to restart the `inetd` server.

Configuring the xinetd server is a bit more complicated. The xinetd server reads a configuration file named /etc/xinetd.conf at startup. This file, in turn, refers to configuration files stored in the /etc/xinetd.d directory. The configuration files in /etc/xinetd.d tell xinetd which ports to listen to and which server to start for each port. Type **ls /etc/xinetd.d** to see a list of the files in the /etc/xinetd.d directory on your system. Each file represents a service that xinetd can start. To turn off any of these services, edit the file in a text editor and add a disable = yes line in the file. After you make any changes to the xinetd configuration files, you must restart the xinetd server; otherwise, the changes don't take effect. To restart the xinetd server, type **/etc/init.d/xinetd restart**. This command stops the xinetd server and then starts it again. When it restarts, it reads the configuration files, and the changes take effect.

Configuring TCP wrapper security

A security feature of both inetd and xinetd is their use of the TCP wrapper to start various services. The *TCP wrapper* is a block of code that provides an access-control facility for Internet services, acting like a protective package for your message. The TCP wrapper can start other services, such as FTP and TELNET; but before starting a service, it consults the /etc/hosts.allow file to see whether the host requesting service is allowed that service. If nothing appears in /etc/hosts.allow about that host, the TCP wrapper checks the /etc/hosts.deny file to see if it denies the service. If both files are empty, the TCP wrapper provides access to the requested service.

Here are the steps to follow to tighten the access to the services that inted or xinetd are configured to start:

1. **Use a text editor to edit the /etc/hosts.deny file, adding the following line into that file:**

   ```
   ALL:ALL
   ```

   This setting denies all hosts access to any Internet services on your system.

2. **Edit the /etc/hosts.allow file and add to it the names of hosts that can access services on your system.**

   For example, to enable only hosts from the 192.168.1.0 network and the localhost (IP address 127.0.0.1) to access the services on your system, place the following line in the /etc/hosts.allow file:

   ```
   ALL: 192.168.1.0/255.255.255.0 127.0.0.1
   ```

3. **If you want to permit access to a specific Internet service to a specific remote host, you can do so by using the following syntax for a line in /etc/hosts.allow:**

   ```
   server_program_name: hosts
   ```

Here *server_program_name* is the name of the server program, and *hosts* is a comma-separated list of hosts that can access the service. You may also write *hosts* as a network address or an entire domain name, such as .mycompany.com.

Using Secure Shell (SSH) for Remote Logins

Linux comes with the *Open Secure Shell* (OpenSSH) software, a suite of programs that provides a secure replacement for the Berkeley r commands: rlogin (remote login), rsh (remote shell), and rcp (remote copy). OpenSSH uses public-key cryptography to authenticate users and to encrypt the communication between two hosts, so users can securely log in from remote systems and copy files securely.

In this section, I briefly describe how to use the OpenSSH software in Linux. To find out more about OpenSSH and read the latest news about it, visit www.openssh.com or www.openssh.org.

The OpenSSH software is installed during Linux installation. Table 3-1 lists the main components of the OpenSSH software.

Table 3-1 Components of the OpenSSH Software

Component	*Description*
/usr/sbin/sshd	This Secure Shell daemon must run on a host if you want users on remote systems to use the ssh client to log in securely. When a connection from an ssh client arrives, sshd performs authentication using public-key cryptography and establishes an encrypted communication link with the ssh client.
/usr/bin/ssh	Users can run this Secure Shell client to log in to a host that is running sshd. Users can also use ssh to execute a command on another host.
/usr/bin/slogin	A symbolic link to /usr/bin/ssh.
/usr/bin/scp	The secure-copy program that works like rcp, but securely. The scp program uses ssh for data transfer and provides the same authentication and security as ssh.
/usr/bin/ssh-keygen	You use this program to generate the public- and private-key pairs you need for the public-key cryptography used in OpenSSH. The ssh-keygen program can generate key pairs for both RSA and DSA (Digital Signature Algorithm) authentication. (The RSA algorithm is named after the initials of Ron Rivest, Adi Shamir, and Leonard Adleman — the developers of that algorithm.)

Component	Description
`/etc/ssh/sshd_config`	This configuration file for the `sshd` server specifies many parameters for `sshd` — including the port to listen to, the protocol to use (there are two versions of SSH protocols, SSH1 and SSH2, both supported by OpenSSH), and the location of other files.
`/etc/ssh/ssh_config`	This configuration file is for the `ssh` client. Each user can also have a `ssh` configuration file named `config` in the `.ssh` subdirectory of the user's home directory.

OpenSSH uses public-key encryption where the sender and receiver both have a pair of keys — a public key and a private key. The public keys are freely distributed, and each party knows the other's public key. The sender encrypts data by using the recipient's public key. Only the recipient's private key can then decrypt the data.

To use OpenSSH, you first need to start the `sshd` server and then generate the host keys. Here's how:

✦ If you want to support SSH-based remote logins on a host, start the `sshd` server on your system. Type **ps ax | grep sshd** to see if the server is already running. If not, log in as `root`, and turn on the SSH service.

  In Fedora Core and SUSE, type **chkconfig --level 35 sshd on**. In Debian and Xandros, type **update-rc.d ssh defaults**. To start the `sshd` server immediately, type **/etc/init.d/ssh start** in Debian and Xandros or type **/etc/init.d/sshd start** in Fedora Core and SUSE.

✦ Generate the host keys with the following command:

```
ssh-keygen -d -f /etc/ssh/ssh_host_key -N ''
```

  The `-d` flag causes the `ssh-keygen` program to generate DSA keys, which the SSH2 protocol uses. If you see a message saying that the file `/etc/ssh/ssh_host_key` already exists, that means that the key pairs were generated during Linux installation. You can then use the existing file without having to regenerate the keys.

A user who wants to log in using `ssh` must also generate the public- and private-key pair. For example, here is what I do so that I can log in from another system on my Linux system using SSH:

1. I type the following command to generate the DSA keys for use with SSH2:

```
ssh-keygen -d
```

   I am prompted for a passphrase and the last message informs me that my public key is saved in `/home/naba/.ssh/id_dsa.pub`.

2. I copy my public key — the /home/naba/.ssh/id_dsa.pub file — to the remote system and save it as the ~/.ssh/authorized_keys2 file. (This name refers to the authorized_keys2 file in the .ssh subdirectory of the other system, assuming that the remote system is also another Linux system.) Note that the 2 in the name of the authorized_keys2 file refers to the SSH2 protocol.
3. To log in to my account on my Linux system (with hostname lnbp200), I type the following command on the remote system:

   ```
   ssh lnbp200 -l naba
   ```

4. When prompted for my password on the lnbp200 host, I enter the password. I can also log in to this account with the following equivalent command:

   ```
   ssh naba@lnbp200
   ```

If I simply want to copy a file securely from the lnbp200 system, I can use scp like this:

```
scp lnbp200:/etc/ssh/ssh_config .
```

This command securely copies the /etc/ssh/ssh_config file from the lnbp200 host to the system from which I type the command.

Setting Up Simple Firewalls

A *firewall* is a network device or host with two or more network interfaces — one connected to the protected internal network and the other connected to unprotected networks, such as the Internet. The firewall controls access to and from the protected internal network.

If you connect an internal network directly to the Internet, you have to make sure that every system on the internal network is properly secured — which can be nearly impossible because only one careless user can render the entire internal network vulnerable. A firewall is a single point of connection to the Internet: You can direct all your efforts toward making that firewall system a daunting barrier to unauthorized external users. Essentially, a firewall is like a protective fence that keeps unwanted external data and software out and sensitive internal data and software in. (See Figure 3-1.)

The firewall runs software that examines the network packets arriving at its network interfaces and takes appropriate action based on a set of rules. The idea is to define these rules so that they allow only authorized network traffic to flow between the two interfaces. Configuring the firewall involves setting up the rules properly. A configuration strategy is to reject all network traffic and then enable only a limited set of network packets to go through the firewall. The authorized network traffic would include the connections necessary to enable internal users to do things such as visiting Web sites and receiving electronic mail.

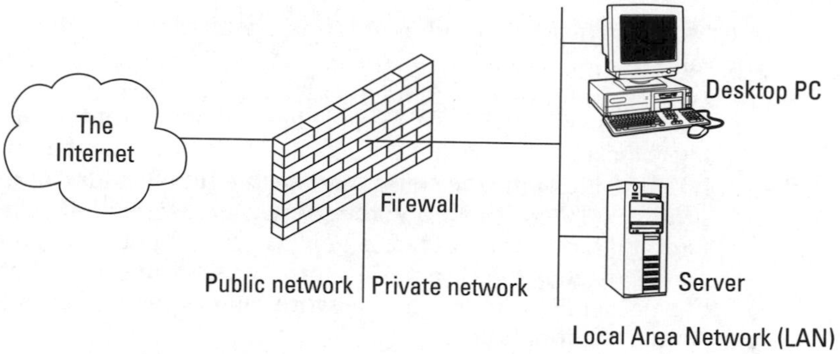

Figure 3-1: A firewall protects hosts on a private network from the Internet.

To be useful, a firewall has the following general characteristics:

- ✦ It must control the flow of packets between the Internet and the internal network.
- ✦ It must *not* provide dynamic routing because dynamic routing tables are subject to route *spoofing* — use of fake routes by intruders. Instead, the firewall uses static routing tables (which you can set up with the `route` command on Linux systems).
- ✦ It must not allow any external user to log in as `root`. That way, even if the firewall system is compromised, the intruder is blocked from using `root` privileges from a remote login.
- ✦ It must be kept in a physically secure location.
- ✦ It must distinguish between packets that come from the Internet and packets that come from the internal protected network. This feature allows the firewall to reject packets that come from the Internet, but have the IP address of a trusted system on the internal network.
- ✦ It acts as the SMTP mail gateway for the internal network. Set up the sendmail software so that all outgoing mail appears to come from the firewall system.
- ✦ Its user accounts are limited to a few user accounts for those internal users who need access to external systems. External users who need access to the internal network should use SSH for remote login (see discussion of SSH earlier in this chapter).
- ✦ It keeps a log of all system activities, such as successful and unsuccessful login attempts.

- It provides DNS name-lookup service to the outside world to resolve any host names that are known to the outside world.
- It provides good performance so that it doesn't hinder the internal users' access to specific Internet services (such as HTTP and FTP).

A firewall can take many different forms. Here are three common forms of a firewall:

- **Packet filter firewall:** This simple firewall uses a router capable of filtering (blocking or allowing) packets according to a number of their characteristics, including the source and destination IP addresses, the network protocol (TCP or UDP), and the source and destination port numbers. Packet filter firewalls are usually placed at the outermost boundary with an untrusted network, and they form the first line of defense. An example of a packet filter firewall is a network router that employs filter rules to screen network traffic.

  Packet filter firewalls are fast and flexible, but they cannot prevent attacks that exploit application-specific vulnerabilities or functions. They can log only a minimal amount of information, such as source IP address, destination IP address, and traffic type. Also, they are vulnerable to attacks and exploits that take advantage of flaws within the TCP/IP protocol, such as IP address spoofing, which involves altering the address information in network packets in order to make packets appear to come from a trusted IP address.
- **Stateful inspection firewall:** In this case, the firewall keeps track of network connections that network applications are using. When an application on an internal system uses a network connection to create a session with a remote system, a port is also opened on the internal system. This port receives network traffic from the remote system. For successful connections, packet filter firewalls must permit incoming packets from the remote system. Opening up many ports to incoming traffic creates a risk of intrusion by unauthorized users who abuse the expected conventions of network protocols such as TCP. Stateful inspection firewalls solve this problem by creating a table of outbound network connections, along with each session's corresponding internal port. This "state table" is then used to validate any inbound packets. This stateful inspection is more secure than a packet filter because it tracks internal ports individually rather than opening all internal ports for external access.
- **Application-proxy gateway firewall:** This firewall acts as an intermediary between internal applications that attempt to communicate with external servers such as a Web server. For example, a Web proxy receives requests for external Web pages from Web browser clients running inside the firewall and relays them to the exterior Web server as though the firewall was the requesting Web client. The external Web server responds to

the firewall and the firewall forwards the response to the inside client as though the firewall was the Web server. No direct network connection is ever made from the inside client host to the external Web server.

Application-proxy gateway firewalls have some advantages over packet filter firewalls and stateful inspection firewalls. First, application-proxy gateway firewalls examine the entire network packet rather than only the network addresses and ports. This enables these firewalls to provide more extensive logging capabilities than packet filters or stateful inspection firewalls. Another advantage is that application-proxy gateway firewalls can authenticate users directly, while packet filter firewalls and stateful inspection firewalls normally authenticate users based on the IP address of the system (that is, source, destination, and protocol type). Given that network addresses can be easily spoofed, the authentication capabilities of application-proxy gateway firewall are superior to those found in packet filter or stateful inspection firewalls.

The advanced functionality of application-proxy gateway firewalls, however, results in some disadvantages when compared with packet filter or stateful inspection firewalls. First, because of the "full packet awareness" found in application-proxy gateways, the firewall is forced to spend significant time reading and interpreting each packet. Therefore, application proxy gateway firewalls are generally not well suited to high-bandwidth or real-time applications. To reduce the load on the firewall, a dedicated proxy server can be used to secure less time-sensitive services, such as e-mail and most Web traffic. Another disadvantage is that application-proxy gateway firewalls are often limited in terms of support for new network applications and protocols. An individual, application-specific proxy agent is required for each type of network traffic that needs to go through the firewall. Most vendors of application-proxy gateways provide generic proxy agents to support undefined network protocols or applications. However, those generic agents tend to negate many of the strengths of the application-proxy gateway architecture, and they simply allow traffic to "tunnel" through the firewall.

Most firewalls implement a combination of these firewall functionalities. For example, many vendors of packet filter firewalls or stateful inspection firewalls have also implemented basic application-proxy functionality to offset some of the weaknesses associated with their firewalls. In most cases, these vendors implement application proxies to provide better logging of network traffic and stronger user authentication. Nearly all major firewall vendors have introduced multiple firewall functions into their products in some manner.

TIP

In a large organization, you may also have to isolate smaller internal networks from the corporate network. You can set up such internal firewalls the same way that you set up Internet firewalls.

Using NATs

Network Address Translation (NAT) is an effective tool that enables you to "hide" the network addresses of an internal network behind a firewall. In essence, NAT allows an organization to use private network addresses behind a firewall while still maintaining the ability to connect to external systems through the firewall.

There are three methods for implementing NAT:

- **Static:** In static NAT, each internal system on the private network has a corresponding external, routable IP address associated with it. This particular technique is seldom used because unique IP addresses are in short supply.
- **Hiding:** With hiding NAT, all systems behind a firewall share the same external, routable IP address, while the internal systems use private IP addresses. Thus, with a hiding NAT, a number of systems behind a firewall will still appear to be a single system.
- **Port Address Translation:** With port address translation, it is possible to place hosts behind a firewall system and still make them selectively accessible to external users.

In terms of strengths and weaknesses, each type of NAT — static, hiding, or port address translation — is applicable in certain situations; the variable is the amount of design flexibility offered by each type. Static NAT offers the most flexibility, but it is not always practical because of the shortage of IP addresses. Hiding NAT technology is seldom used because port address translation offers additional features. Port address translation is often the most convenient and secure solution.

Enabling packet filtering on your Linux system

Your Linux system comes with built-in packet-filtering software in the form of something called `netfilter` that's in the Linux kernel. All you have to do is use the `iptables` command to set up the rules for what happens to the packets based on the IP addresses in their header and the network connection type.

TIP

To find out more about `netfilter` and `iptables`, visit the documentation section of the `netfilter` Web site at `www.netfilter.org/documentation`.

The built-in packet-filtering capability is handy when you don't have a dedicated firewall between your Linux system and the Internet. This is the case, for example, when you connect your Linux system to the Internet through a DSL or cable modem. You can essentially have a packet-filtering firewall inside your Linux system, sitting between the kernel and the applications.

Using the security level configuration tool

Some Linux distributions, such as Fedora Core and SUSE, include GUI tools to turn on a packet filtering firewall.

In Fedora Core, you can turn on different levels of packet filtering through the graphical Security Level Configuration tool. To run the tool, log in as `root` and select Main Menu⇨System Settings⇨Security Level. The Security Level Configuration dialog box appears, as shown in Figure 3-2.

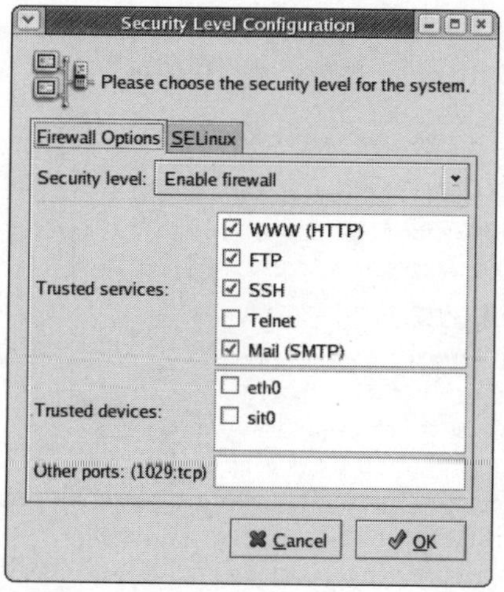

Figure 3-2: In Fedora Core, you can set up packet filtering with this tool.

From the Firewall Options tab in the Security Level Configuration dialog box (refer to Figure 3-2), you can select two predefined levels of simple firewalling (more precisely, packet filtering) with the Security Level Configuration tool:

- **Disable Firewall:** Does not perform any filtering, and all connections are allowed. (You can still turn off Internet services by not running the servers or disabling them in the `xinetd` configuration files.) This security level is fine if your Linux system is inside a protected local area network or if you have a separate firewall device.
- **Enable Firewall:** Turns on packet filtering. You can then select the services that you want to allow and the network devices that you trust.

You can allow incoming packets meant for specific Internet services such as SSH, TELNET, and FTP. If you select a network interface such as `eth0` (the first Ethernet card) as trusted, all network traffic over that interface is allowed without any filtering.

Fedora Core's Security Level Configuration tool has another tab — the SELinux tab (refer to Figure 3-2) — that enables you to turn on or off the mandatory access control provided by SELinux.

In SUSE, to set up a firewall, select Main Menu➪System➪YaST. In the YaST Control Center window that appears, click Security and Users on the left-hand side of the window and then click Firewall on the right-hand side. YaST opens a window (see Figure 3-3) that you can use to configure the firewall in four steps.

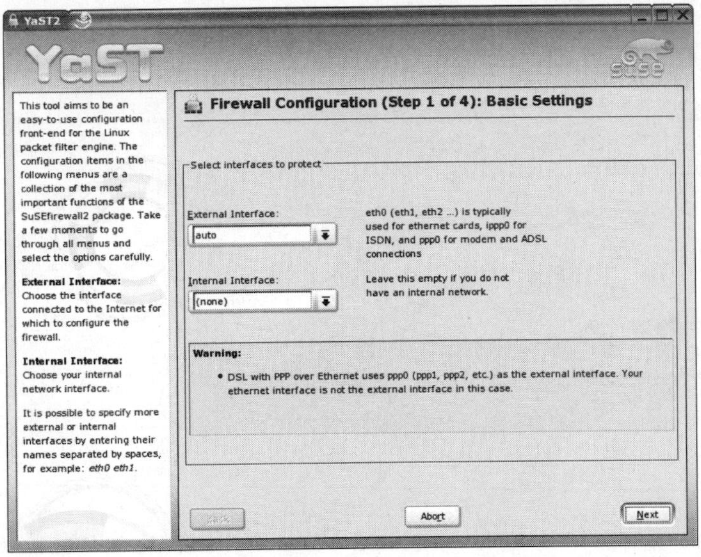

Figure 3-3: In SUSE, configure firewall in four steps through this GUI tool.

The first step selects the network interface (by device name such as `eth0`, `ppp0`, and so on). In Step 2, you select services (such as HTTP and FTP) that your SUSE system should be allowed to provide. Step 3 is for configuring a few more features such as forwarding packets between network interfaces and for not allowing any services except those explicitly enabled in Step 2. Finally, in Step 4, you turn on different levels of logging. (For example, logging all dropped packets that attempted connection at specific ports).

Using the iptables command

The GUI firewall configuration tools use the `iptables` command to implement the firewall. If your Linux system does not have a GUI tool, you can use `iptables` directly to configure firewalling on your Linux system. I introduce you to `iptables` in this section.

Using the `iptables` command is somewhat complex. `iptables` uses the concept of a chain, which is a sequence of rules. Each rule says what to do with a packet if the header contains certain information (such as the source or destination IP address). If a rule does not apply, `iptables` consults the next rule in the chain. By default, there are three chains:

- **INPUT chain:** The first set of rules against which packets are tested. The packets continue to the next chain only if the input chain does not specify `DROP` or `REJECT`.
- **FORWARD chain:** Contains the rules that apply to packets attempting to pass through this system to another system. (When you use your Linux system as a router between your LAN and the Internet, for example.)
- **OUTPUT chain:** Includes the rules applied to packets before they are sent out (either to another network or to an application).

Figure 3-4 shows a high-level depiction of how IP packets are processed by `iptables` through these three chains.

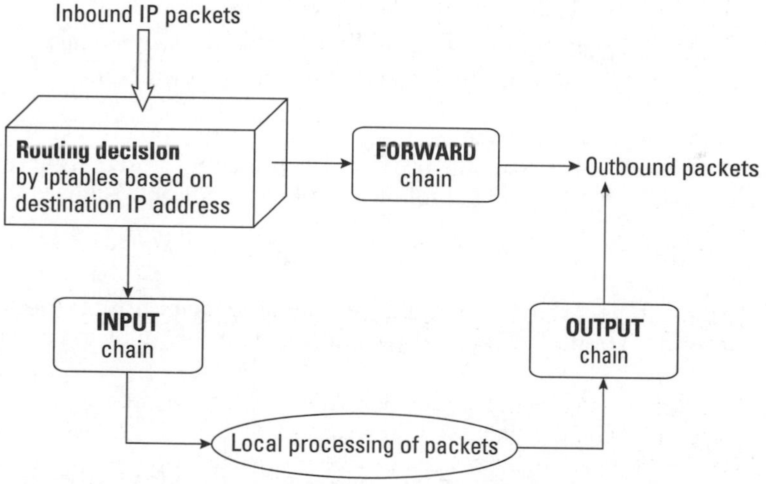

Figure 3-4: Simplified view of `iptables` processing chains.

When an incoming packet arrives, the kernel uses `iptables` to make a routing decision based on the destination IP address of the packet. If the packet is for this server, the kernel passes the packet to the INPUT chain. If the packet satisfies all the rules in the INPUT chain, then the packet is processed by local processes such as an Internet server that is listening for packets of this type.

If the kernel had IP forwarding enabled and the packet has a destination IP address of a different network, the kernel passes the packet to the FORWARD chain. If the packet satisfies the rules in the FORWARD chain, it's sent out to the other network. If the kernel does not have IP forwarding enabled and the packet's destination address is not for this server, then the packet is dropped.

If the local processing programs that receive the input packets want to send network packets out, then those packets pass through the OUTPUT chain. If those packets are accepted by the OUTPUT chain, they are sent out to the specified destination network.

You can view the current chains, add rules to the existing chains, or create new chains of rules by using the `iptables` command. When you view the current chains, you can also save them to a file. For example, if you have done nothing else and your system has no firewall configured, typing **iptables -L** command should show the following:

```
Chain INPUT (policy ACCEPT)
target     prot opt source               destination

Chain FORWARD (policy ACCEPT)
target     prot opt source               destination

Chain OUTPUT (policy ACCEPT)
target     prot opt source               destination
```

In this case, all three chains — `INPUT`, `FORWARD`, and `OUTPUT` — show the same `ACCEPT` policy, which means everything is wide-open.

If you're setting up a packet filter, the first thing you do is specify the packets that you want to accept. For example, to accept packets from the 192.168.0.0 network address, add the following rule to the input chain:

```
iptables -A INPUT -s 192.168.0.0/24 -j ACCEPT
```

Now add a rule to drop everything except local loopback (the `lo` network interface) traffic and stop all forwarding with the following commands:

```
iptables -A INPUT -i ! lo -j REJECT
iptables -A FORWARD -j REJECT
```

The first `iptables` command, for example, appends to the input chain (`-A INPUT`) the rule that if the packet does not come from the `lo` interface (`-i ! lo`), `iptables` rejects the packet (`-j REJECT`).

Before rejecting all other packets, you may also add more rules to each INPUT chain to allow specific packets in. You can select packets to accept or reject based on many different parameters, such as IP addresses, protocol types (TCP, UDP), network interface, and port numbers.

You can do all sorts of specialized packet filtering with `iptables`. For example, suppose you are setting up a Web server and you want to accept packets meant for only HTTP (port 80) and secure shell (SSH) services. The secure shell service (port 22) is for you to securely log in and administer the server. Suppose the server's IP address is 192.168.0.10. Here is how you might set up the rules for this server:

```
iptables -P INPUT DROP
iptables -A INPUT -s 0/0 -d 192.168.0.10 -p tcp --dport 80 -j ACCEPT
iptables -A INPUT -s 0/0 -d 192.168.0.10 -p tcp --dport 22 -j ACCEPT
```

In this case, the first rule sets up the default policy of the INPUT chain to DROP, which means that if none of the specific rules match, the packet will be dropped. The next two rules say that packets addressed to 192.168.0.10 and meant for ports 80 and 22 are accepted.

WARNING!

Don't type `iptables` commands from a remote login session. A rule that begins denying packets from all addresses can also stop what you type from reaching the system; once that happens, you may have no way of accessing the system over the network. To avoid unpleasant surprises, always type `iptables` rules at the console — the keyboard and monitor connected directly to your Linux PC that is running the packet filter. If you want to delete all filtering rules in a hurry, type **iptables -F** to flush them. To change the default policy for the INPUT chain (see Figure 3-4) to ACCEPT, type **iptables -t filter -P INPUT ACCEPT**. This causes `iptables` to accept all incoming packets by default.

REMEMBER

I don't provide all the details of the `iptables` commands in this section. Suffice it to say that you can type **man iptables** to read a summary of the commands. You can also read about `netfilter` and `iptables` at `www.iptables.org`.

After you define the rules by using the `iptables` command, they are in the memory and are gone when you reboot the system. To save them, use the `iptables-save` command to store the rules in a file. For example, you can save the rules in a file named `iptables.rules` by using the following command:

```
iptables-save > iptables.rules
```

Here's a listing of the `iptables.rules` file, generated on a Fedora Core system:

```
# Generated by iptables-save v1.2.11 on Fri Sep 24 08:25:36 2004
*filter
:INPUT ACCEPT [8462:758156]
:FORWARD ACCEPT [0:0]
:OUTPUT ACCEPT [331623:35762727]
:RH-Firewall-1-INPUT - [0:0]
-A INPUT -s 192.168.0.0/255.255.255.0 -j ACCEPT
-A INPUT -i ! lo -j REJECT --reject-with icmp-port-unreachable
-A FORWARD -j REJECT --reject-with icmp-port-unreachable
COMMIT
# Completed on Fri Sep 24 08:25:36 2004
```

In case you're curious, these rules correspond to the following `iptables` commands I use to configure the filter:

```
iptables -A INPUT -s 192.168.0.0/24 -j ACCEPT
iptables -A INPUT -i ! lo -j REJECT
iptables -A FORWARD -j REJECT
```

If you want to load these saved rules into `iptables`, use the following command:

```
iptables-restore < iptables.rules
```

Unless you use `iptables` commands directly to configure a firewall, the exact details of the firewall configuration depend on any GUI utility that your Linux distribution provides for setting up the firewall. For example, the SUSE firewall utility changes the default policy for the INPUT and FORWARD chains (see Figure 3-4) from ACCEPT to DROP, which means that in the absence of any rules, all packets are dropped. Contrast this to Fedora Core's firewall utility that leaves the default policy for INPUT and FORWARD chains as ACCEPT. This means that if no rules are defined, Fedora Core would accept a packet. You should be aware of these differences when you use the firewall utilities in various Linux distributions.

On a Fedora Core system, the process of saving and restoring firewall rules is automated by saving the `iptables` rules in the file `/etc/sysconfig/iptables` and by enabling `iptables` with the following command:

```
chkconfig iptables on
```

That ensures the `/etc/init.d/iptables start` command executes at the system startup. The `/etc/init.d/iptables` script then runs the `/sbin/iptables-restore` command to restore the `iptables` rules from the `/etc/sysconfig/iptables` file.

Chapter 4: Performing Computer Security Audits

In This Chapter

- ✔ **Understanding computer security audits**
- ✔ **Learning a security test methodology**
- ✔ **Reviewing host and network security**
- ✔ **Exploring security testing tools**

You see the term "audit" and you think tax audit, right? Well, there are many different types of audits, and one of them is a *computer security audit*. The purpose of a computer security audit is to basically test your system and network security. For larger organizations, an independent auditor (much like the auditing of financial statements) can do the security audit. If you have only a few Linux systems or a small network, you can do the security audit as a self-assessment, just to figure out if you're doing everything okay or not.

In this chapter, I explain how to perform computer security audits and show you a number of free tools and resources to help you test your system's security.

Understanding Security Audits

An *audit* is simply an independent assessment of whatever it is you're auditing. So a *computer security audit* is an independent assessment of computer security. If someone is conducting a computer security audit of your organization, he or she focuses typically on two areas:

- ✦ Independent verification of whether your organization is complying with its existing policies and procedures for computer security. This part is the non-technical aspect of the security audit.
- ✦ Independent testing of how effective your security controls (any hardware and software mechanisms you use to secure the system) are. This part is the technical aspect of the security audit.

Why do you need security audits? For the same reason you need financial audits — mainly to verify that everything is being done the way it's supposed to be done. For public as well as private organizations, management may want independent security audits to assure themselves that their security is A-okay. Irrespective of your organization's size, you can always perform security audits on your own, either to prepare for independent security audits or simply to know that you're doing everything right.

No matter whether you have independent security audits or a self-assessment, here are some of the benefits you get from security audits:

- Periodic risk assessments that consider internal and external threats to systems and data.
- Periodic testing of the effectiveness of security policies, security controls, and techniques.
- Identification of any significant deficiencies in your system's security (so you know what to fix).
- In the case of self-assessments, preparation for any annual independent security testing that your organization might have to face.

Non-technical aspects of security audits

The non-technical side of computer security audits focuses on your organization-wide security framework. The audit examines how well the organization has set up and implemented the policies, plans, and procedures for computer security. Some of the items to be verified include

- Evidence that risks are periodically assessed.
- The existence of an entity-wide security program plan.
- A security program-management structure is in place.
- Computer security responsibilities are clearly assigned.
- Effective security-related personnel policies are in place.
- The security program's effectiveness is monitored and changes are made when needed.

As you may expect, the non-technical aspects of the security audit involve reviewing documents and interviewing appropriate individuals to find out how the organization manages computer security. Of course, for a small organization or a home PC, expecting plans and procedures in documents is ridiculous. In those cases, all you have to make sure is that you have some technical controls in place to secure your system and your network connection.

Technical aspects of security audits

The technical side of computer security audits focuses on testing the technical controls that secure your hosts and network. The testing involves determining

- **How well the host is secured.** Are all operating system patches applied? Are the file permissions set correctly? Are user accounts protected? Are file changes monitored? Are log files monitored? And so on.
- **How well the network is secured.** Are unnecessary Internet services turned off? Is a firewall installed? Are remote logins secured with tools such as SSH? Are TCP wrapper access controls used? And so on.

Typically, security experts use automated tools to perform these two security reviews for both individual hosts and the entire network.

Implementing a Security Test Methodology

A key element of a computer security audit is a security test that checks the technical mechanisms used to secure a host and the network. The security test methodology follows these high-level steps:

1. Take stock of the organization's networks, hosts, network devices (routers, switches, firewalls, and so on), and how the network connects to the Internet.
2. If there are many hosts and network connections, determine what are the important hosts and network devices that need to be tested. The importance of a host depends on the kinds of applications it runs. For example, a host that runs the corporate database would be more important than the hosts that serve as the desktop systems.
3. Test the hosts individually. Typically, this step involves logging in as a system administrator and then checking various aspects of host security, from passwords to system log files.
4. Test the network. This step is usually done by attempting to break through the network defenses from another system on the Internet. If there is a firewall, the testing checks that the firewall is indeed configured correctly.
5. Analyze the test results of both host and network tests to determine the vulnerabilities and risks.

Each of the two types of testing — host and network — focuses on three areas that comprise overall computer security:

- **Prevention:** Includes the mechanisms (non-technical and technical) that help prevent attacks on the system and the network.
- **Detection:** Refers to techniques such as monitoring log files, checking file integrity, and intrusion detection systems that can detect when someone is about to or has already broken into your system.
- **Response:** Includes the steps such as reporting an incident to authorities and restoring important files from backup that you perform when a computer security incident occurs.

For host and network security, each of these areas has some overlaps. For example, prevention mechanisms for host security (such as good passwords or file permissions) can also provide network security. Nevertheless, thinking in terms of the three areas — prevention, detection, and response — does help.

Before you can think of prevention, however, you have to know the types of problems you're trying to prevent. In other words, what are the common security vulnerabilities? The prevention and detection steps typically depend on what these vulnerabilities are.

Some common computer vulnerabilities

The specific tests of the host and network security depend on the common vulnerabilities. Basically, the idea is to check if a host or a network has the vulnerabilities that crackers are most likely to exploit.

Online resources on computer vulnerabilities

Several online resources identify and categorize computer security vulnerabilities:

- **SANS Institute** publishes a list of the top 20 most critical Internet security vulnerabilities at `www.sans.org/top20`.
- **CVE** (Common Vulnerabilities and Exposures) is a list of standardized names of vulnerabilities. For more information on CVE, see `cve.mitre.org`. (The list has over 7,200 unique names of vulnerabilities.) Using the CVE name to describe vulnerabilities is common practice.
- **ICAT Metabase** is a searchable index of information on computer vulnerabilities, published by the National Institute of Standards and Technology (NIST), a United States government agency. The ICAT vulnerability index is online at `icat.nist.gov`. ICAT lists over 6,900 vulnerabilities, and it provides links to vulnerability advisory and patch information for each vulnerability. ICAT also has a top 10 list that lists the vulnerabilities that were most queried during the past year.

Typical top 20 computer vulnerabilities

The SANS Top 20 Internet security vulnerabilities list includes two types of vulnerabilities — Windows and UNIX. Of these, the UNIX vulnerabilities are relevant to Linux. Table 4-1 summarizes some common UNIX vulnerabilities that apply to Linux. You can read the complete details about these vulnerabilities at www.sans.org/top20.

Table 4-1 Some Common Vulnerabilities to UNIX Systems

Vulnerability Type	*Description*
BIND/DNS	Berkeley Internet Name Domain (BIND) is a package that implements Domain Name System (DNS), the Internet's name service that translates a name to an IP address. Some versions of BIND have vulnerabilities.
Remote Procedure Calls (RPC)	Services such as Network File System (NFS) and Network Information System (NIS) use remote procedure calls (RPC) and some known vulnerabilities are in RPC.
Apache Web server	Some Apache Web server modules (such as mod_ssl) have known vulnerabilities. Any vulnerability in common gateway interface (CGI) programs used with Web servers to process interactive Web pages can provide attackers a way to gain access to a system.
General UNIX Authentication — Accounts with No Passwords or Weak Passwords	User accounts often have no passwords or weak pass words (passwords that are easily cracked by password-cracking programs).
Clear-text Services	Many network services (such as TELNET and FTP, among others) transmit a username and password in the clear, so attackers may be able to pick these up by eavesdropping.
sendmail	sendmail is a complex program used to send, receive, and forward most electronic mail messages on UNIX and Linux systems. Older versions of sendmail have vulnerabilities, such as buffer overflow and bad configurations that allow anyone to relay mail through the system.
Simple Network Management Protocol (SNMP)	SNMP is used to remotely monitor and administer various network-connected systems ranging from routers to computers. SNMP lacks good access control, so if SNMP is running on a system, an attacker may be able to use SNMP to reconfigure or shut down the system.
Secure Shell (SSH)	SSH is used for securely logging in, executing commands, and transferring files across a network. Some SSH implementations have vulnerabilities.
Network File System (NFS) and Network Information Service (NIS)	Both NFS and NIS have many security problems (for example, buffer overflow, potential for denial-of-service attacks, and weak authentication). Also, NFS and NIS are often misconfigured, which could allow the security holes to be exploited by local and remote users.

(continued)

Table 4-1 *(continued)*

Vulnerability Type	*Description*
Open Secure Sockets Layer (OpenSSL)	Many applications such as Apache Web server use OpenSSL to provide cryptographic security for a network connection. Unfortunately, some versions of OpenSSL have known vulnerabilities that could be exploited.

Host-security review

When reviewing host security, focus on assessing the security mechanisms in each of the following areas:

- **Prevention:** Install operating system updates, secure passwords, improve file permissions, set up a password for a boot loader, and use encryption.
- **Detection:** Capture log messages and check file integrity with Tripwire (a tool that can detect changes to system files).
- **Response:** Make routine backups and develop incident response procedures.

I review a few of these host-security mechanisms in the upcoming sections.

Operating-system updates

Linux distributions release updates soon after security vulnerabilities are found. Many distributions offer online updates that you can enable and use to keep your system up to date. The exact details of updating the operating system depend on the distribution. See Book V, Chapter 4 for information on how to update Linux online.

File permissions

Key system files need to be protected with appropriate file ownerships and file permissions. The key procedures in assigning file-system ownerships and permissions are as follows:

- Figure out which files contain sensitive information and why. Some files may contain sensitive data related to your work or business, whereas many other files are sensitive because they control the Linux system configuration.
- Maintain a current list of authorized users and what they are authorized to do on the system.
- Set up passwords, groups, file ownerships, and file permissions to allow only authorized users to access the files.

Table 4-2 lists some important system files in Linux, showing the numeric permission setting for each file. (See Chapter 2 of this minibook for more on numeric permission settings.)

Table 4-2 Important System Files and Their Permissions

File Pathname	*Permission*	*Description*
`/boot/grub/menu.lst`	600	GRUB bootloader menu file
`/etc/cron.allow`	400	List of users permitted to use `cron` to submit periodic jobs
`/etc/cron.deny`	400	List of users who cannot use `cron` to submit periodic jobs
`/etc/crontab`	644	System-wide periodic jobs
`/etc/hosts.allow`	644	List of hosts allowed to use Internet services that are started using TCP wrappers
`/etc/hosts.deny`	644	List of hosts denied access to Internet services that are started using TCP wrappers
`/etc/logrotate.conf`	644	File that controls how log files are rotated
`/etc/pam.d`	755	Directory with configuration files for pluggable authentication modules (PAMs)
`/etc/passwd`	644	Old-style password file with user-account information but not the passwords
`/etc/rc.d`	755	Directory with system-startup scripts
`/etc/securetty`	600	TTY interfaces (terminals) from which `root` can log in
`/etc/security`	755	Policy files that control system access
`/etc/shadow`	400	File with encrypted passwords and password-expiration information
`/etc/shutdown.allow`	400	Users who can shut down or reboot by pressing Ctrl+Alt+Delete
`/etc/ssh`	755	Directory with configuration files for the Secure Shell (SSH)

(continued)

Table 4-2 (continued)

File Pathname	*Permission*	*Description*
/etc/ssh	755	Directory with configuration files for the Secure Shell (SSH)
/etc/sysconfig	755	System-configuration files
/etc/sysctl.conf	644	Kernel-configuration parameters
/etc/syslog.conf	644	Configuration file for the syslogd server that logs messages
/etc/udev/udev.conf	644	Configuration file for udev — the program that provides the ability to dynamically name hot-pluggable devices and create the device files in the /dev directory
/etc/vsftpd	600	Configuration file for the Very Secure FTP server
/etc/vsftpd.ftpusers	600	List of users who cannot use FTP to transfer files
/etc/xinetd.conf	644	Configuration file for the xinetd server
/etc/xinetd.d	755	Directory containing configuration files for specific services that the xinetd server can start
/var/log	755	Directory with all log files
/var/log/lastlog	644	Information about all previous logins
/var/log/messages	644	Main system message log file
/var/log/wtmp	664	Information about current logins

Another important check is to look for executable program files that have the setuid permission. If a program has setuid permission and it's owned by root, then the program runs with root privileges, no matter who is actually running the program. You can find all setuid programs with the following find command:

```
find / -perm +4000 -print
```

You may want to save the output in a file (just append > *filename* to the command) and then examine the file for any unusual setuid programs. For example, a setuid program in a user's home directory is unusual.

Password security

Verify that the password, group, and shadow password files are protected. In particular, the shadow password file has to be write-protected and readable only by `root`. The filenames and their recommended permissions are shown in Table 4-3.

Table 4-3 Ownership and Permission of Password Files

File Pathname	*Ownership*	*Permission*
`/etc/group`	`root.root`	644
`/etc/passwd`	`root.root`	644
`/etc/shadow`	`root.root`	400

Incident response

Incident response is the policy that answers the question of what to do if something unusual does happen to the system — it tells you how to proceed if someone has broken into your system.

Your response to an incident depends on how you use your system and how important it is to you or your business. For a comprehensive incident response, here are some key points to remember:

- Figure out how critical and important your computer and network are and identify who or what resources can help you protect your system.
- Take steps to prevent and minimize potential damage and interruption.
- Develop and document a comprehensive contingency plan.
- Periodically test the contingency plan and revise the procedures as appropriate.

Network-security review

Network-security review focuses on assessing the security mechanisms in each of the following areas:

- **Prevention:** Set up a firewall, enable packet filtering, disable unnecessary `inetd` or `xinetd` services, turn off unneeded Internet services, use TCP wrappers for access control, and use SSH for secure remote logins.
- **Detection:** Use network intrusion detection and capture system logs.
- **Response:** Develop incident-response procedures.

I briefly describe some key steps in assessing the network security in the following three subsections.

Services started by inetd or xinetd

Depending on your distribution, the `inetd` or `xinetd` server may be configured to start some Internet services such as TELNET and FTP. The decision to turn on some of these services depends on factors such as how the system connects to the Internet and how the system is being used. You can usually turn off most `inetd` and `xinetd` services.

Debian and Xandros use `inetd` to start some services. Look at the `/etc/inetd.conf` file to see what services `inetd` is configured to start. You can turn off services by commenting out the line in `/etc/inetd.conf` — just place a hash mark (#) at the beginning of the line.

Fedora Core and SUSE use `xinetd` as the server that starts other Internet services on demand. To see which `xinetd` services are turned off, check the configuration files in the `/etc/xinetd.d` directory for all the configuration files that have a `disable = yes` line. (The line does not count if it's commented out by placing a # at the beginning of the line.) You can add a `disable = yes` line to the configuration file of any service that you want to turn off.

Also check the following files for any access controls used with the `inetd` or `xinetd` services:

- `/etc/hosts.allow` lists hosts allowed to access specific services.
- `/etc/hosts.deny` lists hosts denied access to services.

Standalone services

Many services such as `apache` or `httpd` (Web server) and `sendmail` (mail server) start automatically at boot time, assuming they are configured to start that way.

In Fedora Core and SUSE, you can use the `chkconfig` command to check which of these standalone servers are set to start at various run levels. (See Book V, Chapter 1 for more about run levels.) Typically, your Fedora Core or SUSE system starts up at run level 3 (for text login) or 5 (for graphical login). Therefore, what matters is the setting for the servers in levels 3 and 5. To view the list of servers, type **chkconfig --list | more**. If you're doing a self-assessment of your network security and you find that some servers should not be running, you can turn them off for run levels 3 and 5 by typing **chkconfig --level 35 *servicename* off** where ***servicename*** is the name of the service you want to turn off.

In some distributions, you can use a GUI tool to see which services are enabled and running at any run level. In Fedora Core, select Main Menu➪System Settings➪Server Settings➪Services. In SUSE, select Main Menu➪System➪YaST, then click System on the left side of the window and Runlevel Editor on the right side of the window.

If you're auditing network security, make a note of all the servers that are turned on — and then try to determine whether they should really *be* on, according to what you know about the system. The decision to turn a particular service on depends on how your system is used (for example, as a Web server or as a desktop system) and how it's connected to the Internet (say, through a firewall or directly).

Penetration test

A penetration test is the best way to tell what services are really running on a Linux system. *Penetration testing* involves trying to get access to your system from an attacker's perspective. Typically, you perform this test from a system on the Internet and try to see if you can break in or, at a minimum, get access to services running on your Linux system.

Knoppix running on a laptop is ideal for performing penetration tests because Knoppix is a Live CD distribution that comes bundled with scanning tools such as `nmap` and Nessus. All you have to do is boot from the Knoppix CD, and you are ready to do the penetration test.

One aspect of penetration testing is to see what ports are open on your Linux system. The port number is simply a number that identifies specific TCP/IP network connections to the system. The attempt to connect to a port succeeds only if a server is running on that port (or put another way, if a server is "listening on that port"). A port is considered to be open if a server responds when a connection request for that port arrives.

The first step in penetration testing is to perform a port scan. The term *port scan* is used to describe the automated process of trying to connect to each port number to see if a valid response comes back. Many available automated tools can perform port scanning — you can install and use a popular port-scanning tool called `nmap` (which I describe later in this chapter).

After performing a port scan, you know which ports are in fact open and could potentially be exploited. Not all servers have security problems, but many servers have well-known vulnerabilities, and an open port provides a cracker a way to attack your system through one of the servers. In fact, you can use automated tools called *vulnerability scanners* to identify vulnerabilities that exist in your system. (I describe some vulnerability scanners in the following sections.) Whether your Linux system is connected to the Internet directly (through DSL or cable modem) or through a firewall, use the port-scanning and vulnerability-scanning tools to figure out if you have any holes in your defenses. Better you than them!

Exploring Security Testing Tools

Many automated tools are available to perform security testing. Some of these tools are meant for finding the open ports on every system in a range of IP addresses. Others look for the vulnerabilities associated with open ports. Yet other tools can capture (or *sniff*) those weaknesses and help you analyze them so that you can glean useful information about what's going on in your network.

You can browse a list of the top 75 security tools (based on an informal poll of `nmap` users) at `www.insecure.org/tools.html`. Table 4-4 lists a number of these tools by category. I describe a few of the freely available vulnerability scanners in the next few sections.

Table 4-4 Some Popular Computer Security Testing Tools

Type	*Names of Tools*
Port scanners	`nmap`, Strobe
Vulnerability scanners	Nessus Security Scanner, SAINT, SARA, Whisker (CGI scanner), ISS Internet Scanner, CyberCop Scanner, Vetescan, Retina Network Security Scanner
Network utilities	Netcat, `hping2`, Firewalk, Cheops, `ntop`, `ping`, `ngrep`, AirSnort (802.11 WEP encryption cracking tool)
Host-security tools	Tripwire, lsof
Packet sniffers	`tcpdump`, Ethereal, `dsniff`, `sniffit`
Intrusion-detection systems (IDSs)	Snort, Abacus `portsentry`, `scanlogd`, NFR, LIDS
Password-checking tools	John the Ripper, LC4
Log-analysis and monitoring tools	`logcolorise`, `tcpdstats`, `nlog`, `logcheck`, LogWatch, Swatch

nmap

`nmap` (short for *network mapper*) is a port-scanning tool. It can rapidly scan large networks and determine what hosts are available on the network, what services they are offering, what operating system (and the operating system version) they are running, what type of packet filters or firewalls are in use, and dozens of other characteristics. You can read more about `nmap` at `www.insecure.org/nmap`.

If it's not already installed, you can easily install `nmap` on your distribution. Fedora Core and Knoppix come with `nmap`. In Debian, you can install it with the command `apt-get install nmap`. In SUSE, click the Install and Remove Software from the Software category in YaST Control Center (Main Menu➪System➪YaST) and then use the software search facility of YaST to find `nmap` and install it. In Xandros, you can use the `apt-get install nmap` command; after you run Xandros Networks, select Edit➪Set Application Sources, and click the Debian Unsupported Site link as a source.

If you want to try out `nmap` to scan your local area network, just type a command similar to the following (replace the IP address range with addresses appropriate for your network):

```
nmap -O -sS 192.168.0.4-8
```

Here's a typical output listing from that command:

```
Starting nmap 3.55 ( http://www.insecure.org/nmap/ ) at 2004-09-23 20:30 EDT
Interesting ports on 192.168.0.4:
(The 1657 ports scanned but not shown below are in state: closed)
PORT     STATE SERVICE
21/tcp   open  ftp
22/tcp   open  ssh
111/tcp  open  rpcbind
Device type: general purpose
Running: Linux 2.4.X|2.5.X|2.6.X
OS details: Linux 2.5.25 - 2.6.3 or Gentoo 1.2 Linux 2.4.19 rc1-rc7)
Uptime 10.097 days (since Thu Sep 13 18:10:55 2004)

Warning:  OS detection will be MUCH less reliable because we did not find at
least 1 open and 1 closed TCP port
All 1660 scanned ports on 192.168.0.5 are: filtered
MAC Address: 00:30:AB:06:E2:D5 (Delta NETWORKS)
Too many fingerprints match this host to give specific OS details
... Lines deleted ...
Nmap run completed -- 5 IP addresses (5 hosts up) scanned in 254.162 seconds
```

As you can see, `nmap` displays the names of the open ports and hazards a guess at the operating system name and version number.

Nessus

The Nessus Security Scanner is a modular security auditing tool that uses plugins written in the Nessus scripting language to test for a wide variety of network vulnerabilities. Nessus uses a client-server software architecture with a server called `nessusd` and a client called `nessus`.

Knoppix already comes with Nessus, so you don't have to download or install anything. To start Nessus, select Main Menu➪System➪Security➪NESSUS Security Tool.

To install Nessus, first try your Linux distribution's usual method for installing new software packages. In Debian, type **apt-get install nessus nessusd** to install the packages. In SUSE, click the Install and Remove Software from the Software category in YaST Control Center (Main Menu⇨System⇨YaST) and then use YaST's search facility to find the `nessus` packages, select them, and click Accept to install them. In Xandros, select Edit⇨Set Application Sources, and click the Debian Unsupported Site link as a source. Then type **apt-get install nessus nessusd**.

For Fedora Core, you have to download Nessus from `www.nessus.org/download.html` and install it. Before you try to install Nessus, you must install the `sharutils` RPM. That package includes the `uudecode` utility that the Nessus installation script needs. The `sharutils` package isn't installed with any of the standard package groups in Fedora Core, so you have to install it yourself. To install `sharutils`, mount the companion DVD and install it with the following commands:

```
cd /mnt/cdrom/Fedora/RPMS
rpm -ivh sharutils*.rpm
```

To download and install Nessus, follow these steps (these instructions work on all Linux distributions):

1. **Read the instructions at `www.nessus.org/download.html`. Then follow the link to the package you want to download. Follow the instructions and download the files `nessus-installer.sh` and `MD5`.**
2. **Type the following command to install Nessus (you must have the development tools, including the GIMP Toolkit, installed):**

   ```
   sh nessus-installer.sh
   ```

   Respond to the prompts from the installer script to finish the installation. You can usually press Enter to accept the default choices.

After the installation is complete, follow these steps to use Nessus (in Knoppix, select Main Menu⇨System⇨Security⇨NESSUS Security Tool, and then go to Step 8):

1. **Log in as `root` and type the following command to create the Nessus SSL certificate used for secure communication between the Nessus client and the Nessus server:**

   ```
   nessus-mkcert
   ```

2. **Provide the requested information to complete the certificate generation process.**
3. **Create a `nessusd` account with the following command:**

   ```
   nessus-adduser
   ```

4. **When prompted, enter your username, password, and any rules. (Press Ctrl+D if you don't know what rules to enter.) Then press the Y key.**
5. **If you want to, you can configure** `nessusd` **by editing the configuration file** `/usr/local/etc/nessus/nessusd.conf`.

   If you want to try out Nessus, you can proceed with the default configuration file.
6. **Start the Nessus server with this command:**

   ```
   nessusd -D
   ```
7. **Run the Nessus client by typing the following command in a terminal window:**

   ```
   nessus
   ```

   The Nessus Setup window appears.
8. **Type a** `nessusd` **username and password, and then click the Log In button. (See Figure 4-1.)**
9. **When Nessus displays the certificate used to establish the secure connection and asks if you accept it, click Yes.**

   After the client connects to the server, the Log In button changes to Log Out, and a Connected label appears at its left.

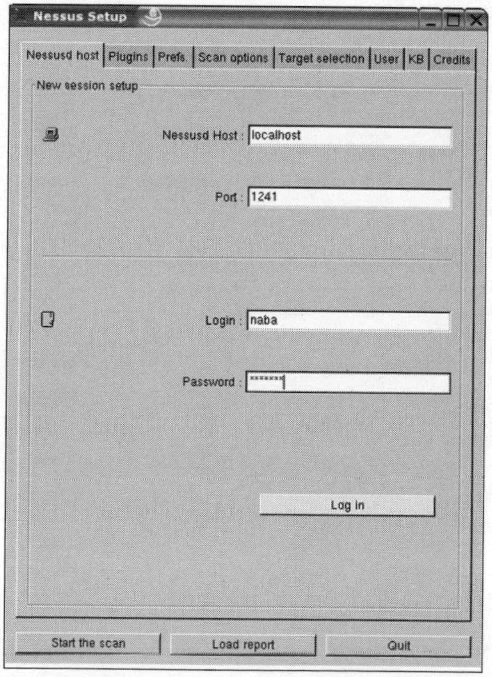

Figure 4-1: The Nessus client screen looks like this before a user logs in.

`nessud` gives you an option to enable plugins that can scan for specific vulnerabilities, but some of these may crash hosts and disrupt your network during the scan. If you want to try any of the plugins, select and enable them. If you want to be safe, click the Enable All but Dangerous Plugins link.

10. **Click the Target Selection tab and enter a range of IP addresses to scan all hosts in a network.**

    For example, to scan the first eight hosts in a private network 192.168.0.0, I enter the address as:

    ```
    192.168.0.0/29
    ```

    WARNING!

    Don't use Nessus to scan any network that you do not own. Scanning other networks is usually against the law and there could be serious consequences if you break the applicable laws.

11. **Click Start the Scan.**

    Nessus starts scanning the IP addresses and checks for many different vulnerabilities. Progress bars show the status of the scan.

After Nessus completes the vulnerability scan of the hosts, it displays the result in a nice combination of graphical and text formats , as shown in Figure 4-2. The report is interactive — you can select a host address to view the report on that host, and you can drill down on a specific vulnerability to find details, such as the CVE number that identifies the vulnerability and a description of the vulnerability.

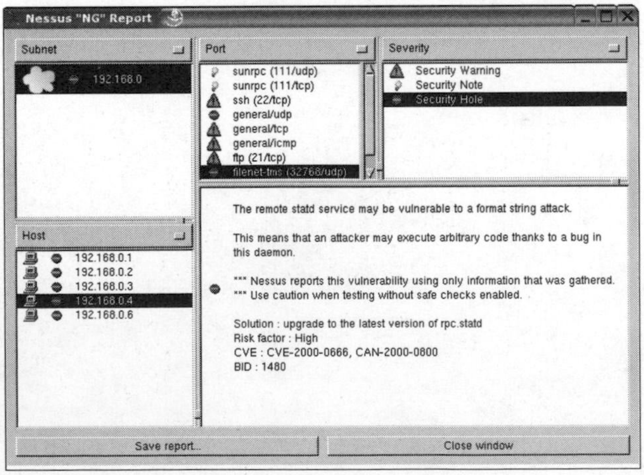

Figure 4-2: Nessus displays results of scanning in an interactive report.

Book VII

Internet Servers

"Well, let's look in the Registry and see what your life preferences have been."

Contents at a Glance

Chapter 1: Managing Internet Services

In This Chapter

- **Understanding Internet services**
- **Controlling servers through** `inetd` **or** `xinetd`
- **Using** `chkconfig` **or** `update-rc.d` **to manage servers**
- **Using GUI utilities to configure services to start at boot time**

The Internet is a world of clients and servers. Clients make requests to servers, and servers respond to the requests. For example, your Web browser is a client that downloads information from Web servers and displays it to you. Of course, the clients and servers are computer programs that run on a wide variety of computers. A Linux system is an ideal system to run a wide variety of servers — from a Web server to a Windows file and print server. In this chapter, I provide an overview of a typical Internet service, its client/server architecture, and how to manage the servers in Linux. You can use the information in this chapter to manage any server running on your Linux system.

Understanding Internet Services

Internet services are network applications designed to deliver information from one system to another. By design, each Internet service is implemented in two parts — a *server* that provides information and one or more *clients* that request information.

Such a *client/server* architecture is the most common way to build distributed information systems. The clients and servers are computer programs that run on these computers and communicate through the network. The neat part is that you can run a client at your desktop computer and access information from a server running on a computer anywhere in the world (as long as it's on the Internet).

The Web itself, e-mail, and FTP (File Transfer Protocol) are examples of Internet services that use the client/server model. For example, when you use the Web, you use the Web-browser client to download and view Web pages from the Web server.

Client/server architecture requires clients to communicate with the servers. That's where the *Transmission Control Protocol/Internet Protocol* — TCP/IP — comes in. TCP/IP provides a standard way for clients and servers to exchange packets of data. In the next few sections, I explain how TCP/IP-based services communicate.

TCP/IP and sockets

Client/server applications such as the Web and FTP use TCP/IP for data transfers between client and server. These Internet applications typically use TCP/IP communications utilizing the *Berkeley Sockets interface* (so named because the socket interface was introduced in Berkeley UNIX around 1982). The sockets interface is nothing physical — it's simply some computer code that a computer programmer can use to create applications that can communicate with other applications on the Internet.

Even if you don't write network applications using sockets, you may have to use or set up many network applications. Knowledge of sockets can help you understand how network-based applications work, which in turn helps you find and correct any problems with these applications.

Socket definition

Network applications use sockets to communicate over a TCP/IP network. A *socket* represents one end-point of a connection. Because a socket is bidirectional, data can be sent as well as received through it. A socket has three attributes:

- The *network address* (the IP address) of the system
- The *port number,* identifying the process (a *process* is a computer program running on a computer) that exchanges data through the socket
- The *type of socket,* identifying the protocol for data exchange

Essentially, the IP address identifies a computer (host) on the network; the port number identifies a process (server) on the node; and the socket type determines the manner in which data is exchanged — through a connection-oriented (stream) or connectionless (datagram) protocol.

Connection-oriented protocols

The socket type indicates the protocol being used to communicate through the socket. A connection-oriented protocol works like a normal phone conversation. When you want to talk to your friend, you have to dial your friend's phone number and establish a connection before you can have a conversation. In the same way, connection-oriented data exchange requires both the sending and receiving processes to establish a connection before data exchange can begin.

In the TCP/IP protocol suite, TCP — *Transmission Control Protocol* — supports a connection-oriented data transfer between two processes running on two computers on the Internet. TCP provides reliable two-way data exchange between processes.

As the name TCP/IP suggests, TCP relies on IP — *Internet Protocol* — for delivery of packets. IP does not guarantee delivery of packets; nor does it deliver packets in any particular sequence. IP does, however, efficiently move packets from one network to another. TCP is responsible for arranging the packets in the proper sequence, detecting whether errors have occurred, and requesting retransmission of packets in case of an error.

TCP is useful for applications intended to exchange large amounts of data at a time. In addition, applications that need reliable data exchange use TCP. (For example, FTP uses TCP to transfer files.)

In the sockets model, a socket that uses TCP is referred to as a *stream socket.*

Connectionless protocols

A *connectionless* data-exchange protocol does not require the sender and receiver to explicitly establish a connection. It's like shouting to your friend in a crowded room — you can't be sure that your friend hears you.

In the TCP/IP protocol suite, the *User Datagram Protocol* (UDP) provides connectionless service for sending and receiving packets known as *datagrams.* Unlike TCP, UDP does not guarantee that datagrams ever reach their intended destinations. Nor does UDP ensure that datagrams are delivered in the order they are sent.

UDP is used by applications that exchange small amounts of data at a time, or by applications that don't need the reliability and sequencing of data delivery. For example, SNMP (Simple Network Management Protocol) uses UDP to transfer data.

In the sockets model, a socket that uses UDP is referred to as a *datagram socket.*

Sockets and the client/server model

Two sockets are needed to complete a communication path. When two processes communicate, they use the client/server model to establish the connection. Figure 1-1 illustrates the concept. The server application listens on a specific port on the system — the server is completely identified by the IP address of the system where it runs and the port number where it listens for connections. The client initiates a connection from any available port and tries to connect to the server (identified by the IP address and port number). When the connection is established, the client and the server can exchange data according to their own protocol.

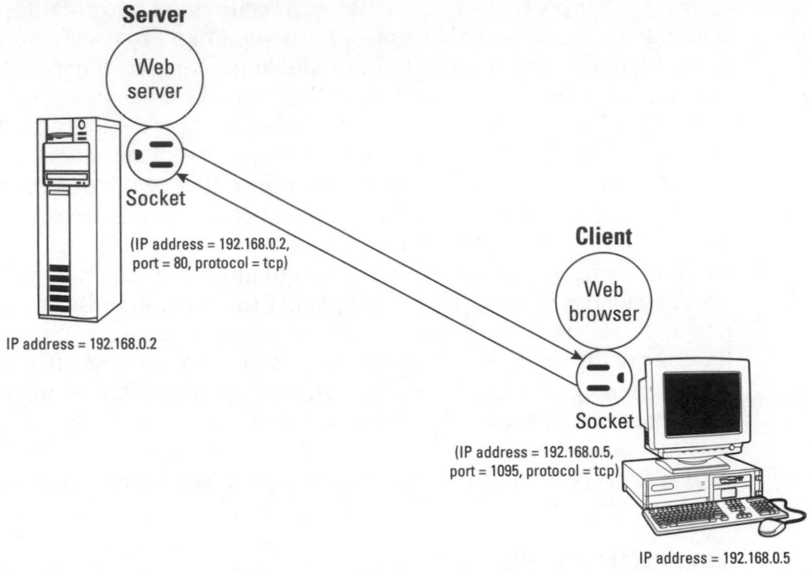

Figure 1-1: Client and server processes use two sockets to communicate.

The sequence of events in socket-based data exchanges depends on whether the transfer is connection-oriented (TCP) or connectionless (UDP).

For a connection-oriented data transfer using sockets, the server "listens" on a specific port, waiting for clients to request connection. Data transfer begins only after a connection is established.

For connectionless data transfers, the server waits for a datagram to arrive at a specified port. The client does not wait to establish a connection; it simply sends a datagram to the server.

Regardless of whether it's a server or a client, each application first creates a socket. Then it *associates* (binds) the socket with the local computer's IP address and a port number. The IP address identifies the machine (where the application is running), and the port number identifies the application using the socket.

REMEMBER

Servers typically listen to a well-known port number so that clients can connect to that port to access the server. For a client application, the process of binding a socket to the IP address and port is the same as that for a server, but the client can use 0 as the port number — the sockets library automatically uses an unused port number for the client.

For a connection-oriented stream socket, the communicating client and server applications have to establish a connection. The exact steps for establishing a connection depend on whether the application is a server or a client.

In the client/server model, the server has to be up and running before the client can run. After creating a socket and binding the socket to a port, the server application sets up a queue of connections, which determines how many clients can connect to the server. Typically, a server listens to anywhere from one to five connections. However, the size of the listen queue is one of the parameters you can adjust (especially for a Web server) to ensure that the server responds to as many clients as possible. After setting up the listen queue, the server waits for a connection from a client.

Establishing the connection from the client side is somewhat simpler. After creating a socket and binding the socket to an IP address, the client establishes a connection with the server. To make the connection, the client must know the host name or IP address of the server, as well as the port on which the server accepts connection. All Internet services have well-known standard port numbers.

After a client establishes a connection to a server via a connection-oriented stream socket, the client and server can exchange data by calling the appropriate sockets' API functions. Like a conversation between two persons, the server and client alternately send and receive data — the meaning of the data depends on the message protocol that the server and clients use. Usually, a server is designed for a specific task; inherent in that design is a message protocol that the server and clients use to exchange necessary data. For example, the Web server and the Web browser (client) communicate using HTTP (HyperText Transfer Protocol).

Internet services and port numbers

The TCP/IP protocol suite is the *lingua franca* of the Internet because the Internet services "speak" TCP/IP. These services make the Internet tick by making possible the transfer of mail, news, and Web pages. Each Internet service has its own protocol that relies on TCP/IP for the actual transfer of the information. Each service also has one or more assigned port numbers that it uses to do whatever it's designed to do. Here are some well-known Internet services and their associated protocols:

- **DHCP (Dynamic Host Configuration Protocol)** is for dynamically configuring TCP/IP network parameters on a computer. DHCP is primarily used to assign dynamic IP addresses and other networking information such as name server, default gateway, and domain names that are needed to configure TCP/IP networks. The DHCP server listens on port 67.
- **FTP (File Transfer Protocol)** is used to transfer files between computers on the Internet. FTP uses two ports — data is transferred on port 20; control information is exchanged on port 21.
- **HTTP (HyperText Transfer Protocol)** is for sending documents from one system to another. HTTP is the underlying protocol of the Web. By default, the Web server and client communicate on port 80.

- **SMTP (Simple Mail Transfer Protocol)** is for exchanging e-mail messages between systems. SMTP uses port 25 for information exchange.
- **NNTP (Network News Transfer Protocol)** is for the distribution of news articles in a store-and-forward fashion across the Internet. NNTP uses port 119.
- **SSH (Secure Shell)** is a protocol for secure remote login and other secure network services over an insecure network. SSH uses port 22.
- **TELNET** enables a user on one system to log into another system on the Internet. (The user must provide a valid user ID and password to log into the remote system.) TELNET uses port 23 by default. However, the TELNET client can connect to any specified port.
- **NFS (Network File System)** is for sharing files among computers. NFS uses Sun's Remote Procedure Call (RPC) facility, which exchanges information through port 111.
- **NTP (Network Time Protocol)** is used by client computers to synchronize the system time with that on a server (one with a more accurate clock). NTP uses port 123.
- **SNMP (Simple Network Management Protocol)** is for managing all types of network devices on the Internet. Like FTP, SNMP uses two ports: 161 and 162.
- **TFTP (Trivial File Transfer Protocol)** is for transferring files from one system to another (typically used by X terminals and diskless workstations to download boot files from another host on the network). TFTP data transfer takes place on port 69.

Each service is provided by a *server process* — a computer program that runs on a system awaiting client requests that arrive at the well-known port associated with its service. Thus the Web server expects client requests at port 80, the standard port for HTTP service.

The `/etc/services` text file on your Linux system stores the association between a service name and a port number (as well as a protocol). Here is a small subset of entries in the `/etc/services` file from a Linux system:

```
ftp-data        20/tcp
ftp             21/tcp
fsp             21/udp          fspd
ssh             22/tcp                          # SSH Remote Login Protocol
ssh             22/udp
telnet          23/tcp
smtp            25/tcp          mail
time            37/tcp          timserver
time            37/udp          timserver
rlp             39/udp          resource        # resource location
nameserver      42/tcp          name            # IEN 116
whois           43/tcp          nicname
tacacs          49/tcp                          # Login Host Protocol (TACACS)
```

A quick look through the entries in the `/etc/services` file shows the breadth of networking services available under TCP/IP.

Note: Port number 80 is designated for Web services. In other words, if you set up a Web server on your system, that server listens to port 80. By the way, IANA — the Internet Assigned Numbers Authority (`www.iana.org`) — is the organization responsible for coordinating the assignment of port numbers below 1,024.

Using the Internet Super Server

The client/server architecture of Internet services requires that the server be up and running before a client makes a request for service. It would probably be a bad idea to run all the servers all the time — impractical because each server process would use up system resources in the form of memory and processor time. Besides, you don't really need *all* the services up and ready at all times. A smart solution to this problem is to run a single server that listens to all the ports and then starts the appropriate server when a client request comes in. Such a server is known as the *Internet super server* because it starts various services on demand.

There are two Internet super servers — `inetd` and `xinetd`. The `inetd` server was the older one and is still used in some Linux distributions such as Debian, Knoppix, and Xandros. The `xinetd` server is a replacement for `inetd`, offering improved access control and logging. The name `xinetd` stands for *extended* `inetd`. Distributions such as Fedora Core and SUSE use `xinetd`.

Using inetd

In Linux distributions that use `inetd`, the system starts `inetd` when the system boots. The `inetd` server reads a configuration file named `/etc/inetd.conf` at startup. This file tells `inetd` which ports to listen to and what server to start for each port. For example, on one of my Linux systems, the entry in the `/etc/inetd.conf` file that starts the FTP server looks like this:

```
ftp     stream  tcp    nowait  root    /usr/sbin/tcpd  /usr/sbin/proftpd
```

The first item on this line, `ftp`, tells `inetd` the name of the service. `inetd` uses this name to look up the port number from the `/etc/services` file. If you type **grep ftp /etc/services**, you find that the port number of the FTP service is 21. This tells `inetd` to listen to port 21 for FTP service requests.

The rest of the fields on the FTP entry have the following meanings:

✦ The second and third fields of the entry, `stream` and `tcp`, tell `inetd` that the FTP service uses a connection-oriented TCP socket to communicate with the client. For services that use the connectionless UDP sockets, these two fields say `dgram` and `udp`.

✦ The fourth field, `nowait`, tells `inetd` to start a new server for each request. If this field says `wait`, `inetd` waits until the server exits before starting the server again.

✦ The fifth field provides the user ID that `inetd` uses to run the server. In this case, the server runs the FTP server as `root`.

✦ The sixth field specifies the program to run for this service and the last field is the argument that `inetd` passes to the server program. In this case, the `/usr/sbin/tcpd` program is provided `/usr/sbin/ftpd` as argument.

The `/usr/sbin/tcpd` program is an access control facility — called *TCP wrapper* — for Internet services. Because unnecessary Internet services are often the sources of security vulnerabilities, you may want to turn off any unneeded services or at least control access to the services. The `tcpd` program can start other services such as FTP and TELNET, but before starting the service, `tcpd` consults the `/etc/hosts.allow` file to see if the host requesting service is allowed that service. If there is nothing in `/etc/hosts.allow` about that host, `tcpd` checks the `/etc/hosts.deny` file to see if the service should be denied. If both files are empty, `tcpd` allows the host access to the requested service. You can place the line `ALL:ALL` in the `/etc/hosts.deny` file to deny all hosts access to any Internet services.

Browse through the `/etc/inetd.conf` file on your system to find out the kinds of services that `inetd` is set up to start. Nowadays, most `inetd` services are turned off and many others such as FTP are started by standalone servers. In any case, if you should see any services that you want to turn off, simply place a hash mark (#) at the beginning of the lines that start these services. When you make such a change to the `/etc/inetd.conf` file, type **/etc/init.d/inetd restart** to restart the `inetd` server.

Using xinetd

Linux distributions that use `xinetd` start `xinetd` when the system boots. The `xinetd` server reads a configuration file named `/etc/xinetd.conf` at startup. This file tells `xinetd` which ports to listen to and what server to start for each port. The file can contain instructions that include other configuration files. In Linux, the `/etc/xinetd.conf` file looks like the following:

```
# Simple configuration file for xinetd
#
# Set some defaults and include /etc/xinetd.d/

defaults
```

```
{
        instances               = 30
        log_type                = FILE /var/log/xinetd.log
        log_on_success          = HOST EXIT DURATION
        log_on_failure          = HOST ATTEMPT
        cps                     = 50 10
}
includedir /etc/xinetd.d
```

Comment lines begin with the hash mark (#). The `defaults` block of attributes, enclosed in curly braces (`{ . . . }`), specifies default values for some attributes. These default values apply to all other services in the configuration file. The `instances` attribute is set to 30, which means, at most, 30 servers can be simultaneously active for any service.

The last line in the `/etc/xinetd.conf` file uses the `includedir` directive to include all files inside the `/etc/xinetd.d` directory, excluding files that begin with a period (`.`). The idea is that the `/etc/xinetd.d` directory contains all service-configuration files — one file for each type of service the `xinetd` server is expected to manage. Type **ls /etc/xinetd.d** to see the `xinetd` configuration files for your system. Each file in `/etc/xinetd.d` specifies attributes for one service that `xinetd` can start.

For example, SUSE Linux uses `xinetd` to start some services, including the `vsftpd` FTP server. Type **cat /etc/xinetd.d/vsftpd** to see the `xinetd` configuration for the `vsftpd` service. Here's a typical listing of that file on a SUSE system:

```
# default: off
# description:
#   The vsftpd FTP server serves FTP connections. It uses
#   normal, unencrypted usernames and passwords for authentication.
# vsftpd is designed to be secure.
service ftp
{
        socket_type     = stream
        protocol        = tcp
        wait            = no
        user            = root
        server          = /usr/sbin/vsftpd
}
```

The filename (in this case, `vsftpd`) can be anything; what matters is the service name that appears next to the `service` keyword in the file. In this case, the line `service ftp` tells `xinetd` the name of the service. `xinetd` uses this name to look up the port number from the `/etc/services` file.

The attributes in `/etc/xinetd.d/vsftpd`, enclosed in curly braces (`{ . . . }`), have the following meanings:

✦ The socket_type attribute is set to stream, which tells xinetd that the FTP service uses a connection-oriented TCP socket to communicate with the client. For services that use the connectionless UDP sockets, this attribute is set to dgram.

✦ The wait attribute is set to no, which tells xinetd to start a new server for each request. If this attribute is set to yes, xinetd waits until the server exits before starting the server again.

✦ The user attribute provides the user ID that xinetd uses to run the server. In this case, the server runs the TELNET server as root.

✦ The server attribute specifies the program to run for this service. In this case, xinetd runs the /usr/sbin/vsftpd program to provide the FTP service.

Browse through the files in the /etc/xinetd.d directory on your Linux system to find out the kinds of services xinetd is set up to start. If you want to turn any service off (many are already disabled), you can do so by editing the configuration file for that service and adding the following line inside the curly braces that enclose all attributes:

```
disable          = yes
```

When you make such a change to the xinetd configuration files, you must restart the xinetd server by typing the following command:

```
/etc/init.d/xinetd restart
```

Note: You can typically configure services to run under xinetd or as a standalone service. For example, SUSE starts the Very Secure FTP server (vsftpd) under the control of xinetd. Debian and Fedora Core, however, run vsftpd as a standalone server.

Running Standalone Servers

Starting servers through inetd or xinetd is a smart approach, but it's not efficient if a service has to be started very often. If the Web server were controlled by inetd or xinetd, you'd have a situation in which that server is started often because every time a user clicks a link on a Web page, a request arrives for the Web service. For such high-demand services, starting the server in a standalone manner is best. In standalone mode, the server can run as a *daemon* — a process that runs continuously and never dies. That means the server listens on the assigned port, and whenever a request arrives, the server handles it by making a copy of itself. In this way, the server keeps running as long as the machine is running — in theory, forever. A more efficient strategy, used for Web servers, is to run multiple copies of the server and let each copy handle some of the incoming requests.

You can easily configure your Linux system to start various standalone servers automatically. I show you how in this section.

Starting and stopping servers manually

To start a service that's not running, use the server command. For example, if the Web server (called `httpd` in Fedora Core) isn't running, you can start it by running a special shell script with the following command:

```
/etc/init.d/httpd start
```

That command runs the `/etc/init.d/httpd` script with `start` as the argument. If the `httpd` server is already running and you want to stop it, run the same command with `stop` as the argument, like this:

```
/etc/init.d/httpd stop
```

To stop and start a server again, just use `restart` as the argument:

```
/etc/init.d/httpd restart
```

In Debian and SUSE, where the Web server program is called `apache2`, type **/etc/init.d/apache2 start** to start the Web server. In Knoppix and Xandros, type **/etc/init.d/apache start**. Use that same command with arguments `stop` or `restart` to stop the Web server or restart it.

What are all the services that you can start and stop? Well, the answer is in the files in the `/etc/init.d` directory. To get a look at it, type the following command:

```
ls /etc/init.d
```

All the files you see listed in response to this command are the services installed on your Linux system — and you can start and stop them as needed. You typically find 65 to 70 services listed in the `/etc/init.d` directory.

Starting servers automatically at boot time

You can start, stop, and restart servers manually by using the scripts in the `/etc/init.d` directory, but you want some of the services to start as soon as you boot the Linux system. You can configure servers to start automatically at boot time by using a graphical server-configuration utility or a command.

The command for configuring services to start automatically depends on the distribution. In Debian, Knoppix, and Xandros, use the `update-rc.d` command. In Fedora Core and SUSE, use the `chkconfig` command. I explain both commands in the following sections.

Using the chkconfig command in Fedora Core and SUSE

The chkconfig program is a command-line utility in Fedora Core and SUSE for checking and updating the current setting of servers in Linux. Various combinations of servers are set up to start automatically at different run levels. Each *run level* represents a system configuration in which a selected set of processes runs. You're usually concerned about run levels 3 and 5 because run level 3 is for text-mode login and run level 5 is for logging in through a graphical interface.

The chkconfig command is simple to use. For example, suppose that you want to automatically start the named server at run levels 3 and 5. All you have to do is log in as root and type the following command at the shell prompt:

```
chkconfig --level 35 named on
```

To see the status of the named server, type the following command:

```
chkconfig --list named
```

You see a line of output similar to the following:

```
named    0:off  1:off  2:off  3:on   4:off  5:on   6:off
```

The output shows you the status of the named server at run levels 0 through 6. As you can see, named is set to run at run levels 3 and 5.

If you want to turn named off, you can do so with this command:

```
chkconfig --level 35 named off
```

You can use chkconfig to see the status of all services, including the ones started through xinetd. For example, you can view the status of all services by typing the following command:

```
chkconfig --list | more
```

The output shows the status of each service for each of the run levels from 0 through 6. For each run level, the service is either on or off. At the very end of the listing, chkconfig displays a list of the services that xinetd controls. Each xinetd-based service is also marked on or off, depending on whether or not xinetd is configured to start the service.

Using the update-rc.d command in Debian, Knoppix, and Xandros

In Debian, Knoppix, and Xandros, you can use the update-rc.d command to set up services that should start when the system boots at specific boot levels. The easiest way to set up is to use the `defaults` option in a command of this form:

```
update-rc.d service defaults
```

where *`service`* is the name of the script file in the `/etc/init.d` directory that starts and stops the service, among other things.

When you use the `defaults` option, `update-rc.d` sets up *symbolic links* — shortcuts, in other words — to start the service in run levels 2, 3, 4, and 5 and stop the service in run levels 0, 1, and 6. A sequence number controls the order in which each service is started. (Services with smaller sequence numbers start before those with larger sequence numbers, and the numbers typically range from 00 through 99.) If you do not specify a sequence number explicitly, `update-rc.d` uses a sequence number of 20 when you use the `defaults` option.

You can also start and stop a service at specific run levels as well as in a specific sequence. For example, to start a service at run levels 2 and 5 at a sequence number of 85 and stop it at run levels 0, 1, and 6 at a sequence of 90, use the following command.

```
update-rc.d service start 85 2 5 . stop 90 0 1 6 .
```


Remember that *`service`* must be the name of a script file in the `/etc/init.d` directory.

TIP

If you need to stop a service from starting at system startup, type **update-rc.d -f *service* remove** in a terminal window, where ***service*** is the name of the script file in `/etc/init.d` that starts or stops that service.

Using a GUI service configuration utility

If you don't like typing commands, you may be able to use a GUI tool to configure the services. Fedora Core and SUSE include such tools to manage the services.

DISTRIBUTION SPECIFIC

In Fedora Core, log in as `root` and choose Main Menu⇨System Settings⇨Server Settings⇨Services from the GUI desktop. You can then turn services on or off from the Service Configuration window, as shown in Figure 1-2.

The Service Configuration utility shows the names of services in a scrolling list. Each line in the list shows the name of a service with a check box in front of the name. A check mark in the box indicates that the service is already selected to start at boot time for the current run level. When the dialog box first appears, many services are already selected.

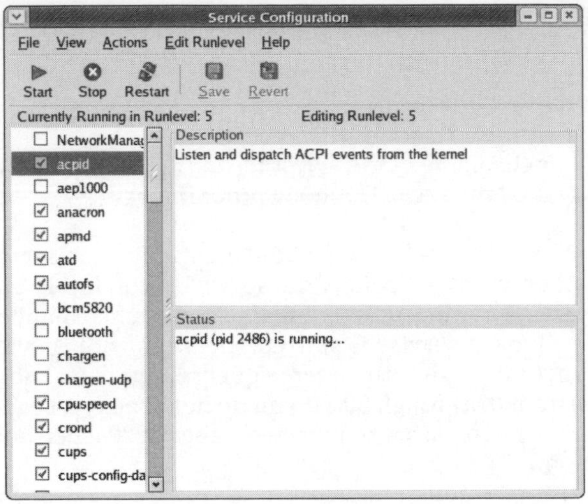

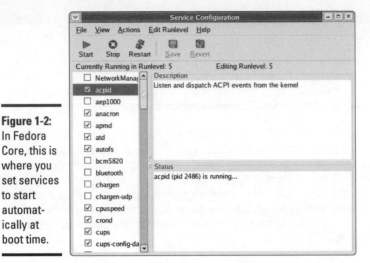

Figure 1-2: In Fedora Core, this is where you set services to start automatically at boot time.

You can scroll up and down the list and click the check box to select or deselect a service. If you click the check box, the check mark alternately turns on and off. To find out more about a service, click the service name to display a brief description in the right-hand side of the window. For example, Figure 1-2 shows the help text for the `acpid` service. Additionally, the utility also shows you whether the selected service is currently running or not.

After you select all the servers you want to start when the system boots, click the Save button on the toolbar to save the changes. Then choose File⇨Quit to exit.

By default, the service configuration utility configures the selected services for the current run level. That means if you're selecting services from the graphical desktop, the system is in run level 5 and the services you configure are set to start at run level 5. If you want to set up the services for a different level, select that run level from the Edit Runlevel menu.

In SUSE, you can configure the services from YaST Control Center (Main Menu⇨System⇨YaST). Click System in the left-hand window and then click Runlevel Editor. YaST opens the Runlevel Editor window (see Figure 1-3), where you can enable or disable services. To enable or disable services at specific run levels, click the Expert Mode button and edit the services in the new list that appears.

Table 1-1 shows a list of the services, along with a brief description of each one. The first column shows the name of the service, which is the same as the name of the program that has to run to provide the service. You may not see all these services listed when you run the GUI service configuration utility on your system because the exact list of services depends on what is installed on your Linux system.

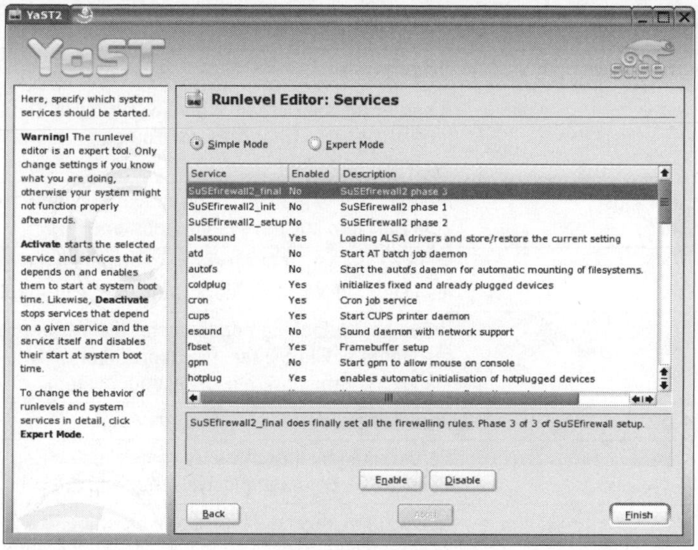

Figure 1-3: In SUSE, use the Runlevel Editor to specify services that start at boot time.

Table 1-1 Some Common Services in Linux

Service Name	*Description*
`acpid`	Listens to Advanced Configuration and Power Interface (ACPI) events from the kernel and notifies other programs when such events occur. ACPI events can occur when the kernel puts the computer into a low-power state (for example, standby mode) to save energy.
`apache`, `apache2`, or `httpd`	The Apache World Wide Web (WWW) server.
`apmd`	Monitors the Advanced Power Management (APM) BIOS and logs the status of electric power (AC or battery backup).
`atd`	Runs commands scheduled by the `at` and `cron` commands.
`autofs`	Automatically mounts file systems (for example, when you insert a CD-ROM in the CD-ROM drive).
`cron` or `crond`	Runs user-specified programs according to a periodic schedule set by the `crontab` command.
`gpm`	Enables use of the mouse in text-mode screens.
`innd`	The InterNetNews daemon — the Internet news server you can use to support local newsgroups on your system.
`isdn`	Starts and stops ISDN (Integrated Services Digital Network) services — a digital communication service over regular phone lines (enable only if you have ISDN service).

(continued)

Table 1-1 *(continued)*

Service Name	*Description*
`named`	A server for the Domain Name System (DNS) that translates host names into IP addresses. You can run a copy on your system if you want.
`network` or `networking`	Enables you to activate or deactivate all network interfaces configured to start at system boot time.
`nfs` or `nfsserver`	Enables sharing of file systems specified in the `/etc/exports` file using the Network File System (NFS) protocol.
`nfslock`	Provides file-locking capability for file systems exported using the Network File System (NFS) protocol, so other systems (running NFS) can share files from your system.
`pcmcia`	Provides support for PCMCIA devices.
`portmap`	Server used by any software that relies on Remote Procedure Calls (RPC). For example, NFS requires the `portmap` service.
`sendmail`	Moves mail messages from one machine to another. Start this service if you want to send mail from your Linux system. If you don't plan to use your Linux system as a mail server, don't start the `sendmail` server because it can slow down the booting process and consume unnecessary resources.
`samba`, `smb`, or `smbfs`	Starts and stops the Samba `smbd` and `nmbd` services that support LAN Manager services on a Linux system.
`snmpd`	Simple Network Management Protocol (SNMP) service used for network-management functions.
`spamassassin`	Runs `spamd` — the SpamAssassin mail filter program.
`ssh` or `sshd`	Server for the OpenSSH (Secure Shell) secure remote login facility.
`syslog` or `sysklogd`	Service used by many other programs (including other services) to log various error and status messages in a log file (usually, the `/var/log/messages` file). Always run this service.
`vsftpd`	Very Secure FTP daemon for file transfers using the File Transfer Protocol (FTP).
`winbind`	Starts and stops the Samba `winbindd` server that provides a name-switch capability similar to that provided by the `/etc/nsswitch.conf` file.
`xfs`	Server that starts and stops the X Font Server.
`xinetd`	The Internet super server, a replacement for the older `inetd`. It starts other Internet services, such as TELNET and FTP, whenever they are needed.
`ypbind`	Service that runs on Network Information System (NIS) clients and binds the clients to a NIS domain. You don't have to start `ypbind` unless you're using NIS.

Chapter 2: Running a Web Server

In This Chapter

- ✔ **Understanding HTTP**
- ✔ **Installing the Apache Web server**
- ✔ **Configuring the Apache Web server**
- ✔ **Supporting virtual hosts with the Apache Web server**

The World Wide Web (*WWW* or the *Web*) has catapulted the Internet into the mainstream because Web browsers make browsing documents stored on various Internet hosts easy for users. Whether you run a small business or manage computer systems and networks for a large company, chances are good that you have to set up and maintain a Web server. Because it has built-in networking support, a Linux PC makes an affordable Web server. This chapter describes how to configure the Apache Web server on a Linux PC.

Understanding HTTP

Web servers provide information using HTTP. Web servers are also known as *HTTP daemons* (because continuously running server processes are called daemons in UNIX), or *HTTPD* for short. The Web server program is usually named `apache`, `apache2`, or `httpd`, depending on your Linux distribution.

HTTP stands for *HyperText Transfer Protocol*. The *HyperText* part refers to the fact that Web pages include hypertext links. The *Transfer Protocol* part refers to the standard conventions for transferring a Web page across the network from one computer to another. Although you really don't have to understand HTTP to set up a Web server or use a Web browser, taking a look at its workings does help you understand how the Web works.

You can get a firsthand experience with HTTP by using the TELNET program to connect to the port where a Web server listens. On most systems, the Web server listens to port 80 and responds to any HTTP requests sent to that port. Therefore, you can use the TELNET program to connect to port 80 of a system (if it has a Web server) and try some HTTP commands.

Is HTTP an Internet standard?

Despite its widespread use in the Web since 1990, HTTP was not an Internet standard until fairly recently. All Internet standards are first distributed as a *Request for Comment* (RFC). The first HTTP-related RFC was RFC 1945, "HyperText Transfer Protocol — HTTP/1.0" (T. Berners-Lee, R. Fielding, and H. Frystyk, May 1996). However, RFC 1945 is considered an informational document, not a standard.

RFC 2616, "HyperText Transfer Protocol — HTTP/1.1" (R. Fielding, J. Gettys, J. Mogul, H. Frystyk, L. Masinter, P. Leach, T. Berners-Lee, June 1999) is the Draft Internet standard for HTTP.

To read these RFCs, point your Web browser to either `www.apps.ietf.org/rfc/` or `www.faqs.org/rfcs`.

To find out more about HTTP/1.1 and other Web-related standards, use a Web browser to access `www.w3.org/Protocols`.

To see an example of HTTP at work, follow these steps:

1. **Make sure that your Linux PC's connection to the Internet is up and running.**

   If you use PPP, for example, make sure that you have established a connection. If you have a broadband cable or DSL connection, chances are your connection is always on.

2. **Type the following command (I am using a U.S. government Web site's URL to illustrate how the HTTP protocol works):**

   ```
   telnet www.firstgov.gov 80
   ```

3. **After you see the `Connected...` message, type the following HTTP command and then press Enter twice:**

   ```
   GET / HTTP/1.0
   ```

   In response to this HTTP command, the Web server returns some useful information, followed by the contents of the default HTML file (usually called `index.html`).

The following is what I get when I try the `GET` command on a U.S. government Web site:

```
Trying 199.107.69.75...
Connected to www.firstgov.gov.
Escape character is '^]'.
HTTP/1.0 200 OK
Date: Sat, 25 Sep 2004 16:43:19 GMT
Server: Apache/1.3.27 (Unix) mod_ssl/2.8.14 OpenSSL/0.9.7b
Set-Cookie: SessionID=13183109613059925166 9; path=/;
```

```
Connection: close
Content-Type: text/html

<html lang="en"><head>
<title>FirstGov.gov: The U.S. Government's Official Web
 Portal</title>
...... (lines deleted)
</head><body alink="#990000" bgcolor="#ffffff" leftmargin="3"
    link="#000066" marginheight="0" marginwidth="3"
    onunload="Poll(); return true;" text="#000000"
    topmargin="0" vlink="#990000">
...... (lines deleted)
</body> </html>

Connection closed by foreign host.
```

When you try this example with TELNET, you see exactly what the Web server sends back to the Web browser. The first few lines are administrative information for the browser. The server returns this information:

- A line that shows that the server uses HTTP protocol version 1.0 and a status code of 200 indicating success:

  ```
  HTTP/1.0 200 OK
  ```

- The current date and time. A sample date and time string looks like this:

  ```
  Date: Sat, 25 Sep 2004 16:43:19 GMT
  ```

- The name of the Web-server software. For example, for a site running the Apache Web server, the server returns the following string:

  ```
  Server: Apache/1.3.27 (Unix) mod_ssl/2.8.14
      OpenSSL/0.9.7b
  ```

  The server suppresses the version number and other details so crackers cannot easily exploit known security holes in specific versions of Apache Web server.

- The type of document the Web server returns. For HTML documents, the content type is reported as follows:

  ```
  Content-type: text/html
  ```

The document itself follows the administrative information. An HTML document has the following general layout:

```
<title>Document's title goes here</title>
<html>
<body optional attributes go here >
... The rest of the document goes here
</body>
</html>
```

You can identify this layout by looking through the listing that shows what the Web server returns in response to the `GET` command. Because the example uses a `telnet` command to get the document, you see the HTML content as lines of text. If you were to access the same Web site (`www.firstgov.gov`) with a Web browser (such as Mozilla), you see the page in its graphical form, as shown in Figure 2-1.

Figure 2-1: The `www.firstgov.gov` Web site as viewed with a Web browser.

The example of HTTP commands shows the result of the `GET` command. `GET` is the most common HTTP command; it causes the server to return a specified HTML document or image.

The other two HTTP commands are `HEAD` and `POST`. The `HEAD` command is almost like `GET`: It causes the server to return everything in the document except the body. The `POST` command sends information to the server; it's up to the server to decide how to act on the information.

Exploring the Apache Web Server

You probably already know how to use the Web, but you may not know how to set up a Web server so that you, too, can provide information to the world through Web pages. To become an information provider on the Web, you have to run a Web server on your Linux PC on the Internet. You also have to prepare the Web pages for your Web site — a task that may be more demanding than the Web server setup.

Among the available Web servers, the Apache Web server is the most popular, and it's available for all Linux distributions. The Apache Web server started out as an improved version of the NCSA HTTPD server, but soon grew into a separate development effort. Like NCSA HTTPD, the Apache server is developed and maintained by a team of collaborators. Apache is freely available over the Internet.

Installing the Apache Web server

Depending on the choices you made when you installed your Linux distribution, the Apache Web server may be already installed in your system. If it's installed, it may already be running or you may have to start it. For example, the Apache Web server is already installed in Knoppix and Xandros, but it's not turned on by default.

The Apache Web server package name varies among distributions — Fedora Core calls it `httpd` whereas Knoppix and Xandros call it `apache`. Debian and SUSE call the package `apache2`. To see if the Apache Web server is installed, type **dpkg -l apache*** in Debian, Knoppix, and Xandros. If you see `ii` or `pn` in the first column of the output showing package names that begin with `apache`, then it's fully or partially installed. In Fedora Core, type **rpm -q httpd**. In SUSE, type **rpm -q apache2**.

If the Web server is not installed, you can install it easily. The steps depend on your Linux distribution. In Debian, type **apt-get install apache2**. In Fedora Core, mount the companion DVD and install the Apache Web server by typing the following commands:

```
cd /mnt/cdrom/Fedora/RPMS
rpm -ivh httpd*
```

In SUSE, click Install and Remove Software from the Software category in YaST Control Center (Main Menu➪System➪YaST), and then use YaST's search capability to find `apache`. When you find the packages you want, select them and click Accept to install them.

That's it! After you have installed the Apache Web server, you can run it.

Starting the Apache Web server

Even if the Apache Web server is installed, it may not be set up to start at boot time. If you want to try it out, you have to start the server.

To start the Apache Web server, log in as `root` and type **/etc/init.d/apache2 start** in Debian and SUSE. In Fedora Core, type **service httpd start**. In Knoppix and Xandros, type **/etc/init.d/apache start**. If you want to start the Apache Web server automatically at boot time, type **update-rc.d apache2 defaults** in

Debian. In Knoppix and Xandros, type **update-rc.d apache defaults**. In Fedora Core, type **chkconfig --levels 35 httpd on**. In SUSE, type **chkconfig --levels 35 apache2 on**.

To see whether the server is running, type **ps ax | grep *processname*** where ***processname*** is `httpd` in Fedora Core and SUSE and `apache` in Debian, Knoppix, and Xandros. If you see a number of Web server processes in the output, then everything is fine. Running several Web server processes — one parent and several child processes — is a common approach so that several HTTP requests can be handled efficiently by assigning each request to a Web server process.

If the output of `ps ax` does not show any Web server processes, errors may be lurking in the Apache configuration file. If this is the case, you have to fix any problems in the configuration file and start the server again.

If the Web server is up and running, you can use the TELNET program to connect to port 80 and see if the server works. Begin by typing the following command in a terminal window:

```
telnet localhost 80
```

After you get the `Connected` message, type

```
HEAD / HTTP/1.0
```

Why is it called Apache?

According to the information about the Apache Web server project on `www.apache.org/foundation/faq.html`, the Apache group was formed in March 1995 by a number of people who provided patch files that had been written to fix bugs in NCSA HTTPD 1.3. The result after applying the patches to NCSA HTTPD was what they called *a patchy server* (that's how the name Apache came about). The Apache Group has now evolved into The Apache Software Foundation (ASF), a nonprofit corporation that was incorporated in Delaware, U.S.A., in June 1999. ASF has a number of other ongoing projects. You can read about these projects at `www.apache.org`. In particular, visit `httpd.apache.org` for more information about the Apache Web server project.

According to the September 2004 Netcraft Web Server Survey at `news.netcraft.com/archives/web_server_survey.html`, the Apache Web server is the most popular Web server out there — 67.85 percent of the 54,407,216 sites reported using the Apache server. Microsoft Internet Information Server (IIS) is a distant second, with 21.14 percent of the sites.

Then press Enter twice. You get a response that looks similar to the following (with different dates and numbers, of course):

```
HTTP/1.1 200 OK
Date: Sat, 25 Sep 2004 16:22:10 GMT
Server: Apache/2.0.49 (Linux/SuSE)
Content-Location: index.html.en
Vary: negotiate,accept-language,accept-charset
TCN: choice
Last-Modified: Fri, 04 May 2001 00:01:18 GMT
ETag: "1a4ef-5b0-40446f80;1a505-961-8562af00"
Accept-Ranges: bytes
Content-Length: 1456
Connection: close
Content-Type: text/html; charset=ISO-8859-1
Content-Language: en
Expires: Sat, 25 Sep 2004 16:22:10 GMT

Connection closed by foreign host.
```

The response shows some information about the Web server and the default home page. You can also check out the Web server by using a Web browser, such as Mozilla, running on your Linux system. Use the URL `http://localhost/` and see what happens.

Configuring the Apache Web Server

The Apache Web server program files and configuration files are stored in different locations in different distributions. The Apache Web server configuration file is named `httpd.conf` in Fedora Core, Knoppix, SUSE, and Xandros, but in Debian it's named `apache2.conf`. The configuration file is a text file with directives that specify various aspects of the Web server.

In Debian and SUSE, the configuration file is in the `/etc/apache2` directory. In Fedora Core, the `httpd.conf` file is in the `/etc/httpd/conf` directory. In Knoppix and Xandros, the file is in the `/etc/apache` directory.

The directory with the `httpd.conf` file also contains information about the Secure Sockets Layer (SSL) implementation needs. (The SSL implementation comes as part of the Apache Web server.)

Using Apache configuration tools

In some Linux distributions, you can use a GUI tool to configure the Apache Web server. In particular, Fedora Core and SUSE come with GUI tools for configuring the Apache Web server. I introduce you to these GUI tools in this section.

In Fedora Core, log in as `root` and select Main Menu➪System Settings➪Server Settings➪HTTP from the GUI desktop. The Apache Configuration dialog box appears, as shown in Figure 2-2.

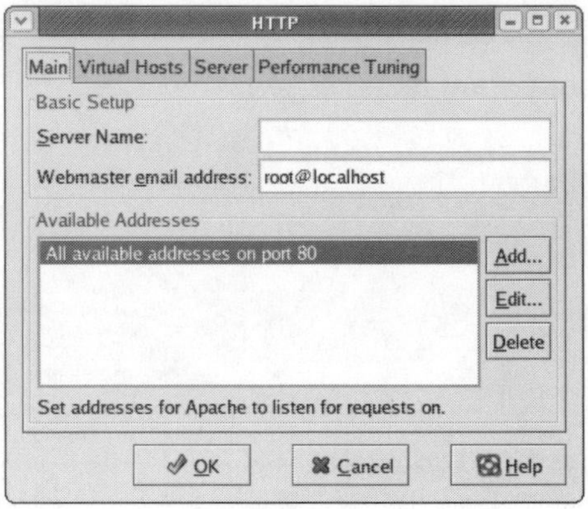

Figure 2-2: In Fedora Core, configure the Apache HTTP server from this dialog box.

The Apache Configuration dialog box is organized into four tabs. You can set various options from each of these tabs:

- **Main:** From this tab, you can specify the IP addresses and port number where Apache expects requests for Web service. You can also set the e-mail address of the Webmaster.
- **Virtual Hosts:** Here you can set up virtual hosts. (I discuss the options for virtual hosts later in this chapter.) You can also edit the default settings that apply to all virtual hosts. Clicking the Edit Default Settings button on the Virtual Hosts tab brings up another dialog box (shown in Figure 2-3) from which you can set a number of different options.
- **Server:** This tab has settings for the server such as the user and group names under which the HTTP server runs and the locations of the file where the process ID is stored.
- **Performance Tuning:** On this tab, you can set some parameters that control overall performance. You can set the maximum number of connections allowed, the timeout period for connections, and the maximum number of requests per connection.

Initially the configuration window displays the default values from the configuration file `/etc/httpd/conf/httpd.conf`. After you make any changes, click the OK button. The configuration tool prompts you to ask whether you really want to save the changes and exit. If you do, click Yes and you are done.

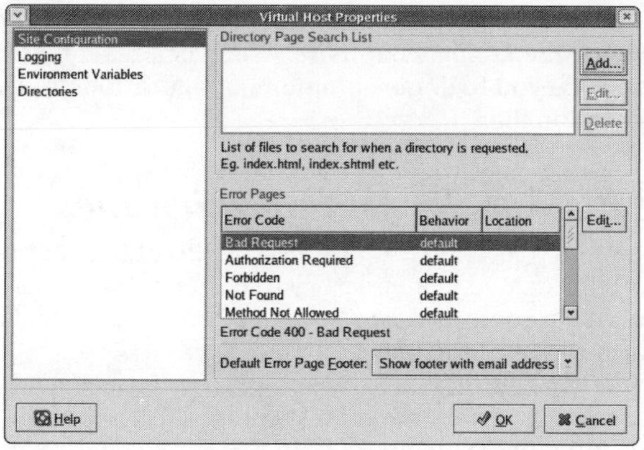

Figure 2-3: You can configure the virtual host properties from Fedora Core's GUI utility.

In SUSE, select Main Menu⇨System⇨YaST to open the YaST Control Center. Click Network Services in the left-hand side of the window and click HTTP Server in the right-hand side. YaST opens the HTTP Server Configuration window, as shown in Figure 2-4. You can then configure the properties of the server from the configuration window.

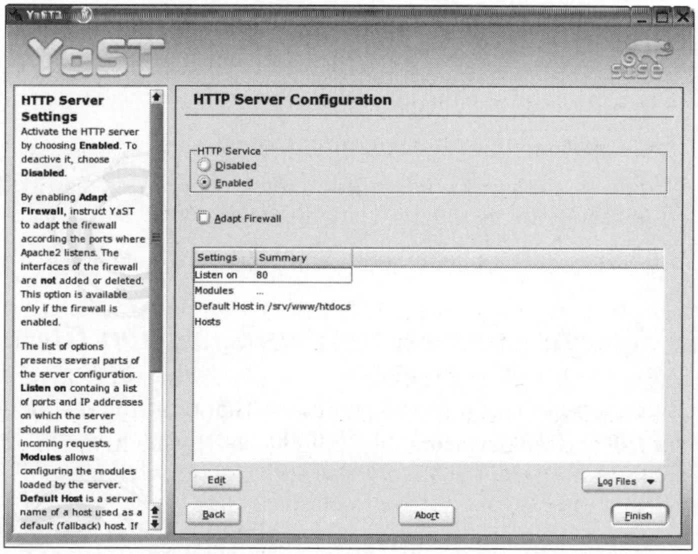

Figure 2-4: In SUSE, YaST enables you to configure the Apache HTTP server.

When you configure the Apache HTTP server by using a GUI configuration tool, all you're doing is changing options and attributes stored in the Apache Web server configuration file (`/etc/apache2/httpd.conf` in Debian, `/etc/httpd/conf/httpd.conf` in Fedora Core, `/etc/apache/httpd.conf` in Knoppix and Xandros, and in SUSE, `/etc/apache2/httpd.conf` and all the

.conf files in the /etc/apache2 directory). You can just as easily make the changes by editing the configuration file, which is a plain text file. In the next sections, I introduce you to some common configuration directives in the Apache configuration file.

Syntax of the Apache configuration files

The Apache server's operation is controlled by the httpd.conf (or apache2.conf in Debian) file located in a directory that depends on your distribution. The configuration file controls how the server runs, what documents it serves, and who can access these documents.

In the next few sections, I summarize key information about the Apache Web server configuration file. Typically, you don't have to change anything in the configuration files to run the Apache Web server. However, knowing the format of the configuration files and the meaning of the various keywords used in them is useful.

As you study the Apache Web server configuration files, keep these syntax rules in mind:

- Each configuration file is a text file that you can edit with your favorite text editor and view with the more command.
- All comment lines begin with a #.
- Each line can have only one directive.
- Extra spaces and blank lines are ignored.
- Typically, the main configuration file incorporates many other configuration files by using the Include directive.
- All entries, except pathnames and URLs, are case insensitive.

The Apache Web server configuration file

The httpd.conf file (or apache2.conf in Debian) is the main HTTP-daemon configuration file — it includes directives that control how the Apache Web server runs. Often, the configuration file incorporates several other configuration files by referencing them with a directive called Include.

The configuration file specifies the port number the server uses, the name of the Web site, and the e-mail address to which mail is sent in case of any problems with the server. In addition, the configuration file specifies where the Web pages are located and who can access what directories.

In the following sections, I present the Apache directives grouped in three separate categories: general HTTPD directives, resource-configuration directives, and access-control directives. Finally, I explain how virtual hosts can be set up in Apache Web server so a single Web server can handle Web requests sent to several IP addresses or host names.

TIP

To browse the Apache HTTPD documentation online, visit `httpd.apache.org/docs-2.0`. Specifically, you can look up information on configuration directives at `httpd.apache.org/docs-2.0/mod/directives.html`.

General HTTPD directives

Some interesting items from the Apache Web server configuration file are

- `ServerAdmin` is the e-mail address that the Web server provides to clients in case any errors occur. The default value for `ServerAdmin` is `root@localhost`. Set this address to a valid e-mail address that anyone on the Internet can use to report any errors that your Web site may contain.
- `Include` loads more configuration directives from a specified file. For example, in Fedora Core, the default `/etc/httpd/conf/httpd.conf` file loads all the configuration files from the `/etc/httpd/conf.d` directory by using the following `Include` directive:

  ```
  Include conf.d/*.conf
  ```

  This command means that you can load another set of configurations by simply adding a file to the `/etc/httpd/conf.d` directory. In fact, that's the directory where you find the configuration files for various Apache HTTPD modules, such as Perl, PHP, and SSL. In Fedora Core, study the configuration file in the `/etc/httpd/conf.d` directory to find out more about the total set of directives that affect the Apache Web server's behavior.

Many more directives control the way that the Apache Web server works. The following list summarizes some of the directives you can use in the `httpd.conf` file. You can leave most of these directives in their default settings, but knowing about them if you're maintaining a Web server is important.

- `Listen` *`IP-Address:Port`*: Forces the Web server to listen to a specific IP address and port number. By default, the Web server responds to all IP addresses associated with the host.
- `User` *`name [ #id]`*: Specifies the username (or ID) the HTTP daemon uses. You can leave this directive at the default setting (`apache`). If you specify a user ID, use a hash (#) prefix for the numeric ID.
- `Group` *`name [ #id]`*: Specifies the group name (or ID) of the HTTP daemon when running in standalone mode. The default group name is `apache`.
- `ServerRoot` *`pathname`*: Specifies the directory where the Web server's configuration and log files are expected to reside. In Debian and SUSE,

ServerRoot is /etc/apache2. In Fedora Core, ServerRoot is set to /etc/httpd. In Knoppix and Xandros, ServerRoot is /etc/apache.

- ServerName *www.company.com*:80: Sets the server's host name to *www.company.com* and the port number to 80. ServerName is used only when redirecting a Web page to another.
- ServerTokens Major|Minor|Min|Prod|OS|Full: Controls how much information is sent back to the client in the Server field of the header. Set the directive to Prod for a Server response that simply identifies the product name (in this case, Apache).
- StartServers *num*: Sets the number of child processes that start as soon as the Apache Web server runs. The default value is 8.
- MaxSpareServers *num*: Sets the desired maximum number of idle child-server processes. (A child process is considered idle if it's not handling an HTTP request.) The default value is 20.
- MinSpareServers *num*: Sets the desired minimum number of idle child server processes. (A child process is considered idle if it's not handling an HTTP request.) A new spare process is created every second if the number falls below this threshold. The default value is 5.
- Timeout *numsec*: Sets the number of seconds that the server waits for a client to send a query after the client establishes connection. The default Timeout is 300 seconds (five minutes).
- ErrorLog *filename*: Sets the file where httpd logs the errors it encounters. If the filename does not begin with a slash (/), the name is taken to be relative to ServerRoot. The default ErrorLog is /var/log/httpd/error_log in Fedora Core and /var/log/apache2/error_log in SUSE. In Debian, the error log is in /var/log/apache2/error.log. In Knoppix and Xandros, the error log is in /var/log/apache/error.log. Typical error log entries include events, such as server restarts, and any warning messages.
- TransferLog *filename*: Sets the file where httpd records all client accesses (including failed accesses).
- LogFormat *formatstring formatname*: Specifies the format of log-file entries for the TransferLog. The CustomLog directive also uses this format to produce logs in a specific format.
- CustomLog *filename formatname*: Sets the name of the custom log file where httpd records all client accesses (including failed accesses) in a format specified by *formatname* (which you define using a LogFormat directive).
- PidFile *filename*: Sets the file where httpd stores its process ID.
- MaxClients *num*: Sets the limit on the number of clients that can simultaneously connect to the server. The default value is 150. The value of MaxClients cannot be more than 256.

- LoadModule *module* modules/modfile.so: Loads a module that was built as a Dynamic Shared Object (DSO). You have to specify the module name and the module's object file. Because the order in which modules are loaded is important, leave these directives as they appear in the default configuration file. ***Note:*** The mod_ssl module provides support for encryption using the Secure Sockets Layer (SSL) protocol.

Resource configuration directives

The resource configuration directives specify the location of the Web pages, as well as how to specify the data types of various files. To get started, you can leave the directives at their default settings. These are some of the resource configuration directives for the Apache Web server:

- DocumentRoot *pathname*: Specifies the directory where the HTTP server finds the Web pages. In Debian, the default DocumentRoot is /var/www/apache2-default. In Fedora Core, DocumentRoot is /var/www/html. In SUSE, DocumentRoot is /srv/www/htdocs. In Knoppix and Xandros, DocumentRoot is /var/www. If you place your HTML documents in another directory, set DocumentRoot to that directory.
- UserDir *dirname*: Specifies the subdirectory below a user's home directory where the HTTP server looks for Web pages when a username appears in the URL (in an URL such as http://www.xyz.net/~naba, for example, which includes a username with a tilde prefix). By default, the UserDir feature is turned off by setting *dirname* to disable. If you want it enabled, you can set it to public_html, which means that a user's Web pages are in the public_html subdirectory of that user's home directory.
- DirectoryIndex *filename1 filename2 ...*: Indicates the server return default file or files when the client does not specify a document. The default DirectoryIndex is index.html. If the Apache Web server does not find this file, it returns an index (basically, a nice-looking listing of the files) of that directory, provided indexing is allowed for that directory.
- AccessFileName *filename*: Specifies the name of the file that may appear in each directory that contains documents and that indicates who has permission to access the contents of that directory. The default AccessFileName is .htaccess. The syntax of this file is the same as that of Apache access-control directives, which I discuss in the next section.
- AddType *type/subtype extension*: Associates a file extension with a MIME data type (of the form *type/subtype*, such as text/plain or image/gif). Thus, to have the server treat files with the .lst extension as plain-text files, specify the following:

  ```
  AddType text/plain .lst
  ```

  The default MIME types and extensions are listed in the /etc/mime.types file.

- `AddEncoding` *`type extension`*: Associates an encoding type with a file extension. To have the server mark files ending with `.gz` or `.tgz` as encoded with the `x-gzip` encoding method (the standard name for the GZIP encoding), specify the following:

  ```
  AddEncoding x-gzip gz tgz
  ```

- `DefaultType` *`type/subtype`*: Specifies the MIME type that the server uses if it cannot determine the type from the file extension. If you don't specify `DefaultType`, the Apache Web server assumes the MIME type to be `text/html`. In the default `httpd.conf` file, `DefaultType` is specified as `text/plain`.

- `Redirect` *`requested-file actual-URL`*: Specifies that any requests for *`requested-file`* be redirected to *`actual-URL`*.

- `Alias` *`requested-dir actual-dir`*: Specifies that the server use *`actual-dir`* to locate files in the *`requested-dir`* directory (in other words, *`requested-dir`* is an alias for *`actual-dir`*). To have requests for the `/icons` directory go to `/usr/share/apache2/icons/`, specify the following:

  ```
  Alias /icons/ "/usr/share/apache2/icons/"
  ```

- `ScriptAlias` *`requested-dir actual-dir`*: Specifies the real name of the directory where scripts for the Common Gateway Interface (CGI) are located. The default configuration file contains this directive:

  ```
  ScriptAlias /cgi-bin/ "/srv/www/cgi-bin/"
  ```

  This directive means that when a Web browser requests a script, such as `/cgi-bin/test-cgi`, the HTTP server runs the script `/srv/www/cgi-bin/test-cgi`.

- `DefaultIcon` *`iconfile`*: Specifies the location of the default icon that the server uses for files that have no icon information.

- `ReadmeName` *`filename`*: Specifies the name of a `README` file whose contents are added to the end of an automatically generated directory listing. The default `ReadmeName` is `README`.

- `HeaderName` *`filename`*: Specifies the name of a header file whose contents are prepended to an automatically generated directory listing. The default `HeaderName` is `HEADER`.

- `AddDescription` *`"file description" filename`*: Specifies that the *`file description`* string display next to the specified filename in the directory listing. You can use a wildcard, such as `*.html`, as the filename. For example, the following directive describes files ending with `.tgz` as GZIP compressed tar archives:

  ```
  AddDescription "GZIP compressed tar archive" .tgz
  ```

✦ `AddIcon` *`iconfile extension1 extension2 ...`*: Associates an icon with one or more file extensions. The following directive associates the icon file `/icons/text.gif` with the file extension `.txt`:

```
AddIcon /icons/text.gif .txt
```

✦ `AddIconByType` *`iconfile MIME-types`*: Associates an icon with a group of file types specified as a wildcard form of MIME types (such as `text/*` or `image/*`). To associate an icon file of `/icons/text.gif` with all `text` types, specify the following:

```
AddIconByType (TXT,/icons/text.gif) text/*
```

This directive also tells the server to use `TXT` in place of the icon for clients that cannot accept images. (Browsers tell the server what types of data they can accept.)

✦ `AddIconByEncoding` *`iconfile encoding1 encoding2 ...`*: Specifies an icon to display for one or more encoding types (such as `x-compress` or `x-gzip`).

✦ `IndexIgnore` *`filename1 filename2 ...`*: Instructs the server to ignore the specified filenames (they typically contain wildcards) when preparing a directory listing. To leave out `README`, `HEADER`, and all files with names that begin with a period (`.`), a trailing tilde (~), or a trailing hash mark (`#`), specify the following:

```
IndexIgnore .??* *~ *# HEADER* README* RCS CVS *,v *,t
```


✦ `IndexOptions` *`option1 option2 ...`*: Indicates the options you want in the directory listing prepared by the server. Options can include one or more of the following:

- `FancyIndexing` turns on the fancy directory listing that includes filenames and icons representing the files' types, sizes, and last-modified dates.
- `IconHeight=N` specifies that icons are `N` pixels tall.
- `IconWidth=N` specifies that icons are `N` pixels wide.
- `NameWidth=N` makes the filename column `N` characters wide.
- `IconsAreLinks` makes the icons act like links.
- `ScanHTMLTitles` shows a description of HTML files.
- `SuppressHTMLPreamble` does not add a standard HTML preamble to the header file (specified by the `HeaderName` directive).
- `SuppressLastModified` stops display of the last date of modification.
- `SuppressSize` stops display of the file size.
- `SuppressDescription` stops display of any file description.
- `SuppressColumnSorting` stops the column headings from being links that enable sorting the columns.

✦ `ErrorDocument` *`errortype filename`*: Specifies a file that the server sends when an error of a specific type occurs. You can also provide a text message for an error. Here are some examples:

```
ErrorDocument 403 "Sorry, no access to this directory"
ErrorDocument 403 /error/noindex.html
ErrorDocument 404 /cgi-bin/bad_link.pl
ErrorDocument 401 /new_subscriber.html
```

If you don't have the `ErrorDocument` directive, the server sends a built-in error message. The *`errortype`* can be one of the following `HTTP/1.1` error conditions (see RFC 2616 at `www.ietf.org/rfc/rfc2616.txt` or `www.faqs.org/rfcs/rfc2616.html` for more information):

- 400: Bad Request
- 401: Unauthorized
- 402: Payment Required
- 403: Forbidden
- 404: Not Found
- 405: Method Not Allowed
- 406: Not Acceptable
- 407: Proxy Authentication Required
- 408: Request Timeout
- 409: Conflict
- 410: Gone
- 411: Length Required
- 412: Precondition Failed
- 413: Request Entity Too Large
- 414: Request-URI Too Long
- 415: Unsupported Media Type
- 416: Requested Range Not Satisfiable
- 417: Expectation Failed
- 500: Internal Server Error
- 501: Not Implemented
- 502: Bad Gateway
- 503: Service Unavailable
- 504: Gateway Timeout
- 505: HTTP Version Not Supported

- `TypesConfig` *`filename`*: Specifies the file that contains the mapping of file extensions to MIME data types. (MIME stands for *Multipurpose Internet Mail Extensions,* a way to package attachments in a single message file.) The server reports these MIME types to clients. If you don't specify a `TypesConfig` directive, `httpd` assumes that the `TypesConfig` file is `/etc/mime.types`. The following are a few selected lines from the default `/etc/mime.types` file:

  ```
  application/msword              doc
  application/pdf                 pdf
  application/postscript          ai eps ps
  application/x-tcl               tcl
  audio/mpeg                      mpga mp2 mp3
  audio/x-pn-realaudio            ram rm
  audio/x-wav                     wav
  image/gif                       gif
  image/jpeg                      jpeg jpg jpe
  image/png                       png
  text/html                       html htm
  text/plain                      asc txt
  video/mpeg                      mpeg mpg mpe
  ```

  Each line shows the MIME type (such as `text/html`), followed by the file extensions for that type (`html` or `htm`).

Access-control directives

Access-control directives enable you to control who can access different directories in the system. These are the global access-configuration directives. You can also have another access-configuration file that uses a name specified by the `AccessFileName` directive in every directory from which the Apache Web server can serve documents. (That *per-directory* access-configuration file is named `.htaccess` by default.)

Stripped of most of its comment lines, the access-control directive has this format:

```
# First, we configure the "default" to be a
# very restrictive set of permissions.
<Directory />
    Options FollowSymLinks
    AllowOverride None
</Directory>

# The following directory name should
# match DocumentRoot in httpd.conf
<Directory /var/www/html>
    Options Indexes FollowSymLinks
    AllowOverride None
    order allow,deny
    allow from all
</Directory>
```

```
# The directory name should match the
# location of the cgi-bin directory
<Directory "/srv/www/cgi-bin">
    AllowOverride None
    Options None
    Order allow,deny
    Allow from all
</Directory>
```

Access-control directives use a different syntax from the other Apache directives. The syntax is like that of HTML. Various access-control directives are enclosed within pairs of tags, such as `<Directory> ... </Directory>`.

The following list describes some of the access-control directives. In particular, notice the `AuthUserFile` directive; you can have password-based access control for specific directories.

- `Options` *`opt1 opt2`* `...`: Specifies the access-control options for the directory section in which this directive appears. The options can be one or more of the following:
  - `None` disables all access-control features.
  - `All` turns on all features for the directory.
  - `FollowSymLinks` enables the server to follow symbolic links (shortcuts, in other words).
  - `SymLinksIfOwnerMatch` follows symbolic links, only if the same user of the directory owns the linked directory.
  - `ExecCGI` enables execution of CGI scripts in the directory.
  - `Includes` enables server-side include files in this directory. (The term *server-side include* refers to directives, placed in an HTML file, that the Web server processes before returning the results to the Web browser.)
  - `Indexes` enables clients to request indexes (directory listings) for the directory.
  - `IncludesNOEXEC` disables the `#exec` command in server-side includes.
- `AllowOverride` *`directive1 directive2`* `...`: Specifies which access-control directives can be overridden on a per-directory basis. The directive list can contain one or more of the following:
  - `None` stops any directive from being overridden.
  - `All` enables overriding of any directive on a per-directory basis.

  - Options enables the use of the Options directive in the directory-level file.
  - FileInfo enables the use of directives controlling document type, such as AddType and AddEncoding.
  - AuthConfig enables the use of authorization directives, such as AuthName, AuthType, AuthUserFile, and AuthGroupFile.
  - Limit enables the use of Limit directives (allow, deny, and order) in a directory's access-configuration file.

- AuthName *name*: Specifies the authorization name for a directory.
- AuthType *type*: Specifies the type of authorization to be used. The only supported authorization type is Basic.
- AuthUserFile *filename*: Specifies the file in which usernames and passwords are stored for authorization. For example, the following directive sets the authorization file to /etc/httpd/conf/passwd:

  ```
  AuthUserFile /etc/httpd/conf/passwd
  ```

  You have to create the authorization file with the /usr/bin/htpasswd support program. To create the authorization file and add the password for a user named jdoe, specify the following:

  ```
  /usr/bin/htpasswd -c /etc/httpd/conf/passwd jdoe
  ```

  When prompted for the password, enter the password and then confirm it by typing it again.
- AuthGroupFile *filename*: Specifies the file to consult for a list of user groups for authentication.
- order *ord*: Specifies the order in which two other directives — allow and deny — are evaluated. The order is one of the following:
  - deny,allow causes the Web server to evaluate the deny directive before allow.
  - allow,deny causes the Web server to evaluate the allow directive before deny.
  - mutual-failure enables only hosts in the allow list.
- deny from *host1 host2...*: Specifies the hosts denied access.
- allow from *host1 host2...*: Specifies the hosts allowed access. To enable all hosts in a specific domain to access the Web documents in a directory, specify the following:

  ```
  order deny,allow
  allow from .nws.noaa.gov
  ```

✦ `require entity en1 en2...`: This directive specifies which users can access a directory. `entity` is one of the following:

- `user` enables only a list of named users.
- `group` enables only a list of named groups.
- `valid-user` enables all users listed in the `AuthUserFile` access to the directory (provided they enter the correct password).

Virtual host setup

A useful feature of the Apache HTTP server is that it can handle virtual Web servers. *Virtual hosting* simply means that a single Web server can respond to many different IP addresses and serve Web pages from different directories, depending on the IP address. That means you can set up a single Web server to respond to both `www.big.org` and `www.tiny.com` and serve a unique home page for each host name. A server with this capability is known as a *multi-homed* Web server, a *virtual* Web server, or a server with *virtual host support.*

As you might guess, Internet Service Providers (ISPs) use the virtual host feature of Apache Web server to offer virtual Web sites to their customers. You need the following to support virtual hosts:

✦ The Web server must be able to respond to multiple IP addresses (each with a unique domain name) and must enable you to specify document directories, log files, and other configuration items for each IP address.

✦ The host system must be able to associate multiple IP addresses with a single physical network interface. Linux can do so.

✦ Each domain name associated with the IP address must be a unique, registered domain name with proper DNS entries.

For the latest information on how to set up virtual hosts in an Apache HTTP server, consult the following URL:

```
http://httpd.apache.org/docs-2.0/vhosts
```

The Apache HTTP server can respond to different host names with different home pages. You have two options when supporting virtual hosts:

✦ **Run multiple copies of the `httpd` program, one for each IP address:** In this case, you create a separate copy of the `httpd.conf` configuration file for each host and use the `Listen` directive to make the server respond to a specific IP address.

✦ **Run a single copy of the `httpd` program with a single `httpd.conf` file:** In the configuration file, set `Listen` to a port number only (so the server responds to any IP address associated with the host), and use the `VirtualHost` directive to configure the server for each virtual host.

Run multiple HTTP daemons only if you don't expect heavy traffic on your system; the system may not be able to respond well because of the overhead associated with running multiple daemons. However, you may need multiple HTTP daemons if each virtual host has a unique configuration need for the following directives:

- ✦ `UserId` and `GroupId` (the user and group ID for the HTTP daemon)
- ✦ `ServerRoot` (the `root` directory of the server)
- ✦ `TypesConfig` (the MIME type configuration file)

For a site with heavy traffic, configure the Web server so that a single HTTP daemon can serve multiple virtual hosts. Of course, this recommendation implies that there is only one configuration file. In that configuration file, use the `VirtualHost` directive to configure each virtual host.

Most ISPs use the `VirtualHost` capability of Apache HTTP server to pro vide virtual Web sites to their customers. Unless you pay for a dedicated Web host, you typically get a virtual site where you have your own domain name, but share the server and the actual host with many other customers.

The syntax of the `VirtualHost` directive is as follows:

```
<VirtualHost hostaddr>
    ... directives that apply to this host
    ...
</VirtualHost>
```

With this syntax, you use `<VirtualHost>` and `</VirtualHost>` to enclose a group of directives that applies only to the particular virtual host identified by the *`hostaddr`* parameter. The *`hostaddr`* can be an IP address or the fully qualified domain name of the virtual host.

You can place almost any Apache directive within the `<VirtualHost>` block. At a minimum, Webmasters include the following directives in the `<Virtual Host>` block:

- ✦ `DocumentRoot`, which specifies where this virtual host's documents reside
- ✦ `Servername`, which identifies the server to the outside world (this name is a registered domain name that DNS supports)
- ✦ `ServerAdmin`, the e-mail address of this virtual host's Webmaster
- ✦ `Redirect`, which specifies any URLs to be redirected to other URLs
- ✦ `ErrorLog`, which specifies the file where errors related to this virtual host are to be logged

- CustomLog, which specifies the file where accesses to this virtual host are logged

When the server receives a request for a document in a particular virtual host's DocumentRoot directory, it uses the configuration parameters within that server's <VirtualHost> block to handle that request.

Here is a typical example of a <VirtualHost> directive that sets up the virtual host www.lnbsoft.com:

```
<VirtualHost www.lnbsoft.com>
    DocumentRoot    /home/naba/httpd/htdocs
    ServerName   www.lnbsoft.com
    ServerAdmin   webmaster@lnbsoft.com
    ScriptAlias   /cgi-bin/   /home/naba/httpd/cgi-bin/
    ErrorLog  /home/naba/httpd/logs/error_log
    CustomLog   /home/naba/httpd/logs/access_log common
</VirtualHost>
```

Here the name common in the CustomLog directive refers to the name of a format defined earlier in the httpd.conf file by the LogFormat directive, as follows:

```
LogFormat "%h %l %u %t \"%r\" %>s %b" common
```

This format string for the log produces lines in the log file that look like this:

```
dial236.dc.psn.net - - [13/Jul/2004:18:09:00 -0500] "GET /
   HTTP/1.0" 200 1243
```

The format string contains two letter tokens that start with a percent sign (%). The meaning of these tokens is shown in Table 2-1.

Table 2-1 LogFormat Tokens

Token	*Meaning*
%b	The number of bytes sent to the client, excluding header information
%h	The host name of the client machine
%l	The identity of the user, if available
%r	The HTTP request from the client (for example, GET / HTTP/1.0)
%s	The server response code from the Web server
%t	The current local date and time
%u	The username the user supplies (only when access-control rules require username/password authentication)

Chapter 3: Setting Up the FTP Server

In This Chapter

- **Installing the FTP server**
- **Configuring the FTP server**

File Transfer Protocol (FTP) is a popular Internet service for transferring files from one system to another. *Anonymous FTP* is another popular Internet service for distributing files. The neat thing about anonymous FTP is that if a remote system supports anonymous FTP, anyone can use FTP with the `anonymous` user ID and can download files from that system. Although anonymous FTP is useful for distributing data, it poses a security risk if it's not set up properly.

Linux distributions typically come with several FTP clients and the Very Secure FTP daemon (`vsftpd`), written by Chris Evans. The FTP server typically includes the files you need to support anonymous FTP. In this chapter, I show you how to configure the `vsftpd` FTP server through text configuration files and how to control access to the FTP server.

Installing the FTP Server

Depending on the choices you made during Linux installation, the FTP server `vsftpd` and its configuration files may already be installed on your system. If `vsftpd` is not installed, you can easily install it.

In Debian and Xandros, type **dpkg -l *ftp*** to see if the FTP server is installed. In Fedora Core and SUSE, type **rpm -qa | grep vsftp** and see if the `vsftpd` package is installed.

In Debian, type **apt-get install vsftpd** to install the FTP server. In Fedora Core, log in as `root`, mount the DVD, and type **cd /mnt/cdrom/Fedora/RPMS** followed by **rpm -ivh vsftpd***. In SUSE, click Install and Remove Software in the YaST Control Center's Software category. Then use YaST's search capability to find `vsftpd` and install it. In Xandros, first run Xandros Networks, select Edit⇨Set Application Sources, and click the Debian Unsupported Site link as a source; then you can use the **apt-get install vsftpd** command to install the Very Secure FTP server.

Configuring the FTP Server

The Very Secure FTP daemon (vsftpd) uses a number of configuration files in the /etc directory (and in the /etc/vsftpd directory in Fedora Core). By default, the vsftpd server is disabled — and if you want to use the FTP server, first you have to enable it. In this section, I show you how.

The vsftpd server can be configured to run in standalone mode or under the control of the xinetd server. In Debian and Fedora Core, vsftpd is set to run as a standalone. In SUSE, vsftpd runs under the control of xinetd. In Debian and Fedora Core, you can start vsftpd by typing **/etc/init.d/vsftpd start**. In SUSE, edit the file /etc/xinetd.d/vsftpd — making sure that it does not have a disable = yes line — then type **/etc/init.d/xinetd restart** to restart xinetd.

To start the vsftpd when the system boots, type **update-rc.d vsftpd defaults** in Debian. In Fedora Core, enable vsftpd for automatic start by typing **chkconfig --level 35 vsftpd on**.

After you start the vsftpd server, the default settings are good enough for the server to be useful. That's because other FTP clients can now connect and request files from your FTP server. However, you need to know about the configuration files in case you have to customize them some other time.

vsftpd configuration files

The vsftpd server consults the vsftpd.conf file (located in /etc in Debian, SUSE, and Xandros and in the /etc/vsftpd directory in Fedora Core — remember that you must first install vsftpd in Xandros). That configuration file may refer to other files in the /etc directory. The vsftpd.conf file controls many aspects of the FTP server, such as whether it runs in standalone mode, who can download files, and whether to allow anonymous FTP. The key configuration files for vsftpd are the following:

- /etc/vsftpd.conf or /etc/vsftpd/vsftpd.conf controls how the vsftpd server works (for example, whether it allows anonymous logins, allows file uploads, and so on).
- /etc/vsftpd.ftpusers, if it exists, lists names of users who cannot access the FTP server.
- /etc/vsftpd.user_list, if it exists, lists names of users who are denied access (not even prompted for password). However, if the userlist_deny option is set to NO in /etc/vsftpd/vsftpd.conf, these users are allowed to access the FTP server.

In Debian, SUSE, and Xandros, vsftpd uses a single configuration file — /etc/vsftpd.conf. In Fedora Core, the default installation of vsftpd uses the /etc/vsftpd/vsftpd.conf file, as well as /etc/vsftpd.ftpusers and /etc/vsftpd.user_list.

You can usually leave most of the vsftpd configuration files with their default settings. However, just in case you have to change something to make vsftpd suit your needs, I explain the configuration files briefly in the next few sections.

The vsftpd.conf file

To find out what you can have in the vsftpd.conf file and how these lines affect the vsftpd server's operation, start by looking at the vsftpd.conf file that's installed by default. The comments in this file tell you what each option does.

By default, vsftpd allows almost nothing. By editing the options in vsftpd.conf, you can loosen the restrictions so that users can use FTP. You can decide how loose the settings are.

Here are some of the options that you can set in the vsftpd.conf file:

- anon_mkdir_write_enable=YES enables anonymous FTP users to create new directories. This option is risky because a malicious user may use up all of your hard drive space by creating too many directories. Therefore, you may want to set this option to NO, even if you allow anonymous users to upload files.
- anon_upload_enable=YES means anonymous FTP users can upload files. This option takes effect only if write_enable is already set to YES and the directory has write permissions for everyone. ***Remember:*** Allowing anonymous users to write on your system can be very risky because the users could fill up the disk or use your disk for their personal storage.
- anonymous_enable=YES enables *anonymous FTP.* (Users can log in with the username anonymous and provide their e-mail address as a password.) Comment out this line if you don't want anonymous FTP.
- ascii_download_enable=YES enables file downloads in ASCII mode. Unfortunately, a malicious remote user can issue the SIZE command with the name of a huge file and essentially cause the FTP server to waste huge amounts of resources opening that file and determining its size. This technique is used in a Denial of Service attack. (For more information about Denial of Service [DOS] attacks, see Chapter 1 of Book VI.)
- ascii_upload_enable=YES enables file uploads in ASCII mode (for text files).

- async_abor_enable=YES causes vsftpd to recognize ABOR (abort) requests that arrive at any time. You may have to enable it to allow older FTP clients to work with vsftpd.
- banned_email_file=/etc/vsftpd.banned_emails specifies the file with the list of banned e-mail addresses (used only if deny_email_enable is set to YES).
- chown_uploads=YES causes uploaded anonymous files to be owned by a different user specified by the chown_username option. Don't enable this option unless absolutely necessary — and don't specify root as the chown_username (that's a disaster just waiting to happen). You may need to enable this if a process running under a specific username uses the uploaded files, which means that no matter who uploads the files, the owner has to be changed to the username that the process expects.
- chown_username=*name* specifies the username that owns files uploaded by anonymous FTP users.
- chroot_list_enable=YES causes vsftpd to confine all users except those on a list specified by the chroot_list_file to their home directories when they log in for FTP service. This option prevents these users from getting to any other files besides what's in their home directories.
- chroot_list_file=/etc/vsftpd.chroot_list is the list of users who are either confined to their home directories or not, depending on the setting of chroot_local_user.
- connect_from_port_20=YES causes vsftpd to make sure that data transfers occur through port 20 (the FTP data port).
- data_connection_timeout=120 is the time in seconds after which an inactive data connection is timed out.
- deny_email_enable=YES causes vsftpd to check a list of banned e-mail addresses and deny access to anyone who tries to log in anonymously with a banned e-mail address as a password.
- dirmessage_enable=YES causes vsftpd to display messages when FTP users change to certain directories.
- ftpd_banner=Welcome to my FTP service sets the banner that vsftpd displays when a user logs in. You can change the message to anything you want.
- idle_session_timeout=600 is the time (in seconds) after which an *idle session* (refers to the situation where someone connects and does not do anything) times out and vsftpd logs the user out.
- listen=YES causes vsftpd to listen for connection requests and, consequently, run in standalone mode. Set this option to NO if you want to run vsftpd under xinetd.

- `local_enable=YES` causes `vsftpd` to grant local users access to FTP.
- `local_umask=022` means that whatever files FTP writes have a permission of 644 (read access for everyone, but write access for owner only). You can set it to any file permission mask setting you want. For example, if you want no permissions for anyone but the owner, change this option to 077. (To learn more about file permission masks, consult Book VI, Chapter 2.)
- `ls_recurse_enable=YES` enables FTP users to recursively traverse directories by using the `ls -R` command.
- `nopriv_user=ftp` identifies an unprivileged user account that the FTP server can use.
- `pam_service_name=vsftpd` is the name of the Pluggable Authentication Module (PAM) configuration file that is used when `vsftpd` must authenticate a user. By default, the PAM configuration files are in the `/etc/pam.d` directory. That means `vsftpd`'s PAM configuration file is `/etc/pam.d/vsftpd`.
- `tcp_wrappers=YES` enables support for access control through the TCP wrapper that consults the files `/etc/hosts.allow` and `/etc/hosts.deny`. (For more information about the TCP wrapper, see Book VI, Chapter 3.)
- `userlist_deny=YES` causes `vsftpd` to deny access to the users listed in the `/etc/vsftpd.user_list` file. These users are not even prompted for a password.
- `write_enable=YES` causes `vsftpd` to allow file uploads to the host.
- `xferlog_enable=YES` turns on the logging of file downloads and uploads (always a good idea, but takes disk space).
- `xferlog_file=/var/log/vsftpd.log` specifies the full pathname of the `vsftpd` log file. The default is `/var/log/vsftpd.log`.
- `xferlog_std_format=YES` causes `vsftpd` to generate log files in a standard format used by other FTP daemons.

/etc/vsftpd.ftpusers file

The `vsftpd` server uses the *Pluggable Authentication Module* (PAM) to authenticate users when they try to log in (just as the normal login process uses PAM to do the job). The PAM configuration file for `vsftpd` is `/etc/pam.d/vsftpd`. That PAM configuration file refers to `/etc/vsftpd.ftpusers` like this:

```
auth    required    /lib/security/pam_listfile.so item=user sense=deny file=/etc/
    vsftpd.ftpusers onerr=succeed
```

This command basically says that anyone listed in the /etc/vsftpd.ftpusers file is denied login. The default /etc/vsftpd.ftpusers file contains the following list of users:

```
root
bin
daemon
adm
lp
sync
shutdown
halt
mail
news
uucp
operator
games
nobody
```

/etc/vsftpd.user_list file

If the userlist_deny option is set to YES, vsftpd does not allow users listed in the /etc/vsftpd.user_list file any access to FTP services. It does not even prompt them for a password. However, if userlist_deny is set to NO, the meaning is reversed and these users are the only ones allowed access (but the PAM configuration still denies anyone on the /etc/vsftpd.ftpusers list).

Chapter 4: Managing Mail and News Servers

In This Chapter

- **Installing and using** `sendmail`
- **Testing mail delivery manually**
- **Configuring** `sendmail`
- **Installing the InterNetNews (INN) server**
- **Configuring and starting INN**
- **Setting up local newsgroups**

Electronic mail (e-mail) is one of the popular services available on Internet hosts. E-mail software comes in two parts: a mail-transport agent (MTA), which physically sends and receives mail messages; and a mail-user agent (MUA), which reads messages and prepares new messages. In this chapter, I describe the e-mail service and show you how to configure the `sendmail` server on a Linux PC.

Internet newsgroups provide another convenient way, besides e-mail, to discuss various topics and to share your knowledge with others. Linux comes with the software you need to read newsgroups and to set up your own system as a news server. In this chapter, I describe how to configure and run the InterNetNews server, a popular news server. I also show you how to set up local newsgroups for your corporate intranet (or even your home network).

Installing the Mail Server

Depending on the choices you made during Linux installation, you may have already installed the mail server software on your system. You can choose from several mail servers such as `exim`, `postfix`, and `sendmail` — I briefly cover `sendmail` in this chapter. If `sendmail` is not installed, you can easily install it.

In Debian and Xandros, type **dpkg -l sendmail*** to see if `sendmail` is installed. In Fedora Core and SUSE, type **rpm -qa | grep sendmail** and see if the `sendmail` package is installed.

In Debian, type **apt-get install sendmail** to install the `sendmail` server. In Fedora Core, log in as `root`, mount the DVD, and type **cd /mnt/cdrom/ Fedora/RPMS** followed by **rpm -ivh sendmail***. In SUSE, click Install and Remove Software in the YaST Control Center's Software category. Then use YaST's search facility to find the `sendmail` packages and install them.

Using sendmail

To set up your system as a mail server, you must configure the `sendmail` mail-transport agent properly. `sendmail` has the reputation of being a complex but complete mail-delivery system. Just one look at `sendmail`'s configuration file — `/etc/mail/sendmail.cf`, in Fedora Core and `/etc/sendmail.cf` in SUSE — can convince you that `sendmail` is indeed complex. Luckily, you don't have to be an expert on the `sendmail` configuration file. All you need is one of the predefined configuration files — like the one that's installed on your system — to use `sendmail`.

Your system already has a working `sendmail` configuration file — `/etc/mail/sendmail.cf`. The default file assumes you have an Internet connection and a name server. Provided that you have an Internet connection and that your system has an official domain name, you can send and receive e-mail from your Linux PC.

To ensure that mail delivery works correctly, your system's name must match the system name that your ISP has assigned to you. Although you can give your system any host name you want, other systems can successfully deliver mail to your system only if your system's name is in the ISP's name server.

A mail-delivery test

To try out the `sendmail` mail-transfer agent, you can use the `mail` command to compose and send a mail message to any user account on your Linux system. For example, here's how I send myself a message using the `mail` command:

```
mail naba
Subject: Testing e-mail
This is from my Linux system.
.
```

The `mail` command is a simple mail-user agent. In the preceding example, I specify the addressee — `naba` — in the command line. The `mail` program prompts for a subject line. Following the subject, I enter my message and end it with a line that contains only a period. After I end the message, the mail-user agent passes the message to `sendmail` — the mail-transport agent — for delivery to the specified address. `sendmail` delivers the mail message immediately. To verify the delivery of mail, I type **mail** to run the `mail` command again and read the message.

Thus, the initial `sendmail` configuration file is adequate for sending and receiving e-mail, at least within your Linux system. External mail delivery also works, provided that your Linux system has an Internet connection and a registered domain name.

REMEMBER

If you have an ISP account that provides your Linux system with a dynamic IP address, you have to use mail clients such as Evolution or Mozilla Mail that contact your ISP's mail server to deliver outbound e-mail.

The mail-delivery mechanism

On an Internet host, the `sendmail` mail-transport agent delivers mail using the Simple Mail Transfer Protocol (SMTP). SMTP-based mail-transport agents listen to the TCP port 25 and use a small set of text commands to exchange information with other mail-transport agents. In fact, SMTP commands are simple enough that you can use them manually from a terminal to send a mail message. The following example shows how I use SMTP commands to send a mail message to my account on the Linux PC from a `telnet` session running on the same system:

```
telnet localhost 25
Trying 127.0.0.1...
Connected to localhost.
Escape character is '^]'.
220 linux.site ESMTP Sendmail 8.12.10/8.12.10/SuSE Linux 0.7; Sun, 26 Sep 2004
    10:40:02 -0400
help
214-2.0.0 This is sendmail version 8.12.10
214-2.0.0 Topics:
214-2.0.0       HELO    EHLO    MAIL    RCPT    DATA
214-2.0.0       RSET    NOOP    QUIT    HELP    VRFY
214-2.0.0       EXPN    VERB    ETRN    DSN     AUTH
214-2.0.0       STARTTLS
214-2.0.0 For more info use "HELP <topic>".
214-2.0.0 To report bugs in the implementation send email to
214-2.0.0       sendmail-bugs@sendmail.org.
214-2.0.0 For local information send email to Postmaster at your site.
214 2.0.0 End of HELP info
help DATA
214-2.0.0 DATA
214-2.0.0       Following text is collected as the message.
214-2.0.0       End with a single dot.
214 2.0.0 End of HELP info
HELO localhost
250 linux.site Hello localhost [127.0.0.1], pleased to meet you
MAIL FROM: naba
553 5.5.4 naba... Domain name required for sender address naba
MAIL FROM: naba@localhost
250 2.1.0 naba@localhost... Sender ok
RCPT TO: naba
250 2.1.5 naba... Recipient ok
DATA
354 Enter mail, end with "." on a line by itself
Testing... 1 2 3
Sending mail by telnet to port 25
.
250 2.0.0 i8QEe2sY014906 Message accepted for delivery
```

```
quit
221 2.0.0 localhost.localdomain closing connection
Connection closed by foreign host.
```

The `telnet` command opens a TELNET session to port 25 — the port on which `sendmail` expects SMTP commands. The `sendmail` process on the Linux system immediately replies with an announcement.

I type `HELP` to view a list of SMTP commands. To get help on a specific command, I can type `HELP` *`commandname`*. The listing shows the help information `sendmail` prints when I type `HELP DATA`.

I type `HELO localhost` to initiate a session with the host. The `sendmail` process replies with a greeting. To send the mail message, I start with the `MAIL FROM:` command that specifies the sender of the message. (I enter the username on the system from which I am sending the message.) `sendmail` requires a domain name along with the username.

Next, I use the `RCPT TO:` command to specify the recipient of the message. If I want to send the message to several recipients, all I have to do is provide each recipient's address with the `RCPT TO:` command.

To enter the mail message, I use the `DATA` command. In response to the `DATA` command, `sendmail` displays an instruction that I have to end the message with a period on a line by itself. I enter the message and end it with a single period on a separate line. The `sendmail` process displays a message indicating that the message is accepted for delivery. Finally, I quit the `sendmail` session with the `QUIT` command.

Afterward, I log in to my Linux system and check mail with the `mail` command. The following is the session with the `mail` command when I display the mail message I sent through the sample SMTP session with `sendmail`:

```
mail
Mail version 8.1 6/6/93.  Type ? for help.
"/var/spool/mail/naba": 1 message 1 new
>N  1 naba@localhost.local  Sun Mar 14 15:16  12/479
& 1
Message 1:
From naba@localhost.localdomain  Sun Mar 14 15:16:31 2004
Date: Sun, 14 Mar 2004 15:14:38 -0500
From: Naba Barkakati <naba@localhost.localdomain>

Testing... 1 2 3
Sending mail by telnet to port 25

& q
Saved 1 message in mbox
```

Here, I type **mail** to start the mail program. It displays a numbered list of new messages (in this case, there is only one message) and a prompt (&). I type **1** — the message number of the message I want to read. The mail program displays the message and waits for my input again. I type **q** to quit the program.

As this example shows, the SMTP commands are simple enough for humans to understand. This example helps you understand how a mail-transfer agent uses SMTP to transfer mail on the Internet. Of course, e-mail programs usually automate this whole process — and so does the `sendmail` program (through settings in the `sendmail` configuration file `sendmail.cf`).

The sendmail configuration file

You don't have to understand everything in the `sendmail` configuration file, `sendmail.cf`, but you need to know how that file is created. That way, you can make minor changes if necessary and regenerate the `sendmail.cf` file.

DISTRIBUTION SPECIFIC

In SUSE, you can configure `sendmail` through the YaST Control Center (select Main Menu⇨System⇨YaST) — click the Network Services in the left-hand side of the window and then click Mail Transfer Agent in the right-hand side of the window. YaST displays a window (see Figure 4-1) that you can use to configure `sendmail`. First you specify the general settings, then the settings for outgoing mail, and finally the settings for incoming mail. After you exit the mail configuration utility, YaST stores the mail settings in the files `/etc/sysconfig/sendmail` and `/etc/sysconfig/mail` and updates the `sendmail` configuration file — `/etc/sendmail.cf` — by running `SuSEconfig`.

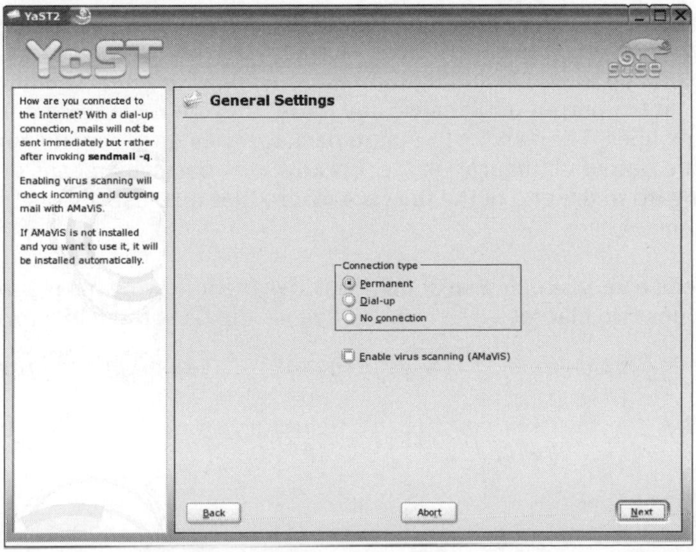

Figure 4-1: In SUSE, you can configure `sendmail` through YaST.

You can also generate the `sendmail.cf` file from a number of *m4 macro files* (text files in which each line eventually expands to multiple lines that mean something to some program). These macro files are organized into a number of subdirectories in the `/usr/share/sendmail-cf` directory in Fedora Core or the `/usr/share/sendmail` directory in SUSE. You can read the `README` file in that directory to find out more about the creation of `sendmail` configuration files.

m4 macro processor

The m4 macro processor generates the `sendmail.cf` configuration file, which comes with the `sendmail` package in Linux. The main macro file, named variously `sendmail.mc` or `linux.mc`, is included with the `sendmail` package.

So what's a macro? A *macro* is basically a symbolic name for code that handles some action, usually in a shorthand form that substitutes for a long string of characters. A *macro processor* such as m4 usually reads its input file and copies it to the output, processing the macros along the way. The processing of a macro generally involves performing some action and generating some output. Because a macro generates a lot more text in the output than merely the macro's name, the processing of macros is referred to as *macro expansion*.

The m4 macro processor is *stream-based*. That means it copies the input characters to the output while it's busy expanding any macros. The m4 macro processor does not have any concept of lines, so it copies newline characters (that mark the end of a line) to the output. That's why you see the word `dnl` in most m4 macro files; `dnl` is an m4 macro that stands for "delete through newline." The `dnl` macro deletes all characters starting at the `dnl` up to and including the next newline character. The newline characters in the output don't cause any harm; they merely create unnecessary blank lines. The `sendmail` macro package uses `dnl` to avoid such blank lines in the output configuration file. Because `dnl` basically means delete everything up to the end of the line, m4 macro files also use `dnl` as the prefix for comment lines.

To see a very simple use of m4, consider the following m4 macro file that defines two macros — `hello` and `bye` — and uses them in a form letter:

```
dnl ###################################################################
dnl #  File: ex.m4
dnl #  A simple example of m4 macros
dnl ###################################################################
define('hello', 'Dear Sir/Madam')dnl
define('bye',
'Sincerely,
```

```
Customer Service')dnl
dnl Now type the letter and use the macros
hello,

This is to inform you that we received your recent inquiry.
We will respond to your question soon.

bye
```

Type this text (using your favorite text editor) and save it in a file named `ex.m4`. You can name a macro file anything you like, but using the `.m4` extension for m4 macro files is customary.

Before you process the macro file by using m4, note the following key points about the example:

- Use the `dnl` macro to start all the comment lines (for example, the first four lines in the example).
- End each macro definition with the `dnl` macro. Otherwise, when m4 processes the macro file, it produces a blank line for each macro definition.
- Use the built-in m4 command `define` to define a new macro. The macro name and the value are both enclosed between a pair of left and right quotes (' . . . '). Note that you cannot use the plain single quote to enclose the macro name and definition.

Now process the macro file `ex.m4` by typing the following command:

```
m4 ex.m4
```

m4 processes the macros and displays the following output:

```
Dear Sir/Madam,

This is to inform you that we received your recent inquiry.
We will respond to your question soon.

Sincerely,


Customer Service
```

Sounds just like a typical customer service form letter, doesn't it?

If you compare the output with the `ex.m4` file, you see that m4 prints the form letter on standard output, expanding the macros `hello` and `bye` into their defined values. If you want to save the form letter in a file called `letter`, use the shell's output redirection feature, like this:

```
m4 ex.m4 > letter
```

What if you want to use the word `hello` or `bye` in the letter without expanding them? You can do so by enclosing these words in a pair of quotes ('. . .'). You have to do so for other predefined m4 macros, such as `define`. To use *define* as a plain word, not as a macro to expand, type **'define'**.

The sendmail macro file

The simple example in the preceding section gives you an idea of how m4 macros are defined and used to create configuration files such as the `sendmail.cf` file. You find many complex macros stored in files in the `/usr/share/sendmail-cf` directory in Fedora Core or the `/usr/share/sendmail` directory in SUSE. A top-level macro file — called `sendmail.mc` in Fedora Core and `linux.mc` in SUSE — described later in this section, brings in these macro files with the `include` macro (used to copy a file into the input stream).

To avoid repeatedly mentioning different file and directory names for different distributions such as Fedora Core and SUSE, I use the file and directory names for Fedora Core in the following discussions. The general discussions apply to `sendmail` in all Linux distributions, but you have to replace the file and directory names with those for your specific distribution.

By defining its own set of high-level macros in files located in the `/usr/share/sendmail-cf` directory, `sendmail` essentially creates its own macro language. The `sendmail` macro files use the `.mc` extension. The primary `sendmail` macro file you configure is `sendmail.mc`, located in the `/etc/mail` directory.

Unlike the `/etc/mail/sendmail.cf` file, the `/etc/mail/sendmail.mc` file is short and easier to work with. Here are some lines from the `/etc/mail/sendmail.mc` file that comes with Fedora Core:

```
divert(-1)dnl
dnl #
dnl # This is the sendmail macro config file for m4. If you make changes to
dnl # /etc/mail/sendmail.mc, you will need to regenerate the
dnl # /etc/mail/sendmail.cf file by confirming that the sendmail-cf package is
dnl # installed and then performing a
dnl #
dnl #     make -C /etc/mail
dnl #
include('/usr/share/sendmail-cf/m4/cf.m4')dnl
VERSIONID('setup for Red Hat Linux')dnl
OSTYPE('linux')dnl
dnl #
dnl # default logging level is 9, you might want to set it higher to
dnl # debug the configuration
dnl #
dnl define('confLOG_LEVEL', '9')dnl
dnl #
```

```
dnl # Uncomment and edit the following line if your outgoing mail needs to
dnl # be sent out through an external mail server:
dnl #
dnl define('SMART_HOST','smtp.your.provider')

...lines deleted ...

dnl #
dnl # The following example makes mail from this host and any additional
dnl # specified domains appear to be sent from mydomain.com
dnl #
dnl MASQUERADE_AS('mydomain.com')dnl
dnl #
dnl # masquerade not just the headers, but the envelope as well
dnl #
dnl FEATURE(masquerade_envelope)dnl
dnl #
dnl # masquerade not just @mydomainalias.com, but @*.mydomainalias.com as well
dnl #
dnl FEATURE(masquerade_entire_domain)dnl
dnl #
dnl MASQUERADE_DOMAIN(localhost)dnl
dnl MASQUERADE_DOMAIN(localhost.localdomain)dnl
dnl MASQUERADE_DOMAIN(mydomainalias.com)dnl
dnl MASQUERADE_DOMAIN(mydomain.lan)dnl
MAILER(smtp)dnl
MAILER(procmail)dnl
```

If you make changes to the /etc/mail/sendmail.mc file, you must generate the /etc/mail/sendmail.cf file by running the sendmail.mc file through the m4 macro processor with the following command (you have to log in as root):

```
m4 /etc/mail/sendmail.mc > /etc/mail/sendmail.cf
```

The comments also tell you that you need the sendmail-cf package to process this file.

From the previous section's description of m4 macros, you can see that the sendmail.mc file uses define to create new macros. You can also see the liberal use of dnl to avoid inserting too many blank lines into the output.

The other uppercase words (such as OSTYPE, FEATURE, and MAILER) are sendmail macros. These are defined in the .m4 files located in the subdirectories of the /usr/share/sendmail-cf directory and are incorporated into the sendmail.mc file with the following include macro:

```
include('/usr/share/sendmail-cf/m4/cf.m4')dnl
```

The /usr/share/sendmail-cf/m4/cf.m4 file, in turn, includes the cfhead.m4 file, which includes other m4 files, and so on. The net effect is that, as the m4 macro processor processes the sendmail.mc file, the macro processor incorporates many m4 files from various subdirectories of /usr/share/sendmail-cf.

Here are some key points to note about the /etc/mail/sendmail.mc file:

- ✦ VERSIONID('setup for Red Hat Linux') macro inserts the version information enclosed in quotes into the output.
- ✦ OSTYPE('linux') specifies Linux as the operating system. You have to specify this macro early to ensure proper configuration.

  Placing this macro right after the VERSIONID macro is customary.
- ✦ MAILER(smtp) describes the mailer. According to instructions in the /usr/share/sendmail-cf/README file, MAILER declarations are always placed at the end of the sendmail.mc file, and MAILER(smtp) always precedes MAILER(procmail). The mailer smtp refers to the SMTP mailer.
- ✦ FEATURE macros request various special features. For example, FEATURE ('blacklist_recipients') turns on the capability to block incoming mail for certain usernames, hosts, or addresses. The specification for what mail to allow or refuse is placed in the access database (/etc/mail/access.db file). You also need the FEATURE('access_db') macro to turn on the access database.
- ✦ MASQUERADE_AS('mydomain.com') causes sendmail to label outgoing mail as having come from the host mydomain.com (replace with your domain name). The idea is for a large organization to set up a single sendmail server that handles the mail for many subdomains and makes everything appear to come from a single domain (for example, mail from many departments in a university appear to come from the university's main domain name).
- ✦ MASQUERADE_DOMAIN(subdomain.mydomain.com) instructs sendmail to send mail from an address such as user@subdomain.mydomain.com as having originated from the same username at the domain specified by the MASQUERADE_AS macro.

The sendmail macros such as FEATURE and MAILER are described in the /usr/share/sendmail-cf/README file. Consult that file to find out more about the sendmail macros before you make changes to the sendmail.mc file.

Typically, you have to add your system's host name in the last line of the /etc/mail/sendmail.mc file. Follow these steps to add the host name:

1. **If the host name is mycompany.com, edit the Cw line in /etc/mail/sendmail.mc as follows:**

   ```
   Cwlocalhost.localdomain mycompany.com mycompany
   ```

2. **Rebuild the /etc/mail/sendmail.cf file with this command:**

   ```
   m4 /etc/mail/sendmail.mc > /etc/mail/sendmail.cf
   ```

3. **Restart** `sendmail` **with the following command:**

   ```
   service sendmail restart
   ```

sendmail.cf file syntax

The `sendmail.cf` file's syntax is designed to be easy to parse by the `sendmail` program because `sendmail` reads this file whenever it starts. Human readability was not a primary consideration when the file's syntax was designed. Still, with a little explanation, you can understand the meaning of the control lines in `sendmail.cf`.

Each `sendmail` control line begins with a single-letter operator that defines the meaning of the rest of the line. A line that begins with a space or a tab is considered a continuation of the previous line. Blank lines and lines beginning with a pound sign (#) are comments.

Often, no space is between the single-letter operator and the arguments that follow the operator, which makes the lines even harder to understand. For example, `sendmail.cf` uses the concept of a *class* — essentially a collection of phrases. You can define a class named `P` and add the phrase `REDIRECT` to that class with the following control line:

```
CPREDIRECT
```


Because everything is jumbled together, the command is hard to decipher. On the other hand, to define a class named `Accept` and set it to the values `OK` and `RELAY`, write the following:

```
C{Accept}OK RELAY
```

This command may be slightly easier to understand because the delimiters (such as the class name, `Accept`) are enclosed in curly braces.

Other — more recent — control lines are even easier to understand. For example, the line

```
O HelpFile=/etc/mail/helpfile
```

defines the option `HelpFile` as the filename `/etc/mail/helpfile`. That file contains help information `sendmail` uses when it receives a `HELP` command.

Table 4-1 summarizes the one-letter control operators used in `sendmail.cf`. Each entry also shows an example of that operator. This table helps you understand some of the lines in `sendmail.cf`.

Table 4-1 Control Operators Used in sendmail.cf

Operator	*Description*
C	Defines a class; a variable (think of it as a set) that can contain several values. For example, `Cwlocalhost` adds the name `localhost` to the class `w`.
D	Defines a macro, a name associated with a single value. For example, `DnMAILER-DAEMON` defines the macro `n` as `MAILER-DAEMON`.
F	Defines a class that's been read from a file. For example, `Fw/etc/mail/local-host-names` reads the names of hosts from the file `/etc/mail/local-host-names` and adds them to the class `w`.
H	Defines the format of header lines that `sendmail` inserts into a message. For example, `H?P?Return-Path: <$g>` defines the `Return-Path:` field of the header.
K	Defines a map (a key-value pair database). For example, `Karith arith` defines the map named `arith` as the compiled-in map of the same name.
M	Specifies a mailer. The following lines define the `procmail` mailer: `Mprocmail,P=/usr/bin/procmail, F=DFMSPhnu9,S=EnvFromSMTP/HdrFromSMTP,R=EnvToSMTP/HdrFromSMTP,T=DNS/RFC822/X-Unix, A=procmail -Y -m $h $f $u`.
O	Assigns a value to an option. For example, `O AliasFile=/etc/aliases` defines the `AliasFile` option to `/etc/aliases`, which is the name of the `sendmail` alias file.
P	Defines values for the precedence field. For example, `Pjunk=-100` sets to `-100` the precedence of messages marked with the header field `Precedence: junk`.
R	Defines a rule (a rule has a left-hand side and a right-hand side; if input matches the left-hand side, the right-hand side replaces it — this rule is called *rewriting*). For example, the rewriting rule `R$* ;    $1` strips trailing semicolons.
S	Labels a ruleset you can start defining with subsequent R control lines. For example, `Scanonify=3` labels the next ruleset as `canonify` or ruleset 3.
T	Adds a username to the trusted class (class `t`). For example, `Troot` adds `root` to the class of trusted users.
V	Defines the major version number of the configuration file. For example, `V10/Berkeley` defines the version number as 10.

Other sendmail files

The `/etc/mail` directory contains other files that `sendmail` uses. These files are referenced in the `sendmail` configuration file, `/etc/mail/sendmail.cf` in Fedora Core and `/etc/sendmail.cf` in SUSE. (Debian, Knoppix, and

Xandros do not use `sendmail` by default.) For example, here's how you can search for the `/etc/mail` string in the `/etc/mail/sendmail.cf` file in Fedora Core:

```
grep "\/etc\/mail" /etc/mail/sendmail.cf
```

Here's what the `grep` command displays as a result of the search on my Fedora Core system:

```
Fw/etc/mail/local-host-names
FR-o /etc/mail/relay-domains
Kmailertable hash -o /etc/mail/mailertable.db
Kvirtuser hash -o /etc/mail/virtusertable.db
Kaccess hash -T<TMPF> -o /etc/mail/access.db
#O ErrorHeader=/etc/mail/error-header
O HelpFile=/etc/mail/helpfile
O UserDatabaseSpec=/etc/mail/userdb.db
#O ServiceSwitchFile=/etc/mail/service.switch
#O DefaultAuthInfo=/etc/mail/default-auth-info
Ft/etc/mail/trusted-users
```

You can ignore the lines that begin with a hash mark or number sign (#) because `sendmail` treats those lines as comments. The other lines are `sendmail` control lines that refer to other files in the `/etc/mail` directory.

Here's what some of these `sendmail` files are supposed to contain (note that not all of these files have to be present in your `/etc/mail` directory and even when present, some files may be empty):

- `/etc/mail/access`: Names and/or IP addresses of hosts allowed to send mail (useful in stopping *spam* — unwanted e-mail)
- `/etc/mail/access.db`: Access database generated from the `/etc/mail/access` file
- `/etc/mail/helpfile`: Help information for SMTP commands
- `/etc/mail/local-host-names`: Names by which this host is known
- `/etc/mail/mailertable`: Mailer table used to override how mail is routed (for example, the entry `comcast.net smtp:smtp.comcast.net` tells `sendmail` that mail addressed to `comcast.net` has to be sent to `smtp.comcast.net`)
- `/etc/mail/relay-domains`: Hosts that permit relaying
- `/etc/mail/trusted-users`: List of users allowed to send mail using other user's names without a warning
- `/etc/mail/userdb.db`: User database file containing information about each user's login name and real name
- `/etc/mail/virtusertable`: Database of users with virtual-domain addresses hosted on this system

The /etc/mail directory sometimes contains other files — /etc/mail/certs and the files with the .pem extension — that are meant for supporting privacy enhanced mail (PEM) in sendmail by using the STARTTLS extension to SMTP. The STARTTLS extension uses TLS (more commonly known as SSL — Secure Sockets Layer) to authenticate the sender and encrypt mail. RFC 2487 describes STARTTLS. (This RFC is available online at ietf.org/rfc/rfc2487.txt.)

If you edit the /etc/mail/mailertable file, you have to type the following command before the changes take effect:

```
makemap hash /etc/mail/mailertable < /etc/mail/mailertable
```

Here is an easier way to make sure that you rebuild everything necessary after making any changes — just type the following commands while logged in as root:

```
cd /etc/mail
make
```

The first command changes the current directory to /etc/mail and the second command runs the make command, which reads a file named Makefile in /etc/mail to perform the steps necessary to rebuild everything. (To learn more about make and Makefile, see Book VIII, Chapter 1.)

The .forward file

Users can redirect their own mail by placing a .forward file in their home directory. The .forward file is a plain-text file with a comma-separated list of mail addresses. Any mail sent to the user is then forwarded to these addresses. If the .forward file contains a single address, all e-mail for that user is redirected to that single e-mail address. For example, suppose a .forward file containing the following line is placed in the home directory of a user named emily:

```
ashley
```

This line causes sendmail to automatically send all e-mail addressed to emily to the username ashley on the same system. User emily does not receive mail at all.

You can also forward mail to a username on another system by listing a complete e-mail address. For example, I added a .forward file with the following line to send my messages (addressed to my username, naba) to the mail address naba@comcast.net:

```
naba@comcast.net
```

Now suppose I want to keep a copy of the message on the original system, in addition to forwarding to the address `naba@comcast.net`. I can do so by adding the following line to the `.forward` file:

```
naba@comcast.net, naba\
```

I simply append my username and end the line with a backslash. The backslash (\) at the end of the line stops `sendmail` from repeatedly forwarding the message (because when a copy is sent to my username on the system, `sendmail` would normally process my `.forward` file again — the backslash tells `sendmail` not to forward the message repeatedly).

The sendmail alias file

In addition to the `sendmail.cf` file, `sendmail` also consults an alias file named `/etc/aliases` to convert a name into an address. The location of the alias file appears in the `sendmail` configuration file.

Each *alias* is typically a shorter name for an e-mail address. The system administrator uses the `sendmail` alias file to forward mail, to create mailing lists (a single alias that identifies several users), or to refer to a user by several different names. For example, here are some typical aliases:

```
barkakati: naba
naba: naba@lnbsoft
all: naba, leha, ivy, emily, ashley
```


The first line says that mail addressed to `barkakati` is delivered to the user named `naba` on the local system. The second line indicates that mail for `naba` really is sent to the username `naba` on the `lnbsoft` system. The last line defines `all` as the alias for the five users `naba`, `leha`, `ivy`, `emily`, and `ashley`. That means mail sent to `all` goes to these five users.

After defining any new aliases in the `/etc/aliases` file, you must log in as `root` and make the new alias active by typing the following command:

```
sendmail -bi
```

Installing the INN Server

In this section, I describe how to configure the InterNetNews (INN) — a TCP/IP-based news server. First you have to install INN.

In Debian and Xandros, type **dpkg -l inn*** to see if `inn` is installed. In Fedora Core and SUSE, type **rpm -q inn** and see if the `inn` package is installed.

In Debian, type **apt-get install inn** to install the INN server. In Fedora Core, log in as `root`, mount the DVD, and type **cd /mnt/cdrom/Fedora/RPMS** followed by **rpm -ivh inn***. In SUSE, click Install and Remove Software in the YaST Control Center's Software category. Then use YaST's search feature to look for `inn`, select the relevant packages from the search results, and install them. In Xandros, first run Xandros Networks, select Edit⇨Set Application Sources, and click the Debian Unsupported Site link as a source; then type **apt-get install inn** to install the INN server.

Configuring and Starting the INN Server

Much of the *InterNetNews* (INN) software is ready to go as soon as you install the software. All you need is to brush up a bit on the various components of INN, edit the configuration files, and start `innd` — the INN server. By the way, sometimes I refer to the INN server as the *news server.*

If you want to run a news server that supports a selection of Internet newsgroups, you also have to arrange for a *news feed* — the source from which your news server gets the newsgroup articles. Typically, you can get a news feed from an ISP, but the ISP charges an additional monthly fee to cover the cost of resources required to provide the feed. (Your normal ISP charges cover reading news from the ISP's server; you have to pay additional charges only if you want to run your own server and get a news feed.) You need the name of the upstream server that provides the news feed, and you have to provide that server with your server's name and the newsgroups you want to receive.

By the way, you don't need any external news feed if you are running a news server to support local newsgroups that are available only within your organization's network. I describe how to set up local newsgroups in the "Setting Up Local Newsgroups" section of this chapter.

Depending on the newsgroups you want to receive and the number of days you want to retain articles, you have to set aside appropriate disk space to hold the articles. The newsgroups are stored in a directory hierarchy (based on the newsgroup names) in the `/var/spool/news` directory of your system. If you're setting up a news server, you may want to devote a large disk partition to the `/var/spool/news` directory.

In your news server's configuration files, enter the name of the server providing the news feed. At the same time, add to the configuration files the names of any downstream news servers (if any) that receive news feeds from your server. Then you can start the news server and wait for news to arrive. Monitor the log files to ensure that the news articles sort and store properly in the `/var/spool/news` directory on your system.

In the following sections, I introduce you to INN setup, but you can find out more about INN from the Internet Software Consortium (ISC), a nonprofit corporation dedicated to developing and maintaining open source Internet software, such as BIND (an implementation of Domain Name System), DHCP (Dynamic Host Configuration Protocol), and INN. Rich Salz originally wrote INN; ISC took over the development of INN in 1996. You can find out more about INN and can access other resources at ISC's INN Web page at `www.isc.org/products/INN`.

InterNetNews components

INN includes several programs that deliver and manage newsgroups. It also includes a number of files that control how the INN programs work. The most important INN programs are the following:

- `innd`: The news server. It runs as a *daemon* — a background process that keeps itself running to provide a specific service — and listens on the NNTP port (TCP port 119). The `innd` server accepts connections from other feed sites, as well as from local newsreader clients, but it hands off local connections to the `nnrpd`.
- `nnrpd`: A special server invoked by `innd` to handle requests from local newsreader clients.
- `expire`: Removes old articles based on the specifications in the text file `/etc/news/expire.ctl`.
- `nntpsend`: Invokes the `innxmit` program to send news articles to a remote site by using NNTP. The configuration file `/etc/news/nntpsend.ctl` controls the `nntpsend` program.
- `ctlinnd`: Enables you to control the `innd` server interactively. The `ctlinnd` program can send messages to the control channel of the `innd` server.

The other vital components of INN are the control files. Most of these files are in the `/etc/news` directory of your Linux system, although a few are in the `/var/lib/news` directory. Between those two directories, you have more than 30 INN control files. Some important files include the following:

- `/etc/news/inn.conf`: Specifies configuration data for the `innd` server. (To view online help for this file, type **man inn.conf**.)
- `/etc/news/newsfeeds`: Specifies what articles to feed downstream to other news servers. (The file is complicated, but you can get help by typing **man newsfeeds**.)
- `/etc/news/incoming.conf`: Lists the names and addresses of hosts that provide news feeds to this server. (To view online help for this file, type **man incoming.conf**.)

- /etc/news/storage.conf: Specifies the storage methods to be used when storing news articles. (To view online help for this file, type **man storage.conf**.)
- /etc/news/expire.ctl: Controls expiration of articles, on a per-newsgroup level, if desired. (To view online help for this file, type **man expire.ctl**.)
- /var/lib/news/active: Lists all active newsgroups, showing the oldest and newest article number for each, and each newsgroup's posting status. (To view online help for this file, type **man active**.)
- /var/lib/news/newsgroups: Lists newsgroups, with a brief description of each.
- /etc/news/readers.conf: Specifies hosts and users who are permitted to read news from this news server and post news to newsgroups. The default file allows only the localhost to read news; you have to edit it if you want to allow other hosts in your local area network to read news. (To view online help for this file, type **man readers.conf**.)

In the next few sections, I describe how to set up some of the important control files.

The inn.conf file

This file holds configuration data for all INN programs — which makes it the most important file. Each line of the file has the value of a parameter in the following format:

```
parameter:      value
```

Depending on the parameter, the value is a string, a number, or true or false. As in many other configuration files, comment lines begin with a number or pound sign (#).

Most of the parameters in the default inn.conf file in the /etc/news directory do not require changes. You may want to edit one or more of the parameters shown in Table 4-2.

Table 4-2 Configuration Parameters in /etc/news/inn.conf

Parameter Name	*Description*
mta	Set this parameter to the command used to start the mail transfer agent that is used by innd to transfer messages. The default is to use sendmail.

Parameter Name	Description
organization	Set this parameter to the name of your organization in the way you want it to appear in the Organization: header of all news articles posted from your system. Users may override this parameter by defining the ORGANIZATION environment variable.
ovmethod	Sets the type of overview storage method. (The *overview* is an index of news articles in the newsgroup.) The default method is tradindexed, which is fast for reading news, but slow for storing news items.
pathhost	Set this parameter to the name of your news server as you want it to appear in the Path header of all postings that go through your server. If pathhost isn't defined, the fully qualified domain name of your system is used.
pathnews	Set this parameter to the full pathname of the directory that contains INN binaries and libraries. The default pathnews is set to /usr/lib/news.
domain	Set this parameter to the domain name for your server.
allownewnews	Set this parameter to true if you want INN to support the NEWNEWS command from newsreaders. In the past, this option was set to false because the NEWNEWS command used to reduce the server's performance, but nowadays the default is set to true because modern servers can easily handle the NEWNEWS command.
hiscachesize	Set this parameter to the size in kilobytes that you want INN to use for caching recently received message IDs that are kept in memory to speed history lookups. This cache is used only for incoming feeds, and a small cache can hold quite a few history file entries. The default setting of 0 disables history caching. If you have more than one incoming feed, you may want to set this parameter to a value of 256 (for 256KB).
innflags	Set this parameter to any flags you want to pass to the INN server process when it starts up.

The newsfeeds file

The newsfeeds file specifies how incoming news articles are redistributed to other servers and to INN processes. If you provide news feeds to other servers, you have to list these news feeds in this file. (You also must have an entry labeled ME, which serves a special purpose that I explain later in this section.)

The newsfeeds file contains a series of entries, one for each feed. Each feed entry has the following format:

```
site[/exclude,exclude...]\
      :pattern,pattern...[/distrib,distrib...]\
      :flag,flag...\
      :param
```

Each entry has four fields separated by colons (:). Usually, the entries span multiple lines, and a backslash (\) at the end of the line is used to continue a line to the next. Here's what the four fields mean:

- ✦ The first field, *site*, is the name of the feed. Each name must be unique, and for feeds to other news servers, the name is set to the host name of the remote server. Following the name is an optional slash and an exclude list (*/exclude,exclude...*) consisting of a list of names. If any of the names in this list appear in the Path line of an article, that article isn't forwarded to the feed. You can use an exclude list if you don't want to receive articles from a specific source.
- ✦ The second field consists of a comma-separated list of newsgroup patterns, such as *,@alt.binaries.warez.*,!control*,!local*, followed by an optional distribution list. The distribution list is a list of comma-separated keywords, with each keyword specifying a specific set of sites to which the articles are distributed. The newsgroup patterns essentially define a subscription list of sites that receive this news feed. An asterisk matches all newsgroups. A pattern beginning with an @ causes newsgroups matching that pattern to be dropped. A pattern that begins with an exclamation mark (!) means the matching newsgroups are not sent. By the way, the simple pattern-matching syntax used in INN configuration files is referred to as a *wildmat* pattern.
- ✦ The third field is a comma-separated list of *flags* — fields that determine the feed-entry type and set certain parameters for the entry. You see numerous flags; type **man newsfeeds** and read the man page for more information about the flags.
- ✦ The fourth field is for parameters whose values depend on the settings in the third field. Typically, this field contains names of files or external programs that the INN server uses. You can find more about this field from the newsfeeds man page.

Now that you know the layout of the /etc/news/newsfeeds file, you can study that file as an example. The default file contains many sample feed entries, but only two are commented out:

- ✦ ME is a special feed entry that's always required. It serves two purposes. First, the newsgroup patterns listed in this entry are used as a prefix for all newsgroup patterns in all other entries. Second, the ME entry's distribution list determines what distributions your server accepts from remote sites.
- ✦ The controlchan feed entry is used to set up INN so that an external program is used to handle control messages. (These messages are used to create new newsgroups and remove groups.) For example, the following controlchan entry specifies the external program /usr/lib/news/bin/controlchan to handle all control messages, except cancel messages (meant for canceling an article):

```
controlchan!\
                  :!*,control,control.*,!control.cancel\
                  :Tc,Wnsm:/usr/lib/news/bin/controlchan
```

In addition to these feed entries, you add entries for any actual sites to which your news server provides news feeds. Such entries have the format

```
feedme.domain.com\
          :!junk,!control/!foo\
          :Tm:innfeed!
```

where *feedme.domain.com* is the fully qualified domain name of the site to which your system sends news articles.

The incoming.conf file

The `incoming.conf` file describes which hosts are allowed to connect to your host to feed articles. For a single feed, you can add an entry like

```
peer mybuddy {
    hostname: a-feed-site.domain.com
}
```

where *mybuddy* is a label for the peer and *a-feed-site.domain.com* identifies the site that feeds your site.

Keep in mind that simply adding a site's name in the `incoming.conf` file does not cause that remote site to start feeding news to your site — it simply enables your server to accept news articles from the remote site. At the remote site, your buddy has to configure his or her server to send articles to your site.

The readers.conf file

This file specifies the host names or IP addresses from which newsreader clients (such as Mozilla) can retrieve newsgroups from your server. For example, the following `readers.conf` file allows *read access* and *post access* (meaning you can submit articles) from `localhost` and from any host in the network 192.168.0.0:

```
auth "localhost" {
    hosts: "localhost, 127.0.0.1, stdin"
    default: "<localhost>"
}
access "localhost" {
    users: "<localhost>"
    newsgroups: "*"
    access: RPA
}
```

```
auth "localnet" {
    hosts: 192.168.0.0/24
    default: "<localnet>"
}
access "localnet" {
    users: "<localnet>"
    newsgroups: "*"
    access: RPA
}
```

InterNetNews startup

In addition to the configuration files, you also have to initiate `cron` jobs that perform periodic maintenance of the news server. In Fedora Core, these `cron` jobs are already set up. Therefore, you're now ready to start the INN server — `innd`.

Before you start `innd`, you must run `makehistory` and `makedbz` to initialize and rebuild the INN history database. Type **man makehistory** and **man makedbz** to find out more about these commands. Type the following commands to create an initial history database, associated indexes, and set the ownerships and permissions of some files:

```
/usr/lib/news/bin/makehistory -b -f history -O -l 30000 -I
cd /var/lib/news
/usr/lib/news/bin/makedbz -s 'wc -l < history' -f history
chown news.news *
chown news.news /var/spool/news/overview/group.index
chmod 664 /var/spool/news/overview/group.index
```

In Fedora Core, to start `innd`, log in as `root` and type **/etc/init.d/innd start**. In Debian, SUSE, and Xandros, type **/etc/init.d/inn start**. To ensure that `innd` starts at boot time, type **chkconfig --level 35 innd on** in Fedora Core and **chkconfig --level 35 inn on** in SUSE. In Debian and Xandros, type **update-rc.d inn defaults**.

If you make any changes to the INN configuration files, remember to restart the server by invoking the `/etc/init.d` script with `restart` as the argument.

Setting Up Local Newsgroups

If you want to use newsgroups as a way to share information within your company, you can set up a hierarchy of local newsgroups. Then you can use these newsgroups to create virtual communities within your company, where people with shared interests can informally discuss issues and exchange knowledge.

Defining a newsgroup hierarchy

The first task is to define a hierarchy of newsgroups and decide what each newsgroup will discuss. For example, if your company name is XYZ Corporation, here's a partial hierarchy of newsgroups you might define:

- `xyz.general`: General items about XYZ Corporation
- `xyz.weekly.news`: Weekly news
- `xyz.weekly.menu`: The weekly cafeteria menu and any discussions about it
- `xyz.forsale`: A listing of items offered for sale by employees
- `xyz.jobs`: Job openings at XYZ Corporation
- `xyz.wanted`: Wanted (help, items to buy, and so on) postings by employees
- `xyz.technical.hardware`: Technical discussions about hardware
- `xyz.technical.software`: Technical discussions about software

Updating configuration files

Here are the steps you follow to update the configuration files for your local newsgroups and then restart the news server:

1. **Add descriptive entries for each of these newsgroups to the `/var/lib/news/newsgroups` file.**

   Add to this file a line for each local newsgroup — type its name, followed by a brief description. For example, here's what you might add for the `xyz.general` newsgroup:

   ```
   xyz.general        General items about XYZ Corporation
   ```

2. **Edit the `ME` entry in the `/etc/news/newsfeeds` file and add the phrase `,!xyz.*` to the comma-separated list of newsgroup patterns.**

   This step ensures that your local newsgroups are not distributed outside your site.

3. **Add a storage method to be used for the local newsgroups.**

   For example, you can add the following lines in `/etc/news/storage.conf` to define the storage method for the new `xyz` hierarchy of newsgroups (change `xyz` to whatever you name your local newsgroups):

   ```
   method tradspool {
       class: 1
       newsgroups: xyz.*
   }
   ```

4. **To make these changes effective, restart the news server (type** /etc/init.d/innd restart **in Fedora Core or** /etc/init.d/inn restart **in Debian, SUSE, and Xandros).**

Adding the newsgroups

The final step is to add the newsgroups. After you update the configuration files and have `innd` running, adding a local newsgroup is easy. Log in as `root` and use `ctlinnd` to perform this task. For example, here's how you add a newsgroup named `xyz.general`:

```
/usr/lib/news/bin/ctlinnd newgroup xyz.general
```

That's it! That command adds the `xyz.general` newsgroup to your site. If you use the traditional storage method, the `innd` server creates the directory `/var/spool/news/articles/xyz/general` and stores articles for that newsgroup in that directory. (This happens the first time someone posts a news article to that newsgroup.)

After you create all the local newsgroups, users from your intranet can post news articles and read articles in the local newsgroups. If they have problems accessing the newsgroups, make sure that the `/etc/news/readers.conf` file contains the IP addresses or names of the hosts that have access to the `innd` server.

Testing your newsgroups

For example, I add a newsgroup named `local.news` on an INN server running on my Linux system by using the instructions explained in the previous sections. Then I start Mozilla on another Linux system on the LAN and set up a new news account with the news server set to my INN server. Next, I access the `local.news` newsgroup by typing **news:local.news** as the URL. Try it! I bet you'll like it.

Chapter 5: Managing DNS

In This Chapter

- **Understanding DNS**
- **Exploring BIND**
- **Configuring DNS**
- **Setting up a caching name server**
- **Configuring a primary name server**

Domain Name System (DNS) is an Internet service that converts a fully qualified domain name, such as `www.debian.org`, into its corresponding IP address, such as `194.109.137.218`. You can think of DNS as the directory of Internet hosts — DNS is the reason why you can use easy-to-remember host names even though TCP/IP requires numeric IP addresses for data transfers. DNS is basically a hierarchy of distributed DNS servers. In this chapter, I provide an overview of DNS and show you how to set up a caching DNS server on your Linux system.

Understanding Domain Name System (DNS)

In TCP/IP networks, each network interface (for example, an Ethernet card or a dialup modem connection) is identified by an IP address. Because IP addresses are hard to remember, an easy-to-remember name is assigned to the IP address — much like the way a name goes with a telephone number. For example, instead of having to remember that the IP address of Red Hat's Web server is `194.109.137.218`, you can simply refer to that host by its name, `www.debian.org`. When you type `www.debian.org` as the URL in a Web browser, the name `www.debian.org` is translated into its corresponding IP address. This is where the concept of DNS comes in.

What is DNS?

Domain Name System is a distributed, hierarchical database that holds information about computers on the Internet. That information includes host name, IP address, and mail-routing specifications. Because this information resides on many DNS hosts on the Internet; DNS is called a *distributed* database. The primary job of DNS is to associate host names to IP addresses and vice versa.

In ARPANET — the precursor to today's Internet — the list of host names and corresponding IP addresses was maintained in a text file named `HOSTS.TXT`, which was managed centrally and periodically distributed to every host on the network. As the number of hosts grew, this static host table quickly became unreasonable to maintain. DNS was proposed by Paul Mockapetris to alleviate the problems of a static host table. As formally documented in Request for Comment (RFC) 882 and 883 (published in November 1983, see `www.faqs.org/rfcs/rfc882.html` and `www.faqs.org/rfcs/rfc883.html`), the original DNS introduced two key concepts:

- The use of hierarchical domain names, such as `www.ee.umd.edu` and `www.debian.org`
- The use of DNS servers throughout the Internet — a form of *distributed responsibility* — as a means of managing the host database

Today, DNS is an Internet standard documented in RFCs 1034 and 1035. The standard has been updated and extended by several other RFCs — 1101, 1183, 1348, 1876, 1982, 1996, 2065, 2181, 2136, 2137, 2308, 2535, 2845, and 2931. The earlier updates define data encoding, whereas later ones focus on improving DNS security. To read these and other RFCs online, visit the RFC page at the Internet Engineering Task Force (IETF) Web site:

`www.ietf.org/rfc.html`

DNS defines the following:

- A hierarchical domain-naming system for hosts
- A distributed database that associates every domain name with an IP address
- Library routines (resolvers) that network applications can use to query the distributed DNS database (this library is called the *resolver library*)
- A protocol for DNS clients and servers to exchange information about names and IP addresses

Nowadays, all hosts on the Internet rely on DNS to access various Internet services on remote hosts. As you may know from personal experience, when you obtain Internet access from an Internet Service Provider (ISP), your ISP provides you with the IP addresses of *name servers* — the DNS servers your system accesses whenever host names are mapped to IP addresses.

If you have a small LAN, you may decide to run a DNS server on one of the hosts or to use the name servers provided by the ISP. For medium-sized networks with several subnets, you can run a DNS server on each subnet to provide efficient DNS lookups. On a large corporate network, the corporate domain (such as `microsoft.com`) is further subdivided into a hierarchy of subdomains; several DNS servers may be used in each subdomain.

In the following sections, I provide an overview of the hierarchical domain-naming convention and describe BIND — the DNS software used on most UNIX systems, including Linux.

Discovering hierarchical domain names

DNS uses a hierarchical tree of domains to organize the *namespace* — the entire set of names. Each higher-level domain has authority over its lower-level subdomains. Each domain represents a distinct block of the namespace and is managed by a single administrative authority. Figure 5-1 illustrates the hierarchical organization of the DNS namespace.

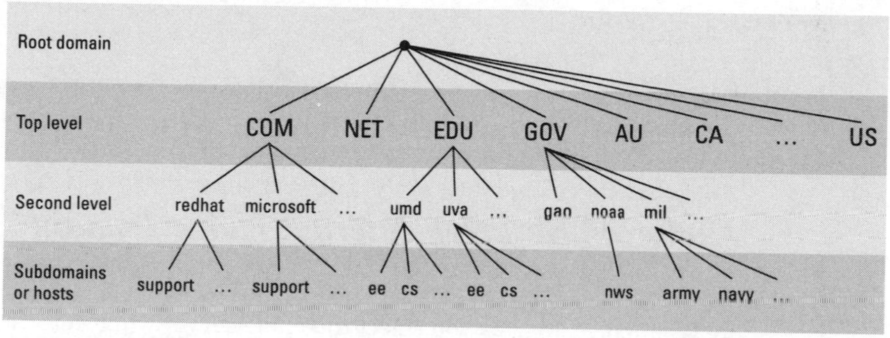

Figure 5-1: The DNS namespace is organized in a hierarchy.

The root of the tree is called the *root domain* and is represented by a single dot (.). The top-level, or root-level, domains come next. The top-level domains are further divided into second-level domains, which, in turn, can be broken into further subdomains.

The top-level domains are relatively fixed and include well-known domains such as `COM`, `NET`, `ORG`, `EDU`, `GOV`, and `MIL`. These are the commonly used top-level domains in the United States. These top-level domains came about as the Internet came to widespread use in the early 1990s.

Another set of top-level domain names is for the countries. These domain names use the two-letter country codes assigned by the International Organization for Standardization (abbreviated as ISO, see `www.iso.ch`). For example, the top-level country code domain for the United States is `US`. In the United States, many local governments and organizations use the `US` domain. For example, `mcps.k12.md.us` is the domain name of the Montgomery County Public Schools in the state of Maryland, USA.

The *fully qualified domain name* (FQDN) is constructed by stringing together the subdomain names, from lower- to higher-level, using dots (.) as separators. For example, `REDHAT.COM` is a fully qualified domain name; so is `EE.UMD.EDU`.

Note that each of these may also refer to a specific host computer. Figure 5-2 illustrates the components of a fully qualified domain name.

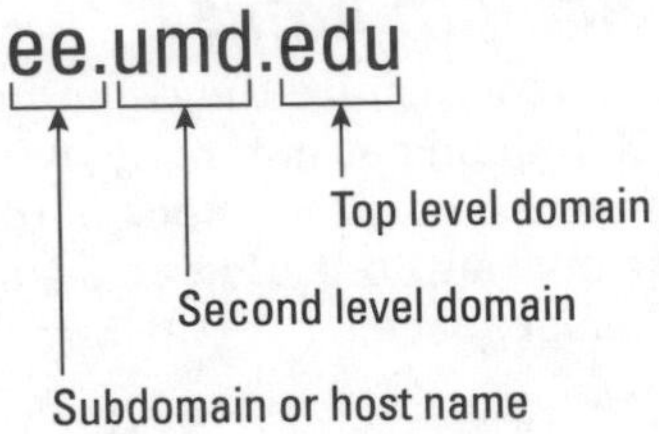

Figure 5-2: A fully qualified domain name has a hierarchy of components.

Domain names are case insensitive. Therefore, as far as DNS is concerned, the domains `UMD.EDU` and `umd.edu` both represent University of Maryland's domain. The norm, however, is to type domain names in all lowercase.

Exploring Berkeley Internet Name Domain (BIND)

Most UNIX systems, including Linux, come with the BIND system — a well-known implementation of DNS. The BIND software is installed during Linux installation, as long as you select the name server when selecting the packages for installation.

In Debian and Xandros, type **dpkg -l bind*** to see if BIND is installed. In Fedora Core and SUSE, type **rpm -q bind** and see if the `bind` package is installed.

In Debian, type **apt-get install bind9** to install BIND. In Fedora Core, log in as `root`, mount the DVD, and type **cd /mnt/cdrom/Fedora/RPMS** followed by **rpm -ivh bind***. In SUSE, click Install and Remove Software in the YaST Control Center's Software category. Then use YaST's search facility to look for `bind`, select the relevant packages, and install them. In Xandros, first run Xandros Networks, select Edit⇨Set Application Sources, and click the Debian Unsupported Site link as a source; then type **apt-get install bind9** to install the INN server.

BIND includes three major components:

- ✦ The `named` daemon — the name server — that responds to queries about host names and IP addresses
- ✦ A resolver library that applications can use to resolve host names into IP addresses (and vice versa)
- ✦ Command-line DNS utility programs (DNS clients), such as `dig` (Domain Internet Groper) and `host`, that users can use to query DNS

I describe these components of BIND in the next few sections. In later sections, I explain how to configure the resolver and the name server.

named — the BIND name server

The `named` daemon is the name server that responds to queries about host names and IP addresses. Based on the configuration files and the local DNS database, `named` either provides answers to queries or asks other servers and caches their responses. The `named` server also performs a function referred to as *zone transfer,* which involves copying data among the name servers in a domain.

The name server operates in one of three modes:

- **Primary or Master:** In this case, the name server keeps the master copy of the domain's data on disk. One primary server is for each domain or subdomain.
- **Secondary or Slave:** A secondary name server copies its domain's data from the primary server using a zone transfer operation. You can have one or more secondary name servers for a domain.
- **Caching:** A caching name server loads the addresses of a few authoritative servers for the root domain, and gets all domain data by caching responses to queries it has resolved by contacting other name servers. Primary and secondary servers also cache responses.

A *name server* can be authoritative or not, depending on what information it's providing. As the term implies, the response from an authoritative name server is supposed to be accurate. The primary and secondary name servers are authoritative for their own domains, but they are not authoritative for responses provided from cached information.

REMEMBER

Caching name servers are never authoritative because all their responses come from cached information.

To run a name server on your Linux system, you have to run `named` with the appropriate configuration files. Later in this chapter, you find out about the configuration files and data files that control how the name server operates.

Resolver library

Finding an IP address for a host name is referred to as *resolving the host name*. Network-aware applications, such as a Web browser or an FTP client, use a *resolver library* to perform the conversion from the name to an IP address. Depending on the settings in the `/etc/host.conf` file, the resolver library consults the `/etc/hosts` file or makes a DNS query to resolve a host name to its IP address. The resolver library queries the name servers listed in the `/etc/resolv.conf` file.

You don't have to know much about the resolver library unless you're writing network-aware applications. To run Internet services properly, all you have to know is how to configure the resolver. Later in this chapter, I show you how to configure the server and other aspects of DNS.

DNS utility programs

You can use the DNS utility programs — `dig` and `host` — to try out DNS interactively from the shell prompt. These utility programs are DNS clients. You can use them to query the DNS database and debug any name server you may set up on your system. By default, these programs query the name server listed in your system's `/etc/resolv.conf` file.

You can use `dig`, the Domain Internet Groper program, to look up IP addresses for a domain name or vice versa. For example, to look up the IP address of `ftp.redhat.com`, type

```
dig ftp.redhat.com
```

`dig` prints the results of the DNS query in great detail. Look in the part of the output labeled `ANSWER SECTION:` for the result. For example, here's what that section looks like for this sample query:

```
;; ANSWER SECTION:
ftp.redhat.com.         212     IN      A       66.187.224.30
ftp.redhat.com.         212     IN      A       209.132.176.30
```

This output means that the name `ftp.redhat.com` refers to both IP addresses — 66.187.224.30 and 209.132.176.30.

Reverse lookups (finding host names for IP addresses) are also easy with `dig`. For example, to find the host name corresponding to the IP address 209.132.176.30, type the following:

```
dig -x 209.132.176.30
```

Again, the answer appears in the `ANSWER SECTION` of the output, which, for this example, looks like this:

```
;; ANSWER SECTION:
30.176.132.209.in-addr.arpa.. 600 IN      PTR     ftp.redhat.com.
```

In this case, the host name corresponding to the IP address 209.132.176.30 happens to be `ftp.redhat.com`.

You can also query DNS by using the `host` program. The `host` program produces output in a compact format. For example, here's a typical use of `host` to look up an IP address for a host name:

```
host www.gao.gov
```

This command generates the following one-liner:

```
www.gao.gov has address 161.203.16.2
```

By default, `host` prints the IP address and any *MX record.* (These records list the names of mail handlers for the host.)

For a reverse lookup, use the `-t ptr` option, along with the IP address as an argument, like this:

```
host -t ptr 161.203.16.2
```

Here's the relay from `host`:

```
2.16.203.161.in-addr.arpa domain name pointer www.gao.gov.
```

In this case, `host` prints the PTR record (from the DNS database) that shows the host name corresponding to the IP address. (PTR refers to "pointer" and the PTR record specifies the name corresponding to an address.)

You can also try other types of records, such as `CNAME` (for canonical name), as follows:

```
host -t cname www.ee.umd.edu
```

The response from `host` says

```
www.ee.umd.edu is an alias for edison.eng.umd.edu.
```

This output indicates that the *canonical name* (or alias) for `www.ee.umd.edu` is `edison.eng.umd.edu`.

Configuring DNS

You configure DNS by using a number of configuration files. The exact set of files depends on whether or not you're running a name server and, if so, the type of name server — caching or primary. Some configuration files are needed whether you run a name server or not.

Configuring the resolver

You don't need a name server running on your system to use the DNS clients (`dig` and `host`). You can use them to query your domain's name server. Typically, your ISP provides you with this information. You have to list the IP addresses of these name servers in the `/etc/resolv.conf` file — the resolver library reads this file to determine how to resolve host names. The format of this file is

```
domain your-domain.com
search your-domain.com
nameserver A.B.C.D
nameserver X.Y.Z.W
```

where `A.B.C.D` and `X.Y.Z.W` are the IP addresses (dot-separated numeric addresses, such as 192.168.0.1) of the primary and secondary name servers that your ISP provides you.

The `domain` line lists the local domain name. The `search` line specifies the domains on which a host name is searched first (usually, you put your own domain in the search line). The domain listed on the `search` line is appended to any host name before the resolver library tries to resolve it. For example, if you look for a host named `mailhost`, the resolver library first tries `mailhost.your-domain.com`; if that fails, it tries `mailhost`. The `search` line applies to any host name that you try to access. For example, if you're trying to access `www.redhat.com`, the resolver first tries `www.redhat.com.your-domain.com` and then `www.redhat.com`.

Another important configuration file is `/etc/host.conf` — this file tells the resolver what to do when attempting to resolve a host name. A typical `/etc/host/conf` file contains the following line:

```
order hosts,bind
```

This command tells the resolver to consult the `/etc/hosts` file first and, if that fails, to query the name server listed in the `/etc/resolv.conf` file. The `/etc/hosts` file usually lists any local host names and their IP addresses. Here's a typical line from the `/etc/hosts` file:

```
127.0.0.1    lnbp200  localhost.localdomain  localhost
```

This line says that the IP address `127.0.0.1` is assigned to the host names `lnbp200`, `localhost.localdomain`, and `localhost`.

In the latest version of the Linux kernel — the one that uses GNU C Library version 2 (glibc 2) or later — the name service switch (NSS) file, `/etc/nsswitch.conf`, controls how services such as the resolver library, NIS, NIS+, and local files such as `/etc/hosts` and `/etc/shadow` interact. For example, the following `hosts` entry in the `/etc/nsswitch.conf` file specifies that the resolver library first try the `/etc/hosts` file, then try NIS+, and finally try DNS:

```
hosts:      files nisplus dns
```

To find more about the `/etc/nsswitch.conf` file and what it does, type **man nsswitch.conf** in a terminal window.

Configuring a caching name server

A simple, but useful, name server is one that finds answers to host-name queries by using other name servers and then remembers the answer (by saving it in a cache) for the next time you need it. This caching name server can shorten the time it takes to access hosts you have accessed recently; the answer is already in the cache.

When you install BIND, the configuration files for a caching name server are also installed. That means you can start running the caching name server without much work on your part. This section describes the configuration files and what you have to do to start the caching name server.

The /etc/named.conf file

The first configuration file you need is `/etc/named.conf`. (Actually, that's the name in Fedora Core and SUSE; in Debian and Xandros, the BIND configuration file is called `/etc/bind/named.conf`.) The `named` server reads this configuration file when it starts. You already have this file if you installed BIND. Here's a `/etc/named/conf` file from Fedora Core:

```
options {
    directory "/var/named";
    /*
     * If there is a firewall between you and nameservers you want
     * to talk to, you might need to uncomment the query-source
     * directive below.
     */
    // query-source address * port 53;
};

//
// A caching only nameserver configuration
//
controls {
    inet 127.0.0.1 allow { localhost; } keys { rndckey; };
};
zone "." IN {
    type hint;
    file "named.ca";
};

zone "localhost" IN {
    type master;
    file "localhost.zone";
    allow-update { none; };
};

zone "0.0.127.in-addr.arpa" IN {
    type master;
    file "named.local";
    allow-update { none; };
};

include "/etc/rndc.key";
```

Comments are C-style (`/* ... */`) or C++-style (starts with `//`). The file contains block statements enclosed in curly braces (`{ . . . }`) and terminated by a semicolon (`;`). A block statement, in turn, contains other statements, each ending with a semicolon.

This `/etc/named.conf` file begins with an `options` block statement with a number of option statements. The `directory` option statement tells `named` where to look for all other files that appear on file lines in the configuration file. In this case, `named` looks for the files in the `/var/named` directory.

In SUSE, the `directory` option in `/etc/named.conf` refers to the `/var/lib/named` directory, which means that all other BIND configuration files are in `/var/lib/named`. In Debian and Xandros, the configuration files are explicitly specified to be in the `/etc/bind` directory.

The `controls` statement in `/etc/named.conf` contains security information so that the `rndc` command can connect to the `named` service at port 953 and interact with `named`. In this case, the `controls` statement contains the following line:

```
inet 127.0.0.1 allow { localhost; } keys { rndckey; };
```

This command says that `rndc` can connect from `localhost` with the key named `rndc`. (The file `/etc/rndc.key` defines the key and the encryption algorithm to be used.)

The `rndc` (remote name daemon control) utility is a successor to the older `ndc` (for *name daemon controller*) utility used to control the `named` server by sending it messages over a special control channel, a TCP port where `named` listens for messages. The `rndc` utility uses a cryptographic key to authenticate itself to the `named` server. The `named` server has the same cryptographic key so that it can decode the authentication information sent by `rndc`.

After the `options` statement, the `/etc/named.conf` file contains several `zone` statements, each enclosed in curly braces and terminated by a semicolon. Each `zone` statement defines a zone. The first zone is named `.` (root zone); it's a hint zone that specifies the root name servers. (When the DNS server starts, it uses the hint zone to find a root name server and get the most recent list of root name servers.)

The next two `zone` statements in `/etc/named.conf` are master zones. (A *master zone* is simply the master copy of data for a domain.) The syntax for a *master zone statement* for an Internet class zone (indicated by the `IN` keyword) is as follows:

```
zone "zone-name" IN {
        type master;
        file "zone-file";
        [...other optional statements...]
};
```

The zone-name is the name of the zone, and zone-file is the zone file that contains the resource records (RR) — the database entries — for that zone. I describe zone file formats and resource record formats in the next two sections.

Zone file formats

The zone file typically starts with a number of directives, each of which begins with a dollar sign ($) followed by a keyword. Two commonly used directives are $TTL and $ORIGIN.

For example, the line

```
$TTL    86400
```

uses the $TTL directive to set the default Time To Live (TTL) for subsequent records with undefined TTLs. The value is in seconds, and the valid TTLs are in the range 0 to 2147483647 seconds. In this case, the directive sets the default TTL as 86400 seconds (or one day).

The $ORIGIN directive sets the domain name that is appended to any unqualified records. For example, the following $ORIGIN directive sets the domain name to localhost:

```
$ORIGIN localhost.
```

If there is no $ORIGIN directive, the initial $ORIGIN is the same as the zone name that comes after the zone keyword in the /etc/named.conf file.

After the directives, the zone file contains one or more resource records. These records follow a specific format, which I outline in the next section.

Resource record (RR) formats

You have to understand the format of the resource records before you can understand and intelligently work with zone files. Each resource record has the following format (the optional fields are shown in square brackets):

```
[domain] [ttl] [class] type data [;comment]
```

The fields are separated by tabs or spaces and may contain some special characters, such as an @ symbol for the domain and a semicolon (;) to indicate the start of a comment.

The first field, which must begin at the first character of the line, identifies the domain. You can use the @ symbol to use the current `$ORIGIN` for the domain name for this record. If you have multiple records for the same domain name, leave the first field blank.

The optional `ttl` field specifies the Time To Live — the duration for which the data can be cached and considered valid. You can specify the duration in one of the following formats:

- `N`, where *N* is a number meaning *N* seconds
- `NW`, where *N* is a number meaning *N* weeks
- `ND`, where *N* is a number meaning *N* days
- `NH`, where *N* is a number meaning *N* hours
- `NM`, where *N* is a number meaning *N* minutes
- `NS`, where *N* is a number meaning *N* seconds

The letters `W`, `D`, `H`, `M`, and `S` can also be in lowercase. Thus, you can write `86400` or `1D` (or `1d`) to indicate a duration of one day. You can also combine these to specify more precise durations, such as `5w6d16h` to indicate 5 weeks, 6 days, and 16 hours.

The `class` field specifies the network type. The most commonly used value for this field is `IN` for Internet.

Next in the resource record is the `type` field, which denotes the type of record (such as `SOA`, `NS`, `A`, or `PTR`). Table 5-1 lists the DNS resource record types. The data field comes next, and it depends on the type field.

Table 5-1 DNS Resource Record Types

Type	*Name*	*Description*
`SOA`	Start of Authority	Indicates that all subsequent records are authoritative for this zone.
`NS`	Name Server	Identifies authoritative name servers for a zone.
`A`	Address	Specifies the IP address corresponding to a host name.
`PTR`	Pointer	Specifies the name corresponding to an address (used for reverse mapping — converting an IP address to a host name).

Type	Name	Description
MX	Mail Exchanger	Identifies the host that accepts mail meant for a domain (used to route e-mail).
CNAME	Canonical Name	Defines the nickname or alias for a host name.
KEY	Public Key	Stores a public key associated with a DNS name.
CERT	Digital Certificate	Holds a digital certificate.
HINFO	Host Info	Identifies the hardware and operating system for a host.
RP	Responsible Person	Provides the name of a technical contact for a domain.
SRV	Services	Lists well-known network services provided by the domain.
TXT	Text	Used to include comments and other information in the DNS database.

Read the resource records in the zone files, at least the ones of type SOA, NS, A, PTR, and MX, which are some of the most commonly used. (You'll find the zone files in the /etc/bind directory in Debian and Xandros; the /var/named directory in Fedora Core; and the /var/lib/named directory in SUSE.) Next, I briefly describe these records, illustrating each record type through an example.

A typical SOA record has the following format:

```
@     1D IN SOA       @ root (
                      42                ; serial
                      3H                ; refresh -- 3 hours
                      15M               ; retry -- 15 minutes
                      1W                ; expiry -- 1 week
                      1D )              ; minimum -- 1 day
```

The first field specifies the domain as an @, which means the current domain (by default, the zone name, as shown in the /etc/named.conf file). The next field specifies a TTL of one day for this record. The class field is set to IN, which means the record is for Internet. The type field specifies the record type as SOA. The rest of the fields constitute the data for the SOA record. The data includes the name of the primary name server (in this case, @, or the current domain), the e-mail address of the technical contact, and five different times enclosed in parentheses.

The NS record specifies the authoritative name servers for a zone. A typical NS record looks like the following:

```
.         3600000  IN   NS    A.ROOT-SERVERS.NET.
```

In this case, the `NS` record lists the authoritative name server for the root zone. (Notice that the name of the first field is a single dot.) The Time-To-Live field specifies that the record is to be valid for 1,000 hours (3600000 seconds). The class is `IN`, for Internet; and the record type is `NS`. The final field lists the name of the name server (`A.ROOT-SERVERS.NET.`), which ends with a dot.

An `A` record specifies the address corresponding to a name. For example, the following `A` record shows the address of `A.ROOT-SERVERS.NET.` as `198.41.0.4`:

```
A.ROOT-SERVERS.NET.        3600000       A      198.41.0.4
```

In this case, the network class isn't specified because the field is optional, and the default is `IN`.

`PTR` records are used for reverse mapping — converting an address to a name. Consider the following example:

```
1        IN      PTR      localhost.
```

This record comes from a file for a zone named `0.0.127.in-addr.arpa.` Therefore, this record says that the name associated with the address `127.0.0.1` is `localhost.`

An `MX` record specifies the name of a host that accepts mail on behalf of a specific domain. For example, here's a typical `MX` record:

```
naba     IN     MX     10     mailhub.lnbsoft.com.
```

This record says that mail addressed to the host named `naba` in the current domain is sent to `mailhub.lnbsoft.com.` (This host is called a mail exchanger.) The number `10` is the preference value. For a list of multiple `MX` records with different preference values, the ones with lower preference values are tried first.

Armed with this bit of information about resource records, you can go through the zone files for the caching name server.

The root zone file

Information about the thirteen root name servers is in the zone file referenced in the zone statement for the root zone in the `/etc/named.conf` file. (In Fedora Core the root zone file is `/var/named/named.ca`, in Debian and Xandros it's `/etc/bind/db.root`, and in SUSE it's `/var/lib/named/root.hint`.) The following listing shows the root zone file:

```
;       This file holds the information on root name servers needed to
;       initialize cache of Internet domain name servers
;       (e.g. reference this file in the "cache  .  <file>"
```

```
;       configuration file of BIND domain name servers).
;
;       This file is made available by InterNIC
;       under anonymous FTP as
;          file                /domain/named.cache
;          on server           FTP.INTERNIC.NET
;       -OR-                   RS.INTERNIC.NET
;
;       last update:    Jan 29, 2004
;       related version of root zone:   2004012900
;
;
; formerly NS.INTERNIC.NET
;
.                        3600000  IN  NS    A.ROOT-SERVERS.NET.
A.ROOT-SERVERS.NET.      3600000      A     198.41.0.4
;
; formerly NS1.ISI.EDU
;
.                        3600000      NS    B.ROOT-SERVERS.NET.
B.ROOT-SERVERS.NET.      3600000      A     192.228.79.201
;
; formerly C.PSI.NET
;
.                        3600000      NS    C.ROOT-SERVERS.NET.
C.ROOT-SERVERS.NET.      3600000      A     192.33.4.12
;
; formerly TERP.UMD.EDU
;
.                        3600000      NS    D.ROOT-SERVERS.NET.
D.ROOT-SERVERS.NET.      3600000      A     128.8.10.90
;
; formerly NS.NASA.GOV
;
.                        3600000      NS    E.ROOT-SERVERS.NET.
E.ROOT-SERVERS.NET.      3600000      A     192.203.230.10
;
; formerly NS.ISC.ORG
;
.                        3600000      NS    F.ROOT-SERVERS.NET.
F.ROOT-SERVERS.NET.      3600000      A     192.5.5.241
;
; formerly NS.NIC.DDN.MIL
;
.                        3600000      NS    G.ROOT-SERVERS.NET.
G.ROOT-SERVERS.NET.      3600000      A     192.112.36.4
;
; formerly AOS.ARL.ARMY.MIL
;
.                        3600000      NS    H.ROOT-SERVERS.NET.
H.ROOT-SERVERS.NET.      3600000      A     128.63.2.53
;
; formerly NIC.NORDU.NET
;
.                        3600000      NS    I.ROOT-SERVERS.NET.
I.ROOT-SERVERS.NET.      3600000      A     192.36.148.17
;
; operated by VeriSign, Inc.
;
.                        3600000      NS    J.ROOT-SERVERS.NET.
J.ROOT-SERVERS.NET.      3600000      A     192.58.128.30
;
```

```
; operated by RIPE NCC
;
.                       3600000      NS    K.ROOT-SERVERS.NET.
K.ROOT-SERVERS.NET.     3600000      A     193.0.14.129
;
; operated by ICANN
;
.                       3600000      NS    L.ROOT-SERVERS.NET.
L.ROOT-SERVERS.NET.     3600000      A     198.32.64.12
;
; operated by WIDE
;
.                       3600000      NS    M.ROOT-SERVERS.NET.
M.ROOT-SERVERS.NET.     3600000      A     202.12.27.33
; End of File
```

This file contains NS and A resource records that specify the names of authoritative name servers and their addresses for the root zone (indicated by the . in the first field of each NS record).

The comment lines in the file begin with a semicolon. These comments give you hints about the location of the root name servers. There are 13 root name servers for the Internet; most root servers are located in the United States. This file is a necessity for any name server because the name server has to be able to reach at least one root name server.

The localhost.zone file

The /etc/named.conf file includes a zone statement for the localhost zone that specifies the zone file as localhost.zone. That file is located in the /var/named directory in Fedora Core, in the /var/local/named directory in SUSE, and in /etc/bind/db.local in Debian and Xandros. Here's a listing of what the localhost.zone file contains:

```
$TTL    86400
$ORIGIN localhost.
@             1D IN SOA      @ root (
                             42            ; serial (d. adams)
                             3H            ; refresh
                             15M           ; retry
                             1W            ; expiry
                             1D )          ; minimum

              1D IN NS       @
              1D IN A        127.0.0.1
```

This zone file starts with a $TTL directive that sets the default TTL (Time To Live) to one day (86400 seconds) for subsequent records with undefined TTLs. Next, a $ORIGIN directive sets the domain name to localhost.

After these two directives, the localhost.zone file contains three resource records (RRs): an SOA record, an NS record, and an A record. The SOA and the

NS records specify `localhost` as the primary authoritative name server for the zone. The A record specifies the address of `localhost` as `127.0.0.1`.

The zone file for reverse mapping 127.0.0.1

The third `zone` statement in the `/etc/named.conf` file specifies a reverse-mapping zone named `0.0.127.in-addr.arpa`. For this zone, the zone file is `/var/named/named.local` in Fedora Core, `/var/lib/named/127.0.0.zone` in SUSE, and `/etc/bind/db.127` in Debian and Xandros. This zone file contains the following:

```
$TTL    86400
@       IN      SOA     localhost. root.localhost.  (
                                   1997022700 ; Serial
                                   28800      ; Refresh
                                   14400      ; Retry
                                   3600000    ; Expire
                                   86400 )    ; Minimum
        IN      NS      localhost.
1       IN      PTR     localhost.
```

The SOA and NS records specify `localhost` as the primary name server. The PTR record specifies `localhost` as the name corresponding to the address `127.0.0.1`.

The SOA record also shows `root.localhost.` as the e-mail address of the technical contact for the domain. Note that the DNS zone files use a `user.host.` (notice the ending period) format for the e-mail address. When sending any e-mail to the contact, you have to replace the first dot with an @ and remove the final dot.

Caching name server: Startup and test

After you've studied the configuration files for the caching name server, you can start the name server and see it in operation.

To start the name server, log in as `root` and type **/etc/init.d/named start** in Fedora Core and SUSE. To ensure that the `named` server starts every time you reboot the system, type **chkconfig --level 35 named on** in Fedora Core and SUSE. In Debian and Xandros, type **/etc/init.d/bind9 start** to start the `named` server.

The `named` server writes diagnostic log messages in the `/var/log/messages` file. After you start `named`, you can check the log messages by opening `/var/log/messages` in a text editor. If no error messages are from `named`, you can proceed to test the name server.

Before you try the caching name server, you have to specify that name server as your primary one. To do so, make sure that the first line in the `/etc/resolv.conf` file is the following:

```
nameserver 127.0.0.1
```

Now you can use `host` to test the name server. For example, to look up the IP address of `www.gao.gov` by using the caching name server on `localhost`, type the following command:

```
host www.gao.gov localhost
```

Here's the resulting output from the `host` command:

```
Using domain server:
Name: localhost
Address: 127.0.0.1#53
Aliases:
www.gao.gov. has address 161.203.16.2
```

As the output shows, the `host` command uses `localhost` as the DNS server and returns the IP address of `www.gao.gov`. If you get an output similar to this, the caching name server is up and running.

Configuring a primary name server

The best way to configure a primary name server is to start by configuring a caching name server (as explained in the previous sections). Then, add master zones for the domains for which you want this name server to be the primary name server. For example, suppose that I want to define a primary name server for the `naba.net` domain. Here are the steps I go through to configure that primary name server on a Fedora Core system (after I log in as `root`):

1. **Add the following zone statements to the `/etc/named.conf` file:**

    ```
    zone "naba.net" IN {
        type master;
        file "naba.zone";
    };
    zone "0.168.192.in-addr.arpa" IN {
        type master;
        file "0.168.192.zone";
    };
    ```

2. **Create the zone file `/var/named/naba.zone` with the following lines in it:**

    ```
    $TTL    86400
    $ORIGIN naba.net.
    ```

```
@               1D IN SOA          @ root.naba.net (
                                   100                 ; serial
                                   3H                  ; refresh
                                   15M                 ; retry
                                   1W                  ; expiry
                                   1D )                ; minimum

                1D IN NS           @
                1D IN A            192.168.0.7

wxp    IN    A    192.168.0.2
```

3. Create the zone file `/var/named/0.168.192.zone` with the following lines in it:

```
$TTL    86400
; Remember zone name is: 0.168.192.in-addr.arpa
@       IN      SOA     naba.net. root.naba.net  (
                                      1          ; Serial
                                      28800       ; Refresh
                                      14400       ; Retry
                                      3600000     ; Expire
                                      86400 )     ; Minimum
        IN      NS      naba.net.

7       IN      PTR     naba.net.
2       IN      PTR   wxp.naba.net.
```

4. To test the new configuration, restart the `named` server with the following command:

```
/etc/init.d/named restart
```

5. Use `dig` or `host` to query the DNS server.

For example, here's how I use `host` to check the address of the host `wxp.naba.net` at the DNS server running on `localhost`:

```
host wxp.naba.net localhost
```

This command results in the following output:

```
Using domain server:
Name: localhost
Address: 127.0.0.1#53
Aliases:

wxp.naba.net has address 192.168.0.2
```

If you want to use `dig` to check the DNS server, type the following command:

```
dig @localhost wxp.naba.net
```

That `@localhost` part specifies the DNS server that `dig` contacts.

When you successfully use `dig` to contact a DNS server, you can get a bit fancier with what you ask that server to do. Here, for example, is the command I type to try a reverse lookup with the IP address `192.168.0.2`:

```
host 192.168.0.2 localhost
```

This command displays the following output:

```
Using domain server:
Name: localhost
Address: 127.0.0.1#53
Aliases:

2.0.168.192.in-addr.arpa domain name pointer wxp.naba.net
```

Chapter 6: Using Samba and NFS

In This Chapter

- **Sharing files with NFS**
- **Installing and configuring Samba**
- **Setting up a Windows server using Samba**

If your local area network is like many others, it needs the capability to share files between systems that run Linux and other systems that don't. Thus, Linux includes two prominent file-sharing services:

- **Network File System (NFS)** is for sharing files with other UNIX systems (or PCs with NFS client software).
- **Samba** is for file sharing and print sharing with Windows systems.

In this chapter, I describe how to share files using both NFS and Samba.

Sharing Files with NFS

Sharing files through NFS is simple and involves two basic steps:

- On the Linux system that runs the NFS server, you export (share) one or more directories by listing them in the `/etc/exports` file and by running the `exportfs` command. In addition, you must start the NFS server.
- On each client system, you use the `mount` command to mount the directories that your server has exported.

The only problem in using NFS is that each client system must support it. Microsoft Windows doesn't come with NFS. That means you have to buy NFS software separately if you want to share files by using NFS. However, using NFS if all systems on your LAN run Linux (or other variants of UNIX with built-in NFS support) makes sense.

NFS has security vulnerabilities. Do not set up NFS on systems directly connected to the Internet.

In the next few sections, I walk you through NFS setup, using an example of two Linux PCs on a LAN.

Exporting a file system with NFS

Start with the server system that *exports* — makes available to the client systems — the contents of a directory. On the server, you must run the NFS service and also designate one or more file systems to export.

To export a file system, you have to add an appropriate entry to the `/etc/exports` file. For example, suppose that you want to export the `/home` directory and want to enable the host named `LNBP75` to mount this file system for read and write operations. You can do so by adding the following entry to the `/etc/exports` file:

```
/home LNBP75(rw,sync)
```

If you want to give access to all hosts on a LAN such as `192.168.0.0`, you could change this line to

```
/home 192.168.0.0/24(rw,sync)
```

Every line in the `/etc/exports` file has this general format:

```
directory    host1(options)  host2(options)  ...
```

The first field is the directory being shared via NFS, followed by one or more fields that specify which hosts can mount that directory remotely and a number of options within parentheses. You can specify the hosts with names or IP addresses, including ranges of addresses.

The options within parentheses denote the kind of access each host is granted and how user and group IDs from the server are mapped to ID the client. (For example, if a file is owned by `root` on the server, what owner is that on the client?) Within the parentheses, commas separate the options. For example, if a host is allowed both read and write access — and all IDs are to be mapped to the `anonymous` user (by default this is the user named `nobody`) — then the options look like this:

```
(rw,all_squash)
```

Table 6-1 shows the options you can use in the `/etc/exports` file. You find two types of options — general options and user ID mapping options.

Table 6-1 Options in /etc/exports

This Option	*Does the Following*
General Options	
secure	Allows connections only from ports 1024 or lower (default).
insecure	Allows connections from 1024 or higher.
ro	Allows read-only access (default).
rw	Allows both read and write access.
sync	Performs write operations (writing information to the disk) when requested (by default).
async	Performs write operations when the server is ready.
no_wdelay	Performs write operations immediately.
wdelay	Waits a bit to see whether related write requests arrive, and then performs them together (by default).
hide	Hides an exported directory that's a subdirectory of another exported directory (by default).
no_hide	Behaves exactly the opposite of hide.
subtree_check	Performs subtree checking, which involves checking parent directories of an exported subdirectory whenever a file is accessed (by default).
no_subtree_check	Turns off subtree checking (opposite of subtree_check)
insecure_locks	Allows insecure file locking.
User ID Mapping Options	
all_squash	Maps all user IDs and group IDs to the anonymous user on the client.
no_all_squash	Maps remote user and group IDs to similar IDs on the client (by default).
root_squash	Maps remote root user to the anonymous user on the client (by default).
no_root_squash	Maps remote root user to the local root user.
anonuid=UID	Sets the user ID of anonymous user to be used for the all_squash and root_squash options.
anongid=GID	Sets the group ID of anonymous user to be used for the all_squash and root_squash options.

After adding the entry in the /etc/exports file, manually export the file system by typing the following command in a terminal window:

```
exportfs -a
```

This command exports all file systems defined in the /etc/exports file.

Now you can start the NFS server processes.

In Debian, start the NFS server by logging in as root and typing **/etc/init.d/nfs-kernel-server start** in a terminal window. In Fedora Core, type **/etc/init.d/nfs start**. In SUSE, type **/etc/init.d/nfsserver start**. If you want the NFS server to start when the system boots, type **update-rc.d nfs-kernel-server defaults** in Debian. In Fedora Core, type **chkconfig --level 35 nfs on**. In SUSE, type **chkconfig --level 35 nfsserver on**. In Xandros, type **update-rc.d nfs-user-server defaults**.

When the NFS service is up, the server side of NFS is ready. Now you can try to mount the exported file system from a client system, and then access the exported file system as needed.

If you ever make any changes to the exported file systems listed in the /etc/exports file, remember to restart the NFS service. To restart a service, invoke the script in /etc/init.d directory with restart as the argument (instead of the start argument that you use to start the service).

Mounting an NFS file system

To access an exported NFS file system on a client system, you have to mount that file system on a mount point. The *mount point* is nothing more than a local directory. For example, suppose that you want to access the /home directory exported from the server named LNBP200 at the local directory /mnt/lnbp200 on the client system. To do so, follow these steps:

1. **Log in as root and create the directory with this command:**

   ```
   mkdir /mnt/lnbp200
   ```

2. **Type the following command to mount the directory from the remote system (LNBP200) on the local directory /mnt/lnbp200:**

   ```
   mount lnbp200:/home /mnt/lnbp200
   ```

After completing these steps, you can then view and access exported files from the local directory /mnt/lnbp200.

To confirm that the NFS file system is indeed mounted, log in as root on the client system and type **mount** in a terminal window. You see a line similar to the following about the NFS file system:

```
lnbp200:/home/public on /mnt/lnbp200 type nfs (rw,addr=192.168.0.4)
```

Setting Up a Windows Server Using Samba

If you rely on Windows for file sharing and print sharing, you probably use Windows in your servers and clients. If so, you can still move to a Linux PC as your server without losing Windows file- and print-sharing capabilities; you can set up Linux as a Windows server. When you install Linux from this book's companion DVD-ROM, you also get a chance to install the Samba software package, which performs that setup. All you have to do is select the Windows File Server package group during installation.

After you install and configure Samba on your Linux PC, your client PCs — even if they're running the old Windows for Workgroups operating system or the more recent Windows 95/98/NT/2000/XP versions — can access shared disks and printers on the Linux PC. To do so, they use the Server Message Block (SMB) protocol, the underlying protocol in Windows file and print sharing.

With the Samba package installed, you can make your Linux PC a Windows client, which means that the Linux PC can access the disks and printers that a Windows server manages.

The Samba software package has these major components:

- `/etc/samba/smb.conf`: The Samba configuration file that the SMB server uses.
- `/etc/samba/smbusers`: This Samba configuration file shows the Samba usernames corresponding to usernames on the local Linux PC.
- `nmbd`: This is the NetBIOS name server, which clients use to look up servers. (NetBIOS stands for *Network Basic Input/Output System* — an interface that applications use to communicate with network transports, such as TCP/IP.)
- `nmblookup`: This command returns the IP address of a Windows PC identified by its NetBIOS name.
- `smbadduser`: This program adds users to the SMB (Server Message Block) password file.
- `smbcacls`: This program manipulates Windows NT access control lists (ACLs) on shared files.
- `smbclient`: This is the Windows client, which runs on Linux and allows Linux to access the files and printer on any Windows server.
- `smbcontrol`: This program sends messages to the `smbd`, `nmbd`, or `winbindd` processes.
- `smbd`: This is the SMB server, which accepts connections from Windows clients and provides file- and print-sharing services.
- `smbmount`: This program mounts a Samba share directory on a Linux PC.

- smbpasswd: This program changes the password for an SMB user.
- smbprint: This script enables printing on a printer on an SMB server.
- smbstatus: This command lists the current SMB connections for the local host.
- smbtar: This program backs up SMB shares directly to tape drives on the Linux system.
- smbumount: This program unmounts a currently mounted Samba share directory.
- testparm: This program ensures that the Samba configuration file is correct.
- winbindd: This server resolves names from Windows NT servers.

In the following sections, I describe how to configure and use Samba.

Installing Samba

You may have already installed Samba when you installed Linux. You can check first and, if you don't find Samba on your system, you can easily install it.

In Debian and Xandros, type **dpkg -l samba*** to see if Samba is installed. In Fedora Core and SUSE, type **rpm -q samba** and see if the samba package is installed.

In Debian, type **apt-get install samba** to install Samba. In Fedora Core, log in as root, mount the DVD, and type **cd /mnt/cdrom/Fedora/RPMS** followed by **rpm -ivh samba***. In SUSE, click Install and Remove Software in the YaST Control Center's Software category. Then use YaST's search facility to look for samba, select the relevant packages, and install them. As for Xandros, you get Samba when you install Xandros.

After installing the Samba software, you have to configure Samba before you can use it.

Configuring Samba

To set up the Windows file-sharing and print-sharing services, you can either edit the configuration file manually or use a GUI tool. Of course, the GUI tool is much easier than having to edit a configure file. Fedora Core and SUSE come with GUI tools for configuring the Samba server.

In Fedora Core, choose Main Menu➪System Settings➪Server Settings➪Samba to open the Samba Server Configuration window. Click Add and fill in information about a directory that you want to share with Windows systems, as shown in Figure 6-1. Click the Access tab to specify which users can access the shared directory. The Samba Server Configuration tool creates the Samba share by adding entries in the configuration file /etc/samba/smb.conf.

In SUSE, you can configure Samba through the YaST Control Center (select Main Menu⇨System⇨YaST) — click the Network Services in the left-hand side of the window and then click Samba Server in the right-hand side of the window. YaST displays a window (see Figure 6-2) through which you can configure Samba. First you enable the server, set the workgroup name, and give the Samba server a name. Then you can select what you want to share. After you exit the Samba server configuration utility, YaST stores the Samba settings in configuration files in the /etc/samba directory.

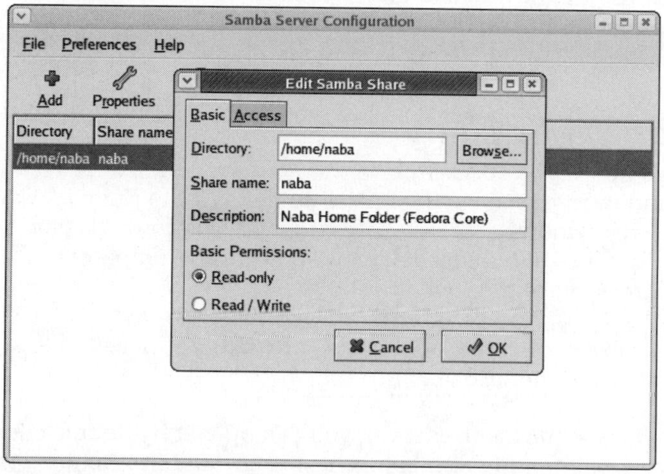

Figure 6-1: Adding a Samba share in Fedora Core.

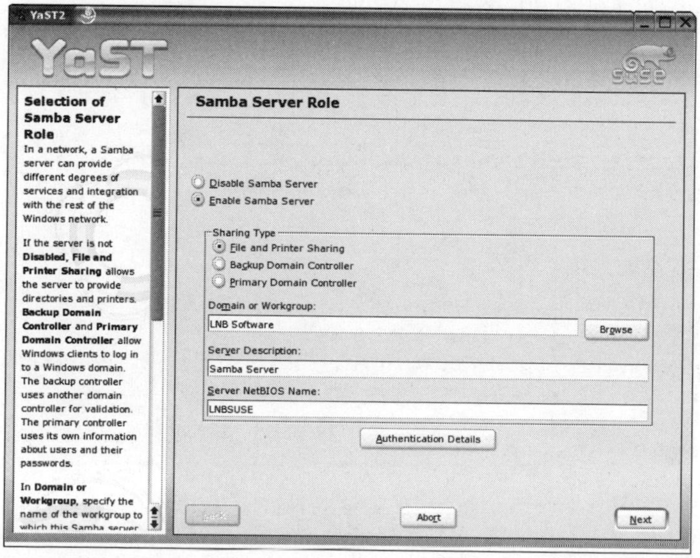

Figure 6-2: In SUSE, you can configure the Samba server through YaST.

After adding a Samba share, type the following command in a terminal window to verify that the Samba configuration file is okay:

```
testparm
```

If the command says that it loaded the files okay, you're all set to go. The `testparm` command also displays the contents of the Samba configuration file.

To start the Samba services automatically when the system reboots, type **update-rc.d samba defaults** in Debian and Xandros. In Fedora Core and SUSE, type **chkconfig --level 35 smb on**.

Trying out Samba

You can now try to access the Samba server on the Linux system from one of the Windows systems on the LAN. Double-click the Network Neighborhood icon on the Windows 95/98/ME desktop. On Windows XP, choose Start⇨My Network Places and then click View Workgroup Computers. All the computers on the same workgroup are shown.

As you can see from the label (see Figure 6-3), the selected icon represents a Linux system running Samba.

When you see the Samba server, you can open it by double-clicking the icon. You are prompted for your Samba username and the Samba password and, after you enter that information correctly, you can access the folders and printers (if any) on the Samba share.

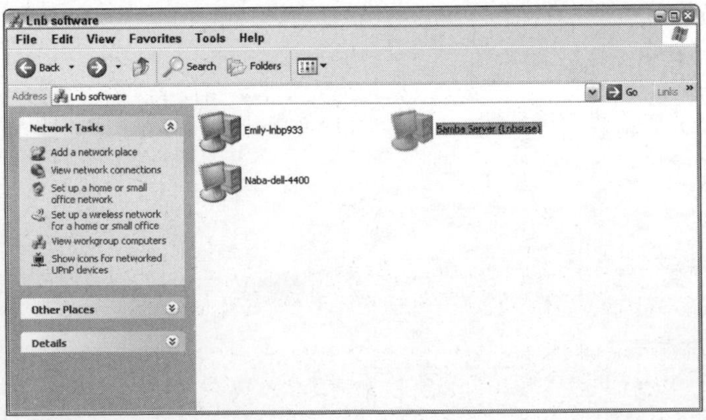

Figure 6-3: You can view the Linux Samba server from Windows XP.

Book VIII

Programming

The 5th Wave By Rich Tennant

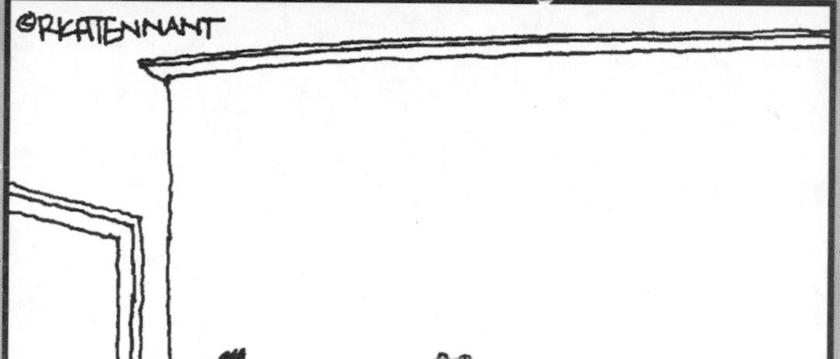

"When we started the company, we weren't going to call it 'Red Hat'. But eventually we decided it sounded better than 'Beard of Bees Linux'."

Contents at a Glance

Chapter 1: Programming in Linux

In This Chapter

- Learning programming
- Exploring the software development tools in Linux
- Compiling and linking programs with GCC
- Using `make`
- Debugging programs with `gdb`
- Understanding the implications of GNU GPL and LGPL

Linux comes loaded with all the tools you need to develop software. (All you have to do is install them.) In particular, it has all the GNU software-development tools, such as GCC (C and C++ compiler), GNU `make`, and the GNU debugger. In this chapter, I introduce you to programming, describe these software-development tools, and show you how to use them. Although I use examples in the C and C++ programming languages, the focus is not on showing how to program in those languages, but on showing you how to use various software-development tools (such as compilers, `make`, and debugger).

I also briefly explain how the Free Software Foundation's GNU General Public License (GPL) may affect any plans you might have to develop Linux software. You need to know this because you use GNU tools and GNU libraries to develop software in Linux.

An Overview of Programming

If you've written computer programs in any programming language, you can start writing programs on your Linux system very quickly. If you've never written a computer program, however, you need two basic resources before you get into it: a look at the basics of programming, and a quick review of computers and the major parts that make them up. In this section, I give you an overview of computer programming — just enough to get you going.

A simplified view of a computer

Before you get a feel for computer programming, you need to understand where computer programs fit into the rest of your computer. Figure 1-1 shows a simplified view of a computer, highlighting the major parts that are important to a programmer.

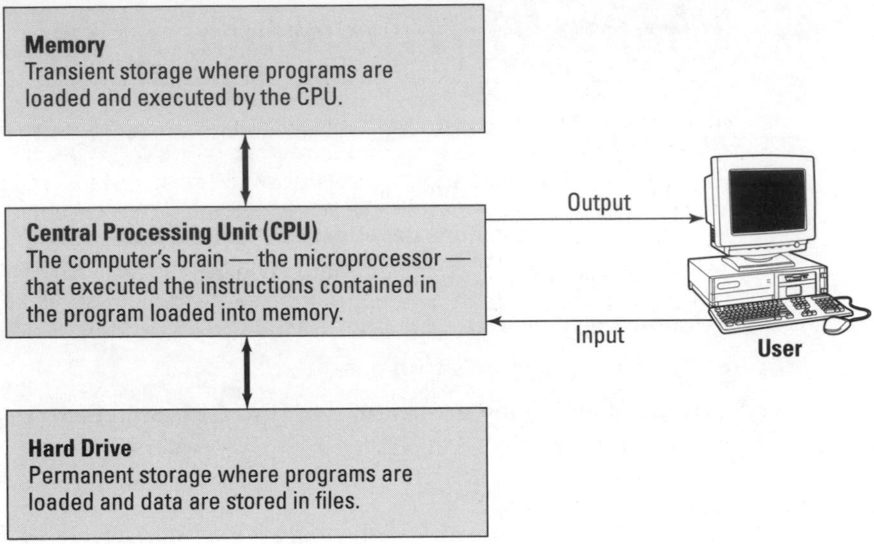

Figure 1-1: A simplified view of a computer and how it runs programs.

At the heart of a computer is the *central processing unit* (CPU) that performs the instructions contained in a computer program. The specific piece of hardware that does the job (which its makers call a *microprocessor* and the rest of us call a *chip*) varies by system: In a Pentium PC, it's a Pentium; in a Sun SPARC workstation, it's a SPARC chip; in an HP UNIX workstation, it's a PA-RISC chip. These microprocessors have different capabilities but the same mission: Tell the computer what to do.

Random Access Memory (RAM), or just *memory,* serves as the storage for computer programs while the CPU executes them. If a program works on some data, that data is also stored in the memory. The contents of the memory are not permanent; they go away (never to return) when the computer is shut down or when a program is no longer running.

The *hard drive* (also referred to as the *hard disk* or *disk*) serves as the permanent storage space for computer programs and data. The hard drive is organized into files, which are in turn organized in hierarchical directories and subdirectories (somewhat like organizing paper folders into the drawers in a file cabinet). Each file is essentially a block of storage capable of holding a variety of information. For example, a file may be a human-readable text file — or it may be a collection of computer instructions that makes sense only to the CPU. When you create computer programs, you work a lot with files.

For a programmer, the other two important items are the *input* and *output* — the way a program gets input from the user and displays output to the user. The user provides input through the keyboard and mouse and output appears on the monitor. However, a program may also accept input from a file and send output to a file.

Role of the operating system

The *operating system* is a special collection of computer programs whose primary purpose is to load and run other programs. The operating system also acts as an interface between the software and the hardware. All operating systems include one or more command processors (called *shells* in Linux) that allow users to type commands and perform tasks such as running a program or printing a file. Most operating systems also include a graphical user interface (such as GNOME and KDE in Linux) that allows the user to perform most tasks by clicking on-screen icons. Linux, Windows (whether the NT, 2000, or XP version), and various versions of UNIX, including Linux, are examples of operating systems.

It's the operating system that gives a computer its personality. For example, you can run Windows 2000 or Windows XP on a PC. On that same PC, you can also install and run Linux. That means, depending on the operating system installed on it, the selfsame PC could be a Windows 2000, Windows XP, or a Linux system.

Computer programs are built "on top of" the operating system. That means a computer program must make use of the capabilities that the operating system includes. For example, computer programs read and write files by using built-in capabilities of the operating system. (And if the operating system can't make coffee, no program can tell it to and still expect positive results.)

Although the details vary, most operating systems support a number of similar concepts. As a programmer, you need to be familiar with the following handful of concepts:

- A *process* is a computer program that is currently running in the computer. Most operating systems allow multiple processes to run simultaneously.
- A *command processor,* or *shell,* is a special program that allows the user to type commands and perform various tasks, such as run any program, look at a host of files, or print a file. In Windows 2000 or Windows XP, you can type commands in a Command Prompt window.
- The term *command line* refers to the commands that a user types to the command processor. Usually a command line contains a command and one or more *options* — the command is the first word in the line and the rest are the options (specific behaviors demanded of the computer).
- *Environment variables* are essentially text strings with a name. For example, the `PATH` environment variable refers to a string that contains the names of directories. Operating systems use environment variables to provide useful information to processes. To see a list of environment variables in a Windows 2000 or Windows XP system, type **set** in the Command Prompt window. In Linux, you can type **printenv** to see the environment variables.

Basics of computer programming

A *computer program* is a sequence of instructions for performing a specific task, such as adding two numbers or searching for some text in a file. Consequently, computer programming involves *creating* that list of instructions, telling the computer how to complete a specific task. The exact instructions depend on the programming language that you use. For most programming languages, you have to go through the following steps to create a computer program:

1. Use a text editor to type in the sequence of commands from the programming language.

   This sequence of commands accomplishes your task. This human-readable version of the program is called the *source file* or *source code*. You can create the source file using any application (such as a word processor) that can save a document in plain-text form.

   Always save your source code as plain text. (The filename depends on the type of programming language.) Word processors can sometimes put extra instructions in their documents that tell the computer to display the text in a particular font or other format. Saving the file as plain text deletes any and all such extra instructions. Trust me, your program is much better off without such stuff.

2. Use a *compiler* program to convert that text file — the source code — from human-readable form into machine-readable *object code*.

   Typically, this step also combines several object code files into a single machine-readable computer program, something that the computer can actually run.

3. Use a special program called a *debugger* to track down any errors and find which lines in the source file might have caused the errors.

4. Go back to Step 1 and use the text editor to fix the errors and repeat the rest of the steps.

These steps are referred to as the *Edit-Compile-Debug cycle* of programming because most programmers have to repeat this sequence several times before a program works correctly.

In addition to knowing the basic programming steps, you also need to be familiar with the following terms and concepts:

- *Variables* are used to store different types of data. You can think of each variable as being a placeholder for data — kind of like a mailbox, with a name and room to store data. The content of the variable is its value.
- *Expressions* combine variables by using operators. An expression may add several variables; another may extract a part of a string.

✦ *Statements* perform some action, such as assigning a value to a variable or printing a string.

✦ *Flow-control statements* allow statements to execute in various orders, depending on the value of some expression. Typically, flow-control statements include `for`, `do-while`, `while`, and `if-then-else` statements.

✦ *Functions* (also called *subroutines* or *routines*) allow you to group several statements and give them a name. This feature allows you to execute the same set of statements by invoking the function that represents those statements. Typically, a programming language provides many predefined functions to perform tasks such as opening (and reading from) a file.

Exploring the Software Development Tools in Linux

Linux includes these traditional UNIX software-development tools:

✦ Text editors such as `vi` and `emacs` for editing the source code. (To find out more about `vi`, see Book II, Chapter 5.)

✦ A C compiler for compiling and linking programs written in C — the programming language of choice for writing UNIX applications (though nowadays, many programmers are turning to C++ and Java). Linux includes the GNU C and C++ compilers. Originally, the GNU C Compiler was known as GCC — which now stands for *GNU Compiler Collection.* (See a description at `gcc.gnu.org`.)

✦ The GNU `make` utility for automating the software *build process* — the process of combining object modules into an executable or a library. (The operating system can load and run an executable, and a *library* is a collection of binary code that can be used by executables.)

✦ A debugger for debugging programs. Linux includes the GNU debugger `gdb`.

✦ A version-control system to keep track of various revisions of a source file. Linux comes with RCS (Revision Control System) and CVS (Concurrent Versions System). Nowadays, most open-source projects use CVS as their version-control system, but a recent version control system called Subversion is being developed as a replacement for CVS.

You can install these software development tools in any Linux distribution. Xandros should have the tools already installed. In Fedora Core, select the Development Tools package during installation. In Debian, type **apt-get install gcc** and then **apt-get install libc6-dev** in a terminal window. In SUSE, select Main Menu⇨System⇨YaST, click Software on the left-hand side of the window, and then click Install and Remove Software. Type **gcc** in the search field in YaST, select the relevant packages from the search results, and click Accept to install. If you find any missing packages, you can install them in a similar manner.

In the next few sections, I briefly describe how to use these software-development tools to write applications for Linux.

GNU C and C++ compilers

The most important software-development tool in Linux is GCC — the GNU C and C++ compiler. In fact, GCC can compile three languages: C, C++, and Objective-C (a language that adds object-oriented programming capabilities to C). You use the same `gcc` command to compile and link both C and C++ source files. The GCC compiler supports ANSI standard C, making it easy to port any ANSI C program to Linux. In addition, if you've ever used a C compiler on other UNIX systems, you should feel right at home with GCC.

Using GCC

Use the `gcc` command to invoke GCC. By default, when you use the `gcc` command on a source file, GCC preprocesses, compiles, and links to create an executable file. However, you can use GCC options to stop this process at an intermediate stage. For example, you might invoke `gcc` by using the `-c` option to compile a source file and to generate an object file, but not to perform the link step.

Using GCC to compile and link a few C source files is very simple. Suppose you want to compile and link a simple program made up of two source files. I use the following program source for this task; it's stored in the file `area.c`, and it's the main program that computes the area of a circle whose radius is specified through the command line:

```
#include <stdio.h>
#include <stdlib.h>

/* Function prototype */
double area_of_circle(double r);

int main(int argc, char **argv)
{
  if(argc < 2)
  {
    printf("Usage: %s radius\n", argv[0]);
    exit(1);
  }
  else
  {
    double radius = atof(argv[1]);
    double area = area_of_circle(radius);
    printf("Area of circle with radius %f = %f\n",
        radius, area);
  }
  return 0;
}
```

You need another file that actually computes the area of a circle. Here's the listing for the file `circle.c`, where I define a function that computes the area of a circle:

```
#include <math.h>

#define SQUARE(x) ((x)*(x))

double area_of_circle(double r)
{
  return 4.0 * M_PI * SQUARE(r);
}
```

For such a simple program, of course, I could have placed everything in a single file, but I needed this contrived example to show you how to handle multiple files.

To compile these two files and to create an executable file named `area`, you use this command:

```
gcc -o area area.c circle.c
```

This invocation of GCC uses the `-o` option to specify the name of the executable file. (If you don't specify the name of an output file with the `-o` option, GCC saves the executable code in a file named `a.out`.)

If you have too many source files to compile and link, you can compile the files individually and generate *object files* (that have the `.o` extension). That way, when you change a source file, you need to compile only that file — you just link the compiled file to all the object files. The following commands show how to separate the compile and link steps for the sample program:

```
gcc -c area.c
gcc -c circle.c
gcc -o area area.o circle.o
```

The first two commands run `gcc` with the `-c` option compiling the source files. The third `gcc` command links the object files into an executable named `area`.

In case you are curious, here's how you run the `area` program (to compute the area of a circle with a radius of 1):

```
./area 1
```

The program generates the following output:

```
Area of circle with radius 1.000000 = 12.566371
```

Incidentally, you have to add the `./` prefix to the program's name (`area`) only if the current directory is not in the `PATH` environment variable. You do no harm in adding the prefix, even if your `PATH` contains the current directory.

Compiling C++ programs

GNU CC is a combined C and C++ compiler, so the `gcc` command also can compile C++ source files. GCC uses the file extension to determine whether a file is C or C++. C files have a lowercase `.c` extension, whereas C++ files end with `.C` or `.cpp`.

Although the `gcc` command can compile a C++ file, that command does not automatically link with various class libraries that C++ programs typically require. That's why compiling and linking a C++ program by using the `g++` command is easy, which, in turn, runs `gcc` with appropriate options.

Suppose that you want to compile the following simple C++ program stored in a file named `hello.C` (using an uppercase C extension for C++ source files is customary):

```
#include <iostream>

int main()
{
  using namespace std;
  cout << "Hello from Linux!" << endl;
}
```

To compile and link this program into an executable program named `hello`, use this command:

```
g++ -o hello hello.C
```

The command creates the `hello` executable, which you can run as follows:

```
./hello
```

The program displays the following output:

```
Hello from Linux!
```

A host of GCC options controls various aspects of compiling C and C++ programs.

Exploring GCC options

Here is the basic syntax of the `gcc` command:

```
gcc options filenames
```

Each option starts with a hyphen (-) and usually has a long name, such as `-funsigned-char` or `-finline-functions`. Many commonly used options are short, however, such as `-c`, to compile only, and `-g`, to generate debugging information (needed to debug the program by using the GNU debugger, `gdb`).

You can view a summary of all GCC options by typing the following command in a terminal window:

```
man gcc
```

Then you can browse through the commonly used GCC options. Usually, you do not have to provide GCC options explicitly because the default settings are fine for most applications. Table 1-1 lists some of the GCC options you may use.

Table 1-1 Commonly Used GCC Options

Option	*Meaning*
`-ansi`	Support ANSI standard C (ISO C89) syntax only. (This option disables some GNU C-specific features, such as the `asm` and `typeof` keywords.)
`-c`	Compile and generate object file only.
`-D`*`MACRO`*	Define the macro with the string `"1"` as its value.
`-D`*`MACRO=DEFN`*	Define the macro as `DEFN` where `DEFN` is some text string.
`-E`	Run only the C preprocessor.
`-fallow-single-precision`	Perform all math operations in single precision.
`-fpcc-struct-return`	Return all `struct` and `union` values in memory, rather than return in registers. (Returning values this way is less efficient, but at least it's compatible with other compilers.)
`-fPIC`	Generate position-independent code (PIC) suitable for use in a shared library.
`-freg-struct-return`	When possible, return `struct` and `union` values in registers.
`-g`	Generate debugging information. (The GNU debugger can use this information.)
`-I` *`DIRECTORY`*	Search the specified directory for files that you include by using the `#include` preprocessor directive.
`-L` *`DIRECTORY`*	Search the specified directory for libraries.
`-l` *`LIBRARY`*	Search the specified library when linking.
`-mcpu=`*`cputype`*	Optimize code for a specific processor (*`cputype`* can take many different values — some common ones are `i386`, `i486`, `i586`, and `i686`).

(continued)

Table 1-1 *(continued)*

Option	*Meaning*
`-o` *`FILE`*	Generate the specified output file (used to designate the name of an executable file).
`-O0` (two zeros)	Do not optimize.
`-O` or `-O1` (letter O)	Optimize the generated code.
`-O2` (letter O)	Optimize even more.
`-O3` (letter O)	Perform optimizations beyond those done for `-O2`.
`-Os` (letter O)	Optimize for size (to reduce the total amount of code).
`-pedantic`	Generate errors if any non-ANSI standard extensions are used.
`-pg`	Add extra code to the program so that, when run, it generates information the `gprof` program can use to display timing details for various parts of the program.
`-shared`	Generate a shared object file (typically used to create a shared library).
`-U`*`MACRO`*	Undefine the specified macro.
`-v`	Display the version number of GCC.
`-w`	Don't generate any warning messages.
`-Wl,`*`OPTION`*	Pass the *`OPTION`* string (containing multiple comma-separated options) to the linker. To create a shared library named `libXXX.so.1`, for example, use the following flag: `-Wl,-soname,libXXX.so.1`.

The GNU make utility

When an application is made up of more than a few source files, compiling and linking the files by manually typing the `gcc` command can get very tiresome. Also, you do not want to compile every file whenever you change something in a single source file. These situations are where the GNU `make` utility comes to your rescue.

The `make` utility works by reading and interpreting a *makefile* — a text file that describes which files are required to build a particular program, as well as how to compile and link the files to build the program. Whenever you change one or more files, `make` determines which files to recompile — and it issues the appropriate commands for compiling those files and rebuilding the program.

Makefile names

By default, GNU `make` looks for a makefile that has one of the following names, in the order shown:

- GNUmakefile
- makefile
- Makefile

In UNIX systems, using Makefile as the name of the makefile is customary because it appears near the beginning of directory listings where the uppercase names appear before the lowercase names.

When you download software from the Internet, you usually find a Makefile, together with the source files. To build the software, you have only to type **make** at the shell prompt and make takes care of all the steps necessary to build the software.

If your makefile does not have a standard name (such as Makefile), you have to use the -f option with make to specify the makefile's name. If your makefile is called myprogram.mak, for example, you have to run make using the following command line:

```
make -f myprogram.mak
```

The makefile

For a program made up of several source and header files, the makefile specifies the following:

- The items that make creates — usually the object files and the executable. Using the term *target* to refer to any item that make has to create is common.
- The files or other actions required to create the target.
- Which commands to execute to create each target.

Suppose that you have a C++ source file named form.C that contains the following preprocessor directive:

```
#include "form.h"  // Include header file
```

The object file form.o clearly depends on the source file form.C and the header file form.h. In addition to these dependencies, you must specify how make converts the form.C file to the object file form.o. Suppose that you want make to invoke g++ (because the source file is in C++) with these options:

- -c (compile only)
- -g (generate debugging information)
- -O2 (optimize some)

In the makefile, you can express these options with the following rule:

```
# This a comment in the makefile
# The following lines indicate how form.o depends
# on form.C and form.h and how to create form.o.

form.o: form.C form.h
        g++ -c -g -O2 form.C
```

In this example, the first noncomment line shows `form.o` as the target and `form.C` and `form.h` as the dependent files.

The line following the dependency indicates how to build the target from its dependents. This line must start with a tab. Otherwise, the `make` command would exit with an error message and you'd be left scratching your head because when you look at the makefile in a text editor you can't tell the difference between tab and space. Now that you know the secret, the fix is to replace the spaces at the beginning of the offending line with a single tab.

The benefit of using `make` is that it prevents unnecessary compilations. After all, you can run `g++` (or `gcc`) from a shell script to compile and link all the files that make up your application, but the shell script compiles everything, even if the compilations are unnecessary. GNU `make`, on the other hand, builds a target only if one or more of its dependents have changed since the last time the target was built. `make` verifies this change by examining the time of the last modification of the target and the dependents.

`make` treats the target as the name of a goal to be achieved; the target does not have to be a file. You can have a rule such as this one:

```
clean:
        rm -f *.o
```

This rule specifies an abstract target named `clean` that does not depend on anything. This dependency statement says that to create the target `clean`, GNU `make` invokes the command `rm -f *.o`, which deletes all files that have the `.o` extension (namely the object files). Thus, the net effect of creating the target named `clean` is to delete the object files.

Variables (or macros)

In addition to the basic capability of building targets from dependents, GNU `make` includes many nice features that make expressing the dependencies and rules for building a target from its dependents easy for you. If you need to compile a large number of C++ files by using GCC with the same options, for example, typing the options for each file is tedious. You can avoid this repetitive task by defining a variable or macro in `make` as follows:

```
# Define macros for name of compiler
CXX= g++

# Define a macro for the GCC flags
CXXFLAGS= -O2 -g -mcpu=i686

# A rule for building an object file
form.o: form.C form.h
        $(CXX) -c $(CXXFLAGS) form.C
```

In this example, `CXX` and `CXXFLAGS` are `make` variables. (GNU `make` prefers to call them *variables,* but most UNIX `make` utilities call them *macros.*)

To use a variable anywhere in the makefile, start with a dollar sign (`$`) followed by the variable within parentheses. GNU `make` replaces all occurrences of a variable with its definition; thus it replaces all occurrences of `$(CXXFLAGS)` with the string `-O2 -g -mcpu=i686`.

GNU `make` has several predefined variables that have special meanings. Table 1-2 lists these variables. In addition to the variables listed in Table 1-2, GNU `make` considers all environment variables (such as `PATH` and `HOME`) to be predefined variables as well.

Table 1-2 Some Predefined Variables in GNU make

Variable	*Meaning*
`$%`	Member name for targets that are archives. If the target is `libDisp.a(image.o)`, for example, `$%` is `image.o`.
`$*`	Name of the target file without the extension.
`$+`	Names of all dependent files with duplicate dependencies, listed in their order of occurrence.
`$<`	The name of the first dependent file.
`$?`	Names of all dependent files (with spaces between the names) that are newer than the target.
`$@`	Complete name of the target. If the target is `libDisp.a(image.o)`, for example, `$@` is `libDisp`.
`$^`	Names of all dependent files, with spaces between the names. Duplicates are removed from the dependent filenames.
`AR`	Name of the archive-maintaining program (default value: `ar`).
`ARFLAGS`	Flags for the archive-maintaining program (default value: `rv`).
`AS`	Name of the assembler program that converts the assembly language to object code (default value: `as`).
`ASFLAGS`	Flags for the assembler.

(continued)

Table 1-2 *(continued)*

Variable	*Meaning*
CC	Name of the C compiler (default value: cc).
CFLAGS	Flags that are passed to the C compiler.
CO	Name of the program that extracts a file from RCS (default value: co).
COFLAGS	Flags for the RCS co program.
CPP	Name of the C preprocessor (default value: $(CC) -E).
CPPFLAGS	Flags for the C preprocessor.
CXX	Name of the C++ compiler (default value: g++).
CXXFLAGS	Flags that are passed to the C++ compiler.
FC	Name of the FORTRAN compiler (default value: f77).
FFLAGS	Flags for the FORTRAN compiler.
LDFLAGS	Flags for the compiler when it is supposed to invoke the linker ld.
RM	Name of the command to delete a file (Default value: rm -f).

A sample makefile

You can write a makefile easily if you use the predefined variables of GNU make and its built-in rules. Consider, for example, a makefile that creates the executable xdraw from three C source files (xdraw.c, xviewobj.c, and shapes.c) and two header files (xdraw.h and shapes.h). Assume that each source file includes one of the header files. Given these facts, here is what a sample makefile may look like:

```
#######################################################################
# Sample makefile
# Comments start with '#'
#
#######################################################################

# Use standard variables to define compile and link flags

CFLAGS= -g -O2
# Define the target "all"
all: xdraw

OBJS=xdraw.o xviewobj.o shapes.o

xdraw: $(OBJS)

# Object files
xdraw.o: Makefile xdraw.c xdraw.h
```

```
xviewobj.o: Makefile xviewobj.c xdraw.h

shapes.o: Makefile shapes.c shapes.h
```

This makefile relies on GNU `make`'s implicit rules. The conversion of `.c` files to `.o` files uses the built-in rule. Defining the variable `CFLAGS` passes the flags to the C compiler.

The target named `all` is defined as the first target for a reason — if you run GNU `make` without specifying any targets in the command line (see the `make` syntax described in the following section), the command builds the first target it finds in the makefile. By defining the first target `all` as `xdraw`, you can ensure that `make` builds this executable file, even if you do not explicitly specify it as a target. UNIX programmers traditionally use `all` as the name of the first target, but the target's name is immaterial; what matters is that it is the first target in the makefile.

How to run make

Typically, you run `make` by simply typing the following command at the shell prompt:

```
make
```

When run this way, GNU `make` looks for a file named `GNUmakefile`, `makefile`, or `Makefile` — in that order. If `make` finds one of these makefiles, it builds the first target specified in that `makefile`. However, if `make` does not find an appropriate makefile, it displays the following error message and then exits:

```
make: *** No targets specified and no makefile found.  Stop.
```

If your makefile happens to have a different name from the default names, you have to use the `-f` option to specify the makefile. The syntax of the `make` command with this option is

```
make -f filename
```

where *`filename`* is the name of the makefile.

Even when you have a makefile with a default name such as `Makefile`, you may want to build a specific target out of several targets defined in the makefile. In that case, you have to use the following syntax when you run `make`:

```
make target
```

For example, if the makefile contains the target named clean, you can build that target with this command:

```
make clean
```

Another special syntax overrides the value of a make variable. For example, GNU make uses the CFLAGS variable to hold the flags used when compiling C files. You can override the value of this variable when you invoke make. Here is an example of how you can define CFLAGS as the option -g -O2:

```
make CFLAGS="-g -O2"
```

In addition to these options, GNU make accepts several other command-line options. Table 1-3 lists the GNU make options.

Table 1-3 Options for GNU make

Option	*Meaning*
-b	Ignore but accept for compatibility with other versions of make.
-C DIR	Change to the specified directory before reading the makefile.
-d	Print debugging information.
-e	Allow environment variables to override definitions of similarly named variables in the makefile.
-f *FILE*	Read *FILE* as the makefile.
-h	Display the list of make options.
-i	Ignore all errors in commands executed when building a target.
-I *DIR*	Search specified directory for included makefiles. (The capability to include a file in a makefile is unique to GNU make.)
-j NUM	Specify the number of commands that make can run simultaneously.
-k	Continue to build unrelated targets, even if an error occurs when building one of the targets.
-l *LOAD*	Don't start a new job if load average is at least *LOAD* (a floating-point number).
-m	Ignore but accept for compatibility with other versions of make.
-n	Print the commands to execute, but do not execute them.
-o *FILE*	Do not rebuild the file named *FILE*, even if it is older than its dependents.
-p	Display the make database of variables and implicit rules.
-q	Do not run anything, but return 0 (zero) if all targets are up to date; return 1 if anything needs updating; and 2 if an error occurs.

Option	*Meaning*
`-r`	Get rid of all built-in rules.
`-R`	Get rid of all built-in variables and rules.
`-s`	Work silently (without displaying the commands as they execute).
`-t`	Change the timestamp of the files.
`-v`	Display the version number of `make` and a copyright notice.
`-w`	Display the name of the working directory before and after processing the makefile.
`-W FILE`	Assume that the specified file has been modified (used with `-n` to see what happens if you modify that file).

The GNU debugger

Although `make` automates the process of building a program, that part of programming is the least of your worries when a program does not work correctly or when a program suddenly quits with an error message. You need a debugger to find the cause of program errors. Linux includes `gdb` — the versatile GNU debugger with a command line interface.

Like any debugger, `gdb` lets you perform typical debugging tasks, such as the following:

- ✦ Set the breakpoint so that the program stops at a specified line.
- ✦ Watch the values of variables in the program.
- ✦ Step through the program one line at a time.
- ✦ Change variables in an attempt to fix errors.

The `gdb` debugger can debug C and C++ programs.

Preparing to debug a program

If you want to debug a program by using `gdb`, you have to ensure that the compiler generates and places debugging information in the executable. The debugging information contains the names of variables in your program and the mapping of addresses in the executable file to lines of code in the source file. `gdb` needs this information to perform its functions, such as stopping after executing a specified line of source code.

TIP

To ensure that the executable is properly prepared for debugging, use the `-g` option with GCC. You can do this task by defining the variable `CFLAGS` in the makefile as

```
CFLAGS= -g
```

Running gdb

The most common way to debug a program is to run gdb by using the following command:

```
gdb progname
```

progname is the name of the program's executable file. After it runs, gdb displays the following message and prompts you for a command:

```
GNU gdb 6.1-debian
Copyright 2004 Free Software Foundation, Inc.
GDB is free software, covered by the GNU General Public License, and you are
welcome to change it and/or distribute copies of it under certain conditions.
Type "show copying" to see the conditions.
There is absolutely no warranty for GDB.  Type "show warranty" for details.
This GDB was configured as "i386-linux".
(gdb)
```

You can type gdb commands at the (gdb) prompt. One useful command is help — it displays a list of commands as the next listing shows:

```
 (gdb) help
List of classes of commands:

aliases -- Aliases of other commands
breakpoints -- Making program stop at certain points
data -- Examining data
files -- Specifying and examining files
internals -- Maintenance commands
obscure -- Obscure features
running -- Running the program
stack -- Examining the stack
status -- Status inquiries
support -- Support facilities
tracepoints -- Tracing of program execution without stopping the program
user-defined -- User-defined commands

Type "help" followed by a class name for a list of commands in that class.
Type "help" followed by command name for full documentation.
Command name abbreviations are allowed if unambiguous.
(gdb)
```

To quit gdb, type **q** and then press Enter.

gdb has a large number of commands, but you need only a few to find the cause of an error quickly. Table 1-4 lists the commonly used gdb commands.

Table 1-4 Commonly Used gdb Commands

This Command	*Does the Following*
`break` *NUM*	Sets a *breakpoint* at the specified line number. (The debugger stops at breakpoints.)
`bt`	Displays a trace of all stack frames. (This command shows you the sequence of function calls so far.)
`clear` *FILENAME:NUM*	Deletes the breakpoint at a specific line in a source file. For example, `clear xdraw.c:8` clears the breakpoint at line 8 of file `xdraw.c`.
`continue`	Continues running the program being debugged. (Use this command after the program stops due to a signal or breakpoint.)
`display` *EXPR*	Displays the value of expression (consisting of variables defined in the program) each time the program stops.
`file` *FILE*	Loads a specified executable file for debugging.
`help` *NAME*	Displays help on the command named *NAME*.
`info break`	Displays a list of current breakpoints, including information on how many times each breakpoint is reached.
`info files`	Displays detailed information about the file being debugged.
`info func`	Displays all function names.
`info local`	Displays information about local variables of the current function.
`info prog`	Displays the execution status of the program being debugged.
`info var`	Displays all global and static variable names.
`kill`	Ends the program you're debugging.
`list`	Lists a section of the source code.
`make`	Runs the `make` utility to rebuild the executable without leaving `gdb`.
`next`	Advances one line of source code in the current function without stepping into other functions.
`print EXPR`	Shows the value of the expression *EXPR*.
`quit`	Quits `gdb`.
`run`	Starts running the currently loaded executable.
`set variable` *VAR=VALUE*	Sets the value of the variable *VAR* to *VALUE*.
`shell` *CMD*	Executes a UNIX command *CMD*, without leaving `gdb`.
`step`	Advances one line in the current function, stepping into other functions, if any.
`watch` *VAR*	Shows the value of the variable named *VAR* whenever the value changes.

(continued)

Table 1-4 *(continued)*

This Command	*Does the Following*
`where`	Displays the call sequence. Use this command to locate where your program died.
`x/F ADDR`	Examines the contents of the memory location at address *ADDR* in the format specified by the letter *F*, which can be `o` (octal); `x` (hex); `d` (decimal); `u` (unsigned decimal); `t` (binary); `f` (float); `a` (address); `i` (instruction); `c` (char); or `s` (string). You can append a letter indicating the size of data type to the format letter. Size letters are `b` (byte); `h` (halfword, 2 bytes), `w` (word, 4 bytes); and `g` (giant, 8 bytes). Typically, *ADDR* is the name of a variable or pointer.

Finding bugs by using gdb

To understand how you can find bugs by using `gdb`, you need to see an example. The procedure is easiest to show with a simple example, so I start with a rather contrived program that contains a typical bug.

The following is the contrived program, which I store in the file `dbgtst.c`:

```
#include <stdio.h>

static char buf[256];
void read_input(char *s);

int main(void)
{
  char *input = NULL; /* Just a pointer, no storage for
    string */

  read_input(input);

/* Process command. */
  printf("You typed: %s\n", input);

/* ... */
  return 0;
}

void read_input(char *s)
{
  printf("Command: ");
  gets(s);
}
```

This program's `main` function calls the `read_input` function to get a line of input from the user. The `read_input` function expects a character array in which it returns what the user types. In this example, however, main calls read_input with an uninitialized pointer — that's the bug in this simple program.

Build the program by using gcc with the -g option:

```
gcc -g -o dbgtst dbgtst.c
```

Ignore the warning message about the gets function being dangerous; I'm trying to use the shortcoming of that function to show how you can use gdb to track down errors.

To see the problem with this program, run it and type **test** at the Command: prompt:

```
./dbgtst
Command: test
Segmentation fault
```

The program dies after displaying the Segmentation fault message. For such a small program as this one, you can probably find the cause by examining the source code. In a real-world application, however, you may not immediately know what causes the error. That's when you have to use gdb to find the cause of the problem.

To use gdb to locate a bug, follow these steps:

1. **Load the program under gdb. To load a program named dbgtst in gdb, type the following:**

   ```
   gdb dbgtst
   ```

2. **Start executing the program under gdb by typing the run command. When the program prompts for input, type some input text.**

   The program fails as it did previously. Here's what happens with the dbgtst program:

   ```
   (gdb) run
   Starting program: /home/naba/swdev/dbgtst
   Command: test

   Program received signal SIGSEGV, Segmentation fault.
   0x4008888a in gets () from /lib/tls/libc.so.6
   (gdb)
   ```

3. **Use the where command to determine where the program died.**

   For the dbgtst program, this command yields this output:

   ```
   (gdb) where
   ```

```
#0  0x4008888a in gets () from /lib/tls/libc.so.6
#1  0x080483ed in read_input (s=0x0) at dbgtst.c:22
#2  0x080483b6 in main () at dbgtst.c:10
(gdb)
```

The output shows the sequence of function calls. Function call `#0` — the most recent one — is to a C library function, `gets`. The `gets` call originates in the `read_input` function (at line 22 of the file `dbgtst.c`), which in turn is called from the `main` function at line 10 of the `dbgtst.c` file.

4. **Use the `list` command to inspect the lines of suspect source code.**

   In `dbgtst`, you may start with line 22 of `dbgtst.c` file, as follows:

```
(gdb) list dbgtst.c:22
17      }
18
19      void read_input(char *s)
20      {
21        printf("Command: ");
22        gets(s);
23      }
24
(gdb)
```

   After looking at this listing, you can tell that the problem may be the way `read_input` is called. Then you list the lines around line 10 in `dbgtst.c` (where the `read_input` call originates):

```
(gdb) list dbgtst.c:10
5
6       int main(void)
7       {
8         char *input = NULL; /* Just a pointer, no
   storage for string */
9
10        read_input(input);
11
12      /* Process command. */
13        printf("You typed: %s\n", input);
14
(gdb)
```

   At this point, you can narrow the problem to the variable named `input`. That variable is an array, not a `NULL` (which means zero) pointer.

Fixing bugs in gdb

Sometimes you can fix a bug directly in `gdb`. For the example program in the preceding section, you can try this fix immediately after the program dies after displaying an error message. Because the example is contrived, I have an extra buffer named `buf` defined in the `dbgtst` program, as follows:

```
static char buf[256];
```

I can fix the problem of the uninitialized pointer by setting the variable `input` to `buf`. The following session with `gdb` corrects the problem of the uninitialized pointer (this example picks up immediately after the program runs and dies, due to the segmentation fault):

```
 (gdb) file dbgtst
A program is being debugged already.  Kill it? (y or n) y

Load new symbol table from "dbgtst"? (y or n) y
Reading symbols from dbgtst...done.
(gdb) list
1       #include <stdio.h>
2
3       static char buf[256];
4       void read_input(char *s);
5
6       int main(void)
7       {
8         char *input = NULL; /* Just a pointer, no storage
   for string */
9
10        read_input(input);
(gdb) break 9
Breakpoint 1 at 0x80483ab: file dbgtst.c, line 9.
(gdb) run
Starting program: /home/naba/swdev/dbgtst

Breakpoint 1, main () at dbgtst.c:10
10                read_input(input);
(gdb) set var input=buf
(gdb) cont
Continuing.
Command: test
You typed: test

Program exited normally.
(gdb)q
```

As the previous listing shows, if I stop the program just before `read_input` is called and set the variable named `input` to `buf` (which is a valid array of characters), the rest of the program runs fine.

After finding a fix that works in `gdb`, you can make the necessary changes to the source files and make the fix permanent.

Understanding the Implications of GNU Licenses

You have to pay a price for the bounty of Linux — to protect its developers and users, Linux is distributed under the GNU GPL (General Public License), which stipulates the distribution of the source code.

The GPL does not mean, however, that you cannot write commercial software for Linux that you want to distribute (either for free or for a price) in binary form only. You can follow all the rules and still sell your Linux applications in binary form.

When writing applications for Linux, be aware of two licenses:

- The GNU General Public License (GPL), which governs many Linux programs, including the Linux kernel and GCC
- The GNU Library General Public License (LGPL), which covers many Linux libraries

The following sections provide an overview of these licenses and some suggestions on how to meet their requirements. Because I am not a lawyer, however, don't take anything in this book as legal advice. The full text for these licenses is in text files on your Linux system; show these licenses to your legal counsel for a full interpretation and an assessment of applicability to your business.

The GNU General Public License

The text of the GNU General Public License (GPL) is in a file named `COPYING` in various directories in your Linux system. For example, type the following command to find a copy of that file in your Linux system:

```
find /usr -name "COPYING" -print
```

After you find the file, you can change to that directory and type **more COPYING** to read the GPL. If you cannot find the COPYING file, just turn to the back of this book to read the GPL.

The GPL has nothing to do with whether you charge for the software or distribute it for free; its thrust is to keep the software free for all users. GPL requires that the software is distributed in source-code form and by stipulating that any user can copy and distribute the software in source-code form to anyone else. In addition, everyone is reminded that the software comes with absolutely no warranty.

The software that the GPL covers is not in the public domain. Software covered by GPL is always copyrighted and the GPL spells out the restrictions on the software's copying and distribution. From a user's point of view, of course,

GPL's restrictions are not really restrictions; the restrictions are really benefits because the user is guaranteed access to the source code.

If your application uses parts of any software the GPL covers, your application is considered a *derived work,* which means that your application is also covered by the GPL, and you must distribute the source code to your application.

Although the GPL covers the Linux kernel, the GPL does not cover your applications that use the kernel services through system calls. Those applications are considered normal use of the kernel.

If you plan to distribute your application in binary form (as most commercial software is distributed), you must make sure that your application does not use any parts of any software the GPL covers. Your application may end up using parts of other software when it calls functions in a library. Most libraries, however, are covered by a different GNU license, which I describe in the next section.

You have to watch out for only a few library and utility programs the GPL covers. The GNU `dbm` (`gdbm`) database library is one of the prominent libraries GPL covers. The GNU `bison` parser-generator tool is another utility the GPL covers. If you allow `bison` to generate code, the GPL covers that code.

Other alternatives for the GNU `dbm` and GNU `bison` are not covered by GPL. For a database library, you can use the Berkeley database library `db` in place of `gdbm`. For a parser-generator, you may use `yacc` instead of `bison`.

The GNU Library General Public License

The text of the GNU Library General Public License (LGPL) is in a file named `COPYING.LIB`. If you have the kernel source installed, a copy of `COPYING.LIB` file is in one of the source directories. To locate a copy of the `COPYING.LIB` file on your Linux system, type the following command in a terminal window:

```
find /usr -name "COPYING*" -print
```

This command lists all occurrences of `COPYING` and `COPYING.LIB` in your system. The `COPYING` file contains the GPL, whereas `COPYING.LIB` has the LGPL.

The LGPL is intended to allow use of libraries in your applications, even if you do not distribute source code for your application. The LGPL stipulates, however, that users must have access to the source code of the library you use and that users can make use of modified versions of those libraries.

The LGPL covers most Linux libraries, including the C library (`libc.a`). Thus, when you build your application on Linux by using the GCC compiler, your application links with code from one or more libraries the LGPL covers. If you want to distribute your application in binary form only, you need to pay attention to LGPL.

One way to meet the intent of the LGPL is to provide the object code for your application and a makefile that relinks your object files with any updated Linux libraries the LGPL covers.

A better way to satisfy the LGPL is to use *dynamic linking,* in which your application and the library are separate entities, even though your application calls functions in the library when it runs. With dynamic linking, users immediately get the benefit of any updates to the libraries without ever having to relink the application.

Chapter 2: Programming in C

In This Chapter

- **Understanding the basics of C programming**
- **Discovering the features of the C programming language**
- **Taking stock of the standard C library**
- **Using shared libraries in Linux applications**

The composition of the C programming language — a sparse core with a large support library — makes it an ideal language for developing software. The core offers a good selection of data types and control structures while all additional tasks, including input and output (I/O), math computations, and access to peripheral devices, are relegated to a library of functions. Basically, C allows you to get to anything you want in a system. That means you can write anything from device drivers to graphical applications in C. In this chapter, I introduce you to C programming. I also briefly explain the importance of shared libraries and how to create one in Linux using the C programming language.

The Structure of a C Program

A typical C program is organized into one or more source files, or modules. (See Figure 2-1.) Each file has a similar structure with comments, preprocessor directives, declarations of variables and functions, and their definitions. You usually place each group of related variables and functions in a single source file.

Some files are simply a set of declarations that are used in other files through the `#include` directive of the C preprocessor. These files are usually referred to as *header files* and have names ending with the `.h` extension. In Figure 2-1, the file `shapes.h` is a header file that declares common data structures and functions for the program. Another file, `shapes.c`, defines the functions. A third file, `shapetest.c`, implements the `main` function — the execution of a C program begins in this function. These files with names ending in `.c` are the source files where you define the functions needed by your program. Although Figure 2-1 shows only one function in each source file, in typical programs many functions are in a source file.

shapes.h

```
/* File: shapes.h
 * Header file for data structures
 */
#ifndef _SHAPES_H
#define _SHAPES

enum shape_type{T_CIRCLE, T_RECTANGLE};
typedef struct RECTANGLE
{
  double x1, y1, x2, y2;
} RECTANGLE;
typedef struct CIRCLE
{
  double xc, yc, radius;
} CIRCLE
typedef struct SHAPE
{
  enum shape_type type;
  union
  {
    RECTANGLE r;
    CIRCLE c;
  } u;
} SHAPE;

/* Function prototypes */
double compute_area(SHAPE *p_s);
#endif
```

shapes.c

```
/* File: shapes.c
 * Function that computes area of shapes
 */
#include <math.h>
#include "shapes.h"
double compute_area(SHAPE *p_s);
{
  switch(p_s->type)
  {
    case T_CIRCLE:
    {
      CIRCLE *p_c = &(p_s->u.c);
      return M_PI* p_c->radius * p_c ->radius;
    }
  case T_RECTANGLE:
  {
        RECTANGLE *p_r = &(p_s-u.r);
        return fabs (p_r->x2 - p_r->x1) *
                     (p_r->y2 - p_r-y1));
    }
  }
}
```

shapetest.c

```
/* File: shapetest.c
 * Main program to test shapes.c
 */
#include <stdio.h>
#include "shapes.h"

int main(void)
{
  SHAPE s;
  CIRCLE *p_c = &(s.u.c];
  s.type = T_CIRCLE;
  p_c->radius = 50.0
  p_c->xc = p_c->yc = 100.0;
  printf("Area of circle = #f/n",
compute_area(&s));
  return 0;
}
```

Figure 2-1: Typically, several source files make up a C program.

To create an executable program, you must compile and link the source files. The exact steps for building programs from C source files depend on the compiler and the operating system. For example, in Linux, you can compile and link the files shown in Figure 2-1 with the following command:

```
gcc -o shapetest shapetest.c shapes.c
```

This command creates an executable file named `shapetest`. You can then run that file with the command

```
./shapetest
```

Here is the output the program displays:

```
Area of circle = 7853.981634
```

Declaration versus definition

A *declaration* determines how the program interprets a symbol. A *definition*, on the other hand, actually creates a variable or a function. Definitions cause the compiler to set aside storage for data or code, but declarations do not. For example,

```
Int x, y, z;
```

is a definition of three distinct integer variables, but

```
Extern int x, y, z;
```

is a declaration, indicating that the three integer variables are defined in another source file.

Within each source file, the components of the program are laid out in a standard manner. As the files illustrated in Figure 2-1 show, the typical components of a C source file follow a certain order if you scroll down through them on-screen:

1. The file starts with some comments that describe the purpose of the module and provide some other pertinent information, such as the name of the author and revision dates. In C, comments start with `/*` and end with `*/`.
2. Commands for the preprocessor, known as *preprocessor directives,* follow the comments. The first few directives typically are for including header files and defining constants.
3. Declarations of variables and functions that are visible throughout the file come next. In other words, the names of these variables and functions may be used in any of the functions in this file. Here, you also define variables needed within the file.
4. The rest of the file includes definitions of functions. Inside a function's body, you can define variables that are local to the function and that exist only while the function's code is being executed.

Preprocessor Directives

Preprocessing refers to the first step in translating or compiling a C file into machine instructions. The preprocessor processes the source file and acts on certain commands (called *preprocessor directives*) embedded in the program. These directives begin with the hash mark (#) followed by a keyword. Usually, the compiler automatically invokes the preprocessor before beginning compilation, but most compilers give you the option of invoking the preprocessor alone. You can utilize three major capabilities of the preprocessor to make your programs modular, more readable, and easier to customize:

- You can use the `#include` directive to insert the contents of a file into your program. With this directive, you can place common declarations in one location and use them in all source files through file inclusion. The result is a reduced risk of mismatches between declarations of variables and functions in separate program modules.
- Through the `#define` directive, you can define macros that enable you to replace one string with another. You can use the `#define` directive to give meaningful names to numeric constants, thus improving the readability of your source files.
- With directives such as `#if`, `#ifdef`, `#else`, and `#endif`, you can compile only selected portions of your program. You can use this feature to write source files with code for two or more systems, but compile only those parts that apply to the computer system on which you compile the program. With this strategy, you can maintain multiple versions of a program using a single set of source files.

Including files

You can write modular programs by exploiting the `#include` directive. This directive is possible because the C preprocessor enables you to keep commonly used declarations in a single file that you can insert in other source files as needed. ANSI C supports three forms of the `#include` directive. As a C programmer, you need to be familiar with the first two forms:

```
#include <stdio.h>
#include "shapes.h"
```

You use the first form of `#include` to read the contents of a file — in this case, the standard C header file `stdio.h` from the default location where all the header files reside. Put the filename within double quotes when the file (for example, `shapes.h`) is in the current directory. The exact conventions for locating the included files depend on the compiler.

Defining macros

A *macro* is essentially a short name for a reusable block of C code. The code can be as simple as a numerical constant or as complicated as many lines of detailed C code. The idea is that after you define a macro, you can use that macro wherever you want to use that code in your program. When the source file is preprocessed, every occurrence of a macro's name is replaced with its definition.

A common use of macros is to define a symbolic name for a numerical constant and then use the symbol instead of the numbers in your program. A macro improves the readability of the source code; with a descriptive name, you aren't left guessing why a particular number is being used in the program. You can define such macros in a straightforward manner using the #define directive. Here are some examples:

```
#define PI           3.14159
#define GRAV_ACC     9.80665
#define BUFSIZE      512
```

After these symbols are defined, you can use PI, GRAV_ACC, and BUFSIZE instead of the numerical constants throughout the source file.

Macros, however, can do much more than simply replace a symbol for a constant or some block of code. A macro can accept a parameter and replace each occurrence of that parameter with the provided value when the macro is used in a program. Thus, the code that results from the expansion of a macro can change, depending on the parameter you use when running the macro. For example, here is a macro that accepts a parameter and expands to an expression designed to calculate the square of the parameter:

```
#define square(x) ((x)*(x))
```

If you use square(z) in your program, it becomes ((z)*(z)) after the source file is preprocessed. In effect, this macro is equivalent to a function that computes the square of its arguments — except you don't call a function. Instead, the expression generated by the macro is placed directly in the source file.

Conditional directives

You can use the conditional directives, such as #if, #ifdef, #ifndef, #else, #elif, and #endif, to control which parts of a source file are compiled and under what conditions. With this feature, you maintain a single set of source files that can be selectively compiled with different compilers and in different environments. (Another common use is to insert printf statements for debugging that are compiled only if a symbol named DEBUG is defined.) Conditional directives start with #if, #ifdef, or #ifndef — and may be followed by any number of #elif directives (or by none at all). Next comes an optional #else, followed by an #endif directive that marks the end of that conditional block. Here are some common ways of using conditional directives.

To include a header file only once, you can use the following:

```
#ifndef _ _PROJECT_H
#define _ _PROJECT_H
/*  Declarations to be included once */
/* ... */

#endif
```

The following prints a diagnostic message during debugging (when the symbol DEBUG is defined):

```
#ifdef DEBUG
    printf("In read_file: bytes_read = %d\n", bytes_read);
#endif
```

The following example shows how you can include a different header file depending on the type of system for which the program is being compiled. To selectively include a header file, you can use the following:

```
#if CPU_TYPE == I386
    #include <i386\sysdef.h>
#elif CPU_TYPE == M68K
    #include <m68k\sysdef.h>
#else
    #error Unknown CPU type.
#endif
```

The `#error` directive is used to display error messages during preprocessing.

Other directives

Several other preprocessor directives perform miscellaneous tasks. For example, you can use the `#undef` directive to remove the current definition of a symbol. The `#pragma` directive is another special purpose directive that you can use to convey information to the C compiler. You can use `pragma` to access the special features of a compiler — and those vary from one compiler to another.

C compilers provide several predefined macros (see Table 2-1). Of these, the macros `_ _FILE_ _` and `_ _LINE_ _`, respectively, refer to the current source filename and the current line number being processed. You can use the `#line` directive to change these. For example, to set `_ _FILE_ _` to `"file_io.c"` and `_ _LINE_ _` to 100, you say:

```
#line 100 "file_io.c"
```

Table 2-1 Predefined Macros in C

Macro	*Definition*
`_ _DATE_ _`	This string contains the date when you invoke the C compiler. It is of the form `MMM DD YYYY` (for example, `Oct 26 2004`).
`_ _FILE_ _`	This macro expands to a string containing the name of the source file.
`_ _LINE_ _`	This macro is a decimal integer with a value equal to the line number within the current source file.

Macro	Definition
`__STDC__`	This macro expands to the decimal constant 1 to indicate that the C compiler conforms to the ANSI standard.
`__TIME__`	This string displays the time when you started compiling the source file. It is of the form `HH:MM:SS` (for example, `21:59:45`).

Declaration and Definition of Variables

In C, you must either define or declare all variables and functions before you use them. The definition of a variable specifies three things:

- Its *visibility,* which indicates exactly where the variable can be used. (Is it defined for all files in a program, the current file, or only in a function?)
- Its *lifetime,* which determines whether the variable exists temporarily (for example, a local variable in a function) or permanently (as long as the program is running)
- Its *type* (and, in some cases, its *initial value*). For example, an integer variable `x` initialized to `1` is defined this way:

```
int  x = 1;
```

If you're using a variable defined in another source file, you declare the variable with an `extern` keyword, like this:

```
extern int message_count;
```

You must define this variable without the `extern` qualifier in at least one source file. When the program is built, the linker resolves all references to the `message_count` variable and ensures that they all use the same variable.

Basic data types

C has four basic data types: `char` and `int` are for storing characters and integers, and `float` and `double` are for floating-point numbers. You can define variables for these basic data types in a straightforward manner:

```
char   c;
int    i, j, bufsize;
float  volts;
double mean, variance;
```

You can expand the basic data types into a much larger set by using the `long`, `short`, and `unsigned` qualifiers as prefixes. The `long` and `short` qualifiers are size modifiers. For example, a `long int` is at least 4 bytes long, whereas a `short int` has a minimum size of only 2 bytes. The size of an `int` is system dependent, but it definitely is at least as large as a `short`.

The `unsigned` qualifier is reserved for `int` and `char` types only. Normally, each of these types hold negative as well as positive values. This qualifier is the default signed form of these data types. You can use the `unsigned` qualifier when you want the variable to hold positive values only. Here are some examples of using the `short`, `long`, and `unsigned` qualifiers:

```
unsigned char mode_select, printer_status;
short      record_number;               /* Same as "short int"           */
long       offset;                      /* Same as "long int"            */
unsigned     i, j, msg_id;              /* Same as "unsigned int"        */
unsigned short width, height;           /* Same as "unsigned short int" */
unsigned long file_pos;                 /* Same as "unsigned long int"  */
long double  result;
```

When the `short`, `long`, and `unsigned` qualifiers are used with `int` types, you can drop the `int` from the declaration. You can also extend the `double` data type with a `long` prefix.

GCC comes with the predefined header files — `limits.h` and `float.h` — that define exact sizes of the various data types — and ranges of values — in those header files. You can examine these files in the `/usr/include` directory of your Linux system to determine the sizes of the basic data types that the GCC compiler supports.

Enumerations

You can use the `enum` data type to define your own enumerated list — a fixed set of named integer constants. For example, you can declare a Boolean data type named `BOOLEAN` by using `enum` as follows:

```
/* Declare an enumerated type named BOOLEAN */
    enum BOOLEAN {false = 0, true = 1, stop = 0, go = 1,
                  off = 0, on = 1};

/* Define a BOOLEAN called "status" and initialize it */
    enum BOOLEAN status = stop;
```

This example first declares `BOOLEAN` to be an enumerated type. The list within the braces shows the enumeration constants that are valid values of an `enum BOOLEAN` variable. You can initialize each constant to a value of your choice, and several constants can use the same value. In this example, the constants `false`, `stop`, and `off` are set to `0`, while `true`, `go`, and `on` are initialized to `1`. The example then defines an enumerated `BOOLEAN` variable named `status`, which is initially set to the constant `stop`.

Structures, Unions, and Bit Fields

Use `struct` to group related data items together, and refer to that group by a name. For example, the declaration of a structure to hold variables of a queue may look like this:

```
/* Declare a structure */
struct QUEUE
{
    int  count;     /* Number of items in queue      */
    int  front;     /* Index of first item in queue */
    int  rear;      /* Index of last item in queue  */
    int  elemsize;  /* Size of each element of data */
    int  maxsize;   /* Maximum capacity of queue     */
    char *data;     /* Pointer to queued data        */
};

/* Define two queues */
struct QUEUE rcv_q, xmit_q;
```

The elements inside the `QUEUE` structure are called its *members*. You can access these members by using the member selection operator (`.`). For instance, `rcv_q.count` refers to the `count` member of the `rcv_q` structure.

A `union` is like a `struct`, but instead of grouping related data items together (as `struct` does), a `union` allocates storage for several data items starting at the same location. Thus, all members of a `union` share the same storage location. You can use `union`s to view the same data item in different ways. Suppose that you are using a compiler that supports 4-byte `long` numbers, and you want to access the 4 individual bytes of a single `long` integer. Here is a `union` that enables you to accomplish just that:

```
union
{
    long  file_type;
    char  bytes[4];
} header_id;
```

With this definition, `header_id.file_type` refers to the `long` integer, while `header_id.bytes[0]` is the first byte of that `long` integer.

Arrays

An *array* is a collection of one or more identical data items. You can declare arrays of any type of data, including structures and types defined by `typedef`. For example, to define an array of 80 characters, you write the following:

```
char    string[80];
```

The characters in the string array occupy successive storage locations, beginning with location 0. Thus in this example, string[0] refers to the first character in this array, while string[79] refers to the last one. You can define arrays of other data types and structures similarly:

```
struct Customer          /* Declare a structure    */
{
  int id;
  char first_name[40];
  char last_name[40];
};

struct Customer customers[100]; /* Define array of structures */
int      index[64];             /* An array of 64 integers    */
```

You can also define multidimensional arrays. For example, to represent an 80-column-by-25-line text-display screen, you can use a two-dimensional array as follows:

```
unsigned char text_screen[25][80];
```

Each item of text_screen is an array of 80 unsigned chars, and text_screen contains 25 such arrays. In other words, the two-dimensional array is stored by laying out one row after another in memory. You can use expressions such as text_screen[0][0] to refer to the first character in the first row and text_screen[24][79] to refer to the last character of the last row of the display screen. Higher-dimensional arrays are defined similarly:

```
float coords[3][2][5];
```

This example defines coords as a three-dimensional array of three data items: Each item is an array of two arrays, each of which, in turn, is an array of five float variables. Thus, you interpret a multidimensional array as an "array of arrays."

Pointers

A *pointer* is a variable that can hold the address of any type of data except a bit field. For example, if p_i is a pointer to an integer variable, you can define and use it as follows:

```
/* Define an int pointer and an integer */
   int *p_i, count;

/* Set pointer to the address of the integer "count" */
    p_i = &count;
```

In this case, the compiler allocates storage for an int variable count and a pointer to an integer p_i. The number of bytes necessary to represent a pointer depends on the underlying system's addressing scheme.

TIP

Don't use a pointer until it contains the address of a valid object.

The example shows p_i being initialized to the address of the integer variable count using the & operator, which provides the address of a variable. After p_i is initialized, you can refer to the value of count with the expression *p_i, which is read as "the contents of the object with its address in p_i."

Pointers are useful in many situations; an important one is the dynamic allocation of memory. The standard C libraries include functions such as malloc and calloc, which you can call to allocate storage for arrays of objects. After allocating memory, these functions return the starting address of the block of memory. Because this address is the only way to reach that memory, you must store it in a variable capable of holding an address — a pointer.

Suppose that you allocated memory for an array of 50 integers and saved the returned address in p_i. Now you can treat this block of memory as an array of 50 integers with the name p_i. Thus, you can refer to the last element in the array as p_i[49], which is equivalent to *(p_i+49). Similarly, C treats the name of an array as a pointer to the first element of the array. The difference between the name of an array and a pointer variable is that the name of the array is a constant without any explicit storage necessary to hold the address of the array's first element. The pointer, on the other hand, is an actual storage location capable of holding the address of any data.

In addition to storing the address of dynamically allocated memory, pointers are also commonly used as arguments to functions. When a C function is called, all of its arguments are passed by value — that is, the function gets a copy of each argument, not the original variables appearing in the argument list of the function call. Thus, a C function cannot alter the value of its arguments. Pointers provide a way out. To change the value of a variable in a function, you can pass the function a pointer to the variable; the function can then alter the value through the pointer.

Type definitions

Through the typedef keyword, C provides you with a convenient way of assigning a new name to an existing data type. You can use the typedef facility to give meaningful names to data types used in a particular application. For example, a graphics application might declare a data type named Point as follows:

```
/* Declare a Point data type */
    typedef struct Point
    {
        short x;
        short y;
    } Point;
```

```
/* Declare PointPtr to be pointer to Point types */
    typedef Point *P_PointPtr;

/* Define some instances of these types
 * and initialize them */
    Point      a = {0, 0};
    PointPtr  p_a = &a;
```

As shown by the Point and PointPtr types, you can use typedef to declare complex data types conveniently.

Type qualifiers: const and volatile

Two type qualifiers, const and volatile, work this way in a declaration:

- The const qualifier in a declaration tells the compiler that the program must not modify the particular data object. The compiler must not generate code that might alter the contents of the location where that data item is stored.
- The volatile qualifier specifies that factors beyond the program's control may change the value of a variable.

You can use both const and volatile keywords on a single data item to mean that, although your program must not modify the item, some other process may alter it. The const and volatile keywords always qualify the item that immediately follows (to the right). The information provided by the const and the volatile qualifiers is supposed to help the compiler optimize the code it generates. For example, suppose that the variable block_size is declared and initialized as follows:

```
const int block_size = 512;
```

In this case, the compiler does not need to generate code to load the value of block_size from memory. Instead, it can use the value 512 wherever your program uses block_size. Now suppose that you add volatile to the declaration and change the declaration to

```
volatile const int block_size = 512;
```

This declaration says that some external process can change the contents of block_size. Therefore, the compiler cannot optimize away any reference to block_size. You may need to use such declarations when referring to an I/O port or video memory because these locations can be changed by factors beyond your program's control.

Expressions

An *expression* is a combination of variables, function calls, and operators that results in a single value. For example, here is an expression with a value that is the number of bytes needed to store the *null-terminated string* str (that is, an array of char data types with a zero byte at the end):

```
(strlen(str) * sizeof(char) + 1)
```

This expression involves a function call — strlen(str) – and the multiplication (*), addition (+), and sizeof operators.

C has a large number of operators that are an important part of expressions. Table 2-2 provides a summary of the operators in C.

Table 2-2 Summary of C Operators

Name of Operator	*Syntax*	*Result*
Arithmetic Operators		
Addition	x+y	Adds x and y.
Subtraction	x-y	Subtracts y from x.
Multiplication	x*y	Multiplies x and y.
Division	x/y	Divides x by y.
Remainder	x%y	Computes the remainder that results from dividing x by y.
Preincrement	++x	Increments x before use.
Postincrement	x++	Increments x after use.
Predecrement	--x	Decrements x before use.
Postdecrement	x--	Decrements x after use.
Minus	-x	Negates the value of x.
Plus	+x	Maintains the value of x unchanged.
Relational and Logical Operators		
Greater than	x>y	Value is 1 if x exceeds y; otherwise, value is 0.
Greater than or equal to	x>=y	Value is 1 if x exceeds or equals y; otherwise, value is 0.
Less than	x<y	Value is 1 if y exceeds x; otherwise, value is 0.
Less than or equal to	x<=y	Value is 1 if y exceeds or equals x; otherwise, value is 0.

(continued)

<table>
<tr><th colspan="3">Table 2-2 (continued)</th></tr>
<tr><th>Name of Operator</th><th>Syntax</th><th>Result</th></tr>
<tr><td>Equal to</td><td><code>x==y</code></td><td>Value is 1 if x equals y; otherwise, value is 0.</td></tr>
<tr><td>Not equal to</td><td><code>x!=y</code></td><td>Value is 1 if x and y are unequal; otherwise, value is 0.</td></tr>
<tr><td>Logical NOT</td><td><code>!x</code></td><td>Value is 1 if x is 0; otherwise, value is 0.</td></tr>
<tr><td>Logical AND</td><td><code>x&&y</code></td><td>Value is 0 if either x or y is 0.</td></tr>
<tr><td>Logical OR</td><td><code>x||y</code></td><td>Value is 0 if both x and y are 0.</td></tr>
<tr><td colspan="3">Assignment Operators</td></tr>
<tr><td>Assignment</td><td><code>x=y</code></td><td>Places the value of y into x.</td></tr>
<tr><td>Compound Assignment</td><td><code>x 0=y</code></td><td>Equivalent to x = x 0 y, where 0 is one of the following operators: +, -, *, /, %, <<, >, &, ^, or |.</td></tr>
<tr><td colspan="3">Data Access and Size Operators</td></tr>
<tr><td>Subscript</td><td><code>x[y]</code></td><td>Selects the y-th element of array x.</td></tr>
<tr><td>Member selection</td><td><code>x.y</code></td><td>Selects member y of structure (or union) x.</td></tr>
<tr><td>Member selection</td><td><code>x->y</code></td><td>Selects the member named y from a structure or union with x as its address.</td></tr>
<tr><td>Indirection</td><td><code>*x</code></td><td>Contents of the location with x as its address.</td></tr>
<tr><td>Address of</td><td><code>&x</code></td><td>Address of the data object named x.</td></tr>
<tr><td>Size of</td><td><code>sizeof(x)</code></td><td>Size (in bytes) of the data object named x.</td></tr>
<tr><td colspan="3">Bitwise Operators</td></tr>
<tr><td>Bitwise NOT</td><td><code>~x</code></td><td>Changes all 1s to 0s and 0s to 1s.</td></tr>
<tr><td>Bitwise AND</td><td><code>x&y</code></td><td>Result is the bitwise AND of x and y.</td></tr>
<tr><td>Bitwise OR</td><td><code>x|y</code></td><td>Result is the bitwise OR of x and y.</td></tr>
<tr><td>Bitwise exclusive OR</td><td><code>x^y</code></td><td>Result contains 1s where corresponding bits of x and y differ.</td></tr>
<tr><td>Left shift</td><td><code>x<<y</code></td><td>Shifts the bits of x to the left by y bit positions. Fills 0s in the vacated bit positions.</td></tr>
<tr><td>Right shift</td><td><code>x>>y</code></td><td>Shifts the bits of x to the right by y bit positions. Fills 0s in the vacated bit positions.</td></tr>
</table>

Name of Operator	Syntax	Result
Miscellaneous Operators		
Function call	`x(y)`	Result is the value returned (if any) by function x, which is called with argument y.
Type cast	`(type)x`	Converts the value of x to the type named in parentheses.
Conditional	`z?x:y`	If z is not 0, evaluates x; otherwise, evaluates y.
Comma	`x,y`	Evaluates x first and then y.

Operator Precedence

Typical C expressions consist of several operands and operators. When writing complicated expressions, you must be aware of the order in which the compiler evaluates the operators. For example, suppose a program uses an array of pointers to integers defined as follows:

```
typedef int *IntPtr;/* Use typedef to simplify declarations*/
IntPtr  iptr[10];   /* An array of 10 pointers to int      */
```

Now suppose that you encounter the expression `*iptr[4]`. Does it refer to the value of the `int` with the address in `iptr[4]`, or is this the fifth element from the location with the address in `iptr`? What you really need to know is whether the compiler evaluates the subscript operator (`[]`) before the indirection operator (*) — or does it work the other way around? To answer questions such as these, you need to know the *precedence* — the order in which the program applies the operators.

Table 2-3 summarizes C's precedence rules. The table shows the operators in order of decreasing precedence. The operators with highest precedence — those applied first — are shown first. The table also shows *associativity* — the order in which operators at the same level are evaluated.

Table 2-3 Precedence and Associativity of C Operators

Operator Group	Operator Name	Notation	Associativity
Postfix	Subscript	`x[y]`	Left to right
	Function call	`x(y)`	
	Member selection	`x.y`	
	Member selection	`x->y`	

(continued)

Table 2-3 (continued)

<table>
<tr><th>Operator Group</th><th>Operator Name</th><th>Notation</th><th>Associativity</th></tr>
<tr><td>Unary</td><td>Postincrement</td><td>x++</td><td>Right to left</td></tr>
<tr><td></td><td>Postdecrement</td><td>x--</td><td></td></tr>
<tr><td></td><td>Preincrement</td><td>++x</td><td></td></tr>
<tr><td></td><td>Predecrement</td><td>--x</td><td></td></tr>
<tr><td></td><td>Address of</td><td>&x</td><td></td></tr>
<tr><td></td><td>Indirection</td><td>*x</td><td></td></tr>
<tr><td></td><td>Plus</td><td>+x</td><td></td></tr>
<tr><td></td><td>Minus</td><td>-x</td><td></td></tr>
<tr><td></td><td>Bitwise NOT</td><td>~x</td><td></td></tr>
<tr><td></td><td>Logical NOT</td><td>!x</td><td></td></tr>
<tr><td></td><td>Sizeof</td><td>sizeof x</td><td></td></tr>
<tr><td></td><td>Type cast</td><td>(type)x</td><td></td></tr>
<tr><td>Multiplicative</td><td>Multiply</td><td>x*y</td><td>Left to right</td></tr>
<tr><td></td><td>Divide</td><td>x/y</td><td></td></tr>
<tr><td></td><td>Remainder</td><td>x%y</td><td></td></tr>
<tr><td>Additive</td><td>Add</td><td>x+y</td><td>Left to right</td></tr>
<tr><td></td><td>Subtract</td><td>x-y</td><td></td></tr>
<tr><td>Shift</td><td>Left shift</td><td>x<<y</td><td>Left to right</td></tr>
<tr><td></td><td>Right shift</td><td>x>>y</td><td></td></tr>
<tr><td>Relational</td><td>Greater than</td><td>x>y</td><td>Left to right</td></tr>
<tr><td></td><td>Greater than or equal to</td><td>x>=y</td><td></td></tr>
<tr><td></td><td>Less than</td><td>x<y</td><td></td></tr>
<tr><td></td><td>Less than or equal to</td><td>x<=y</td><td></td></tr>
<tr><td>Equality</td><td>Equal to</td><td>x==y</td><td>Left to right</td></tr>
<tr><td></td><td>Not equal to</td><td>x!=y</td><td></td></tr>
<tr><td>Bitwise</td><td>Bitwise AND</td><td>x&y</td><td>Left to right</td></tr>
<tr><td></td><td>Bitwise exclusive OR</td><td>x^y</td><td></td></tr>
<tr><td></td><td>Bitwise OR</td><td>x|y</td><td></td></tr>
<tr><td>Logical</td><td>Logical AND</td><td>x&&y</td><td>Left to right</td></tr>
<tr><td></td><td>Logical OR</td><td>x||y</td><td></td></tr>
<tr><td>Conditional</td><td>Conditional</td><td>z?x:y</td><td>Right to left</td></tr>
<tr><td>Assignment</td><td>Assignment</td><td>x=y</td><td>Right to left</td></tr>
<tr><td></td><td>Multiply assign</td><td>x *= y</td><td></td></tr>
</table>

Operator Group	Operator Name	Notation	Associativity
	Divide assign	`x /= y`	
	Remainder assign	`x %= y`	
	Add assign	`x += y`	
	Subtract assign	`x -= y`	
	Left shift assign	`x <<= y`	
	Right shift assign	`x >>= y`	
	Bitwise AND assign	`x &= y`	
	Bitwise XOR assign	`x ^= y`	
	Bitwise OR assign	`x |= y`	
Comma	Comma	`x,y`	Left to right

Getting back to the question of interpreting `*iptr[4]`, a quick look at Table 2-3 tells you that the `[]` operator has precedence over the `*` operator. Thus, when the compiler processes the expression `*iptr[4]`, it evaluates `iptr[4]` first, and then it applies the `indirection` operator, resulting in the value of the `int` with the address in `iptr[4]`.

Statements

You use statements to represent the actions C functions perform and to control the flow of execution in the C program. A *statement* consists of keywords, expressions, and other statements. Each statement ends with a semicolon (`;`).

A special type of statement — the *compound statement* — is a group of statements enclosed in a pair of braces (`{. . .}`). The body of a function is a compound statement. Such compound statements (also known as *blocks*) can contain local variables.

In the following sections — which are alphabetically arranged — I briefly describe the types of statements available in C.

The break statement

You use the `break` statement to jump to the statement following the innermost `do`, `for`, `switch`, or `while` statement. It is also used to exit from a `switch` statement. Here is an example that uses `break` to exit a `for` loop:

```
for(i = 0; i < ncommands; i++)
{
     if(strcmp(input, commands[i]) == 0) break;
}
```

The case statement

The `case` statement marks labels in a `switch` statement. Here is an example (here `interrupt_id` is an integer variable):

```
switch (interrupt_id)
{
     case XMIT_RDY:
          transmit();
          break;

     case RCV_RDY:
          receive();
          break;
}
```

A compound statement or block

A *compound statement* or block is a group of declarations followed by statements, all enclosed in a pair of braces ({ . . . }). Typical compound statements are the body of a function and the block of code following an `if` statement. In the following example, everything that appears within the braces — the declarations and the statements — constitutes a compound statement:

```
if(theEvent.xexpose.count == 0)
{
     int i;
/* Clear the window and draw the figures
 * in the "figures" array
 */
     XClearWindow(theDisplay, dWin);
     if(numfigures > 0)
          for(i=0; i<numfigures; i++)
               draw_figure(theDisplay, dWin, theGC, i);
}
```

The continue statement

The `continue` statement begins the next iteration of the innermost `do`, `for`, or `while` statement in which it appears. You can use `continue` when you want to skip the execution of the loop. For example, to add the numbers from 1 to 10, excluding 5, you can use a `for` loop that skips the body when the loop index (`i`) is `5`:

```
for(i=0, sum=0; i <= 10, i++)
{
      if(i == 5) continue;    /* Exclude 5 */
      sum += i;
}
```

The default label

You use `default` as the label in a `switch` statement to mark code that executes when none of the case labels match the `switch` expression.

The do statement

The `do` statement, together with `while`, forms iterative loops with the following structure:

```
do
  statement
  while(expression);
```

statement (usually a compound statement) executes until the *expression* in the `while` statement evaluates to `0`. The expression is evaluated after each execution of the statement — thus a `do-while` block *always executes at least once*. For example, to add the numbers from 1 to 10, you can use the following `do` statement:

```
sum = 0;
do
{
    sum += i;
    i++;
}
while(i <= 10);
```

Expression statements

Expression statements are evaluated for their side effects. Some typical uses of expression statements include calling a function, incrementing a variable, and assigning a value to a variable. Here are some examples:

```
printf("Hello, World!\n");
i++;
num_bytes = length * sizeof(char);
```


The for statement

Use the `for` statement to execute a statement any number of times (basing that number on the value of an expression). The syntax is as follows:

```
for (expr_1; expr_2; expr_3) statement
```

The *expr_1* is evaluated once at the beginning of the loop, and the statement executes until the expression *expr_2* evaluates to 0. The third expression, *expr_3*, is evaluated after each execution of the statement. All three expressions are optional and the value of *expr_2* is assumed to be 1 if it is omitted. Here is an example that uses a `for` loop to add the numbers from 1 to 10:

```
for(i=0, sum=0; i <= 10; sum += i, i++);
```

In this example, the actual work of adding the numbers is done in the third expression, and the statement controlled by the `for` loop is a `null` statement (a lone ;).

The goto statement

The `goto` statement transfers control to a statement label. Here is an example that prompts the user for a value and repeats the request if the value is not acceptable:

```
ReEnter:
    printf("Enter offset: ");
    scanf(" %d", &offset);
    if(offset < 0 || offset > MAX_OFFSET)
    {
        printf("Bad offset: %d Please reenter:\n",
               offset);
        goto ReEnter;
    }
```

The if statement

You can use the `if` statement to test an expression and execute a statement only when the expression is not zero. An `if` statement takes the following form:

```
if ( expression )  statement
```

The statement following the `if` statement executes only if the expression in parentheses evaluates to a non-zero value. That statement is usually a compound statement. Here is an example:

```
if(mem_left < threshold)
{
    Message("Low on memory! Close some windows.\n");
}
```

The if-else statement

The `if-else` statement is a form of the `if` statement coupled with an `else` clause. The statement has the syntax

```
if ( expression )
     statement_1
else
     statement_2
```

statement_1 executes if the *expression* within the parentheses is not zero. Otherwise, *statement_2* executes. Here is an example that uses `if` and `else` to pick the smaller of two variables:

```
if ( a <= b)
     smaller = a;
else
     smaller = b;
```

The null statement

The `null` statement, represented by a solitary semicolon, does nothing. You use `null` statements in loops when all processing is done in the loop expressions rather than in the body of the loop. For example, to locate the zero byte marking the end of a string, you may use the following:

```
char str[80] = "Test";
int i;

for (i=0; str[i] != '\0'; i++)
                                  ;  /* Null statement */
```

The return statement

The `return` statement stops executing the current function and returns control to the calling function. The syntax is

```
return expression;
```

where the value of the *expression* is returned as the value of the function. For a function that does not return a value, use the `return` statement without the expression as follows:

```
return;
```

The switch statement

The `switch` statement performs a multiple branch, depending on the value of an expression. It has the following syntax:

```
switch (expression)
{
     case value1:
          statement_1
```

```
            break;
        case value2:
            statement_2
            break;
               .
               .
               .
        default:
            statement_default
    }
```

If the *expression* being tested by `switch` evaluates to *value1*, *statement_1* executes. If the expression is equal to *value2*, *statement_2* executes. The value is compared with each case label and the statement following the matching label executes. If the value does not match any of the case labels, the block *statement_default* following the default label executes. Each statement ends with a `break` statement that separates the code of one case label from another. Here is a `switch` statement that calls different routines, depending on the value of an integer variable named `command`:

```
switch (command)
{
        case 'q':
            quit_app(0);

            case 'c':
            connect();
            break;

        case 's':
            set_params();
            break;

        case '?':
        case 'H':
            print_help();
            break;

        default:
            printf("Unknown command!\n");
}
```

The while statement

The `while` statement is used in the form

```
while (expression) statement
```

The *statement* executes until the *expression* evaluates to `0`. A `while` statement evaluates the expression before each execution of the statement. Thus, a `while` loop executes the statement zero or more times. Here is a `while` statement for copying one array to another:

```
i = length;
while (i >= 0)  /* Copy one array to another */
{
     array2[i] = array1[i];
     i--;
}
```

Functions

A *function* is a collection of declarations and statements. As such, functions are the building blocks of C programs. Each C program has at least one function — the *main function,* where the execution of a C program begins. The C library contains mostly functions, although it contains quite a few macros as well.

Function prototypes

In C, you must declare a function before using it. The function declaration tells the compiler the type of value that the function returns and the number and type of arguments it takes. Declare a function as a complete *function prototype,* showing the return type as well as a list of arguments. The `calloc` function in the C library returns a void pointer and accepts two arguments, each of type `size_t`, which is an unsigned integer type of sufficient size to hold the value of the `sizeof` operator. Thus, the function prototype for `calloc` is the following:

```
void *calloc(size_t, size_t);
```

This prototype shows the type of each argument in the argument list. You can also include an identifier for each argument. In that case, you write the prototype as follows:

```
void *calloc(size_t num_elements, size_t elem_size);
```

Here the prototype looks exactly like the first line in the definition of the function, except you stop short of defining the function and end the line with a semicolon. With well-chosen names for arguments, this form of prototype can provide a lot of information about the function's use. For example, one look at the prototype of `calloc` tells you that its first argument is the number of elements to allocate, and the second argument is the size of each element.

Prototypes also help the compiler check function arguments and generate code that may use a faster mechanism for passing arguments. From the prototype, the compiler can determine the exact number and type of arguments to expect. Therefore, the prototype enables the compiler to catch any mistakes that you might make when calling a function, such as passing the wrong number of arguments (when the function takes a fixed number of arguments) or passing a wrong type of argument to a function.

The void type

What do you do when a function doesn't return anything nor accept any parameters? To handle these cases, C provides the `void` type, which is useful for declaring functions that return nothing and for describing pointers that can point to any type of data. For example, you can use the `void` return type to declare a function such as `exit` that does not return anything:

```
void exit(int status);
```

On the other hand, if a function doesn't accept any formal parameters, its list of arguments is represented by a `void`:

```
FILE *tmpfile(void);
```

The `void` pointer is useful for functions that work with blocks of memory. For example, when you request a certain number of bytes from the memory allocation routine `malloc`, you can use these locations to store any data that fits the space. In this case, the address of the first location of the allocated block of memory is returned as a `void` pointer. Thus, the prototype of `malloc` is written as follows:

```
void *malloc(size_t numbytes);
```

Functions with a variable number of arguments

If a function accepts a variable number of arguments, you can indicate this by using an ellipsis (`...`) in place of the argument list; however, you must provide at least one argument before the ellipsis. A good example of such functions is the `printf` family of functions defined in the header file `stdio.h`. The prototypes of these functions are as follows:

```
int fprintf(FILE *stream, const char *format, ...);
int printf(const char *format, ...);
int sprintf(char *buffer, const char *format, ...);
```

The C Library

The ANSI and ISO standards for C define all aspects of C — the language, the preprocessor, and the library. The prototypes of the functions in the library, as well as all necessary data structures and preprocessor constants, are defined in a set of standard header files. Table 2-4 lists the standard header files, including a summary of their contents.

If you're going to write applications in C, you have to become familiar with many of the standard libraries, because that's where much of C's programming prowess lies. If you are writing graphical applications, you also must be familiar with other libraries such as the GIMP toolkit.

Table 2-4 Standard Header Files in C

Header File	*Purpose*
`<assert.h>`	Defines the `assert` macro. Used for program diagnostics.
`<ctype.h>`	Declares functions for classifying and converting characters.
`<errno.h>`	Defines macros for error conditions, `EDOM` and `ERANGE`, and the integer variable `errno` where library functions return an error code.
`<float.h>`	Defines a range of values that can be stored in floating-point types.
`<iso646.h>`	Defines a number of macros that are helpful when writing C programs in non-English languages that may use character combinations such as `&` and ~ for other purposes.
`<limits.h>`	Defines the limiting values of all integer data types.
`<locale.h>`	Declares the `lconv` structure and the functions necessary for customizing a C program to a particular locale.
`<math.h>`	Declares common mathematical functions and the `HUGE_VAL` macro.
`<setjmp.h>`	Defines the `setjmp` and `longjmp` functions that can transfer control from one function to another without relying on normal function calls and returns. Also defines the `jmp_buf` data type used by `setjmp` and `longjmp`.
`<signal.h>`	Defines symbols and routines necessary for handling exceptional conditions.
`<stdarg.h>`	Defines macros that provide access to the unnamed arguments in a function that accepts a varying number of arguments.
`<stddef.h>`	Defines the standard data types `ptrdiff_t`, `size_t`, `wchar_t`; the symbol `NULL`; and the macro `offsetof`.
`<stdio.h>`	Declares the functions and data types necessary for input and output operations. Defines macros such as `BUFSIZ`, `EOF`, `SEEK_CUR`, `SEEK_END`, and `SEEK_SET`.
`<stdlib.h>`	Declares many utility functions, such as the string conversion routines, random number generator, memory allocation routines, and process control routines (such as `abort`, `exit`, and `system`).
`<string.h>`	Declares the string manipulation routines such as `strcmp` and `strcpy`.

(continued)

Table 2-4 (continued)

Header File	*Purpose*
`<time.h>`	Defines data types and declares functions that manipulate time. Defines the types `clock_t` and `time_t` and the `tm` data structure.
`<wchar.h>`	Defines data types and declares functions for working with wide character data types (`wchar_t`).
`<wctype.h>`	Defines data types and declares functions for classifying and converting wide character data types (`wchar_t`).

Shared Libraries in Linux Applications

Most Linux programs use shared libraries. At a minimum, most C programs use the C shared library `libc.so.`*`X`*, where *`X`* is a version number. Using shared libraries is desirable because many executable programs can share the same shared library — you need only one copy of the shared library loaded into memory. Also, *dynamic linking* (wherein a program loads code modules and links with them at runtime) is becoming increasingly popular because it enables an application to load blocks of code only when needed, thus reducing the memory requirement of the application.

When a program uses one or more shared libraries, you need the program's executable file, as well as all the shared libraries, to run the program. In other words, your program doesn't run if all shared libraries are not available on a system.

If you sell an application that uses shared libraries, make sure all necessary shared libraries are distributed with your software.

The subject of shared libraries is of interest to Linux programmers because use of shared libraries reduces the size of executables. In the following sections, I briefly describe how to create and use a shared library in a sample program.

Examining the shared libraries that a program uses

Use the `ldd` utility to determine which shared libraries an executable program needs. Type the following `ldd` command to see the shared libraries used by a program (that was stored by GCC in the default file named `a.out`):

```
ldd a.out
```

Here is what `ldd` reports for a typical C program:

```
        libc.so.6 => /lib/tls/libc.so.6 (0x40024000)
/lib/ld-linux.so.2 => /lib/ld-linux.so.2 (0x40000000)
```

A more complex program, such as the GIMP (an Adobe Photoshop-like program) uses many more shared libraries. To view its shared library needs, type the following command:

```
ldd /usr/bin/gimp
```

Here's the list displayed on a Debian system:

```
        libgtk-1.2.so.0 => /usr/lib/libgtk-1.2.so.0 (0x40024000)
libgdk-1.2.so.0 => /usr/lib/libgdk-1.2.so.0 (0x4016c000)
libgmodule-1.2.so.0 => /usr/lib/libgmodule-1.2.so.0 (0x401a5000)
libglib-1.2.so.0 => /usr/lib/libglib-1.2.so.0 (0x401a8000)
libdl.so.2 => /lib/tls/libdl.so.2 (0x401c9000)
libXi.so.6 => /usr/X11R6/lib/libXi.so.6 (0x401cc000)
libXext.so.6 => /usr/X11R6/lib/libXext.so.6 (0x401d4000)
libX11.so.6 => /usr/X11R6/lib/libX11.so.6 (0x401e2000)
libm.so.6 => /lib/tls/libm.so.6 (0x402aa000)
libc.so.6 => /lib/tls/libc.so.6 (0x402cd000)
/lib/ld-linux.so.2 => /lib/ld-linux.so.2 (0x40000000)
```

In this case, the program uses quite a few shared libraries, including the X11 library (`libX11.so.6`), the GIMP toolkit (`libgtk-1.2.so.0`), the General Drawing Kit (GDK) library (`libgdk-1.2.so.0`), the Math library (`libm.so.6`), and the C library (`libc.so.6`).

Almost any Linux application requires shared libraries to run.

Creating a shared library

Creating a shared library for your own application is fairly simple. Suppose that you want to implement an object in the form of a shared library. (Think of an object as a bunch of code and data.) A set of functions in the shared library represents the object's interfaces. To use the object, you load its shared library and invoke its interface functions. (I show you how to load a library in the following section.)

Here is the C source code for this simple object, implemented as a shared library (you might also call it a *dynamically linked library*) — save this code in a file named `dynobj.c`:


```
/*-------------------------------------------------------*/
/* File: dynobj.c
 *
 * Demonstrate use of dynamic linking.
 * Pretend this is an object that can be created by calling
 * init and destroyed by calling destroy.
 */
#include <stdio.h>
#include <stdlib.h>
#include <string.h>

/* Data structure for this object */
```

```
typedef struct OBJDATA
{
  char *name;
  int version;
} OBJDATA;

/*---------------------------------------------------------*/
/* i n i t
 *
 * Initialize object (allocate storage).
 *
 */
void* init(char *name)
{
  OBJDATA *data = (OBJDATA*)calloc(1, sizeof(OBJDATA));
  if(name)
    data->name = malloc(strlen(name)+1);
  strcpy(data->name, name);

  printf("Created: %s\n", name);

  return data;
}
/*---------------------------------------------------------*/
/* s h o w
 *
 * Show the object.
 *
 */
void show(void *data)
{
  OBJDATA *d = (OBJDATA*)data;
  printf("show: %s\n", d->name);
}
/*---------------------------------------------------------*/
/* d e s t r o y
 *
 * Destroy the object (free all storage).
 *
 */
void destroy(void *data)
{
  OBJDATA *d = (OBJDATA*)data;
  if(d)
  {
    if(d->name)
    {
      printf("Destroying: %s\n", d->name);
      free(d->name);
    }
    free(d);
  }
}
```

The object offers three interface functions:

- `init` to allocate any necessary storage and initialize the object
- `show` to display the object (here, it simply prints a message)
- `destroy` to free any storage

To build the shared library named `libdobj.so`, follow these steps:

1. **Compile all source files with the `-fPIC` flag. In this case, compile the `dynobj.c` file by using this command:**

   ```
   gcc -fPIC -c dynobj.c
   ```

2. **Link the objects into a shared library with the `-shared` flag, and provide appropriate flags for the linker. To create the shared library named `libdobj.so.1`, use the following:**

   ```
   gcc -shared -Wl,-soname,libdobj.so.1 -o libdobj.so.1.0
       dynobj.o
   ```

3. **Set up a sequence of symbolic links so that programs using the shared library can refer to it with a standard name.**

   For the sample library, the standard name is `libdobj.so`, and the following commands set up the symbolic links:

   ```
   ln -sf libdobj.so.1.0 libdobj.so.1
   ln -sf libdobj.so.1 libdobj.so
   ```

4. **When you test the shared library, define and export the `LD_LIBRARY_PATH` environment variable by using the following command:**

   ```
   export LD_LIBRARY_PATH=`pwd`:$LD_LIBRARY_PATH
   ```

After you test the shared library and you're satisfied that the library works, copy it to a standard location, such as `/usr/local/lib`, and run the `ldconfig` utility to update the link between `libdobj.so.1` and `libdobj.so.1.0`. These are the commands that you use to install your shared library for everyone's use (you have to be `root` to perform these steps):

```
cp libdobj.so.1.0 /usr/local/lib
/sbin/ldconfig
cd /usr/local/lib
ln -s libdobj.so.1 libdobj.so
```


Dynamically loading a shared library

Loading a shared library in your program and using the functions within the shared library is simple. In this section, I demonstrate the way you do this action. The header file `<dlfcn.h>` (that's a standard header file in Linux) declares the functions for loading and using a shared library. Four functions are declared in the file `dlfcn.h` for dynamic loading:

- `void *dlopen(const char *filename, int flag);`: Loads the shared library specified by the filename and returns a handle for the library. The flag can be `RTD_LAZY` (resolve undefined symbols as the library's code executes); or `RTD_NOW` (resolve all undefined symbols before `dlopen` returns and fail if all symbols are not defined). If `dlopen` fails, it returns `NULL`.
- `const char *dlerror (void);`: If `dlopen` fails, call `dlerror` to get a string that contains a description of the error.
- `void *dlsym (void *handle, char *symbol);`: Returns the address of the specified symbol (function name) from the shared library identified by the handle (that was returned by `dlopen`).
- `int dlclose (void *handle);`: Unloads the shared library if no one else is using it.

When you use any of these functions, include the header file `dlfcn.h` with this preprocessor directive:

```
#include <dlfcn.h>
```

Finally, here is a simple test program — `dltest.c` — that shows how to load and use the object defined in the shared library `libdobj.so`, which you create in the preceding section:

```
/*-------------------------------------------------------*/
/* File: dltest.c
 *
 * Test dynamic linking.
 *
 */
#include <dlfcn.h>  /* For the dynamic loading functions */
#include <stdio.h>

int main(void)
{
  void *dlobj;
  void * (*init_call)(char *name);
  void (*show_call)(void *data);
  void (*destroy_call)(void *data);

/* Open the shared library and set up the function pointers
   */
  if(dlobj = dlopen("libdobj.so.1",RTLD_LAZY))
  {
    void *data;

    init_call=dlsym(dlobj,"init");
    show_call=dlsym(dlobj,"show");
    destroy_call=dlsym(dlobj,"destroy");

/* Call the object interfaces */
```

```
        data = (*init_call)("Test Object");
        (*show_call)(data);
        (*destroy_call)(data);
    }
    return 0;
}
```

The program is straightforward: It loads the shared library, gets the pointers to the functions in the library, and calls the functions through the pointers.

You can compile and link this program in the usual way, but you must link with the `-ldl` option so that you can use the functions declared in `dlfcn.h`. Here is how you build the program `dltest`:

```
gcc -o dltest dltest.c -ldl
```

To see the program in action, run `dltest` by typing the following command:

```
./dltest
```

It displays the following lines of output:

```
Created: Test Object
show: Test Object
Destroying: Test Object
```

Although this sample program is not exciting, you now have a sample program that uses a shared library.

To see the benefit of using a shared library, return to the preceding section and make some changes in the shared library source file — `dynobj.c`. For example, you could print some other message in a function so that you can easily tell that you have made some change. Rebuild the shared library alone. Then run `dltest` again. The resulting output shows the effect of the changes you make in the shared library, which means you can update the shared library independently of the application.

A change in a shared library can affect many applications installed on your system. Therefore, be careful when making changes to *any* shared library. By the same token, shared libraries can be a security risk if someone manages to replace one with some malicious code.

Chapter 3: Writing Shell Scripts

In This Chapter

- **Trying out simple shell scripts**
- **Discovering the basics of shell scripting**
- **Exploring Bash's built-in commands**

Linux gives you many small and specialized commands, along with the plumbing necessary to connect these commands. By *plumbing,* I mean the way in which one command's output can be used as a second command's input. Bash (short for Bourne Again SHell) — the default shell in most Linux systems — provides this plumbing in the form of I/O redirection and pipes. Bash also includes features such as the `if` statement that you can use to run commands only when a specific condition is true and the `for` statement that repeats commands a specified number of times. You can use these features of Bash when writing programs called *shell scripts*.

In this chapter, I show you how to write simple *shell scripts* — task-oriented collections of shell commands stored in a file. Shell scripts are used to automate various tasks. For example, when your Linux system boots, many shell scripts stored in various subdirectories in the `/etc` directory (for example, `/etc/init.d`) perform many initialization tasks.

Trying Out Simple Shell Scripts

If you are not a programmer, you may feel apprehensive about programming. But shell *scripting* (or programming) can be as simple as storing a few commands in a file. In fact, you can have a useful shell program that has a single command.

While writing this book, for example, I captured screens from the X Window System and used the screen shots in figures. I used the X screen-capture program, `xwd`, to store the screen images in the X Window Dump (XWD) format. The book's production team, however, wanted the screen shots in TIFF format. Therefore, I used the Portable Bitmap (PBM) toolkit to convert the XWD images to TIFF format. To convert each file, I've run two programs and deleted a temporary file, as follows:

```
xwdtopnm < file.xwd > file.pnm
pnmtotiff < file.pnm > file.tif
rm file.pnm
```

These commands assume that the `xwdtopnm` and `pnmtotiff` programs are in the `/usr/bin` directory — one of the directories listed in the `PATH` environment variable. By the way, `xwdtopnm` and `pnmtotiff` are two programs in the PBM toolkit.

After converting a few XWD files to TIFF format, I get tired of typing the same sequence of commands for each file, so I prepare a file named `totif` and save the following lines in it (the first line with the magic incantation `#!/bin/sh` starts the Bash program that then executes the remaining lines in the file — you need that first line in every shell script):

```
#!/bin/sh
xwdtopnm < $1.xwd > $1.pnm
pnmtotiff < $1.pnm > $1.tif
rm $1.pnm
```

Then I make the `totif` file executable by using this command:

```
chmod +x totif
```

The `chmod` command enables you to change the permission settings of a file. One of those settings determines whether the file is executable. The `+x` option means that you want to mark the file as executable. You do have to mark it that way because Bash runs only executable files.

Now when I want to convert the file `figure1.xwd` to `figure1.tif`, I can do so by typing the following command:

```
./totif figure1
```

The `./` prefix indicates that the `totif` file is in the current directory — you don't need the `./` prefix if the `PATH` environment variable includes the current directory. The `totif` file is a shell script (also called a *shell program*). When you run this shell program with the command `totif figure1`, the shell substitutes `figure1` for each occurrence of `$1`. (Note that `$1` refers to the first option that the user types on the command used to execute the script.)

Shell scripts are popular among system administrators. If you are a system administrator, you can build a collection of custom shell scripts that help you automate tasks you perform often. If a hard drive seems to be getting full, for example, you may want to find all files that exceed some size (say, 1MB) and that have not been accessed in the past 30 days. In addition, you may want to send an e-mail message to all users who have large files, requesting that they archive and clean up those files. You can perform all these tasks with a shell script. You might start with the following `find` command to identify large files:

```
find / -type f -atime +30 -size +1000k -exec ls -l {} \; > /tmp/largefiles
```

This command creates a file named /tmp/largefiles, which contains detailed information about old files taking up too much space. After you get a list of the files, you can use a few other Linux commands — such as sort, cut, and sed — to prepare and send mail messages to users who have large files to clean up. Instead of typing all these commands manually, place them in a file and create a shell script. That, in a nutshell, is the essence of shell scripts — to gather shell commands in a file so that you can easily perform repetitive system administration tasks.

Just as most Linux commands accept command-line options, a Bash script also accepts command-line options. Inside the script, you can refer to the options as $1, $2, and so on. The special name $0 refers to the name of the script itself.

Here's a typical Bash script that accepts arguments:

```
#!/bin/sh
echo "This script's name is: $0"
echo Argument 1: $1
echo Argument 2: $2
```

The first line runs the /bin/sh program, which subsequently processes the rest of the lines in the script. The name /bin/sh traditionally refers to the Bourne shell — the first UNIX shell. In most Linux systems, /bin/sh is a symbolic link to /bin/bash, which is the executable program for Bash.

Save this simple script in a file named simple, and make that file executable with the following command:

```
chmod +x simple
```

Now run the script as follows:

```
./simple
```

It displays the following output:

```
This script's name is: ./simple
Argument 1:
Argument 2:
```

The first line shows the script's name. Because you have run the script without arguments, the script displays no values for the arguments.

Now try running the script with a few arguments, like this:

```
./simple "This is one argument" second-argument third
```

This time the script displays more output:

```
This script's name is: ./simple
Argument 1: This is one argument
Argument 2: second-argument
```

As the output shows, the shell treats the entire string within the double quotation marks as a single argument. Otherwise, the shell uses spaces as separators between arguments on the command line.

This sample script ignores the third argument because the script is designed to print only the first two arguments. The script ignores all arguments after the first two.

Exploring the Basics of Shell Scripting

Like any programming language, the Bash shell supports the following features:

- ✦ Variables that store values, including special built-in variables for accessing command-line arguments passed to a shell script and other special values.
- ✦ The capability to evaluate expressions.
- ✦ Control structures that enable you to loop over several shell commands or to execute some commands conditionally.
- ✦ The capability to define functions that can be called in many places within a script. Bash also includes many built-in commands that you can use in any script.

In the next few sections, I illustrate some of these programming features through simple examples. (I'm assuming that you're already running Bash, in which case, you can try the examples by typing them at the shell prompt in a terminal window. Otherwise, all you have to do is open a terminal window and Bash would run and display its prompt in that window.)

Storing stuff

You define variables in Bash just as you define environment variables. Thus, you may define a variable as follows:

```
count=12  # note no embedded spaces allowed
```

To use a variable's value, prefix the variable's name with a dollar sign ($). For example, `$PATH` is the value of the variable `PATH`. (This variable is the famous PATH environment variable that lists all the directories that Bash searches when trying to locate an executable file.) To display the value of the variable count, use the following command:

```
echo $count
```

Bash has some special variables for accessing command-line arguments. In a shell script, $0 refers to the name of the shell script. The variables $1, $2, and so on refer to the command-line arguments. The variable $* stores all the command-line arguments as a single variable, and $? contains the exit status of the last command the shell executes.

From a Bash script, you can prompt the user for input and use the read command to read the input into a variable. Here is an example:

```
echo -n "Enter value: "
read value
echo "You entered: $value"
```

When this script runs, the read value command causes Bash to read whatever you type at the keyboard and store your input in the variable called value.

Note: The -n option prevents the echo command from automatically adding a new line at the end of the string that it displays.

Calling shell functions

You can group a number of shell commands that you use consistently into a *function* and assign it a name. Later, you can execute that group of commands by using the single name assigned to the function. Here is a simple script that illustrates the syntax of shell functions:

```
#!/bin/sh

hello() {
        echo -n "Hello, "
        echo $1 $2
}

hello Jane Doe
```

When you run this script, it displays the following output:

```
Hello, Jane Doe
```

This script defines a shell function named `hello`. The function expects two arguments. In the body of the function, these arguments are referenced by `$1` and `$2`. The function definition begins with `hello()` — the name of the function, followed by parentheses. The body of the function is enclosed in curly braces — `{ . . . }`. In this case, the body uses the `echo` command to display a line of text.

The last line of the example shows how a shell function is called with arguments. In this case, the `hello` function is being called with two arguments: `Jane` and `Doe`. The `hello` function takes these two arguments and prints out a line that says `Hello, Jane Doe`.

Controlling the flow

In Bash scripts, you can control the flow of execution — the order in which the commands are executed — by using special commands such as `if`, `case`, `for`, and `while`. These control statements use the exit status of a command to decide what to do next. When any command executes, it returns an exit status — a numeric value that indicates whether or not the command has succeeded. By convention, an exit status of zero means the command has succeeded. (Yes, you read it right: Zero indicates success!) A nonzero exit status indicates that something has gone wrong with the command.

For example, suppose that you want to make a backup copy of a file before editing it with the `vi` editor. More importantly, you want to avoid editing the file if a backup can't be made. Here's a Bash script that takes care of this task:

```
#!/bin/sh
if cp "$1" "#$1"
then
    vi "$1"
else
    echo "Failed to create backup copy"
fi
```

This script illustrates the syntax of the `if-then-else` structure and shows how the exit status of the `cp` command is used by the `if` command to determine the next action. If `cp` returns zero, the script uses `vi` to edit the file; otherwise, the script displays an error message and exits. By the way, the script saves the backup in a file whose name is the same as that of the original, except for a hash mark (#) added at the beginning of the filename.

Don't forget the final `fi` that terminates the `if` command. Forgetting `fi` is a common source of errors in Bash scripts.

You can use the test command to evaluate any expression and to use the expression's value as the exit status of the command. Suppose that you want a script that edits a file only if it already exists. Using test, you can write such a script as follows:

```
#!/bin/sh
if test -f "$1"
then
    vi "$1"
else
    echo "No such file"
fi
```

A shorter form of the test command is to place the expression in square brackets ([. . .]). Using this shorthand notation, you can rewrite the preceding script like this:

```
#!/bin/sh
if [ -f "$1" ]
then
    vi "$1"
else
    echo "No such file"
fi
```

Note: You must have spaces around the two square brackets.

Another common control structure is the for loop. The following script adds the numbers 1 through 10:

```
#!/bin/sh
sum=0
for i in 1 2 3 4 5 6 7 8 9 10
do
    sum=`expr $sum + $i`
done
echo "Sum = $sum"
```


This example also illustrates the use of the expr command to evaluate an expression.

The case statement is used to execute a group of commands based on the value of a variable. For example, consider the following script:

```
#!/bin/sh
echo -n "What should I do -- (Y)es/(N)o/(C)ontinue? [Y] "
read answer
case $answer in
    y|Y|"")
      echo "YES"
```

```
    ;;
    c|C)
      echo "CONTINUE"
    ;;
    n|N)
      echo "NO"
    ;;
    *)
      echo "UNKNOWN"
    ;;
esac
```

Save this code in a file named `confirm` and type **chmod +x confirm** to make it executable. Then try it out like this:

```
./confirm
```

When the script prompts you, type one of the characters **y**, **n**, or **c** and then press Enter. The script displays `YES`, `NO`, or `CONTINUE`. For example, here's what happens when I type **c** (and then press Enter):

```
What should I do -- (Y)es/(N)o/(C)ontinue? [Y] c
CONTINUE
```

The script displays a prompt and reads the input you type. Your input is stored in a variable named `answer`. Then the `case` statement executes a block of code based on the value of the answer variable. For example, when I type **c**, the following block of commands execute:

```
    c|C)
      echo "CONTINUE"
    ;;
```

The `echo` command causes the script to display `CONTINUE`.

From this example, you can see that the general syntax of the `case` command is as follows:

```
case $variable in
     value1 | value2)
     command1
     command2
     ...other commands...
     ;;

     value3)
     command3
     command4
     ...other commands...
     ;;
esac
```

Essentially, the `case` command begins with the word `case` and ends with `esac`. Separate blocks of code are enclosed between the values of the variable, followed by a closing parenthesis and terminated by a pair of semicolons (;;).

Exploring Bash's built-in commands

Bash has more than 50 built-in commands, including common commands such as `cd` and `pwd`, as well as many others that are used infrequently. You can use these built-in commands in any Bash script or at the shell prompt. Table 3-1 describes most of the Bash built-in commands and their arguments. After looking through this information, type **help *cmd*** to read more about a specific built-in command. For example, to find out more about the built-in command `test`, type the following:

```
help test
```

Doing so displays the following information:

```
test: test [expr]
  Exits with a status of 0 (true) or 1 (false) depending on
  the evaluation of EXPR. Expressions may be unary or binary. Unary
  expressions are often used to examine the status of a file. There
  are string operators as well, and numeric comparison operators.

  File operators:

    -a FILE     True if file exists.
    -b FILE     True if file is block special.
    -c FILE     True if file is character special.
    -d FILE     True if file is a directory.
    -e FILE     True if file exists.
    -f FILE     True if file exists and is a regular file.
    -g FILE     True if file is set-group-id.
    -h FILE     True if file is a symbolic link.
    -L FILE     True if file is a symbolic link.
    -k FILE     True if file has its 'sticky' bit set.
    -p FILE     True if file is a named pipe.
    -r FILE     True if file is readable by you.
    -s FILE     True if file exists and is not empty.
    -S FILE     True if file is a socket.
    -t FD       True if FD is opened on a terminal.
    -u FILE     True if the file is set-user-id.
    -w FILE     True if the file is writable by you.
    -x FILE     True if the file is executable by you.
    -O FILE     True if the file is effectively owned by you.
    -G FILE     True if the file is effectively owned by your group.
(... Lines deleted ...)
```

Where necessary, the online help from the `help` command includes a considerable amount of detail.

Some external programs may have the same name as Bash built-in commands. If you want to run any such external program, you have to specify explicitly the full pathname of that program. Otherwise, Bash executes the built-in command of the same name.

Table 3-1 Summary of Built-in Commands in Bash Shell

This Function	*Does the Following*
`. `*filename* [*arguments*]	Reads and executes commands from the specified file using the optional arguments. (Works the same way as the `source` command.)
`: `[*arguments*]	Expands the arguments but does not process them.
[*expr*]	Evaluates the expression *expr* and returns zero status if *expr* is true.
`alias` [*name*[=*value*] ...]	Defines an alias.
`bg` [*job*]	Puts the specified job in the background. If no job is specified, it puts the currently executing command in the background.
`bind` [-m *keymap*] [-lvd] [-q *name*]	Binds a key sequence to a macro.
`break` [*n*]	Exits from a `for`, `while`, or `until` loop. If *n* is specified, the *n*-th enclosing loop is exited.
`builtin` *builtin_command* [*arguments*]	Executes a shell built-in command.
`cd` [*dir*]	Changes the current directory to *dir*.
`command` [-pVv] *cmd* [*arg* ...]	Runs the command *cmd* with the specified arguments (ignoring any shell function named *cmd*).
`continue` [*n*]	Starts the next iteration of the `for`, `while`, or `until` loop. If *n* is specified, the next iteration of the *n*-th enclosing loop is started.
`declare` [-frxi] [*name*[=*value*]]	Declares a variable with the specified name and, optionally, assigns it a value.
`dirs` [-l] [+/-*n*]	Displays the list of currently remembered directories.
`echo` [-neE] [*arg* ...]	Displays the arguments on standard output.
`enable` [-n] [-all] [*name* ...]	Enables or disables the specified built-in commands.
`eval` [*arg* ...]	Concatenates the arguments and executes them as a command.
`exec` [*command* [*arguments*]]	Replaces the current instance of the shell with a new process that runs the specified command.
`exit` [*n*]	Exits the shell with the status code *n*.

This Function	*Does the Following*
export [-nf] [*name*[=*word*]] ...	Defines a specified environment variable and exports it to future processes.
fc -s [*pat*=*rep*] [*cmd*]	Re-executes the command after replacing the pattern *pat* with *rep*.
fg [*jobspec*]	Puts the specified job in the foreground. If no job is specified, it puts the most recent job in the foreground.
getopts *optstring name* [*args*]	Gets optional parameters (which are called in shell scripts to extract arguments from the command line).
hash [-r] [*name*]	Remembers the full pathname of a specified command.
help [*cmd* ...]	Displays help information for specified built-in commands.
history [*n*]	Displays past commands or past *n* commands, if you specify a number *n*.
jobs [-lnp] [*jobspec* ...]	Lists currently active jobs.
kill [-s *sigspec* | -*sigspec*] [*pid* | *job spec*]...let *arg* [*arg* ...]	Evaluates each argument and returns 1 if the last *arg* is 0.
local [*name*[=*value*] ...]	Creates a local variable with the specified name and value (used in shell functions).
logout	Exits a login shell.
popd [+/-*n*]	Removes entries from the directory stack.
pushd [*dir*]	Adds a specified directory to the top of the directory stack.
pwd	Prints the full pathname of the current working directory.
read [-r] [*name* ...]	Reads a line from standard input and parses it.
readonly [-f] [*name* ...]	Marks the specified variables as read-only, so that the variables cannot be changed later.
return [*n*]	Exits the shell function with the return value *n*.
set [--abefhkmnptuvxl dCHP] [-o *option*] [*arg* ...]	Sets various flags.
shift [*n*]	Makes the *n+1* argument $1, the *n+2* argument $2, and so on.
source *filename* [*arguments*]	Reads and executes commands from a file.
suspend [-f]	Stops execution until a SIGCONT signal is received.
test expr	Evaluates the expression expr and returns zero if expr is true.

(continued)

Table 3-1 *(continued)*

This Function	*Does the Following*
`times`	Prints the accumulated user and system times for processes run from the shell.
`trap [-l] [`*`cmd`*`] [`*`sigspec`*`]`	Executes `cmd` when the signal `sigspec` is received.
`type [-all] [-type | -path]` *`name`* `[`*`name`* `...]`	Indicates how the shell interprets each name.
`ulimit [-SHacdfmstpnuv [limit]]`	Controls resources available to the shell.
`umask [-S] [`*`mode`*`]`	Sets the file creation mask — the default permission for files.
`unalias [-a] [`*`name`* `...]`	Undefines a specified alias.
`unset [-fv] [`*`name`* `...]`	Removes the definition of specified variables.
`wait [`*`n`*`]`	Waits for a specified process to terminate.

Chapter 4: Programming in Perl

In This Chapter

- Writing your first Perl program
- Getting an overview of Perl
- Understanding Perl packages and modules
- Using objects in Perl

When it comes to writing scripts, the Perl language is very popular among system administrators, especially on UNIX and Linux systems. System administrators use Perl to automate routine system administration tasks such as looking for old files that could be archived and deleted to free up disk space.

Perl is a scripting language, which means that you do not have to compile and link a Perl script (a text file containing Perl commands). Instead, an interpreter executes the Perl script. This capability makes writing and testing Perl scripts easy because you do not have to go through the typical edit-compile-link cycles to write Perl programs.

Besides ease of programming, another reason for Perl's popularity is that Perl is distributed freely and is available for a wide variety of operating systems, including Linux and many others such as UNIX, Windows 95/98/NT/2000/XP, and Apple Mac OS X.

In this chapter, I introduce you to Perl scripting.

Understanding Perl

Officially, Perl stands for *Practical Extraction Report Language*, but Larry Wall, the creator of Perl, says people often refer to Perl as *Pathologically Eclectic Rubbish Lister*. As these names suggest, Perl was originally designed to extract information from text files and to generate reports.

Perl began life in 1986 as a system administration tool created by Larry Wall. Over time, Perl grew by accretion of many new features and functions. The latest version — Perl 5.8 — supports object-oriented programming and allows anyone to extend Perl by adding new modules in a specified format.

True to its origin as a system administration tool, Perl has been popular with UNIX system administrators for many years. More recently, when the World Wide Web (or Web for short) became popular and the need for Common Gateway Interface (CGI) programs arose, Perl became the natural choice for those already familiar with the language. The recent surge in Perl's popularity is primarily due to the use of Perl in writing CGI programs for the Web. Of course, as people pay more attention to Perl, they discover that Perl is useful for much more than CGI programming. That, in turn, has made Perl even more popular among users.

Perl is available on a wide variety of computer systems because, like the Linux operating system, Perl can be distributed freely.

If you are familiar with shell programming or the C programming language, you can pick up Perl quickly. If you have never programmed, becoming proficient in Perl may take a while. I encourage you to start with a small subset of Perl's features and to ignore anything you don't immediately understand. Then, slowly add Perl features to your repertoire.

Determining Whether You Have Perl

Before you proceed with the Perl tutorial, check whether you have the `perl` program installed on your Linux system. Type the following command:

```
which perl
```

The `which` command tells you whether it finds a specified program in the directories listed in the `PATH` environment variable. If `perl` is installed, you see the following output:

```
/usr/bin/perl
```

You should find Perl already installed in all Linux distributions.

Another way to check for Perl is to type the following command to see its version number:

```
perl -v
```

Here is typical output from that command:

```
This is perl, v5.8.4 built for i386-linux-thread-multi

Copyright 1987-2004, Larry Wall

Perl may be copied only under the terms of either the Artistic License or the
GNU General Public License, which may be found in the Perl 5 source kit.
```

```
Complete documentation for Perl, including FAQ lists, should be found on
this system using 'man perl' or 'perldoc perl'.  If you have access to the
Internet, point your browser at http://www.perl.com/, the Perl Home Page.
```

This output tells you that you have Perl Version 5.8, patch Level 4, and that Larry Wall, the originator of Perl, holds the copyright. (Remember, however, that Perl is distributed freely under the GNU General Public License.)

REMEMBER

You can get the latest version of Perl by pointing your World Wide Web browser to the Comprehensive Perl Archive Network (CPAN). The following address connects you to the CPAN site nearest to you:

```
www.perl.com/CPAN
```

Writing Your First Perl Script

Perl has many features of C, and, as you may know, most books on C start with an example program that displays `Hello, World!` on your terminal. Because Perl is an interpreted language, as opposed to C and C++ which require compiling before the program can be run, you can accomplish this task directly from the command line. If you enter

```
perl -e 'print "Hello, World!\n";'
```

Perl responds with the following:

```
Hello, World!
```

This command uses the `-e` option of the `perl` program to pass the Perl program as a command-line argument to the Perl interpreter. In this case, the following line constitutes the Perl program:

```
print "Hello, World!\n";
```

To convert this line to a Perl script, simply place the line in a file and start the file with a directive to run the `perl` program (as you do in shell scripts, when you place a line such as `#!/bin/sh` to run the shell to process the script).

To try this Perl script, follow these steps:

1. **Use a text editor to type and save the following lines as a file named `hello.pl`:**

   ```
   #!/usr/bin/perl
   # This is a comment.
   print "Hello, World!\n";
   ```

2. **Make the** `hello.pl` **file executable by using the following command:**

   ```
   chmod +x hello.pl
   ```

3. **Run the Perl script by typing the following at the shell prompt:**

   ```
   ./hello.pl
   ```

   It displays the following output:

   ```
   Hello, World!
   ```

That's it! You have written and tried your first Perl script.

Notice that the first line of a Perl script starts with `#!`, followed by the full pathname of the `perl` program. If the first line of a script starts with `#!`, the shell simply strips off the `#!`, appends the script file's name to the end, and runs the script. Thus, if the script file is named `hello.pl` and the first line is `#!/usr/bin/perl`, the shell executes the following command:

```
/usr/bin/perl hello.pl
```

Getting an Overview of Perl

Most programming languages, including Perl, have some common features:

- **Variables** store different types of data. You can think of each variable as a placeholder for data — kind of like a mailbox, with a name and room to store data. The content of the variable is its value.
- **Expressions** combine variables by using operators. One expression may add several variables; another might extract a part of a string.
- **Statements** perform some action, such as assigning a value to a variable or printing a string.
- **Flow-control statements** enable statements to execute in various orders, depending on the value of some expression. Typically, flow-control statements include `for`, `do-while`, `while`, and `if-then-else` statements.
- **Functions** (also called *subroutines* or *routines*) enable you to group several statements and give them a name. Using this feature, you can execute the same set of statements by invoking the function that represents those statements. Typically, a programming language provides some predefined functions.
- **Packages** and **modules** that enable you to organize a set of related Perl subroutines that are designed to be reusable. (Modules were introduced in Perl 5.)

In the next few sections, I provide an overview of these major features of Perl and illustrate the features through simple examples.

Basic Perl syntax

Perl is free-form, like C. There are no constraints on the exact placement of any keyword. Often, Perl programs are stored in files with names that end in `.pl`, but there is no restriction on the filenames you use.

As in C, each Perl statement ends with a semicolon (`;`). A hash mark or pound sign (#) marks the start of a comment; the `perl` program disregards the rest of the line beginning with the hash mark.

Groups of Perl statements are enclosed in braces (`{. . .}`). This feature also is similar in C.

Variables

You don't have to declare Perl variables before using them, as you do in the C programming language. You can recognize a variable in a Perl script easily because each variable name begins with a special character: an at symbol (@), a dollar sign ($), or a percent sign (%). These special characters denote the variable's type. The three variable types are as follows:

- **Scalar variables** represent the basic data types: integer, floating-point number, and string. A dollar sign ($) precedes a scalar variable. Following are some examples:

```
$maxlines = 256;
$title = "Linux All-in-One Desk Reference For Dummies";
```

- **Array variables** are collections of scalar variables. An array variable has an at symbol (@) as a prefix. Thus, the following are arrays:

```
@pages = (62, 26, 22, 24);
@commands = ("start", "stop", "draw", "exit");
```

- **Associative arrays** are collections of key-value pairs, in which each key is a string and the value is any scalar variable. A percent-sign (%) prefix indicates an associative array. You can use associative arrays to associate a name with a value. You may store the amount of disk space each user occupies in an associative array, such as the following:

```
%disk_usage = ("root", 147178, "naba", 28547,
               "emily", 55, "ashley", 40);
```

Because each variable type has a special character prefix, you can use the same name for different variable types. Thus, `%disk_usage`, `@disk_usage`, and `$disk_usage` can appear within the same Perl program.

Scalars

A *scalar variable* can store a single value, such as a number or a text string. Scalar variables are the basic data type in Perl. Each scalar's name begins with a dollar sign ($). Typically, you start using a scalar with an assignment statement that initializes it. You can even use a variable without initializing it; the default value for numbers is zero, and the default value of a string is an empty string. If you want to see whether a scalar is defined, use the `defined` function as follows:

```
print "Name undefined!\n" if !(defined $name);
```

The expression (`defined $name`) is 1 if `$name` is defined. You can "undefine" a variable by using the `undef` function. You can undefine `$name`, for example, as follows:

```
undef $name;
```

Variables are evaluated according to context. Following is a script that initializes and prints a few variables:

```
#!/usr/bin/perl
$title = "Linux All-in-One Desk Reference For Dummies";
$count1 = 650;
$count2 = 166;

$total = $count1 + $count2;

print "Title: $title -- $total pages\n";
```

When you run the preceding Perl program, it produces the following output:

```
Title: Linux All-in-One Desk Reference For Dummies -- 816
   pages
```

As the Perl statements show, when the two numeric variables are added, their numeric values are used; but when the `$total` variable prints, its string representation displays.

Another interesting aspect of Perl is that it evaluates all variables in a string within double quotation marks ("..."). However, if you write a string inside single quotation marks ('...'), Perl leaves that string untouched. If you write

```
print 'Title: $title -- $total pages\n';
```

with single quotes instead of double quotes, Perl displays

```
Title: $title -- $total pages\n
```

and does not generate a new line.

A useful Perl variable is `$_` (the dollar sign followed by the underscore character). This special variable is known as the *default argument.* The Perl interpreter determines the value of `$_` depending on the context. When the Perl interpreter reads input from the standard input, `$_` holds the current input line; when the interpreter is searching for a specific pattern of text, `$_` holds the default search pattern.

Arrays

In Perl, an *array* is a collection of scalars. The array name begins with an at symbol (@). As in C, array subscripts start at zero. You can access the elements of an array with an index. Perl allocates space for arrays dynamically.

Consider the following simple script:

```
#!/usr/bin/perl
@commands = ("start", "stop", "draw" , "exit");

$numcmd = @commands;
print "There are $numcmd commands.\n";
print "The first command is: $commands[0]\n";
```

When you run the script, it produces the following output:

```
There are 4 commands.
The first command is: start
```

As you can see, equating a scalar to the array sets the scalar to the number of elements in the array. The first element of the `@commands` array is referenced as `$commands[0]` because the index starts at zero. Thus, the fourth element in the `@commands` array is `$commands[3]`.

Two special scalars are related to an array. The `$[` variable is one of them, and it's the current base index (the starting index), which is zero by default. The other scalar is `$#arrayname` (in which `arrayname` is the name of an array variable), which has the last array index as the value. Thus, for the `@commands` array, `$#commands` is 3.

You can print an entire array with a simple `print` statement like this:

```
print "@commands\n";
```

When Perl executes this statement, it displays the following output:

```
start stop draw exit
```

Associative arrays

Associative array variables, which are declared with a percent sign (%) prefix, are unique features of Perl. Using associative arrays, you can index an array with a string, such as a name. A good example of an associative array is the `%ENV` array that Perl automatically defines for you. In Perl, `%ENV` is the array of environment variables that you can access by using the environment variable name as an index. The following Perl statement prints the current `PATH` environment variable:

```
print "PATH = $ENV{PATH}\n";
```

When Perl executes this statement, it prints the current setting of `PATH`. In contrast to indexing regular arrays, you have to use braces to index an associative array.

Perl has many built-in functions — such as `delete`, `each`, `keys`, and `values` — that enable you to access and manipulate associative arrays.

Predefined variables in Perl

Perl has several predefined variables that contain useful information you may need in a Perl script. Following are a few important predefined variables:

- `@ARGV` is an array of strings that contains the command-line options to the script. The first option is `$ARGV[0]`, the second one is `$ARGV[1]`, and so on.
- `%ENV` is an associative array that contains the environment variables. You can access this array by using the environment variable name as a key. Thus `$ENV{HOME}` is the home directory, and `$ENV{PATH}` is the current search path that the shell uses to locate commands.
- `$_` is the default argument for many functions. If you see a Perl function used without any argument, the function probably is expecting its argument to be contained in the `$_` variable.
- `@_` is the list of arguments passed to a subroutine.
- `$0` is the name of the file containing the Perl program.
- `$^V` is the version number of Perl you are using. (For example, if you use Perl Version 5.8.3, `$^V` is `v5.8.3`.)
- `$<` is the user ID (an identifying number) of the user running the script.
- `$$` is the script's process ID.
- `$?` is the status the last system call has returned.

Operators and expressions

Operators are used to combine and compare Perl variables. Typical mathematical operators are addition (+), subtraction (-), multiplication (*), and division (/). Perl and C provide nearly the same set of operators. When you use operators to combine variables, you end up with expressions. Each expression has a value.

Here are some typical Perl expressions:

```
error < 0
$count == 10
$count + $i
$users[$i]
```

These expressions are examples of the comparison operator (the first two lines), the arithmetic operator, and the array-index operator.

In Perl, don't use the == operator to determine whether two strings match; the == operator works only with numbers. To test the equality of strings, Perl includes the FORTRAN-style `eq` operator. Use `eq` to see whether two strings are identical, as follows:

```
if ($input eq "stop") { exit; }
```

Other FORTRAN-style, string-comparison operators include `ne` (inequality), `lt` (less than), `gt` (greater than), `le` (less than or equal to), and `ge` (greater than or equal to). Also, you can use the `cmp` operator to compare two strings. The return value is –1, 0, or 1, depending on whether the first string is less than, equal to, or greater than the second string.

Perl also provides the following unique operators. C lacks an exponentiation operator, which FORTRAN includes; Perl uses ** as the exponentiation operator. Thus, you can write the following code in Perl:

```
$x = 2;
$y = 3;
$z = $x**$y;  # z should be 8 (2 raised to the power 3)
$y **= 2; # y is now 9 (3 raised to the power 2)
```

You can initialize an array to `null` by using `()` — the null-list operator — as follows:

```
@commands = ();
```

The dot operator (`.`) enables you to concatenate two strings, as follows:

```
$part1 = "Hello, ";
$part2 - "World!";
$message = $part1.$part2;  # Now $message = "Hello, World!"
```

The repetition operator, denoted by `x=`, is interesting and quite useful. You can use the `x=` operator to repeat a string a specified number of times. Suppose that you want to initialize a string to 65 asterisks (*). The following example shows how you can initialize the string with the `x=` operator:

```
$marker = "*";
$marker x= 65;  # Now $marker is a string of 65 asterisks
```

Another powerful operator in Perl is range, which is represented by two periods (`..`). You can initialize an array easily by using the range operator. Following are some examples:

```
@numerals = (0..9); # @numerals = 0, 1, 2, 3, 4, 5, 6, 7, 8 , 9
@alphabet = ('A'..'Z'); # @alphabet = capital letters A through Z
```

Regular expressions

If you have used any UNIX or Linux system for a while, you probably know about the `grep` command, which enables you to search files for a pattern of strings. Following is a typical use of `grep`:

```
cd /usr/src/linux*/drivers/cdrom
grep "[bB]laster"  *.c
```

The preceding `grep` command finds all occurrences of `blaster` and `Blaster` in the files with names ending in `.c`.

The `grep` command's `"[bB]laster"` argument is known as a *regular expression,* a pattern that matches a set of strings. You construct a regular expression with a small set of operators and rules that resemble the ones for writing arithmetic expressions. A list of characters inside brackets (`[...]`), for example, matches any single character in the list. Thus, the regular expression `"[bB]laster"` is a set of two strings, as follows:

```
blaster   Blaster
```

Perl supports regular expressions, just as the `grep` command does. Many other Linux programs, such as the `vi` editor and `sed` (the stream editor), also support regular expressions. The purpose of a regular expression is to search for a pattern of strings in a file. That's why editors support regular expressions.

You can construct and use complex regular expressions in Perl. The rules for these regular expressions are fairly simple. Essentially, the regular expression is a sequence of characters in which some characters have special meaning. Table 4-1 summarizes the basic rules for interpreting the characters used to construct a regular expression.

Table 4-1 Rules for Interpreting Regular Expression Characters

Expression	*Meaning*
.	Matches any single character except a newline.
x*	Matches zero or more occurrences of the character x.
x+	Matches one or more occurrences of the character x.
x?	Matches zero or one occurrence of the character x.
[...]	Matches any of the characters inside the brackets.
x{n}	Matches exactly n occurrences of the character x.
x{n,}	Matches n or more occurrences of the character x.
x{,m}	Matches zero or, at most, m occurrences of the character x.
x{n,m}	Matches at least n occurrences, but no more than m occurrences of the character x.
$	Matches the end of a line.
\0	Matches a null character.
\b	Matches a backspace.
\B	Matches any character not at the beginning or end of a word.
\b	Matches the beginning or end of a word — when not inside brackets.
\cX	Matches Ctrl-X (where X is any alphabetic character).
\d	Matches a single digit.
\D	Matches a nondigit character.
\f	Matches a form feed.
\n	Matches a newline (line-feed) character.
\ooo	Matches the octal value specified by the digits ooo (where each o is a digit between 0 and 7).
\r	Matches a carriage return.
\S	Matches a nonwhite space character.
\s	Matches a white space character (space, tab, or newline).
\t	Matches a tab.
\W	Matches a nonalphanumeric character.
\w	Matches an alphanumeric character.
\xhh	Matches the hexadecimal value specified by the digits hh (where each h is a digit between 0 and f).
^	Matches the beginning of a line.

If you want to match one of the characters $, |, *, ^, [,], \, and /, you have to place a backslash before the character you want to match. Thus you type these characters as \$, \|, *, \^, \[, \], \\, and \/. Regular expressions often look confusing because of the preponderance of strange character sequences and the generous sprinkling of backslashes. As with anything else, however, you can start slowly and use only a few of the features in the beginning.

So far, I have summarized the syntax of regular expressions. But I haven't yet shown how to use regular expressions in Perl. Typically, you place a regular expression within a pair of slashes and use the match (=~) or not-match (!~) operators to test a string. You can write a Perl script that performs the same search as the one done with grep earlier in this section. Follow these steps to complete this task:

1. **Use a text editor to type and save the following script in a file named lookup:**

```
#!/usr/bin/perl

while (<STDIN>)
{
    if ( $_ =~ /[bB]laster/ ) { print $_; }
}
```

2. **Make the lookup file executable by using the following command:**

```
chmod +x lookup
```

3. **Try the script by using the following command:**

```
cat /usr/src/linux*/drivers/cdrom/sbpcd.c | ./lookup
```

   In this case, the cat command feeds the contents of a specific file (which, as you know from the grep example, contains some lines with the regular expression) to the lookup script. The script simply applies Perl's regular expression-match operator (=~) and prints any matching line. The output is similar to what the grep command displays with the following command:

```
grep "[bB]laster"  /usr/src/linux*/drivers/cdrom/sbpcd.c
```

The $_ variable in the lookup script needs some explanation. The <STDIN> expression gets a line from the standard input and, by default, stores that line in the $_ variable. Inside the while loop, the regular expression is matched against the $_ string. The following single Perl statement completes the lookup script's work:

```
if ( $_ =~ /[bB]laster/ ) { print $_; }
```

This example illustrates how you might use a regular expression to search for occurrences of strings in a file.

After you use regular expressions for a while, you can better appreciate their power. The trick is to find the regular expression that performs the task you want. For example, here is a search that looks for all lines that begin with exactly seven spaces and end with a closing parenthesis:

```
while (<STDIN>)
{
      if ( $_ =~ /\)\n/ && $_ =~ /^ {7}\S/ )  { print $_; }
}
```

Flow-control statements

So far, you have seen Perl statements intended to execute in a serial fashion, one after another. Perl also includes statements that enable you to control the flow of execution of the statements. You already have seen the `if` statement and a `while` loop. Perl includes a complete set of flow-control statements just like those in C, but with a few extra features.

In Perl, all conditional statements take the following form:

```
conditional-statement
{ Perl code to execute if conditional is true }
```

Notice that you must enclose within braces (`{ . . . }`) the code that follows the conditional statement. The conditional statement checks the value of an expression to determine whether to execute the code within the braces. In Perl, as in C, any nonzero value is considered logically true, whereas a zero value is false.

Next, I briefly describe the syntax of the major conditional statements in Perl.

if and unless

The Perl `if` statement resembles the C `if` statement. For example, an `if` statement may check a count to see whether the count exceeds a threshold, as follows:

```
if ( $count > 25 ) { print "Too many errors!\n"; }
```

You can add an `else` clause to the `if` statement, like this:

```
if ($user eq "root")
{
     print "Starting simulation...\n";
}
else
{
     print "Sorry $user, you must be \"root\" to run this
    program.\n";
     exit;
}
```

If you know C, you can see that Perl's syntax looks quite a bit like that in C. Conditionals with the `if` statement can have zero or more `elsif` clauses to account for more alternatives, as in the following:

```
print "Enter version number:"; # prompt user for version number
$os_version = <STDIN>;      # read from standard input
chop $os_version; # get rid of the newline at the end of the line
# Check version number
if ($os_version >= 10 ) { print "No upgrade necessary\n";}
elsif ($os_version >= 6 && $os_version < 9)
                  { print "Standard upgrade\n";}
elsif ($os_version > 3 && $os_version < 6) { print "Reinstall\n";}
else { print "Sorry, cannot upgrade\n";}
```

The `unless` statement is unique to Perl. This statement has the same form as `if`, including the use of `elsif` and `else` clauses. The difference is that `unless` executes its statement block only if the condition is false. You can, for example, use `unless` in the following code:

```
unless ($user eq "root")
{
    print "You must be \"root\" to run this program.\n";
    exit;
}
```

In this case, unless the string `user` is `"root"`, the script exits.

while

Use Perl's `while` statement for *looping* — the repetition of some processing until an existing condition becomes logically false. To read a line at a time from standard input and to process that line, you may use the following `while` loop:

```
while ($in = <STDIN>)
{
# Code to process the line
    print $in;
}
```

If you read from the standard input without any argument, Perl assigns the current line of standard input to the $_ variable. Thus, you can write the preceding `while` loop as follows:

```
while (<STDIN>)
{
# Code to process the line
    print $_;
}
```

Perl's `while` statements are more versatile than those of C because you can use almost anything as the condition to be tested. If you use an array as the condition, for example, the `while` loop executes until the array has no elements left, as in the following example:

```
# Assume @cmd arg has the current set of command arguments
while (@cmd arg)
{
    $arg = shift @cmd arg;  # this extracts one argument
# Code to process the current argument
    print $arg;
}
```

The `shift` function removes the first element of an array and returns that element.

You can skip to the end of a loop with the `next` keyword; the `last` keyword exits the loop. For example, the following `while` loop adds the numbers from 1 to 10, skipping 5:

```
while (1)
{
  $i++;
  if($i == 5) { next;} # Jump to the next iteration if $i is 5
  if($i > 10) { last;} # When $i exceeds 10, end the loop
  $sum += $i;      # Add the numbers
}
# At this point $sum should be 50
```

for and foreach

Perl and C's `for` statements have similar syntax. Use the `for` statement to execute a statement any number of times, based on the value of an expression. The syntax is as follows:

```
for (expr_1; expr_2; expr_3) { statement block }
```

expr_1 is evaluated one time, at the beginning of the loop; the statement block executes until *expr_2* evaluates to zero. The third expression, *expr_3*, is evaluated after each execution of the statement block. You can omit any of the expressions, but you must include the semicolons. In addition, the braces around the statement block are required. Following is an example that uses a `for` loop to add the numbers from 1 to 10:

```
for($i=0, $sum=0; $i <= 10; $sum += $i, $i++) {}
```

In this example, the actual work of adding the numbers is done in the third expression, and the statement the `for` loop controls is an empty block (`{}`).

The `foreach` statement is most appropriate for arrays. Following is the syntax:

```
foreach Variable (Array) { statement block }
```

The `foreach` statement assigns to *`Variable`* an element from the *`Array`* and executes the statement block. The `foreach` statement repeats this procedure until no array elements remain. The following `foreach` statement adds the numbers from 1 to 10:

```
foreach $i (1..10) { $sum += $i;}
```

Notice that I declare the array by using the range operator (`..`). You also can use a list of comma-separated items as the array.

If you omit the *`Variable`* in a `foreach` statement, Perl implicitly uses the `$_` variable to hold the current array element. Thus you can use the following:

```
foreach (1..10) { $sum += $_;}
```

goto

The `goto` statement causes Perl to jump to a statement identified by a label. Here is an example that prompts the user for a value and repeats the request if the value is not acceptable:

```
ReEnter:
print "Enter offset: ";
$offset = <STDIN>;
chop $offset;
unless ($offset > 0 && $offset < 512)
{
    print "Bad offset: $offset\n";
    goto ReEnter;
}
```

Accessing Linux commands

You can execute any Linux command from Perl in several ways:

- ✦ Call the `system` function with a string that contains the Linux command that you want to execute.
- ✦ Enclose a Linux command within backquotes (`), which also are known as *grave accents*. You can run a Linux command this way and capture its output.
- ✦ Call the `fork` function to copy the current script and process new commands in the child process. (If a process starts another process, the new one is known as a *child* process.)
- ✦ Call the `exec` function to overlay the current script with a new script or Linux command.
- ✦ Use `fork` and `exec` to provide shell-like behavior. (Monitor user input and process each user-entered command through a child process.) In this section, I present a simple example of how to accomplish this task.

The simplest way to execute a Linux command in your script is to use the `system` function with the command in a string. After the `system` function returns, the exit code from the command is in the `$?` variable. You can easily write a simple Perl script that reads a string from the standard input and processes that string with the `system` function. Follow these steps:

1. **Use a text editor to enter and save the following script in a file named `rcmd.pl`:**

```
#!/usr/bin/perl
# Read user input and process command

$prompt = "Command (\"exit\" to quit): ";
print $prompt;

while (<STDIN>)
{
    chop;
    if ($_ eq "exit") { exit 0;}

# Execute command by calling system
    system $_;
    unless ($? == 0) {print "Error executing: $_\n";}
    print $prompt;
}
```

2. **Make the `rcmd.pl` file executable by using the following command:**

```
chmod +x rcmd.pl
```

3. **Run the script by typing `./rcmd.pl` at the shell prompt.**

   Here's a sample output from the `rcmd.pl` script (the output depends on what commands you enter):

```
Command ("exit" to quit): ps
  PID TTY          TIME CMD
 3128 pts/2    00:00:00 bash
 3314 pts/2    00:00:00 rcmd.pl
 3315 pts/2    00:00:00 ps
Command ("exit" to quit): exit
```


You can also run Linux commands by using `fork` and `exec` in your Perl script. Following is an example script — `psh.pl` — that uses `fork` and `exec` to execute commands the user enters:

```
#!/usr/bin/perl

# This is a simple script that uses "fork" and "exec" to
# run a command entered by the user

$prompt = "Command (\"exit\" to quit): ";
print $prompt;
```

```
while (<STDIN>)
{
    chop;    # remove trailing newline
    if($_ eq "exit") { exit 0;}

    $status = fork;
    if($status)
    {
# In parent... wait for child process to finish...
        wait;
        print $prompt;
        next;
    }
    else
    {
        exec $_;
    }
}
```

The following sample output shows how the `psh.pl` script executes the `ps` command:

```
Command ("exit" to quit): ps
  PID TTY          TIME CMD
 3128 pts/2    00:00:00 bash
 3321 pts/2    00:00:00 psh.pl
 3322 pts/2    00:00:00 ps
Command ("exit" to quit): exit
```

Shells (such as Bash) use the `fork` and `exec` combination to run commands.

File access

You may have noticed the `<STDIN>` expression used in various examples in this chapter. That's Perl's way of reading from a file. In Perl, a *file handle,* also known as an *identifier,* gives a file a distinct identity while it's being read. Usually, file handles are in uppercase characters. `STDIN` is a predefined file handle that denotes the standard input — by default, the keyboard. `STDOUT` and `STDERR` are the other two predefined file handles. `STDOUT` is used for printing to the terminal, and `STDERR` is used for printing error messages.

To read from a file, write the file handle inside angle brackets (`<>`). Thus, `<STDIN>` reads a line from the standard input.

You can open other files by using the `open` function. The following example shows you how to open the `/etc/passwd` file for reading and how to display the lines in that file:

```
open (PWDFILE, "/etc/passwd"); # PWDFILE is the file handle
while (<PWDFILE>) { print $_;} # By default, input line is in $_
close PWDFILE;          # Close the file
```

By default, the `open` function opens a file for reading. You can add special characters at the beginning of the filename to indicate other types of access. A > prefix opens the file for writing, whereas a >> prefix opens a file for appending. Following is a short script that reads the `/etc/passwd` file and creates a new file, named `output`, with a list of all users who lack shells (the password entries for these users have : at the end of each line):

```
#!/usr/bin/perl
# Read /etc/passwd and create list of users without any shell

open (PWDFILE, "/etc/passwd");
open (RESULT, ">output");     # open file for writing

while (<PWDFILE>)
{
    if ($_ =~ /:\n/) {print RESULT $_;}
}

close PWDFILE;
close RESULT;
```

After you execute this script, you find a file named `output` in the current directory. Here's what the `output` file contains when I run this script on a Fedora Core system:

```
news:x:9:13:news:/etc/news:
```

Filename with pipe prefix

One interesting filename prefix is the *pipe character* — the vertical bar (|). If you call `open` with a filename that begins with |, the rest of the filename is treated as a command. The Perl interpreter executes the command, and you can use `print` calls to send input to this command. The following Perl script sends a mail message to a list of users by using the `mail` command:

```
#!/usr/bin/perl
# Send mail to a list of users

foreach ("root", "naba")
{
  open (MAILPIPE, "| mail -s Greetings $_");
  print MAILPIPE "Remember to send in your weekly report today!\n";
  close MAILPIPE;
}
```


If a filename ends with a pipe character (|), that filename executes as a command; you can read that command's output with the angle brackets (<. . .>), as shown in the following example:

```
open (PSPIPE, "ps ax |");
while (<PSPIPE>)
{
```

```
# Process the output of the ps command
# This example simply echoes each line
    print $_;
}
```

Subroutines

Although Perl includes a large assortment of built-in functions, you can add your own code modules in the form of *subroutines*. In fact, Perl comes with a large set of these programs-within-programs. Here's a simple script that illustrates the syntax of subroutines in Perl:

```
#!/usr/bin/perl
sub hello
{
# Make local copies of the arguments from the @_ array
    local ($first,$last) = @_;

    print "Hello, $first $last\n";
}

$a = Jane;
$b = Doe;

&hello($a, $b);      # Call the subroutine
```

When you run the preceding script, it displays the following output:

```
Hello, Jane Doe
```

Note the following points about subroutines:

- The subroutine receives its arguments in the array @_ (the at symbol, followed by an underscore character).
- Variables used in subroutines are global by default. Use the `local` function to create a local set of variables.
- Call a subroutine by placing an ampersand (&) before its name. Thus, the subroutine `hello` is called by typing `&hello`.

If you want, you can put a subroutine in its own file. The `hello` subroutine, for example, can reside in a file named `hello.pl`. When you place a subroutine in a file, remember to add a return value at the end of the file — just type **1;** at the end to return `1`. Thus, the `hello.pl` file appears as follows:

```
sub hello
{
# Make local copies of the arguments from the @_ array
    local ($first,$last) = @_;
```

```
    print "Hello, $first $last\n";
}
1;      # return value
```

Then, you have to write the script that uses the `hello` subroutine, as follows:

```
#!/usr/bin/perl
require 'hello.pl';  # include the file with the subroutine

$a = Jane;
$b = Doe;

&hello($a, $b);      # Call the subroutine
```

This script uses the `require` function to include the `hello.pl` file that contains the definition of the `hello` subroutine.

Built-in functions in Perl

Perl has nearly 200 built-in functions (also referred to as *Perl functions*), including functions that resemble the ones in the C Run-Time Library, as well as functions that access the operating system. You really need to go through the list of functions to appreciate the breadth of capabilities available in Perl. I don't have enough space in this book to cover these functions, but you can find out about the Perl built-in functions by pointing your Web browser to the following address:

```
www.perldoc.com/perl5.8.0/pod/perlfunc.html
```

This address connects you to the Perl 5.8.0 documentation page so that you can get an overview of the Perl built-in functions. On that page, click a function's name to view more detailed information about that function.

Understanding Perl Packages and Modules

A *Perl package* is a way to group together data and subroutines. Essentially, it's a way to use variable and subroutine names without conflicting with any names used in other parts of a program. The concept of a package has existed in Perl since version 4.

The package provides a way to control the *namespace* — a term that refers to the collection of variable and subroutine names. Although you may not be aware of this, when you write a Perl program, it automatically belongs to a package named `main`. Besides `main`, other Perl packages are in the Perl library (in the `/usr/lib/perl5` directory of your Linux system), and you can define your own package, as well.

Perl *modules* are packages that follow specific guidelines.

Perl packages

You can think of a Perl package as a convenient way to organize a set of related Perl subroutines. Another benefit is that variable and subroutine names defined in a package do not conflict with names used elsewhere in the program. Thus, a variable named `$count` in one package remains unique to that package and does not conflict with a `$count` used elsewhere in a Perl program.

A Perl package is in a single file. The `package` statement is used at the beginning of the file to declare the file as a package and to give the package a name. For example, the file `timelocal.pl` defines a number of subroutines and variables in a package named `timelocal`. (Note that the `Time::Local module` supercedes the `timelocal.pl` file.) The `timelocal.pl` file has the following `package` statement in various places:

```
package timelocal;
```

The effect of this package declaration is that all subsequent variable names and subroutine names are considered to be in the `timelocal` package. You can put such a package statement at the beginning of the file that implements the package.

What if you are implementing a package and you need to refer to a subroutine or variable in another package? As you might guess, all you need to do is specify both the package name and the variable (or subroutine) name. Perl provides the following syntax for referring to a variable in another package:

```
$Package::Variable
```

Here *`Package`* is the name of the package, and *`Variable`* is the name of the variable in that package. If you omit the package name, Perl assumes that you're referring to a variable in the `main` package.

To use a package in your program, you can simply call the `require` function with the package filename as an argument. For example, a package named `ctime` is defined in the file `ctime.pl`. That package includes the `ctime` subroutine that converts a binary time into a string. The following simple program uses the `ctime` package from the `ctime.pl` file:

```
#!/usr/bin/perl -w

# Use the ctime package defined in ctime.pl file
require 'ctime.pl';

# Call the ctime subroutine
$time = ctime(time());

# Print the time string
print $time;
```

As you can see, this program uses the `require` function to bring the `ctime.pl` file into the program. When you run this program, it prints the current date and time formatted as shown in the following sample output:

```
Tue Aug 31 20:59:16 2004
```

Note that the first line of this script uses the `-w` option. That option causes the Perl interpreter to print warning messages about any bad constructs in the Perl script. Including the `-w` option on the line that invokes the Perl interpreter is a good idea.

If you want to check the syntax of a Perl program without actually running it, run the Perl interpreter with the `-c` option, like this (*filename* is the name of the Perl program whose syntax you want to check):

```
perl -c filename
```

Perl modules

Perl 5 took the concept of a package one step further and introduced the *module*, a package that follows certain guidelines and is designed to be reusable. Each module is a package that is defined in a file with the same name as the package but with a `.pm` extension. Each Perl object is implemented as a module. For example, the `CGI` object (for use in Web servers) is implemented as the `CGI` module, stored in the file named `CGI.pm`.

Nowadays, Perl comes with many modules. You find these modules in the `/usr/lib/perl5` directory as well as `/usr/share/perl/X.Y.Z` where `X.Y.Z` is the Perl version number. In these directories, look for files with names that end in `.pm` (which stands for *Perl module*).

Using a module

You can call the `require` function, or the `use` function, to include a Perl module in your program. For example, a Perl module named `Cwd` (defined, as expected, in the `Cwd.pm` file) provides a `getcwd` subroutine that returns the current directory. You can call the `require` function to include the `Cwd` module and call `getcwd` as follows:

```
require Cwd;  # You do not need the full filename
$curdir = Cwd::getcwd();
print "Current directory = $curdir\n";
```

The first line brings the `Cwd.pm` file into this program — you do not have to specify the full filename; the `require` function automatically appends `.pm` to the module's name to figure out which file to include. The second line shows how you call a subroutine from the `Cwd` module. When you use `require` to include a module, you must invoke each subroutine with the *`Module::subroutine`* format.

If you rewrite this example program with the `use` function in place of `require`, it takes the following form:

```
use Cwd;
$curdir = getcwd(); # no need for Cwd:: prefix
print "Current directory = $curdir\n";
```

The most significant difference is that you no longer need to qualify a subroutine name with the module name prefix (such as `Cwd::`).

You can call either `require` or `use` to include a module in your program. Just remember the following nuances when you use these functions:

- When you include a module by calling `require`, the module is included only when the `require` function is invoked as the program runs. You must use the *`Module::subroutine`* syntax to invoke any subroutines from a module that you include with the `require` function.
- When you include a module by calling `use`, the module is included in the program as soon as the `use` statement is processed. Thus, you can invoke subroutines and variables from the module as if they are part of your program. You do not need to qualify subroutine and variable names with a *`Module::`* prefix.

You may want to stick to the `use` *`Module;`* syntax to include modules in your program because this syntax lets you use a simpler syntax when you call subroutines from the module.

Using Objects in Perl

An *object* is a data structure together with the functions that operate on that data. Each object is an instance of a class that defines the object's type. For example, a rectangle class may have the four corners of the rectangle as data; functions such as one that computes the rectangle's area; and another that draws the rectangle. Then, each rectangle object can be an *instance* of the rectangle *class,* with different coordinates for each of the four corners. In this sense, an object is an instance of a class.

The functions (or subroutines) that implement the operations on an object's data are known as *methods*. That's terminology borrowed from Smalltalk, one of the earliest object-oriented programming languages.

Classes also suggest the notion of inheritance. You can define a new class of objects by extending the data or methods (or both) of an existing class. A common use of inheritance is to express the IS A relationship among various classes of objects. Consider, for example, the geometric shapes. Because a circle IS A shape and a rectangle IS A shape, you can say that the circle and rectangle classes inherit from the shape class. In this case, the shape class is called a parent class or base class.

The basic idea behind *object-oriented programming* is that you can package the data and the associated methods (subroutines) of an object so that they work like a *black box* — input generates output, without your having to specify every detail of how to get the job done. Programmers access the object only through advertised methods, without having to know the inner workings of the methods. Typically, a programmer can create an object, invoke its methods to get or set attributes (that's another name for the object's data), and destroy the object. In this section, I show you how to use objects in Perl. With this knowledge in hand, you can exploit objects as building blocks for your Perl programs.

Understanding Perl Objects

Perl implements objects by using modules, which package data and subroutines in a file. Perl presents the following simple model of objects:

- An *object* is denoted by a reference. (Objects are implemented as references to a hash.)
- A *class* is a Perl module that provides the methods to work with the object.
- A *method* is a Perl subroutine that expects the object reference as the first argument.

Object implementers have to follow certain rules and provide certain methods in a module that represents a class. However, you really don't need to know much about an object's implementation to use it in your Perl program. For practical purposes, all you need to know are the steps you have to follow when you use an object.

Creating and accessing Perl objects

An especially useful Perl object is the `Shell` object, which is implemented by the Perl module `Shell.pm`. That module comes with the Perl distribution and is in the `/usr/share/perl/5.8.4` directory (for Perl Version 5.8.4).

As the name implies, the `Shell` object is meant for running shell commands from within Perl scripts. You can create a `Shell` object and have it execute commands.

To use the Shell object, follow these general steps:

1. **Place the following line to include the Shell module in your program:**

   ```
   use Shell;
   ```

   You must include this line before you create a Shell object.

2. **To create a Shell object, use the following syntax:**

   ```
   my $sh = Shell->new;
   ```

   where $sh is the reference to the Shell object.

3. **Run Linux commands by using the Shell object and capture any outputs by saving to an appropriate variable. For example, to save the directory listing of the /usr/share/perl/5.8.4 directory in an array named @modules, write the following:**

   ```
   @modules = $sh->ls("/usr/lib/perl/5.8.4/*.pm");
   ```

   Then you can work with this array of Perl module filenames (that's what *.pm files are) any way you want. For example, to simply go through the array and print each string out, use the following while loop:

   ```
   while(@modules)
   {
     $mod = shift @modules;
     # Do whatever you want with the module name
     print $mod;
   }
   ```

How do you know which methods to call and in what order to call them? You have to read the object's documentation before you can use the object. The method names and the sequences of method invocation depend on what the object does.

Using the English module

Perl includes several special variables with strange names, such as $_ (for the default argument) and $! (for error messages corresponding to the last error). When you read a program, guessing what a special variable means can be difficult. The result is that you may end up avoiding a special variable that could be useful in your program.

As a helpful gesture, Perl 5 provides the English module (English.pm), which enables you to use understandable names for various special variables in Perl. To use the English module, include the following line in your Perl program:

```
use English;
```

After that, you can refer to `$_` as `$ARG` and `$!` as `$ERRNO` (these "English" names can still be a bit cryptic, but they're definitely better than the punctuation marks).

The following program uses the English module — and prints a few interesting variables:

```
#!/usr/bin/perl -w
# File: english.pl

use English;
print "Perl executable = $EXECUTABLE_NAME\n";
print "Script name = $PROGRAM_NAME\n";
```

Run this script with the following command:

```
./english.pl
```

When I run this script, here's what I get as output:

```
Perl executable = /usr/bin/perl
Script name = ./english.pl
```

The English module is handy because it lets you write Perl scripts in which you can refer to special variables by meaningful names. To find out more about the Perl special variables and their English names, type **man perlvar** in a terminal window — or, better yet, point your Web browser to

```
www.perldoc.com/perl5.8.0/pod/perlvar.html
```

Appendix: About the DVD

In This Appendix

- **System requirements**
- **DVD installation instructions**
- **What you'll find on the DVD**
- **Troubleshooting**

This book's companion DVD includes five prominent Linux distributions — Debian GNU/Linux, Fedora Core, Knoppix, SUSE, and Xandros Desktop OS — to get you started on your Linux journey. This appendix briefly describes the DVD and tells you how to get started with the installation.

System Requirements

Make sure that your computer meets the minimum system requirements shown in the following list. If your computer doesn't match up to most of these requirements, you may have problems using the software and files on the DVD:

- A PC with processor running at 400 MHz or faster for graphical installation
- At least 192MB of total RAM installed on your computer for graphical installation (256MB recommended)
- At least 520MB free space on your hard drive for a minimal installation; 5GB of free space recommended if you plan to install most packages so that you can try out everything covered in this book
- A DVD-ROM drive and a CD burner (see Book I, Chapter 2 for instructions on burning installation CDs)
- A graphics card and a monitor capable of displaying at least 256 colors
- A sound card
- Ethernet network interface card (NIC) or modem with a speed of at least 56 Kbps

On some PCs, after booting from the companion DVD, Knoppix and Fedora Core installation may not work. If you have such problems with the DVD, you can burn a Knoppix Live CD from the ISO image in the DVD's `distros` directory. For Fedora Core, please visit `www.dummies.com/go/linux3sourcecoupon` to obtain the CD set. Note that this problem does not affect the other distributions' ISO images that are in the DVD's `distros` directory.

DVD Installation Instructions

To install a Linux distribution from the companion DVD, follow these steps. (Consult Book I, Chapter 2 for details.)

1. **Gather information about your PC's hardware, such as graphics card, network card, and SCSI card, before you install Linux.**
2. **Use a partitioning program such as PartitionMagic or the FIPS program to create room on your hard drive for Linux.**

   Skip this step if you plan to use Linux as the sole operating system on your PC or if you plan to install it on an empty second hard drive.
3. **Burn CDs for your distribution. (Skip this step if you are installing Fedora Core.)**

   Consult Book I, Chapter 2 for instructions specific to each distribution.
4. **Boot your PC with the DVD (for Fedora Core and Knoppix) or the first CD (for Debian, SUSE, and Xandros).**

   Knoppix is a Live CD distribution, so this step should get you the Knoppix desktop. For other distributions, this step runs that distribution's installation program. From this point on, respond to the questions and choices as the installation program takes you through the steps. Here are some of the typical installation steps:

   - Prepare the hard drive partitions for Linux. If you have created space by reducing the size of an existing Windows partition, this step enables you to create the partitions for Linux.
   - Configure the Ethernet network, if any. Typically, you configure the network automatically by using DHCP.
   - Specify the local time zone and set the `root` password.
   - Install a boot loader program on your hard drive so that you can boot Linux when you power up your PC after shutting it down.
   - Select the specific software packages that you want to install, such as the X Window System and the GNOME or KDE graphical desktop.

What You'll Find on the DVD

This section provides a summary of the software and other goodies you find on the DVD. If you need help with installing the items provided on the DVD, refer back to the installation instructions in the preceding section.

Shareware programs are fully functional, free, trial versions of copyrighted programs. If you like particular programs, register with their authors for a nominal fee and receive licenses, enhanced versions, and technical support.

Freeware programs are free, copyrighted games, applications, and utilities. You can copy them to as many PCs as you like — for free — but they offer no tech support.

Trial, demo, or *evaluation* versions of software are usually limited by time or functionality (such as not letting you save a project after you create it).

GNU software is governed by its own license, which is included in the folder of the GNU software. There are no restrictions on distribution of GNU software. See the GNU license at the root of the DVD or back of this book for details. As required by the GNU license, this book includes the source code for Fedora Core. As for the source code for Debian, Knoppix, SUSE, and Xandros, here's how you can get the source code from the Internet for each application:

- **Debian:** Go through the list of mirror sites at `www.debian.org/mirror/list` and click the URL for the site nearest you. After the site loads, go to the `pool` directory and then look for source code files in one of the three directories — `main`, `contrib`, and `non-free`. The files are further organized into separate directories according to the first letter of the package's name. For example, the source code for the `sendmail` package is in the `s` directory. (See `www.debian.org/doc/FAQ/ch-ftparchives.en.html#s-pools` for more information about the `pool` directory.)
- **Knoppix:** Many packages for Knoppix are from the Debian project and their source code is available from the Debian Web site. (See the previous bullet for information on downloading Debian source code.) Download the Knoppix-specific source code from `www.knopper.net/download/knoppix`.
- **SUSE:** Download the source package for SUSE Linux from the FTP server at `ftp://ftp.suse.com/pub/suse/i386/9.2/suse/src`.
- **Xandros:** Download the source code for the free and open-source components of Xandros from `www.xandros.com/support/source_code.html`.

If you want the source code sent to you, please compete the on-line coupon at www.dummies.com/go/linux3sourcecoupon.

The DVD includes the Linux distributions in several different formats:

- **Full distribution:** You can boot from the DVD and install a full distribution. With a full distribution, you don't have to do anything special other than boot from the DVD. You can then simply proceed to install the Linux distribution.
- **Ready-to-run Live CD:** You can boot a Live CD by booting your PC from the DVD. After you boot a ready-to-run Live CD, you should get a Linux GUI desktop that you can begin using immediately without having to install anything on the hard drive.
- **ISO images:** You have to burn CDs from the ISO images and then install from the CDs. Although you can download ISO images yourself, the files are quite big — each ISO image is about 700MB — and having them on the DVD eliminates the hassles of downloading huge files from the Internet. Some of the ISO images are Live CD images. After you burn a CD from a Live CD ISO, you can boot from the CD and get a Linux system without having to install anything on the hard drive.

TIP

If you don't have a DVD drive, please use the coupon at the back of the book to order the CD set that provides everything that the DVD includes.

Here are the Linux distributions that the DVD includes:

- **Debian:** Provided in the form of ISO images. Burn the CDs and you are ready to install Debian.
- **Fedora Core:** Included as a full distribution with the source code. Simply boot from the DVD and you get the option of installing Fedora Core. Use the graphical installer to complete the installation steps.
- **Knoppix:** Included as a ready-to-run Live CD. Boot from the DVD and you get the option to start Knoppix. After it starts, you get the Knoppix desktop without having to install anything on the hard drive.
- **SUSE:** Provided as a single CD ISO image. Burn the CD and then boot from the CD to get a SUSE Linux system. As with other Live CD distributions, you don't need to install anything on the hard drive.
- **Xandros Open Circulation Edition:** Provided as a single CD ISO image. Burn the CD and then install Xandros.

The detailed software list for each Linux distribution varies somewhat, but most of the distributions include the following:

- ✦ Linux kernel 2.6.x with driver modules for major PC hardware configurations, including IDE/EIDE and SCSI drives, PCMCIA devices, CD drives and DVD drives
- ✦ A complete set of installation and configuration tools for setting up devices and services
- ✦ A graphical user interface based on the X Window System, with GNOME 2.8 and KDE 3.3 graphical desktops
- ✦ Full TCP/IP networking for Internet, LANs, and intranets
- ✦ Tools for connecting your PC to your Internet Service Provider (ISP) using PPP, DSL, or dial-up serial communications programs
- ✦ A complete suite of Internet applications, including electronic mail (`sendmail`, `mail`), news (INN), TELNET, FTP, DNS, and NFS
- ✦ Ximian Evolution or equivalent e-mail and calendar application
- ✦ OpenOffice.org 1.1.2 office suite with word processor, spreadsheet, presentation software, and more
- ✦ Apache Web server 2.0.51 (to turn your PC into a Web server) and Mozilla 1.7 (to surf the Net)
- ✦ Samba 3.0.7 LAN Manager software for Microsoft Windows connectivity
- ✦ Several text editors (for example, GNU Emacs 21.3; `vim`)
- ✦ Graphics and image manipulation software, such as The GIMP, Xfig, Gnuplot, Ghostscript, Ghostview, and ImageMagick
- ✦ Programming languages (GNU C and C++ 3.4, Perl 5.8.5, Tcl/Tk 8.4.7, Python 2.3.4, GNU AWK 3.1.3) and software development tools (GNU Debugger 6.1, CVS 1.11, RCS 5.7, GNU Bison 1.875, flex 2.5.4a, TIFF, and JPEG libraries)
- ✦ Support for industry standard Executable and Linking Format (ELF) and Intel Binary Compatibility Specification (iBCS)
- ✦ A complete suite of standard UNIX utilities from the GNU project
- ✦ Tools to access and use DOS files and applications (`mtools` 3.9.9)
- ✦ Text formatting and typesetting software (`groff`, TeX, and LaTeX)

Troubleshooting

If you have difficulty installing or using the materials on the companion DVD, consult the detailed installation and troubleshooting instructions in Book I.

If you still have trouble with the DVD-ROM, please call the Wiley Product Technical Support phone number: (800) 762-2974. Outside the United States, call 1(317) 572-3994. You can also contact Wiley Product Technical Support through the Internet at `www.wiley.com/techsupport`. Wiley Publishing will provide technical support only for installation and other general quality control items; for technical support on the applications themselves, consult the program's vendor or author.

To place additional orders or to request information about other Wiley products, please call (800) 225-5945.

Index

Symbols & Numerics

A

B

C

D

E

F

G

H

I

J

K

L

M

N

O

P

S

U

V

W

X

Y

Z

Notes

ISO Distribution: This book includes an ISO copy of Fedora Core 3 Linux from the Fedora Project, which you may use in accordance with the license agreements accompanying the software. For more information, see the Fedora Project Web site (`http://fedora.redhat.com/`). Red Hat does not provide support services for Fedora Core. You may purchase Red Hat® Enterprise Linux® and technical support from Red Hat through its Web site (`www.redhat.com`) or its toll-free number (1-888-2REDHAT).

Limited Warranty: (a) WPI warrants that the Software and Software Media are free from defects in materials and workmanship under normal use for a period of sixty (60) days from the date of purchase of this Book. If WPI receives notification within the warranty period of defects in materials or workmanship, WPI will replace the defective Software Media. (b) WPI AND THE AUTHOR(S) OF THE BOOK DISCLAIM ALL OTHER WARRANTIES, EXPRESS OR IMPLIED, INCLUDING WITHOUT LIMITATION IMPLIED WARRANTIES OF MERCHANTABILITY AND FITNESS FOR A PARTICULAR PURPOSE, WITH RESPECT TO THE SOFTWARE, THE PROGRAMS, THE SOURCE CODE CONTAINED THEREIN, AND/OR THE TECHNIQUES DESCRIBED IN THIS BOOK. WPI DOES NOT WARRANT THAT THE FUNCTIONS CONTAINED IN THE SOFTWARE WILL MEET YOUR REQUIREMENTS OR THAT THE OPERATION OF THE SOFTWARE WILL BE ERROR FREE. (c) This limited warranty gives you specific legal rights, and you may have other rights that vary from jurisdiction to jurisdiction.

Wiley Publishing, Inc.

Fedora™ Core 3 Linux® CD-ROM Offer

If you do not have access to a PC with a DVD drive, we are offering the complete set on CD-ROMs for a nominal shipping-and-materials fee. If you'd like the CDs sent to you, please follow the instructions below to order by phone, online, or coupon.

For each ordering method, please use ISBN: 0764588214 and Promo Code LAIOF when prompted. The cost is $11.00 (USD) plus shipping.

Terms: Void where prohibited or restricted by law. Allow 2-4 weeks for delivery.

To order by phone:

1. Call toll free in the United States – 1-877-762-2974. International customers, dial 1-317-572-3994.
2. Give the operator the appropriate ISBN and Promo Code. Please have your credit card ready.

To order online:

1. Go to `http://www.wiley.com/`.
2. Use the Product Search feature to search for RHFLinux 3 Multipack or 0764588214.
3. Place the item in the shopping cart and use the Promo Code (LAIOF) when prompted.

To order by coupon:

1. Complete the coupon below.
2. Include a check or money order for $11.00 (USD) plus shipping. To find out the shipping costs, call 1-877-762-2974 in the US or 1-317-572-3994 for international customers.
3. Send it to us at the address listed at the bottom of the coupon.

Name ____________________

Company ____________________

Address ____________________

City __________ **State** __________ **Postal Code** __________ **Country** __________

E-mail ____________________ **Telephone** ____________________

Place where book was purchased ____________________

❑ Check here to find out what we're up to by joining our e-mail list—a convenient way to receive news about our products and events as well as about special discount offers.

Return this coupon with the appropriate U.S. funds to:
Wiley Publishing, Inc.
Customer Care
RHFLinux 3 Multipack, 0764588214 Promo: LAIOF
10475 Crosspoint Blvd.
Indianapolis, IN 46256

Terms: Wiley is not responsible for lost, stolen, late, or illegible orders. For questions regarding this fulfillment offer, please call us at 1-877-762-2974 or 1-317-572-3994.

BUSINESS, CAREERS & PERSONAL FINANCE

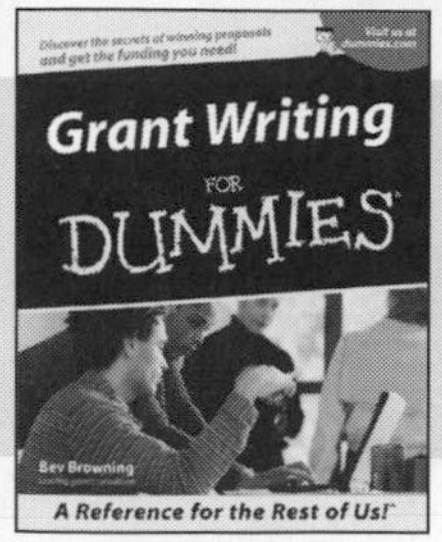

0-7645-5307-0

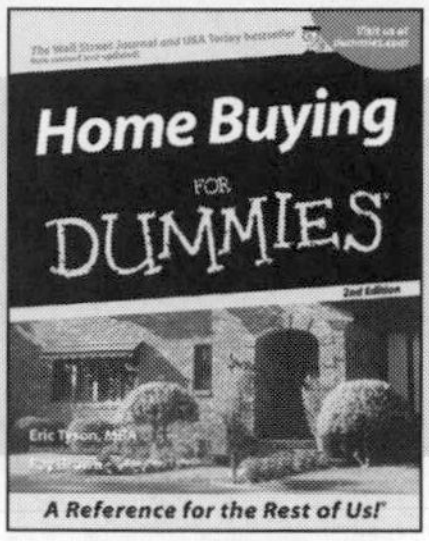

0-7645-5331-3 *†

Also available:

- Accounting For Dummies † 0-7645-5314-3
- Business Plans Kit For Dummies † 0-7645-5365-8
- Cover Letters For Dummies 0-7645-5224-4
- Frugal Living For Dummies 0-7645-5403-4
- Leadership For Dummies 0-7645-5176-0
- Managing For Dummies 0-7645-1771-6
- Marketing For Dummies 0-7645-5600-2
- Personal Finance For Dummies * 0-7645-2590-5
- Project Management For Dummies 0-7645-5283-X
- Resumes For Dummies † 0-7645-5471-9
- Selling For Dummies 0-7645-5363-1
- Small Business Kit For Dummies *† 0-7645-5093-4

HOME & BUSINESS COMPUTER BASICS

0-7645-4074-2

0-7645-3758-X

Also available:

- ACT! 6 For Dummies 0-7645-2645-6
- iLife '04 All-in-One Desk Reference For Dummies 0-7645-7347-0
- iPAQ For Dummies 0-7645-6769-1
- Mac OS X Panther Timesaving Techniques For Dummies 0-7645-5812-9
- Macs For Dummies 0-7645-5656-8
- Microsoft Money 2004 For Dummies 0-7645-4195-1
- Office 2003 All-in-One Desk Reference For Dummies 0-7645-3883-7
- Outlook 2003 For Dummies 0-7645-3759-8
- PCs For Dummies 0-7645-4074-2
- TiVo For Dummies 0-7645-6923-6
- Upgrading and Fixing PCs For Dummies 0-7645-1665-5
- Windows XP Timesaving Techniques For Dummies 0-7645-3748-2

FOOD, HOME, GARDEN, HOBBIES, MUSIC & PETS

0-7645-5295-3

0-7645-5232-5

Also available:

- Bass Guitar For Dummies 0-7645-2487-9
- Diabetes Cookbook For Dummies 0-7645-5230-9
- Gardening For Dummies * 0-7645-5130-2
- Guitar For Dummies 0-7645-5106-X
- Holiday Decorating For Dummies 0-7645-2570-0
- Home Improvement All-in-One For Dummies 0-7645-5680-0
- Knitting For Dummies 0-7645-5395-X
- Piano For Dummies 0-7645-5105-1
- Puppies For Dummies 0-7645-5255-4
- Scrapbooking For Dummies 0-7645-7208-3
- Senior Dogs For Dummies 0-7645-5818-8
- Singing For Dummies 0-7645-2475-5
- 30-Minute Meals For Dummies 0-7645-2589-1

INTERNET & DIGITAL MEDIA

0-7645-1664-7

0-7645-6924-4

Also available:

- 2005 Online Shopping Directory For Dummies 0-7645-7495-7
- CD & DVD Recording For Dummies 0-7645-5956-7
- eBay For Dummies 0-7645-5654-1
- Fighting Spam For Dummies 0-7645-5965-6
- Genealogy Online For Dummies 0-7645-5964-8
- Google For Dummies 0-7645-4420-9
- Home Recording For Musicians For Dummies 0-7645-1634-5
- The Internet For Dummies 0-7645-4173-0
- iPod & iTunes For Dummies 0-7645-7772-7
- Preventing Identity Theft For Dummies 0-7645-7336-5
- Pro Tools All-in-One Desk Reference For Dummies 0-7645-5714-9
- Roxio Easy Media Creator For Dummies 0-7645-7131-1

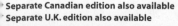

*** Separate Canadian edition also available**
† Separate U.K. edition also available

Available wherever books are sold. For more information or to order direct: U.S. customers visit www.dummies.com or call 1-877-762-2974. U.K. customers visit www.wileyeurope.com or call 0800 243407. Canadian customers visit www.wiley.ca or call 1-800-567-4797.

WILEY

SPORTS, FITNESS, PARENTING, RELIGION & SPIRITUALITY

0-7645-5146-9

0-7645-5418-2

Also available:

- Adoption For Dummies 0-7645-5488-3
- Basketball For Dummies 0-7645-5248-1
- The Bible For Dummies 0-7645-5296-1
- Buddhism For Dummies 0-7645-5359-3
- Catholicism For Dummies 0-7645-5391-7
- Hockey For Dummies 0-7645-5228-7
- Judaism For Dummies 0-7645-5299-6
- Martial Arts For Dummies 0-7645-5358-5
- Pilates For Dummies 0-7645-5397-6
- Religion For Dummies 0-7645-5264-3
- Teaching Kids to Read For Dummies 0-7645-4043-2
- Weight Training For Dummies 0-7645-5168-X
- Yoga For Dummies 0-7645-5117-5

TRAVEL

0-7645-5438-7

0-7645-5453-0

Also available:

- Alaska For Dummies 0-7645-1761-9
- Arizona For Dummies 0-7645-6938-4
- Cancún and the Yucatán For Dummies 0-7645-2437-2
- Cruise Vacations For Dummies 0-7645-6941-4
- Europe For Dummies 0-7645-5456-5
- Ireland For Dummies 0-7645-5455-7
- Las Vegas For Dummies 0-7645-5448-4
- London For Dummies 0-7645-4277-X
- New York City For Dummies 0-7645-6945-7
- Paris For Dummies 0-7645-5494-8
- RV Vacations For Dummies 0-7645-5443-3
- Walt Disney World & Orlando For Dummies 0-7645-6943-0

GRAPHICS, DESIGN & WEB DEVELOPMENT

0-7645-4345-8

0-7645-5589-8

Also available:

- Adobe Acrobat 6 PDF For Dummies 0-7645-3760-1
- Building a Web Site For Dummies 0-7645-7144-3
- Dreamweaver MX 2004 For Dummies 0-7645-4342-3
- FrontPage 2003 For Dummies 0-7645-3882-9
- HTML 4 For Dummies 0-7645-1995-6
- Illustrator CS For Dummies 0-7645-4084-X
- Macromedia Flash MX 2004 For Dummies 0-7645-4358-X
- Photoshop 7 All-in-One Desk Reference For Dummies 0-7645-1667-1
- Photoshop CS Timesaving Techniques For Dummies 0-7645-6782-9
- PHP 5 For Dummies 0-7645-4166-8
- PowerPoint 2003 For Dummies 0-7645-3908-6
- QuarkXPress 6 For Dummies 0-7645-2593-X

NETWORKING, SECURITY, PROGRAMMING & DATABASES

0-7645-6852-3

0-7645-5784-X

Also available:

- A+ Certification For Dummies 0-7645-4187-0
- Access 2003 All-in-One Desk Reference For Dummies 0-7645-3988-4
- Beginning Programming For Dummies 0-7645-4997-9
- C For Dummies 0-7645-7068-4
- Firewalls For Dummies 0-7645-4048-3
- Home Networking For Dummies 0-7645-42796
- Network Security For Dummies 0-7645-1679-5
- Networking For Dummies 0-7645-1677-9
- TCP/IP For Dummies 0-7645-1760-0
- VBA For Dummies 0-7645-3989-2
- Wireless All In-One Desk Reference For Dummies 0-7645-7496-5
- Wireless Home Networking For Dummies 0-7645-3910-8

EALTH & SELF-HELP

0-7645-6820-5 *†

0-7645-2566-2

Also available:

- Alzheimer's For Dummies 0-7645-3899-3
- Asthma For Dummies 0-7645-4233-8
- Controlling Cholesterol For Dummies 0-7645-5440-9
- Depression For Dummies 0-7645-3900-0
- Dieting For Dummies 0-7645-4149-8
- Fertility For Dummies 0-7645-2549-2
- Fibromyalgia For Dummies 0-7645-5441-7
- Improving Your Memory For Dummies 0-7645-5435-2
- Pregnancy For Dummies † 0-7645-4483-7
- Quitting Smoking For Dummies 0-7645-2629-4
- Relationships For Dummies 0-7645-5384-4
- Thyroid For Dummies 0-7645-5385-2

DUCATION, HISTORY, REFERENCE & TEST PREPARATION

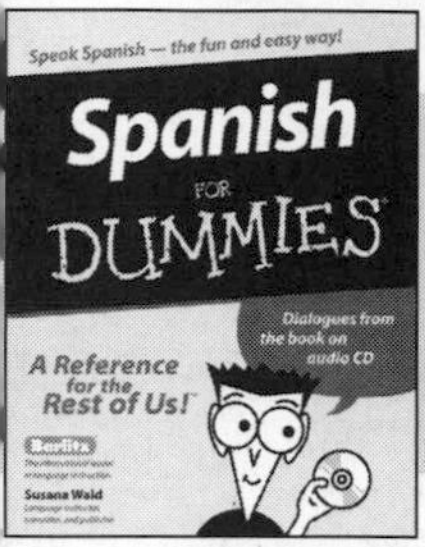

0-7645-5194-9

0-7645-4186-2

Also available:

- Algebra For Dummies 0-7645-5325-9
- British History For Dummies 0-7645-7021-8
- Calculus For Dummies 0-7645-2498-4
- English Grammar For Dummies 0-7645-5322-4
- Forensics For Dummies 0-7645-5580-4
- The GMAT For Dummies 0-7645-5251-1
- Inglés Para Dummies 0-7645-5427-1
- Italian For Dummies 0-7645-5196-5
- Latin For Dummies 0-7645-5431-X
- Lewis & Clark For Dummies 0-7645-2545-X
- Research Papers For Dummies 0-7645-5426-3
- The SAT I For Dummies 0-7645-7193-1
- Science Fair Projects For Dummies 0-7645-5460-3
- U.S. History For Dummies 0-7645-5249-X

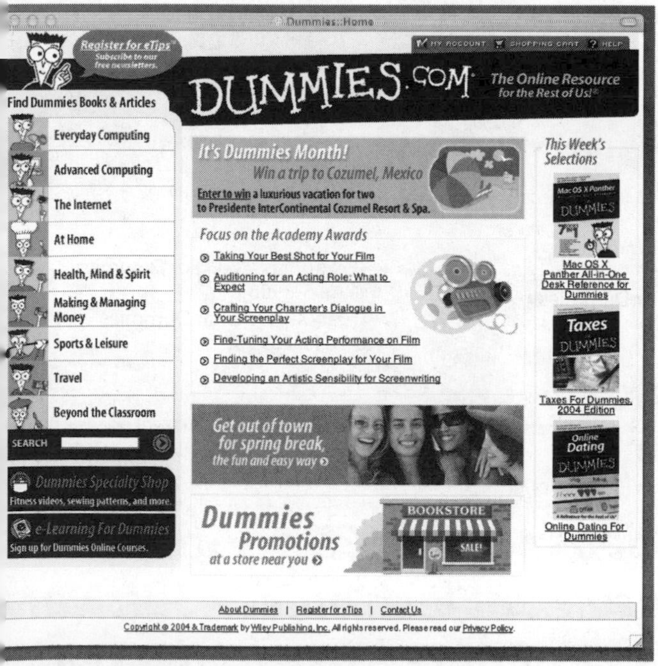

Get smart @ dummies.com®

- **Find a full list of Dummies titles**
- **Look into loads of FREE on-site articles**
- **Sign up for FREE eTips e-mailed to you weekly**
- **See what other products carry the Dummies name**
- **Shop directly from the Dummies bookstore**
- **Enter to win new prizes every month!**

Separate Canadian edition also available
Separate U.K. edition also available

vailable wherever books are sold. For more information or to order direct: U.S. customers visit www.dummies.com or call 1-877-762-2974.
K. customers visit www.wileyeurope.com or call 0800 243407. Canadian customers visit www.wiley.ca or call 1-800-567-4797.

Do More with Dummies Products for the Rest of Us!

From hobbies to health, discover a wide variety of fun products

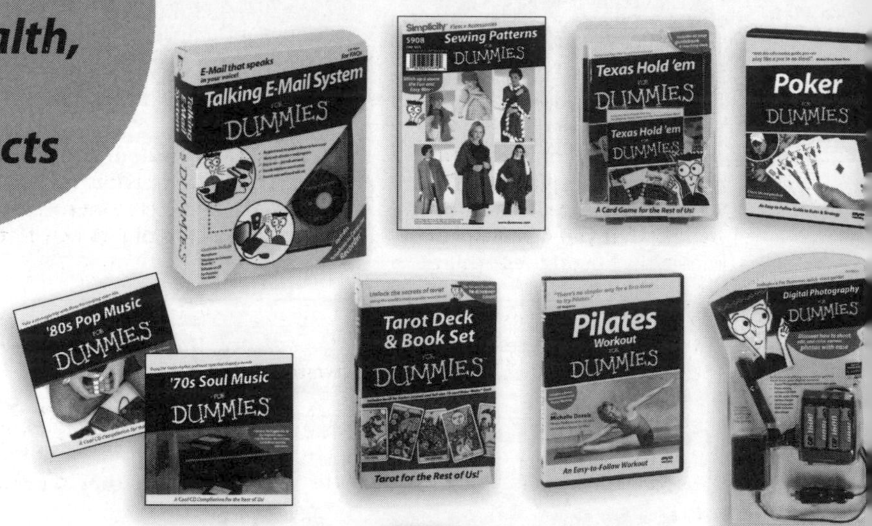

DVDs/Videos • Music CDs • Games
Consumer Electronics • Softwar
Craft Kits • Culinary Kits • and More!

Check out the Dummies Specialty Shop at www.dummies.com for more information!

WILEY

GNU General Public License

Version 2, June 1991
Copyright © 1989, 1991 Free Software Foundation, Inc.
59 Temple Place, Suite 330, Boston, MA 02111-1307, USA

Everyone is permitted to copy and distribute verbatim copies of this license document, but changing it is not allowed.

Preamble

The licenses for most software are designed to take away your freedom to share and change it. By contrast, the GNU General Public License is intended to guarantee your freedom to share and change free software-to make sure the software is free for all its users. This General Public License applies to most of the Free Software Foundation's software and to any other program whose authors commit to using it. (Some other Free Software Foundation software is covered by the GNU Library General Public License instead.) You can apply it to your programs, too.

When we speak of free software, we are referring to freedom, not price. Our General Public Licenses are designed to make sure that you have the freedom to distribute copies of free software (and charge for this service if you wish), that you receive source code or can get it if you want it, that you can change the software or use pieces of it in new free programs; and that you know you can do these things.

To protect your rights, we need to make restrictions that forbid anyone to deny you these rights or to ask you to surrender the rights. These restrictions translate to certain responsibilities for you if you distribute copies of the software, or if you modify it.

For example, if you distribute copies of such a program, whether gratis or for a fee, you must give the recipients all the rights that you have. You must make sure that they, too, receive or can get the source code. And you must show them these terms so they know their rights.

We protect your rights with two steps: (1) copyright the software, and (2) offer you this license which gives you legal permission to copy, distribute and/or modify the software.

Also, for each author's protection and ours, we want to make certain that everyone understands that there is no warranty for this free software. If the software is modified by someone else and passed on, we want its recipients to know that what they have is not the original, so that any problems introduced by others will not reflect on the original authors' reputations.

Finally, any free program is threatened constantly by software patents. We wish to avoid the danger that redistributors of a free program will individually obtain patent licenses, in effect making the program proprietary. To prevent this, we have made it clear that any patent must be licensed for everyone's free use or not licensed at all.

The precise terms and conditions for copying, distribution and modification follow.

Terms and Conditions for Copying, Distribution and Modification

0. This License applies to any program or other work which contains a notice placed by the copyright holder saying it may be distributed under the terms of this General Public License. The "Program", below, refers to any such program or work, and a "work based on the Program" means either the Program or any derivative work under copyright law: that is to say, a work containing the Program or a portion of it, either verbatim or with modifications and/or translated into another language. (Hereinafter, translation is included without limitation in the term "modification".) Each licensee is addressed as "you".

   Activities other than copying, distribution and modification are not covered by this License; they are outside its scope. The act of running the Program is not restricted, and the output from the Program is covered only if its contents constitute a work based on the Program (independent of having been made by running the Program). Whether that is true depends on what the Program does.

1. You may copy and distribute verbatim copies of the Program's source code as you receive it, in any medium, provided that you conspicuously and appropriately publish on each copy an appropriate copyright notice and disclaimer of warranty; keep intact all the notices that refer to this License and to the absence of any warranty; and give any other recipients of the Program a copy of this License along with the Program.

   You may charge a fee for the physical act of transferring a copy, and you may at your option offer warranty protection in exchange for a fee.

2. You may modify your copy or copies of the Program or any portion of it, thus forming a work based on the Program, and copy and distribute such modifications or work under the terms of Section 1 above, provided that you also meet all of these conditions:

   a) You must cause the modified files to carry prominent notices stating that you changed the files and the date of any change.

   b) You must cause any work that you distribute or publish, that in whole or in part contains or is derived from the Program or any part thereof, to be licensed as a whole at no charge to all third parties under the terms of this License.

   c) If the modified program normally reads commands interactively when run, you must cause it, when started running for such interactive use in the most ordinary way, to print or display an announcement including an appropriate copyright notice and a notice that there is no warranty (or else, saying that you provide a warranty) and that users may redistribute the program under these conditions, and telling the user how to view a copy of this License. (Exception: if the Program itself is interactive but does not normally print such an announcement, your work based on the Program is not required to print an announcement.)

   These requirements apply to the modified work as a whole. If identifiable sections of that work are not derived from the Program, and can be reasonably considered independent and separate works in themselves, then this License, and its terms, do not apply to those sections when you distribute them as separate works. But when you distribute the same sections as part of a whole which is a work based on the Program, the distribution of the whole must be on the terms of this License, whose permissions for other licensees extend to the entire whole, and thus to each and every part regardless of who wrote it.

Thus, it is not the intent of this section to claim rights or contest your rights to work written entirely by you; rather, the intent is to exercise the right to control the distribution of derivative or collective works based on the Program.

In addition, mere aggregation of another work not based on the Program with the Program (or with a work based on the Program) on a volume of a storage or distribution medium does not bring the other work under the scope of this License.

3. You may copy and distribute the Program (or a work based on it, under Section 2) in object code or executable form under the terms of Sections 1 and 2 above provided that you also do one of the following:

   a) Accompany it with the complete corresponding machine-readable source code, which must be distributed under the terms of Sections 1 and 2 above on a medium customarily used for software interchange; or,

   b) Accompany it with a written offer, valid for at least three years, to give any third party, for a charge no more than your cost of physically performing source distribution, a complete machine-readable copy of the corresponding source code, to be distributed under the terms of Sections 1 and 2 above on a medium customarily used for software interchange; or,

   c) Accompany it with the information you received as to the offer to distribute corresponding source code. (This alternative is allowed only for noncommercial distribution and only if you received the program in object code or executable form with such an offer, in accord with Subsection b above.)

   The source code for a work means the preferred form of the work for making modifications to it. For an executable work, complete source code means all the source code for all modules it contains, plus any associated interface definition files, plus the scripts used to control compilation and installation of the executable. However, as a special exception, the source code distributed need not include anything that is normally distributed (in either source or binary form) with the major components (compiler, kernel, and so on) of the operating system on which the executable runs, unless that component itself accompanies the executable.

   If distribution of executable or object code is made by offering access to copy from a designated place, then offering equivalent access to copy the source code from the same place counts as distribution of the source code, even though third parties are not compelled to copy the source along with the object code.

4. You may not copy, modify, sublicense, or distribute the Program except as expressly provided under this License. Any attempt otherwise to copy, modify, sublicense or distribute the Program is void, and will automatically terminate your rights under this License. However, parties who have received copies, or rights, from you under this License will not have their licenses terminated so long as such parties remain in full compliance.

5. You are not required to accept this License, since you have not signed it. However, nothing else grants you permission to modify or distribute the Program or its derivative works. These actions are prohibited by law if you do not accept this License. Therefore, by modifying or distributing the Program (or any work based on the Program), you indicate your acceptance of this License to do so, and all its terms and conditions for copying, distributing or modifying the Program or works based on it.

6. Each time you redistribute the Program (or any work based on the Program), the recipient automatically receives a license from the original licensor to copy, distribute or modify the Program subject to these terms and conditions. You may not impose any further restrictions on the recipients' exercise of the rights granted herein. You are not responsible for enforcing compliance by third parties to this License.

7. If, as a consequence of a court judgment or allegation of patent infringement or for any other reason (not limited to patent issues), conditions are imposed on you (whether by court order, agreement or otherwise) that contradict the conditions of this License, they do not excuse you from the conditions of this License. If you cannot distribute so as to satisfy simultaneously your obligations under this License and any other pertinent obligations, then as a consequence you may not distribute the Program at all. For example, if a patent license would not permit royalty-free redistribution of the Program by all those who receive copies directly or indirectly through you, then the only way you could satisfy both it and this License would be to refrain entirely from distribution of the Program.

   If any portion of this section is held invalid or unenforceable under any particular circumstance, the balance of the section is intended to apply and the section as a whole is intended to apply in other circumstances.

   It is not the purpose of this section to induce you to infringe any patents or other property right claims or to contest validity of any such claims; this section has the sole purpose of protecting the integrity of the free software distribution system, which is implemented by public license practices. Many people have made generous contributions to the wide range of software distributed through that system in reliance on consistent application of that system; it is up to the author/donor to decide if he or she is willing to distribute software through any other system and a licensee cannot impose that choice.

   This section is intended to make thoroughly clear what is believed to be a consequence of the rest of this License.

8. If the distribution and/or use of the Program is restricted in certain countries either by patents or by copyrighted interfaces, the original copyright holder who places the Program under this License may add an explicit geographical distribution limitation excluding those countries, so that distribution is permitted only in or among countries not thus excluded. In such case, this License incorporates the limitation as if written in the body of this License.

9. The Free Software Foundation may publish revised and/or new versions of the General Public License from time to time. Such new versions will be similar in spirit to the present version, but may differ in detail to address new problems or concerns.

   Each version is given a distinguishing version number. If the Program specifies a version number of this License which applies to it and "any later version", you have the option of following the terms and conditions either of that version or of any later version published by the Free Software Foundation. If the Program does not specify a version number of this License, you may choose any version ever published by the Free Software Foundation.

10. If you wish to incorporate parts of the Program into other free programs whose distribution conditions are different, write to the author to ask for permission. For software which is copyrighted by the Free Software Foundation, write to the Free Software Foundation; we sometimes make exceptions for this. Our decision will be guided by the two goals of preserving the free status of all derivatives of our free software and of promoting the sharing and reuse of software generally.

NO WARRANTY

11. BECAUSE THE PROGRAM IS LICENSED FREE OF CHARGE, THERE IS NO WARRANTY FOR THE PROGRAM, TO THE EXTENT PERMITTED BY APPLICABLE LAW. EXCEPT WHEN OTHERWISE STATED IN WRITING THE COPYRIGHT HOLDERS AND/OR OTHER PARTIES PROVIDE THE PROGRAM "AS IS" WITHOUT WARRANTY OF ANY KIND, EITHER EXPRESSED OR IMPLIED, INCLUDING, BUT NOT LIMITED TO, THE IMPLIED WARRANTIES OF MERCHANTABILITY AND FITNESS FOR A PARTICULAR PURPOSE. THE ENTIRE RISK AS TO THE QUALITY AND PERFORMANCE OF THE PROGRAM IS WITH YOU. SHOULD THE PROGRAM PROVE DEFECTIVE, YOU ASSUME THE COST OF ALL NECESSARY SERVICING, REPAIR OR CORRECTION.

12. IN NO EVENT UNLESS REQUIRED BY APPLICABLE LAW OR AGREED TO IN WRITING WILL ANY COPYRIGHT HOLDER, OR ANY OTHER PARTY WHO MAY MODIFY AND/OR REDISTRIBUTE THE PROGRAM AS PERMITTED ABOVE, BE LIABLE TO YOU FOR DAMAGES, INCLUDING ANY GENERAL, SPECIAL, INCIDENTAL OR CONSEQUENTIAL DAMAGES ARISING OUT OF THE USE OR INABILITY TO USE THE PROGRAM (INCLUDING BUT NOT LIMITED TO LOSS OF DATA OR DATA BEING RENDERED INACCURATE OR LOSSES SUSTAINED BY YOU OR THIRD PARTIES OR A FAILURE OF THE PROGRAM TO OPERATE WITH ANY OTHER PROGRAMS), EVEN IF SUCH HOLDER OR OTHER PARTY HAS BEEN ADVISED OF THE POSSIBILITY OF SUCH DAMAGES.

END OF TERMS AND CONDITIONS